FOUNDATIONS OF LAW:
CASES, COMMENTARY, AND ETHICS

The West Paralegal Series

Your options keep growing with West Publishing.

Each year our list continues to offer you more options for every course, new or existing, and on-the-job reference materials. We now have over 140 titles from which to choose.

We are pleased to offer books in the following subject areas:

Administrative Law
Alternative Dispute Resolution
Bankruptcy
Business Organizations/Corporations
Civil Litigation and Procedure
CLA Exam Preparation
Client Accounting
Computer in the Law Office
Constitutional Law
Contract Law
Criminal Law and Procedure
Document Preparation
Environmental Law
Ethics

Family Law
Federal Taxation
Intellectual Property
Introduction to Law
Introduction to Paralegalism
Law Office Management
Law Office Procedures
Legal Research, Writing, and Analysis
Legal Terminology
Paralegal Employment
Real Estate Law
Reference Materials
Torts and Personal Injury Law
Will, Trusts, and Estate Administration

You will find unparalleled, practical teaching support.

Each text is enhanced by instructor and student supplements to ensure the best learning experience possible to prepare for this field. We also offer custom publishing and other benefits such as West's Student Achievement Award. In addition, our sales representatives are ready to provide you with needed and dependable service.

We want to hear from you.

The most important factor in improving the quality of our paralegal texts and teaching packages is active feedback from educators in the field. If you have a question, concern, or observation about any of our materials or you have written a proposal or manuscript, we want to hear from you. Please do not hesitate to contact your local representative or write us at the following address:

West Paralegal Series, 3 Columbia Circle, P.O. Box 15015, Albany, NY 12212-5015.

For additional information point your browser to
http://www.westpub.com/Educate and **http://www.delmar.com**

West Publishing — *Your Paralegal Publisher*
an imprint of Delmar Publishers

an International Thomson Publishing company I(T)P®

FOUNDATIONS OF LAW:
CASES, COMMENTARY,
AND ETHICS

The West Paralegal Series

Your options keep growing with West Publishing.

Each year our list continues to offer you more options for every course, new or existing, and on-the-job reference materials. We now have over 140 titles from which to choose.

We are pleased to offer books in the following subject areas:

Administrative Law	Family Law
Alternative Dispute Resolution	Federal Taxation
Bankruptcy	Intellectual Property
Business Organizations/Corporations	Introduction to Law
Civil Litigation and Procedure	Introduction to Paralegalism
CLA Exam Preparation	Law Office Management
Client Accounting	Law Office Procedures
Computer in the Law Office	Legal Research, Writing, and Analysis
Constitutional Law	Legal Terminology
Contract Law	Paralegal Employment
Criminal Law and Procedure	Real Estate Law
Document Preparation	Reference Materials
Environmental Law	Torts and Personal Injury Law
Ethics	Will, Trusts, and Estate Administration

You will find unparalleled, practical teaching support.

Each text is enhanced by instructor and student supplements to ensure the best learning experience possible to prepare for this field. We also offer custom publishing and other benefits such as West's Student Achievement Award. In addition, our sales representatives are ready to provide you with needed and dependable service.

We want to hear from you.

The most important factor in improving the quality of our paralegal texts and teaching packages is active feedback from educators in the field. If you have a question, concern, or observation about any of our materials or you have written a proposal or manuscript, we want to hear from you. Please do not hesitate to contact your local representative or write us at the following address:

West Paralegal Series, 3 Columbia Circle, P.O. Box 15015, Albany, NY 12212-5015.

For additional information point your browser to
http://www.westpub.com/Educate and **http://www.delmar.com**

West Publishing — *Your Paralegal Publisher*
an imprint of Delmar Publishers

an International Thomson Publishing company I⟨T⟩P

FOUNDATIONS OF LAW: CASES, COMMENTARY, AND ETHICS

SECOND EDITION

Ransford C. Pyle

WEST PUBLISHING

an International Thomson Publishing company I**T**P®

Albany • Bonn • Boston • Cincinnati • Detroit • London • Madrid
Melbourne • Mexico City • Minneapolis/St. Paul • New York • Pacific Grove
Paris • San Francisco • Singapore • Tokyo • Toronto • Washington

NOTICE TO THE READER

Cover Background by Jennifer McGlaughlin
Cover Design by Douglas J. Hyldelund/Linda C. DeMasi

Delmar Staff

Acquisitions Editor: Christopher Anzalone
Developmental Editor: Jeffrey D. Litton
Hyldelund
Project Editor: Eugenia L. Orlandi

Production Coordinator: Jennifer Gaines
Art & Design Coordinator: Douglas J.

COPYRIGHT © 1996
By West Publishing
an imprint of Delmar Publishers
a division of International Thomson Publishing
The ITP logo is a trademark under license.

Printed in the United States of America

For more information, contact:

Delmar Publishers
3 Columbia Circle , Box 15015
Albany, New York 12212-5015

International Thomson Publishing – Europe
Berkshire House
168-173 High Holborn
London, WC1V 7AA
England

Thomas Nelson Australia
102 Dodds Street
South Melbourne, 3205
Victoria, Australia

Nelson Canada
1120 Birchmount Road
Scarborough, Ontario
Canada M1K 5G4

International Thomson Editores
Campos Eliseos 385, Piso 7
Col Polanco
11560 Mexico D F Mexico

International Thomson Publishing GmbH
Königswinterer Strasse 418
53227 Bonn
Germany

International Thomson Publishing – Asia
221 Henderson Road
#05 -10 Henderson Building
Singapore 0315

International Thomson Publishing – Japan
Hirakawacho Kyowa Building, 3F
2-2-1 Hirakawacho
Chiyoda-ku, Tokyo 102 Japan

5 6 7 8 9 10 XXX 03 02 01 00 99 98

Library of Congress Cataloging-in-Publication Data

Pyle, Ransford Comstock, 1936-
 Foundations of lawfor paralegals: cases, commentary, and ethics
 /Ransford Pyle. —2nd ed.
  p. cm.
 Includes index.
 ISBN 0-8273-7194-2
  1. Legal assistants—United States—Handbooks, maunuals, etc. 2. Law—United States
I. Title.
KF320.L4P9535 1996
 349.73—dc20
 [347.3]
                                                              95-19605
                                                                    CIP

CONTENTS

CHAPTER 3:   Ethics   47

CHAPTER 4:   Sources of the Law: Cases   79

CHAPTER 5: Legislation   99

CHAPTER 6: Trial and Appellate Courts   119

CHAPTER 7:   State and Federal Courts   137

CHAPTER 8:   Procedure in Civil Cases   167

CHAPTER 10: Criminal Law   229

CHAPTER 11:   Torts, Personal Injury, and Compensation   251

CHAPTER 12: Contracts and Commercial Law   281

CHAPTER 13:   The Law of Property   315

CHAPTER 14: Family Law 341

APPENDICES   401

PREFACE

Philosophically, the second edition of *Foundations of Law* has not changed from the first. *Foundations of Law* has received widespread acceptance in each region of the country, and the author has received a favorable response from students as well. A new chapter on family law has been added based on suggestions from a number of users. A wealth of smaller suggestions from reviewers have also been adopted, making many improvements in the text itself. The temptation to be all things to all people was avoided; this would have entailed doubling the size of the book. The aim in the beginning was to make the text long enough to cover all major areas of American law and the American legal system without becoming encyclopedic.

The major change to *Foundations of Law* is the addition of many new cases. Experience revealed that a number of cases in the first edition required too much explanation for students who had no prior legal training. Although the newly added cases tend to be recent, they were chosen primarily for instructive value rather than recency. (All the cases have been edited for ease of comprehension, and internal citations have been omitted almost entirely.)

All the cases, new and old, now have case questions, which substantially improves the instructional value of the book. The questions have several purposes. They allow a check on the reader's comprehension of the case and direct attention to the purpose for including that particular case in the text. An additional purpose was to pose general questions to provoke thought about the law and perhaps furnish a basis for class discussion. The cases and the questions that follow them should help students increase their issue awareness, an attitude essential to understanding American law to its fullest that is not necessarily engendered by reading texts or rules.

I have added a sample complaint and sample answer taken from Carol Bast's text *Legal Research and Writing* (Delmar/Lawyers' Coop 1995). Dr. Bast is a colleague who has also used this text and offered numerous suggestions as well as encouragement in writing this second edition.

TABLE OF CASES

WHAT PARALEGALS WILL BE DOING TOMORROW

Chere B. Estrin

What's clear about the paralegal profession of the future is that it will differ from the present. Just two decades old, it has already undergone extraordinary changes, and that will only continue.

Just how it will change is the million dollar question. Interviews with a wide array of experts and managers in the field certainly suggests no unanimity of prognostication. ... [C]lients are already aware of paralegal capabilities. "Savvy clients are recognizing the cost savings and specifically requesting paralegal services." In an effort to compete for clients, law firms are marketing their paralegal programs in ... collateral materials such as brochures and firm resumes.

But what if the legal industry continues to contract and is forced to become far more cost effective, as so many experts suggest? ... [T]hat's likely to reduce the number of attorneys rather than paralegals. If potential attorneys believe they face careers without partnership, doing work that does not use their education, and pays at paralegal levels, law school enrollments will drop. At the same time, almost all the experts agreed that stiffer educational demands will be made on the paralegal.

But in the name of efficiency alone, firms will still have to use paralegals. ... [L]ike attorneys, paralegals will need to cross-train into other specialties to follow the legal action. With transactional work drying up, they will move into health care, aviation, and environmental law.

... [A] recruiter ... predicts that the economic realities of the future will stymie what has been the continual expansion of the paralegal role. "Paralegals may not necessarily get more sophisticated assignments ... ; rather, the role of the executive will emerge. Paralegals possess extraordinary organization and management skills which will not only finally be recognized but utilized appropriately as the practice of law changes."

But whether that actually occurs ... will depend largely on the severity of constriction in legal practice. It is quite possible, for instance, that while paralegals will be pulled back from attorney-like tasks, such as drafting complaints, they may well move into other areas like marketing, budgeting, and other management tasks. The role may evolve into an administrative role, such as litigation executive or case manager.

"With the globalization of the American economy, there will be far more demand for paralegals with foreign language skills to work internationally ... ." [One] paralegal coordinator sees paralegals becoming more heavily involved in law firm computerization, specifically in the areas of management, human resources, case management, and information management. "The paralegal without computer skills will become obsolete."

... [T]he movement of paralegals into the corporate environment will not only continue but increase to the point that many positions will require a paralegal background but not necessarily carry the title, such as the contracts administrator position. [Also,] corporations will increasingly use paralegals in nontraditionally law related areas. "Banks are now innovators using paralegals. However, this wasn't always the case. They may have done better in the past if all of their loan officers were paralegals."

[Paralegals may play] an increasingly important role in entertainment. With their legal knowledge and comparatively low cost, they will be perfectly suited to handle an increasingly wide array of negotiations. [I]ndependent entertainment paralegal firms [could profit] handsomely by providing lower cost legal services in an industry that historically pays highly for them.

[Some have] doubts about the continued upgrading of the paralegal role in the law firm environment, [but see] them increasingly providing a wide array of affordable legal services to the American public. "The future of the paralegal movement lies in providing certain routine legal services and other legal information services directly to the public without supervision of attorneys. New computer-based legal expert systems will enable paralegals to create and operate 'Legal Information Centers' as a practical and economical alternative to the present patterns of legal service delivery."

"The way we practice law has changed drastically. ... But's what clear to me is that the role of the paralegal will continue to evolve. It is a profession that's here to stay."

Reprinted from *Everything You Need to Know About Being a Legal Assistant*, © 1995, Delmar Publishers.

CHAPTER 1

PARALEGALS

CHAPTER OUTLINE

Introduction

Although lawyers must be licensed, those who assist lawyers in their legal work do not as yet need to be licensed. The position of legal assistant or paralegal has in recent years become fairly well defined, but because its definition is unofficial, anyone may use this designation in most states. Nevertheless, the advent of numerous respected paralegal training programs and the growing employment of paralegals in law firms have contributed to defining a paralegal. Although the American Bar Association (ABA) definition comes from a lawyers' group and reflects lawyers' concerns, it demonstrates that paralegals have come to occupy a recognized place of importance in the legal profession. Like lawyers, paralegals perform a broad range of tasks, only some of which will be performed by any one paralegal. This makes the field exciting; there is a place for anyone willing to work and learn. Because the law touches every aspect of human life, the opportunities are limitless.

This chapter attempts to define paralegals and describe some of the tasks they perform.

Origins

The terms *paralegal* and *legal assistant* are today used interchangeably, though only a few years ago there was some debate over which term was more descriptive. Whichever term is used, the paralegal/legal assistant career has become clearly defined in the last twenty years.

In general, paralegals do not perform any tasks that were not performed in law offices prior to the rise in importance of their field. In fact, paralegals do not perform any tasks that lawyers did not perform in the past. Paralegals assist lawyers in providing legal services to clients, but there are a number of things paralegals cannot do because they are not licensed to practice law, a matter discussed later in this chapter. Because paralegals are employees of lawyers and law firms, the nature of their work depends largely on how their work is defined by their employers, but the types of tasks they perform have become increasingly standardized, in part because of the uniformity of the formal training they are receiving in educational institutions.

Although the paralegal profession is relatively recent in origin, lawyers have been using legal assistants in some form since the founding of our republic. Before bar associations, bar examinations, and law schools, it was the custom in the legal profession to learn law by apprenticeship in a law office, often called "reading the law." Except for those affluent enough to study law at the **Inns of Court** in London, early nineteenth-century lawyers learned law by assisting lawyers for a period of time, taking what opportunities they could to read cases and treatises about the law. This often took on an aspect of exploitation at low wages, but eventually the novice was sponsored by his employer to be accepted into practice by the courts of his jurisdiction. This form of legal education qualified bar applicants in most states well into the twentieth century, and contemporary law school students continue to serve much the same function when they work as law clerks in law offices during summer vacations from law school. It would be appropriate to refer to these students as paralegals, though many of them might not be comfortable with such a designation. In communities with large law schools, law students and paralegals often compete for employment.

Before the rise of paralegalism, many lawyers trained their legal secretaries to perform legal tasks beyond the usual scope of secretarial work, and some attorneys still prefer this approach to hiring formally trained assistants. Many present-day paralegals were trained in this way. As the attorney's practice increased, the secretary was gradually converted into a full-time paralegal, and a new secretary was hired to do the secretarial work. The advantage of such an arrangement was that the lawyer was able to take an employee with whom a good working relationship had been established and train that person to do the specific auxiliary tasks the lawyer needed. The disadvantage was that both the lawyer and the secretary took time away from their work for the training.

The paralegal position would never have been invented if it had not proven economically advantageous to law firms. The prime movers in paralegalism have been the largest law firms in the largest American cities. In large law firms, attorneys tend to be highly specialized, which tends to produce attorneys very knowledgeable and competent within their field of practice. They charge premium fees because they can provide quick delivery of high-quality legal services to large corporate and affluent private clients. But this can be accomplished effectively only if the firm is a well-managed business. The lawyers are freed to concentrate on important tasks by the assistance of a competent staff, consisting primarily of law office managers, paralegals, and secretaries. The more support staff a lawyer has, the more time the lawyer can

---

BALLENTINE'S

Inns of Court   For centuries, English lawyers were trained in the Inns of Court, where students learned the law in association with legal scholars, lawyers, and judges. (The reputation of these institutions had its ups and downs, at times appearing more like young gentlemen's clubs than legal institutions.) English lawyers are divided into two groups: *barristers*, roughly equivalent to our trial lawyers, and the more numerous *solicitors*, who handle legal matters other than trial work. The Inns of Court were the traditional training ground for barristers.

devote to delivering legal services and the more money can be brought into the firm. In many instances this benefits the clients, who can be billed for paralegal research, for example, at a significantly lower rate than the attorney's hourly rate. In short, paralegals came to occupy defined positions in large law firms simply because they were part of a rational allocation of work that improved the quality of legal services at the same time that it increased profit for the firm.

Paralegal Training

Because paralegals are as yet unlicensed, no formal training is required. As mentioned, many paralegals have been trained at work by their supervising attorney; some have even trained themselves. While we may call some persons paralegals by virtue of the completion of formal training, others are best defined by the nature of the work they do. In addition, many individuals working in law firms perform secretarial work as well as legal work that goes beyond what would normally be expected of a legal secretary. Whether we call such individuals legal secretaries or paralegals is presently a matter of choice.

In their book *Paralegals,* Johnstone and Wenglinsky provide an insightful sketch of the plight of paralegal schools in attempting to develop quality curricula and graduate employable paralegals. They compiled questionnaires and conducted interviews with hundreds of paralegals in New York City. *Paralegals* is not only an excellent source of data on paralegals but also a very thoughtful analysis of the field. Although published in 1985 and focused on New York City, the book provides an interesting background against which to compare today's figures. Johnstone and Wenglinsky found that a minority (36%) of their subjects working as paralegals had formal paralegal training, but the proliferation of paralegal courses in recent years has pushed this figure upward as more trained paralegals have entered the market. This impact is most evident among younger and less experienced paralegals. The lowest percentage figures for formal training were encountered in governmental law offices (14%) and large firms (18%), while the largest was in medium-sized firms (64%). The low percentages come from large, bureaucratic offices, which are best able to organize training programs and are most likely to require specialized expertise that is still difficult to obtain in a paralegal school. The federal government has also been under budgetary restraints for a number of years and has tended to recruit paralegals from within rather than add new personnel.

Many of the entry-level positions are now called "clerkships" or "case clerks," indicating the clerical nature of such positions. Many major law firms look for experience and specialization and prefer lateral hires to making major investments in training. The recession that

bottomed out in 1991 witnessed layoffs in the legal community along with the rest of the business world, but the recovery from recession has seen a reversal in legal employment. At this point, the future looks bright, but newcomers to the field should take heed and develop valuable skills to enhance their marketability.

The number of paralegals with formal training will vary considerably locally, as many cities do not have or have only recently developed paralegal schools. In response to Department of Labor projections for increases in paralegal employment, paralegal schools blossomed over the American landscape.

All it takes to obtain a job as a paralegal is to convince an employer to hire you. The only qualifications needed are those the particular law firm requires. Nevertheless, we live in a society that cherishes credentials in the workplace. It seems inevitable that the paralegal field, like the legal profession before it, will gravitate toward formal training, certificates, and degrees. Paralegal schools will be ranked by reputation, and the graduates of a "good" school will have an edge over others.

Paralegal Schools

Paralegal training is not currently monopolized by any one type of institution. This is unusual because training in most fields is clearly either vocational or academic. Paralegals should be viewed as professionals who must possess not only technical skills but also a firm grounding in the subject matter of their field, which is law. A *professional* is a person who applies a body of knowledge to aid people in solving their problems.

Perhaps an analogy with the English legal profession will be helpful. In England, the legal profession is divided into barristers and solicitors. Solicitors perform the day-to-day tasks of handling commercial transactions and advising clients with legal problems. Barristers are similar to what we in America call *trial lawyers*; they take from solicitors cases that cannot be resolved by negotiation and must be decided by trial in court. Although English solicitors have broader authority than American paralegals, the two are similar in the sense that their authority stops short of representation in court. Nevertheless, paralegals, like solicitors, are often present during trials to advise and assist the trial attorney. Solicitors are not merely technicians but must have an intimate knowledge of the law in order to adequately represent the interests of their clients.

Parallels with the English system are obvious, and recognition of paralegalism as a profession in its own right is imminent. To take their place beside the time-honored professions, paralegals must possess more than technical skills. They must also acquire a broad body of knowledge to help them exercise wise and effective judgments. With this in view, paralegal training takes on a serious mission.

Who can claim a legitimate role in training paralegals? Should traditional academic programs in colleges and universities enjoy a monopoly, or should technical and vocational schools do the training? Both have legitimate claims because of the need for both technical and academic training appropriate to the field. Fortunately, both kinds of programs usually employ practitioners who have an understanding of the needs of the profession and endeavor to impart the skills and knowledge necessary.

Academic institutions conform to the traditions of academic training and the requirements of regional accrediting agencies, which monitor the activities of the institutions that seek continuing approval. The ABA has added its own approval process, which entails a detailed initial approval application and periodic review to maintain approval. Any program that has obtained ABA approval has received careful attention to ensure that it meets stringent requirements. At this writing, the ABA is the only body that sets standards for paralegal programs and gives or refuses its stamp of approval. Because the process is voluntary as well as costly and time-consuming, many fine programs have declined to seek ABA approval. The American Association for Paralegal Education (AAfPE) has grown significantly in recent years and may play a significant role in setting future standards, perhaps in cooperation with the ABA.

Regional accreditation subjects an educational institution as a whole to intense scrutiny, but does not necessarily subject its paralegal program to the same scrutiny, which is largely up to the institution itself. An institution like a community college or university that has both regional accreditation and ABA approval has undergone scrutiny through two processes. Though neither of these guarantees high quality, they demonstrate that a program has met important minimal standards. A less formal, but nonetheless important, measure of any program is its reputation among local attorneys. Good programs that graduate good paralegals will ultimately be recognized through the legal grapevine, because attorneys have a serious interest in hiring competent paralegals. Nevertheless, a good job placement program at a paralegal school is essential to promote both the school and its graduates.

Paralegal training programs can also be divided into degree programs and certificate programs. Degree programs are more typical of traditional academic programs, like those found in community college, college, and university settings, where a degree such as Associate of Science, Associate of Arts, or Bachelor of Arts is awarded. In these programs, the institution usually requires that the academic training meet a general standard that may require courses in addition to paralegal courses. In certificate programs, a certificate of satisfactory completion is conferred, and the programs usually limit themselves to the particular field of study. *Certificate programs* should not be confused with *certification* by the National Association of Legal Assistants (NALA), which conducts an optional examination of qualified paralegals leading to the designation *Certified Legal Assistant*. Although this designation has no official legal status, NALA was an early entry into the paralegal field, assigning itself the mission of establishing standards for practicing paralegals; certification, like passing a bar exam, is evidence of professional knowledge and competence.

There are literally hundreds of paralegal schools, and the number has been growing consistently in recent years in response to predictions of continually rising paralegal employment through the end of the century. Two-year programs are the most numerous, but four-year colleges and universities that offer paralegal training are on the increase. There are a number of proprietary schools unaffiliated with colleges that offer only paralegal training.

The quality of training is difficult to measure for a number of reasons. First, it is not clear exactly what should be taught. A primary issue is whether training should be general or specific. Although law firms frequently want specialists for whom they do not need to provide extensive training, few schools can afford to offer many specialized courses. Training a student in bankruptcy or government contracts has minimal usefulness if that student is hired by a personal injury firm. Unless the locality has a clearly defined specialized need or the students have already obtained employment, highly specialized courses are simply not economically justifiable. As paralegal employment expands and competition increases, individual schools, when feasible, will develop one or two specialties they have determined to be marketable.

A second factor making curriculum planning difficult is the diverse nature of paralegal students. Some are young, seeking their first career employment; many are older, seeking a career change or returning to the workforce after a period of child-rearing. Many paralegal students are legal secretaries or office-trained paralegals who are attempting to upgrade their skills and their employment. Many have college degrees or some college training, whereas others have none. Some schools have resolved the problem of diversity by requiring prior college training, but the typical community college program cannot logically limit admittance on this basis.

In 1988, a group of attorneys, paralegals, and educators called The Conclave made recommendations for paralegal education that may spell a trend toward more extensive education. The group recommended that programs include a minimum of thirty hours of general education courses, including math and accounting, computers, history, and government. Note that these recommendations include both business skills (accounting, computers) and background (history and government) courses. The Conclave and the legal profession in general have apparently concluded that paralegals, like lawyers, should have more than vocationally specific skills training. Paralegals planning to rise above case clerk should acquire the credentials and experience that will convince a law firm that more important duties should be assigned. Of course, the demands of the firms present a contradiction: though looking for specialists with technical expertise, the firms are also requiring general knowledge and education. What may be appropriate for an entry-level position may not lead to the specialization desired for advancement. The solution to the problem requires individuals to take responsibility for continuing to educate themselves and positioning themselves to acquire marketable experience.

A third factor for paralegal training programs is faculty. The typical paralegal instructor is a full-time practicing attorney teaching in a paralegal school on a part-time basis. The advantage of this arrangement is that the schools can recruit attorneys who specialize in the field that they teach and are up-to-date on the law and practices of their field. The disadvantage is that part-time academic salaries are low, especially when compared with the compensation received by a successful specialist practitioner. Part-time instructors are rarely available to students outside of class and have a limited commitment to the institution, which in turn may often find it difficult to assess the quality of the instruction.

It is particularly difficult for the paralegal student who has no prior experience in a law office to assess the quality of a school or the quality of individual courses. The competent paralegal must have practical skills as well as a general knowledge of the law, but must rely on the instructors to decide how much of either is desirable in any given course. Paralegal students commonly experience a high level of anxiety about what they are learning and whether they will be competent to perform the tasks they will be assigned once they obtain employment. Understanding a few simple facts can reduce this anxiety:

1. No one knows all the law or even a major part of it—not paralegals, not lawyers, not even the Chief Justice of the United States Supreme Court.

2. With a general understanding of the law and the legal system, skills and specifics can always be learned. It is up to the individual to ask, study, and learn. Nothing contributes more to success in law than thoroughness and perseverance.

3. Every case has something unique about it; something that the lawyer or paralegal must think about for the first time; something they could not have been prepared for.

Legal study often seems overwhelming, but the student should learn to enjoy the challenge of the law. There is always more to be learned, but it is never enough.

Curriculum

Paralegal schools vary significantly in their curricula, though a number of courses are offered nearly universally. Curricula are planned by program administrators to fulfill their perceptions of the needs of the local market, student needs, and the basic core of American law. The curricula resemble law school curricula, but with a different emphasis. This is partly because lawyers typically design the programs and partly because law school curricula reflect market needs and essential subject areas of law. When considering curriculum requirements, keep in mind that acquiring a general knowledge of American law is itself a rather daunting task. This book, for example, merely scratches the surface of the legal universe.

ABA-approved and regionally accredited paralegal schools must have an advisory board composed of lawyers and paralegals who provide input into the perceived needs of the local bar. Curricula can be separated into the areas of **substantive law, procedure**, research and writing, office skills, and miscellaneous courses.

Substantive law curricula frequently begin with an overview course on American law and the American legal system. This course introduces students to substantive law and the court system and provides a basic introduction to fundamental legal concepts and the vocabulary that expresses them.

More specific subject areas are always included in the substantive law curriculum under a variety of names. Two subject areas are almost universally included, property law and contract law, though the former is commonly called "Real Estate Transactions" and the latter "Business Law." The difference in terminology reflects a philosophical difference between paralegal training, which is directed primarily to law office tasks, and law school training, which is geared to analytical reasoning and general knowledge of the law. Other subject areas commonly offered are **torts**, often referred to as personal injury law; **domestic relations** (family law); and criminal law. The field of business law often includes a course on business organizations, likely to be called "Corporations" or "Corporate Law," which usually also covers partnerships and sole

---
BALLENTINE'S
---

substantive law   Area of the law that defines right conduct, as opposed to *procedural law*, which governs the process by which rights are adjudicated.

procedure   1. The means or method by which a court adjudicates cases, as distinguished from the substantive law by which it determines legal rights. 2. A specific course of action; a particular method for doing something.

tort   A wrong involving a breach of duty and resulting in an injury to the person or property of another. ... [A] violation of a duty established by law ... . [A] private wrong that must be pursued by the injured party in a civil action.

domestic relations   The field of law relating to domestic matters, such as marriage, divorce, support, custody, and adoption; family law.

proprietorships. Advanced study in property law typically includes a course in **estates** and **trusts** and sometimes a course in estate planning. Property and business law courses tend to dominate the substantive law curriculum because these fields offer a great deal of paralegal work.

Procedural law is traditionally divided into **civil procedure** and **criminal procedure**, though a course in the latter is rarely required because it may be included in a criminal law course. Criminal law constitutes a small portion of legal practice and has not kept pace with civil law in terms of paralegal employment. Civil procedure is sometimes called *litigation* and is likely to overlap with other areas of the curriculum by requiring extensive drafting of litigation forms and management of case materials. Legal research is an essential paralegal course that familiarizes students with the law library and teaches how to look for the law. Legal writing may be included in the research course or may form a separate course; it instructs the student in legal writing format and style. Although paralegals are usually not hired primarily for research and writing, skills in these areas are expected of them.

Law office skills courses may be organized in many different combinations, but include law office management and computer literacy. Programs at four-year colleges and programs requiring college degrees may expect students to have already acquired basic keyboarding skills or to learn them outside the curriculum.

Among miscellaneous courses, legal ethics is commonly offered, in part because it has been mandated by the American Bar Association for ABA approval. Interviewing and counseling courses are sometimes offered. Many schools provide credit for internships in law offices. Specialty courses are offered where the local market provides special opportunities for employment.

What Paralegals May Not Do

Before we discuss what paralegals actually do, it may be helpful to clarify what they may *not* do. This summary does not include all the areas

---

BALLENTINE'S

estate   The right, title, and interest a person has in real or personal property, either tangible or intangible.

trust   A fiduciary relationship involving a trustee who holds trust property for the benefit or use of a beneficiary.

civil procedure   The rules of procedure by which private rights are enforced; the rules by which civil actions are governed.

criminal procedure   The rules of procedure by which criminal prosecutions are governed.

in which paralegals may run into difficulties, such as fee-splitting with attorneys, soliciting business for attorneys, and other ethical problems covered in Chapter Three; for now we confine the discussion to work tasks.

Problem areas are found under what is called *unauthorized practice of law*. Some things may be done legally only by licensed attorneys, and most states have a statute that restricts the practice of law to attorneys. Limited exceptions may be made for realtors and accountants, for example, within their respective fields, and paralegals may enjoy limited privileges if the state has specifically authorized them. Those few states that have addressed this issue by statute have been largely concerned with what paralegals cannot do rather than with what they can do. It is incumbent upon paralegals to become familiar with restrictions and privileges in effect in their state. Because many states are currently investigating the need for and desirability of regulating and licensing paralegals, we can anticipate that the range of permissible activities for paralegals will vary widely among the states and gradually settle into basic principles recognized nationally. Several national paralegal associations and the American Bar Association encourage uniformity among the states. In the meantime, individual paralegals must stay informed of the requirements of their states.

Despite variations among the states, it is possible to arrive at general principles, because there is a consensus on what an attorney's license permits. Lawyers are privileged to provide legal advice and legal representation to clients. Legal advice means advising a client about legal rights and duties and especially about the proper course of action as it relates to the law. For instance, a paralegal may properly advise someone, "I think you ought to see a lawyer," but it would not be proper to say, "I think you ought to file a motion to dismiss." This extends even to matters of law clearly within the paralegal's knowledge and competence. *The temptation to advise must be resisted.* This proscription extends beyond actual clients—whenever a paralegal gives legal advice, she may be engaged in the unauthorized practice of law. The line is not always easy to draw. Consider the example of a friend laboring under the misconception that the **statute of limitations** is four years when the paralegal knows it to be only two. Should she quietly sit by and let her friend lose a suit? Without advising the friend on a course of legal action, the paralegal can certainly question the friend's knowledge and suggest a visit to an attorney or provide a copy of pertinent state statutes, without interpretation that might constitute legal advice.

BALLENTINE'S

statutes of limitations   Federal and state statutes prescribing the maximum period of time during which various types of civil actions and criminal prosecutions can be brought after the occurrence of the injury or the offense.

Legal representation includes a number of important activities, including representation before a court, which is the privileged domain of attorneys. This monopoly of the bar is necessary to exercise control over attorneys who act improperly and to enable clients who are improperly represented to sue their attorneys for malpractice. Nonlawyers may not represent others in court, may not sign documents submitted to the court in any proceeding, nor sign any documents that call for attorneys' signatures. The paralegal is not an agent of a client and must avoid any appearance of being one. There may be limited exceptions to this rule, but paralegals act at their peril in such matters and must be very clear on state law when interviewing clients or engaging in negotiations.

Observing two cardinal rules can avoid the dangers of legal representation by the paralegal. First, the client must always be aware that the paralegal is not an attorney. In any consultations with a client in which the paralegal may participate, especially in initial contacts, the status of paralegal should be clear to the client. Letters written on law firm stationery (some states do not allow paralegals' names on the letterhead) should make clear that the letter is not from an attorney, e.g., "As Mr. Clinton's paralegal, I have been asked to write concerning ... [signed] Erin Summer, Paralegal." Even this might not be sufficient if legal advice is offered. Many clients do not know that paralegals are not lawyers.

The second rule concerns attorney supervision. As long as the paralegal is under the control and supervision of an attorney and the attorney exercises supervision properly, nearly all potential problems are avoided. Many legal documents, including **pleadings**, are prepared by paralegals and signed by lawyers. The attorney is responsible for ascertaining the paralegal's competence to prepare the documents and must review and amend the documents before signing them. Responsibility rests with the supervising attorney, who may be disciplined by the court or the bar association for problems created by a failure to supervise properly, but the paralegal must be aware of the dangers of such situations. Other activities that could constitute unauthorized practice of law include:

1. Negotiating fees or legal representation on behalf of the attorney.
2. Discussing the merits of a case with attorneys for the other side.
3. Assisting others in the unauthorized practice of law.

Legal Technicians

The terms *paralegal* and *legal assistant* both imply attorney supervision. There are also a number of persons now calling themselves *legal technicians,*

BALLENTINE'S

pleadings Formal statements by the parties to an action setting forth their claims or defenses.

who provide legal services without attorney supervision. A movement toward licensing appears to have started in California, where a significant number of independent paralegals risked legal sanctions for providing services to the public. Although the California Bar Association disapproved the proposed licensing of paralegals in November 1990, the issue survives. Several states have formalized licensing bills in the state legislatures, including Illinois, Minnesota, Washington, and Oregon. In 1994, Arizona followed other states in postponing comprehensive regulation and licensing. Until a consensus is built in the bar of at least one state, or until someone frames a case for the courts, the problem of regulation is likely to be tabled for the time being, but it will not go away as long as the number of nonlawyers offering legal services continues to increase. The issue of the 1990s is likely to shift from *whether* to license paralegals to who will be responsible for regulating them.

Rosemary Furman Fights the Florida Bar Association

On April 26, 1984, the Florida Supreme Court, in *Florida Bar v. Furman*, 451 So. 2d 808 (Fla. 1984), sentenced Rosemary Furman to thirty days in jail for contempt of court. The contempt charge was based on her violation of a 1979 order from the same court enjoining her from engaging in the unauthorized practice of law. In her long-standing fight with the Florida Bar, Furman had become a folk hero to many. Governor Bob Graham excused her from serving the jail sentence.

Rosemary Furman is outspoken in her criticisms of the legal profession. Her primary complaint concerns the excessive fees many lawyers charge people of modest means for providing routine legal services. Prior to her difficulties with the Florida Bar, she had served for more than twenty years as a court stenographer. In 1972, she assisted in creating a house for battered wives. The women who came to this house were typically without financial resources, and Ms. Furman began to help them obtain divorces. Eventually she opened her own office, offering services primarily for obtaining divorces. For her services the charges generally ranged from fifty to one hundred dollars.

Ms. Furman was not a member of the bar, not licensed to practice law. While she maintained that she was simply helping people to fill out forms for routine legal matters, the Florida Bar thought otherwise, contending that she was giving legal advice constituting unauthorized practice of law. Subsequent to the 1979 order of the Florida Supreme Court, Furman continued in her business and was again pursued by the Florida Bar. The matter was referred by the Florida Supreme Court to a referee, who concluded from the evidence presented by the Bar that Furman was practicing law in violation of the court order and recommended a four-month prison term. The court accepted the referee's findings but reduced the term to thirty days on condition that she comply with the original court order for two years. Under Florida law, Furman was not entitled to and did not receive a jury trial.

In finding her in contempt of court, the Florida Supreme Court cited evidence of several instances in which Furman had advised clients to distort what they put in their petitions for divorce and how to proceed. Evidence cited by the referee included occasions on which Furman advised clients to submit inaccurate information. In holding against Ms. Furman, the Florida Supreme Court emphasized its responsibility under the law to ensure that competent legal services be provided to the public.

In commuting Ms. Furman's sentence, with assurances that she would not continue her business, Governor Graham emphasized the continuing need for inexpensive public access to the courts.

Case Questions

1. Because it is the ethical duty of the bar to ensure that legal services are provided to the public, did the Florida Bar draw the lines of permissible nonlawyer activities too harshly?
2. To what extent is the Florida Bar acting in its own self-interest, and to what extent is it protecting the public?

Case Glossary

contempt of court Conduct that tends to bring the authority and administration of the law into disrepect or that embarrasses or obstructs the court's discharge of its duties.

enjoin To restrain by injunction. ... To command; to order.

commutation of sentence The substitution of a less severe punishment for a more severe punishment.

What Paralegals Do

Once impermissible tasks are eliminated, paralegals may do anything from typing and filing to preparing appellate **briefs**. An efficiently run law office will clarify the boundaries between paralegal work and the work of the rest of the office staff. Routine typing and filing should be assigned to the secretarial staff simply because such tasks do not effectively utilize the knowledge and skills of the paralegal. Appellate briefs probably should be written by attorneys, though paralegals can provide valuable assistance.

Rather than catalog the myriad tasks that a paralegal can do, it is more instructive to consider what a paralegal might do in a case. In a complex case that may result in litigation, a paralegal may be assigned extensive duties of management and coordination. A supervising attorney can delegate tasks to a trusted and experienced paralegal to free the attorney from time-consuming, routine activities. In our hypothetical case, the attorney is working on a **contingency fee** basis, so the final fee will be the same regardless of who performs the work. In such a situation, the use of paralegals, who presumably earn considerably less

———————————BALLENTINE'S———————————

brief A written statement submitted to a court for the purpose of persuading it of the correctness of one's position. A brief argues the facts of the case and the applicable law, supported by citations of authority.

contingent (contingency) fee A fee for legal services, calculated on the basis of an agreed-upon percentage of the amount of money recovered for the client by his or her attorney.

than the supervising attorney, is very cost-efficient. Keep in mind that consultations with the attorney should be frequent, and the attorney should directly supervise the paralegal's work. Depending on the complexity of the case, a paralegal may actually supervise other paralegals.

Hypothetical case: The parents of a five-year-old boy who has a rare form of cancer consult a personal injury firm concerning a possible lawsuit against a business adjacent to their residence that has been investigated for and charged with dumping toxic waste in back of the business premises. It has been determined by a public investigating agency that some of the effluent has caused contamination of the well water serving the surrounding neighborhood. The parents have received information that the particular chemicals disposed of have been linked elsewhere with their son's form of cancer. After a preliminary investigation, the law firm decides that the business wrongfully dumped toxic waste that caused contamination of the water supply, that a strong case can be made for a causal connection between the contamination and the child's cancer, and that the injuries sustained were sufficient to pursue the case on a contingency fee basis. What are some of the tasks that might be assigned to the paralegal working on the case?

Numerous tasks could be performed by a paralegal assigned as case manager. A paralegal may be put in charge of many tasks and report directly to a supervising attorney. Some tasks may be delegated to a secretary or another assisting paralegal. Without a paralegal, some tasks, such as telephone calls to collect information and arrange meetings, would be performed by a legal secretary, while others would be performed by an attorney.

An attorney may prefer to have the paralegal present from the outset in any consultations with a client. In fact, the client may see the paralegal first in an interview to determine the nature of the case. All this depends on the practices of the firm and the relationship between attorney and paralegal. An advantage of having a paralegal present is that the client can be introduced in a setting in which the client perceives the paralegal as a trusted assistant to the attorney. In addition, the paralegal can take notes, thus freeing the attorney from talking and taking notes at the same time. If the paralegal is not present, the attorney must later take time to explain the case to the paralegal.

The paralegal will engage in some investigative activities. The facts as represented by a client are necessarily incomplete. Facts must thus be collected from other sources to get a complete picture and also to minimize any distortions the client may have conveyed. A report of the agency investigating the dumping of wastes will be sought. Any action taken against the business will be researched and its status followed through any final decision. The paralegal may make a visit to the site to take pictures of the client's property and its relation to the property on which the chemicals were dumped. The paralegal may question neighbors named by the client who have suffered illness they believe to be caused by the dumping of waste. In short, a full picture of the background in which these events took place should be established, both through informal investigation and questioning and through public and private records.

Pretrial preparation also involves formal devices for collecting information from the opposing party, called **discovery**. The paralegal can be instrumental in the pretrial process. He can arrange for depositions to be taken of the employees of the business and any other witnesses for the opposition. During the case, the attorney will develop what is often loosely called the "theory" of the case, that is, the most probable legal basis for winning the case, tying it into the facts of the case. It is called *theory* for two reasons: First, no one can be certain that the judge or jury will agree until the final decision. Second, the approach and even the basis for the lawsuit may change as the factual basis becomes clearer. Like a scientific theory, the theory of the case is a tentative explanation or working hypothesis that remains to be proved and may be adjusted if it is not working.

In a good working relationship, attorney and paralegal share the story of a case and develop a strategy to deal with it. If a paralegal enjoys the confidence of the attorney, the paralegal can formulate questions for depositions, draft **interrogatories** to opposing counsel to obtain basic information, and participate in and sometimes direct other discovery processes such as requesting documents from the other side. The fact that the attorney is responsible for reviewing and approving or signing appropriate documents does not prevent the paralegal from doing most of the work. Oral depositions must be arranged at times convenient to attorneys for both sides as well as the person to be deposed. It is more economical for a paralegal or secretary to make such arrangements than an attorney. The case manager can track the process on the attorney's calendar to see that these tasks are completed. Obviously secretaries can perform such tasks, but it is more efficient to have someone in charge of the loose ends of a particular case to ensure that everything has been done.

Whether or not the paralegal is directly involved in the deposition itself, in a complicated case it is essential that the deposition be summarized and indexed. The court reporter typically reduces the deposition to a verbatim written **transcript**, which can often run to several

---

BALLENTINE'S

discovery　A means for providing a party, in advance of trial, with access to facts that are within the knowledge of the other side, to enable the party to better try his or her case.

interrogatories　Written questions put by one party to another, or, in limited situations, to a witness in advance of trial. Interrogatories are a form of discovery and are governed by the rules of civil procedure.

transcript　A typewritten copy of the court reporter's stenographic notes of a trial ... [;] a record of the proceedings.

hundred pages. Long transcripts are unmanageable without summaries and references to the pages of important topics discussed. Summarizing and indexing should be done by someone familiar with the case and its theory. This is a time-consuming job that can be accomplished by a paralegal, allowing better time management by the attorney.

Extensive legal research will be necessary in the case. As much as possible, the client's legal position must be bolstered by persuasive legal authority. This is not only important to persuade the trial judge but is also instrumental in negotiations with opposing counsel. If a defendant's attorney is convinced that, under the law, his client has a losing case, focus will change from fighting the case to saving the client money by a favorable negotiation. A strong case built on solid research is an essential part of the negotiation process. Although some attorneys insist on doing most or all of the legal research, many paralegals are accomplished researchers. The most important ingredients in good research are thoroughness and perseverance.

Management of a complex case requires an orderly filing system. The many documents that accumulate in the course of the case must be readily available for review and preparation for trial. In our computer age, file management has been made much easier. Many software packages are available for litigation files, and a program can be tailored for specific styles of organization. Material can be stored by computers in ways that make retrieval fast and efficient. Nevertheless, a human being is still necessary to record and file the material on the computer, and paralegal case managers often perform or delegate these responsibilities.

Writing can also be an important activity for the paralegal. In complex litigation, a paralegal case manager may at many points in the case have a greater mastery of the legal and factual details of the case than the attorney, who as the decision-maker has an overview of the case. The attorney may ask the paralegal to write memoranda about the case, and especially the legal issues of the case, so that the major issues are summarized in an analytical form that makes a quick review of the case and its status possible. Although analysis and writing require more skill than does research, experience is a great teacher. The fortunate paralegal works for an attorney who will take time to help build these skills.

Paralegals can also be instrumental in maintaining good client relations. One of the most frequent client complaints is difficulty in reaching attorneys by phone and in receiving return calls. Paralegals often have direct contact with clients and may have a better feel for clients' concerns. Clients may be reluctant to discuss all their concerns with the attorney, especially if they think of that two-dollar-a-minute clock ticking. The paralegal is often a more sympathetic and patient listener and can reassure the client that the case is proceeding in a timely fashion, as well as relay the client's concerns to the attorney. Clients often feel that nothing is happening in their case if their attorney has not corresponded with them for some time. It is helpful for a client to know that more than one person is concerned about the case. The paralegal can call, receive calls, make sure that copies of letters and legal documents are sent to the client, and in other ways make the client appreciate that the case is receiving attention. The paralegal can also alert the attorney to angry clients and help head off unpleasant confrontations.

The tasks performed by paralegals are too numerous to catalog completely, but the following lists give some indication of paralegal duties in two specialized areas of the law. They borrow heavily from lists prepared by the Subcommittee on Legal Assistance of the New York State Bar Association:

Real Estate Transactions

1. Review the contract for sale of real property.
2. Request and obtain title searches.
3. Request and obtain survey of the property.
4. Prepare deeds.
5. Review title opinion and/or title insurance documents.
6. Prepare and review closing statements.
7. Forward, receive, and track documents for closing.
8. Monitor closing file for completeness and accuracy.
9. Track deadlines.

Wills and Trusts

1. Maintain files and indexes.
2. Initial interview with fiduciary.
3. Prepare and file probate documents.
4. Arrange for publication and service of citation.
5. Prepare application for tax identification number.
6. Value assets.
7. Transfer property to trust.
8. Prepare decedent's final income tax return.
9. Prepare estate tax return.
10. Prepare applications for life insurance benefits.
11. Inventory investments, bank accounts, etc.
12. Pay decedent's debts and costs of administration.
13. Cancel credit cards.
14. Prepare final accounting.
15. Prepare final probate petition.

Similar lists could be compiled for corporate paralegals, tax paralegals, bankruptcy paralegals, or virtually any other specialty using paralegals. The lists indicate the variety of formal document preparation and management required for activities involving property transfers. A great deal of work is required to ensure that these events are handled accurately, completely, and in a timely fashion.

The *Winder* case draws a fine line between what is the practice of law and what is not. In drawing its conclusions, it cites a case involving a well-known book titled *How to Avoid Probate!*, which caused considerable consternation among state bar associations. **Probate** is the court procedure whereby the **estate** of a deceased person is administered and distributed. When poorly planned by the **decedent**, the estate may be subject

---

The STATE of New York, Respondent,
v.
James A. WINDER, Individually and dba
Divorce Yourself,
Do It Yourself Divorce Kits and Divorce Aid
Service Enterprises, Appellant.
Supreme Court, Appellate Division,
Fourth Dept.
348 N.Y.S.2d 270 (1973)

The Divorce Yourself Kit offered for sale by defendant, a layman, purports to offer forms and instructions in law and procedure in certain areas of matrimonial law and the judicial process. In *Matter of New York Co. Lawyers' Ass'n v. Dacey*, 28 A.D.2d 161 ... , the court dealt with the publishing of a book "How to Avoid Probate!" consisting of 55 pages of text and 310 pages of forms. In the dissenting opinion adopted by the Court of Appeals, Justice Stevens, analyzing the pertinent rules of law, stated ... : "It cannot be claimed that the publication of a legal text which purports to say what the law is amounts to legal

practice. And the mere fact that the principles or rules stated in the text may be accepted by a particular reader as a solution to his problem does not affect this. ... Apparently it is urged that the conjoining of these two, that is, the text and the forms, with advice as to how the forms should be filled out, constitutes the unlawful practice of law. But that is the situation with many approved and accepted texts. Dacey's book is sold to the public at large. There is no personal contact or relationship with a particular individual. Nor does there exist that relation of confidence and trust so necessary to the status of attorney and client. This is the essential of legal practice—the representation and the advising of a particular person in a particular situation. ... At most the book assumes to offer general advice on common problems, and does not purport to give personal advice on a specific problem peculiar to a designated or readily identified person." Similarly the defendant's publication does not purport "to give personal advice on a specific problem peculiar to a designated or readily identified person," and because

---

BALLENTINE'S

probate 1. The judicial act whereby a will is adjudicated to be valid. 2. A term that describes the functions of the probate court, including the probate of wills and the supervision of the accounts and actions of administrators and executors of decedents' estates.

decedent's estate The total property, real or personal, that a decedent owns at the time of his or her death.

decedent A legal term for a person who has died.

of the absence of the essential element of "legal practice—the representation and the advising of a particular person in a particular situation" in the publication and sale of the kits, such publication and sale did not constitute the unlawful practice of law in violation of Sec. 478 of the Judiciary Law and was improperly enjoined by paragraph I of the judgment appealed from. There being no legal impediment under the statute to the sale of the kit, there was no proper basis for the injunction in paragraph G against defendant maintaining an office for the purpose of selling to persons seeking a divorce, separation, annulment or separation agreement any printed material or writings relating to matrimonial law or the prohibition in the memorandum of modification of the judgment against defendant having an interest in any publishing house publishing his manuscript on divorce and against his having any personal contact with any prospective purchaser. The record does fully support, however, the finding of the court that for the charge of $75 or $100 for the kit, the defendant gave legal advice in the course of personal contacts concerning particular problems which might arise in the reparation and presentation of the purchaser's asserted matrimonial cause of action or pursuit of other legal remedies and assistance in the preparation of necessary documents. The ordering paragraphs of the injunction A through F, H and J all enjoin conduct constituting the practice of law, particularly with reference to the giving of advice and counsel by the defendant relating to specific problems of particular individuals in connection with a divorce, separation, annulment of [sic] sought and should be affirmed.

Judgment unanimously modified on the law and facts in accordance with Memorandum and as modified affirmed without costs.

Case Questions

1. What does the court describe as the essential ingredient of legal practice?
2. Why may a nonlawyer give advice in a book but not in person?

to significant costs during the probate process, which in some jurisdictions has been abused by lawyers and judges. In writing his book, Dacey appealed to the fears of those who had heard horror stories of probate. There are a number of legal devices for passing on property without going through probate. Members of the legal profession, nevertheless, were properly concerned that a general book about probate failed to take into account the peculiarities of various state laws and the individualized needs of those who sought a proper division of their property.

Summary

Paralegals perform a variety of tasks in law offices that depend largely on the needs of the firm. It is easier to say what paralegals cannot do than what they can do. Because legal advice and legal representation are restricted to licensed members of the bar, paralegals must be careful not to cross the line into these areas, but they may do virtually anything else that lawyers have traditionally done. When paralegal work is supervised by an attorney, most potential problems of unauthorized practice of law and malpractice suits against the attorney are minimized.

Paralegal training is available at a variety of schools, and many paralegals are trained by their firms or attorneys. Paralegals are distinguished from other law office staff by specialized legal knowledge and skills and the manner in which they apply these.

Review Questions

1. Check the want ads in the local newspaper for paralegals. What qualifications are mentioned? If you have access to a newsletter of a local city or county bar association, check to see if it has advertisements for paralegals. Also see if it mentions local paralegal associations.

2. Find out if your state has a state paralegal association and if your city or county (or region) has a paralegal association. See what information you can obtain from these groups. The National Association of Legal Assistants also has representatives in most metropolitan areas.

LAND OF THE GIANTS

Steven Cohn

Nationwide, about 14 percent of paralegals work for law firms of more than 100 attorneys (according to the most recent National Association of Legal Assistants *National Utilization and Compensation Survey Report for the Legal Assistant Profession*), and interview responses indicate that large-firm paralegals are taking on more responsibilities, working much more closely with clients, doing more supervising of less-senior paralegals, receiving overtime (for the most part), and participating in outstanding benefit and bonus programs.

More Responsibility, Changing Roles

[T]he use of legal assistants has changed quite a bit during the past few years. "I would say today's paralegals are yesterday's associates ... . I was a litigator for 11 years. I utilized the services of paralegals in a way that I encourage at the firm—bringing them into trial, giving them substantive things to do. My senior legal assistants here train associates. That's part of their job description. As technology improves and our cases are managed technologically, the paralegals are better able to handle the technology than attorneys; hence, they become more substantively involved."

Some also see more legal assistants moving into duties formerly taken by associates. "For instance, five years ago, in the real estate practice group, attorneys would handle in-house residential real estate work. Now it's being handled by two legal assistants. These two career legal assistants are obviously supervised by an attorney, but nonetheless deal with the clients. They handle much of the work on the refinancing of people's co-op loans, second mortgages etc., so obviously that's a tremendous savings to the firm and to the clients as well.

"There's also been a general move among a lot of large firms to have more specialized paralegals ... . Litigation paralegals now do trademark work exclusively as opposed to five years ago when they would have been a kind of 'jack of all trades.'"

"Have things changed? I would definitely say yes in all departments, especially in litigation. [T]hey've really effectively utilized their paralegals. We've got folks who are drafting sections of briefs, who are doing a lot of legal research. A lot of this heretofore had been considered first- and second-year associate work, now it's a standard expectation of the paralegals. They're expected to know how to do it, if not when they walk through the door, then shortly thereafter."

Additional responsibility for paralegals at these large law firms has come in the area of technology, an area in which attorneys seem more than happy to allow paralegals to take the lead. "The technology is available to everybody and to everybody's advantage and the legal assistants have totally embraced available applications ... . It impacts their lives maybe even more than the attorneys.

"(Legal assistants) are moving into different roles ... . Our litigation support department was initially staffed by legal assistants who learned new technology and implemented that service for our clients. We have also had legal assistants involved in the conflicts process, all of which helps them to develop different skills."

"Legal assistants are encouraged to be computer literate ... . Many areas rely extensively on specialized software to efficiently handle the needs of our clients."

[T]he increase in technological expertise among legal assistants has changed the way litigation departments works. "We don't do the same things we used to do, like digest depositions or index boxes of documents anymore. We scan documents in-house, we do searches with the computer, we have all kinds of software for searching information. We put the material on disk and run it through a Windows program."

Technology has also had an impact on utilization of legal assistants. "Much of the voluminous and tedious manipulation of paper associated with large complex litigation has been reduced by document imaging and full-text search capability."

"Cases in the firm are staffed by one or two highly experienced legal assistants who work on the more substantive aspects of document production, deposition preparation and brief preparation. Now legal assistants have to really know and understand all of the factual materials associated with their cases. They must have a thorough understanding of the litigation process and they must be able to interact with attorneys to integrate the factual record into the overall litigation strategy for the case."

CHAPTER 2

LAWYERS

CHAPTER OUTLINE

Introduction

One generation after the founding of the Virginia and Massachusetts Bay colonies, private lawyers were forbidden to practice before their courts. As the legal historian Lawrence M. Friedman remarked, the American lawyer "has played a useful role, sometimes admired, but rarely loved." Suspicion, distrust, and outright hostility toward lawyers is still much a part of American folklore. "Lawyer-bashing" has become a concern to the profession, and popular media are rife with lawyer jokes. The very word *lawyers,* when uttered with a certain intonation, connotes greed and chicanery. The truth is, however, that few outside the legal profession understand exactly what lawyers do or why they do what they do. The aim of this chapter, in discussing lawyers and the legal profession, is to arrive at a basic understanding of their place in our legal system and our society.

The Law and the Lawyer

Lawyers are named after the subject matter of the profession, the law. Unfortunately, the field of law is not as easily described as, say, electrical engineering. The problem of precisely defining law may be left to legal philosophers and scholars of **jurisprudence**. The primary concern of this study is with law in operation or "in practice." Lawyers are called professionals, but are also referred to as *practitioners*, referring to the professional application of learned skills. The practice of law includes a great variety of services furnished by lawyers to their clients.

For practical purposes, law may be defined as a process, a system, or a set of rules governing society. As a process, law can be viewed as the means by which rights and duties are created and exercised. As a system, law interconnects rules governing society with a hierarchy of courts served by the legal profession and the police. As a set of rules, law is a complex code of conduct and values formally established and published, backed by the threat of enforcement. This last view of law as rules is what law students regularly study and what the public generally views as the law.

Failure to understand law as system and process, however, leads to a distorted view of law and lawyers. For example, nonlawyers often

---

jurisprudence   The science of law; legal philosophy.

regard **plea bargaining** as an unethical device used by criminal defense lawyers to circumvent justice. Plea bargaining only makes sense in the context of the pressures and problems inherent in the administration of criminal justice. It has become an indispensable aid, some might say a necessary evil, in resolving criminal cases in the context of overcrowded jails, overburdened court **dockets**, and overworked **prosecutors**.

One must never forget that law continually undergoes change. Not only do the rules change, but the legal system also changes. As society changes, so must law. Law has a particularly important place in American society, which is extremely diverse and complex in comparison with other societies. The various parts of American society express differing and often conflicting values, so a major task of law is to convert values into functioning rules. In the last thirty years, America has encountered major value confrontations over racial integration, civil disobedience in the Vietnam era, gays in the military, and abortion. Although these are social, political, and even spiritual issues, Americans have looked to law and the legal system for their resolution.

The law we discuss in the following chapters is American law, the law of the American legal system as practiced by the legal profession. It might be more properly labeled "Anglo-American law," since we have more than nine hundred years of unbroken legal tradition from England. The severing of political bonds with England in 1776 did not bring a corresponding break with the English legal tradition. In fact, it has been argued convincingly that the American colonials were fighting for the rights normally accorded Englishmen in England but denied to Americans by colonial governments.

Law is concerned with rights, duties, obligations, and privileges and their enforcement. Under the U.S. constitutional model, political authority is divided among the executive, legislative, and judicial branches of government. The study of law generally focuses on the judiciary, because the courts in our system are entrusted with interpreting the law, and it is in the courts that disputes between opposing sides are resolved.

Disputes form the heart of our legal system, which has evolved as an **adversarial system** in which legal battle is waged by conflicting

---

BALLENTINE'S

plea bargain   An agreement between the prosecutor and a criminal defendant under which the accused agrees to plead guilty, usually to a lesser offense, in exchange for receiving a lighter sentence than he or she would likely have received had he or she been found guilty after trial on the original charge.

docket   A list of cases for trial or other disposition; a court calendar.

prosecutor   A public official, elected or appointed, who conducts criminal prosecutions on behalf of his or her jurisdiction.

adversary system   The system of justice in the United States. Under the adversary system, the court hears the evidence presented by adverse parties and decides the case.

parties employing legal counsel to take their sides before an impartial judge and, if necessary, an impartial jury. The practice of law commonly involves advancing and protecting the interests of a client in a dispute, but equally important is preventing disputes. No ethical lawyer would write a **will** or **contract** or close a real estate transaction hoping that **litigation** would result. The test of a well-written will is whether its provisions are carried out uncontested; the test of a good contract is whether it has resolved all reasonably foreseeable conflicts in advance and allows the contracting parties to perform their obligations to their mutual satisfaction. Perhaps it is in this area of preventive law, in which lawyers foresee and avoid future problems, that they do their best work and provide their most valuable services. The public rarely recognizes that lawyers routinely perform this function. The **uncontested** will, the contract that is not **breached**, and the transaction that runs smoothly do not make headlines. For most lawyers, however, an appreciative and satisfied client is one of the frequent personal rewards of the practice of law.

Becoming a Lawyer

In order to represent a client before a court, a person must become a member of the bar. In a general sense of the term, the bar refers to licensed members of the legal profession, the community of American lawyers, just as the bench refers to all judges collectively. Requirements for membership, however, differ from state to state, and membership in one state bar does not confer membership in another state. In most states, licensing is regulated by a state bar association to which members pay annual dues. The state bar associations are responsible for maintaining standards of conduct within the profession and for determining misconduct or assisting the court in disciplining members for misconduct with a variety of sanctions, the most severe of which is **disbarment**.

BALLENTINE'S

will   An instrument by which a person (the testator) makes a disposition of his or her property, to take effect after his or her death.

contract   An agreement entered into, for adequate consideration, to do, or refrain from doing, a particular thing. The Uniform Commercial Code defines a contract as the total legal obligation resulting from the parties' agreement.

litigation   A legal action; a lawsuit.

uncontested   Not disputed; unopposed; not defended against; not litigated.

breach of contract   Failure, without legal excuse, to perform any promise that forms a whole or a part of a contract, including the doing of something inconsistent with its terms.

disbarment   The revocation of an attorney's right to practice law.

Bar disciplinary boards are particularly concerned with misconduct in relations with clients, such as misuse of client funds or the failure to provide promised services. Bar associations also engage in review and reform of laws and provide a sounding board and even lobbying activities for the legal profession. If a state attempts to place new restrictions or taxes on lawyers, they will be quick to respond through their respective bar associations. The authority and activities of the different associations vary considerably from state to state.

Admission to the bar requires passing a bar examination and submission to scrutiny by the bar association. Traditionally, bar membership has required that each candidate be approved on the basis of moral character, as determined by the licensing association. In earlier times, the character and competence of an applicant for admission to the bar was vouched for by members of the bar; today some states conduct extensive inquiry into each applicant's background.

Approval of an application to take the bar examination generally requires completion of law school and the receipt of a law degree, usually called a J.D. (Juris Doctor) or LL.B. (Bachelor of Laws), although some states allow senior law students to take the examination prior to graduation. Admission to law school normally requires completion of a four-year undergraduate degree.

Law School

To understand how lawyers think, some appreciation of the law school experience is helpful. Law school provides a rigorous training that formally and informally molds a certain sort of thinking. Strict emphasis on critical and analytical reasoning sets a high standard for legal debate and discussion, but some, such as Michael W. Gordon, of the University of Florida College of Law, have argued that the focus is too narrow: "One thing that has always troubled me with doctors and lawyers is the fact that we take the brightest people in America and send them into these disciplines and turn them into workaholics and some of the most narrow-minded people in the world."

Admission to law school is highly competitive. Prestige and reputation are important in the legal profession and equally so to the law student, because placement and salary upon graduation from law school depend upon the prestige of the law school and performance in law school. Entry to law school is based principally on undergraduate grade point average and scores obtained on the Law School Admissions Test (LSAT). The more prestigious the law school, the higher grades and scores must be to obtain admission. Intense competition is characteristic of law students and happily encouraged by their professors, most of whom were once law school achievers.

Among law schools, the most elite are considered "national law schools" because their orientations as well as their reputations are national. Yale Law School in New Haven, Connecticut, for example, is not a training ground for Connecticut lawyers but an entree to large New York law firms, the so-called "Wall Street firms," which represent national business interests. The archetype of the perfect new **associate** just hired by a law firm went to Harvard Law School, became editor of the **Harvard Law Review**, and served a year or two as a law **clerk** for a United States Supreme Court **Justice**. Such credentials would guarantee a handsome salary at a top law firm.

Law school training continues to follow a model established in the 1890s by Dean Christopher Columbus Langdell of the Harvard Law School. He invented the *case method* in which students read judicial opinions, or cases, rather than treatises about law, formerly the dominant method of studying law. Langdell reasoned that the practice of law in the United States was based on discovering the law through judicial decisions, because it was in the courts that law was interpreted and explained. A natural corollary to the case method is the *Socratic dialogue* between professor and student. Instead of lecturing, the law professor asks questions of the students about cases they have been assigned to read in order to determine the issues and reasoning in the opinions. For the freshman law student, this is a grueling and often humiliating experience and has been called a "game that only one (the professor) can play." It is a rite of passage in which students are forced to shed their former ways of thinking and reacting to issues and problems and begin to "think like lawyers." This method of teaching has been seriously criticized as promoting tunnel vision, but it succeeds in its goal of fostering analytical thinking and objective argument. Because of this criticism, however, many law schools have in recent years shown a greater sensitivity to the needs of students, offering counseling and tutoring by staff and peers.

The product of an American law school has read hundreds of judicial opinions and spent countless hours finding the way through an extensive law library, but may never have been in a courtroom and may not know the difference between a **bailiff** and a **court reporter**. In recent

---

BALLENTINE'S

associate   A person engaged in the practice of law with another attorney or attorneys, but not as a partner or member of the firm.

law reviews   A publication containing articles by law professors and other authorities, with respect to legal issues of current interest, and summaries of significant recent cases, written by law students.

clerkship   Employment of a law student or a graduate attorney as a clerk by a licensed attorney or a judge.

Justice   The title of a judge, especially the judge of an appellate court.

bailiff   A court attendant charged with maintaining order in the courtroom.

court reporter   A person who stenographically or by "voice writing" records court proceedings, from which, when necessary, he or she prepares a transcript that becomes a part of the record in the case.

years law schools have initiated or expanded the number of clinical programs in which students practice law under the supervision of an instructor. In addition, many law students gain experience by serving as law clerks for law firms during the summers between academic years. Despite this occasional practical education, law schools focus on developing an attitude of mind that seeks the relevant legal issue in each human transaction and applies a technical analytical approach to solving problems.

Obtaining a License to Practice Law

To represent a client in legal matters, an attorney must be licensed in the jurisdiction in which he or she practices. Each state has its own requirements for admission to practice, and the federal courts have their own requirements. Many states relax their requirements for long-term members of the bar of other states, but the process by which the newly graduated law student becomes an attorney follows a similar pattern in most states.

Application for licensing generally requires graduation from a law school approved by the American Bar Association (in some states nonapproved law schools are allowed). The applicant must also show good moral character, but the extent to which this is scrutinized depends on the state. Moral fitness is difficult to define and must be determined on a case-by-case basis; but bar examiners are especially concerned about defects in character that suggest a potential for betraying a client's trust or deceiving a court. For example, an individual previously convicted of **perjury** would be a poor candidate for the practice of law, having demonstrated a disregard for the integrity of the justice system. Finally, admission is usually predicated on a passing score on the bar examination.

Bar Examination

Upon completion of law school or just before graduation, aspiring candidates face the dreaded ordeal of the bar examination. This generally consists of two or three days of a written examination, which in most states consists of two parts. One part is the Multistate Bar Examination, a standardized national test that contains two hundred multiple-choice questions based on general legal topics such as property, contracts, and constitutional law. Each question is based on a hypothetical

---

BALLENTINE'S

perjury   Giving false testimony in a judicial proceeding or an administrative proceeding; lying under oath as to a material fact; swearing to the truth of anything one knows or believes to be false.

fact situation, and the examination requires a thorough knowledge of **black letter law**. This mentally exhausting part of the examination lasts six hours.

The Multistate is based on general principles of law, but most states require a second part that addresses law specific to the state administering the examination. This part of the examination often requires written essay questions based on hypothetical legal disputes and resembles the sorts of examinations typically given as final examinations in law school. Applicants must then wait several weeks, even months, to receive the final results. Each state licensing board is free to establish its own standards, so a passing grade on the Multistate in one state may be a failing grade in another. In most states between 65 and 90 percent of examinees pass. A failing candidate can usually retake the examination, though some states limit the number of times the examination can be taken.

The bar examination not only establishes a minimum standard of competence for lawyers, but it also represents a psychological ordeal shared by attorneys; most recall vividly the examination. The Multistate in particular calls for an approach for which law students have not been prepared, namely, to command a broad knowledge of the law and apply it all at once to a series of multiple-choice questions. For this reason, most applicants take a bar review course lasting several weeks prior to the examination itself. Whereas law students have been accustomed to limiting their study to a particular subject over the course of an academic term, the bar examination requires the applicant to recall the sum of three years of legal study.

In most states, a license to practice law is predicated on membership in the state bar association. This signifies an **integrated bar**. Because the bar also acts as a lobbying organization, some members may object when their dues are spent on political efforts with which they disagree.

Attorney Employment

The vast majority of new bar members join private law firms, but significant numbers obtain employment as government attorneys or as **house counsel** for private corporations. A few brave souls decide

---

————————————————BALLENTINE'S————————————————

black letter law   Fundamental and well-established rules of law.

integrated bar   A type of involuntary bar association that exists in some states, to which all attorneys practicing in the state must belong. Created by statute or rule of court, it is, in effect, a governmental body.

house counsel   An attorney who represents a single client, usually on a full-time basis.

John CROSETTO, et al., Plaintiffs-Appellants,
v.
STATE BAR OF WISCONSIN, et al.,
Defendants-Appellees.
United States Court of Appeals,
Seventh Circuit
12 F.3d 1396 (7th Cir. 1994)

I. Background ... .

In 1943, the Wisconsin legislature enacted a bill directing that there "shall be an association ... composed of persons licensed to practice law in this state, and membership in the association shall be a condition precedent to the right to practice law in Wisconsin." Construing the statute to be merely advisory, the Wisconsin Supreme Court initially declined to integrate the State's bar, and allowed bar association membership to remain voluntary.

By 1956, the Wisconsin Supreme Court had become concerned that "too many lawyers have refrained or refused to join [the voluntary bar association], ... and that [a] substantial minority of the lawyers in the state [were] not associated with the State Bar Association." ... [A]fter a two year trial period, the Court permanently integrated the State's bar.

A significant portion of Wisconsin lawyers opposed the Wisconsin Supreme Court's decision and filed a lawsuit alleging that Wisconsin's integrated bar violated the First Amendment. This lawsuit ultimately reached the Supreme Court of the United States. *Lathrop v. Donahue,* 367 U.S. 820 (1961). In *Lathrop,* [the justices] ... concluded that Wisconsin's integrated bar did not violate Wisconsin lawyers' First Amendment rights. ... [Nevertheless, b]y the late 1970s, resistance to Wisconsin's integrated bar became so pronounced, as the State Bar became increasingly involved in advocating various political policies, that the Wisconsin Supreme Court decided to allow all attorneys who objected to the Bar's political expenditures to reduce their membership dues according to that portion of dues spent on the objectionable political activities.

Unsatisfied by the Wisconsin Supreme Court's dues-reduction compromise, a Wisconsin lawyer filed a federal **class action** suit challenging the ... constitutionality of Wisconsin's integrated bar. *Levine v. Supreme Court of Wisconsin,* 679 F. Supp. 1478 (W.D. Wis. 1988) (hereinafter "*Levine I*"). ... [T]he district court declared that Wisconsin's mandatory bar membership rule and its Bar dues requirement facially violated all Wisconsin lawyers' First and Fourteenth Amendment rights. The district court awarded the plaintiff both compensatory and punitive damages, and enjoined the State Bar from enforcing its mandatory bar-membership rule. ... To comply with *Levine I,* the Wisconsin Supreme Court suspended enforcement of the mandatory membership rule. Following the victory in *Levine I,* the opposition lawyers filed the case here before us ... hoping to curb further the State's integrated bar.

[*Crosetto* was delayed first by *Levine II,* the appeal reversing *Levine I* and upholding *Lathrop,* and further by *Keller v. State Bar of California* in the U.S. Supreme Court, which attacked California's integrated bar.]

After the Court in *Keller* upheld California's integrated bar, the Wisconsin Bar began the process of re-integrating. ... [and] the Wisconsin Supreme Court reestablished the integrated bar, effective July 1, 1992 ... .

[*Crosetto* was disposed of because of the absolute immunity from suit of the justices of the Wisconsin Supreme Court and the qualified immunity of defendant Smay, the Executive Director of the Wisconsin Bar Association. Injunctive relief was denied largely on the grounds that the bar's procedures provided adequate means for members to file grievances with regard to dues. The case was remanded, however, on the issue of whether the state bar was in fact sufficiently vested with characteristics of state actin to qualify for **sovereign (governmental) immunity** to exempt it from being sued in federal court. The court strongly hinted that it was.]

The Wisconsin rules follow the law of *Keller* and *Hudson* in the following ways: (1) [they require] that the Bar provide written notice to all members before the beginning of each fiscal year, describing those activities the Bar has determined are chargeable and those which are non-chargeable, informing members as to the cost of those activities and describing how those amounts were calculated; (2) [they set up procedures for challenging the calculation and arbitration of disputes.] ...

Therefore because Plaintiffs have failed to identify any defect in the Wisconsin Bar's compulsory dues plan, we hold this plan constitutional both facially and as applied, and thus affirm the district court's denial of Plaintiffs' motion for injunctive relief. ...

Affirmed in part, **vacated** in part, and **remanded**.

Case Questions

1. Would an integrated bar be better than a voluntary bar at policing itself?
2. Was the failure of a minority of lawyers to join the bar a sufficient reason for integration?
3. State bar associations often engage in lobbying activities and legal activism which are opposed by some of the members. Should those members be required to subsidize political and legal activities with which they disagree?

Case Glossary

class action An action brought by one or several plaintiffs on behalf of a class of persons. A class action may be appropriate when there has been injury to so many people that their voluntarily and unanimously joining in a lawsuit is improbable and impracticable. In such a situation, injured parties who wish to do so may, with the court's permission, sue on behalf of all.

sovereign immunity The principle that the government—specifically, the United States or any state of the United States—is immune from suit except when it consents to be sued.

affirm [T]o uphold the decision or judgment of the lower court after an appeal.

vacate As applied to a judgment, decree, or other order of a court, to annul, set aside, void, or cancel.

remand The return of a case by an appellate court to the trial court for further proceedings, for a new trial, or for entry of judgment in accordance with an order of the appellate court. To return or send back.

to "hang out their shingles" and begin practicing law as sole practitioners or jointly with one or more law school colleagues. Despite three years of intensive training, few law school graduates are prepared for the demands of practice. They are unfamiliar with law office routine and management, the peculiarities of court systems, interviewing clients, negotiating settlements, and collecting for services. Successful practice requires interpersonal skills that are sorely neglected in law school. In addition, law school focuses on major legal issues presented in casebooks with national distribution. A law school graduate, before preparing for the bar exam, is likely to be totally ignorant of many areas of state law. A new lawyer is unlikely to know how to process a **bankruptcy**, do a tenant eviction, get a **zoning variance** from a city, or even conduct a real estate **closing**. Because of unfamiliarity with so many features of day-to-day practice, the new lawyer is most comfortable in the company of more experienced practitioners and their legal staff.

The competitive spirit of law school also directs many new lawyers to large firms. Already oriented toward achievement and success, graduating law students often measure themselves by starting salaries and the prestige of the law firms they join. Big city law firms compete with each other for top law school graduates, and the largest Wall Street firms offer starting salaries more than twice the average.

Fortunately for our society, not all law graduates are driven to enrich themselves. It is very common for a graduate to return to his or her home town to assume a respected position among friends and associates. Lawyers who choose this path inevitably find that the rewards of service to the community outweigh monetary compensation. The practice of law, like most other professions, offers an opportunity for personal satisfaction difficult to find in other kinds of employment.

Some law school graduates have specific goals for their training, such as preserving the environment, providing legal services to the poor, prosecuting criminals, or serving as elected legislators. The legal profession provides a unique foundation for contributing to change or improvement of one's society.

Obtaining prestigious employment, however, does not guarantee a successful career. New attorneys in a firm are called *associates*, a position from which they may never graduate. The traditional course of a legal career in a private firm entails working for a few years as an associate until invited to become a partner in the firm, which means moving from a salary to sharing in the profits of the firm. In the largest firms, only a small number of associates are ever asked to become partners. Associates who do not make partner commonly move to other firms or set up their own practices. This brutally competitive system has been improved somewhat by many firms by establishing intermediate positions like senior associate or junior

---

BALLENTINE'S

bankruptcy   The system under which a debtor may come into court or be brought into court by his or her creditors, either seeking to have his or her assets administered and sold for the benefit of ... creditors and to be discharged from his or her debts, or to have his or her debts reorganized.

zoning   The creation and application of structural, size, and use restrictions imposed upon the owners of real estate within districts or zones in accordance with ... regulations or ordinances. ... [A] form of land use regulation.

variance   In zoning law, an exception from the strict application of a zoning ordinance, granted to relieve a property owner of unnecessary hardship.

closing   Completing a transaction, particularly a contract for the sale of real estate.

partner. This allows firms to reward attorneys without forcing a partnership decision.

The pressures on attorneys to perform do not consist simply of providing good services to clients. A law firm is also a business, and attorneys who do not add significant profits to the business by way of new clients and many hours of work billable to clients are unlikely to become partners in a firm. For some, the advantage of employment with government or a private corporation is that an attorney is more often measured by the quality of work rather than the quantity of business generated.

Paralegals must understand the stresses involved in the work of attorneys in order to work better with their employers. One of the advantages of paralegal work over that of an attorney is that paralegals do not bear ultimate responsibility for the outcome of clients' problems. The difference in stress can be great. Paralegals occupy a position similar to corporate lawyers in that performance is measured by the quality of their work.

What Lawyers Do

The United States has more than a half a million lawyers. They are assisted by over one hundred thousand paralegals, whose numbers are projected to double by the year 2000. Obviously, a great deal of legal work exists to support this workforce. What exactly do lawyers do?

Acquisition of knowledge in law school is merely the first step in becoming a competent attorney; this knowledge must be put into practice. Just as the LSAT is an imprecise predictor of performance in law school, law school grades are an imperfect predictor of success in the practice of law. Even the bar examination fails to measure many qualities essential to future success. An attorney is not simply a repository of legal knowledge and technical skills. An attorney is a problem solver who must rely on imagination, creativity, common sense, and psychology as well as the analytical skills learned in school. The rules that make up the body of the law are abstractions that only take on meaning in the course of human events. Attorneys are frequently addressed as "counselor," and this perhaps comes closer than any other word to the nature of their work. Attorneys act as providers of legal services, advisors, counselors, negotiators, and agents for their clients.

The following case illustrates several features of the attorney-client relationship. Pay particular attention to how power and authority are allocated between attorney and client.

DAGNEY MANAGEMENT CORP., et al., Respondents.

v.

OPPENHEIM & MELTZER et al., Appellants.
Supreme Court, Appellate Division, Third Department.
199 A.D.2d 711, 606 N.Y.S.2d 337 (1993)

In May 1986, Stephen L. Oppenheim and Perry E. Meltzer, practicing law under the name of Oppenheim & Meltzer (hereinafter the firm), were retained by Dennis Pemberton and Dagney Management Corporation (hereinafter collectively referred to as the client) to assist in obtaining certain real property from Dolphin Development Corporation. During the course of the firm's representation of the client, the firm, inter alia, commenced an action for **specific performance** on behalf of the client against Dolphin and continued a related proceeding commenced by Pemberton before the State Human Rights Commission. In accordance with the **retainer** agreement between the client and the firm, the firm was to receive an hourly fee of $100 per hour and a **contingency fee** of 25% of any recovery of damages as counsel fees.

The client and Dolphin thereafter reached a tentative settlement whereby the property in question would be conveyed to a third party and the client would receive $75,000 out of the proceeds of the sale as damages. The firm, however, apparently believing that the client's recovery under the tentative settlement consisted of more than the sum of money disclosed, interfered with the closing on the property and, as a result, was discharged from service. The client then obtained substitute counsel, settled the underlying actions, closed on the property and received proceeds from the sale in accordance with the terms of the settlement agreement. The firm thereafter commenced actions seeking, inter alia, a judgment determining the amount of fees due from the client. The client also commenced actions against the firm, and all actions were joined for trial. At the conclusion of the nonjury trial, Supreme Court determined that the firm was discharged for cause and,

therefore, was not entitled to compensation from the client. This appeal by the firm followed.

It is well settled that "notwithstanding the terms of the agreement between them, a client has an absolute right, at any time, with or without cause, to terminate the attorney-client relationship by discharging the attorney." Where such discharge is without cause, the attorney is entitled to recover in **quantum meruit** the fair and reasonable value of the services rendered. On the other hand, "[w]here the discharge is for cause, the attorney has no right to compensation or a retaining lien, notwithstanding a specific retainer agreement."

The record ... reveals that the firm, whether in an effort to protect its contingent fee or under the guise of safeguarding its client's interests, plainly frustrated and interfered with the client's attempt to settle the underlying actions and close on the property in question. Although the firm was aware that the client had negotiated directly with the other parties involved, the firm's associate appeared at the closing and, without the client's knowledge or consent, circulated a letter directing the parties involved to immediately cease communications with the client. Additionally, the record indicates that although the firm had been advised that the entire settlement was in peril if the closing did not take place in a timely fashion, the firm nevertheless insisted that the closing not take place unless it was allowed to participate and until it was advised of the final settlement figure, thereby enabling it to calculate its contingency fee. The record further reveals that the firm refused to disclose its fee and insisted, in contravention of the client's wishes and the proposed settlement agreement, that all settlement proceeds be deposited into the firm's escrow account to be distributed by the firm at a later date.

Unquestionably, a client has the right to settle his or her cause of action with or without the attorney's consent. An attorney, by virtue of his general authority as such, has exclusive control in the conduct of the litigation in which he represents his client; his client, on the other hand, is generally conceded to have control over the subject matter of the litigation, and may at any time before judgment, if acting in good faith, compromise, settle, or adjust his cause of action out of court without his attorney's intervention, knowledge, or consent, notwithstanding any contingent fee agreement and even though he has agreed with his attorney not to do so. Based upon our review of the record as a whole, we are of the view that the firm's interference with the client's right to settle constitutes misconduct sufficient to rise to a level warranting discharge for cause and forfeiture of its fee.

Case Questions

1. What are the justifications for giving the client an absolute right to discharge the attorney?
2. What difference does it make whether an attorney is discharged for cause or without cause?
3. What is under the control of the attorney in a lawsuit and what is under the control of the client?

Case Glossary

specific performance The equitable remedy of compelling performance of a contract, as distinguished from an action at law for damages for breach of contract due to nonperformance. Specific performance may be ordered in circumstances where damages are an inadequate remedy.

retainer A preliminary fee paid to an attorney at the time he or she is retained in order to secure her services.

contingent (contingency) fee A fee for legal services, calculated on the basis of an agreed-upon percentage of the amount of money recovered for the client by his or her attorney.

quantum meruit Means "as much as is merited" or "as much as is deserved." The doctrine of *quantum meruit* makes a person liable to pay for services or goods that he or she accepts while knowing that the other party expects to be paid, even if there is no express contract. In such circumstances, the law creates an implied contract to avoid unjust enrichment.

The Lawyer as Provider of Legal Services

The public most commonly pictures the lawyer as a furnisher of services in legal problem solving. Although this may be the primary function of an attorney, the following sections reveal that attorneys also play many other roles.

The dramatic popular image of the lawyer focuses on the trial lawyer, when in actuality very few attorneys spend a significant portion of their time in court. Many lawyers never try cases, and most trial lawyers spend most of their time preparing for trial. Lawyers are basically problem solvers. Sometimes the problems are actual disputes that may lead to lawsuits and eventually to trial. Most disputes never reach the trial stage, but are settled with the lawyer acting principally as negotiator or conciliator.

Much of the work that lawyers do has nothing to do with disputes. Many client problems do not involve an adversary, but range from matters as simple as changing one's legal name to something as complicated as obtaining approval for a major airport. Potential adversaries may be lurking on the sidelines, but most problems require legal help largely because they have legal consequences. Incorporating a business must be accomplished in accordance with state law; writing a will must be done with formalities dictated by state law. Although these may be done without an attorney, it is wiser and safer to employ professional services.

Most lawyers are specialists, whether they realize it or not. Some, for instance, handle only tax matters; others, who may call themselves general practitioners, may refuse to handle criminal or divorce cases. The body of the law is immense and constantly growing. No lawyer can adequately keep up with the changes in all areas of the law. If a lawyer accepts a case in an area in which she is not expert, it is her duty to educate herself before proceeding.

Because of specialization, the distribution of legal work for any particular lawyer varies considerably, but we may make some generalizations about how lawyers spend their time. They talk with clients, first to understand the problem, then to explain its legal ramifications to the client. They write many letters—to clients, to other attorneys, to a variety of sources to request information. They are constantly reading. They read contracts furnished by their clients; they read wills and deeds and many other legal documents to assess their clients' duties, rights, and risks. They read a lot of "law," which may be focused on research for a problem or a dispute or may be designed to keep them current on areas of law of particular concern. Lawyers must be well informed about matters affecting their clients. It has been said that some lawyers specializing in **medical malpractice** cases know more about many fields of medicine than the average physician. In short, the attorney must know enough to provide competent legal representation to a client, an ethical duty imposed by the ABA Canons of Ethics and every state bar association. (See Chapter 3 on current ethical codes.)

In short, lawyers must rely on their communication skills; they talk, they write, and they read. Those who view lawyers as merely clever manipulators of words fail to recognize that a primary function of law in our society is to reduce rules of conduct to precise language that can be applied to real situations. Lawyers exercise their verbal skills with a knowledge of the law and supported by analytical training. In a legal context, words simply may not be used in the manner of casual speech. The attorney must use not only legal terms in a precise way but ordinary words as well. When dealing with the written word, attorneys read with a verbal microscope, analyzing

---
BALLENTINE'S

medical malpractice   A physician's negligent failure to observe the appropriate standard of care in providing services to a patient; also, misconduct while engaging in the practice of medicine.

each word and phrase for its legal implications. They are adept at what we might call "legal semantics." Anyone can memorize rules or fill out forms, but training, experience, and intelligence are required to use the special language of the law.

Lawyers are also organizers. Many transactions require detail and coordination. The merger of two corporations, for example, is a complex transaction that should be performed without leaving loose ends. Lawyers serve in such transactions to ensure that no legal problems will arise that could have been foreseen and avoided during the negotiations. They establish an orderly process to facilitate a smooth transition. Similarly, preparation for trial requires a step-by-step process in which all necessary information is collected and organized in a way that builds a logical and convincing presentation of the client's side of the lawsuit. As the case is built, it must be constantly reevaluated; lack of proper organization will produce poor results.

The Lawyer as Advisor

Clients consult lawyers when they feel they need legal advice. Many transactions and events take place in our society that have legal significance, and common sense dictates that they be entrusted at least in part to someone knowledgeable in their legal ramifications. Probably most of these involve property transactions in some way, but those who are accused of a crime or are seeking compensation for injury can best protect their interests by employing an attorney.

A person making a will or buying a residence is involved in important property planning. For most, purchasing a home constitutes the largest investment of a lifetime, and the consequences of such a transaction should not be left to chance and ignorance. This transaction involves two principal areas of law—the law of real property and the law of contracts. Property law has evolved over many centuries and contains many relics of the past that present hidden traps for the unwary. The buyer may be presented with a standard contract for sale that provides reasonable protections for buyer and seller, or may be confronted with a contract that was designed primarily for the benefit of the seller. In either case, it is unlikely that the buyer understands the full import of the many clauses contained in the document. An attorney well-versed in property law can explain the contract and advise the client about its possible dangers and how to deal with them.

As an advisor in these circumstances, the attorney does not give only legal advice. The attorney is likely to have a wealth of practical knowledge that has nothing to do with law, strictly speaking, such as the current state of local real estate prices, the most favorable mortgage rates, and planned or proposed development in the area. The attorney may know that the airport is about to change its flight paths in such a way that flights will pass directly over the home in question. Such information may be more valuable to a client than the explanation of rights and duties or the legal consequences of the contract itself.

Attorneys may be successful for many reasons, including politics and even luck, but most attorneys succeed because they provide valuable services. They are in a position to acquire a great deal of practical knowledge because they deal on a daily basis with countless problems that arise in the course of practice. An attorney who specializes in wills and **trusts**, for example, has seen countless examples of what can happen when someone dies if relatives and in-laws fight over the deceased's **estate**. Writing a will for a client may appear to be a technical legal matter, yet an attorney's knowledge of human nature will influence the legal advice given.

This role of the lawyer as personal, practical advisor is also important with business clients. Many businesses frequently require legal help. Not only are they concerned with making contracts and buying and selling, but they must also be concerned with employee relations, government regulation, and taxation, not to mention the type of business organization that is appropriate to the enterprise. It is common for a close relationship to develop between an attorney and a business client. The attorney comes to understand the business and its needs, and the client often turns to the attorney for advice of a business and personal nature. The client also enjoys the **attorney-client privilege**, which allows the client to treat the attorney as a confidante who may be told matters that could not be disclosed to anyone else.

The Lawyer as Counselor

The role of counselor includes the role of advisor and more. The term is commonly used to refer to legal counsel, but in fact attorneys are often called upon to do much more. Certain areas of the practice of law entail personal counseling skills beyond legal skills, most notably divorce law. Lawyers must be prepared for the fact that clients deliver problems to them that the clients are not competent to handle themselves. When dealing with a client seeking divorce or one accused of a crime, the lawyer must be aware that the client is dealing with intensely emotional personal

---

————BALLENTINE'S————

trust   A fiduciary relationship involving a trustee who holds trust property for the benefit or use of a beneficiary.

estate   The right, title, and interest a person has in real or personal property, either tangible or intangible.

attorney-client privilege   Most information a client tells his or her attorney in connection with his or her case cannot be disclosed by the attorney, or anyone employed by the attorney or the attorney's firm, without the client's permission.

problems as well as immediate legal problems. Law school training rarely prepares the new attorney for this kind of conflict.

Although the function of the lawyer is to resolve a client's legal difficulties, the close personal and confidential relationship that often develops between lawyer and client can put the attorney in a role similar to that of a mental health counselor. Some lawyers avoid this role by taking a distant, strictly professional attitude toward their clients, but others feel that this can seem callous and insensitive to a client who may be very much in need of caring and understanding. To a person who may be full of guilt and pain and have low self-esteem, personal rejection by the person they are looking to for solutions can make them feel very alone.

On the surface, the lawyer's responsibility would seem to end with the furnishing of legal services, but the nature of the relationship between attorney and client affects the quality of the services rendered. A divorcing spouse or an incarcerated person may well be in an emotional state that weakens his or her ability to achieve a reasonable legal solution. Persons suing for compensation for personal injury often face loss of work, medical expenses, and other financial difficulties that render them vulnerable to unfair negotiations with an insurance company or corporation that views the dispute as merely a business transaction. An attorney insensitive to these personal problems may do a client a disservice.

Attorneys must also learn that a fine line must be drawn between caring and understanding and emotional involvement with a client's problems. It is one thing to have a personal relationship with a client and quite another to have a social or even romantic relationship. Taking a cue from mental health counselors, the lawyer should maintain a professional attitude without losing sight of the fact that clients are human beings deserving respect and understanding.

The Lawyer as Negotiator

The attorney must give a client the best representation possible. In the adversarial legal system, a lawyer often appears to be the "hired gun," using all the tricks of the trade to destroy the opposing party. This picture misrepresents the role of the lawyer, who is more often a negotiator, mediator, and conciliator. In a personal injury case, for example, the attorney must weigh a number of factors besides winning. If a person injured in an auto accident is suing an insurance company, both sides will have made an estimate of reasonable compensation. Their estimates are based on past experience, both in negotiations and with awards made by juries and judges. If the initial estimates, which are kept secret, are close, it is likely that the two sides can come to an early agreement. If this happens, a number of advantages accrue to the client.

First, the client will not experience the considerable unpleasantness of a trial. Second, the client will not endure prolonged negotiations. Third, the expenses, including attorneys' fees, will be minimized.

The client in this case is best served by an attorney who is a persuasive negotiator and can convince the other parties that it is in their best interests to present reasonable offers of compensation. The attorney not only negotiates with the insurance company's attorney but must also apprise the client of the risks and strategies on both sides, so that the client has reasonable expectations. Although the client must make the final decision to accept or reject an offer of settlement, the attorney commonly acts as a mediator between the two sides, ultimately persuading the client that an offer should be accepted. It should be noted, however, that some insurance companies adopt a strategy of nonnegotiation, in which case the plaintiff's attorney must assume an aggressive and threatening posture.

The adversarial role is especially problematic in divorce cases. The legal process of divorce tends to aggravate an already painful and frequently hostile relationship between husband and wife. The best interests of clients go beyond maximizing economic benefits and parental rights. If minor children are involved, the divorcing couple need to establish at least a minimal basis of cooperation for the children's sake. A court battle is likely to leave everyone severely scarred emotionally. Nowhere are ethical and professional duties more perplexing than in divorce law. Divorce does not make unhappy people happy. Perhaps no area of the practice of law produces so many dissatisfied clients. Interpersonal skills in negotiation, mediation, and conciliation are just as essential as legal skills in this field.

Negotiating skills are essential in commercial law as well. In business and real estate transactions, in contracts, and in structuring business organizations, the objective is usually to establish agreement among all concerned within the requirements of the law. Though different parties have different self-interests, business transactions are normally entered into because everyone benefits. The attorney acts as a facilitator and negotiator, at the same time protecting the client's interests. In some long-standing business relationships based on personal trust, legal counsel may actually be intrusive. If agreements have been customarily cemented with a handshake, the sudden appearance of a contract written by an attorney may be insulting and could damage the relationship. Again, the lawyer's legal skills must be tempered with sensitivity.

It has often been said that the attorney who represents himself has a fool for a lawyer. How much more foolish it is when a nonlawyer attempts to represent herself. The *Blair* case gives some inkling of the procedural pitfalls of representing oneself. Although this case speaks for the right to represent oneself in court, note that historically the greater struggle was to obtain the right to counsel.

Myrtle Sue BLAIR
v.
Elliott E. MAYNARD, Judge.
Supreme Court of Appeals of West Virginia
174 W. Va. 247, 324 S.E.2d 391 (1984)

1. Under [the state constitution], the right of self-representation in civil proceedings is a fundamental right which cannot be arbitrarily or unreasonably denied.

2. The fundamental right of self-representation recognized in [the state constitution] may not be denied without a clear showing in the record that the **pro se** litigant is engaging in a course of conduct which demonstrates a clear intention to obstruct the administration of justice.

[T]he petitioner, Myrtle Sue Blair, seeks a **writ of mandamus** to compel the respondent, Judge Elliott E. Maynard of the Circuit Court of Mingo County, to allow her to appear pro se in a civil action brought by the petitioner in that court. A trial in this case was previously begun in which the petitioner was acting as her own counsel. An early **mistrial** resulted, however, when the petitioner made certain improper remarks in her **opening statement** to the jury. ... Subsequently, the respondent informed the petitioner that the case would be set again for trial only when she had an attorney to assist her. The respondent maintains that, due to the petitioner's limited experience and the legal complexities of this particular case, allowing the petitioner to continue to appear as her own counsel will likely result in more mistrials, unfairly imposing additional burden and expense upon the defendants. The petitioner, also citing economic reasons, wishes to continue pro se.

I

Self-representation by a litigant was formerly a duty rather than a privilege or right. Preceding the gradual evolution of the legal profession, the common law requirement was that a party "should appear and conduct his own cause in his own words." Even long after the establishment of the legal profession, self-representation often maintained a preferred, if not mandatory, status. ...

For a variety of legal and cultural reasons, "it was only gradually that an attorney was allowed to take the place of his client for all purposes."

Justice Stewart, in *Faretta v. California*, 422 U.S. 806, 95 S. Ct. 2525, 45 L. Ed. 2d 562 (1975), concisely summarized the early American experience. In the American Colonies the insistence upon a right of self-representation was, if anything, more fervent than in England. The colonists brought with them an appreciation of the virtues of self-reliance and a traditional distrust of lawyers. ... This prejudice gained strength in the Colonies where "distrust of lawyers became an institution." ... The prejudice persisted into the 18th century as "the lower classes came to identify lawyers with the upper class." The years of Revolution and Confederation saw an upsurge of antilawyer sentiment, a "sudden revival, after the War of Revolution, of the old dislike and distrust of lawyers as a class." In the heat of these sentiments the Constitution was forged. This is not to say that the Colonies were slow to recognize the value of counsel in criminal cases. Colonial judges soon departed from ancient English practice and allowed accused felons the aid of counsel for their defense. At the same time, however, the basic right of self-representation was never questioned. We have found no instance where a colonial court required a defendant in a criminal case to accept as his representative an unwanted lawyer. Indeed, even where counsel was permitted, the general practice continued to be self-representation. ...

The right, claimed by the petitioner herein, to act as her own attorney in civil proceedings, although derived from a different source, stands on equal footing with the parallel right accorded the criminally accused under [the state constitution]. ... This provision "contemplates that every person ... shall have recourse to the courts to seek redress of his injuries." This constitutional right of access to the courts is not limited to those persons able and willing to employ an attorney. Litigants who, by choice or necessity, seek to advocate their own cause cannot be denied this fundamental right. As observed by another court, "the right to self-representation embodies one of the most cherished ideals of our culture; the right of an individual to determine his own destiny." "Like most fundamental freedoms, the right to proceed pro se derives from the belief that respect for human dignity is best served by respect for individual freedom of choice." ...

Today ... we hold that under [the state constitution], the right of self-representation in civil proceedings is a fundamental right which cannot be arbitrarily or unreasonably denied.

II

Although the right to appear pro se is available to all **natural persons** wishing to exercise this option, it cannot be employed in a manner which unreasonably interferes with the duty of the trial court to supervise and control judicial proceedings to ensure fairness to all parties. The countervailing interests which are present in any adversarial proceeding pose special circumstances for a trial court when a party chooses to appear pro se. Furthermore, these concerns are particularly heightened when the right to a jury trial is demanded, as is the case here.

However, trial courts possess a discretionary range of control over parties and proceedings which will allow reasonable accommodations to pro se litigants without resultant prejudice to adverse parties. Pro se parties, like other litigants, should be provided the opportunity to have their cases "fully and fairly heard so far as such latitude is consistent with the just rights of any adverse party."

We are not proposing that trial judges should become surrogate attorneys for pro se litigants. The fundamental tenet that the rules of procedure should work to do substantial justice, however, commands that judges painstakingly strive to insure that no person's cause or defense is defeated solely by reason of their unfamiliarity with procedural or evidentiary rules.

Of course, the court must not overlook the rules to the prejudice of any party. The court should strive, however, to ensure that the diligent pro se party does not forfeit any substantial rights by inadvertent omission or mistake. Cases should be decided on the merits, and to that end, justice is served by reasonably accommodating all parties, whether represented by counsel or not. This "reasonable accommodation" is purposed upon protecting the meaningful exercise of a litigant's constitutional right of access to the courts. Therefore, ultimately, the pro se litigant must bear the responsibility and accept the consequences of any mistakes and errors. ...

In the underlying case, the petitioner's remarks which precipitated the declaration of a mistrial have not been shown to be anything other than an excusable mistake. While it may be more likely that such a mistake would be committed by a pro se litigant, similar errors are not uncommonly committed by even experienced attorneys. Prohibiting this petitioner from again appearing to present her case is an unreasonably harsh measure under these circumstances.

Accordingly ... , we grant the writ of mandamus.

Case Questions

1. How does a judge ensure fairness when one party is represented by legal counsel and the other is pro se?
2. Why are some matters kept from the jury?
3. What reason does the court give for granting the writ of mandamus?

Case Glossary

pro se Means "for one's self." Refers to appearing on one's own behalf in either a civil action or a criminal prosecution, rather than being represented by an attorney.

writ A written order issued by a court directing the person to whom it is addressed to do a specified act.

mandamus Means "we command." A writ issuing from a court of competent jurisdiction, directed to an inferior court, board, or corporation, or to an officer of a branch of government ... , requiring the performance of some ministerial act.

mistrial A trial that has been terminated by the judge prior to its conclusion ... because of prejudicial error that cannot be corrected or eliminated by any action the court might take ... . A mistrial is the equivalent of no trial having been held.

opening statement A statement made by the attorney for each party at the beginning of a trial, outlining to the judge and jury the issues in the case and the facts that each side intends to prove.

natural person A human being, as distinguished from an artificial person created by law, such as a corporation.

Summary

In this chapter we have seen that law school training and admission to the bar are merely the first steps in becoming a competent attorney. Although law school imparts a basic knowledge of important fields of the law, it emphasizes the development of analytical skills and does not provide either training for the daily tasks of the practice of law or the communication skills necessary for rendering valuable legal services.

Attorneys are paid for their communication skills. Most of their time is spent talking, writing, and reading, but law is a specialized language that must be used with care and precision. Words have legal implications often fully appreciated only by lawyers. Clients' goals are facilitated by lawyers who rephrase their wishes in language that establishes legal rights and duties, whether in a business contract, a will, or a divorce settlement.

Lawyers are problem-solvers; they help remove the legal hurdles from a client's path. Sometimes this means fighting a legal battle in court to protect a client's interests, but more often it involves resolving a dispute without going to trial. Perhaps attorneys spend an even greater portion of their time preventing disputes and aiding in personal and business transactions by anticipating potential conflicts and either eliminating them or providing for their amicable resolution.

The practice of law entails many skills that are not taught in law school and are often absent from the popular image of the lawyer.

These are primarily interpersonal communication skills that cast the attorney in the role of advisor, counselor, and negotiator. Lawyers regularly find themselves in difficult and complex situations that call for stamina, intelligence, patience, creativity, and, most of all, an understanding of human nature.

CONFIDENTIALITY AND THE CORPORATE PARALEGAL

Angela Schneeman

Maintaining client confidentiality is one of the most important rules of ethics that paralegals must follow. Information revealed by a client to an attorney during the course of a legal consultation is privileged and may only be disclosed with the consent of the client, or when special circumstances provide an exception to the rule. Keeping client information confidential is a basic concept, but practical application of the rule often proves to be more complex. A demanding client or a pushy reporter can further complicate matters. Corporate paralegals face ethical dilemmas dealing with client confidentiality daily.

Considerations Unique to Corporate Paralegals

In addition to concerns faced by all paralegals, corporate paralegals must concern themselves with questions of confidentiality unique to the representation of corporations. The corporate paralegal's duty to maintain client confidentiality is complicated by the fact that the client is an entity and not an individual.

As a corporate paralegal, you may from time to time be involved in facilitating corporate mergers and acquisitions, anything from the sale of a small family-held business to the merger of two or more mega-corporations. The slightest hint of a merger or acquisition can lead reporters, employees, and others who may be affected by the transaction to seek out information that must be kept confidential until the appropriate time. Rumors regarding mergers and acquisitions can have a devastating effect on the outcome of a proposed transaction, as well as an effect on the price of the stock of either or both of the companies involved.

Paralegals who work in the securities area must also be aware of the damage that can be done by leaking even the smallest piece of information concerning their clients. Unauthorized leaks of information from a law firm representing publicly held corporations, or corporations that are planning public offerings, can have significant financial implications for the client. All information regarding a publicly held corporation must be carefully monitored and released only with forethought. Information passed on to third parties regarding publicly held corporations may be considered "insider information" and could subject individuals purchasing stock based on that information to civil suits, criminal prosecution, or both.

The very nature of the corporate client complicates the requirement of maintaining client confidentiality. A corporation is not an individual with whom you may have confidential discussions. It is important that the attorney who represents the corporation keep you informed about whom you may communicate with within the corporation.

While it would be a safe approach not to release corporate client information to anyone, it would make the corporate paralegal's job impossible. As a corporate paralegal, you must assume a certain degree of responsibility for the client information entrusted to you. The best course of action to take when beginning work for a new client or on a new file is to specifically address client confidentiality with the responsible attorney by having the following questions answered:

- Who will your contacts within the corporation be?
- Are there any other individuals or organizations involved with whom you may discuss the client's file (such as accountants, etc.)?
- Are there other attorneys and paralegals with whom you may discuss the client's file (in-house or outside counsel)?
- Is there any specific information that may not be discussed with your contacts?
- Is there any specific type of documentation that may not be released to your contacts?

Getting these questions answered will give you the information you need to make responsible decisions to maintain client confidentiality. When in doubt, it is always best to ask.

CHAPTER 3

ETHICS

Introduction

The study of ethics is a branch of philosophy. The ethics discussed in this chapter is more appropriately labeled *legal ethics*, which has developed over the last century from an intuitive sense of duty and responsibility to an explicit set of rules governing the professional conduct of attorneys. Violation of the rules subjects attorneys to disciplinary action.

Because paralegals are not members of the bar, they have no licenses that can be suspended or revoked. An understanding of ethical principles is nonetheless vitally important for paralegals because unethical conduct may result in serious problems for them, the attorneys they work for, and the clients they serve. For example, a paralegal who gives legal advice may be prosecuted by the state for unauthorized practice of law, and the paralegal's supervising attorney may be disciplined for negligent supervision. If the advice is faulty, the client receiving that advice may suffer a detriment, the supervising lawyer and law firm may be sued for malpractice, and the paralegal's career may come to a sudden end.

It must be cautioned at the outset that a strong sense of right and wrong will not guarantee avoidance of the violation of professional ethics, though it certainly minimizes the danger. The practice of law involves duties to clients, to the public, to the courts, and to colleagues. Lawyers have access to sensitive, confidential information about their clients, information that must often necessarily be shared with law office staff. In the representation of clients, attorneys are frequently faced with ethical dilemmas that are not easily solved. Ethical codes are designed to provide answers to most of these dilemmas, but they cannot precisely address every possible situation. Clients can be unpredictable and even unscrupulous, consciously or unconsciously putting attorneys in positions that lead to unfavorable outcomes. It is only by strictly following the ethical codes and acting in utmost good faith that attorneys can avoid the many traps that the practice of law entails.

In the last two decades, the legal profession has expended great effort to define and refine the principles governing the ethical conduct of attorneys. More than any other profession, the legal profession has embarked on a campaign to identify and police unethical conduct and fulfill its primary duty of serving the public and the legal system.

In the discussion that follows, the subject of legal ethics in general is covered, but greatest attention is given to those areas of particular concern to paralegals.

History of Ethical Rules

Formulating ethical principles has been an ongoing task of the American Bar Association, which established Canons of Ethics as early as 1908. The ABA has no disciplinary authority, but it is the appropriate forum for discussing ethical principles because it represents the bar nationwide. The Canons are general statements of principle urging proper conduct. They have been elaborated over the years through the addition and amendment of *Disciplinary Rules* and *Ethical Considerations,* which describe more specifically conduct that is subject to discipline (Disciplinary Rules) and conduct that, though improper, is not subject to discipline (Ethical Considerations).

In 1970, these principles crystallized in the ABA's *Model Code of Professional Responsibility* and were quickly adopted by nearly all states. Once these principles were adopted, the Multistate Bar Examination devised a separate ethics test, which most states then made a part of their state bar examination. The ABA additionally provided advisory opinions on specific applications of the *Model Code,* and many state bar associations have similarly answered ethical questions posed by their members in formal opinions.

In 1983, after several years of intense study and dialogue, the ABA reformulated legal ethics in the *Model Rules of Professional Conduct.* The *Model Rules* (as distinguished from the earlier *Model Code*) attempted to reflect changes in the legal profession; for instance, the former prohibition against advertising legal services was found by the U.S. Supreme Court to be an unconstitutional invasion of freedom of speech. The *Model Rules* also addressed conduct more specifically, narrowing the principles to increase clarity and enforceability. The *Model Rules* did away with *Disciplinary Rules* and *Ethical Considerations,* substituting "shall" and "shall not" ("a lawyer shall not seek to influence a judge, juror ... except as permitted by law or the rules of court") as language warranting disciplinary action and "may" ("a lawyer may refuse to offer evidence that the lawyer reasonably believes is false") as language expressing conduct that is discretionary and not subject to disciplinary action.

The *Model Code* must be discussed along with the more recent *Model Rules* for three reasons:

1. The basic principles are quite similar.
2. Because the *Model Code* was the initial set of rules adopted in the states, a host of opinions and judicial decisions serve as precedents for interpretations of the *Rules.*

3. The *Model Rules* have not received the same degree of acceptance from state bar associations as the *Model Code* enjoyed previously.

The Model Code and the Model Rules

The Canons of Professional Responsibility of the *Model Code* are listed here with corresponding sections of the *Model Rules*. Although the same issues are addressed, a comparison reveals a distinct difference. The Canons somewhat resemble the Ten Commandments, a moral code to live by, whereas the *Model Rules* reflect a more sophisticated legislative approach, organized into related subject areas with specific proscriptions that provide better guidance to disciplinary boards and tribunals. The *Model Rules* are eminently more practical, both in terms of enforcement and in terms of the clarity provided to attorneys.

Keep in mind that the Canons were extensively supplemented by *Disciplinary Rules* and *Ethical Considerations* that spelled out specific problems. Nor does displaying the *Model Rules* in this way show their higher degree of organization. The *Model Rules* were published with supplementary comments that address problems routinely confronted by attorneys and are a practical improvement over the *Model Code* as guidelines for attorneys. Nevertheless, because the *Model Rules* are more specific and more clearly enforceable, not all sectors of the bar have been satisfied with them, and the states have not received the *Model Rules* with the same wholehearted approval that the *Model Code* received.

Codes for Legal Assistants

Legal assistant organizations have also formulated ethical codes designed specifically for paralegals. Deborah Orlik in *Ethics for the Legal Assistant* (1986) describes these as "overly broad and moralistic." This is undoubtedly due to their lack of enforceability, as they have no official or legal force. Making specific prohibitions that cannot be enforced is problematic. Additionally, the paralegal associations must as yet function reactively to the bar associations, which set the standards for lawyers, including the lawyers' responsibility for supervision of their legal staffs.

The National Association of Legal Assistants (NALA) followed its earlier *Code of Ethics and Professional Responsibility* with the 1984 *Model Standards and Guidelines for Legal Assistants*. The National Federation of

Paralegal Associations (NFPA) published an *Affirmation of Responsibility.* In general, the substantive sections of both codes are derivative of the ethical principles embodied by the ABA codes. As a practical matter, the paralegal should concentrate on the ABA codes, because the paralegal is not simply concerned about ethical conduct but also is concerned about conduct that would put a supervising attorney in an ethical dilemma.

MODEL CODE AND MODEL RULES COMPARED

Model Code of Professional Responsibility	*Model Rules of Professional Conduct*
Canons:	**Rules:**
1. A lawyer should assist in maintaining the integrity and competence of the legal profession.	*8 Maintaining the integrity of the profession.*
	8.3 Reporting professional misconduct. (a) A lawyer having knowledge that another lawyer has committed a violation of the Rules of Professional Conduct ... shall inform the appropriate professional authority.
2. A lawyer should assist the legal profession in fulfilling its duty to make legal counsel available.	*6 Public service.* *6.1 Pro bono publico service.* A lawyer should render public interest legal service ...
	6.2 Accepting appointments. A lawyer shall not seek to avoid appointment by a tribunal to represent a person except for good cause ...
3. A lawyer should assist in preventing the unauthorized practice of law.	*5.5 Unlicensed (or unauthorized?) practice of law.* A lawyer shall not: (a) practice in a jurisdiction where doing so violates the regulation of the legal profession in that jurisdiction; or (b) assist a person who is not a member of the bar in the performance of activity that constitutes the unauthorized practice of law.
4. A lawyer should preserve the confidences and secrets of a client.	*1.6 Confidentiality of information.* (a) A lawyer shall not reveal information relating to representation of a client ... unless the client consents after disclosure to the client.

5. A lawyer should exercise independent professional judgment on behalf of a client.

5.4 Professional independence of a lawyer.

(a) A lawyer or law firm shall not share legal fees with a nonlawyer, except ...

(b) A lawyer shall not form a partnership with a nonlawyer if any of the activities of the partnership consist of the practice of law.

(c) A lawyer shall not permit a person who recommends, employs, or pays the lawyer to render legal services for another to direct or regulate the lawyer's professional judgment in rendering such legal services.

6. A lawyer should represent a client competently.

1.1 Competence. A lawyer shall provide competent representation to a client. Competent representation requires the legal knowledge, skill, thoroughness, and preparation reasonably necessary for the representation.

7. A lawyer should represent a client zealously within the bounds of the law.

[Canon 7 is arguably spread among the many subsections of Rules 1 (Client-Lawyer Relationship), 2 (Counselor), and 3 (Advocate).]

8. A lawyer should assist in improving the legal system.

[Canon 8 is primarily exhortatory rather than disciplinary and is implied in many of the Rules and the Preamble.]

9. A lawyer should avoid even the appearance of professional impropriety.

[The vagueness of Canon 9 has been resolved by addressing specific improprieties within the Rules.]

Disclosure

Many ethical problems can be resolved or mitigated by full disclosure to clients. Many conflict-of-interest situations may be eliminated by disclosure of the conflict to the client and opposing party and consent by both to continued representation. Even if an attorney represents a client in the mistaken belief that the ethical problem has been resolved, evidence of full disclosure indicates a good faith attempt by the attorney to resolve the ethical problem and may mitigate any resulting disciplinary action.

In addition to disclosure to the parties, ethical questions over which some uncertainty exists may be addressed to an appropriate state bar ethics committee for an opinion on the ethical issues, if such a procedure is available.

Defining the Practice of Law

The practice of law may be defined in two ways as it relates to professional ethics. The first definition addresses the question of whether an attorney is rendering legal services. For example, a lawyer may engage in mediation activities (see Chapter 15), which does not entail providing legal services and therefore is not covered by legal ethics per se, but any linkage of mediation services and the practice of law raises ethical problems. For example, an attorney might mediate a divorce between husband and wife and then represent one of them in the divorce or refer them to the attorney's firm for representation. Such action would invoke ethical problems of conflict of interest and confidentiality constituting a serious breach of ethics. Thus, an attorney may engage in activities other than the practice of law, but such activities must be consistent with the attorney's professional responsibilities.

The practice of law is defined differently when addressing the question of the unauthorized practice of law. In this instance, it is not so much what lawyers do as what may be done *only* by lawyers that defines the practice of law. For ethical purposes, the practice of law is best defined in the context of unauthorized practice of law, which is subject to criminal and civil sanctions by the court. In applying these sanctions, the courts have been forced to address the definition of the practice of law.

Unauthorized Practice of Law

The following discussion should be supplemented with a review of the comments already made on this subject in Chapter 1.

Each state restricts the practice of law to licensed attorneys and provides for a penalty, commonly criminal, to enforce these prohibitions. The problem lies in defining what constitutes the practice of law, which varies widely among the states. From an ethical standpoint, the restrictions on providing legal services can be justified only by an interest in protecting the public and not in preserving a professional monopoly. There are two issues in protecting the public: (1) the public should be protected against incompetence, and (2) some agency, usually a court, must have the power to protect the public. Licensing protects the public by requiring a level of competence necessary to obtain the license and by establishing authority to revoke the license for misconduct. Those without licenses can be punished for practicing law.

Lawyers are agents of their clients; they can represent clients before the court, sign certain documents on behalf of their clients, and act as direct contacts in matters in which they represent their clients. Because of this agency relationship, the lawyer is held to ethical standards in representing clients and can be disciplined for misconduct, even sued by the client for breach of the limits of the relationship. Abuse of the representation can have serious consequences to the client and so justifies this control over attorney misconduct. Unlicensed persons providing legal services are much less subject to the scrutiny of the court and the profession.

The practice of law is much less narrow than the practice of other professions, such as medicine and dentistry. For example, lawyers give advice on the conduct of personal and business affairs, but so do many others, such as accountants, real estate brokers, stock brokers, insurance agents, bankers, etc. These persons commonly give advice concerning the legal consequences of their clients' personal and business decisions. In fact, advice that could be considered legal is furnished by just about everyone. Anyone arrested for speeding, anyone buying land, or anyone getting a divorce can find many people offering advice on the legal aspects of each of these. When are such people practicing law?

The answer to this question is by no means easy, as a review of court cases on unauthorized practice of law attests. It is not sufficient to define the practice of law, as some early cases did, as what lawyers traditionally do. Lawyers do a great many things that do not require legal expertise. For the purposes of unauthorized practice of law, the issue has come down to identifying what it is that only lawyers may do. Although the states vary considerably on the specific activities restricted to lawyers, three activities are universally identified:

1. Legal representation before a court.
2. Preparation of legal documents.
3. Giving legal advice.

Note that the first two categories relate to the attorney-client agency relationship under control of the court, whereas the third category is concerned with legal competence.

For instance, Louisiana regulates the practice of law with the following statutes:

> It is a crime for a non-lawyer to practice law, hold himself out as an attorney, or advertise that he alone or jointly has an office for the practice of law.

La. Rev. Stat. Ann. § 37:213.

> The practice of law is defined as appearing as an advocate, drawing papers, pleadings or documents, performing any act in connection with pending or prospective court proceedings or, if done for consideration, the advising on the "secular" law and doing any act on behalf of another tending to obtain or secure the prevention or redress of a wrong or the enforcement or establishment of a right.

La. Rev. Stat. Ann. § 37:212.

Legal Representation Before a Court

Because of the technical requirement of procedural law, as well as the intricacies of specific kinds of lawsuits, a litigant without a lawyer is severely disadvantaged, especially if the opposing party has legal representation. In our legal system, it is not required that a person have an attorney to bring or defend a suit, but a person may not be represented by someone other than a licensed attorney. The court relies on the competence and accountability of attorneys.

A successful outcome to a trial generally requires legal skills, experience, and knowledge of a high order; the adversarial system does not work fairly when one of the parties lacks legal representation. However, many nontrial court appearances involve routine matters that do not involve legal argument or expertise and could easily be managed by legal staff acting on behalf of an attorney at a great savings to clients without risk.

The appearance of the attorney in court is certainly necessary when a legal argument may ensue or rights and duties of clients are decided, otherwise the court need only be reassured that an attorney is ultimately responsible for the action taken. The legal system and the practice of law would be more efficient and less costly if paralegals were authorized to perform a number of routine tasks. Nevertheless, no paralegal should ever appear in court to represent a client unless absolutely certain that this is permissible.

Many administrative agencies, like the Social Security Administration, permit representation by any person of the claimant's choosing. Before undertaking such representation, a paralegal should ascertain the extent and scope of such representation under the agency's rules and regulations and make certain the person represented consents (in writing) to such representation with full knowledge that the paralegal is not a member of the bar.

Although the *Alexander* case is more than thirty years old, the court struggles with a continuing problem: What is, and what is not, the practice of law? The law student clerk charged with unauthorized practice of law might today be described as a paralegal. The trial court took a broad view of the practice of law, a protectionist attitude toward the bar, and was perhaps affronted by the appearance of a nonlawyer in

**PEOPLE of the State of Illinois,
Plaintiff—Appellee,
v.
Walton ALEXANDER, Defendant-
Appellant.
Appellate Court of Illinois, First District,
Fourth Division
53 Ill. App. 2d 299, 202 N.E.2d 841 (1964)**

This is an appeal from a judgment order adjudging defendant guilty of contempt of court for the unauthorized practice of law. The Supreme Court transferred this case to our court and it is to be considered here as a direct contempt.

Defendant is a clerk employed by a firm of attorneys and is not licensed as a lawyer, although he is studying to be an attorney. On October 19, 1962, defendant was present in court when the case of *Ryan v. Monson* was called. Thereafter, he prepared an order spreading of record the fact that after a trial of the case of *Ryan v. Monson* the jury had disagreed and continuing the case until October 22. The trial judge added to that order "a mistrial declared."

Before entering the contempt order, the court issued a rule to **show cause** and a hearing was held at which only defendant testified. He was examined by his attorney, cross-examined and also interrogated by the judge. ...

In his testimony defendant stated that after the case was called on October 19, he and plaintiff's attorney in the *Ryan v. Monson* case stepped up; that the judge inquired whether they knew of the disagreement by the jury; that the court requested that an order be prepared spreading the mistrial of record; that both defendant and plaintiff's lawyer sat down at a counsel's table and defendant wrote the order which they then presented to the judge in **chambers**.

An order of court reciting the verdict of a jury or setting out its failure to agree on a verdict is the responsibility of the court and the court clerk is usually ordered by the court to enter an order showing the result of a jury's deliberations. This is reflected in *Freeport Motor Casualty Co. v. Tharp,* 406 Ill. 295, at 299, 94 N.E.2d 139, at 141... .

The preparation of an order, in the instant case, with the collaboration of opposing counsel was a ministerial act for the benefit of the court and a mere recordation of what had transpired. We cannot hold that this conduct of defendant constituted the unauthorized practice of law.

The opinion of the trial court also states as a basis for contempt that on October 22 the judge inquired of defendant whether the case of *Ryan v. Monson* was settled and that defendant answered in the negative. It appears that on that date the court held the case for trial. Defendant testified that he advised the court that the trial attorney was actually engaged in a trial in the Federal Court. The court held that the appearance of defendant constituted the unauthorized practice of law.

Plaintiff contends that any appearance by a non-lawyer before a court for the purpose of apprising the court of an engagement of counsel or transmitting to the court information supplied by the attorney in the case regarding the availability of counsel or the status of the case is the unauthorized practice of law.

... In the case of *People ex rel. Illinois State Bar Ass'n v. People's Stock Yards State Bank,* 344 Ill. 462, at page 476, 176 N.E. 901, at page 907, wherein a bank was prosecuted for the unauthorized practice of law, the following quotation is relied upon:

> "According to the generally understood definition of the practice of law in this country, it embraces the preparation of pleadings, and other papers incident to actions and special proceedings, and the management of such actions and proceedings on behalf of clients before judges and courts * * *."

Since this statement relates to the appearance and management of proceedings in court on behalf of a client, we do not believe it can be applied to a situation where a clerk hired by a law firm presents information to the court on behalf of his employer.

We agree with the trial judge that clerks should not be permitted to make **motions** or participate in other proceedings which can be considered as "managing" the litigation. However, if apprising the court of an employer's engagement or inability to be present constitutes the making of a motion, we must hold that clerks may make such motions for continuances without being guilty of the unauthorized practice of law. Certainly with the large volume of cases appearing on the trial calls these days, it is imperative that this practice be followed.

Case Questions

1. The court distinguishes between appearance in court "in behalf of a client" and appearance "in behalf of the attorney-employer." Is this a relevant distinction?
2. Is there an implied distinction between "management of proceedings" and routine clerical activities? What is meant by "ministerial act"?

Case Glossary

show cause To comply with an order to show cause by appearing before the court and presenting facts and legal arguments for the purpose of influencing the court not to take a certain action adverse to the party making the appearance.

chambers The private office of a judge, where parties are heard and orders are entered in matters not required to be brought into open court.

motion An application made to a court for the purpose of obtaining an order or rule directing something to be done in favor of the applicant. The types of motions available to litigants, as well as their form and the matters they appropriately address, are set forth in detail in the Federal Rules of Civil Procedure and the rules of civil procedure of the various states, as well as in the Federal Rules of Criminal Procedure and the various states' rules of criminal procedure. Motions may be written or oral, depending on the type of relief sought and on the court in which they are made.

the courtroom. The appellate court, however, showed a progressive attitude toward the allocation of legal services benefiting the bench, the bar, and the public.

Note that the individual in question was not prosecuted for unauthorized practice of law but was disciplined by the court for contempt of court, a sanction available to a judge for punishing misconduct in court.

Preparation of Legal Documents

This category refers to "preparation of legal instruments and contracts by which legal rights are secured." A major function of paralegals is the preparation of such documents; real estate agents ordinarily prepare contracts for sale that allocate legal rights and duties in great detail; and accountants prepare tax forms. So the word "preparation" may be a poor choice, as it is not the preparation per se that is at issue but the final product at the time it takes legal effect. The person who takes ultimate responsibility for the document must be licensed to practice law.

In many instances, paralegals prepare documents that are signed by attorneys. There is no ethical problem with this as long as the supervising attorney reads and approves the document prior to signing. Many documents require little skill in draftsmanship, sometimes only requiring that names, dates, and the like be inserted into a standard form. Nevertheless, the attorney is responsible for the legal sufficiency of documents prepared for clients. There is a danger that an attorney with a large workload assisted by a seasoned, competent paralegal may place too much reliance on the paralegal and begin signing documents without reading them, even when the documents are not standard forms. The concern here is not the competence of the paralegal but a proper allocation of responsibility.

In reality, a paralegal may be more knowledgeable about a particular legal matter than an attorney, but in theory the paralegal is a trained technician while the attorney is a legal analyst. This is an excellent combination of skills to serve clients; paralegal and attorney working as a team provide legal services of high quality. If the attorney, however, relies on the paralegal entirely, the equation fails; the client has not received the services contracted.

As an employee of an attorney, a paralegal is understandably reluctant to criticize the boss; but it is important to ensure that the attorney reads a document before signing. The paralegal can tactfully express doubts about a document and thereby urge the attorney to read with care. In fact, if the paralegal has any doubts about the form of the document, its legal consequences, or the propriety of the language used, these doubts should be brought to the attention of the attorney, who may then take special care in reading relevant parts of the document. Even though the paralegal is not legally accountable for a document signed by a supervising attorney, the paralegal's ethical duty does not end with the exercise of technical skills. Service to client and service to attorney require attention to these details.

Despite their best urging and protestations, many paralegals work for attorneys who do not read many of the documents prepared by the paralegals. Despite confidence in the quality of the documents, the paralegal may nonetheless have the uncomfortable feeling that the process is not as it should be. The paralegal faces an ethical dilemma because of the attorney's lack of diligence. It may be that no one is harmed in that the legal documents are sound. But a fraud has been perpetrated on the client, who has contracted and dearly paid for the legal expertise of a licensed member of the bar. On these occasions, a paralegal should seek counsel from an appropriate source, such as a trusted member of the firm.

It is anticipated that in the 1990s legal technicians will come to enjoy limited authority to help individuals fill out legal forms, much as H & R Block helps individuals fill out tax forms. If the bar makes good on its commitment to ensure that legal services are provided to the public, such a development should be one of the consequences, as numerous legal documents require little or no advice necessitating an attorney and can be completed by legal technicians (independent paralegals) at minimal cost to the client.

Giving Legal Advice

Paralegals must be careful not only to refrain from giving legal advice but also to avoid even giving that impression. It is important that each client clearly understand that the paralegal is not a lawyer and is not licensed to practice law. Clients will often seek advice from paralegals, especially when the attorney is temporarily unavailable. Paralegals possess a competence and knowledge of the law that tends to encourage clients and friends to ask for legal advice.

Defining *legal advice* is not an easy task because there is a fine line between providing information and giving advice. For example, it is neither unethical nor an unauthorized practice of law to sell standard legal forms (office supply stores regularly sell legal forms). Nor is furnishing typing services improper. A logical conclusion might be that assisting a person in typing in the blanks on a standard legal form is not improper or illegal. In the course of filling out a form, however, a client may ask a question concerning the legal consequences of an item in the form. Rosemary Furman (see Chapter 1) was accused of telling her clients to include or exclude information on the divorce forms. The most serious charges against her concerned encouraging her clients to lie on the forms. The *Furman* case presents some legitimate concerns of the bar—it is not the giving of legal advice per se that is wrong but the giving of incompetent or inaccurate advice. Because the bar and the courts have little control over nonlawyers, the public has little protection against incompetents and charlatans.

As a practical matter, the paralegal should be alert to making statements to a client. Statements that may induce the client to do or refrain from doing something that may have legal consequences may be construed as legal advice. There is a big difference between saying "Don't do that" and "You ought to talk to an attorney before doing that." When pressed for advice, the paralegal must always refer the questions to the attorney. Although often a conduit or messenger between attorney and client, the paralegal must exercise care in conveying information or advice. Even when instructions are unambiguous, such as "Tell the client to go ahead and sign the contract," a paralegal should ascertain the exact instructions to be conveyed and indicate to the client that the instructions are those of the attorney. Of course, it is far better for the attorney to communicate directly with the client.

Ironically, a paralegal is more constrained in giving legal advice than is the man-in-the-street. The justification for this is that the paralegal is knowledgeable in the law, so paralegal advice is likely to be construed as correct and thus be acted upon. Presumably, individuals understand that legal advice from the man-in-the-street has no authority behind it. Paralegals must be aware of their special vulnerability in this regard. In coming years the boundaries of paralegal responsibilities will undoubtedly undergo significant clarification. It should be noted that at present the states differ significantly in where they draw these boundaries.

Confidentiality

Perhaps the most important topic in legal ethics is confidentiality. In the course of legal consultation, a client typically reveals information that is personal, private, and often secret. Legal services are predicated on the assurance that none of these private facts will be disclosed to third parties beyond the attorney and the attorney's staff. To deal effectively with client affairs, the attorney must be fully informed about all matters relating to the client's need for legal service and advice. For this reason, statements made in confidence to an attorney by a client are privileged and may be disclosed only with the consent of the client or when special circumstances provide clear exceptions to the rule.

The privilege extends to law firm employees who necessarily have access to confidential material in order to provide legal services, including especially legal secretaries, clerks, and paralegals. Although paralegals are not subject to disciplinary actions for improper disclosures, a supervising attorney can be held responsible both by attorney disciplinary rules and by a possible suit by the client.

The paralegal must be scrupulous in protecting clients' confidences. It is a great temptation for attorneys and paralegals alike to relate the facts of an interesting case to friends and associates outside the law firm, but any disclosure incurs the risk that the listener may identify a client and thereby learn facts that are privileged. If third parties not covered by the privilege learn confidential communications, the disclosures may lose their confidential status. Extreme caution must be exercised in discussing specific matters involving specific clients. Attorneys and law firms routinely warn staff about confidentiality, but paralegals must also constantly remind themselves of their responsibilities toward the clients.

Confidentiality can lead to bizarre predicaments, as illustrated by the following real-life situation. A woman was working as an intake paralegal for a Legal Aid office that provided legal services in civil cases for indigents. As such, she interviewed prospective clients for the office. A woman seeking divorce came to the office and was accepted as a client. The attorney in charge of the case was encountering difficulties finding the woman's husband to serve notice of the pending divorce action. It so happened that the husband later came to the office for legal representation. In the course of collecting intake information, the paralegal recognized that the man was the husband of a client of the office. Although the office could not represent both husband and wife, it was now in possession of the husband's address and telephone number—but that information was now considered privileged information because the husband had furnished it in confidence in attempting to establish a lawyer-client relationship.

Although the attorney for the wife was informed that the husband had furnished this information, she and the paralegal concluded that it might be improper to give it to the wife's attorney, so the husband's file was locked away where the attorney did not have access to it. (Fortunately, the husband's whereabouts were discovered through another source.) The lesson, however, is that the paralegal and the attorney were appropriately sensitive to the confidentiality question.

A client's actions may render disclosures nonconfidential. Statements made before third parties who are not covered by confidentiality are disclosable. If, for instance, the client brings a friend along to a meeting with the attorney and the friend has no relation to the case, statements made are not confidential. Attorneys and paralegals are careful to exclude third parties from discussions, especially when confidential statements are expected. The problem with nonconfidential statements is that their content is subject to discovery by the opposing side, and in criminal cases, the third parties may be required to disclose the statements on the witness stand.

Whether or not the confidential attorney-client relationship applies depends on the circumstances. Even though an attorney may have represented a client in the past, statements made with regard to an unrelated current problem may not be confidential if the client has not expressed an intention to retain the attorney in the current matter.

In contrast, the attorney-client relationship may be understood to be ongoing. A client who employs an attorney on all business matters may implicitly intend all business statements to be confidential. A client may also pay an attorney a general retainer with the understanding that the attorney and client have a continuing relationship. Once confidentiality is established, the confidentiality does not end with the termination of client representation, though it may not extend to subsequent nonconfidential information.

The PEOPLE of the State of New
York, Respondent,
v.
John C. MITCHELL, Appellant.
Court of Appeals of New York
58 N.Y.2d 368, 448 N.E.2d 121 (1983)

Defendant was a resident of Waterloo, New York, and, at the time these events occurred, he was under **indictment** for causing the stabbing death of his girlfriend, Audrey Miller, in February, 1976. He was represented on that charge by Rochester attorney Felix Lapine. In January, 1977, defendant went to Rochester to take care of some personal matters and registered at the Cadillac Hotel. On the evening of January 5 while sitting at the hotel bar, he met O'Hare McMillon. They had two or three highballs and then were seen to leave the bar about 11:00 p.m. and take the elevator to the floor on which Mitchell's room was located. No one saw either of them leave defendant's room that night or the next morning, but in the afternoon of January 6, on a tip from attorney Lapine, the police went to defendant's hotel room and found the partially clad dead body of O'Hare McMillon on the bed. She had been stabbed 11–12 times in the face, chest and back. At least four of the wounds were sufficient to cause her death by exsanguination.

After leaving the hotel room that morning, defendant went to attorney Lapine's office. Lapine was not in but defendant met and spoke to a legal secretary, Molly Altman, in the reception area. She testified that he seemed nervous and as if he was looking for someone. Apparently he could not find whomever it was he was looking for so he left only to return a minute later and start telling her about what happened the night before. She testified that he said: "he wanted to go out and have a last fling * * * he had been out drinking and met a girl and then he woke up in the morning and she was dead. He had stayed there all night and then he walked out again."

While he was talking to Ms. Altman, Judith Peacock, another legal secretary, entered the reception area. She testified that defendant was kind of rambling on but he said that: "he had laid next to someone all night and they didn't move, and he [was] in a bar and *** in a hotel *** this person who he had laid next to was black and he was worried because when the black people find out about it, they protect their own and he would be in danger." She also testified that he muttered something about a knife.

Ms. Pope-Johnson entered the room. She asked defendant what was wrong and he told her: "that there was a dead body and he felt that he had done it and that the person was dead, that she was dead because of being stabbed."

Shortly thereafter, Lapine entered the office and talked privately with defendant. After defendant left Lapine called the police and had them check defendant's hotel room. The body was discovered, defendant's identification learned from the hotel registration and defendant found and arrested at a bar near the courthouse.

. . . .

On this state of the record, we conclude that defendant has not met his burden of establishing that when he spoke to these unknown women in a common reception area, his statements were intended to be confidential and made to an employee of his attorney for the purpose of obtaining legal advice. The only evidence identifying the women came from Lapine who responded to a question whether he had "any female employees" by saying "Yes, Robin Pope-Johnson." She, it turns out, was the last woman in the office to hear defendant's inculpatory statements and even if statements made to her at the time could have been privileged, the privilege was lost because of the prior **publication** to nonemployees and the utterance of the statements to Pope-Johnson in front of the nonemployees [Cc.] Taking this view we need not consider whether the statements could be privileged because of an ongoing retainer between defendant and Lapine or if they could be privileged if made to the attorney's employee before a formal retainer was agreed upon.

Case Questions
1. What circumstances argued most strongly for defeating the attorney-client privilege?
2. What argument can be made in Mitchell's behalf?

Case Glossary

indictment A charge made in writing by a grand jury, based upon evidence presented to it, accusing a person of having committed a criminal act, generally a felony. It is the function of the prosecution to bring a case before the grand jury. If the grand jury indicts the defendant, a trial follows.

publication The act of making something known to the public; the act of publishing.

Exceptions to Confidentiality

Rule 1.6 Confidentiality of information.

(a) A lawyer shall not reveal information relating to representation of a client except as stated in paragraphs (b), (c), and (d) unless the client consents after disclosure to the client.

(b) A lawyer shall reveal such information to the extent the lawyer believes necessary:
    (1) To prevent a client from committing a crime; or
    (2) To prevent a death or substantial bodily harm to another.

(c) A lawyer may reveal such information to the extent the lawyer believes necessary:
    (1) To serve the client's interest unless it is information the client specifically requires not to be disclosed;
    (2) To establish a claim or defense on behalf of the lawyer in a controversy between the lawyer and client;
    (3) To establish a defense to a criminal charge or civil claim against the lawyer based upon conduct in which the client was involved;
    (4) To respond to allegations in any proceeding concerning the lawyer's representation of the client; or
    (5) To comply with the *Rules of Professional Conduct*.

(d) When required by a tribunal to reveal such information, a lawyer may first exhaust all appellate remedies.

The exceptions to confidentiality privilege are primarily aimed at protecting the public [(b)(1) and (b)(2)] and protecting the attorney in a conflict with the client [(c)]. Although confidential statements about past crimes and misconduct are privileged, a client's intention to commit a crime in the future is not. An attorney has an ethical duty to attempt to dissuade a client from committing a crime and a duty to inform appropriate authorities if unable to dissuade the client. The most difficult case arises when a client plans to commit perjury at trial and, despite the attorney's admonitions, proceeds to lie on the witness stand. Attempted withdrawal by the attorney at that stage of the process will ordinarily be refused by the court, but the attorney also is not free to disclose the confidences that would reveal the perjury. The complexities of this situation are illustrated by the following:

ABA Project on Standards for Criminal Justice; Proposed Defense Function Standard 4-7.7 (2d ed. 1980).

(a) If the defendant has admitted to defense counsel facts which establish guilt and counsel's independent investigation established that the admissions are true but the defendant insists on the right to trial, counsel must strongly discourage the defendant against taking the witness stand to testify perjuriously.

(b) If, in advance of trial, the defendant insists that he or she will take the stand to testify perjuriously, the lawyer may withdraw from the case, if that is feasible, seeking leave of the court if necessary, but the court should not be advised of the lawyer's reason for seeking to do so.

(c) If withdrawal from the case is not feasible or is not permitted by the court, or if the situation arises immediately preceding trial or during the trial and the defendant insists upon testifying perjuriously in his or her own behalf, it is unprofessional conduct for the lawyer to lend aid to the perjury or use the perjured testimony. Before the defendant takes the stand in these circumstances, the lawyer should make a record of the fact that the defendant is taking the stand against the advice of counsel in some appropriate manner without revealing to the court the client's intent to perjure himself. The lawyer may identify the witness as the defendant and may ask appropriate questions of the defendant when it is believed that the defendant's answers will not be perjurious. As to matters for which it is believed the defendant will offer perjurious testimony, the lawyer should seek to avoid direct examination of the defendant in the conventional manner; instead, the lawyer should ask the defendant if he or she wishes to make any additional statement concerning the case to the trier or triers of the facts. A lawyer may not later argue the defendant's known false version of facts to the jury as worthy of belief, and may not recite or rely upon the false testimony in his or her closing argument.

Conflicts of Interest

A common conflict-of-interest problem arises when an attorney leaves one firm for another and the second firm represents a party suing or being sued by a client of the former firm. The risk of disclosure of attorney-client confidences by the attorney to the new employers raises serious ethical concerns. Extreme cases are not difficult to decide. If the attorney worked on the client's case at his first employment, it would be clearly unethical to work for the opposing party. However, if an attorney moves from one large law firm to another and had no exposure to the case at either firm, the risk of disclosure is minimal. The risk can be further minimized by erecting a "Chinese wall" between the attorney and those dealing with the case, that is, preventing access to the case file and warning all concerned not to discuss the case with the firm-switching attorney. If no exception is made, an attorney working for a large firm becomes a "typhoid Mary," virtually unemployable at other large firms for fear the firm may have or may take on a client who may be involved in a dispute against a client of the other firm.

Because paralegals regularly deal with confidential material, an identical problem arises; the entire firm may be disqualified from representing a client if the court concludes that the risk of improper disclosure cannot be purged. In fact, some paralegals will have contact with a greater number of files than any single attorney.

This particular form of conflict of interest poses a practical as well as an ethical problem, because the firm representing a client can request that the court disqualify an opposing firm's representation. This action has resulted in numerous reported decisions of the courts that not only clarify the ethical principles but also give them the force of law. In *Silver Chrysler Plymouth, Inc. v. Chrysler Motors Corp.*, 518 F.2d 751 (2d Cir. 1975), the court articulated the "substantially related" test subsequently adopted by the courts of many jurisdictions. *Silver Chrysler* distinguished between the activities of a lawyer or law clerk at a former law firm that were substantially related to representation in a current case at a second law firm employing the attorney. The court thereby attempted to distinguish situations in which a distinct risk of confidential disclosures exists from those in which the risk is insignificant.

In the *Gas-A-Tron* case the Ninth Circuit Court of Appeals reiterated the test in *Silver Chrysler*. Note that in both cases, the attorney who switched firms was an associate who had limited access to files and limited decision making in the cases under consideration.

The ABA *Model Rules* adopted the "substantially related" test in 1980:

> **Rule 1.9** A lawyer who has formerly represented a client in a matter shall not thereafter:
> (a) represent another person in the same or a substantially related matter to which that person's interests are materially adverse to the interests of the former client unless the former client consents after consultation; or

**GAS-A-TRON OF ARIZONA and
Coinoco, Plaintiffs-Appellants,
v.
UNION OIL COMPANY OF CALIFORNIA
et al., Defendants-Appellees.**

**PETROL STOPS NORTHWEST,
Plaintiff-Appellant,
v.
CONTINENTAL OIL COMPANY et al.,
Defendants-Appellees.
United States Court of Appeals,
Ninth Circuit
534 F.2d 1322 (1976)**

We recognize that the primary responsibility for controlling the conduct of lawyers practicing before the district court lies with that court, and not with us. We will not disturb the district court's exercise of its discretion in fulfilling that responsibility if the record reveals any sound basis for its discretion disqualifying or refusing to disqualify a lawyer. The record in this case does not support the district court's decision. The district court's disqualification of Mr. Burbidge rested upon its determination that the pending litigation was "substantially related" to the matters in which he had previously represented Shell and Exxon while he was associated with McCutchen. Mr. Burbidge's situation was almost identical to that of the young associates whose claimed disqualification was considered in *Silver Chrysler Plymouth, Inc. v. Chrysler Motors Corp.*, 518 F.2d 751 (2d Cir. 1975), and *Bonus Oil Co. v. American Petrofina Co.*, No. CV—73—L—165 (D.Neb. May 1, 1975). *See*

also Redd v. Shell Oil Co., Civ. No. C—104-71 (D.Utah, Sept. 2, 1974), *rev'd on other grounds* 518 F.2d 311 (10th Cir. 1975) (in another case involving Mr. Burbidge, Berman and McCutchen, district court found motion for disqualification a sham). In each case, the court decided that the associate was not disqualified because no substantial relationship existed between the pending litigation and the matters upon which he had worked for the client during his prior association. We agree with the reasoning in those cases. Here, as in those cases, the associate had not actually obtained any confidential information about either Shell or Exxon that would be relevant to the pending litigation, and he had not worked on matters that were "substantially related" to the pending litigation.

We share the district court's concern for the appearance of impropriety. However, we are convinced that any initial inference of impropriety that arose from Mr. Burbidge's potential physical access to the files of Exxon and Shell and from his association with lawyers who did know confidential information about them was dispelled by evidence that he saw none of the files other than those relating to the cases assigned to him heretofore described and that he heard no confidences about Exxon and Shell from the lawyers with whom he was earlier associated.

Berman's disqualification was based solely on Mr. Burbidge's disqualification, and that disqualification vanishes with Mr. Burbidge's nondisqualification.

Reversed.

Case Questions

1. Apparently the trial court was swayed by the appearance of impropriety, a standard to which attorneys are sometimes held. Under what circumstances would an attorney's assocation with two firms appear truly improper?
2. Does the "substantially related" test help answer question 1?

(b) use information relating to the representation to the disadvantage of the former client except as Rule 1.6 would permit with respect to a client or when the information has become generally known.

The Canons of Ethics, formerly the primary standard in all states, expressed general ethical principles. These gave rise to philosophical discussions in some cases, like the *Horan* case. The conflict of interest appears obvious, yet the attorney involved probably acted decently and in good faith in the matter. The court, however, held him to a higher standard.

STATE v. HORAN
Supreme Court of Wisconsin
21 Wis. 2d 66, 123 N.W.2d 488 (1963)

Mr. Horan, a bachelor 46 years old, has practiced law in Friendship, Wisconsin, for over 20 years. ... He enjoys a good reputation in his community and was a close friend and advisor of Wellington B. Barnes, a widower, who died on October 11, 1959, at the age of 87 leaving an estate of approximately $265,000. Upon Barnes' death the only **heir** at law was Myrtle Marks, a first cousin of the half-blood. He also left a relative Elizabeth Hover, a first cousin once removed. After Mrs. Barnes' death and between April 28, 1955, and November 29, 1958, Horan drew six wills for Barnes and a **codicil** on February 14, 1959. The general scheme of the wills provided specific **bequests** and a proportion of the residuary estate to various friends and to Myrtle Marks, Elizabeth Hover and Horan. The first will contained a bequest to Mr. Horan of $12,633 and a proportional share of the residuary estate. In each succeeding will, as other beneficiaries were eliminated or their share cut down, the specific bequest or the share of the residuary estate to Horan was increased ... . No claim is made the testator was incompetent or the defendant used **undue influence** in procuring the financial benefit to himself under the will.

[The will was entered into probate after an agreement among the various parties which left Horan with a share worth $38,817.22.]

Posed for consideration is the specific question of whether Mr. Horan's conduct subjects him to any disciplinary action and a broader question of whether an attorney under any circumstances may draft and supervise the execution of a will for his client wherein he is named a substantial beneficiary without violating the rules of professional conduct. No claim is made [that] Horan exercised any undue influence in drafting the wills in which he became a substantial beneficiary. If he did, his conduct would involve moral turpitude and would demand that this court impose more severe discipline than it does in this case. ... The practice of the law is not a business but a profession—a form of public trust, the performance of which is entrusted only to those who can qualify by fitness, not the least of which is good moral character. While within his power, an attorney has no right to jeopardize the performance of his duties or the confidence, approval and esteem of the public which the legal profession has traditionally enjoyed. An attorney has a duty not to harm but to maintain the integrity of the legal profession even though this may call for a personal sacrifice of the omission of acts which are not intrinsically bad. "The profession of the law, in its nature the noblest and most beneficial to mankind, is in its abuse and abasement the most sordid and pernicious." [Lord Bolingbroke]. ...

Many lawyers in their practice have been confronted with the situation of drawing a will for a friend or a relative who wishes to make a bequest to him or to a member of his family. Perhaps sufficient consideration of the problem involved has not been given by lawyers or by the bar. The recurrence of the problem in the practice does not dull its serious dangers. The conflict of interests, the incompetency of an attorney-beneficiary to testify because of a transaction with the deceased, the possible jeopardy of the will if its admission to probate is contested, the possible harm done to other beneficiaries and the undermining of the public trust and confidence in the integrity of the legal profession, are only some of the dangers which a lawyer must consider.

The Canons of Professional Ethics, which may be considered as broad but not all-inclusive standards, do not expressly mention the drafting of wills. Canon 6 makes it unprofessional conduct "to represent conflicting interests, except by the express consent of all concerned given after a full disclosure of the facts." Canon 11 requires "The lawyer should refrain from any action whereby for his personal benefit or gain he abuses or takes advantage of the confidence reposed in him by his client." [The Court then discusses meager authorities suggesting that an attorney in this situation advise the client to seek advice of other counsel or have another attorney draw up a codicil to include the attorney's bequest.] ...

[O]rdinary prudence requires that such a will be drawn by some other lawyer of the testator's own choosing so that any suspicion of undue influence is thereby avoided. ...

An attorney's duty of fidelity to his client involves more than refraining from exercising undue influence. A client has a right to full and disinterested advice. The "right to make a will is a sacred and a constitutional right and that right includes a right of equal dignity to have it carried out." When Mr. Horan was drafting the wills for Barnes he failed to recognize the conflict of interests which existed between him as an attorney for his client and his position as a beneficiary of a substantial sum of money. It was his duty to fully advise his client that the will was vulnerable to attack because of the inference of undue influence which arose and his incapacity to give testimony to support it. Nor should he have placed himself in a position of drafting the will where his self-interest might have prevented his giving disinterested advice ... . Because the law on this subject has not been clearly defined or well understood by the members of the legal profession and no undue influence is involved, we deem a reprimand and the payment of costs to be sufficient.

Case Questions

1. Why might Myrtle Marks, the heir, be interested in contesting the will or the attorney's share in the will?
2. How could Horan have handled this matter in such a way as to ethically participate in the distribution of his client's estate?

Case Glossary

heirs Persons who are entitled to inherit real or personal property of a decedent who dies intestate; persons receiving property by descent. ... Although not technically correct, the word is often used to indicate persons who receive property through a decedent's will.

codicil An addition or supplement to a will, which adds to or modifies the will without replacing or revoking it.

bequest Technically, a gift of personal property by will, ... although the term is often loosely used in connection with a testamentary gift of real estate as well.

undue influence Inappropriate pressure exerted on a person for the purpose of causing him or her to substitute his or her will for the will or wishes of another. Undue influence is a form of coercion to which the aged or infirm are particularly vulnerable, especially at the hands of a person whom they feel they have reason to trust.

Solicitation

For many years, the legal profession banned advertising legal services, and many disciplinary cases considered such issues as listings in the yellow pages, the sending of Christmas cards, the size of law office signs, etc. In 1977, the U.S. Supreme Court, in *Bates v. State Bar of Arizona,* 433 U.S. 350, held that the ban on advertising violated First Amendment freedom of speech. Since that time, ethical concerns have aimed at distinguishing advertising from solicitation. The bar continues to attempt to thwart "ambulance chasing," the practice of hunting down injured parties and twisting their arms to hire the attorney. Although *Bates* made it clear that attorneys were free to announce their services to the public in general, the aggressive solicitation of individual clients is still condemned.

> *Model Rules of Professional Conduct:*
> **Rule 7.3** Direct contact with prospective clients.
> A lawyer may not solicit professional employment from a prospective client with whom the lawyer has no family or prior professional relationship, in person or otherwise, when a significant motive for the lawyer's doing so is the lawyer's pecuniary gain. The term "solicit" includes contact in person, by telephone or telegraph, by letter or other writing, or by other communication directed to a specific recipient. ...

An attorney is also prohibited from soliciting through another person, including a paralegal. Paralegals must be careful in generating business for the attorneys for whom they work. It is very tempting, when hearing a story of a personal injury or some other promising legal case, to encourage a visit to the law office, but paralegals must be cautious in their treatment of such situations. Certainly it is unethical to loiter at the hospital handing out business cards to accident victims, but it is not necessary to keep one's employment a secret or, when asked, to recommend an attorney. Suggesting that a person seek legal help is ethical if the paralegal has not sought out clients. The paralegal should not disparage other attorneys nor encourage a person to switch from one attorney to another nor criticize an attorney's handling of a client. When learning of possible misconduct by an attorney, the paralegal should discuss the matter with an attorney associate, who has an ethical duty to address attorney misconduct.

Fees

The *Model Rules* treat fee arrangements with much more specificity than did the *Model Code.* Fees are based on contracts between the attorney and the client and should be specifically discussed by the attorney with the client. Whenever fees have not been adequately explained to a client, a potential conflict emerges. If at all possible, a contract signed by the client should clearly explain the basis on which the fees are established. When the *Model Rules* were debated, the framers wanted to require that all fee arrangements be in writing, but sole practitioners and rural lawyers argued that this would hurt their relationships with many of their clients, so the writing was not made mandatory.

A recurring issue regarding fees concerns contingency fees, whereby the attorney is paid a percentage of the award or recovery received by the client. There is a strong national movement favoring limitations on contingency fees. Personal injury cases are typically based on contingency fees, which are unethical in criminal cases and divorce proceedings. It is essential that the client understand that the percentage does not include costs other than the attorney's services. In cases using expert witnesses, the costs can be quite large; the client must be aware of this and the fact that the client must pay the costs regardless of who wins the case.

Work performed by a paralegal is commonly billed to a client. Ordinarily the paralegal's work is charged at a rate significantly less than that for an attorney, though not necessarily proportional to the compensation paid the paralegal. Clients should not be charged for attorney's work if paralegals actually did the work, nor should they be billed for more time than was actually spent. The latter is not only unethical but illegal as well. Even though paralegals may not be responsible for the billing, they should not participate, actively or passively, in a fraud on the client.

Reporting Misconduct

Model Rules of Professional Conduct:
> **Rule 8.3** Reporting professional misconduct.
> (a) A lawyer having knowledge that another lawyer has committed a violation of the *Rules of Professional Conduct* ... shall inform the appropriate professional authority.

Although lawyers are understandably reluctant to inform on each other, this rule is clear, and failure to report misconduct is an ethical violation. The object is not simply to punish the wrongdoer but to protect the public and the legal system. Choice of the authority to which the misconduct should be reported depends on whether the misconduct is a professional matter or matter before the court.

The duty of paralegals to report misconduct is more problematic. If the misconduct is also criminal, a legal duty to report a crime falls upon the paralegal. If the misconduct is of a professional, noncriminal nature, the duty is less clear. There is an ethical duty in an abstract sense, but not one that subjects the paralegal to discipline, as the paralegal is not a member of the bar. If misconduct results in an injury to a client, the paralegal who overlooks the misconduct may be viewed as contributing to the injury. In any event, such matters must be treated with great delicacy. Accusations of misconduct can have serious ramifications for an attorney. The paralegal is quite vulnerable as well, having a subordinate position in the legal hierarchy. In such a situation, it is to be hoped that the paralegal will know a lawyer who can give counsel. If the misconduct can be corrected, approaching the wrongdoer rather than informing may be the best policy. In any event, diplomacy and caution should be exercised.

Trust Accounts

One of the most common reasons for attorney discipline involves the misuse of client funds. This is considered by disciplinary committees to be one of the most serious transgressions. Clients deposit funds with attorneys for a number of reasons besides paying fees. Money held for a client must never be commingled (mixed) with an attorney's personal accounts, nor should separate trust accounts be commingled in any way. Accurate recordkeeping is essential to properly account for monies received and disbursed.

Misuse of client funds may constitute the crime of embezzlement. A paralegal must not participate or contribute to improper use of client funds.

Malpractice

Disciplinary action is not the only risk facing an attorney. When a client has been injured by the negligence of an attorney, he or she may bring a civil action for **malpractice**, seeking compensation from the attorney for the injury. Malpractice refers to professional negligence, and negligence in turn refers to a cause of action falling in the class of

---

—BALLENTINE'S—

malpractice   The failure of a professional person to act with reasonable care; misconduct by a professional person in the course of engaging in his or her profession.

private suits called torts, explained in greater detail in Chapter 11. Ordinary negligence occurs when a person fails to exercise reasonable care and because of carelessness causes injury to another person or to property. Persons (usually licensed) holding themselves out as professionals are held to a professional rather than an ordinary standard of care. After all, lawyers are hired because of their presumed competence and skill in legal representation. The lawyer who fails to meet the standards of the profession should compensate those injured by this failure. Much of a lawyer's work involves judgments that may prove mistaken but are nevertheless defensible even in retrospect. It may not be difficult in such situations for an attorney to get other attorneys to testify that the judgment was within the standards of the profession. Some mistakes, however, are not easy to defend, as the *Van Berkel* case illustrates. The most provable instance of attorney malpractice occurs when an attorney negligently allows a statute of limitations to run, barring further action on a client's lawsuit. There may be other consequences from such conduct as well.

Mitchell VAN BERKEL, Plaintiff,
v.
FOX FARM AND ROAD MACHINERY,
et al., Defendants.
United States District Court,
District of Minnesota
581 F. Supp. 1248 (D. Minn. 1984)

The principal issue here, occasioned by defendants' motion for **summary judgment** and for reimbursement of costs and attorneys' fees, is whether plaintiff's attorney acted within proper professional standards when he instituted this **products liability** case, and later when he refused to dismiss it upon learning that all the claims were time barred by statutes of limitations.

Plaintiff is a Minnesota farmer who lost his right arm in a farm accident on September 6, 1976 while using a corn chopper manufactured, sold and distributed by defendant foreign corporations. Plaintiff engaged Douglas E. Schmidt ... to represent him. Mr. Schmidt filed this lawsuit on September 2, 1983 on theories of negligence, strict liability and breach of express and implied warranties. The complaint alleged that the accident took place on September 6, *1977*. In actuality, the accident happened on September 6, *1976* ... .

When the lawsuit was filed on September 2, 1983, the Minnesota statutes of limitation on all claims had already run.

Defendants filed their answer on October 7, 1983 alleging, among other defenses, that the claims were time barred by the statutes of limitation. On October 12, 1983, defendants' attorney served a demand for medical disclosure, including a request for medical authorizations. It was not till December 28, 1983, after repeated demands by defendants, that plaintiff's attorney, Mr. Schmidt, provided defendants with the medical authorizations. On January 9, 1984, Mr. Schmidt served a response to the demand for medical disclosure.

On January 24, 1984, defendants' attorney wrote Mr. Schmidt and enclosed copies of the medical records which reflected that the accident happened on September 6, *1976* and hence all claims were time barred, and asked plaintiff's attorney to dismiss the case. Defendants' attorney called Mr. Schmidt on February 1, 1984, asking him to dismiss the case. Defendants' attorney confirmed this phone call by a letter to Mr. Schmidt dated February 2, 1984. Plaintiff's attorney was also furnished a copy of a news article from ... [a] newspaper dated September 15,

1976, reporting that the accident happened on September 6, *1976*. ...

When asked what inquiry he had made before instituting the lawsuit, Mr. Schmidt said he had a competent expert witness check out the machine, talked to plaintiff and family members at their farm home, and received copies of the operators and owners manuals ... . He said he did not obtain or review any medical records before starting the lawsuit and did not see them till they were furnished to him by defendants' counsel in January or February 1984, some four or five months after suit was filed, and apparently over four years after he was retained by his client.

* * *

Rule 11 of the Federal Rules of Civil Procedure provides that the signature of an attorney to a pleading is a certification that he has made reasonable inquiry upon which to base a belief that the allegations of it are well grounded in fact and law and provides for sanctions for its violation. 28 U.S.C. § 1927 authorizes imposition of costs and attorneys' fees upon an attorney who multiplies proceedings unreasonably and vexatiously.

Had Mr. Schmidt made even a minimum investigation into the facts of this case, he would have determined the accurate date of the accident. The hospital and medical records reflected it. The client came to Mr. Schmidt, the affidavits show, sometime before 1980, so he had adequate time to obtain and examine all pertinent records and make additional needful inquiry. Plaintiff's case was put on his law firm's computer in 1980 and Mr. Schmidt was periodically advised of the date of the running of the statute of limitations. Assuming a September 1977 accident date, had Mr. Schmidt filed the action anytime before September 1981, all claims, including the breach of warranty claims which had a four year limitation period, would have been timely.

* * *

Mr. Schmidt's stated justification for not dismissing the lawsuit after learning it was time barred is that he could not dismiss it without his client's approval and that he had "an ethical duty to my client." This was wrong. On the contrary, Mr. Schmidt had a professional duty to dismiss a baseless lawsuit, even over the objection of his client, and to do it promptly when he learned that his client had no case.

Attorneys are officers of the court and their first duty is to the administration of justice. Whenever an attorney's duties to his client conflict with those he owes to the public as an officer of the court, he must give precedence to his duty to the public. Any other view would run counter to a principled system of justice.

* * *

IT IS ORDERED THAT:

1. Defendants' motion for summary judgment is granted.

2. Douglas E. Schmidt, signatory as attorney for plaintiff on the complaint, is *SANCTIONED* and ordered personally to pay defendants' costs, expenses and attorneys' fees occasioned by such conduct, which the court finds to be $2,894.62.

Case Questions

1. Why is failure to file within the time period of a statute of limitations the most provable instance of attorney malpractice?
2. What precisely was the attorney's ethical duty in the course of this case?
3. With the conclusion of this decision, another lawsuit would be appropriate. What would it be and who would be the parties to the suit?

Case Glossary

summary judgment A method of disposing of an action without further proceedings. Under the Federal Rules of Civil Procedure, and the rules of civil procedure of many states, a party ... may file a motion for summary judgment seeking judgment in his or her favor if there is no genuine issue as to any material fact.

product liability The liability of a manufacturer or seller of an article for an injury caused to a person or to property by a defect in the article sold.

Summary

The legal profession is governed by a code of professional ethics that is enforced by the courts and the profession. Each state has an ethical code for lawyers. The ABA has been the leader in developing ethical codes, adopting the *Model Code of Professional Responsibility* in 1970 and the *Model Rules of Professional Conduct* in 1983. Most states have adopted these codes nearly verbatim, so there is considerable uniformity in principle, at least.

The interpretation of the codes in the courts shows some disparities, especially in defining the unauthorized practice of law, which is of special concern to paralegals because they risk unauthorized practice of law if they engage in activities permitted only to licensed attorneys, namely:

1. Legal representation before a court;
2. Preparation of legal documents;
3. Giving legal advice.

The unauthorized practice of law may be prosecuted under criminal statutes or by the court as contempt of court.

Confidentiality of client statements is protected by the attorney-client privilege, which extends to law office personnel. Paralegals must take great pains not to disclose confidential information on clients to persons not covered by the privilege. The attorney-client privilege belongs to the client and not the attorney. Major exceptions to the privilege occur when a client proposes to commit a crime or when the client sues the attorney.

Confidentiality gives rise to problems of conflict of interest when an attorney or a paralegal changes employment from one firm to another. If the new firm represents a party adverse to a party represented by the firm from which the new employee came, the risk that confidential information may be disclosed to the disadvantage of a former client is great. The entire firm may be disqualified. However, in this age of large law firms, lawyers and paralegals frequently have no contact with a client of the firm in which they work. As a result, the courts and the *Model Rules* have adopted the "substantially related" test: The adverse representation must be substantially related to matters with which the attorney dealt in prior employment. Law firms must additionally take pains to isolate the attorney from the case, the so-called "Chinese wall" approach.

Review Questions

Hypothetical 1: You have been working as a paralegal for five years for an attorney specializing in divorce and family law. A close friend comes to you for help. He says that his wife has filed for divorce and has presented him with a **marital settlement agreement** drawn up by her attorney, and he wants you to read it and tell him what you think of it. You have prepared many of these agreements yourself and know that in your jurisdiction the judges routinely approve such agreements when signed by both parties unless they appear grossly unfair to one party. Your friend says that the agreement appears to him to reflect his oral agreements with his wife before she consulted an attorney. He has consulted several attorneys, and all want at least $1,500 to represent him. He says he cannot afford this additional expense and will not hire an attorney unless absolutely necessary. If you do not read the agreement, he says, he will simply take his chances by signing it. He knows you are a paralegal and not licensed to practice law.

What are the ethical considerations?

1. Does it matter whether your friend pays you for this service?

2. Must you advise your friend to consult an attorney?

3. Must you refuse to read the agreement?

4. If you read the agreement and are convinced that it is fair and legally sound, can you so inform your friend?

5. If you read the agreement and have doubts about some of its clauses, what can you tell your friend?

6. Can you advise your friend with a disclaimer to the effect that you are not an attorney, that your advice may be incorrect, and that he should consult an attorney?

────────────────────────BALLENTINE'S────────────────────────

marital agreement   An agreement between two people who are married to each other ... , with respect to the disposition of the marital property or property owned by either spouse before the marriage, with respect to the rights of either in the property of the other, or with respect to support.

Hypothetical 2: You are assisting an attorney in the defense of a man accused of murder. Two days before the trial the client declares that he will perjure himself in order to present a more plausible argument for self-defense.

7. May the attorney withdraw from the case?

8. Must the attorney disclose the perjury?

9. What are the risks to the attorney?

Exercises

1. Find out whether your state has adopted either the *Model Code* or the *Model Rules* or has its own ethical code.

2. Does your state have a statute covering unauthorized practice of law? What does it say?

3. How are attorney grievances processed in your state?

4. Can you find out from a local paralegal association or other source what paralegals are permitted to do and are prohibited from doing in your state?

FAST AND EFFECTIVE CITE CHECKING

Karen Jolly

Paralegal cite checking is the attorney's first line of defense against citation error. Correct citations are important not only to convey information but also for the favorable impression they create in the mind of the reader, whether judge, law clerk, or lawyer. While cite checking can be one of the most exciting tasks performed by a paralegal, it can also be one of the most frustrating. Because it is by its very nature a last-minute activity, speed and efficiency are essential.

Cite checking involves three basic steps: (1) verifying case citations, (2) checking subsequent history, and (3) conforming all citations to standard Blue Book form (*A Uniform System of Citation* by the Harvard Law Review Association). To cite check, you must employ reverse engineering. Where the attorney starts with a legal argument and looks for cases in support, you have the cases in support of the argument and must backtrack to be sure that they are correctly relied upon, accurately quoted and properly cited.

[T]ry these four simple rules to faster and more efficient cite checking.

1. Streamline the Process

Review the pleading before you start cite checking so you know what to expect, but don't read it because you won't have time. Highlight categories to be checked (*e.g.,* yellow for documents to be checked from the file, green for statutes, purple for anything that has to be verified outside the office).

It is especially helpful to have the table of authorities in at least rough draft form before you start to cite check. If it is not available, quickly jot down the cites and, if possible, a partial case name. ... Use this list to run through Autocite or Instacite, and to get an idea of the Shepard's volumes you will need to check.

2. Shepardize by Volume Rather Than Case

Shepardizing is both the most tedious and the most crucial aspect of cite checking. A mistake here could cost the client his case and, at the very least, will cause your attorney considerable professional embarrassment.

While Shepard's is available on-line, ... manual check can be done as quickly and is often more cost-effective. To speed up the manual search, arrange all the Shepard's volumes that you will need in front of you ... . Then, starting at the top of your table of authorities, check all the cases that are covered by each volume of Shepard's. Be sure to include all applicable paper supplements. Copy any Shepard's pages that indicate negative treatment. You can greatly speed up the attorney's review of these cases by highlighting the negative treatment and indicating the name of the case that was Shepardized.

3. Know Where to Look for Miscited Cases

Cases miscited in the brief can slow you down but shouldn't stop you. First, check the table of contents in the volume cited to see if the page number has just been jumbled. If the case doesn't appear there, try a quick name search on LEXIS or Westlaw [or] a manual search ... by using the Table of Cases or Defendant/Plaintiff Table in the appropriate digest. The digest ... will be determined by the court and date of the case as cited (these elements are less often jumbled than the volume and page number).

For recent cases (within the last year), check the closing table in the last digest supplement to determine the extent of coverage for the reporter in which you are interested. Once you have determined the coverage of the digest, start a manual volume-by-volume search through the reporter volumes not covered by the digest. Include all advance sheets (although here, you need only check the cumulative table of cases contained in the last issue of each volume).

4. Know Where to Look for Statutes

Another potentially time-consuming situation arises when statutes are referred to with incomplete or inaccurate cites. To locate a federal statute, go first to *United States Code Annotated* (U.S.C.A.) or *United States Code Service* (U.S.C.S.). These two commercially published codes use the same citation pattern as the *U.S. Code,* but they are updated more frequently, contain case annotations and, most important to the paralegal, have more detailed indexing.

If you are unable to locate the correct cite to the statute through these sources, you can try looking for it by popular name. ... [A]n electronic search should be made only as a last resort.

Reprinted with permission from *Legal Assistant Today* magazine.

CHAPTER 4

SOURCES OF
THE LAW: CASES

Law and the Courts

The law in practice revolves around disputes and problems. The primary forum for dispute resolution is the court. Even though most disputes brought to lawyers do not result in trials, the courts, through their spokespersons, the judges, are the final arbiters of what the law is. Because courts are the last legitimate resort of disputants, judges must decide. No matter how difficult or complex a case, the judge may not plead ignorance, frustration, or indecision. In deciding a case, the judge must provide reasons and rules, the final product of the process of adjudication. Without reasons and rules, decision making is purely political. This is particularly true in our constitutional system in which the lines between the judicial function and the administrative and legislative functions are relatively distinct.

Where does a judge find the rules? The judicial imagination is not sufficient authority, even though some judicial decisions seem to suggest otherwise. There are several sources for the law, the primary ones being the Constitution, legislation, and prior judicial decisions. This last is the subject matter of this chapter.

Judicial Restraint

In the American judiciary, a principle has evolved called *judicial restraint.* The United States Constitution set the stage by separating executive, legislative, and judicial functions into the three basic branches of government. Taking their cues from European Enlightenment thinkers of the eighteenth century, the framers of the Constitution established a political charter designed to break completely from the archaic remnants of feudalism, in which power and status were based on the accident of birth and society was ruled by an aristocracy with ultimate power residing in the monarch. The Constitution, by contrast, attempted to create a "government of laws and not of men" and allocated authority to the three branches of government in such a way that each could serve as a check on the other.

From the beginning, the President and the members of Congress were elected officials and ipso facto involved in politics and the political process. The political nature of the courts was not clearly defined in the Constitution, and it can fairly be said that Chief Justice John Marshall, who dominated the United States Supreme Court during the early nineteenth century, singlehandedly defined the role of the federal judiciary. Among the important doctrines Marshall established, two stand out as fundamental principles that have guided American law ever since:

1. Marshall argued that the U.S. Constitution was the "law of the land," meaning that no law or official act that violated the Constitution was lawful; the Constitution stood as the guiding light superior to every other law. Because the U.S. Supreme Court is the final interpreter of the meaning of the Constitution, this doctrine of constitutional supremacy provided the Supreme Court with great political power. This phrase in the Constitution is referred to as the **supremacy clause**. The power of the court to examine legislative and executive acts is called *judicial review.*

2. This power was severely limited by another principle established by Marshall, which was dubbed *judicial restraint.* Because ultimate authority resides in the Court, which is made up of judges who are appointed for life subject only to removal by impeachment, it is necessary that judges restrain themselves from actively entering the political arena. This can be effectively accomplished by judges devoting themselves to deciding cases according to existing law. In simple terms, this means that judges interpret the law rather than make it, the latter function being reserved to the legislature. Ideally, judicial decisions are based on the authority of legal principles already in existence and not on the moral, political, or social preferences of the judges.

The Common Law

The American legal system is said to follow the common law tradition inherited from England. We are perhaps unique, along with England, Canada, Australia, and New Zealand, in enjoying 900 hundred years of virtually uninterrupted legal evolution since the Norman Conquest of England in 1066. Since that time, England has not been invaded by foreign powers imposing their own legal institutions, nor have political or legal revolutions seriously disrupted the steady development of English law. When the British came to America, they brought their law with them. The American Revolution made a political break with the mother country and established a more democratic political organization, but it did not change the fundamental process of the law. When our judges sought legal authority for their decisions, they logically turned to the basic principles of English law, which they knew and trusted even if they did not trust George III.

When the Normans organized England into a unified kingdom, they eliminated the pockets of local authority and jurisdiction characteristic

---

BALLENTINE'S

supremacy clause   The provision in Article VI of the Constitution that "this Constitution and laws of the United States ... shall be the supreme law of the land, and the judges in every state shall be bound hereby."

of continental European countries at the height of the Middle Ages. Although local legal process continued for a time for purely local matters, England gradually became a nation in the true sense of the word and gave birth to the "common law of England," under which developed a body of law common to all citizens of the nation. This undoubtedly led eventually to the reverence for the rule of law in the minds of the British people.

The common law has come to mean something more than simply English law. In American jurisprudence, the common law refers to judge-made law, distinguishing it from continental European legal systems, which are civil law systems. From the seventeenth century onward, with the rise of European nationhood, centralized governments were formed that required corresponding national legal institutions. Rather than building on existing custom and institutions, these governments compiled sets of laws into codes, borrowing heavily from the *Corpus Juris* of the Roman Emperor Justinian, the first European to attempt to collect and organize legal principles into comprehensive written form. This movement had significantly less impact on England, which had long enjoyed a central government and a national court system.

Although the sources of English law included edicts of the monarch and acts of Parliament, the daily life of the law was conducted in the courts, where pronouncements of the law were made on matters great and small. Today we are accustomed to view the legislature as the source of new law and expect judges to exercise judicial restraint by merely interpreting and enforcing the laws, but this was not always so. Until well into the nineteenth century, the English Parliament, the U.S. Congress, and the various state legislatures were by modern standards virtually inactive. The law was declared by judges in the process of resolving disputes, relying on traditional principles. In modern times society and polity have grown more complex at an accelerating rate, and it is no longer possible to deal with modern problems by relying on slowly evolving legal principles. As a result, modern legislatures have assumed the major burdens of lawmaking, and the courts have assumed a sharply reduced role.

Judges Make Law

It is currently part of the American democratic folklore that judges merely interpret but do not "make" law. The fallacy of this notion lies in the fact that the power to interpret the law inevitably leads to making the law. Every time a judge is called upon to interpret the law, lawmaking occurs. Because judges ordinarily rely on the authority of existing law, judicial interpretation of the law invokes changes that are nearly imperceptible, but when faced with novel or difficult cases, judges occasionally formulate statements of the law that form important new principles.

It may be helpful to give an example of judicial lawmaking. In the landmark case of *MacPherson v. Buick Motor Co.*, 217 N.Y. 382, 111 N.E. 1050 (1916), Justice Cardozo of the New York Court of Appeals wrote an opinion that ushered in a new era in liability of manufacturers for injuries caused by their products, leading many years later to the field of **product liability**. Mr. MacPherson sued for injuries caused by the collapse of a defective wooden spoke wheel on the Buick he had purchased. The company defended against the suit on the grounds that it had sold the car to a dealer, which in turn sold the car to MacPherson. Because Buick did not have a contractual relation with MacPherson, it was not liable, stated attorneys for the company. In a carefully reasoned opinion, Cardozo explained why the company could not be protected by the traditional principle of **privity of contract** and held the company liable. The appearance of the automobile on the American scene put in the hands of the American public a potentially dangerous machine. Cardozo held that the manufacturer was responsible for inspection of the vehicles it sold and refused to allow the manufacturer to pass liability on to the dealer under the guise of privity of contract. In handing down his decision, Cardozo charted a course for compensation law in the United States.

Stare Decisis

Today the importance of the common law tradition lies largely in the principle of *precedent,* or **stare decisis**, by which judicial lawmaking is rendered orderly, predictable, and legitimate. The principle of *stare decisis* dictates that in making decisions judges should follow prior precedents. In practice this means that disputes involving similar fact situations should be decided by similar rules. Former decisions are thus called

---
BALLENTINE'S
---

product liability   The liability of a manufacturer or seller of an article for an injury caused to a person or to property by a defect in the article sold. A product liability suit is a tort action in which strict liability is imposed. The manufacturer or seller of a defective product may be liable to third parties ... as well as to purchasers, as privity of contract is not a requirement in a product liability case.

privity of contract   The legal relationship between the parties to a contract. In some circumstances, a party must be in privity of contract with another party in order to assert a claim.

stare decisis   Means "standing by the decision." ... [T]he doctrine that judicial decisions stand as precedents for cases arising in the future. It is a fundamental policy of our law that, except in unusual circumstances, a court's determination on a point of law will be followed by courts of the same or lower rank in later cases presenting the same legal issue, even though different parties are involved and many years have elapsed.

precedents and are examined for guidance in making present decisions. When the court is faced with a novel fact situation ("case of first impression") and formulates a rule to decide the case, the court "sets a precedent" that should be followed should a similar case arise.

As an example, let us suppose that a state court is faced with the following situation: a man and woman who have been living together for several years without benefit of marriage separate; the woman sues the man for breach of contract, claiming that when they entered into a cohabitation arrangement, the man promised to share his earnings equally with her if she refrained from employment and provided him with homemaking services and companionship, to which she agreed. The man defends on the basis of an established principle of contract law that a contract to perform illegal acts is unenforceable. Because sexual cohabitation is illegal in the state and that was the purpose of any promises that might have been exchanged, claims the man, the contract cannot be enforced.

Assuming the court has never been faced with this precise situation before, it must apply the rules of contract law and set a precedent for cohabitation agreements. Judging from similar cases already decided in several states, the court will probably rule that a cohabitation agreement is enforceable like any other contract unless its purpose is compensation for sexual services. Once this precedent has been set, the next dispute over a cohabitation agreement should be decided by application of the same rule. In this way, the first case is precedent for the second. If the rule is applied in many similar cases over a period of time, the court is likely to refer to it as a "well-established principle of law."

The *Yanakas* case demonstrates the importance which judges attach to precedent. Here the parties were agreeable to dismissing the case without an opinion. The court, however, refused to be manipulated.

The force of a precedent depends upon the court that hands it down. A precedent is considered binding on the court that sets it and all lower courts within its jurisdiction. In a typical state court system, decisions can be rendered at three levels: trial court (lowest), court of appeals (intermediate appellate), and state supreme court (highest). Decisions of the highest state court are binding on all state courts. Decisions of courts of appeals are binding on that court and on lower courts within its jurisdiction. There is frequently more than one court of appeals, each with specific regional jurisdiction within the state. The hierarchy of federal courts also follows this pattern.

It sometimes happens that different courts of appeals within the same system (i.e., a state or the federal system) will formulate different rules for the same fact situation, creating considerable confusion. Trial courts in the First Circuit may feel bound by a different rule than those in the Fifth Circuit, and courts in the Third Circuit, whose court of appeals may not have decided an equivalent case, may be in a quandary about whether to follow the First Circuit rule

MANUFACTURERS HANOVER TRUST COMPANY, Plaintiff-Appellee,
v.
Nicholas YANAKAS, Defendant-Appellant,
Charles Buonincontri and
Camille Buonincontri, Defendants.
United States Court of Appeals,
Second Circuit 11 F.3d 381
(2d Cir. 1993)

The appeal in this matter, in which defendant Nicholas Yanakas challenged the granting of summary judgment to plaintiff Manufacturers Hanover Trust Co. (the Bank) on its claim to enforce certain guarantees, was decided in an opinion filed on October 18, 1993 ... (October judgment). We affirmed in part, reversed in part, and remanded for trial as to certain defenses and **counterclaims** asserted by Yanakas. On October 27, 1993, after the filing of our opinion but before the issuance of the mandate, Yanakas and the Bank jointly moved for **vacatur** of the October judgment on the ground that they have conditionally reached an agreement to settle all of the claims in the suit if this Court will vacate its decision. For the reasons below, we deny the motion.

* * *

Most of the opinions relied on by the parties deal with the course that should be followed when a case becomes **moot** while an appeal is pending. In such circumstances, the appeal itself must of course be dismissed because there is no longer a case or controversy for the appellate court to decide ... .

On the other hand, the appellate court should not vacate the judgment below if the case has become moot due to the voluntary act of the losing party ... . If we were to vacate where the party that lost in the district court has taken action to moot the controversy, the result would be to allow that party to eliminate its loss without an appeal and to deprive the winning party of the judicial protection it has fairly won.

* * *

Nor do we view the granting of such a motion as a wise exercise of discretion, for vacatur of the appellate court's judgment would facilitate two abuses. First, it would allow the parties to obtain an advisory opinion of the court of appeals in a case in which there may not be, or may no longer be, any genuine case or controversy; the federal courts of course have no jurisdiction to render such opinions. Second, even where there was a genuine case or controversy, it would allow a party with a deep pocket to eliminate an unreviewable precedent it dislikes simply by agreeing to a sufficiently lucrative settlement to obtain its adversary's cooperation in a motion to vacate. We do not consider this a proper use of the judicial system. See *Izumi Seimitsu Kogyo Kabushiki Kaisha v. U.S. Philips Corp.*, 62 U.S.L.W. 4007, 4011 (U.S. Nov. 30, 1993) ... (Stevens, J., dissenting from dismissal of certiorari as improvidently granted) ("Judicial precedents are presumptively correct and valuable to the legal community as a whole. They are not merely the property of private litigants and should stand unless a court concludes that the public interest would be served by a vacatur.") ... Although this Circuit's refusal to vacate is limited to judgments as to which there is no right of review, we agree with the Seventh Circuit that [w]hen a clash between genuine adversaries produces a precedent, ... the judicial system ought not allow the social value of that precedent, created at cost to the public and other litigants, to be a bargaining chip in the process of settlement. The precedent, a public act of a public official, is not the parties' property. The Tenth Circuit in *Oklahoma Radio Associates*, after surveying cases from the Supreme Court and all of the Circuits, see 3 F.3d at 1437-44, similarly concluded that

> The furthering of settlement of controversies is important and desirable, but there are significant countervailing considerations which we must also weigh. A policy permitting litigants to use the settlement process as a means of obtaining the withdrawal of unfavorable precedents is fraught with the potential for abuse.

We agree with the Seventh Circuit that an opinion is a public act of the government, which may not be expunged by private agreement. ... We agree with Judge Easterbrook's view that the parties are not free to contract about the existence of these decisions. ...

The joint motion for vacatur of this Court's judgment of October 18, 1993, is DENIED.

Case Questions

1. Why did the parties want this case dismissed short of appeal?
2. The parties wanted to vacate the judgment of the court of appeals because of their mutual agreement. What reasons did the court give for denying their wishes?
3. How does the court recognize a public interest in the outcome of a private lawsuit between two parties?

Case Glossary

counterclaim A cause of action on which a defendant in a lawsuit might have sued the plaintiff in a separate action.

vacatur A rule or order that vacates a proceeding. [To vacate, as] applied to a judgment, decree, or other order of a court, [is] to annul, set aside, void, or cancel.

moot case A case involving only abstract questions; a case without any actual controversy between the parties. Generally, the courts will not hear a case that has become moot.

or the Fifth Circuit rule. The logical solution is to obtain a ruling from the highest court, which is at liberty to adopt either rule or even a different rule, which would then be binding on all the courts within its jurisdiction.

The quagmire of American jurisdiction can be clarified by certain important principles. First, not only are federal and state court systems separate, but state and federal laws are separate as well. Where federal law is concerned, federal courts set the precedents, and the U.S. Supreme Court has final authority in declaring what the law is. In matters of state law, state courts have authority, and the highest court of a state has final authority to declare what the law is. Many Americans labor under the misconception that the U.S. Supreme Court is the final authority for interpreting state law. On the contrary, the highest court of each state is the ultimate authority for the law of that state. One of the reasons for the confusion arises from the supremacy clause of the U.S. Constitution, under which the U.S. Supreme Court may declare state law, whether judicial precedent or state statute, invalid if it is deemed to be in violation of the U.S. Constitution. This power of the U.S. Supreme Court is not derived from any authority to define state law but from authority to interpret the meaning of the U.S. Constitution, which is the "supreme law of the land."

LI
v.
YELLOW CAB COMPANY OF CALIFORNIA
et al., Defendants and
Respondents
13 Cal. 3d 804, 532 P.2d 1226,
119 Cal. Rptr. 858 (1975)

In this case we address the grave and recurrent question [of] whether we should judicially declare no longer applicable in California courts the doctrine of **contributory negligence**, which bars all recovery when the plaintiff's negligent conduct has contributed as a legal cause in any degree to the harm suffered by him, and hold that it must give way to a system of **comparative negligence**, which assesses liability in direct proportion to fault. ...

It is unnecessary for us to catalogue the enormous amount of critical comment that has been directed over the years against the "all-or-nothing" approach of the doctrine of contributory negligence. The essence of that criticism has been constant and clear: the doctrine is inequitable in its operation because it fails to distribute responsibility in proportion to fault.

* * *

It is in view of these theoretical and practical considerations that to this date 25 states have abrogated the "all or nothing" rule of contributory negligence and have enacted in its place general apportionment statutes calculated in one manner or another to assess liability in proportion to fault. In 1973 these states were joined by Florida, which effected the same result by judicial decision. (*Hoffman v. Jones* (Fla. 1973) 280 So.2d 431.) We are likewise persuaded that logic, practical experience, and fundamental justice counsel against the retention of the doctrine rendering contributory negligence a complete bar to recovery—and that it should be replaced in this state by a system under which liability for damage will be borne by those whose negligence caused it in direct proportion to their respective fault. ...

It is urged that any change in the law of contributory negligence must be made by the Legislature, not by this court. Although the doctrine of contributory negligence is of judicial origin ... subsequent cases of this court, it is pointed out, have unanimously affirmed that ... the "all-or-nothing" rule is the law of this state and shall remain so until the Legislature directs otherwise. ...

[There follows a discussion of why the court may nevertheless abolish the doctrine of contributory negligence followed by a discussion of the different forms of comparative negligence adopted in the other states.]

For all of the foregoing reasons we conclude that the "all-or-nothing" rule of contributory negligence as it presently exists in this state should be and is herewith superseded by a system of "pure" comparative negligence, the fundamental purpose of which shall be to assign responsibility and liability for damage in direct proportion to the amount of negligence of each of the parties.

* * *

The judgment is reversed.

* * *

CLARK, J., dissenting. ... [T]he Legislature is the branch best able to effect transition from contributory to comparative or some other doctrine of negligence. Numerous and differing negligence systems have been urged over the years, yet there remains widespread disagreement among both the commentators and the states as to which one is best. ... This court is not an investigatory body, and we lack the means of fairly appraising the merits of these competing systems. Constrained by settled rules of judicial review, we must consider only matters within the record or susceptible to judicial notice. That this court is inadequate to the task of carefully selecting the best replacement system is reflected in the majority's summary manner of eliminating from consideration all but two of the many competing proposals—including models adopted by some of our sister states.

By abolishing this century old doctrine today, the majority seriously erodes our constitutional function. We are again guilty of judicial chauvinism.

Case Questions

1. Is abolishing contributory negligence a question more properly addressed by the legislature than the court? (Consider this question when reading the section below comparing adjudication and legislation.)
2. If the court sets a "bad" precedent, must it wait for the legislature to rectify the mistake?
3. What if the California legislature, after the decision in *Li*, passed a law unequivocally declaring that contributory negligence and not comparative negligence was the law of California? Does a legislature have authority to do this? Must the court follow the statute?

Case Glossary

negligence The failure to do something that a reasonable person would do in the same circumstances, or the doing of something a reasonable person would not do. Negligence is a wrong generally characterized by carelessness, inattentiveness, and neglectfulness rather than by a positive intent to cause injury.

contributory negligence In the law of negligence, a failure by the plaintiff to exercise reasonable care which, in part at least, is the cause of an injury.

comparative negligence The doctrine adopted by most states that requires a comparison of the negligence of the defendant with the negligence of the plaintiff ... . [T]he plaintiff's negligence does not defeat his or her cause of action, but it does reduce the damages he or she is entitled to recover.

The *Li* case is an example of a court overruling a well-established precedent and thus substituting a new rule. The issue facing the Supreme Court of California was whether to abolish the doctrine of contributory negligence and replace it with the doctrine of comparative negligence. Negligence is discussed in some detail in the chapter on torts, but in layman's terms, negligence occurs when one person injures another by failing to exercise care (for example, if someone carelessly causes an auto accident). Because negligence is grounded in fault, the courts in the nineteenth century developed the doctrine of *contributory negligence,* which held that a negligent defendant would not be liable if it could be shown that the plaintiff's negligence also contributed to the injury. It soon became apparent that the doctrine was inequitable in cases in which the defendant's negligence was great and the plaintiff's negligence was minimal. For example, railroad workers commonly worked under dangerously unsafe conditions and sometimes contributed to their own injuries through momentary inattention. Gradually the states began to replace contributory negligence with the doctrine of *comparative negligence,* which apportioned fault between plaintiff and defendant so that the plaintiff, even if also negligent, could recover a diminished amount if the jury found the plaintiff less responsible for the cause of the injury (e.g., plaintiff 20 percent at fault and defendant 80 percent at fault).

In *Li,* the plaintiff made an improper turn through an intersection and was struck by the defendant, who was racing to pass through the intersection while the stoplight was yellow. The case was heard without a jury. The judge found both plaintiff and defendant negligent and entered a judgment in favor of the defendant based on California law. The plaintiff then appealed in the hope that she could persuade the Supreme Court of California to overrule prior precedent, in which effort she was successful.

A careful reading of the case reveals that four of the six justices ruling on the case wanted to change the law. Their decision was complicated by the fact that although contributory negligence originally arose through judicial decision, the California legislature had enacted a statute in 1872 establishing the doctrine of contributory negligence. In a lengthy discussion of the statute and its history (omitted here), the court concluded that the statute had not been intended to permanently establish contributory negligence as the law of the state.

Adjudication versus Legislation

Although judges may be said to "make law," they do so in a way quite unlike that of legislators. Legislation is a very different process with a different orientation. Whereas adjudication can be said to be particularized in the sense that cases focus on particular events and particular parties, legislation is generalized in that it is designed to make rules that apply to everyone.

Adjudication: Narrow Focus on Past Events

Judges resolve disputes between parties; **adjudication** refers to the process of making these decisions. In the American system, a person (which can also be a business, a corporation, or a city) files a lawsuit against another to redress an injury or to establish rights and duties. When a case reaches trial, the judge is faced with past events that have been framed by attorneys for both sides for submission to the judge for resolution. Ordinarily only the facts of the events relating to the dispute are relevant to its resolution. Evidence presented at trial will reveal

---

BALLENTINE'S

adjudication   The final decision of a court, usually made after trial of the case; the court's final judgment.

those facts in great detail in order to determine which rule of law is applicable. The judge will decide which laws are relevant to the facts as determined by the evidence presented in court. Thus, the process of adjudication focuses on past events specific to one dispute, and only the law the judge deems appropriate to that case will be applied.

In short, the judge looks through a magnifying glass at one case and declares what law is applicable. If law is made in the process, it is a byproduct of the case. The function of the judge is to settle the dispute, not to determine how the law applies to other cases in the future. The judge will look to the authority of the past to make the decision.

Legislation: Universal Application and Future Effect

The characteristics of **legislation** are universal application and future effect. Legislators do not resolve individual cases, though they are often motivated by dissatisfaction with the outcomes of cases decided in the courts. For example, the "Baby M" case in New Jersey (*In re Baby M*, 109 N.J. 396, 537 A.2d 1227 [1988]), in which a surrogate mother fought unsuccessfully to gain custody from the couple who had arranged for the baby's adoption, resulted in many legislatures, including New Jersey, enacting laws regulating surrogate mother contracts. But the New Jersey legislature did not decide the *Baby M* case nor change the ruling of the court; its enactment governed contracts between surrogate mothers and adoptive parents in future cases.

The legislative process typically operates by first recognizing a problem and then, through investigation and deliberation, attempting to solve the problem by enacting a law. When the legislative process is complete, the law is a matter of public record, and everyone must comply or risk legal consequences. Only rarely can legislation apply retroactively. The surrogate mother case brought to public attention the moral issues in the commercialization of pregnancy and adoption. Some people felt that such contracts should be illegal or unenforceable, some felt that the natural mother should have the option to revoke the contract, and others felt that ordinary contract law provided sufficient protection. State legislatures deliberated these questions and arrived at laws designed to deal with the question. These laws, however, did not change adoptions that had already taken place, but instead served as the legal standards that would govern surrogate mother contracts subsequent to enactment of law.

The *Colby* and *Higgins* cases illustrate the difference between legislation and adjudication and illuminate the judicial attitude exemplified in the doctrine of stare decisis.

BALLENTINE'S

legislation   Laws ... enacted by a legislative body ... .

Edwin A. COLBY, Administrator

v.

CARNEY HOSPITAL

356 Mass. 527, 254 N.E.2d 407 (1969)

The plaintiff **administrator** brings this action of tort and contract for the death and conscious suffering of his **intestate**. The defendant hospital set up, among other things, the defence of charitable immunity. The plaintiff **demurred** to this part of the answer, stating that it "does not set forth a valid or legal defense, in that said defense as alleged violates and abrogates certain rights, privileges and immunities granted to, and preserved for the citizens of the Commonwealth" under arts. 1, 10, 11, 12, 20, and 30 of our Declaration of Rights and also under the Fifth and Fourteenth Amendments to the Constitution of the United States. A judge in the Superior Court overruled the demurrer, and the plaintiff appealed.

The demurrer was rightly overruled. Nothing has been brought to our attention suggesting that the doctrine of charitable immunity is repugnant to any provision of the Constitutions of the United States and the Commonwealth.

In the past on many occasions we have declined to renounce the defence of charitable immunity set forth in *McDonald v. Massachusetts Gen. Hosp.*, 120 Mass. 432, and *Roosen v. Peter Bent Brigham Hosp.*, 235 Mass. 66, 126 N.E. 392, 14 A.L.R. 563. We took this position because we were of opinion that any renunciation preferably should be accomplished prospectively and that this should be best done by legislative action. Now it appears that only three or four States still adhere to the doctrine. ... It seems likely that no legislative action in this Commonwealth is probable in the near future. Accordingly, we take this occasion to give adequate warning that the next time we are squarely confronted by a legal question respecting the charitable immunity doctrine it is our intention to abolish it.

Order overruling demurrer affirmed.

John HIGGINS

v.

EMERSON HOSPITAL

328 N.E.2d 488 (1975)

This appeal brings before us the issue whether, by reason of the language in *Colby v. Carney Hosp.*, 356 Mass. 527, 528, 254 N.E.2d 407 (1969), we should hold that the defense of charitable immunity is not available to the defendant hospital. ...

The plaintiff brought an action in tort and contract for injuries allegedly sustained by him on June 17, 1970, while he was an inpatient at the defendant hospital. The case was tried on June 20, 1974, before a Superior Court judge and a jury. The plaintiff's attorney made an opening statement that asserted the facts of the plaintiff's accident and injury, including a stipulation that the defendant hospital ... was operated exclusively for charitable purposes. The judge thereupon **directed verdicts** for the defendant as to both counts of the plaintiff's declaration.

... The parties and the judge have clearly considered that the single issue is whether, by reason of the *Colby* case, or any other consideration, we should hold that charitable immunity is not applicable in this case. We hold that the doctrine is applicable and the judge properly directed verdicts for the defendant as to both counts.

The injury here occurred after the date of the decision of the *Colby* case (December 23, 1969), but before the effective date, September 16, 1971, of [the statute] which abolished the doctrine of charitable immunity. We have since held that the statute is not retrospective in effect ... , and it is thus clear that the plaintiff here takes no benefit from the statute.

The plaintiff contends that, because of the intimation in the *Colby* case as to the possible future abolishment of charitable immunity, that doctrine is not applicable in this case. He argues that from the date of the decision the various charitable institutions, as well as the insurance industry and members of the public, were clearly given notice of and could conform their conduct in reliance on the fact that claims of charitable immunity raised with respect to incidents occurring after the date of the decision, December 23, 1969, would be rejected.

He further contends that had the Legislature not acted on the subject matter in 1971 there would be no question that this court would rule the charitable immunity doctrine abolished as to the instant case.

We reject the arguments. In *Colby v. Carney Hosp.,* 356 Mass. 527, 528, 254 N.E.2d 407, 408 (1969), we said that any renunciation of the doctrine of charitable immunity "should be accomplished *prospectively* and that this should be best done by legislative action" (emphasis supplied). At no time has this court abolished the doctrine. In *Ricker v. Northeastern Univ., supra,* _____ at _____, 279 N.E.2d at 672, we said, speaking of the *Colby* case, "This language does not by itself abolish the

doctrine of charitable immunity as of December 23, 1969 ... [the language] makes it clear that no change of the doctrine was then being made." The Legislature chose to act subsequent to the *Colby* decision. We recognize the factual distinction between the instant case and the *Ricker* case, to wit, that the injury to Ricker occurred prior to December 23, 1969, the date of our decision in the *Colby* case, while the injury underlying this action occurred subsequent to that decision. Nevertheless, we see no persuasive reason now to rule, as in practical effect the plaintiff urges here, that the doctrine of charitable immunity does not apply to an injury which occurred after December 23, 1969, but before the effective date of [the statute].

* * *

Judgment affirmed.

Case Questions

1. If the court was so clearly opposed to charitable immunity, why did it not simply abolish it in *Colby?*
2. Since the doctrine of charitable immunity was a judicial creation in the first place, why did the court look to the legislature to abolish it?
3. How do these cases express the judicial attitude toward precedent in Massachusetts?
4. If you had been Higgins's attorney in *Higgins v. Emerson Hospital,* would you have predicted a win or a loss in the Supreme Judicial Court?

Case Glossary

administrator   A person ... appointed by the court to manage the estate of a person either who died without a will or whose will failed to name an executor or named an executor who declined or was ineligible to serve.

intestate   A person who dies without leaving a valid will.

demurrer   A method of raising an objection to the legal sufficiency of a pleading. A demurrer says, in effect, that the opposing party's complaint alleges facts that, even if true, do not add up to a cause of action and that, therefore, the case should be dismissed.

directed verdict   A verdict that a jury returns as directed by the judge. A judge directs a verdict when the party who has the burden of proof has failed to meet that burden.

American courts in the nineteenth century created or expanded immunity to suit for several categories of parties, including charitable institutions, the subject of *Colby* and *Higgins.* Immunity from suit leaves an injured party without a remedy, and in the twentieth century the courts and legislatures of our country began to question the wisdom and legality of immunity to suit. The rise of the insurance industry made such immunities obsolete. Individuals and institutions can protect themselves from catastrophic losses by purchasing insurance. The Supreme Judicial Court of Massachusetts was presented with an archaic principle of charitable immunity that it had created a century before. By the time these cases were decided, nearly every other state had abolished charitable immunity by statute or by the highest state court overruling its own prior decisions.

Even though the court was inclined to abolish charitable immunity, it found itself in a dilemma. Because the precedents were clear (i.e., charitable institutions were immune from suit according to a well-established line of precedents), the Supreme Judicial Court was reluctant to change the rule suddenly, but at the same time the doctrine of charitable immunity had just as clearly been discredited as a principle of American law. Charitable institutions should be able to rely on the law as stated by the courts. Why should a nonprofit hospital buy insurance if it cannot be sued?

Obiter Dictum

Not everything that is expressed in an opinion is precedent. The author of an opinion is free to make comments that go beyond the immediate issues to be decided. The remarks, opinions, and comments in a decision that exceed the scope of the issues and the rules that decide them are called *dictum,* plural **dicta**, from the older Latin phrase *obiter dictum,* and are not binding on future cases. As we have already seen, the process of adjudication commonly results in the making of new rules or the interpretation of existing rules. This is an unavoidable result of the necessity of resolving disputes. However, when a judge attempts to expand an argument to issues or facts not before the court in the dispute, adjudication ends and legislation begins. Although these statements are worthy of consideration in subsequent cases, they are not considered binding precedent and need not be followed; they are *dicta* rather than rule.

Analytically, the way to distinguish *dictum* from the rule of law is to determine the legal and factual issues presented by a dispute and analyze the reasoning that leads to their resolution. Anything outside this reasoning and the rule behind it is *dictum.*

─────────────────────BALLENTINE'S─────────────────────

dicta   Plural of *dictum,* which is short for ... *obiter dictum.* Dicta are expressions or comments in a court opinion that are not necessary to support the decision made by the court; they are not binding authority and have no value as precedent. If nothing else can be found on point, an advocate may wish to attempt to persuade by citing cases that contain dicta.

This can be applied to the *Colby* and *Higgins* cases. In Colby, the court faced the issue of whether charitable immunity was still the rule in Massachusetts. Although the court expressed its disapproval of the rule, it nevertheless followed prior precedent and held that charitable immunity was still in effect, suggesting that it would be better for the legislature to abolish the doctrine. The court added that it intended to abolish the doctrine the next time it was faced with the same issue. This assertion of the court's future intentions was *dictum*. When the trial court in *Higgins* was faced with the same issue five years later, it upheld charitable immunity and directed verdicts in favor of the defendant. The trial court was legally correct, because the Supreme Judicial Court in *Colby* had not abolished the doctrine but merely expressed its intention to do so. The Supreme Judicial Court agreed with the lower court that the doctrine had not been abolished by the court and indicated that its expression of future intentions had no legally binding force on Massachusetts courts. As a practical matter, the fact that the legislature had subsequently abolished charitable immunity meant that the Supreme Judicial Court need not take it upon itself to abolish the doctrine, which only affected those unfortunate few who were injured prior to the legislative act.

The principle of *obiter dictum* thus tells us that not everything written in a judicial opinion is the law. This requires a careful reading of cases before citing them as authority.

Nonbinding Authority

In practical terms, the law consists of state and federal constitutions, statutes, and judicial opinions. If a trial court in Rhode Island is faced with a difficult legal issue, it will attempt to determine the applicable law by resorting to Rhode Island statutes and case law that conforms to mandates of the Rhode Island and federal constitutions. It is bound by these authorities alone. Nevertheless, the court may confront an issue that clearly demands judicial resolution and for which the usual binding sources of the law provide little or no guidance. Typically this arises in a case of first impression in which the factual situation giving rise to the dispute has never been decided by a court of the state nor been addressed by the state legislature.

Reasoning from Authority

To arrive at a reasonable solution, the court will use the best authority it can find. It may reason from existing state law using logic and analogy to infer a rule. For instance, until recently state courts universally rejected the notion that a professional license was property that could be used to establish property settlements upon divorce. This was particularly problematic in cases in which spouses, usually wives, had worked to support their husbands through professional school, only to be divorced soon afterward, when their professional husbands had not yet practiced long enough to acquire much property to be divided between husband and wife. In attempting to classify professional licenses, the courts, though admitting the license clearly had value for its holders, noted that the licenses did not have the usual attributes of property (namely, they could not be transferred, sold, leased, or given away) and noted that they could be revoked by the licensing authority. Although many courts obviously felt that this traditional definition of property resulted in an injustice to many wives, they felt compelled to follow the law. Finally, in *O'Brien v. O'Brien*, 489 N.E.2d 712 (N.Y. 1985), the New York court defined professional licenses as "marital property," justifying its departure from prior law on the basis of recent divorce legislation that provided a broad definition of marital property in divorce.

Law from Sister States

When binding authority is absent, the court often looks to nonbinding authority from other states. An issue unique in one state may very well have been decided in another. It seems reasonable to examine such decisions to see whether the rules handed down and the reasoning behind them are applicable to the law of the state faced with a case of first impression. Often the pioneering state will give its name to the principle; for example, one of the comparative negligence rules mentioned in *Li* as the "50 percent" rule might also be referred to as the "Wisconsin rule," as opposed to the "Florida rule," which is normally referred to as "pure" comparative negligence.

Decisions of other state courts are commonly referred to as *persuasive authority;* they command respect because they represent the law of another American jurisdiction even though they are not binding outside that jurisdiction. The persuasiveness of such authority is greatest in areas of common law, especially torts, and weakest in decisions based on statutory interpretation. For example, in the area of family law, there is considerable variation among the states concerning divorce law, so the reasoning of the court of one state may be considered inappropriate in another by virtue of differences between their respective statutes. For example, California is a **community property**

BALLENTINE'S

community property A system of law under which the earnings of either spouse are the property of both the husband and the wife, and property acquired by either spouse during the marriage (other than by gift, under a will, or through inheritance) is the property of both.

state, whereas New York is an **equitable distribution** state, making California decisions regarding the distribution of property upon divorce often inapplicable to New York cases. In contrast, because the **Uniform Commercial Code** (UCC) has been adopted in every state except Louisiana, decisions interpreting the UCC are often used as persuasive authority.

Secondary Sources

In addition to cases from other states, a vast array of legal materials used in arguments by lawyers and opinions by judges that are not officially the law anywhere are called *secondary authority.* Principal among these are law review articles, **treatises**, and the **Restatements**. Law review articles written by legal scholars commonly address contemporary problems in the law and suggest carefully reasoned solutions. For example, the surrogate motherhood question that arose in New Jersey in the *Baby M* case gave rise to numerous articles critiquing the court's decision and discussing appropriate solutions to the issues raised. Treatises by eminent scholars are often cited in cases, and the Restatements are especially respected because they attempt to provide a general statement of American law rather than focus on any particular state.

In addition to cases of first impression, courts, usually the highest state courts, are sometimes presented with cases that reveal serious weakness in prior precedents and urge their overruling. In rationalizing the departure from what otherwise appears to be binding precedent, the court will muster all the available persuasive authority and secondary authority it can.

Because cases raise serious legal issues and judges are entrusted with the administration of justice, decisions are not mechanical products of legal scholarship. Much attention is given in written opinions to

---
────────────────────────────BALLENTINE'S────────────────────────────

equitable distribution   Some jurisdictions permit their courts, in a divorce case, to distribute all property obtained during the marriage on an "equitable" basis, that is, without regard to whose name the property is in. In deciding what is equitable, the court takes into consideration factors such as the length of the marriage and the contributions of each party, including homemaking.

Uniform Commercial Code   One of the Uniform Laws, which has been adopted in much the same form in every state. It governs most aspects of commercial transactions, including sales, leases, negotiable instruments, deposits and collections, letters of credit, bulk sales, warehouse receipts, bills of lading and other documents of title, investment securities, and secured transactions.

treatise   A book that discusses, in depth, important principles in some area of human activity or interest.

Restatements of the Law   A series of volumes published by the American Law Institute, written by legal scholars, each volume or set of volumes covering a major field of the law. Each of the Restatements is, among other things, a statement of the law as it is generally interpreted and applied by the courts with respect to particular legal principles.

fairness to the parties and the consequences to society of the rules that are constructed or enforced. The search for authority on which to base a rule helps to ensure that judges do not act merely on their own personal value systems but instead reflect a consensus of the wisdom of their peers. This is the legacy of the common law, a system of judicial decision making that has endured many centuries of political and social change and has perhaps greatly assisted in making those changes.

Summary

The Anglo-American legal tradition has a rich history of judge-made law known as the common law. It is governed by the principle of *stare decisis,* which urges that the courts abide by past precedents unless there is a compelling reason to depart from them. The process of adjudication focuses on disputes, in contrast to the legislative process, which enacts general laws for future application.

In determining and interpreting the law, courts base decisions on authority, principally statutes and prior case law. When these do not provide a clear answer to the case at hand, secondary authority may be the source of reasoning and rules.

The statements of the law made in higher courts must be followed by the lower courts, but the force of precedent applies only to that part of the decision pertinent to the facts of the dispute before the court and not to incidental statements of the author of a judicial opinion.

Review Questions

1. Why is the American system called a common law system?

2. What does judicial restraint restrain?

3. Why is *dictum* not binding?

4. What is the difference in process between legislation and adjudication?

5. When may a court overrule a prior precedent?

Exercises

1. Find out what regional reporter publishes your state's appellate decisions. How is the reporter abbreviated in citations?

2. Does your state have a reporter that reports decisions of the trial courts?

TAKE CHARGE OF YOUR CAREER

C.B. Estrin

Learning the Ropes

Whether you are new in the firm or there have been significant changes going on about you, it is imperative that you "learn the ropes." Just about every firm or corporation has some sort of policy manual. Even if your firm's manual doesn't make sense when you first go through it—you may not be familiar with all of the in-house abbreviations—be sure you read it carefully.

Some firms provide in-depth orientations which offer a stockpile of information. Others only allot an hour for this process. Quickly meeting with the human resource director, filling out the W-2 and health insurance forms, and learning about the vacation policy is *not* an orientation.

In such short indoctrinations, employees learn about their firm or corporation only by what is *not* said. They also learn important information only when they've made mistakes "by not following company policy." Ask to read all of the firm's collateral material. Such material includes the firm brochure, annual report, firm résumé, rainmaking letters and even the "face" book (that so-informative directory with everyone's picture and educational background). Also ask for copies of all of the back issues of the firm's newsletter. Reviewing these documents will give you a feel for the progression of the firm, who was promoted from where, what significant clients the firm handles, and who the important players are. If your firm publishes in-house and client newsletters, be sure to get copies of both. Find out whether the firm has a videotape library of previous seminars and other events. There may even be photo albums of past holiday parties and company picnics.

Marketing Your Career

One of the problems paralegals face is being part of the backstage process. When a case is won, a matter settled, a merger completed, it's usually the attorney who is the primary source of praise and attention—not the paralegal. And while many attorneys will acknowledge the help and assistance of the paralegal, more often, paralegals are the "unsung heroes."

If you rarely receive praise for a job well-done, don't be afraid to reach out and claim it. But how you claim your rightful share of the spotlight can be a very sensitive matter. One way is to send a congratulatory memo to the attorney you worked with.

Another simple, yet effective, career marketing tool is to find out who lunches—and get yourself invited. This technique will help you discover what is going on in the organization, communicate to others what you are doing, and give you exposure to other cases and projects.

Communicating to others on what kinds of matters and levels of assignments you handle gives others an opportunity to promote your career for you. Assignments may come up that need additional paralegals. Your colleagues will be able to suggest you because they are familiar with your capabilities.

Have a Plan

Many paralegals feel that moving into upper management would take them away from their preferred hands-on work. However, having a plan of action is just as important for those who seek horizontal moves as for those who want to move up the career ladder. One approach is to target where you would like to be in yearly segments for up to five years.

Don't Be Afraid to Rock the Boat

Wayne Gretzky once said, "You miss 100 percent of the shots you don't take." By not managing your career, you'll miss opportunities. Taking risks may mean that you make a mistake, but making mistakes is a part of life. Hopefully, you'll minimize the results of those mistakes, hurt no one (including yourself) and, in the process, learn not to repeat them.

You must create a positive atmosphere to get rid of nonproductive fears that trap you into becoming a victim of the system. Your career strategy must be constructive, cautious, planned and flexible in order to make quality leaps forward.

CHAPTER 5

LEGISLATION

Introduction

Historically, judicial decisions have played the major role in the evolution of Anglo-American law, but the courts as the source of law have been eclipsed in modern times by the ascendancy of legislatures as primary lawmaking bodies.

Evolution of Legislation

During most of the development of Anglo-American law, the pronouncement of law was accomplished by courts deciding cases in which customs, practices, and informal principles of conduct were formalized in written decisions. Although Anglo-American law largely escaped the **codification** movements that revolutionized continental European law, the nineteenth century brought a new attitude in America with regard to legislation. The English Parliament enacted numerous statutes over the centuries that clarified or changed the common law, but its legislative output was minor in comparison to the courts as a source of law.

The American situation was different. The United States had approved a written federal constitution that allocated political authority among the three branches of government, providing specific important spheres of authority for *Congress*. (See Appendix D; U.S. Const. Art. I, §§ 1 and 8.) The legal profession and the courts were viewed by some with suspicion because of the elitist tradition of these institutions in England and colonial America. Congress, in contrast, was elected by the people and thus viewed as representative of the people. It was natural that antiaristocratic sentiment in the new republic would turn to Congress and the state legislatures for lawmaking, which is their constitutional and customary function.

The last half of the nineteenth century saw a major movement toward codification in the United States. In addition to the reasons previously given for favoring legislation, two others provided impetus. First, Americans had learned through revolution and the establishment of the Constitution that the people could guide their own destiny by making law through their representatives, a democratic and rational process. Second, the country was undergoing rapid change and development,

---

BALLENTINE'S

codification   1. The process of arranging laws in a systematic form covering the entire law of a jurisdiction or a particular area of the law; the process of creating a code. 2. The process of turning a common law rule into a statute.

and Americans were disinclined to preserve ancient customs simply because they were ancient. Americans were ambitious and ready for change. To wait for the evolution of legal principles through the cumbersome and conservative judicial process was probably never truly part of the American character.

The most renowned spokesman for codification was David Dudley Field, a New York lawyer who was appointed to a law revision commission that authored the *Code of Civil Procedure* enacted in 1848, often called simply the "Field Code." Although Field advocated and authored several other codes, their reception in New York and other eastern states was poor. Western states, on the contrary, wholeheartedly jumped at the chance for ready-made law, perhaps because their brief history and lack of tradition made them impatient for a system of laws from which they could set new horizons.

The complex problems of the twentieth century have encouraged timely responses from legislative bodies, which have become politically very powerful, often seeming to eclipse the common law tradition. Although the states differ in the extent to which they have codified state law, every state has enacted a complex body of statutes that serves as a principal source of law. The rise of the power of legislatures is reflected in the courts, which now defer to the statutes. Nevertheless, because disputes over the law must ultimately be resolved in the courts, the meaning of legislation is decided by the courts and applied to specific cases.

The Nature of Legislation

In Chapter 4, legislation was distinguished from judge-made law by its characteristics of "universal application and future effect." The line drawn between the characteristics of legislation and adjudication has not always been clear. In the past, legislatures have often passed special bills to define narrow rights of individuals or local entities, but this practice has always been viewed with suspicion (see the 1851 case of *Ponder v. Graham*). When a legislative body narrows its focus to resolve a particularized dispute, it may be challenged in court as violating the principle of separation of judicial and legislative powers embodied in federal and state constitutions.

Legislation strives to reduce principles of law to a coherent written form in which the intent of the law can be determined from the words alone—statutes are pure rules, often without policy statements or statements of intent. In this respect they differ in nature from the common law, which, while relying on past precedent when available, may be characterized as customary law because it is based on unwritten principles of justice and proper conduct rooted in the values of society and is elaborated in often lengthy critical comments in the decisions. The rules in judicial decisions are formulated to apply to the case before the court and are tailored to that dispute. They express an underlying principle rather than an exact rule, as is the case with legislation. The reasoning is as much a part of the rule as the precise statement of the rule in the decision.

The common law treats law as an evolving process. Ultimately it is what a case comes to stand for rather than what it actually states. For example, the landmark school case *Goss v. Lopez,* 419 U.S. 565 (1975), which defined the rights of public school students in certain disciplinary actions, is frequently cited as establishing a constitutional right to a public education. In fact, *Goss v. Lopez* did not hold that there was such a right in the U.S. Constitution, but rather that once a state (Ohio) established such a right, it could not take that right away without due process of law. Nonetheless, if the U.S. Supreme Court or state courts dealing with state law declare that *Goss v. Lopez* holds that there is a constitutional right to a public education, then that principle becomes the law, regardless of the actual language of the prior case. Because all states provide public education, the distinction is largely academic, but the point here is that judicial statements of law are not always taken literally in the way that statutes are. Because judicial decisions are narrowly framed by reference to particularized disputes, the rules they express frequently require further refinement and explanation when used as precedent for subsequent cases.

This distinction may be shown more simply by the difference in attitude of a court in dealing with legislation as opposed to judicial precedent. The court "interprets" statutes, that is, attempts to determine the meaning of the words and phrases in the statute, whereas the specific rules laid down in cases are examined to determine the underlying principles on which they are based. For example, in *Goss v. Lopez*, the majority concluded with the statement:

> We should also make it clear that we have addressed ourselves solely to the short suspension, not exceeding 10 days. Longer suspensions or expulsions for the remainder of the school term, or permanently, may require more formal procedures.

In so stating, the court made its ruling quite limited, leaving clarification for future cases. Such an imprecise approach would be unacceptable for legislation.

The end result of legislation is the enactment of written laws with an effective date and publication in the statute books. From the lawyer's point of view, the quality of legislation is measured by its clarity and lack of ambiguity. Because lawyers must be able to predict the outcomes of their clients' disputes, carefully framed statutes are an important aid. But legislators are not clairvoyant; they cannot predict every future scenario and provide for every possibility. Numerous cases arise in which the applicability of a statute to a particular case is unclear. A court may ultimately be asked to define the statute with regard to its application to a real-life dispute. Keep in mind, however, that when statutes are later found to be faulty or unclear, the legislature is free to amend or change the statute to reflect its intent.

The *Ponder* case reflects a fundamental difference between legislative and adjudicative functions in our political system, but it also reveals an interesting facet of the history of family law. In England, prior to American independence, family law matters were handled by ecclesiastical courts. There was no divorce in the modern sense, although a cumbersome procedure involving common law courts and an act of Parliament could result in a legal divorce. It was rare and, practically speaking, available only to men of influence and power. Because the United States did not incorporate ecclesiastical courts into the legal system, family law eventually fell within the courts of equity (see Chapter 7 for a discussion of courts of law and equity) rather than the common law courts. In the meantime, several state legislatures borrowed from the English practice of legislative divorce and passed special acts divorcing married couples. In the twentieth century, state legislatures have regulated marriage and divorce through statute, and the courts have assumed the task of granting divorces and determining the rights of divorcing parties. When *Ponder v. Graham* was decided, this separation of function was still evolving.

The Legislative Process

Although individual states are free to regulate and order the process of lawmaking, we find a common pattern by which principles are enacted into law. The following discussion describes a formal political process. It does not take into account the influence on legislation of informal political activities, the conflicts inherent in the two-party system, lobbying, interest groups, constituencies, and the like, because their interaction varies from issue to issue and locality to locality.

The hallmark of the legislative process is discussion and debate. (Note that their absence was criticized implicitly in the legislative divorce that the Supreme Court of Florida invalidated in *Ponder v. Graham*.) Passage of a bill into law ultimately requires open debate within the legislative body, which may be quite extensive with complex or controversial legislation, or quite brief with laws on which there is a general consensus or lack of interest.

Among the many problems that arise in our society, some come to the attention of lawmakers as problems that may be helped by the

William G. PONDER, Executor of Archibald Graham, Appellant

v.

Mary GRAHAM, Appellee
4 Fla. 23 (1851)

[Mary Graham was not satisfied with the provisions made for her by her husband, Archibald Graham, in his will, and petitioned to take her **dower** right to one-third interest in his estate in lieu of the will. Ponder was appointed under the will to distribute Archibald's estate and challenged Mary's right on the grounds that she was not lawfully married to Archibald. The jury found for Mary and the court awarded her a one-third interest in Archibald's real estate.]

The facts of the case are succinctly these: The respondent, then Mary Buccles, about the year 1820, in South Carolina, intermarried with one Solomon Canady. Some time afterwards, they removed to, and resided in Georgia, but soon, in consequence of domestic dissensions, separated. Mary went to reside with Graham, a bachelor, and continued to live with him, under circumstances from which an adulterous **cohabitation** might be inferred.

In 1832, and while the said cohabitation continued, a bill was passed by the Legislative Council of the then Territory of Florida, entitled "An act for the relief of Mary Canady."

By this act, the Legislative Council, for the cause expressed in the preamble, assumed to judge and declare that the said Mary Graham was thereby divorced from her said husband, Solomon, and that the bonds of matrimony subsisting between them, were thereby to be entirely and absolutely dissolved, as if the same had never been solemnized. ... There does not appear to have been any petition, **affidavit**, or proofs—a reference to a committee to ascertain the facts, or any notice to the absent husband. In 1834, the cohabitation between Mary and the testator still subsisting, the ceremony of marriage is celebrated between them, and from the time up to the period of the testator's death, which occurred in 1848, he lived with her, and acknowledged her as his wife, and in his will he provides for her by that name, and in that relation.

* * *

The main question raised in this case, as to the power of a Legislative body, *as such,* to grant divorces, is not altogether a new one. It has been investigated by some of the American Courts, and grave constitutional questions have been necessarily involved in the discussion; and yet the question still remains an open one—opinions clashing—nothing settled. ...

No one doubts the right of the people by their constitution, to invest the power in the Legislature, or any where else; but the question is, when the constitution is silent on the subject, in what department of government does this authority rest? [M]uch, if not the whole difficulty, has arisen from overlooking some of the great principles which enter into the constitutional government of the States, and from not preserving the obvious distinction between legislative and judicial functions—by confounding the *right* which a legislative body has to pass *general laws* on the subject of divorce, with the *power* of dissolving the marriage *contract*.

* * *

[The court goes on to dispute the notion that the English Parliament granted divorces, noting that both ecclesiastical courts and common law courts were required to rule on a divorce before it went for approval by the House of Lords, which served as the English supreme court as well as a legislative body.]

In every respect in which I have been able to see this case, I can find no reason to sustain the act of the legislature. It appears by the record, that the parties were domiciled in the State of Georgia, where, it is alleged, the desertion and ill treatment occurred. The wife, living with the testator, Graham, removed to Florida—while the husband returned to Carolina, his former residence. The bill was introduced into the legislature one day, and passed the next. It is very clear that this divorce would not be recognized by the courts of Georgia or Carolina, were any rights asserted under it in those States. ...

I am, therefore, of opinion that the act of the Legislative Council of February 11th, 1832, was in conflict with the organic law of Florida and the Constitution of the United States, and is, therefore, void.

Per Curiam—Let the judgment of the court below be reversed.

Case Questions

1. What does Mary Graham get as a result of this decision?
2. What are the relative powers of legislature and court with regard to divorce?

Case Glossary

dower The legal right or interest that a wife acquires by marriage in the property of her husband. Dower, which was very important under the common law, ensured that a widow was able to live upon and make use of a portion of her husband's land, usually a third, as long as she lived. Dower, as such, no longer exists or has been substantially modified in most states, but every state retains aspects of the concept for the protection of both spouses.

cohabitation 1. Living together as man and wife, although not married to each other. 2. Living together. 3. Having sexual intercourse.

affidavit Any voluntary statement reduced to writing and sworn to or affirmed before a person legally authorized to administer an oath or affirmation.

---

enactment of laws. Typically, legislators serve on legislative committees that deal with a defined area of interest. These committees are assigned to conduct an examination of proposed legislation and frame the law. In studying the problem, the committee collects a wide range of data and information and often conducts hearings on the subject. The purpose is to frame the legislation in the best way to solve the underlying problem, and this is best accomplished if legislators are fully informed about the problem so they can estimate the effectiveness of the solution. Each legislature has rules by which the proposed legislation reaches the floor of the legislature for open debate and vote. All states except Nebraska have a **bicameral** legislature modeled on the U.S. Senate and House of Representatives; the different views of these two bodies often require compromise for passage of a law.

The process is quite different from adjudication, in that the legislators must view the law in its general effect for the future, taking into consideration the effects on all who may be subject to the law.

BALLENTINE'S

bicameral Two-chambered, referring to the customary division of a legislature into two houses (a Senate and a House of Representatives).

Enactment into law makes a public record and serves as notice to the public of the requirements of the law.

Judicial Invalidation of Legislation

Although the courts are bound to uphold legislation, there are two grounds on which courts have struck down legislation:

1. *Defective procedure.* The passage of the law may have been procedurally defective as measured by state law. Because our legislatures have been operating for many decades, the legal requisites of statutory enactment are well known and generally orderly, so procedural challenges are uncommon.

2. *Unconstitutionality.* The law itself may violate principles of state or federal constitutions. Statutes may also be declared unconstitutional in substance rather than procedure. A statute may be unconstitutional "on its face," meaning that a careful reading of the statute reveals that it violates some constitutional prohibition; or a statute may be unconstitutional in its effects or applications, which is more difficult to establish.

Judicial Deference to Legislation

Our constitutional system allocates legislative powers to Congress and authority to decide cases and "controversies" to the federal judiciary. This constitutional mandate has been followed by state constitutions so that the principle of separation of legislative and judicial functions is a fundamental part of our legal system. Inherent in this scheme is the notion that legislatures make law and courts interpret and enforce them.

The *Papachristou* case held a Jacksonville, Florida, vagrancy ordinance unconstitutional both on its face and in its potential for abuse by the police, an abuse made apparent from the facts of the various parties to the case. Note that local legislative bodies, such as a county commission or a city council, enact legislation, commonly called **ordinances,** which have the force of law and are subject to the same constitutional requirements as state and federal statutes. The principal challenge to the ordinance was based on the principle of *void for vagueness,* which

---

BALLENTINE'S

ordinance   A law of a municipal corporation; a local law enacted by a city council, town council, board of supervisors, or the like.

**Margaret PAPACHRISTOU et al.,
Petitioners,
v.
CITY OF JACKSONVILLE
405 U.S. 156 (1972)**

The facts are stipulated. Papachristou and Calloway are white females. Melton and Johnson are black males. Papachristou was enrolled in a job-training program sponsored by the State Employment Service at Florida Junior College in Jacksonville. Calloway was a typing and shorthand teacher at a state mental institution located near Jacksonville. She was the owner of the automobile in which the four defendants were arrested. Melton was a Vietnam war veteran who had been released from the Navy after nine months in a veterans' hospital. On the date of his arrest he was a part-time computer helper while attending college as a full-time student in Jacksonville. Johnson was a tow-motor operator in a grocery chain warehouse and was a lifelong resident of Jacksonville.

At the time of their arrest the four of them were riding in Calloway's car on the main thoroughfare in Jacksonville. They had left a restaurant owned by Johnson's uncle where they had eaten and were on their way to a night club. The arresting officers denied that the racial mixture in the car played any part in the decision to make the arrest. The arrest, they said, was made because the defendants had stopped near a used-car lot which had been broken into several times. There was, however, no evidence of any breaking and entering on the night in question.

Of these four charged with "prowling by auto" none had been previously arrested except Papachristou who had once been convicted of a municipal offense.

* * *

[The court goes on to describe each of the arrests of the several petitioners—including those in companion cases, which were consolidated upon appeal—none of whom were engaged in conduct that would be criminal except for the ordinance.] ... [Heath and his companion] and the automobile were searched. Although no contraband or incriminating evidence was found, they were both arrested, Heath being charged with being a "common thief" because he was reputed to be a thief. The codefendant was charged with "loitering" because he was standing in the driveway, an act which the officers admitted was done only at their command.

* * *

This ordinance is void-for-vagueness, both in the sense that it "fails to give a person of ordinary intelligence fair notice that his contemplated conduct is forbidden by the statute," *United States v. Harriss*, 347 U.S. 612, 617, and because it encourages arbitrary and erratic arrests and convictions.

Living under a rule of law entails various suppositions, one of which is that "[all persons] are entitled to be informed as to what the State commands or forbids."

* * *

The Jacksonville ordinance makes criminal activities which by modern standards are normally innocent. "Nightwalking" is one. ...

"[P]ersons able to work but habitually living upon the earnings of their wives and minor children"—like habitually living "without visible means of support"—might implicate unemployed pillars of the community who have married rich wives.

"[P]ersons able to work but habitually living upon the earnings of their wives or minor children" may also embrace unemployed people out of the labor market, by reason of a recession or disemployed by reason of technological or so-called structural displacements.

* * *

Another aspect of the ordinance's vagueness appears when we focus, not on the lack of notice given a potential offender, but on the effect of the unfettered discretion it places in the hands of the Jacksonville police. ...

A direction by a legislature to the police to arrest all "suspicious" persons would not pass constitutional muster. A vagrancy prosecution may be merely the cloak for a conviction which could not be obtained on the real but undisclosed grounds for the arrest. ...

The Jacksonville ordinance cannot be squared with our constitutional standards and is plainly unconstitutional.
Reversed.

Case Questions

1. What was the purpose of the Jacksonville ordinance?
2. Why did this decision invalidate vagrancy statutes throughout the United States?
3. What constitutional provision supports the void-for-vagueness doctrine?

applies to a statute that "fails to give a person of ordinary intelligence fair notice that his contemplated conduct is forbidden by the statute." This principle is based on the notion that statutes serve as public notice of the conduct required by law. If a law cannot be understood as written, it does not furnish notice. The void-for-vagueness doctrine is derived from the constitutional requirement in the Fourteenth Amendment that no state shall "deprive any person of life, liberty, or property, without due process of law."

The Jacksonville ordinance included peculiar language that came from much earlier English poor laws used to control the working class:

> Rogues and vagabonds, or dissolute persons who go about begging, common gamblers, persons who use juggling or unlawful games or plays, common drunkards, common night thieves, pilferers or pickpockets, traders in stolen property, lewd, wanton and lascivious persons, keepers of gambling places, common railers and brawlers, persons wandering or strolling around from place to place without any lawful purpose or object, habitual loafers, disorderly persons, persons neglecting all lawful business and habitually spending their time by frequenting houses of ill fame, gaming houses, or places where alcoholic beverages are sold or served, persons able to work but habitually living upon the earnings of their wives or minor children shall be deemed vagrants and, upon conviction in the Municipal court shall be punished as provided for Class D offenses. (Jacksonville Ordinance Code § 26–57.)

This does not abolish the common law system, which is still held in high esteem. Nevertheless, legislatures have surpassed the courts as the major source of new law. The evolution of a complex society and legal system in America brought these two legal institutions into direct and frequent confrontation. The separation of powers and the self-imposed custom of judicial restraint ultimately resulted in judicial subservience to statutes. If a statute is procedurally correct and constitutional in substance, American courts are bound to enforce it. Individual judges and courts have expressed dislike for particular statutes at the same time that they have upheld them. If the legislature passes a "bad" law, it is the job of the legislature, not the courts, to revise the law. Courts often send strong messages to the legislature by way of their written decisions, but the legislature may or may not heed these messages.

In the evolutionary process of defining legislative and judicial functions, legislative bodies have also been subject to certain constraints. Although legislatures enact laws and even provide for the means of enforcement by establishing and funding regulatory, judicial, and law enforcement agencies, the task of enforcement is not a legislative function. The courts are the final arbiters of disputes that arise under the laws, whether common law or legislation. The power of the legislature to make the rules is counterbalanced by the power of the judiciary to interpret and apply them. It is not uncommon for a court to give lip service to the language of a statute at the same time that its interpretation of the statute makes serious inroads into its intended purpose. Lawmaking and interpretation take place in a political, social, and economic environment that is often more influential than legal technicalities or even the Constitution.

Statutory Interpretation

For the legal practitioner, the most important problem with legislation is interpretation. Over the course of many years, a number of principles have been developed to guide the courts in resolving disputes over the meaning of statutes. The principles governing statutory interpretation are commonly called *rules of construction,* referring to the manner in which courts are to *construe* the meaning of statutes. The overriding principle governing statutory interpretation is to determine the intent of the legislature and give force to that intent. The rest of this section discusses some of the rules and priorities employed to further this goal.

Legislative Intent

The underlying purpose behind statutory construction is the search to determine *legislative intent.*

The Plain Meaning Rule

This rule can actually be used to evade legislative intent. The *plain meaning rule* states simply that if the language of a statute is unambiguous and its meaning clear, the terms of the statute should be construed and applied according to their ordinary meaning. Behind this rule is the assumption that the legislature understood the meaning of the words it used and expressed its intent thereby. This rule operates to restrain the court from substituting its notion of what the legislature *really* meant if the meaning is already clear.

The application of the plain meaning rule may in fact undermine legislative intent. Although legislation is usually carefully drafted, language is by its nature susceptible to ambiguity, distortion, or simple lack of clarity. Because legislation is designed to control disputes that have not yet arisen, the "perfect" statute requires a degree of clairvoyance absent in the ordinary human being, including legislators, so that a statute may apply to a situation not foreseen by the legislators, who might have stated otherwise had they imagined such a situation.

The plain meaning rule obviates the need to pursue a lengthy inquiry into intent. Consider the nature of the legislative process. First, legislative intent is difficult to determine. The final product of the legislative process, the statute, would thus seem to be the best evidence of legislative intent. Legislatures are composed of numerous members who intend different things. In many instances, legislators do not even read the laws for which they vote. To believe there is a single legislative intent is to ignore reality. Many statutes are the result of compromise, the politics of which are not a matter of public record and cannot be accurately determined by a court. The precise language of the statute, then, is the best guide to intent. If, in the eyes of the legislature, the court errs in its application of the statute, the legislature may revise the statute for future application.

Limitations on the Plain Meaning Rule

Adherence to the plain meaning rule is neither blind nor simple-minded. A statute that is unambiguous in its language may be found to conflict with other statutes. Statutes are typically enacted in "packages," as part of a legislative effort to regulate a broad area of concern. Thus, alimony is ordinarily defined in several statutes embraced within a package of statutes covering divorce, which in turn may be part of a statutory chapter on domestic relations. The more comprehensive the package, the more likely some of its provisions may prove to be inconsistent. A sentence that seems unambiguous may be ambiguous in relation to a paragraph, a section, or a chapter.

Language must thus be interpreted in its context. In fact, this principle often operates to dispel ambiguity. Comprehensive statutes commonly begin with a preamble or introductory section stating the general purpose of the statutes collected under its heading. This statement of purpose is intended to avoid an overly technical interpretation of the statutes that could achieve results contrary to the general purpose.

The preamble is frequently followed by a section defining terms used in the statutes. This, too, limits the application of the plain meaning rule, but in a different way: The definitions pinpoint terms that have technical or legal significance to avoid what might otherwise be a nontechnical, ordinary interpretation.

On occasion, a provision in a statute may turn out to defeat the purpose of the statute in a particular set of circumstances; the court is then faced with the problem of giving meaning to the purpose of the statute or the language of the clause within the statute. In *Texas & Pacific Railway v. Abilene Cotton Oil Co.*, 204 U.S. 426 (1907), the U.S. Supreme Court was called upon to interpret the Interstate Commerce Act, which set up the Interstate Commerce Commission (ICC) and made it responsible for setting rates and routes for the railroads. A disgruntled shipper sued the railroad under an old common law action for "unreasonable rates." The Act had a provision, commonly included in legislation, stating that the Act did not abolish other existing remedies. However, the court reasoned that if persons were able to bring such actions any time they were unhappy with the rates, the rate structures established by the ICC would have little meaning, depending instead upon what a particular jury or judge considered reasonable. The court limited the effect of the clause and argued that Congress could not have intended for the clause to be used to completely undermine the purpose of the Act; "in other words, the act cannot be held to destroy itself."

The court will not ordinarily disregard the plain meaning of a statute, especially in a criminal case.

Aids to Statutory Interpretation

Single statutes do not exist in a legal vacuum. They are part of a section, chapter, and the state or federal code as a whole. Historically, statutes developed as an adjunct to the traditional common law system that established law from custom.

Like case law, statutory construction relies heavily on *authority*. Interpretation is a formal reasoning process in the law, which in our legal tradition depends less on the creative imagination than on sources of the law. In the reasoning process, an overriding judicial policy insists that the body of laws be as consistent and harmonious as possible. It was for this reason that the court held in *Abilene Oil*, that the statute "cannot be held to destroy itself."

If a clause seems to conflict with its immediate statutory context, it will be interpreted so as to further the general legislative intent, if such can be ascertained. In a sense, this is simply intelligent reading; words and phrases take their meaning from their contexts. The principle can be extended further, however. Statutes taken from different parts of a

The PEOPLE, Plaintiff and Respondent
v.
Dion Bernard BROWN,
Defendant and Appellant.
California Court of Appeal,
Second District
20 Cal. App. 4th 1251,
25 Cal. Rptr. 2d 76 (1993)

A jury convicted appellant of making "terrorist threats" [Cal. Pen. Code § 422], intimidating witnesses, [and] being a felon in possession of a firearm and found true firearm use and prior felony conviction allegations. Appellant was sentenced to a 15-year, 8-month state prison term.

Appellant contends: (1) section 422 prohibits only unconditional threats and therefore he did not violate it. ...

FACTUAL BACKGROUND

Since the only dispute is the meaning of a statute, the facts may be stated simply. Our perspective favors the judgment.

Gloria Ortega, who came to the United States from Guatemala, and Nora Moya, who came to the United States from Mexico, were friends and neighbors. On January 26, 1992, about 6 p.m., they were with their young children walking to Ms. Moya's apartment in the Imperial Court Housing project when Ms. Ortega noticed appellant angrily screaming at someone in the nearby parking lot. When she looked at appellant he approached and said, "What are you looking at, bitch?"

Appellant then walked to where the two women and their children were standing and told them "he didn't want Hispanic people around [here]." As Ms. Moya was trying to open her apartment door appellant again said to Ms. Ortega, "What are you looking at, bitch?" and pulled out a pistol from the small of his back. Appellant, about two feet from Ms. Ortega, pointed the gun at her temple. She asked him why he was doing this since they weren't doing anything to him. Appellant told her to "shut up." The children were crying when Ms. Moya finally unlocked and opened the doors to her apartment.

Appellant, still holding his gun on Ms. Ortega, said "he didn't like having Hispanic people there and that he was going to get us out of there."

After the children ran into the apartment Ms. Moya pulled Ms. Ortega into the apartment. When Ms. Ortega tried to close one of the two doors, the metal door, appellant stuck his foot in the way. Ms. Moya then said "we should call the police." Appellant, holding his pistol in front of him with both hands, said "if we called the police, he would kill us." Appellant then left.

Two days later, in the afternoon, Ms. Ortega saw appellant come from his nearby apartment toward her apartment and fire a pistol shot into the grass.

Thereafter, the women reported the matter to the police and appellant was arrested.

DISCUSSION

Appellant contends his threat to kill the women if they called the police was not an unconditional threat within the meaning of section 422.

Section 422 provides: "Any person who willfully threatens to commit a crime which will result in death or great bodily injury to another person, with the specific intent that the statement is to be taken as a threat, even if there is no intent of actually carrying it out, which, on its face and under the circumstances in which it is made, is so unequivocal, unconditional, immediate, and specific as to convey to the person threatened, a gravity of purpose and an immediate prospect of execution of the threat, and thereby causes that person reasonably to be in sustained fear for his or her own safety or for his or her immediate family's safety, shall be punished by imprisonment in the county jail not to exceed one year, or by imprisonment in the state prison.

* * *

The evidence [that] appellant violated section 422 consisted solely of his statement to Ms. Ortega and Ms. Moya that "if [they] called the police, he would kill [them]."

Appellant's argument is this: although his statement was a threat "of death" that satisfied the statute's requirements of being "unequivocal ... , immediate, and specific," it was a conditional threat, not an "unconditional" one, as expressly required by the statute. As we explain, appellant is correct. ...

"The fundamental rule of statutory interpretation is to 'ascertain the intent of the Legislature so as to effectuate the purpose of the law.'" In determining intent, the court looks first to the words themselves. "When the language is clear and unambiguous, there is no need for construction." The court will decline to follow the plain meaning of a statute only when to do so would inevitably frustrate the manifest purposes of the legislation as a whole or lead to absurd results.

The plain meaning of an "unconditional" threat is that there be no conditions. "If you call the police ..." is a condition.

To—by some linguistic legerdemain—construe "unconditional threat" to include a "conditional threat" would only create "serious constitutional problems." Reasonable certainty in criminal statutes "is a well established element of ... due process of law. No one may be required at peril of life, liberty or property to speculate as to the meaning of penal statutes."

We hold that a conditional threat, such as appellant's, does not violate section 422.

Case Questions

1. Why is the issue of conditional/unconditional threat so important?
2. Under what circumstances may the plain meaning rule be ignored, according to the court?

state or federal code may be found to conflict. The court will interpret the language to harmonize the inconsistency whenever possible. Legislative intent may become quite obscure in such situations because the presumption that the legislature meant what it said is confronted by the problem that it said something different elsewhere. In reconciling the conflict, the court may use its sense of overall legislative policy and even the general history of the law, including the common law. The obvious solution to these conflicts is action by the legislature to rewrite the statutes to resolve the inconsistencies and provide future courts with a clear statement of intent.

Strict Construction

Words by their nature have different meanings and nuances. Shades of meaning change in the context of other words and phrases. Tradition has determined that certain situations call for broad or liberal constructions, whereas others call for narrow or strict construction, meaning that the statute in question will not be expanded beyond a very literal reading of its meaning.

"Criminal statutes are strictly construed." This rule of construction has its source in the evolution of our criminal law, in particular, in the many rights we afford those accused of crime. Out of fear of abuse of the criminal justice system, we have provided protection for the accused against kangaroo courts, overzealous prosecutors, and corrupt police. It is an accepted value of our legal system that the innocent must be protected even if it means that the guilty will sometimes go free.

Although many basic crimes, such as murder, burglary, and assault, were formulated by the common law in the distant past, today most states do not recognize common law crimes but insist that crimes be specified by statute. We consider it unjust for someone to be charged with a crime if the conduct constituting the crime has not been clearly prohibited by statute. Conversely, if a statute defines certain conduct as criminal, "ignorance of the law excuses no one" (*ignorantia legis neminem excusat*). If public notice of prohibited conduct is an essential ingredient of criminal law, strict construction is its logical conclusion. If conduct is not clearly within the prohibitions of a statute, the court will decline to expand its coverage.

A second category of statutes that are strictly construed is expressed by the principle that "statutes in derogation of the common law are strictly construed." State legislatures frequently pass laws that alter, modify, or abolish traditional common law rules. The principle that such changes are narrowly construed not only shows respect for the common law, but also reflects the difference between legislative and judicial decision making. Whereas judicial decisions explain the reasons for the application of a particular rule, allowing for later interpretations and modifications, statutes are presumed to mean what they say. The intent of the legislature is embodied in the language of the statute itself, which if well drafted can be seen to apply to the situations for which it was intended.

A statute should stand alone, its meaning clear. Unfortunately, this is not always possible. If there is some question of meaning, a statute that appears to conflict with prior principles of the common law can be measured against that body of law. In other words, the court has recourse to a wealth of time-tested principles and need not strain to guess legislative intent. This is particularly helpful when the statute neglects to cover a situation that was decided in the past. If the statute is incomplete or ambiguous, the Court will resolve the dispute by following the common law.

Legislative History

If the application of a statute remains unclear in its language and in its written context, the intent of the legislature may be ascertained by researching the statute's legislative history. This includes the records and documents concerning the process whereby the statute became law. The purpose and application of the statute may sometimes become clear with these additional materials. Several committees may have held hearings or discussions on the law during its enactment that have become part of the public record and demonstrate the concerns of legislators and the reasons for enactment. Inferences may be made based on different drafts of the statute and the reasons expressed for the changes. If two houses of the legislature began with different language, the final compromise language may also suggest conclusions. Legislative debates may similarly clarify legislative intent.

Research into legislative history can be a lengthy process involving extensive analytical skills; but an examination of the entire process for a particular enactment will tend to dispel plausible, but incorrect, interpretations of legislative intent. The informal politics of negotiation and compromise, however, are not always reflected in the record, so the reasons for the final decisions on the language of the statute may remain obscure.

A Caveat on Statutory Interpretation

We have touched here on only a few of a multitude of rules of interpretation employed by the courts in resolving issues of statutory meaning. In fact, there are so many rules and exceptions to them that the courts enjoy considerable freedom to select the rules that support the interpretation that a given court or judge favors. For example, any specific rule may be avoided by declaring that it conflicts with the primary intent of the legislature. There is a subjective element to this analysis that provides a court great discretion.

Courts ordinarily attempt to give force to legislative intent. They are assisted by a great variety of technical rules of construction that have been developed in the precedents of prior judges faced with the problem of statutory meaning. But judges differ in their thinking from legislators. They not only deal with abstract rules, but on a daily basis must also resolve difficult problems with justice and fairness. Very few judges will blindly follow a technical rule if the result would be manifestly unfair. They can justly reason that the legislature never intended an unjust result. When arguing the interpretation of a statute, a lawyer or paralegal must keep in mind the importance of persuading the court that the proposed interpretation is not only correct but also fair and just.

Statute and Precedent

It would be a mistake to think that the existence of a statute suspends the common law principle of precedent. Although a statute may supersede a common law rule, the court's interpretation of the statute is law.

When researching a case covered by statute, it is not enough to look merely to the statute. One must look at the cases that have interpreted the statute. In many instances, the application of a statute to a client's case is clear; if any doubt exists, judicial decisions must be examined.

Summary

In modern times, legislation has replaced the common law as the major source of changes in the law. Legislative bodies enact laws to be applied generally to future situations rather than deciding existing disputes, which is the task of the courts. Unless they are procedurally defective or unconstitutional, statutes must be enforced by the court without changing or distorting their language. For cases in which the application of a statute is unclear, the courts have developed a multitude of rules of construction with the purpose of ascertaining the intent of the legislature. Once a higher court has interpreted the meaning of a statute, that decision becomes precedent for it and lower court. The legislature always has the option of rewriting the statute for clarification or revision, or if it objects to the interpretation the court has given it.

Review Questions

1. What statutes are strictly construed?
2. What is the primary goal of statutory interpretation?
3. What is the effect of a state statute found to violate the U.S. Constitution?
4. Which is more binding on a court, judicial precedent or statute?
5. What is legislative history?
6. Why are divorces now granted by courts rather than legislatures?

Exercises

1. Does your state recognize charitable immunity? If not, was it abolished and who abolished it?
2. What are the steps legislation must go through in your state legislature to become law?

SYSTEMATIC TRIAL PREPARATION

Betsy Branyan Kidder, CLA

[T]rial preparation should actually begin when a file is received in the office. Keeping a file well organized, being familiar with the contents of the file and having a good system of preparing for trial are essential. Trials are typically a time of stress and there are steps that can be taken beforehand to ensure that stressful situations are minimized and efficiency is at its peak.

[F]iles have their own individual personality, including a unique set of facts, issues of law and characters. Try to allow some flexibility to be built into your system of trial preparation. Not only do files have their own personalities but so do law firms. The tasks you are asked to accomplish will vary greatly depending upon how many attorneys are in the firm, available support staff, the economic resources available to a case, etc.

Therefore, there are many factors that must be taken into consideration when developing a system for trial preparation. No two cases or law firms are the same. Be patient, no one develops a system of preparing for trial that works immediately. Remember that organization, analysis, and the quick and accurate retrieval of information are goals in any situation.

A trial date is usually established in a scheduling or a pretrial order issued by the court the case is filed in. The date can be scheduled at the court's discretion and, in some cases, is requested by the parties. Once notified of the trial date there are specific steps that need to be undertaken.

A legal assistant can be very useful throughout the life of the case. Trial preparation should begin with the receipt of the case in the office. There are three important things to keep in mind: prepare each case as if it's going to trial (although in reality many do settle or are continued to a later date), keep the file organized, and be familiar with the contents of the file.

Keeping a file organized as a case progresses will save time and avoid confusion and stress as trial approaches. [Y]our goal is to be able to retrieve information quickly, preserve the integrity of documents as received, and avoid losing or misfiling important documents. Keeping things clearly marked and labeled will make them easy to retrieve. Try and coordinate your efforts with the secretaries and file clerks in your office.

[T]he majority of cases settle or the trial date may be continued ... . But in the event this doesn't happen, a well-organized file will allow you to complete your trial preparation more efficiently. Areas where legal assistants can be very useful in trial preparation include:

- notification of trial date,
- review and clean-up,
- pretrial meeting and plan of action,
- pretrial interrogatories,
- depositions,
- pretrial memorandum,
- trial/evidence notebook,
- subpoenas and witness letters,
- exhibits,
- special effects, and
- trial kit.

Include these items in a checklist of things to remember to do and add items such as special assignments requested by attorneys or those things which might pertain to your court system or office. With experience, you will develop a system that will work best for the individual case. Start preparing for trial at least a month before the scheduled date.

First, upon receipt of a pretrial notice, order or scheduling order, calendar all dates immediately, including the date and time of any pretrial conferences, calendar calls or due dates for exhibits, etc.

Each time you go through the experience of preparing for a trial, you'll learn by trial and error what will work for you and will be on your way to developing a system that fits your needs. Use your training, suggested guildelines and form books and you'll be able to face what can be a very difficult task and make it easier.

Involvement in local and national paralegal organizations and review of monthly newsletters and magazines published for legal assistants can keep you informed of the latest developments in the legal profession, especially in the area of litigation support and can also provide a wealth of information in articles written by practicing legal assistants and attorneys. Your local legal assistant organization can also be a very valuable support system in the event you have any questions. Usually, people within the office are also usually quite willing to give assistance when asked. Don't get discouraged. Learn from past experience and don't be afraid to try new ideas.

Reprinted with permission from *Legal Assistant Today* magazine.

CHAPTER 6

TRIAL AND APPELLATE COURTS

The Adversary Process

The American legal system is based on certain assumptions that are responsible for its organization and structure, its strengths and its weaknesses. The system is a competitive one that reflects the political process and the competitive market economy. In the legal arena, this competitive form is referred to as the **adversary system.** Any legitimate legal system must assert justice as its primary goal. Our system maintains that justice can best be achieved on the basis of rules that provide a fair procedure for those engaged in a dispute. The procedure embodies a search for truth by allowing disputing parties to present their cases through partisan, legally competent agents before an impartial tribunal. The agents are duly licensed attorneys, and the impartial tribunal is composed of a disinterested judge and a disinterested jury.

The adversary process has been likened to a game and a fight, but as a game it has serious consequences and as a fight it is controlled by numerous rules that attempt to make the fight fair and civilized. Whichever metaphor is used, the judge may be viewed as an "umpire," ensuring that the rules are followed and each party is treated with fairness.

Although there may be several parties to a lawsuit, there are only two sides. Each side is provided with equal opportunity to present its evidence and arguments and to challenge the evidence and arguments from the other side. It is to be expected that each side will present a very different picture of the dispute, but the underlying assumption is that objective observers will be able to come close to the truth of the events behind the dispute and that the judge, trained and experienced in the law, will be able to weigh the legal arguments of both sides and come to a correct application of the law in each case.

Critics of the adversary system point to certain inherent weaknesses: the partisanship of the attorneys often operates to cloud the truth rather than reveal it; judges and juries are neither objective nor totally disinterested; the competitive market model reflects a patriarchal, elitist, capitalist bias that prevents litigants from obtaining equality before the law; the system is old-fashioned, awkward, and inefficient. There is some truth to all of these criticisms, yet the Anglo-American legal system has made remarkable achievements that have been out of reach for legal systems based on a different model.

Like any human institution, the legal system has its faults, but it has within it the means to diminish or eliminate its own weaknesses.

BALLENTINE'S

adversary system   The system of justice in the United States. Under the adversary system, the court hears the evidence presented by adverse parties and decides the case.

A major means of correcting mistakes in the system lies in the appellate process, which provides the opportunity to litigants to challenge the propriety of the results of trial.

Fact and Law

To understand the difference between trial and appellate courts, an appreciation of the fact/law distinction is necessary. As the modern court system has developed, the functions of judge and jury have become distinct. The word *trial* refers to *trial of fact;* the factfinder at trial is also called the *trier of fact.* In jury cases, the jury is the trier of fact; if there is no jury (for example, if the parties have waived a jury trial), the judge, sometimes simply referred to as the *court,* is the trier of fact. The trier of fact determines, from the evidence presented, the facts of the case in dispute. Once the facts are determined, appropriate law is applied. Decision, declaration, and determination of the law are the sole province of the judge. The jury's factfinding is called the *verdict,* and upon the verdict the judge makes a *judgment,* which determines the respective rights and obligations of the parties.

Facts in a legal case must be distinguished from what is considered fact in the layperson's sense of the word and from what might be considered scientific fact. Although the purpose of trial is to get at facts and truth, neither of these is clear at the outset or there would be no need for a trial; if both parties agree to all the facts relevant to a case, there is nothing left to do but apply the law—no jury is necessary. In a trial, each side presents a different version of the facts. The jury, or the judge in a nonjury trial, must decide what actually happened based on inferences and conclusions drawn from the evidence. The jury (or judge) may believe one side and disbelieve the other, or it may conclude that the truth lies somewhere in between. In many cases, the truth is not readily apparent.

Sometimes fact determinations are supported by very persuasive evidence, but sometimes they are not. Suppose, for example, two litigants were involved in a head-on collision, and each asserts that the other crossed the median line and caused the collision. Assuming one is telling the truth, how is the jury to determine the facts months after the accident? The jury would be very much aided by disinterested eyewitnesses who confirmed one version rather than the other. Expert witnesses may be called upon to reconstruct the accident by skidmarks, the position of the cars after the accident, and the nature of the injuries. But eyewitnesses and expert witnesses can be as equivocal as the participants. Jurors may rely on other inferences—the experience of the drivers, the evidence that one driver had been drinking, and the demeanor of the parties as witnesses (one may seem honest and sincere, the other furtive and evasive). The absolute truth may never be known, but the jury is obliged to draw conclusions about the facts. If standards of scientific proof of fact were required, cases could not be resolved.

Under the adversary system, then, the facts are assumed to be as concluded by the trier of fact. Even though inferences drawn by the trier of fact may differ from the absolute truth, the assumption of the legal system is that when impartial, reasonable persons deliberate about the facts, their conclusions are as close to the truth as possible and that the process of arriving at the facts is fair to both parties.

Distinguishing fact from law is not a simple matter. Generally facts are concerned with what happened—answers to questions of who, when, what, and how. These are questions or issues of fact. A question of law involves the application or meaning of law. As a rule of thumb, questions of law and fact are distinguished by whether a particular question requires legal training or knowledge. For example, whether or not the defendant in an auto accident/negligence case was drinking prior to the accident is a question requiring no special legal training. A judge is no better qualified to answer that question from the evidence presented than a layperson, thus identifying this as a question of fact. In contrast, the issue of whether particular evidence of the defendant's drinking is admissible in court is a question of law; the judge is trained and experienced in the rules of evidence and must decide which evidence may properly be presented and which is inadmissible.

The fact/law distinction is not important only for the assignment of labor between judge and jury; it can be critical on appeal. Once a trial has reached final judgment, a disappointed party may seek reversal on appeal. The appellate courts treat questions of law and questions of fact quite differently. Questions of law decided by the trial court judge are not treated deferentially by an appellate court that disagrees. For example, if the trial judge gave the jury an instruction that the appellate court concludes was an incorrect statement of the law, the appellate court would substitute its judgment for that of the trial court and order a new trial if the improper instructions were **prejudicial**. Factfinding by judge or jury, however, is treated by the appellate court with great deference and will be overturned only if it is **clearly erroneous** or without **substantial evidence** to support it. This standard makes it extremely difficult to challenge factfinding on appeal.

BALLENTINE'S

prejudicial   Detrimental to a party or person or to his or her interests.

clearly erroneous   A standard by which a trial court's findings of fact are reviewed. An appellate court will not set aside a trial court's findings of fact unless they are "clearly erroneous."

substantial evidence   Evidence that a reasonable person would accept as adequate to support the conclusion or conclusions drawn from it; evidence beyond a scintilla.

Questions of law and questions of fact are not always distinct. For example, the meaning of words may be either a law or a fact question. The common meaning of a word is a question of fact; the interpretation of a legal term is a question of law. Although judges may not be more competent than laypersons to define *tree, employee* may be used in either a legal sense or an everyday sense. So if *employee* is used in a statute, its meaning would seem to be a question of law. However, it may not have been used with any particular legal reference and may have been used simply as an ordinary term. Whether a person is an employee for the purposes of inclusion in a collective bargaining unit under the National Labor Relations Act could be treated as either a question of law or a question of fact. Who decides which it is? The judge, of course, or, as put by Isaacs: "Whether a particular question is to be treated as a question of law or a question of fact is not in itself a question of fact, but a highly artificial question of law" [22 *Col. L. Rev.* 1, 11–12 (1922)].

The *Kindle* case is an example of an appellate court reversing a trial court's **factfinding**. Note the short statute of limitations for bringing actions against local government. Note also the standard for mental incapacity, one resembling contractual capacity but different from criminal intent or insanity, as we shall see in later chapters.

Trials and Trial Courts

A trial is an "on-the-record" evidentiary hearing. *On the record* refers to the requirement that the facts be determined exclusively on the basis of evidence presented at trial. Evidence of disputed facts is presented by both sides. The plaintiff attempts to establish facts substantiating claims against the defendant, and the defendant attempts to counter the plaintiff's case by questioning and objecting to the plaintiff's evidence as well as presenting additional evidence. Evidence takes several forms, including witness testimony, **physical evidence**, and documents. The evidence forms the **record**. Naturally the jury will make factual inferences based on common sense and experience gained outside the trial, but it is improper for jurors to use knowledge of events

---

BALLENTINE'S

finding of fact   A conclusion with respect to disputed facts in a legal action, reasoned or inferred from the evidence.

physical evidence   Evidence other than testimony; demonstrative evidence.

record on appeal   The papers a trial court transmits to the appellate court, on the basis of which the appellate court decides the appeal. The record on appeal includes the pleadings, all motions made before the trial court, the official transcript, and the judgment or order appealed from.

**In re Martha KINDLE Claims Against City
and County Employees, Agents and
Officers for Damages Arising From
Assault by Joseph Kindle
Supreme Court of South Dakota
509 N.W.2d 278 (1993)**

Hand County, the City of Miller and agents
and officers thereof appeal a trial court's order
granting Martha Kindle's motion to extend the
time for filing notice of a claim against a public
entity or its employees. We reverse.

FACTS

On May 24, 1991, Martha Kindle (hereinafter
Kindle) was abducted from her job at a Miller,
South Dakota, day-care center by her estranged
husband, Joseph Kindle. [Joseph Kindle beat
Martha, stabbed her with a knife and threatened
to kill her. He was arrested, charged with various
crimes, and eventually pled guilty to kidnapping.]

Kindle sought to file an action against Hand
County, the City of Miller and their agents and officers (hereinafter Defendants). Kindle asserted
that city and county law enforcement officials had
earlier promised her protection after she reported
she had been raped, subjected to physical violence
and threatened by her estranged husband. She
claimed said officials still took no action to safe-
guard her before she was kidnapped and assaulted.

Under [state statute], in order to maintain a
lawsuit against a public entity for an injury caused
by that entity or its employee, a party is required
to serve notice upon the entity within 180 days of
the injury. Defendants did not receive notice by
the time the statute of limitations ... . Kindle
moved the circuit court for an extension of time
to serve notice. She claimed she had been mentally incapacitated by extreme fear, anxiety and
post-traumatic stress syndrome during the time
the statute of limitations was running.

The trial court held a hearing where both
sides presented expert testimony as to mental
incapacity. The court concluded that: "Mental incapacity ... should be defined more narrowly than a
condition where a person cannot generally make
sound decisions concerning the general aspects of

their life." It found Kindle was mentally incapacitated under the statute "to make any decisions
concerning any claims she may have had against
law enforcement officers connected with the assaults upon her" and ordered she be permitted to
file notice on Defendants. This appeal followed.

DECISION

I. THE TRIAL COURT ERRED AS A MATTER OF
LAW IN DEFINING MENTAL INCAPACITY ... . The
legal definition of "mental incapacity" is a question of law. ...

Under South Dakota law, no action for damages may be maintained against a public entity or
official unless written notice of the injury is given
to that entity within 180 days of the injury.

[T]he 180-day notice requirement may be extended for up to two years if the injured party is a minor or mentally incapacitated. ... There is no statutory definition of mental incapacity contained in
[state statute chapter on liability for public officials].
Therefore, we must look to other statutory and case
law to determine what the legislature intended
when it used the term "mentally incapacitated."

This court has never decided a case dealing
specifically with the definition of mental incapacity ... . However, there is one recurrent and prevailing theme to cases dealing with mental
incapacity, mental illness, mental infirmity, unsound mind, or mental impairment as justification
to toll statutes of limitation—did the person understand the nature and consequences of his or her
action? The analysis of whether a person meets this
definition involves an examination of the person's
conduct of his or her everyday affairs.

* * *

In determining whether a person compre-
hends the nature and effect of his or her actions,
a trial court should examine all relevant facts and
circumstances of a person's overall ability to function in society and comprehend and protect his
or her legal rights.

* * *

Defendants attack the sufficiency of the evidence
to support the trial court's findings on the question

CHAPTER 6 TRIAL AND APPELLATE COURTS

of Kindle's mental incapacity. We review a trial court's findings of fact under the clearly erroneous standard. We will not disturb the court's findings unless they are clearly erroneous; the question is whether, after a review of all the evidence, we are left with a definite and firm conviction that a mistake has been made. However, the findings of fact must support the conclusions of law.

* * *

The trial court found that Kindle was able to make decisions concerning the everyday functions of her life but had a tendency to avoid situations involving her abduction. These findings are not clearly erroneous based on the evidence presented. However, the evidence and findings are insufficient to support the trial court's legal conclusion that Kindle was "mentally incapacitated" under the test we have adopted.

Mental incapacity ... means the failure to understand the nature and effect of one's actions. The trial court found Kindle possessed the overall ability to function in society. Kindle exercised her legal rights to the degree she consulted with her attorney, obtained a divorce, and cooperated in the criminal prosecution of Joseph Kindle. Additionally, she was represented by her divorce attorney during at least part of the time the statute of limitations was running. These findings are insufficient to support the legal conclusion that she was "mentally incapacitated"... .

The order of the trial court is reversed.

Case Questions

1. What is the plaintiff claiming she was too mentally incapacitated to do?
2. Has the court enunciated a test for mental incapacity that would make it virtually impossible for someone in the plaintiff's circumstances to bring suit?
3. The 180-day limitation period for suits against a public entity is relatively short. Should this fact influence the interpretation of mental incapacity in this case?

that gave rise to the dispute acquired outside of the record. It would be improper, for instance, for a juror to visit the scene of the crime or ask questions of witnesses or bystanders.

What should the appellate court do when the record from the court below is insufficient? In the *Kingman* case, the trial court did not provide findings of fact on which the appellate court could determine the adequacy of factfinding. The trial court treated this case quite casually, apparently because it seemed a relatively routine exercise of the state's power to take private property for a public use (**eminent domain**). The only requirement placed on the state to obtain judicial approval was to show that the property was being taken for a "public use and necessity." It is usually a fairly easy task to get this rubber-stamped by the court. Apparently the trial judge gave his reasons for denial orally but did not make them part of the record.

—BALLENTINE'S—

eminent domain   The power of the government to take private property for a public use or public purpose without the owners consent, if it pays just compensation.

The STATE of Washington, Petitioner,
v.
W. Kenneth KINGMAN
and Julia E. Kingman,
his wife, et al., Respondents.
Supreme Court of Washington,
Department 1 463 P.2d 638 (1970)

By writ of certiorari, the state seeks review of an order denying its petition for an order of public use and necessity.

* * *

It appears from briefs of counsel (a) that the land to be acquired is a 300 foot strip of waterfront approximately 150 feet wide between the public highway and Lake Chelan; ... specifically, it is to preserve a beautiful view of Lake Chelan and the foothills beyond. Photographs illustrate the state's position.

Except for the phrase "good cause appearing," the trial court, in its order after trial, gives no reasons for denying the certificate of public use and necessity.

* * *

Here we run into a void. For some reason, which does not appear in the record, the trial court did not make and enter findings of fact and conclusions of law.

* * *

A judgment entered in a case tried to the court where findings are required, without findings of fact having been made, is subject to a motion to vacate within the time for the taking of an appeal. After vacation, the judgment shall not be re-entered ... .

The order denying the petition for public use and necessity is set aside; the case is remanded for further proceedings not inconsistent with this opinion.

It is so ordered.

Case Questions

1. Why was the case remanded?
2. When should a court make and enter findings of fact and conclusions of law?

Jury Instructions

The jury is given detailed instructions by the judge about its functions in the lawsuit. Judges vary in their explanations of the proceedings before and during the trial, but the most important instructions are given to the jury at the close of the evidence as the jury prepares to deliberate its verdict. These instructions provide only as much explanation of the law as is needed for the jury to dispose of factual questions. For example, in a lawsuit for slander, the judge would instruct the jury about the facts it would need to find to hold the defendant liable for slander; namely: (1) the utterance alleged to be slanderous was communicated to a third party and (2) injured the reputation of the plaintiff. In addition, the judge would instruct the jury that if it found the statement to be true, the defendant would not be liable. The jury would also be instructed on what would constitute compensation for injuries sustained. The specifics of these instructions could vary considerably from case to case.

In short, the court delineates the facts the jury must decide in making its verdict according to the nature of the case, confining the jury to its factfinding function. When the jury reaches a consensus on the facts and presents the judge with its results, the judge makes conclusions of law and enters a judgment.

Before and during trial, the judge makes a series of decisions on the law, of which the most important concern motions to dismiss the lawsuit in favor of one of the parties, admission of evidence and the propriety of its presentation, and instructions to the jury. In each decision, the judge applies legal principles, which the judge could interpret or apply incorrectly. The correctness of the judge's rulings forms the basis for appeal.

Appellate Courts

The courts above the trial court level to which appeals may be taken are called *appellate courts*. The most common arrangement in the state hierarchy echoes that of the federal court system, with an intermediate appellate court and a court of last resort (e.g., Colorado Court of Appeals, Colorado Supreme Court). Some states have a two-tiered trial court system in which one court handles cases of lesser import, often limited by a dollar amount, and misdemeanor cases, whereas the other court has jurisdiction over felonies and civil cases above the specified dollar amount. In this arrangement the "higher" court may serve as an appellate court for cases decided in the lower court.

Although the drama of the courtroom receives greatest attention from the media and the public, legal professionals are primarily concerned with appellate court decisions because of *stare decisis*. Trial courts interpret and apply the law, but appellate courts state the law with greater authority. Because they establish precedent for future cases, appellate courts not only settle disputes but also have an impact beyond the case at hand.

The appellate process is quite different from trial. The appellate court does not retry facts, does not call witnesses. It receives a record from the trial court, which includes a written transcript of the testimony at trial, exhibits introduced during trial, copies of the pleadings and motions filed with the court before and during trial, and written briefs submitted by the attorneys for **appellant** and **appellee** arguing the issues raised on appeal.

BALLENTINE'S

appellant   A party who appeals from a lower court to a higher court.

appellee   A party against whom a case is appealed from a lower court to a higher court.

Attorneys for the parties are given a limited time to make oral arguments before the appellate court, during which the appellate judges may ask questions concerning the case. Deliberation of the case following oral argument is governed by the customs of the particular court, but at some point a vote is taken and usually a single judge will be assigned to write the opinion for the court in consultation with the other judges. Judges disagreeing with the result may write dissenting opinions; judges agreeing with the result may wish to add comments in a concurring opinion. There can be a considerable lapse of time between the oral argument and the issuance of a written opinion, depending largely on the complexities of the legal issues raised and the extent of disagreement among the judges.

Although the appellate court is limited to the record before it with regard to the dispute, its research of the law and its legal arguments may go beyond the cases and arguments made by attorneys for appellant and appellee in their briefs and oral arguments. Because decisions of the appellate courts may establish precedent for future cases, appellate judges are not concerned simply with resolving the dispute at hand but also with the impact of their interpretation of the law on future cases. At trial, the judge is constrained to proceed in a timely fashion, making rulings that will not delay the process and issuing a decision as soon as possible to define the rights of the parties. By contrast, the appellate process may be described as deliberative. The attorneys representing the parties have the opportunity to reflect on their arguments and craft carefully reasoned briefs, and the appellate court will take the time necessary to examine the law to write a reasoned decision. Steadily rising case loads in appellate courts have put pressure on the courts, but it is fair to say that cases of great import receive corresponding attention by appellate courts.

Appellate courts have two primary functions in deciding appeals: (1) resolve the dispute and (2) state the law. Many cases raise minor issues, dispute well-established rules, or have no particular merit (e.g., many criminal appeals are at government expense, so the convicted party has nothing to lose by appealing). When no significant issue of law is decided, or if prior law is followed, many jurisdictions do not require that the opinion be published. In some instances the court will write a cursory **memorandum** or **per curiam opinion** that disposes of the case without elaborate reasoning. Lengthy reasoning is reserved for cases that raise new or controversial legal issues.

BALLENTINE'S
---

memorandum decision   A court decision, usually consisting of a brief paragraph announcing the court's judgment, without an in-depth opinion.

per curiam opinion   An opinion, usually of an appellate court, in which the judges are all of one view and the legal question is sufficiently clear that a full written opinion is not required and a one- or two-paragraph opinion suffices.

Prejudicial Error

The appellate court examines the record and arguments to determine whether prejudicial, also called *reversible* or *harmful,* error occurred at the lower court level. The court does not impose an impossibly perfect standard on the trial court, but must determine whether mistaken actions constitute grounds for reversal. For example, the court may conclude that one of the instructions to the jury was not an exact statement of the law but, given the facts and circumstances of the case, a precise statement of the law would not have changed the jury's verdict. This would be considered harmless error that did not prejudice the case and would not be grounds for reversal. In some instances the appellate court may agree with the trial court's result but disagree with its reasoning, in which case the court may substitute its reasoning in an affirming opinion or remand the case for the lower court to rewrite the decision in accord with the appellate court's instructions. A remand for a new decision would also be appropriate when no error was committed in factfinding, but there was prejudicial error in application of law. For instance, the appellate court might hold that the trial court had no authority to award **punitive damages**, so that portion of the decision would be deleted, leaving the award of **compensatory damages** intact.

Reversible error may or may not call for a new trial. The appellate court might find, for example, that the trial court was incorrect in ruling that the statute of limitations had not run, thereby barring further suit. The appellate court may conclude that the trial court was wrong in granting plaintiff's motion for judgment notwithstanding the verdict, the effect of which was to reject the verdict in favor of defendant and enter a judgment in favor of plaintiff; the result of the appellate reversal would be to reinstate the jury's verdict and enter a judgment in favor of defendant. In contrast, the appellate court might find that instructions to the jury or a ruling on admissibility of evidence so prejudiced the factfinding process that the error can only be corrected by a new trial.

In short, reversible error refers to the reversal of the *judgment* of the lower court. Because the judgment is based on findings of fact and

---

BALLENTINE'S

punitive damages   Damages that are awarded over and above compensatory damages or actual damages because of the wanton, reckless, or malicious nature of the wrong done by the plaintiff. Such damages bear no relation to the plaintiff's actual loss and are often called exemplary damages, because their purpose is to make an example of the plaintiff to discourage others from engaging in the same kind of conduct in the future.

compensatory damages   Damages recoverable in a lawsuit for loss or injury suffered by the plaintiff as a result of the defendant's conduct. Also called actual damages, they may include expenses, loss of time, reduced earning capacity, bodily injury, and mental anguish.

conclusions of law, either or both could constitute harmful error, and the order of the appellate court is designed to correct the error in the most expeditious manner.

In *Stafford,* the defendant-appellant was convicted of second-degree murder, but a significant portion of the stenographic record of the trial was lost. Errors in serious felony cases are scrutinized much more critically than in lesser crimes and civil cases. The defendant wanted a new trial because of the incomplete record. The defendant also challenged the jury instructions.

STATE of Kansas, Appellee,
v.
Clifton Lorrin STAFFORD, Appellant.
Supreme Court of Kansas
223 Kan. 62, 573 P.2d 970 (1977)

The testimony comprising the state's case came from twelve witnesses. Defendant was the only person to testify on his behalf. Thirty pages of defendant's testimony were transcribed, but another fifty pages were lost. On order of the district court an attempt was made to reconstruct the missing transcript through testimony of defendant's trial attorney. The lost transcript formulates defendant's first point on appeal.

* * *

The inability of the state to provide a full transcript of the trial proceedings does not entitle a defendant to a new trial per se. Before defendant can claim he is entitled to a new trial he must demonstrate that despite a good faith effort it is impossible to reconstruct the missing portion of the record and this precludes effective appellate review of the issues.

* * *

The rest of defendant's claims of error relate to instructions given by the trial court. The trial court instructed on first and second degree murder and voluntary and involuntary manslaughter ... . The court did not define "heat of passion" ... . There was an instruction on the effect of voluntary intoxication. The jury was instructed on defendant's presumption of innocence, weight of the testimony of the witnesses, and the duty to reach a verdict in light of all the evidence.

It is to be noted that none of the objections to instructions now raised were presented to the trial court; therefore, our scope of review is limited to a determination of whether the instructions are "clearly erroneous." An instruction is clearly erroneous when the reviewing court reaches a firm conviction that if the trial error had not occurred there was a real possibility the jury would have returned a different verdict.

* * *

We find no reversible error and the judgment is affirmed.

Case Questions
1. Because the correctness of jury instructions is a question of law rather than a question of fact, why did the reviewing court apply the clearly erroneous test rather than substitution of judgment?
2. Was the loss of the transcript prejudicial to the defendant?

Impact of the Appellate System

Appellate courts serve as a brake on the arbitrariness of trial judges as well as a forum for establishing uniformity in the interpretation of the law. The right to appeal is a fundamental custom of our legal system. Trial court judges naturally dislike being reversed, so the threat of appeal that lurks behind every case encourages them to conform to the law as stated by higher authority. In states having both intermediate courts and courts of last resort, a disappointed litigant has two opportunities for appellate review of the case. Courts of last resort have great discretion in choosing cases for review and decline to hear most cases. Intermediate appellate courts also have significant discretion in the cases they hear and the time they wish to devote to a case.

These factors limit the numbers of appeals, as does the prohibitive cost. Not only are substantial attorney's fees involved in preparing for appeal, but the cost of reproducing the trial transcript in a lengthy trial is an economic burden as well. Appeals therefore tend to involve cases in which the cost of appeal is borne by the government, as in criminal cases, or which involve significant amounts of money. Some appeals are subsidized by outside groups that have an interest in setting a precedent or in representing appellants, such as in a civil rights action. Because of these factors, appeals are not a representative sample of the cases that go to trial.

Appellate decisions also affect lawyers, who must evaluate their client's chances by predicting the outcome of trial and appeal. Most cases are settled without going to trial or appeal; settlement is encouraged by well-established principles of law that allow attorneys to assess whether a case is a winner or a loser. Indirectly, the costs of trial and appeal encourage litigants to make realistic decisions about whether to proceed.

Miscellaneous Judicial Duties

In attempting to learn the law, one tends to concentrate study on appellate decisions, which provide authoritative statements of the law. Most of these are appeals from final judgments from trials, but judges engage in many other duties that consume much time and energy.

Trial Courts

Lower court judges must act on a number of problems that are not truly adversarial in nature but that require orders from a court. The advent of

no-fault divorce, for example, has converted a formerly adversarial proceeding into one that frequently involves a judge simply approving a marital settlement agreement negotiated by the divorcing parties through their attorneys. A five- or ten-minute hearing disposes of the matter. The major purpose of no-fault divorce laws has been to diminish the adversarial aspect of divorce and give the parties rather than the court control over their destinies. Of course, if the parties cannot agree on the distribution of marital assets, alimony, and child support, the proceedings take on the former adversarial character, forcing the judge to decide these issues.

Some actions, like a legal name change, in which no defendant is involved, are rather perfunctory actions requiring a court order. Others, like **garnishment** of wages, can be adversarial but usually are not. In addition, the court must take action on issues prior to trial and enforce judgments after trial. And, depending on the jurisdiction, judges may spend a good deal of time on purely administrative duties.

Appellate Courts

In general, appellate courts are responsible for overseeing the orderly process of the court system. This includes not only hearing appeals, but also ruling on requests for delays in the appellate process, staying decisions of lower courts, applications for bail, and so on. Appellate courts may also be involved in matters relating to admission to the bar and disciplinary actions.

Appellate courts also have responsibility for administrative duties, managing their own activities, as well as some supervisory functions over the lower courts. Onerous administrative duties are often bestowed on the chief judge of a district or circuit, or the chief justice of a supreme court. The time spent in administrative duties may be directly related to the staff available to a judge.

Unlike trials, which are conducted by a single judge, appellate proceedings involve three or more judges, usually an odd number to prevent evenly divided decisions. Assignment of duties also becomes an administrative matter, as someone must make the assignments. Many appellate courts have panels of judges, from which a subset is selected, to hear certain cases. The U.S. Court of Appeals is the most familiar example.

BALLENTINE'S
---

no-fault divorce A term for the requirements for divorce in jurisdictions in which the party seeking the divorce need not demonstrate that the other party is at fault. The requirements differ from state to state.

garnishment A proceeding by a creditor to obtain satisfaction of a debt from money or property of the debtor which is in the possession of a third person or is owed by such a person to the debtor.

The *Lee* case is an example of the regulatory feature of appellate courts. The newspaper in the case was charged with contempt of court for violating a "gag" order of the court in a juvenile case by publishing letters from the parents. The newspaper petitioned for a **writ of prohibition**, which is a common law remedy asking an appellate court to restrain a lower court from doing something it has no authority to do.

MINNEAPOLIS STAR AND TRIBUNE COMPANY,
La Crosse Tribune Company,
and Northwest Publications, Inc.,
Petitioners,
v.
Honorable Robert E. LEE,
Judge of Country Court for Houston County,
Respondent.
Court of Appeals of Minnesota
353 N.W.2d 213 (1984)

FACTS

The petitioners request a writ of prohibition. In June 1984, the trial court issued an order that all parties in what was presumably a juvenile dependency case cease and desist from publishing letters or statements having to do with the proceeding. Subsequently, the minor's parents wrote two letters to the editor of a newspaper in the area. On July 27, 1984, the trial court, believing the letters to be a violation of its order, ordered a contempt hearing ... .

ISSUE

May a court issue an order forbidding publication of information about a juvenile case obtained from involved parties and at the contempt hearing which was open to the public?

ANALYSIS
* * *

Prior restraints of speech have long been deemed unconstitutional except in the most drastic of situations.

* * *

Such a restraint must be "necessitated by a compelling governmental interest, and * * * narrowly tailored to serve that interest."

* * *

In this case, the governmental interest is not constitutional but statutory: privacy in a juvenile proceeding. It is an important and substantial government interest, but also with limits.

* * *

In this case, there has been no showing of any illegality; the trial court simply wanted to stop people from reading about the case. [The trial court judge] said he wanted to protect the child and have a better relationship between Houston County Social Services and the parties. Such an interest does not rise to the level required to justify a prior restraint. The order violated a fundamental constitutional right. Although the court's motives were honorable, nonetheless it was a violation of a fundamental right. There is no adequate remedy at law to redress such a violation and, therefore, the writ must issue.

──────────── BALLENTINE'S ────────────

writ of prohibition   A writ issued by a higher court directing a lower court not to take a certain action, i.e., prohibiting it from attempting to exercise jurisdiction in a matter in which it has no jurisdiction.

DECISION   The writ of prohibition is granted.

The trial court's order was an unconstitutional prior restraint of speech. It is hereby vacated.

Case Questions

1. Why does the court note that there is no adequate remedy at law?
2. Could a court ever use a gag order prior to trial?
3. Under what provision of the Constitution is this case decided?

Case Glossary

prior restraint   The imposition by the government, in advance of publication, of limits that prohibit or restrain speech or publication, as opposed to punishing persons for what they have actually said or written.

Summary

In the United States, the judicial system has a hierarchy that is divided into trial and appellate courts. The function of the trial court is to resolve disputes between parties in an adversarial process in which an impartial and disinterested judge presides over the presentation of evidence of fact by attorneys for the two sides. When a jury is present at trial, it determines issues of fact, whereas the judge applies the law in the conduct of the trial and renders a judgment on the verdict. In a nonjury trial, the judge serves as the trier of fact and then applies the law.

The distinction between law and fact is important on appeal. The appellate court does not try facts, although it is sometimes called upon to determine whether the trial record indicates that factfinding at the trial was clearly erroneous, warranting reversal. This is a much higher standard than the appellate court exercises in reversing an application of law by the trial judge. On questions of law, the appellate court is free to substitute its judgment for that of the lower court and need not show any deference to the lower court. As a result, most reversals are based on legal rather than factual arguments.

For an appellant to win a reversal on appeal, the appellate court must be convinced that there was reversible error at the trial level. Reversible error is a mistake in the law or the facts that was so prejudicial to appellant that a different result might have resulted if the mistake had not occurred. Minor mistakes may be deemed to be nonprejudicial or harmless error. In some cases reversible error requires a new trial; in others the error can be corrected by the appellate court or remanded to the lower court to write a new decision and order.

The appellate process provides a means to make the actions of trial courts consistent with the law, decide new issues of law, and protect litigants from misapplication of the law.

Review Questions

1. What is the policy reason for excluding jurors from a criminal trial if they have observed the defendant being arrested on television?

2. Explain the difference between "substitution of judgment" and "clearly erroneous."

3. Why is it necessary for the judge to give jury instructions?

4. Why is a greater proportion of criminal cases appealed than civil?

5. Why are more cases appealed on questions of law than questions of fact?

6. Does the adversarial system work?

7. Does the truth come out in the course of a trial?

Exercises

1. Determine for each of the following whether it is a question of law or a question of fact. One of the questions could be considered a mixed question of law and fact—can you find it?
   a. Whether the defendant was present at the crime scene.
   b. Whether the proposed evidence is irrelevant and inadmissible.
   c. Whether a juror is disqualified.
   d. Whether the defendant in an auto collision was negligent.
   e. The meaning of the premeditation requirement for a conviction of murder.
   f. Whether the defendant killed with premeditation.
   g. The meaning of "guilt beyond a reasonable doubt."
   h. Whether the defendant was "guilty beyond a reasonable doubt."
   i. The value in dollars of a plaintiff's injuries.
   j. What can be considered in estimating the value of a plaintiff's injuries.

2. How many appellate courts does your state have? What are their names? How many justices are there on the state's highest court?

THE RULES OF COURT

Richard Leiter

Rules of Court are a crucial piece of the litigation puzzle. Court rules set limits on the types and numbers of documents that can be filed in a case, and can also impose other limits on the form of documents. For example, court rules will limit the numbers of interrogatories filed, size of paper used in filings, and set specific time limits on when responses to actions of opposing parties need to be filed or otherwise responded to. Courts may also set rules on courtroom decorum: how attorneys should address the court, how they should approach the bench or the witness box, where they should stand and even how they should stand. What are the consequences of failing to comply with the rules? A critical filing may be ignored or an argument in court may be ignored. Sanctions may also be imposed in some cases.

The obvious question in these cases is where does the researcher go to find court rules that are up-to-date? And, how can one stay up-to-date on the changes that seem to occur almost randomly and without warning?

Getting Rules From the Court

This method of obtaining local court rules can vary greatly in effectiveness and in practicability. This procedure is usually the primary source for local court rules in smaller, rural courts. The first thing that is necessary in order to use this method of obtaining court rules is a good directory of local courts, such as BNA's *Directory of State Courts*. Typically, the clerk of the court is the person who is charged with distributing copies of court rules or amendments. Calling this person to ask for copies to be sent to you can meet with varying results, however. There have been situations where it is possible to actually be placed on a mailing list to receive all updates, and others where you can call and request copies of the currently available rules for free or for a fee.

Commercially Available Compilations

Commercially published compilations can and should be the best way to get current, reliable versions of court rules. However, they are not always available in all jurisdictions. When they are available, the usefulness is sometimes quite lacking. For one thing, most local courts cover relatively small geographic areas and/or small numbers of attorneys, and therefore small markets. In addition, it can be quite costly to compile a set of court rules. [A] call to your local law school library's or county law library's reference desk should provide you with the titles of helpful sources. Another approach would be to call the law librarian at a law firm who practices in your area, who should be able to tell you right away what is available for the jurisdiction that you are interested in.

Advance Sheets, Legal Newspapers and Word of Mouth

Stay up on developments in the area of court rule changes by talking with fellow legal professionals and by reading the local bar journal or legal newspaper. All important changes are sure to meet with some discussion among members of the bar and in newspapers, newsletters, journals or in the court hallways, professional association meeting rooms or taverns where the law is discussed. These can be important ways to keep abreast of the important developments. But, by its nature it can also be unreliable and risky. [T]he advance sheets of the courts are a very effective way of staying abreast of rule changes in many jurisdictions. However, this will require diligently reading the advance sheets on a regular basis and checking specifically for announcements of rule changes.

Online Bulletin Boards

At present, very few courts have the resources to effectively maintain an electronic bulletin board. A court can use such a method to post the full-text of the local court rules, and to announce proposed changes to the rules.

The time to learn the best methods of obtaining the local rules of court is not when you or the attorney you are working for needs them—at that time it is nearly always an emergency—the best time is now. Get familiar with the procedures for updating and disseminating court rule changes, and for publishing and distributing the local court rules before it becomes an emergency. Once you possess a set of local court rules, take systematic steps to keep them current.

Reprinted with permission from *Legal Assistant Today* magazine.

CHAPTER 7

STATE AND FEDERAL COURTS

Introduction

The United States has a unique court system. Whereas most developed countries have a hierarchical court system in which all courts are subordinate to a central supreme court, the United States has two separate court systems, federal and state; also, each state is independent from every other and is free within constitutional limits to make its own laws and administer its own system of justice. This chapter discusses the interrelationships of this court system and its ramifications.

The United States Constitution

The U.S. Constitution allocates power between the federal and state governments. The aspects of the Constitution discussed here are far more important and complex than this summary treatment suggests, but acquaintance with certain constitutional provisions is essential for an understanding of state and federal court systems.

When the American colonies united into a federal republic, their representatives framed a charter, the United States Constitution, which allocated governmental authority between state and federal governments. The Constitution reflects a certain distrust of government based on the experience of abuses of traditional legal principles by the British colonial governors under a monarchy. Not only was there a distrust of government in general but also a degree of mutual distrust among the states due to differences in local economies (e.g., plantation economies of Virginia and the Carolinas versus commercial economies of New York, Massachusetts, and Pennsylvania) and differences in size and population (e.g., Rhode Island versus New York). As a result, the Constitution was framed to limit the power of the federal government while preserving governmental autonomy among the states.

The Constitution was viewed as a granting of power by the states to the federal government such that the federal government's powers were limited to those enumerated in the Constitution. All other governmental authority remained in the states, without need to specify that authority in the Constitution itself. This principle is embodied in the Ninth and Tenth Amendments:

AMENDMENT IX. The enumeration in the Constitution of certain rights shall not be construed to deny or disparage others retained by the people.

AMENDMENT X. The powers not delegated to the United States by the Constitution, nor prohibited by it to the States, are reserved to the States respectively, or to the people.

This language reflects that the federal government exercises its authority "by grant," whereas the states exercise authority "by reservation." Note that this language is the language of property law, such as when a property owner transfers or "grants" property rights to another, "reserving" those rights not granted. Like a property transaction, the grant of power is a contract between the people and the government. This is not merely a philosophical point; constitutional cases may best be conceptualized as enforcing property rights in a contractual relationship in which the federal government is bound by the original bargain.

The scope of federal control over the states can be expanded or restricted by constitutional interpretation. In the twentieth century, it has been greatly expanded by a broad interpretation of the *commerce clause,* Article I, § 8, cl. 3, which gives Congress power to regulate interstate commerce. Because most business is in some way involved in interstate commerce, Congress has allowed pervasive regulation of American business. In contrast, in recent decades the U.S. Supreme Court has recognized inherent privacy rights into which neither the states nor the federal government may intrude (e.g., abortion rights).

Supreme Law of the Land

Article VI, Section 2, of the Constitution provides that the Constitution "shall be the supreme law of the land." It was early established by the U.S. Supreme Court that this clause meant that neither state nor federal legislatures could enact laws in conflict with the Constitution, nor could any official or agency of government act in violation of the Constitution. Because the U.S. Supreme Court is the ultimate authority with regard to the interpretation of the Constitution, it can exercise significant authority over state action.

Due Process

The most important phrase in the Constitution for operation of the legal system is the *due process clause* of the Fifth and Fourteenth Amendments. The Fifth Amendment provides that no person "shall be deprived of life, liberty or property, without due process of law." Because this applied only to the federal government, the Fourteenth Amendment was ratified in 1868, including the language: "nor shall any State deprive any person of life, liberty, or property, without due process of law." In this way actions by state officials, legislatures, and courts become federal constitutional issues if denial of due process is alleged.

Due process is an elusive concept at best. It has been defined as requiring "fundamental fairness" in judicial process and prohibiting legislation that is "unreasonable, arbitrary, or capricious." These are subjective concepts—fairness and reasonableness are in the eyes of the beholder. As long as the court has the last word, what the court says is fair *is* fair, and what the court says is reasonable *is* reasonable. Unbridled power of the judiciary is mitigated, however, because the principles of *stare decisis* and judicial restraint constrain judges from arbitrarily imposing their views on society, and the appellate process encourages trial court judges to stay within the bounds of established law.

Due process has been divided into *procedural* and *substantive* due process. Procedural due process treats the issues of *notice* and *hearing.* Notice requires that a person threatened with legal action or whose legal rights are being affected be notified in such a way as to be able to prepare to protect those rights. *Hearing* requires that the form and nature of legal proceedings be fundamentally fair (e.g., an impartial tribunal, right to counsel, right of cross-examination, etc.). Substantive due process requires that legislation be reasonable, that it have a legitimate purpose, that it use reasonable means to effect a reasonable end, and so on. The void-for-vagueness doctrine is an example of a reasonableness test.

Because the fairness and reasonableness standards of due process are developed on a case-by-case basis, to understand due process one must become acquainted with the principal cases that have interpreted it. But judges tend to perceive as unfair what most citizens perceive as unfair, so the anger and frustration that a person may feel toward treatment at the hands of the law or the courts will often strike a resonant chord in the minds of judges. Whenever the government acts to the detriment of an individual, a due process argument lurks in the background.

It is not possible to catalog all the possibilities for denial of due process, but consider the following in terms of potential lawsuits against government:

1. A state university has a policy not to release course transcripts if a student has a debt outstanding to the university. George Shylock fails to be admitted to law school because his transcripts were not sent due to a $2.00 library fine he failed to pay. George had not been notified of the fine and now must wait an additional year to enter law school.

2. The Town of Uppercrust, Connecticut, passes a new zoning plan that requires residential building lots to be at least half an acre in area. Mohammed Hussein owns a lot that is four tenths of an acre, sufficient under the old ordinance for a building site, but his application for a variance (an exception to the ordinance) is denied, so he cannot build on his lot.

3. Under state law a person can be convicted of manslaughter if involved in a fatal auto accident while driving intoxicated, even if the intoxication did not contribute to the accident.

4. In a rulemaking hearing held by the Interstate Commerce Commission, representatives of the railroad and trucking industries are permitted to offer oral testimony of expert witnesses concerning the impact of proposed transportation regulations but are not permitted to cross-examine witnesses.

These hypothetical situations raise additional constitutional issues. The zoning case would be challenged as taking private property without just compensation under the Fifth Amendment; the manslaughter case would undoubtedly raise the Eighth Amendment issue of cruel and unusual punishment. Due process questions are commonly raised along with other issues.

Equal Protection

The Fourteenth Amendment also prohibits states from denying "any person within its jurisdiction the equal protection of the laws." This language was designed originally to protect former slaves from discriminatory treatment after the Civil War. Its coverage, however, has been expanded to invalidate all laws and procedures that unreasonably discriminate. It has been invoked when classes of persons have been treated unequally by the law; for instance, alimony statutes in many states provided alimony only for women, thus discriminating against men, or public schools budgeted more for male athletics than female athletic programs, discriminating against women. The discriminatory aspect of the law may be more subtle, such as when cable TV companies objected to regulation of their broadcasting that was not also applied to noncable broadcasting. All laws by their nature discriminate—drunkendriving statutes discriminate against drinkers—but such forms of discrimination are benign, protecting society and its members. Equal protection of the laws is designed to protect a stigmatized group from discrimination rather than to control or punish offensive conduct.

Cases and Controversies

Article III of the Constitution vests judicial power in the "Supreme Court, and in such inferior courts as the Congress may from time to time ordain and establish." Article III, Section 2, refers to judicial power over "cases" and "controversies." These words have been interpreted by the U.S. Supreme Court to restrict access to the federal courts in several ways, the most important of which concerns the question of *standing*. In our legal system, not every person may seek redress for every deprivation of a legal right. Standing is a limitation on who may bring an action. In general, only a person who has a "personal stake in the outcome" of a case may bring suit. This gloss on the Constitution encourages litigants to frame their suits in terms of property rights, but even in the violation of abstract rights, such as freedom of speech, suits are limited to those persons directly affected—a person may not sue the government for the abuse of power if that abuse is unrelated to the person desiring to sue.

Case and controversy have also been interpreted as referring to actual disputes between real parties. Not every slight, rebuke, or annoyance is a legal matter. And the courts have refused to hear cases concerning remote or hypothetical questions. This does not mean that some injury or wrong must necessarily have already occurred, but there must at least be an immediate threat of invasion of a right. In the *Waddell* case, a high school referee's call was taken all the way to the Georgia Supreme Court.

GEORGIA HIGH SCHOOL ASSOCIATION
v.
WADDELL et al.
Supreme Court of Georgia
248 Ga. 542, 285 S.E.2d 7 (1981)

On October 23, 1981, a football game was played between R.L. Osborne and Lithia Springs High Schools, members of region 5 AAAA established by the Georgia High School Association. The winner of this game would be in the play-offs, beginning with Campbell High School.

The score was 7 to 6 in favor of Osborne. With 7 minutes, 1 second, remaining in the game, Osborne had the ball on its 47 yard line, 4th down and 21 yards to go for a first down. Osborne punted but "roughing the kicker" was called on Lithia Springs. The referee officiating the game with the approval and sanction of the Georgia High School Association assessed the 15 yard penalty, placed the ball on the Lithia Springs 38 yard line, and declared it was 4th down and 6 yards to go.

The rules of the National Federation of State High School Associations provide that the penalty for roughing the kicker shall be 15 yards *and* 1st down. There is a dispute as to whether the Osborne coaches properly protested to the referee, before the ball was put in play, the error in the referee's failing to declare a 1st down.

From Lithia Springs' 38, Osborne punted again. Lithia Springs received the punt and drove down the field to score a field goal. Now 2 points behind, Osborne passed. Lithia Springs intercepted and scored again. The final score was Lithia Springs over Osborne, 16 to 7.

* * *

On November 12, suit was filed in the Superior Court of Cobb County by parents of Osborne players against the GHSA. Hearing was held on November 13. The court found that it had jurisdiction, found that the referee erred in failing to declare an automatic first down, and found that a protest was lodged with the proper officials of GHSA. The court found that the plaintiffs have a property right in the game of football being played according to the rules and that the referee denied plaintiffs and their sons this property right and equal protection of the laws by failing to correctly apply the rules.

The court then entered its order on November 13 canceling the play-off game between Lithia Springs and Campbell High School scheduled for 8 p.m. that evening and ordered "... that Lithia Springs High School and R.L. Osborne High School meet on the football field on November 14, 1981 at an agreed upon time between the parties and resume play at the Lithia Springs thirty eight yard line with the ball being in the possession of R.L. Osborne High School and it be first down and ten yards to go for a first down and that the clock be set at seven minutes one second to play and that the quarter be designated as the fourth quarter."

Asserting that the trial court's order was erroneous under *Smith v. Crim,* 240 Ga. 390, 240 S.E.2d 884 (1977), and would disrupt the play-off games not only between Lithia Springs and Campbell but succeeding play-offs, the GHSA filed a motion for **supersedeas** in this court on November 13, 1981, and the court entered its order suspending the trial court's order, pending further order of this court.

In *Smith v. Crim, supra,* we held that a high school football player has no right to participate in interscholastic sports and has no protectable property interest which would give rise to a due

process claim. Pretermitting the question of "state action" which is the threshold of the 14th Amendment, we held that Smith was not denied equal protection by the rule of GHSA there involved. Similarly we find no denial of equal protection by the referee's error here. Were our decision to be otherwise, every error in the trial courts would constitute a denial of equal protection. We now go further and hold that courts of equity in this state are without authority to review decisions of football referees because those decisions do not present judicial controversies. The stay granted by this court on November 13, 1981, is hereby reaffirmed.

All the Justices concur.

Case Questions

1. Why is "state action" the threshold question for an inquiry into a denial of equal protection of the law under the Fourteenth Amendment?
2. Why did the football players have no right and no property interest to qualify for due process protection?
3. Did the players receive fair procedure?

Case Glossary

supersedeas A court or writ that stays the power of a lower court to execute on its judgment or decree. An appeal from a trial court to an appellate court automatically serves as a supersedeas of the trial court's judgment.

Full Faith and Credit

Article IV of the Constitution begins: "Full faith and credit shall be given in each State to the public acts, records, and judicial proceedings of every other State." As a practical matter, this means that the courts of each state must recognize the validity of the laws and judicial orders of other states. Divorce provides a useful example. Frequently after divorce, an ex-husband ordered to pay child support or alimony moves to another state and stops making payments. The ex-wife may bring an action in the state to which the former husband has moved to collect arrears in payments. In the action, the court must recognize the validity of the divorce and the order to make payments.

Full faith and credit has some limitations. A court may find that the law or court order of another state is repugnant to public policy, a rare occurrence. One state may conclude that the court of another state did not have jurisdiction over the matter in the first place. A court without jurisdiction has no authority and its orders no validity. For example, husband and wife separate and live in different states. One brings a divorce action in one state and the other in another state. Only one state should have jurisdiction—two conflicting divorce decrees make no legal or practical sense. A court may conclude that the court of another state did not have jurisdiction and refuse to enforce its orders.

This may have unanticipated results; consider the following case. A man from North Carolina obtained a "quickie" divorce in Nevada, immediately remarried in Nevada, and returned to North Carolina with his new wife. North Carolina charged and convicted him of bigamy, and the case went to the U.S. Supreme Court twice. This created the anomalous situation in which a man was a "bigamist for living in one state with the only one with whom the other state would permit him lawfully to live" [Justice Douglas, *Williams v. North Carolina*, 317 U.S. 287 (1942)]. The Court required North Carolina to respect the Nevada decree (with vigorous dissenting opinions). The advent of no-fault divorce has mitigated the need for divorce havens like Nevada, but jurisdictional problems can still create a tangled web in divorce cases.

Subject Matter Jurisdiction

Although jurisdiction may properly be treated as part of civil and criminal procedure, the distinction between federal and state court systems is grounded on jurisdiction as well. The power and authority of a court in a particular dispute are based on jurisdiction. Without jurisdiction, a court has no authority; its orders are not valid. *Subject matter jurisdiction* refers to the kinds of disputes a court has the authority to decide. For example, the Constitution provides that the federal government has exclusive control over **bankruptcy**, **patent**, **trademark**,

---

BALLENTINE'S

bankruptcy The system under which a debtor may come into court ... or be brought into court by ... creditors ... , either seeking to have [the debtor's] assets administered and sold for the benefit of his or her creditors and to be discharged from his or her debts ... , or to have his debts reorganized ... .

patent The exclusive right of manufacture, sale, or use granted by the federal government to a person who invents or discovers a device or process that is new and useful.

trademark A mark, design, title, logo, or motto used in the sale or advertising of products to identify them and distinguish them from the products of others. A trademark is the property of its owner and, when registered under the Trademark Act, is reserved for the exclusive use of its owner.

copyright, and **admiralty**. A state court has no power to decide a bankruptcy case; if it should do so, its orders would have no validity.

General and Limited Jurisdiction

Courts are classified as having *general* or *limited* subject matter jurisdiction. Courts of general jurisdiction have authority to decide a wide variety of cases and apply the full range of judicial remedy and relief. Major trial courts in each jurisdiction fit into this category. However, most states have also established courts of limited jurisdiction to handle only a restricted class of cases. A probate court, for example, handles matters concerning decedents' estates (many probate courts also have jurisdiction over some areas of law relating to juveniles). Thus, a probate court does not hear cases of tenant evictions. Some states divide their courts into criminal and civil courts; Texas even divides appeals into civil and criminal appeals at the supreme court level.

There is a wide variety of lower courts handling minor matters with limited subject matter jurisdiction; one example is small claims court (limited to cases involving a low maximum monetary amount and having limited remedial powers—it cannot grant divorces, issue injunctions, etc.). Municipal courts are common in the United States, typically handling violations of city ordinances and other minor civil and criminal matters. Many of these lesser courts are conducted with less formality than higher trial courts. Small claims courts are designed to provide litigants with an inexpensive means to resolve disputes. Lawyers do not usually participate, court reporters are usually not present (therefore no transcript is made), and court costs are minimal; the judge tends to take a more active role in the process because the litigants are unfamiliar with the technicalities of the law.

Federal Subject Matter Jurisdiction

Federal jurisdiction applies to two categories of cases: (1) federal question cases and (2) diversity of citizenship cases.

------BALLENTINE'S------

copyright   The right of an author, granted by federal statute, to exclusively control the reproduction, distribution, and sale of his or her literary, artistic, or intellectual productions for the period of the copyright's existence. Copyright protection extends to written work, music, films, sound recordings, photographs, paintings, sculpture, and some computer programs and chips.

admiralty   The body of law that regulates the conduct of affairs on navigable waters.

Federal Question Cases

The Constitution provides that the federal courts have jurisdiction over cases arising under the Constitution, laws, and treaties of the United States. These are called *federal question* cases. A case may directly raise a constitutional issue, or it may arise under a federal statute enacted by Congress (e.g., federal civil rights violations, environmental protection issues).

Each state (and the District of Columbia) has at least one U.S. District Court, the federal trial court to which federal question cases are brought. Many cases involve both state law and federal questions and can be brought in state courts, which must then decide issues of both state and federal law. For instance, the drunken driving manslaughter case in our hypothetical situations considered earlier would begin as a state prosecution in which the defendant would raise defense arguments based on the due process and cruel and unusual punishment clauses of the U.S. Constitution, as well as their counterparts in the state constitution (and factual defenses, of course). If convicted, the defendant could appeal to the state court of appeals and the state supreme court, and then petition the U.S. Supreme Court for a writ of certiorari on the federal constitutional issues.

A case originating in the federal district court will stay in the federal system even if an issue of state law must be decided. A case originating in the state courts will remain in the state court system until decided or denied consideration by the state's highest court, from which appeal is made (by way of **certiorari**) to the U.S. Supreme Court. A defendant may challenge federal question jurisdiction in a case in a U.S. District Court, which would force the case into state court if the challenge is successful. Similarly, a defendant may petition the U.S. District Court for removal from state court to the federal court and will succeed if the federal court concludes that the case could have been brought originally in the federal court.

Keep in mind that state courts have the final authority to declare state law, and federal courts have final authority to declare federal law. State courts will thus use federal cases to determine federal law, while federal courts will rely on decisions of state courts where state law is concerned. The exceptions to this are: (1) if state and federal laws overlap and conflict (e.g., certain state and federal labor laws may give rise to an inconsistency between them), state law must yield to federal law; and (2) any state statute or court decision that is held to be in conflict

---

BALLENTINE'S

certiorari   (Latin) A writ issued by a higher court to a lower court requiring the certification of the record in a particular case so that the higher court can review the record and correct any actions taken in the case which are not in accordance with the law. The Supreme Court of the United States uses the writ of certiorari to select the state court cases it is willing to review. Commonly referred to as "cert."

with the U.S. Constitution is invalid and without authority as to the part that is unconstitutional.

Diversity of Citizenship Cases

Article III of the Constitution placed suits between citizens of different states under federal jurisdiction. This jurisdiction is not exclusive, so a plaintiff of Maryland suing a defendant from Virginia may elect to sue in a state court (most likely Virginia) or in a U.S. District Court. The differences in state citizenship are referred to as *diversity of citizenship,* and jurisdiction is based on the status of the parties without regard to the subject matter of the case; that is, no federal law other than the diversity clause of the Constitution is required. Diversity cases additionally require that the amount in controversy exceed $50,000.

Diversity jurisdiction requires total diversity—if there are multiple plaintiffs or defendants and any plaintiff is a citizen of the same state as any defendant, diversity jurisdiction will be denied. Like federal question cases, a petition for removal is available to the defendant if the plaintiff elects to bring the suit in the state court. The petition, however, is not available if suit is brought in the defendant's state. The rationale for this exception is based on the original purpose of the diversity clause. Apparently when the Constitution was framed, it was feared that parties might face prejudice when suing or being sued in a state other than their own. Federal jurisdiction was made available on the belief that federal courts would be less inclined to partiality. Thus, when a defendant is sued at home, the rationale for federal jurisdiction no longer holds.

In the *Fine* case, both sides filed suit on the same day, one in state court and one in federal court. As the case indicates, a corporation may be a "citizen" of more than one state for the purposes of diversity jurisdiction. Although a defendant sued in state court may petition for **removal** to federal court, claiming diversity jurisdiction, a defendant sued in federal court in a diversity case may move to remand to the state court, claiming a lack of diversity jurisdiction. Note that a removal should be distinguished from a *remand,* which in a diversity case would seek a transfer from a federal court back to the state court. Both removal and remand may be distinguished from a motion to dismiss for lack of jurisdiction.

Many have argued that the diversity clause no longer makes sense and unnecessarily clogs federal courts, which ought to be deciding cases of federal rather than state law.

————————————BALLENTINE'S————————————

removal of case   1. In the usual sense, the transfer of a case from a state court to a federal court. 2. In the broad sense of the term, any transfer of a case from one court to another.

William M. FINE, et al., Plaintiffs,
v.
DELALANDE, INC., Defendant.
United States District Court,
S.D. New York
545 F. Supp. 275 (1982)

This lawsuit began on April 1, 1982, in the New York Supreme Court, New York County, the same day on which the defendant Delalande, Inc. filed an action in this Court against the plaintiffs herein based upon claimed diversity of citizenship. Delalande removed this action from the state court on April 20, 1982, pursuant to 28 U.S.C. § 1441(c).

By motion docketed May 5, 1982, the *Fine* plaintiffs seek the remand of this action to the state court as improvidently removed, because

Delalande, Inc. is a citizen of New York by reason of its principal place of business of this state.

For purposes of 18 U.S.C. § 1441, a corporation is deemed to be a citizen of the state wherein it has its principal place of business, and of the state of its incorporation. 28 U.S.C. § 1332(c).

For reasons discussed more fully in this Court's Memorandum and Order of this date in the companion *Delalande* action, 545 F. Supp. 268, familiarity with which is assumed, this Court finds that Delalande has its principal place of business in New York. Accordingly, there is not complete diversity because at least eleven of the plaintiffs are also citizens of New York.

Plaintiff's motion to remand this action to the state court is granted.

Case Questions

1. If Delalande's principal place of business is New York, on what basis was it claiming diversity of citizenship?
2. Why would the plaintiff prefer state court or defendant federal court?

The *Erie* Doctrine

In 1938, the U.S. Supreme Court decided the case of *Erie Railroad v. Tompkins,* 304 U.S. 64, which altered the nature of diversity cases forever. Tompkins was injured by a train while walking along a path beside the railroad tracks, when an open door on a refrigerator car hit him. Tompkins brought a diversity case in federal court and was awarded $30,000 in damages. The Second Circuit Court of Appeals affirmed the award, but the railroad petitioned and received certiorari from the U.S. Supreme Court.

At issue was the substantive law to be followed in a diversity case. The trial judge instructed the jury that the railroad was liable under general law if the jury found simple negligence. The railroad argued from the beginning that the common law of Pennsylvania, the site of the injury, should apply. Under Pennsylvania law, Tompkins would be considered a trespasser, as he was walking on the railroad's right of way, so the railroad would not be liable to a trespasser on the basis of ordinary negligence but only if the jury found gross negligence (i.e., wanton and reckless misconduct). In Pennsylvania, a landowner such as the railroad owes a lower duty of care to a trespasser than to nontrespassers. For this reason, Tompkins's attorneys chose to bring the case in federal court rather than the Pennsylvania state court.

Section 34 of the Federal Judiciary Act of 1789 had provided for the recognition and application of state common law in appropriate cases, but in *Swift v. Tyson,* 41 U.S. 1 (1842), the court had held that the federal courts were free to disregard specific decisions of state common law in favor of general principles of common law.

The effect of *Swift v. Tyson* was to encourage the creation of a general federal common law that could differ significantly from the law of a particular state. This would encourage litigants for whom diversity jurisdiction was available to select the court, state or federal, in which they would have the greatest likelihood of success, precisely what Tompkins's lawyers did. In *Erie* the Supreme Court overruled *Swift v. Tyson* and declared that, henceforth, the federal courts in diversity cases would follow the common law of the state.

Mr. Tompkins lost his case.

Erie has been applied to substantive law but not procedure—when suing in federal court, federal procedure is followed.

In the *Brown* case, like the *Fine* case, the principal issue is diversity jurisdiction. Once the court determines it has jurisdiction, the case is summarily dismissed by interpreting state law as *Erie* requires. The *Brown* plaintiff is suing for wrongful discharge, but she is an "at-will" employee, which means that she does not have an employment contract that guarantees a period of employment, so she can be discharged at any time.

Some states allow suits for wrongful discharge for at-will employees; Missouri does not. Why is the plaintiff trying desperately to get into a Missouri state court? The answer may lie in the Erie doctrine itself. Although the federal court in a diversity case will be extremely reluctant to upset established Missouri precedent, the plaintiff might be able to persuade a Missouri court to overrule precedent in light of a trend in other states to recognize an action for wrongful discharge of an at-will employee.

Bankruptcy

Bankruptcy comes within the exclusive authority of the federal courts because of the provision in the U.S. Constitution, Article I, Section 8, Clause 4, which grants to Congress the power "to establish ... uniform rules on the subject of bankruptcies throughout the United States." Bankruptcy is a means by which an individual or business (or even a municipality) may resolve the problem of overindebtedness. When debts accumulate to the point that they exceed the debtor's ability to

Deborah BROWN, Plaintiff,
v.
SOUTHLAND CORPORATION, et
al., Defendants.
United States District Court,
E.D. Missouri, E.D.
620 F. Supp. 1495 (1985)

Plaintiff, a resident of Missouri, brought this action for damages in the Circuit Court of the City of St. Louis against Southland Corporation, a Texas corporation, and Clyde Tinsley, a resident of Missouri.

The action arises out of the circumstances surrounding plaintiff's discharge from defendant Southland Corporation's (Southland) employment. Plaintiff was employed as the store manager of a "7-Eleven" store owned by defendant Southland at the time of her discharge in May 1980. Plaintiff alleges that she was wrongfully discharged pursuant to a corporate policy implemented to cover-up top-level employees' negligence. ...

28 U.S.C. § 1441(b) gives a defendant who meets certain requirements the right to remove a civil action from a state court to a federal district court on the basis of diversity of citizenship. The requirement of complete diversity between plaintiffs and defendants is fully applicable to § 1441(b). A federal court, however, will not allow removal to be defeated by the collusive or fraudulent joinder of a resident defendant. ...

In the present action, plaintiff's complaint alleges that Tinsley was the zone manager with ultimate supervisory responsibility over the store where plaintiff worked. In support of his removal petition, defendant Tinsley submitted affidavits and plaintiff's own deposition statements to the effect that at the time of the occurrences alleged in plaintiff's complaint, he was not the zone manager of the district in which plaintiff's store was located and that he had no involvement in the said occurrences. Plaintiff states in her deposition that she never spoke with defendant Tinsley. Plaintiff has not disputed this evidence. The Court concludes that defendants have met their burden of proving that defendant Tinsley was improperly joined and dismisses him pursuant to Rule 21, Fed.R.Civ.P. Accordingly, plaintiff's motion to remand is denied.

The next matter for consideration is defendants' motion to dismiss for failure to state a claim. Plaintiff does not allege any contractual or statutory provision that would bar her termination. In Missouri, it is firmly established that an at-will employee cannot maintain an action for wrongful discharge. ...

The above rulings dispose of all claims in plaintiff's complaint against each defendant. Judgment for defendants.

Case Questions

1. Why does the plaintiff want the case remanded to state court?
2. What reasons are given for denial of the petition to remand?
3. What result does *Erie* achieve in this case?

pay (insolvency), bankruptcy is a way to resolve financial distress. It has particular importance to the paralegal field because so much of the work involves administration, preparation of forms and documents, and organization of the bankruptcy process. Although attorneys must advise concerning the initial choice to file for bankruptcy, once the process starts, most of the work follows an orderly procedure that is often somewhat mechanical and clerical in nature. Many paralegals specialize exclusively in bankruptcy, and for that reason it is given special attention here.

The underlying rationale behind bankruptcy is to provide relief for the insolvent debtor and to protect creditors by gathering the debtor's assets and distributing them equitably to the creditors. Although the law strongly favors the full payment of legal debts, individuals and businesses frequently find themselves in a position in which they have no reasonable prospect of becoming solvent and so must default on debts. At that point the debtor or the creditors may decide that the only reasonable method of resolving the problem is to file for bankruptcy, which settles the debts at less than their full value. The old English solution of casting the debtor into prison has been discarded. While imprisonment may satisfy some creditors' desire for punishment, an imprisoned debtor cannot contribute either to paying past debts or to returning to productivity. Nor is insolvency usually the product of bad faith or wrongdoing. Recession, unemployment, and other catastrophes are as much responsible for insolvency as misuse of other people's money.

Current bankruptcy law is based on the Bankruptcy Reform Act of 1978, which forms Title 11 of the United States Code. Individual and commercial bankruptcies fall within Chapters 7, 11, and 13 of Title 11 (the chapters are odd-numbered, Chapter 9 deals with municipalities) and are commonly referred to simply as "Chapter 7," "Chapter 11," etc.

Most bankruptcies are voluntary, that is, the debtor files the petition. Petitions brought by creditors forcing a debtor into bankruptcy are referred to as *involuntary bankruptcy.* Chapter 7 and Chapter 11 petitions may be either voluntary or involuntary, but Chapter 13 proceedings may only be voluntary.

Chapter 7 is titled "Liquidation," which refers to the process of collecting the debtor's assets and distributing them (or the proceeds from their sale) to creditors. A trustee in bankruptcy is appointed to assume control of and distribute the debtor's assets. The trustee has the duty of establishing which claims are valid and payable and of distributing assets according to priorities established by law. Many forms of property interests are exempted from inclusion in the assets, such as $2,400 equity in one motor vehicle and child support payments. Some debts may not be discharged in bankruptcy, such as certain taxes, alimony, and child support. Once the trustee has collected nonexempt property and paid nondischargeable debts, the remainder of the assets, if any, are distributed to creditors and the debts are discharged—a bankrupt individual is no longer legally indebted for discharged debts. Discharge is subject to a number of conditions, one of which is that the bankrupt has not been granted a discharge in bankruptcy within the prior six years.

Chapter 11, titled "Reorganization," is designed principally to save failing business organizations such as corporations and partnerships. Many businesses become financially distressed but are nevertheless worth saving. Liquidation of the business could do much more damage to owners, creditors, and employees than attempting to reorganize the business. Chapter 11 requires that the debtor propose a plan of reorganization, which is subject to acceptance by classes of creditors and classes of interests (e.g., stockholders). Ultimately, the court must decide whether the plan is satisfactory, whether it meets the requirements of the law, and whether acceptance by classes of claims and classes of interests is sufficient. Confirmation of the plan entitles the debtor to a new start, subject to the specific requirements imposed by the decree of the court. Not all Chapter 11 plans are approved, and not all reorganizations result in successful operations.

Chapter 13, titled "Adjustment of Debts of an Individual with Regular Income," allows a voluntary petition designed to defer payments on debts in order to pay them in full under a plan proposed by the debtor and confirmed by the Court. As its title suggests, Chapter 13 applies to individuals and one-owner businesses (sole proprietorships) who are not presently able to pay debts but who have a source of income indicating a future ability to pay. The plan must meet certain statutory requirements, and creditors have the opportunity to accept or reject the plan, though the court has the authority to confirm or reject the plan. Under Chapter 13, creditors should receive more than they would under a Chapter 7 liquidation and may ultimately receive payment in full.

The effect of both voluntary and involuntary petitions is to prevent creditors from bringing or continuing suits to enforce debt. Because of this feature, bankruptcy has occasionally been used as a strategy to stave off enforcement of debts. For example, when Texaco lost a $10 billion dollar judgment to Pennzoil, Texaco filed for bankruptcy, eventually settling for $4 billion; a few years later Texaco was more profitable than ever. It is doubtful that Texaco was ever seriously in danger of going out of business. Frank Lorenzo used bankruptcy to fend off attempts by the unions at Eastern Airlines to take over the company. Eastern, however, was in far more severe financial straits than Texaco had been, and its fortunes proceeded steadily downward.

Conflict of Laws

Separate state jurisdictions within one nation have also presented a special problem called **conflict of laws** or *choice of law*. Suppose two Connecticut residents are involved in an auto accident in Massachusetts.

BALLENTINE'S

conflict of laws (choice of laws)   Area of the law that determines whether the law of some other state or country will be applied in a circumstance where the laws of more than one jurisdiction could apply and are in opposition to each other.

With a Connecticut plaintiff and a Connecticut defendant, suit is logically brought in Connecticut, although it could be brought in Massachusetts where the accident occurred. Should Connecticut or Massachusetts law apply? This is a conflict of laws problem. Whatever state is chosen for the suit (the *forum* state), its procedural laws will be followed; but a question may arise as to which forum's substantive law should apply. In some respects this parallels the issue in *Erie*: the result of the lawsuit should not depend on the choice of the forum. Because of differences in state law, a defendant may be liable under the law of one state but not under the law of another, making the defendant's state of residence the determining factor in the result.

Conflict of laws rules resolve this problem to some extent. Each state has its own rules to decide the choice of law. If the Connecticut plaintiff sues in Connecticut, Connecticut choice of law must apply. Assuming that Connecticut is in no way involved with the accident (i.e., the accident and its causes occurred wholly within Massachusetts), the substantive law of Massachusetts would apply, just as it would if the case were brought in Massachusetts. Connecticut law would require that the substantive law of Massachusetts govern the outcome of the case.

There is logic to this result. Whether conduct is wrongful should be determined by the law of the place where it occurs. The Connecticut driver in Massachusetts must obey Massachusetts law. To illustrate, many states allow a driver to turn right at a red light after stopping and determining it is safe to turn. Suppose a resident of such a state follows this custom in a state that does not allow turning on red. It would certainly be no defense, either civil or criminal, that the driver's home state has a different rule. Suppose that the turn on red caused an accident and that an injured party sued the nonresident in his home state. Should the defendant's conduct be judged differently because it is legal in his home state, the state where the suit was brought? No, wrongful conduct should not be magically transformed into proper conduct by the choice of the forum.

Unfortunately, conflict of laws is not always this simple. Suppose, for example, that the two drivers were crossing the Connecticut–Massachusetts border as the accident occurred. The wrongful act of one driver may have occurred in Connecticut but the injuries inflicted in Massachusetts. Choice of law will depend on the conflict of laws principles of the forum state. In tort cases like an auto accident, two rules are generally applied. The ancient rule, *lex loci delicti,* or "the law of the place of the wrong," holds that choice of law will fall on the site of the last act necessary to make the actor liable, that is, where the tortious act is complete. In recent times another test, called the *significant relationship test,* has been adopted in many states. Under this test, all the circumstances of the tort are considered in deciding which state has the greatest connection with the wrong.

Contract cases present far more problems for conflict of laws. As a somewhat absurd, but not impossible, example, consider the following:

> Two corporations with nationwide activities negotiate a complex contract. One corporation is incorporated in California, the other in New York. The contract is negotiated and signed in Illinois. The contract is to be performed primarily in Texas but is breached in Louisiana. The contract specifically provides, "in case of breach, this contract will be construed under the law of Michigan." The California corporation sues the New York corporation in New Jersey, its principal place of business.

Theoretically, the law of one of several states might be chosen. If suit is brought in New Jersey and the New Jersey court agrees that it has jurisdiction, the choice of law would depend on New Jersey rules on conflict of laws. New Jersey conflict of laws may be very different from those of Texas or Illinois. Most states give great weight to the agreement of the parties to specify the law that governs, here that of Michigan. But many contracts are silent in this regard, and there may be policy reasons for not enforcing that part of the contract.

There are several conflict of laws principles with regard to contracts, and frequently different rules apply to different circumstances. Like torts, there has been a strong trend toward the significant relationship test, which aims at choosing the state having the greatest connection with the contract. Except for those rare experts on conflict of laws, anyone with a problem in this area can anticipate doing considerable research. To achieve the best results, one should consider which state's law might apply; which would be most favorable; and which of the possible forum states has conflict rules that would invoke the favorable state's law.

In the *Newman* case, a conflict of laws problem becomes a pivotal issue, because the plaintiff might well lose in New York and win in Illinois. Note that the case was filed in a federal court in New York, which under *Erie* followed New York law, specifically New York conflict of laws, to determine whether New York or Illinois law should apply. *Newman*, a suit for damages for the cost of recreating a lost manuscript, was decided in the days before photocopying and word processing. Today the court might hold the plaintiff contributorily negligent for not making a copy of the valuable lost manuscript.

Although the court does not discuss them in detail, it uses two of the traditional bases for choice of law in contract cases: (1) the place where the contract was made, and (2) the place where the contract was performed.

NEWMAN
v.
CLAYTON F. SUMMY CO.
Circuit Court of Appeals, Second Circuit
133 F.2d 465 (1943)

Appellee, a composer, sent a manuscript, insured for $500, by Railway Express from Florida to appellant, a music publisher, in Chicago. Appellant later procured appellee's permission to send the manuscript to appellant's New York office. But, unknown to appellee, appellant, in shipping the script to New York, also by Railway Express, described the package as containing merely "sheet music." The script was lost in transit. Appellee, having retained no copy, spent considerable time in reproducing the script and later contracted with another publisher who published it under a royalty agreement.

* * *

The manuscript had no market value and was unique, so that it was proper to measure its value by the reasonable worth of the time and effort spent by appellee in reproducing it. On the basis of evidence, the verdict was not excessive. And appellee's failure to keep a copy of her script did not bar recovery. ...

Appellant asserts that the trial judge erred in instructing the jury as follows: "What is the duty which the bailee, the Summy Company, owed to the bailor, Miss Newman? Being a **bailee**, the Summy Company owed the plaintiff the duty of exercising reasonable care in handling her manuscripts and in dealing with her manuscripts * * * Negligence is usually defined in these words: Negligence is the failure to exercise a care commensurate to the hazard. That is, the amount and kind of care that would be exercised by an ordinarily prudent person in the same or similar circumstances, or that degree of diligence which the manner and the nature of the employment make it reasonable to expect. The question, therefore, that you must decide is whether the defendant failed in its duty to observe that degree of care in looking after the manuscript which had been entrusted to it." Appellant maintains that the judge should have instructed the jury that it was not liable unless it was **grossly negligent** because, appellant claims under *Erie R.R. v. Tompkins,* 304 U.S. 64 ... New York law governs. By the law of New York where the trial was held, appellant was a gratuitous bailee, and a gratuitous bailee is not liable except for gross negligence. There is, however, no need for us to consider what would be the law of New York applicable to such a transaction occurring in New York, for here we must apply the New York doctrine of conflict of laws and that doctrine is to the effect that the applicable legal rules are those of Illinois. There can be no doubt that the arrangements for the bailment were made in Illinois, and that "performance," i.e., the shipment of the manuscripts, occurred in that state. In such circumstances, the New York courts hold that the Illinois law as to bailments should be applied.

Turning then to the Illinois decisions, it appears that the rule is that, regardless of whether or not there was a **gratuitous bailment** or one for "mutual benefit," the bailee must use the same care as he would with respect to his own property; there is no discussion of "gross negligence." ...

The instruction given by the trial court in the instant case was not literally in accord with the language used in those cases. Perhaps the differences are not substantial. But even if they are, that is of no import, since, in the trial court, appellant did not except to the instruction on the ground of any such differences but only because of the failure to give instructions as to gross negligence. Accordingly there was no reversible error.

The judgment of the trial court is affirmed.

Case Questions

1. Why is a different standard of care applied to gratuitous bailment and bailment for hire in New York?
2. To what law (and why) does the federal court look to determine what substantive law to apply?
3. What would be an example of a bailment for hire? A gratuitous bailment?

Case Glossary

bailment   The entrusting of personal property by one person (the bailor) to another (the bailee) for specific purpose, with the understanding that the property will be returned when the purpose is accomplished, the stated duration of the bailment is over, or the bailor reclaims it.

gross negligence   Willfully and intentionally acting, or failing to act, with a deliberate indifference to how others may be affected.

gratuitous bailment   A bailment for the sole benefit of the bailee; that is, one in which no compensation is involved.

Law and Equity

History has left the American legal system with an arbitrary division of remedies into *legal* and *equitable.* Legal remedies refer to relief granted by common law courts, and equitable remedies to those afforded by courts of equity, also called *chancery.* Although this subject is usually treated under the heading of remedies, it is related to jurisdiction, because many states restrict equitable jurisdiction to their highest trial courts.

The existence of legal and equitable remedies can be adequately understood only in historical context. Anglo-American law began with the administrative organization of England in the aftermath of the Norman Conquest. Although the Normans left local tribunals in operation, often applying principles of former English law, the organization of a centralized kingdom included the establishment of laws common to the entire kingdom; hence the name common law. Courts were established that had jurisdiction over the common law. In these courts, actions were initiated by *writs,* a word that does not have an exact counterpart in modern law. A writ stated a cause of action, so it is similar to the modern pleading we now call a *complaint.* But writs had specific names, such as the writ of trespass *quare clausum fregit,* which corresponds to our modern cause of action for trespass to land, or the writ *de ejectione firmæ,* corresponding to modern ejectment or eviction. The writs were essentially formulas applied to recognized legal wrongs, almost like a catalog of actions in which a party would fill in the blanks. Each action was required to fit precisely into a specific writ. In the first years of the common law courts, new writs were constantly created as different disputes arose that varied from already established actions. Gradually, however, the system crystallized, and the common law courts became formal and rigid, resisting the establishment of new writs so that novel cases that did not fall within established writs were rejected by the courts.

This development did not leave litigants without a remedy, however, because from the beginning subjects of the kingdom enjoyed the right of petitioning the king for justice. As more and more cases arose that were not recognized by the common law courts, parties sought relief from the king, who then presented these cases to the chancellor, originally an ecclesiastical office staffed by priests—not to be confused with ecclesiastical courts under the authority of the Church that applied the principles of canon law. Because of a gradually mounting case load, Chancery developed its own courts independent of the common law courts and referred to as courts of equity. Courts of law and equity existed side by side until recent years, when the states merged law and equity into a single court having authority to order both legal and equitable remedies. Despite the merger, features of the historical differences between the two courts remain of importance in modern legal practice.

Courts of equity treated the cases before them somewhat differently than the common law courts. Because petitions in equity sought special justice and presented novel situations, equity courts required greater flexibility and discretion than common law courts. The aim of equity was to provide relief appropriate to merits of the case; thus, courts of equity were described as *courts of conscience,* governed by the moral issues of the case rather than *stare decisis.* Theoretically this is still true today: a judge sitting in equity is not bound by precedent. As a practical matter, modern judges rule in equity on the basis of precedent and expect attorneys to provide precedental authority in their arguments. Nonetheless, since judges sitting in equity sometimes exercise discretion, ignoring precedent, appeal from a case in equity is frequently premised on the basis of "abuse of discretion" by the lower court judge. If a judge departs from well-established principles of equity as revealed by prior cases, an appellant may use this effectively to persuade an appellate court that the lower court judge abused discretion. Thus, justices sitting in equity are urged to follow consistent principles much like the force of precedent in the common law.

Jury Trials

Because courts of equity exercised moral authority and originally were cloaked with the spiritual authority of the clergy and the secular authority of the king, juries were deemed unnecessary and inappropriate. This custom remains today; there is no right to a jury trial in a case seeking equitable relief alone. The merger of law and equity compounds the jury question, as both legal and equitable remedies may be sought in the same suit, and legal as well as equitable issues may be raised in a suit for equitable relief. The *Deborah Leslie* case discusses in some detail the right to a jury trial and the test for determining whether it holds in the context of the modern merger of law and equity.

DEBORAH LESLIE, LTD., Plaintiff,
v.
RONA, INC. and Erwin Rona,
Defendants.
United States District Court, D. Rhode Island
630 F. Supp. 1250 (1986)

The seventh amendment to the federal Constitution is the touchstone of any reasoned analysis anent the availability of civil jury trials in the federal courts. The seventh amendment intones:

> In suits at common law, where the value in controversy shall exceed twenty dollars, the right of trial by jury shall be preserved, and no fact tried by a jury, shall be otherwise reexamined in any Court of the United States, than according to the rules of the common law.

As is clear from the text, the Framers preserved the right to jury trial in all suits at common law. Their basic purpose was to maintain the right to a jury trial as it existed when they adopted the amendment in 1791. Because the seventh amendment speaks in terms of preservation, an historical test has been employed to determine its application. Suits in which traditionally legal rights were to be heard and determined have been jury-eligible; those wherein predominantly equitable remedies were to be administered were thought triable to the court.

The proposition, however, is more easily stated than applied. The dividing line does not depend on the character of the overall action, but instead is determined by "the nature of the issue to be tried." An issue is considered "legal" when its resolution involves the ascertainment and determination of legal rights or when it justifies a remedy traditionally granted by common law courts. An "equitable" issue is one where, whether because of the inadequacy of conventional legal remedies or the need to defeat special kinds of unfairness, courts of chancery have historically intervened. ... Howsoever the standard is phrased, the balance is tilted in favor of trial by jury. ...

[The opinion then addresses the difficult issue of the availability of a jury in a case founded on a cause of action based on a federal statute where Congress has been silent concerning the right to a jury. The court rules in favor of the defendant's demand for a jury trial, applying a test set out by the U.S. Supreme Court in *Ross v. Bernard,* 396 U.S. 531 (1970).]

The Supreme Court has provided direction in these precincts by way of a tripartite test. *Ross,* 396 U.S. at 538 n. 10. In the absence of explicit congressional guidance, a court should consider the following factors to determine if a given case or issue implicates seventh amendment concerns: (i) customs prevailing before the merger of law and equity, (ii) the nature of the remedy sought, and (iii) the practical abilities and limitations of juries. *Id.* The burden of *Ross* is, in effect, to make a "what if?" analysis: had the issue arisen before the historic distinction between law and equity became blurred, which "side" of the tribunal would have entertained it? And, in so doing, the court must factor into the calculus such practical restrictions upon the perceived abilities of jurors as it may deem relevant.

Case Questions

1. What are the two criteria for determining whether an issue is equitable?
2. Why does the court rely so much on tradition?
3. Why do statutes often create special problems with the right to a jury?

Adequacy of Remedy at Law

Equitable jurisdiction was always discretionary. Because equity courts were originally established to provide remedies when the common law was unavailing, the equity courts refused to hear cases if there was an adequate remedy at law. This became the threshold question in every equity action. The usual common law remedy is *damages,* specifically, monetary compensation for an injury or wrong. There are a number of specific common law remedies, such as **replevin** and **ejectment**; various extraordinary remedies titled *writs* (e.g., writ of **mandamus**, writ of prohibition) are common law remedies.

To invoke the equitable jurisdiction of the court, the claim must be based on some special feature that monetary compensation will not redress. A common request for equitable relief is for an *injunction,* usually a prohibitory injunction, which asks the court to order someone *not* to do something. Injunctions are based on an alleged threat of imminent irreparable injury, asking equity to prevent the injury rather than waiting for the injury to occur and then suing for damages. Affirmative injunctions requiring a party to act (e.g., requiring a school to desegregate) are viewed less favorably by the courts, because of enforcement problems.

Inadequacy of legal remedy is often asserted when the subject matter of a contract is unique or irreplaceable. For example, if someone has made a contract to purchase and the seller refuses to deliver the goods, the remedy of specific performance may be sought on the grounds that the goods have some unique quality, such as a family heirloom or a one-of-a-kind classic car. Real property (i.e., land and its improvements) has long been regarded as unique, making available the remedy of specific performance for contracts for the sale of real property. If the goods may be readily purchased elsewhere on the market, however, the remedy is to purchase them and sue the original seller for the difference between the cost of replacement and the cost under the contract. Money damages would then be an adequate remedy, because the final cost would correspond to the price promised under the contract.

Campbell Soup Company had a practice of making **output contracts** with farmers, providing seed and agreeing to purchase the entire

---

BALLENTINE'S

replevin An action by which the owner of personal property taken or detained by another may recover possession of it.

ejectment An action at common law for the right to possession of land.

mandamus (Latin) Means "we command." A writ issuing from a court of competent jurisdiction, directed to an inferior court, board, or corporation, or to an officer of a branch of government (judicial, executive, or legislative), requiring the performance of some ministerial act.

entire output contract A contract in which the seller binds itself to the buyer to sell to the buyer the entire output of a product [the seller] manufactures, and the buyer binds itself to buy all of the product.

crop at prices fixed in advance. The Wentz brothers were Pennsylvania farmers who grew Chantenay carrots for Campbell. During the 1947 season, because of the scarcity of these carrots, the price per ton rose to $90. Because the contract price was $30, the Wentz brothers were not eager to honor the contract and sold 62 of their 100 tons of carrots to Lojeski, who sold half of them to Campbell. Ordinarily, Campbell could pursue a legal remedy by purchasing the carrots elsewhere at the market price and suing for the difference between the market and contact price and so receive the benefit of its bargain. Unfortunately, the

CAMPBELL SOUP CO.
v.
WENTZ et al.

CAMPBELL SOUP CO.
v.
LOJESKI
United States Court of Appeals,
Third Circuit
172 F.2d 80 (1948)

On January 9, 1948, Campbell, suspecting that defendant was selling its "contract carrots," refused to purchase any more, and instituted these suits against the Wentz brothers to enjoin further sale of the contract carrots to others, and to compel specific performance of the contract. ...

We think that on the question of adequacy of the legal remedy, the case is one appropriate for specific performance. It was expressly found that at the time of the trial it was "virtually impossible to obtain Chantenay carrots in the open market." This Chantenay carrot is one which the plaintiff uses in large quantities, furnishing the seed to the growers with whom it makes contracts. It was not claimed that in nutritive value it is any better than other types of carrots. Its blunt shape makes it easier to handle in processing, and its color and texture differ from other varieties. The color is brighter than other carrots. It appears that the plaintiff uses carrots in 15 of its 21 soups. It also appeared that it uses these Chantenay carrots diced in some of them and that the appearance is uniform. ...

The trial court concluded that the plaintiff had failed to establish that the carrots, "judged by objective standards," are unique goods ... . [T]hat the test for specific performance is not necessarily "objective" is shown by the many cases in which equity has given it to enforce contracts for articles—family heirlooms and the like—the value of which was personal to the plaintiff.

... Here the goods of the special type contracted for were unavailable on the open market, the plaintiff had contracted for them long ahead in anticipation of his needs, and had built up general reputation for its products as part of which reputation uniform appearance was important. We think if this were all that was involved in the case, specific performance should have been granted.

The reason that we shall affirm instead of reversing with an order for specific performance is found in the contract itself. We think it is too hard a bargain and too one-sided an agreement to entitle the plaintiff to relief in a court of conscience. ... This form has quite obviously been drawn by skillful draftsmen with the buyer's interests in mind.

[The Court then discusses the contract paragraph by paragraph, demonstrating that it gives Campbell numerous powers and protections while affording no protection to the farmers and concludes the contract is "unconscionable."]

... That equity does not enforce unconscionable bargains is too well established to require elaborate citation.

... As already said, we do not suggest that this contract is illegal. All we say is that the sum total of its provisions drives too hard a bargain for a court of conscience to assist.

The judgments will be affirmed.

Case Questions

1. How is it that the appellate court totally disagreed with the trial court yet affirmed the trial court's decision?
2. What is Campbell Soup's remedy in future cases like this?
3. What is meant by "unconscionable"?

carrots were unavailable on the market. Campbell was also undoubtedly concerned about the possibility of other farmers under contract acting similarly in the future and so a brought suit for specific performance, an equitable remedy asking the court to order performance of the contract.

Clean Hands Principle

Although equity is not bound by *stare decisis*, a number of principles of equity have developed over the years expressed in the form of equitable maxims. One has already been discussed: equity will not intervene if there is an adequate remedy at law. Other maxims reflect the moral basis for equitable relief, one of the important maxims being the *clean hands doctrine*. Because equity is a court of conscience based on moral principles and dispenses special justice, an equity court may refuse to give relief if the petitioner has not acted in good faith or is otherwise undeserving of special consideration.

The *Dixon* case shows an application of the clean hands doctrine. Mother (Dixon) **conveyed** twelve acres of land to Chapman, who used the property as **collateral** for a loan to start a restaurant. Mother and Son (Murphy) assumed Chapman's loan and paid it, at which time Chapman conveyed the property to Son. Meanwhile, Mother declared bankruptcy without indicating any interest in the land. After her assets had been distributed in the bankruptcy proceedings to her creditors, Mother asked Son to reconvey the property, or part of it, to her. Son refused and Mother sued and was awarded two of the acres with a home on it. Mother appealed; Son **cross-appealed**. (Neither of them was happy with the outcome.)

-----------------------BALLENTINE'S-----------------------

convey   To transfer title to property from one person to another by deed, bill of sale, or other conveyance.

collateral   Stocks, bonds, or other property that serve as security for a loan or other obligation; property pledged to pay a debt.

cross-appeal   An appeal filed by the appellee from the same judgment, or some portion of the same judgment, as the appellant has appealed from.

DIXON et al.

v.

MURPHY,

MURPHY

v.

DIXON

Supreme Court of Georgia

259 Ga. 643, 385 S.E.2d 408 (1989)

2. Murphy's defense includes his contention that his mother is barred by the doctrine of unclean hands from seeking equitable relief. We agree.

The evidence is undisputed that Dixon has completed a fraud upon her creditors, by:

(a) swearing in the bankruptcy court that she owned *no* interest in the property;

(b) failing to amend her bankruptcy petition to disclose the interest that she now claims; and

(c) obtaining the discharge of all of her scheduled debts—notwithstanding that, according to her, she owned twelve acres of land during the pendency of the bankruptcy proceeding.

3. (a) What is presented here is more than a case of silence and inaction evidencing intent to defraud; it is a case of success in defrauding.

By extending to her the relief that equity reserves for those whose hands are clean, we can only serve to encourage others to make (or to *say* that they have made) hidden trusts, and then deny their existence in bankruptcy.

(b) The justice system cannot permit itself to become an implement of fraud. The judgment in Case No. S89A0231 is affirmed insofar as it vests title to any of the property in Murphy.

4. As to Murphy's cross-appeal ..., we are aware of no authority that vests in a trial court the power to make equitable distribution in a case of unclean hands. Accordingly, that portion of the judgment awarding the smaller parcel of property to Dixon is reversed.

[The dissenting opinion by Justice Gregory questions the fact-finding by the majority and points out the absurdity of the final result:] Murphy, who paid nothing for the property, now has it all. Dixon, who acquired it twice, paying close to $21,000 the second time, now has nothing. Dixon's fight is not with her creditors, but with Murphy. The creditors, whom the majority thinks were defrauded, also now have nothing, and Murphy, who failed to keep his promise to his mother, gets it all.

Case Questions

1. Is the result just or is the dissent correct?
2. What are the strongest arguments this case gives to justify application of the clean hands doctrine?

Statutes of Limitation and Laches

Another difference between legal and equitable remedies arises in the context of delay in bringing suit. Common law actions may be barred by statutes of limitation. Each state has legislated that suits must be brought within a certain period of time, usually measured in years. Some statutes creating causes of action fix the period within which suit can be brought. Unless the state legislature has otherwise specified a time period, equity follows the maxim expressed by the word *laches*.

Rather than fixing precise periods of time, laches may be used as a defense to an action in equity if the action is unreasonably delayed to the prejudice of a party who has changed position during the delay. Circumstances might dictate that a party bring an action very promptly or, conversely, that because no one was harmed by a long delay, no injustice would occur by allowing the action.

Domestic Relations

Prior to the establishment of the American republic, family law matters fell within the jurisdiction of ecclesiastical courts and were governed by canon law. With the American separation of church and state, the law of domestic relations, having no common law precedent, fell within equity jurisdiction. This has had a profound effect on the law, as equity entails great discretion. This is generally appropriate because, with divorce and custody questions, problems tend to be particularized and each case must be examined on its own merits. No-fault divorce, however, has discouraged divorce contests and encouraged parties to negotiate the conditions of custody and the division of property. State legislatures have been active in recent years in setting the standards for child support and providing the means to collect it.

Language

It is important to note that the historical separation of law and equity has given rise to different terms. Because equity actions are brought by petition, the parties to an action in equity are called *petitioner* and *respondent* rather than their common law equivalents, *plaintiff* and *defendant*. Judges sitting in equity are in some jurisdictions referred to as *chancellor* or *master in equity*.

Summary

The American legal system is complicated by the existence of separate state and federal jurisdictions. Not only do these have different spheres of authority, but the states themselves are also independent jurisdictions. The division of judicial power is expressed in the U.S. Constitution, which grants specific power to the federal government and reserves the remaining authority to the states. The Constitution is the supreme law of the land and no official act, law, or judicial order may violate it. The federal judiciary exercises significant authority over state law under the due process and equal protection clauses of the Fourteenth Amendment. The Constitution also requires that the states honor the acts, laws, and judicial orders of other states under the full faith and credit clause.

The Constitution also dictates subject matter jurisdiction of the federal courts, which have jurisdiction over federal question cases, those arising under the Constitution, laws, and treaties of the federal government, and diversity of citizenship cases, those given federal jurisdiction because of the grant of authority over citizens of different states. In diversity cases, by virtue of the decision in *Erie Railroad v. Tompkins,* the federal courts apply state law rather than developing a general federal common law.

In cases in which there is some question as to which state's substantive law should apply, each state has its own rules, called conflict of laws, to determine whether it should apply its own law or that of a state more closely involved with the facts giving rise to the lawsuit.

A further complication in the American legal system is the historical existence of common law courts and courts of equity. Equity court first arose several centuries ago in England to provide remedies for disputes the common law courts would not hear. Equity developed special remedies differing from the usual common law remedy of monetary compensation (damages) and developed its own principles based on moral principles. As a result, equitable remedies are more flexible and bound less by precedent than legal remedies. One important feature that distinguishes law from equity is the traditional absence of the right to a jury in equity.

Today law and equity have merged, so that American judges provide both equitable and legal relief, and legal and equitable remedies may be requested in the same suit. Nevertheless, many of the traditional differences have been maintained.

Review Questions

1. What is the basis for state power?

2. What establishes the authority of the U.S. Supreme Court?

3. How were U.S. District Courts established?

4. Why does one state enforce decrees of courts of other states?

5. Why do federal courts follow state law in diversity cases?

6. How would a defendant in a diversity case attempt to have the case heard in a state rather than a federal court?

7. What kind of federal jurisdiction requires a minimum amount in controversy to bring a lawsuit?

8. Why did courts of equity first come into existence?

9. What is the threshold question for equity jurisdiction?

10. What is the usual remedy sought in an action at common law?

11. What determines the conflict of laws rules to be followed in a case that requires a choice of law?

12. On what basis does delay in bringing suit bar the suit in law and in equity?

Exercises

1. Of the four hypothetical situations described at the end of the section discussing due process, which would you argue on the basis of substantive due process and which on the basis of procedural due process? Explain.

2. Determine which courts in your state are courts of limited jurisdiction and which are courts of general jurisdiction.

HOW TO SERVE A CIVIL SUMMONS

Lana L. Clark, CLA

An attorney walks into your office, hands you a summons and tells you to "Serve this person." Although serving a civil summons may seem simple, many complex problems can come up. For example, what do you do if the person you're serving is out of the country? Or a state official? Or a minor? While memorizing state and federal regulations is the safest way to go, you can use the following tips as a general guide for what to do when you're faced with a problem, or at least help you locate an answer.

When To Serve a Summons

A summons is not necessary on an amended complaint if you are serving a "Doe" defendant or if the charges to the complaint involve the same individuals previously served and appeared without adding any new defendants. In all other instances (such as adding new parties or changing the name of an unserved defendant), have a summons issued along with the filing of the amended complaint. Cross-complaints or counterclaims need a summons issued at the time of filing.

Who Serves the Summons?

According to the Federal Rules of Civil Procedure (FRCP), which govern services for civil cases on a federal level, a nonparty over the age of 18 may serve the summons and complaint. This person may be an employee of the law firm, a professional process server, peace officer or another individual. There are advantages and disadvantages to consider when utilizing each type of individual for process serving.

The main concern in selecting the proper person is to make sure they are thoroughly familiar with the methods of service, are available to make more than one attempt, can fill out the proof or certificate of service and can testify as a credible witness if the service is challenged. An office employee may not be the best choice if he cannot meet the above requirements or be available to leave the office to take care of serving needs.

By selecting a professional process server, procedures will be performed correctly. While sheriffs and marshals carry a certain authority to serve, they typically have heavy case loads, and the service may not be performed as timely as you would like.

Timing of the service may be an important strategy, so if this is your objective select a professional process server. One attorney, who was owed fees by a delinquent client, timed a service of a complaint to coincide with the client's daughter's wedding reception in order to cause the most humiliation possible. While you may not personally agree with this type of tactic, it was very effective—the client appeared the next day to pay the bill. On the other hand, this method can also antagonize the defendant and set the stage for a long battle.

Because of the complexities of serving a civil summons, it is imperative that you be familiar with the state and federal statutes. Reliance upon statutes is essential as in all other aspects of civil procedure. Keep your code books close by for constant reference.

Mail and Publication

If you have had previous contact with the defendant or his attorney, service by mailing a copy of the summons and complaint along with an acknowledgment of service can be the most inexpensive way. It may, however, delay the calculation of the default date because statutes generally allow the recipient of service by mail 20 days to sign and return the acknowledgment of service before service is deemed complete.

Service by publication is generally more involved because you must first exhaust all other methods and obtain an order from the court authorizing service by publication in a newspaper of general circulation near the defendant's last known address. A declaration detailing the efforts to locate the defendant will be necessary before obtaining a court order.

Attacks on a Service of a Summons

Prior to the time a default judgment is entered, a defendant may challenge the service of the summons by bringing a motion to quash. The defendant must show that the service was improper, taking away the court's jurisdiction over the defendant and preventing any judgment. Oppose the motion by arguing that the service on the defendant was proper and that statutory requirements were met.

After a default judgment has been entered, the defendant will have to bring a motion to set aside the default and challenge the service. If the motion to set aside the default is not granted, the only recourse is an appeal of the denial of the motion.

Reprinted with permission from *Legal Assistant Today* magazine.

CHAPTER 8

PROCEDURE IN CIVIL CASES

CHAPTER OUTLINE

Introduction

Procedural law is the oil that greases the legal machine. No area of law has more theoretical or practical importance. From a theoretical perspective, procedural law informs us about the basic premises of the legal system itself. The adversarial premise of the American legal system maintains that our system is based on competition and that individuals act in their own self-interest and cannot be trusted unless their power positions are equalized by a disinterested and perhaps indifferent tribunal. The fact that we preserve the jury system tells us that we do not even trust the presumed neutrality of the judges. The rules of evidentiary exclusion suggest that we do not trust the capacity of juries to sift good evidence from bad.

The theoretical premise at the heart of our procedure is: If the means by which conflict in society is resolved are fair and equal, justice will, on the whole, be achieved. Acceptance of this premise is a virtual catechism of lawyers. When criminal defense attorneys are asked, "Would you defend a guilty man? Would you help a guilty man be acquitted and go free?", the answer is usually the same: "Every person is entitled to competent legal representation; it is not for the attorney to judge; it is the job of the prosecution to prove guilt beyond a reasonable doubt." This response can only be understood in the context of a system that places procedure on a pedestal.

The practical importance of procedure is equal to its philosophical importance. Rights have no meaning without a means to enforce them. Without a procedure for enforcement, the establishment of a right is merely symbolic.

Each state and the federal system have compiled their own set of rules of civil procedure, which henceforth are referred to as "the rules." These treat some procedural questions with great specificity, allowing little room for interpretation, but other questions may be adequately understood only by researching rules of court, judicial interpretations, or even local procedural customs. The competent practitioner must have a thorough understanding of the rules of the jurisdictions in which practice is to be conducted, but that is beyond the scope of the treatment of civil procedure here. What follows is merely a model and an overview.

Procedure is arbitrary and technical, yet it is always subject to attack for its fairness under the due process clause of the Fourteenth Amendment. Cases concerning procedural due process tend to be exceedingly complex and difficult. One of the reasons may be that the social values underlying the rules are obscure at best. In comparison, substantive areas of law, such as tort and contract, may rely on accepted values. In contract law, it is a premise of our society that a person should fulfill lawful promises; in tort law, it is a premise that a person who wrongfully injures another should compensate the injured party. In contrast, is there any fundamental reason that a jury may not be exposed to hearsay evidence, or that a hearing be adversarial rather than mediatory in nature, or that a complaint must state a cause of action?

Procedural Framework of Legal Disputes

A basic model of the legal processing of a dispute underlies American procedural law. In its minute details, it differs from jurisdiction to jurisdiction, but the basic idea is the same. This chapter delineates its outline, as follows:

1. One who proposes to seek relief through the legal system must formally state to a court the basis for a grievance, and the grounds asserted must amount to a grievance that the law recognizes as enforceable.

2. The opponent in a legal action must be notified of the suit and given the opportunity to prepare for a defense.

3. Parties to a lawsuit will have every reasonable means prior to a trial to become fully informed of the factual and legal arguments of the other side.

4. If a dispute proceeds to trial, it will be conducted as an adversarial proceeding in which each side has every opportunity to challenge the arguments of the other side.

5. In an adversarial trial, decisions of the court must be based on the evidence and arguments presented in court before an adversarial party.

6. Any departure from procedural rules will provide a basis for challenging the fairness of the process.

7. Procedural error takes precedence over substantive goals. The corollary to this is that if the procedure was fair, the results cannot be questioned except in extraordinary circumstances.

Determining the Proper Court for the Suit

In addition to the problems of subject matter jurisdiction discussed in Chapter 7, a number of obstacles may arise concerning the exercise of the court's authority in a particular case.

Service of Process

The notification of the defendant in a lawsuit is accomplished by *service of process.* This refers to the presentation to the defendant of a copy of the complaint, along with a summons, which informs the defendant that an answer to the complaint must be served on the plaintiff's attorney within a specified number of days, commonly twenty. *Service* refers to presentation of the documents; service of the complaint and summons is *original service.* (After original service, documents may be served on the attorneys for the parties by mail.) Process refers to the document commanding a party to do or not do something. At common law, original process was formerly called an original writ or writ of process. In equity, it was called a subpoena. Today original process is usually simply called a summons.

Service of process is effected by filing the complaint and summons with the court, followed by presentation to the defendant of the complaint and summons by one authorized to do so, typically a sheriff or deputy or a U.S. Marshall for federal cases. Private process-servers may also be authorized by the law and are typically used if the defendant may be purposely avoiding service or may be difficult to locate. Deputies and marshalls have many duties and cannot be expected to go to great efforts in serving process in civil cases. Attorneys commonly offer assistance in locating defendants, such as informing the sheriff of the defendant's place of work or the hours the defendant is likely to be at home. The place, time, and manner of service of process must be in accord with the rules or other statutes of the jurisdiction in which process is served.

Presenting the summons and complaint personally to the defendant is called *personal service* and is the ideal form of service, especially in jurisdictions in which the defendant signs a paper, thus assuring the court that the defendant was properly notified of the suit and making it difficult for the defendant to later challenge the service. The rules or statutes also provide for *substituted service* whereby process can be served on someone other than the defendant, such as a relative living at the defendant's abode. Substituted service that does not strictly comply with the law is invalid. Service may also be made by publication in a newspaper of general circulation if a diligent search for the defendant fails to reveal the defendant's whereabouts. *Publication* refers to the publication of a legal notice in an authorized periodical, such as a newspaper of general circulation. Again, the manner of service by publication must strictly follow the law.

The rules provide for service in special situations. Business entities, for example, call for different service—a corporation may be served by service upon an authorized agent of the corporation; partnerships may be served by service upon a partner. Minors, prisoners, military personnel on active duty, legal incompetents, and the like may call for special treatment.

Service of nonresidents is accomplished under the authority of **long-arm statutes**, with the cooperation of the officers of the state of residence of the defendant. If the nonresident is present in the state in which the suit is filed, personal service is effective within the state.

Service other than personal service will be scrutinized carefully by the judge if the defendant does not answer and does not appear for a judicial proceeding. Judges are understandably reluctant to determine the rights of an absent defendant.

The *Wyman* case presents several interesting procedural features, some of which are difficult to reconstruct because of the age of the case. In 1937, personal service of process was preferred even more than today. At that time, the causes of action for **seduction** and breach of promise to marry were recognized in most states as in Florida, which later abolished them, but they were in disrepute, particularly in New York, which may explain why the complaint was filed in Florida rather than New York. (Seduction is one of the so-called *heart balm* suits, along with breach of promise to marry, criminal conversation, and *alienation of affections,* which were designed to compensate for loss of or interference with intimate relationships. Most states have abolished such causes of action through what have come to be known as *anti-heart balm statutes.*) Because the defendant did not answer the Florida complaint, the Florida court entered a **default judgment**, which the plaintiff then attempted to enforce in New York.

In Personam Jurisdiction

In personam, or "personal," jurisdiction refers to the authority of the court to determine the rights of the defendant in a lawsuit. (Personal jurisdiction over the plaintiff results from filing the suit.) When service of process is deficient or not in accordance with law, the court does not have personal jurisdiction over the defendant. The defendant may simply be beyond the reach of the court. If a resident of Oregon is involved in an accident in Oregon with a resident of California, the Oregon resident can object to personal jurisdiction in California—California

---BALLENTINE'S---

long-arm statutes State statutes providing for substituted service of process on a nonresident corporation or individual. Long-arm statutes permit a state's courts to take jurisdiction over a nonresident if he or she has done business in the state (provided the minimum contacts test is met), or has committed a tort or owns property within the state.

seduction [T]he act of inducing a person to have sexual relations, usually through some form of deception. Seduction is a criminal offense in some jurisdictions if it is accomplished by means of a promise of marriage.

default judgment A judgment rendered in favor of a plaintiff based upon a defendant's failure to take a necessary step in a lawsuit within the required time.

WYMAN
v.
NEWHOUSE
Circuit Court of Appeals, Second Circuit
93 F.2d 313 (2d Cir. 1937)

This appeal is from a judgment entered dismissing the complaint on motion before trial. The action is on a judgment entered by default in a Florida state court, a jury having assessed the damages. The recovery there was for money loaned, money advanced for appellee, and for seduction under promise of marriage.

* * *

Appellant and appellee were both married, but before this suit appellant's husband died. They had known each other for some years and had engaged in meretricious relations.

The affidavits submitted by the appellee deemed to be true for the purpose of testing the alleged error of dismissing the complaint established that he was a resident of New York and never lived in Florida. On October 25, 1935, while appellee was in Salt Lake City, Utah, he received a telegram from the appellant, which read: "Account illness home planning leaving. Please come on way back. Must see you." Upon appellee's return to New York he received a letter from appellant stating that her mother was dying in Ireland; that she was leaving the United States for good to go to her mother; that she could not go without seeing the appellee once more; and that she wanted to discuss her affairs with him before she left. Shortly after the receipt of this letter, they spoke to each other on the telephone, whereupon the appellant repeated, in a hysterical and distressed voice, the substance of her letter. Appellee promised to go to Florida in a week or ten days and agreed to notify her when he would arrive. This he did, but before leaving New York by plane he received a letter couched in endearing terms and expressing love and affection for him, as well as her delight at his coming. Before leaving New York, appellee telegraphed appellant, suggesting arrangements for their accommodations together while in Miami. She telegraphed him at a hotel in Washington, D.C., where he was to stop en route, advising him that the arrangements requested had been made. Appellee arrived at 6 o'clock in the morning at the Miami Airport and saw the appellant standing with her sister some 75 feet distant. He was met by a deputy sheriff who, upon identifying appellee, served him with process in a suit for $500,000. A photographer was present who attempted to take his picture. Thereupon a stranger introduced himself and offered to take appellee to his home, stating that he knew a lawyer who was acquainted with the appellant's attorney. The attorney whom appellee was advised to consult came to the stranger's home and seemed to know about the case. The attorney invited appellee to his office, and upon his arrival he found one of the lawyers for the appellant there. Appellee did not retain the Florida attorney to represent him. He returned to New York by plane that evening and consulted his New York counsel, who advised him to ignore the summons served in Florida. He did so, and judgment was entered by default. Within a few days after the service of process, the appellant came to New York and sought an interview with the appellee. It resulted in their meeting at the home of the appellee's attorney. She was accompanied by her Florida counsel.

These facts and reasonable deductions therefrom convincingly establish that fraud perpetrated upon him by the appellant in falsely representing her mother's illness, her intention to leave the United States, and her love and affection for him, when her sole purpose and apparent thought was to induce him to come within the Florida jurisdiction so as to serve him in an action for damages. Appellant does not deny making these representations. All her statements of great and undying love were disproved entirely by her appearance at the airport and participation in the happening there. She never went to Ireland to see her mother, if indeed the latter was sick at all.

In asking for judgment based on these Florida proceedings, appellant relies upon article 4, section 1, of the United States Constitution, providing that "Full Faith and Credit shall be given in each State to the public Acts, Records, and Judicial Proceedings of every other State." ...

This judgment is attacked for fraud perpetrated upon the appellee which goes to the jurisdiction of the Florida court over his person. A judgment procured fraudulently, as here, lacks jurisdiction and is null and void. A fraud affecting the jurisdiction is equivalent to a lack of jurisdiction. The appellee was not required to proceed against the judgment in Florida. ...

Judgment affirmed.

Case Questions

1. Did the Florida trial court have any reason to believe that the service of process was accomplished by fraud?
2. Does the court's opinion suggest a union of a conniving plaintiff and an unscrupulous attorney?

would have personal jurisdiction under its long-arm statute only if the accident occurred in California.

Appearance by the defendant in court confers personal jurisdiction despite deficient service of process. In many jurisdictions, the defendant may enter a special appearance solely for the purpose of contesting personal jurisdiction, and the appearance will not be construed as conferring personal jurisdiction. Challenges to personal jurisdiction must follow the rules to avoid a waiver of defenses to personal jurisdiction. Of course, a nonresident may remain silent and later challenge jurisdiction of the original court if the plaintiff attempts to enforce a judgment under full faith and credit in the defendant's home state, but a significant risk is involved because the defendant's state might reject the defenses and enforce the judgment, leaving the defendant without an opportunity to defend the case on its merits.

In Rem Jurisdiction

Under certain circumstances, the purpose of a suit may be to determine the status of property rather than to determine personal rights, and an *in rem* action may be brought. *Rem* is from the Latin word *res,* roughly translated as "thing." Courts generally have jurisdiction over real and personal property located within their jurisdictions. *In rem* proceedings are often brought to prevent the removal of property from the jurisdiction, typically in **attachment** proceedings to secure court

─────────BALLENTINE'S─────────

attachment The process by which a person's property is figuratively brought into court to ensure satisfaction of a judgment that may be rendered against him or her. In the event judgment is rendered, the property may be sold to satisfy the judgment.

control over property subject to a debt. Some actions involve property but operate only between parties to the suit and are called *quasi in rem*. Conceptually, it is difficult to distinguish *quasi in rem* from *in personam* actions. *In rem* actions are fairly rare because the primary purpose of most lawsuits is to determine the respective rights of persons.

Certain real property actions in equity are *in rem* or *quasi in rem* actions, such as suits to quiet title or to remove a cloud on title. These suits are usually brought in connection with a real estate transaction when an attorney (or title company) discovers some potential defect in the title that should be cleared up prior to completing the transaction. For example, a person can acquire title by adverse possession; that is, someone without rightful possession of real property who nevertheless enters on the land and occupies it for a certain number of years (twenty at common law, less under most state statutes) may acquire title. The presence at some past time of adverse possession may raise doubts about title that can be settled in the suit. Essentially, then, the suit is against the property rather than against specific persons. Whenever the parties are known, caution suggests that they should be included as defendants.

Another example of an *in rem* action is suit for divorce. In theory, the *res* in a divorce action is the marriage—divorce has the effect of changing the status from married to unmarried. In practice, courts are extremely reluctant to treat divorce actions as *in rem* proceedings because ordinarily divorce actions involve the adjudication of personal rights. Alimony and child support, for example, are considered *in personam* questions.

These examples demonstrate that *in rem* proceedings must be restricted to special circumstances; frequently, as in attachment, they are ancillary to a larger *in personam* suit. Whenever a known person's rights are involved, personal jurisdiction should be established to prevent a later attack on the judicial order.

In Personam, in Rem, and Quasi in Rem Compared

In personam, in rem, and *quasi in rem* are difficult to distinguish in the abstract. The cases, the history, and the difference between jurisdictional definitions have left the distinctions quite confused. With this confusion in mind, the following is designed as a rule-of-thumb guide:

In personam jurisdiction has a party—a person—as a defendant.
    Example: Johnson sues Jackson for breach of contract.

In rem jurisdiction has property as a defendant.
    Example: State seizure of property for taxes.

Quasi in rem jurisdiction brings suit against property to satisfy a personal claim.

Example: Plaintiff sues for attachment and sale of property to satisfy a debt owed by another party who has property located within the forum state but is beyond the reach of the personal jurisdiction of the court.

Quasi in rem is used when personal jurisdiction would have been obtained if the defendant could have been served personally. The court has *in rem* jurisdiction over property within the state but does not have *in personam* jurisdiction over out-of-state residents who have no contact with the state other than their ownership of property located within the state.

The distinctions are often obscure, and an inherent due process issue always lurks when rights may be affected without opportunity to be heard. This problem of definition underscores the difficult problems of civil procedure, namely, measuring very technical rules and concepts against the broad, flexible concept of due process.

Venue

Venue refers to the place where jurisdiction is exercised. Venue is easily confused with jurisdiction, but the two must be clearly distinguished. For example, the issue of whether a case should be heard in a state or federal court is a matter of subject matter jurisdiction, as discussed in Chapter 7. Venue concerns the question of which court within a system should be the *place* where jurisdiction is exercised. An example from divorce law in Florida may clarify this problem.

Florida circuit courts have jurisdiction over divorce cases (now called "dissolution of marriage"). The jurisdictional requirement for bringing a divorce action is that the petitioner must have resided in the state for six months prior to bringing the action. The action may be brought in any circuit in the state; in fact, some actions are brought in a venue far from the residences of either party to the action in order to avoid local public scrutiny. However, if the respondent objects to the place where the suit is filed, venue may be challenged, and the court will transfer the case to the circuit in which the respondent resides. It is not that the original court does not have jurisdiction but, rather, that another court with similar jurisdiction is determined to be the more appropriate site of the lawsuit.

The divorce example is based on the allegation of *inconvenient venue*, commonly referred to by the Latin phrase *forum non conveniens*. Another venue challenge is based on the allegation that a party cannot obtain a fair trial where the action has been brought (e.g., the plaintiff may have unusual influence over the local population so that the defendant fears that a fair trial is difficult or impossible).

Pleadings

Many technical problems may arise concerning proper and necessary parties to a lawsuit, that is, who may or must be included in the lawsuit. Problems of multiple plaintiffs or defendants, **class action** suits, and other special problems must be left to a more detailed study of litigation and procedure. Discussion here is limited to the basic documents that frame the issues for trial.

Modern pleading borrows heavily from both law and equity. The basic documents of pleading, the *complaint* and the *answer,* echo the procedure of equity, which required the suitor to file a petition or bill in equity. The petition initiated the suit much like a complaint does today, except that the petition was a lengthy recitation of the facts of the case, much restricted today. After the bill was filed, a subpoena was issued requiring the respondent to appear, and the respondent provided an answer, which presented the respondent's defenses, thereby closing the pleadings and requiring the plaintiff to go forward to prove the allegations.

Equity also provided for *joinder,* which consolidated related claims and related parties, thus avoiding the necessity of hearing numerous cases. If a respondent had a claim against the petitioner, this could be brought through a *cross-bill,* analogous to the modern **counterclaim.**

Equity also provided for petitioner's (and later respondent's) discovery of information possessed by the adverse party in order to prepare for hearing.

All these features of equity procedure were incorporated with changes into modern pleading. Common law procedure, in contrast, was complex and formal. Common law pleading had two principal objects. First, it was necessary for the plaintiff to fit the case into a *form of action* that would support the court's issuing a corresponding writ or order to the sheriff to compel the defendant to satisfy the plaintiff's claim or appear in court to show cause why he or she need not do so. The form of action corresponds to the *cause of action,* still required in modern pleading; the specific facts required by the formula for each form of action correspond to the *elements* presently required to state a cause of action.

————————————BALLENTINE'S————————————

class action   An action brought by one or several plaintiffs on behalf of a class of persons. A class action may be appropriate when there has been injury to so many people that their voluntarily and unanimously joining in a lawsuit is improbable and impracticable. In such a situation, injured parties who wish to do so may, with the court's permission, sue on behalf of all. A class action is sometimes referred to as a *representative action.*

counterclaim   A cause of action on which a defendant in a lawsuit might have sued the plaintiff in a separate action ... [,] stated in a separate division of a defendant's answer ... .

Second, common law pleading was designed to focus the lawsuit on a single issue, and it did this by a series of responsive pleadings back and forth between plaintiff and defendant until the issue was clearly framed. This was a highly technical process with numerous pitfalls. The parties were not allowed to present multiple actions or defenses, and attempt to do so would result in a holding for the other side.

The advantage of common law pleading was its precision; the disadvantages were its inflexibility and technicality. The advantages of equity procedure were its flexibility and attention to substance over technicality; its disadvantage was the time-consuming process of setting the case for hearing—the relative simplicity and flexibility of equity procedure failed to focus the case and restrain the parties.

Modern code pleading attempts to borrow the advantages of both processes while minimizing their disadvantages. Equity pleadings are restricted to the allegation of **ultimate** rather than the more detailed **evidentiary facts**. Rather than focusing on a single issue, the pleadings are designed to establish a cause of action and present defenses. Issues are narrowed largely by the pretrial process, including discovery, a concept borrowed from equity. Liberalized pleading allows complaints to be amended, shifting emphasis toward substantive rather than purely technical issues. It must be noted, however, that civil procedure is by its nature technical, and inattention to the rules can be costly.

The Complaint

The complaint is designed to inform the court and the defendant that a lawsuit has been filed, invoking the attendant legal process. The complaint itself—that is, the document filed with the court and served on the defendant—may be divided into several parts:

1. The *caption* is the heading of the complaint and names the court in which the complaint is filed, the names of the parties to the suit, and the case number of the suit (assigned by the clerk). The caption begins each document filed with the court. Below the case number (on the right underneath the name of the court) or below the caption itself is the label of the document, e.g., "COMPLAINT," "ANSWER," "MOTION FOR SUMMARY JUDGMENT."

2. The first paragraph of the complaint contains the jurisdictional allegation, which states the grounds for subject matter jurisdiction of the court wherein the complaint has been filed.

------------------------------BALLENTINE'S------------------------------

ultimate facts   The facts in a case upon which liability is determined or based.
evidentiary facts   Facts admissible in evidence.

3. The remaining numbered paragraphs of the complaint present a brief allegation of general facts designed to state a cause of action and provide notice to the defendant of the basis for the suit.

4. The complaint ends with a *prayer for relief,* sometimes called the *wherefore clause* because it traditionally begins with something like "WHEREFORE, the Plaintiff prays for judgment ..."

The Answer

To defend the suit, the defendant must file an answer, although other procedural devices to attack the complaint are available at this time. The answer is responsive to the complaint and admits allegations in the complaint that defendant does not wish to contest. It contains denials of allegations in the complaint that the defendant disputes, which allegations then become questions for proof and argument. The answer may also contain *affirmative defenses,* which contain matter not included in the complaint that defendant alleges will prevent the plaintiff from obtaining relief. For example, the defendant may contend that the statute of limitations has run, barring plaintiff's suit. If the plaintiff cannot overcome this defense, the suit must be dismissed. The answer may also present a counterclaim, which is a claim by the defendant against the plaintiff that must contain sufficient allegations to state a cause of action on its own.

The Reply

Although filing an answer usually ends the pleadings, the plaintiff must file a reply if the defendant has made a counterclaim, in order to present denials and defenses to the counterclaim. Affirmative defenses do not necessarily require the filing of a reply, but the cautious attorney may do so to avoid certain technical problems later on.

Discovery

Discovery refers to pretrial devices for obtaining information relevant to the suit. It is a modern adaptation of procedures in equity and has come to play a major role in civil cases. Long delays in bringing suit to trial are most often related to the discovery process, which has been severely criticized for its contribution to delays and the resulting costs that give a significant advantage to wealthy parties. Although it is unethical to delay as a strategy for wearing down an opponent or as leverage to induce settlement, and is subject to sanctions in some states, it is

Sample Complaint

IN THE CIRCUIT COURT
OF THE NINTH JUDICIAL CIRCUIT
IN AND FOR ORANGE COUNTY, FLORIDA

JAKE CARSON,   )
               Plaintiff,)
) CIVIL ACTION
          -vs-   ) No. 94-000-00
)
TOM HARRIS,   )
             Defendant.)[1]

COMPLAINT [2]

Plaintiff, JAKE CARSON, sues defendant, TOM HARRIS, and alleges:[3]

---

[1] The caption contains the name of the court, the names of the parties, and the case number. There is one plaintiff and one defendant in this lawsuit. If there were more parties, all of them would be named in the caption of the initial complaint. In all other documents, only the first party on each side would be named, followed by "*et al.*" replacing all other parties. "*Et al.*" is short for "*et alia,*" meaning "and others." "JAKE CARSON, plaintiff vs. TOM HARRIS, Defendant" is often referred to as the **style** of the case. The case number is supplied by the court clerk. The number "95" indicates the year the case was filed. The next number indicates the order of filing. Cases are given consecutive numbers based on the order filed. For example, "100" would mean that the case was the one hundredth case filed in 1995. The sample complaint is unnumbered—"000"—to show that it is not an actual case.

[2] Rule 1.100 of the Florida Rules of Civil Procedure requires that court documents "indicate clearly the subject matter of the paper and the party requesting or obtaining relief." The form complaints at the end of the Florida Rules of Civil Procedure (see, for example, Forms 1.936–1.942) are simply named "COMPLAINT." Some jurisdictions may require the pleading name to indicate the relief requested, for example, "COMPLAINT FOR DAMAGES."

[3] This introductory clause (also referred to as the *commencement*) states who is suing whom. Notice that the introductory clause is not numbered.

This introductory clause is modeled on the one contained in the forms at the end of the Florida Rules of Civil Procedure: "Plaintiff, A.B., sues defendant, C.D., and alleges:" (see Forms 1.936–1.942). This plain English clause is much easier to read than the traditional introductory clause filled with legalese. For example, the introductory clause rewritten in legalese might look something like this:

Now comes the above-named plaintiff, Jake Carson, by and through his attorney of record, Florida Attorney, and for cause of action and complaint against the defendant herein alleges unto this honorable court:

Write your pleadings in plain English, complying with the court rules of your jurisdiction. Plain English pleadings are easier for the client to understand and are less time-consuming in the long run.

For simplicity's sake, there is one plaintiff and one defendant in this sample complaint. For ease of reference, they are referred to as "Plaintiff" and "Defendant" throughout the complaint. If this were a real complaint, Jake might have also named the Alpha Fraternity and Collegiate University as defendants. Multiple defendants could be referred to by short forms established in the introductory clause. For example:

Plaintiff, JAKE CARSON, sues Defendants, TOM HARRIS ("Defendant Harris"), ALPHA FRA-TERNITY ("Defendant Fraternity"), and COLLEGIATE UNIVERSITY ("Defendant University") and says:

Sample Complaint

COUNT I—DEFAMATION[4]

1. This is an action for damages that exceed $15,000.[5]

2. In October 1993 plaintiff was a student at Collegiate University, a member of the Collegiate Beta Fraternity, and a candidate for student body president of Collegiate University.[6]

3. In October 1993 defendant was a student at Collegiate University, a member of the Collegiate Alpha Fraternity, and a candidate for student body president of Collegiate University.[7]

4. The October 20, 1993, issue of the Collegiate University student newspaper reported that plaintiff and defendant "were running neck and neck" in the student body president race.[8]

5. On October 20, 1993, the day before the student body president election, plaintiff and defendant presented skits to Collegiate University students and faculty at the Collegiate University football stadium.

---

or

Plaintiff, JAKE CARSON, sues Defendants, TOM HARRIS ("Harris"), ALPHA FRATERNITY ("Fraternity"), and COLLEGIATE UNIVERSITY ("University") and says:

Once you establish short forms, you should use them consistently throughout the rest of the complaint. For readability, you may want to put party names in all capital letters.

[4] In a complaint with more than one count, the counts are usually numbered for ease of reference. The count heading may also state the cause of action (here "COUNT I—DEFAMATION" and "COUNT II—FALSE LIGHT INVASION OF PRIVACY") or relief sought. The relief sought in another complaint, for example, might be "SPECIFIC PERFORMANCE" and "DAMAGES." If the complaint contains a single count, the count need not be headed.

In this complaint, the background for both counts is alleged in numbered paragraphs 1 through 8. Paragraph 12 of Count II realleges paragraphs 1 through 8. Another way to organize the complaint is to provide a heading "COMMON ALLEGATIONS" after the introductory paragraph. The "COMMON ALLEGATIONS" section of the complaint would contain numbered paragraphs 1 through 8. Then the complaint would state:

COUNT I—DEFAMATION

9. Plaintiff realleges and incorporates paragraphs 1–8 above.

[5] The paragraphs of the body of the complaint (sometimes referred to as the *charging portion* of the complaint) are numbered consecutively. In the body of the complaint, the plaintiff alleges the plaintiff's ultimate facts. This paragraph establishes the court's jurisdiction. In Florida, the circuit court handles cases with more than $15,000 in controversy.

[6] Paragraphs 2 through 11 contain the evidentiary and ultimate facts on which the plaintiff relies. The two purposes of the body of the complaint are to:

1. give the defendant notice of the plaintiff's claims; and
2. include all the elements of the cause of action that the plaintiff alleges.

Before you write the body of the complaint, make a list of the elements of the cause of action. After you have completed the body of the complaint, double-check to make sure you have included ultimate facts needed for all elements.

[7] Paragraphs 2 and 3 identify the parties. Usually the parties are identified early in the complaint.

[8] Here the plaintiff begins to narrate what happened. The narrative is written in the past tense.

Sample Complaint

6. In defendant's skit, defendant portrayed "plaintiff's doctor" and another student portrayed plaintiff.

7. In defendant's skit, defendant, in the presence and hearing of plaintiff and the students and faculty watching the skit, maliciously and falsely announced that plaintiff had tested HIV positive, saying "you tested HIV positive."

8. In the student body president election on October 21, 1993, plaintiff received 10% of the vote and defendant received 90% of the vote.

9. Plaintiff at the time of defendant's statement was in good health and free from any disease, and the statements of defendant were wholly untrue.

10. As a result of defendant's slanderous statement, plaintiff suffered, and continues to suffer, great nervousness and mental anguish.

11. Plaintiff, as the direct result of defendant's statement, in addition to the nervousness and bodily injury, has been injured in plaintiff's good reputation in the Collegiate University community. Defendant published such false and slanderous statement about plaintiff to numerous students and faculty of Collegiate University, who have changed their attitude toward plaintiff, and who have begun to question plaintiff as to whether plaintiff has tested HIV positive, which the slanderous remark of defendant wrongly, maliciously, and untruthfully imputed to plaintiff.

COUNT II—FALSE LIGHT INVASION OF PRIVACY

12. Plaintiff realleges and incorporates paragraphs 1–8 above.[9]

13. Prior to October 20, 1993, a rumor had circulated on the Collegiate University campus that plaintiff was a homosexual, and this rumor was traced back to defendant's fraternity.

14. Defendant's statement during the skit and the manner of its presentation, in light of the rumor that plaintiff was a homosexual, falsely depicted plaintiff as a homosexual.

15. Plaintiff is not a homosexual and defendant's depiction of plaintiff as a homosexual was highly offensive to plaintiff.

16. Defendant's depiction of plaintiff as a homosexual was done with knowledge of its falsity or reckless disregard whether the depiction gave a false impression or not.

17. As a result of defendant's depiction of plaintiff as a homosexual, plaintiff suffered, and continues to suffer, great nervousness and mental anguish.

18. Plaintiff, as the direct result of defendant's depiction of plaintiff as a homosexual, in addition to the nervousness and bodily injury, has been injured in plaintiff's good reputation in the Collegiate University community. Such false depiction has been circulated also among plaintiff's personal friends, who have changed their attitude toward plaintiff, and who have begun to question whether plaintiff is a homosexual, which depiction defendant wrongly, maliciously, and untruthfully imputed to plaintiff.

---

[9] Paragraph numbering is consecutive from one count to the next.

Sample Complaint

Plaintiff therefore requests judgment granting the following relief as to counts I and II:[10]

A. an award of compensatory damages in an amount to be set at trial;

B. an award of punitive damages in an amount to be set at trial;

C. an award of costs and attorney's fees; and

D. such other relief as the court deems appropriate.[11]

JURY DEMAND

Plaintiff demands trial by jury.[12]

> Florida Attorney
> 101 Main Street
> Anytown, Florida
> Attorney for plaintiff
> (407) 000-0000
> Bar No. 0000000

Sample Answer

IN THE CIRCUIT COURT
OF THE NINTH JUDICIAL CIRCUIT
IN AND FOR ORANGE COUNTY, FLORIDA

JAKE CARSON,		)	
	Plaintiff,	)	
		)	CIVIL ACTION
-vs-		)	No. 94-000-00[13]
		)	
TOM HARRIS,		)	
	Defendant.	)	

ANSWER[14]

---

[10] This is the beginning line of the plaintiff's prayer for relief. The line is not numbered, but the various types of relief sought are lettered with capital letters. Traditionally, the first line of the prayer for relief would have read as follows:

> WHEREFORE, Plaintiff, JAKE CARSON, demands that this honorable court grant judgment for the following relief:

This line has been rewritten in the sample complaint to eliminate legalese. Also, the word "requests" (a word sounding less strident) has been substituted for "demands."

Another way to organize the complaint would be to have two prayer-for-relief sections—one following paragraph 11 and the other (as it is in the sample complaint) following paragraph 18.

[11] This catchall phrase typically is included in the prayer-for-relief because it allows the court to grant relief other than that specifically requested.

[12] Typically the plaintiff requests a jury trial. If the plaintiff decides later against a jury trial, the right may be waived.

[13] The case number is copied from the complaint.

[14] Because there is a single defendant, "ANSWER" is a sufficient title. If there were multiple defendants and the answer was that of all defendants, the pleading would be titled "DEFENDANTS' ANSWER." If the answer was that of less than all the defendants, the title should indicate the party filing the answer, for example, "ANSWER OF DEFENDANT COLLEGIATE UNIVERSITY."

Sample Answer

Defendant TOM HARRIS answers Plaintiff's complaint and says:

1. He admits paragraph 1 for jurisdictional purposes only and otherwise denies it insofar as it is applied to him.

2. He admits paragraph 2.[15]

3. He admits paragraph 3.

4. He admits paragraph 4.

5. He admits paragraph 5.

6. He admits paragraph 6.

7. With respect to paragraph 7, he denies making the quoted statement maliciously or falsely. Otherwise he admits paragraph 7.[16]

8. He is without knowledge of paragraph 8.

9. He is without knowledge of paragraph 9.

10. He is without knowledge of paragraph 10.

11. With respect to paragraph 11, he repeats his response to paragraphs 1 through 7.

12. He is without knowledge of paragraph 12.

13. He denies paragraph 13.

14. He denies paragraph 14.

15. He is without knowledge of paragraph 15.

16. He denies paragraph 16.

17. He is without knowledge of paragraph 17.

18. With respect to paragraph 18, he repeats his response to paragraphs 12 through 17.

FIRST AFFIRMATIVE DEFENSE

19. Defendant's skit was an obvious expression of humor and could not reasonably be understood as describing an actual fact about plaintiff or an actual event in which plaintiff participated.

SECOND AFFIRMATIVE DEFENSE

20. Plaintiff has failed to allege facts showing that defendant's skit was presented with falsity, negligence, actual malice, or reckless disregard for the truth.

---

[15] Here the defendant's numbered paragraphs correspond to the numbering of the paragraphs in the complaint. Another way to organize the answer would be for the defendant to list in a single numbered paragraph the paragraphs of the complaint admitted, to list in a single numbered paragraph the paragraphs of the complaint denied, and to list in a single numbered paragraph the paragraphs of the complaint of which defendant has no knowledge. For example:

    2. He admits paragraphs 2 through 6.
    3. He is without knowledge of paragraphs 8 through 11, 13, 15, 17, and 18.
    4. He denies paragraphs 14 and 16.

[16] Rule 1.110 of the Florida Rules of Civil Procedure requires the defendant to specify which part of the allegation is admitted and which part of the allegation is denied.

Sample Answer

CERTIFICATE OF SERVICE

I furnished a copy of this answer to Florida Attorney, attorney for plaintiff, 101 Main Street, Anytown, Florida, by U.S. mail on _____ , 19___ .

_____
Unnamed Attorney
Attorney for defendant
TOM HARRIS
100 Court Street
Anytown, Florida
(407) 880-0000
Florida Bar No. 100000

---

difficult to prove that attorneys have used procedural devices solely for the purpose of delay. Defense attorneys in personal injury suits have little incentive to effect prompt resolution of a case—their clients are not eager to pay sooner than necessary, and the attorneys continue to receive compensation as the process is prolonged. This is not purely self-serving on the attorneys' part. In the end, the client may save a great deal of money in the settlement, despite increased attorneys' fees. And any eagerness to settle tends to be regarded as weakness by the other side. This is one of the prices we pay for having an adversarial system that encourages both sides to engage in strategies, tricks, and traps to win.

The discovery process involves a great deal of work that is currently accomplished by paralegals. It requires knowledge of the law and the legal system, but does not require the pivotal decision making that is the responsibility of the attorney.

Depositions

A primary tool of discovery is the *deposition.* It consists of an oral questioning of a witness or the parties themselves; present are attorneys for both sides and a court reporter recording verbatim the questions and answers for later transcription. The ostensible purpose of the deposition is to gather information, but it serves also to gauge the credibility of the witness and to make a record of statements under oath to preserve testimony for trial, usually effectively preventing a witness from later changing testimony. The merits of a case are usually reevaluated following the deposition of an important witness, based on the information gathered and the impact the witness is likely to make on judge and jury. Settlement offers are often raised or lowered following a deposition.

Attorneys often arrange for a deposition through their paralegals; scheduling can be difficult because the attorneys and the witness must all be available at the same time. Although several depositions may be taken in succession on the same day, attorneys frequently arrange one deposition at a time, prolonging the pretrial period for several months or even years.

Paralegals frequently draft questions for depositions and may even sit beside an attorney and pass notes concerning objections and follow-up questions to responses made by the deponent.

Interrogatories and Requests for Admissions

Attorneys submit written questions, called *interrogatories,* to the opposing party asking for specific information, usually information not easily denied, such as vital statistics, employment, and historical facts of the case. Time of reply is often protracted, although undue delay may be countered by motions to the court to compel compliance. Requests for admissions ask the opposing party to admit specific facts, which once admitted may no longer be put in dispute, thereby narrowing the issues for trial.

Requests for Documents and Mental and Physical Examinations

A party may demand the production of documents and records relevant to the case (e.g., business records, receipts), as well as mental and physical examinations of a party if it can be shown that an examination is relevant to the case (this is especially common in personal injury actions).

Scope of Discovery

Discovery inquiry is measured by very broad standards and is not limited by the more restrictive standards of admissibility applied to evidence at trial. Discovery is normally conducted through the attorneys without the intervention of the judge, who may have little knowledge of what is happening. The court becomes involved only when the process breaks down and a party seeks an order from the court requiring the other party to comply with the discovery process.

In theory, discovery is based on the rationale that justice is served by both sides being fully informed and prepared for trial. It is a counterpoise to the "gunslinger" approach to trial in which trial is a battle of wits between great performers, a view favored by popular dramatists. In practice, the trial is a performance that has been carefully rehearsed—both sides are aware of the facts and arguments of the other, the only uncertainty being the unpredictability of the jury.

On the surface, discovery appears to be a reasonable feature of the search for truth and the equalization of the positions of the parties. In fact, it is as much subject to subterfuge as any other part of a lawsuit. Deponents are prepared for depositions as are witnesses for trial and are warned by attorneys not to expand on their answers, to answer merely "Yes" or "No" to questions that can be answered simply by yes or no responses. Answers to interrogatories are drafted by attorneys, rather than the parties, to provide as little information as possible. In short, discovery has become a negotiating tool used as much for strategic purposes as for investigation. It is a part of a lengthy pretrial process devoid of judicial scrutiny, encouraging a continual reevaluation of a case for negotiating settlements. It is responsible for pretrial settlements more than any other feature of civil procedure. The question remains whether this mechanism is fairer, more efficient, or more just than procedure without it.

The discovery process typically proceeds without the involvement of the court. When one party is uncooperative, the other may ask for the court's intervention. If this fails to bring the uncooperative party into line, the court may impose sanctions, including dismissal of the case. *Valentine* is one more illustration of the danger of **pro se** litigation. Although the court was patient with the lawyerless plaintiff, it could not rewrite the rules of civil procedure for one individual.

Discovery and the Paralegal

Discovery affords a great deal of work for paralegals, as most of the work of discovery can be accomplished by nonlawyers. Building a theory of a case, determining the information necessary to support that theory, analyzing and indexing transcripts from depositions, drafting interrogatories, and organizing the products of discovery are essential tasks that are efficiently handled by the paralegal–attorney team.

Pretrial Hearing

In a great many cases, a pretrial conference or hearing is held at an advanced stage of the pretrial process. It is frequently held in the judge's chambers rather than in open court and is attended by the judge and attorneys for the parties. A general discussion is held on the issues of the case and the merits of the claim. Matters such as discovery, logistics, and the like are discussed as well. Ostensibly the pretrial hearing helps the judge assess the progress of the pretrial process and plan for trial time. Depending on the judge and the jurisdiction, pretrial is often

----

BALLENTINE'S

pro se Means "for one's self." Refers to appearing on one's own behalf in either a civil action or a criminal prosecution, rather than being represented by an attorney.

Clarence R. VALENTINE, Plaintiff-Appellant,
v.
MUSEUM OF MODERN ART,
Defendant-Appellee.
United States Court of Appeals, Second Circuit
29 F.3d 47 (2d Cir. 1994)

Plaintiff Clarence R. Valentine appeals from a judgment ... dismissing his action on account of Valentine's failure to comply with an order of the court. On appeal, Valentine contends that use of the harsh remedy of dismissal was inappropriate. We disagree and therefore affirm the district court's order of dismissal.

Appearing pro se in the district court, Valentine commenced the present action in 1991 against defendant Museum of Modern Art ("MOMA"), alleging termination of his employment on the basis of his race, in violation of [federal statutes]. During the course of the litigation, MOMA sought discovery from Valentine, with mixed success. Though he appeared for two deposition sessions, he was disruptive on those occasions; on other scheduled occasions he failed to appear.

* * *

On March 25, 1993, Magistrate Judge Kathleen A. Roberts advised Valentine, "As Judge Martin has previously told you, if you don't appear for your deposition, then the case will be dismissed."

On April 22, 1993, Valentine disrupted MOMA's attempt to take his deposition, making "frequent and improper ad hominem remarks disparaging counsel's intelligence, preparation, and personal complicity in what plaintiff views as ongoing discrimination by the Museum and its agents," and forcing MOMA's attorney to halt the deposition and seek intervention by the court. ...

The court directed Valentine to appear for his deposition on October 26 and warned him that if he failed to do so his action would be dismissed. The colloquy was as follows:

THE COURT: Mr. Valentine, ... Judge Roberts' chambers has contacted me. They have been trying to get hold of you to have a deposition concluded. ... Are you available tomorrow morning?

MR. VALENTINE: Sir, I appeal against your decision, and that matter is **sub judice**. I appealed against your decision.

THE COURT: You have the right to appeal. But as far as your deposition, that matter should go forward. I am directing you to go forward.

MR. VALENTINE: I am disagreeing with you, sir. I am saying I appealed against your decision. Your decision in the matter against the Museum of Modern Art, I appealed against your decision, and therefore, having appealed against your decision, the matter is now sub judice, it's out of your hands. You cannot give me any instructions at all.

THE COURT: I am directing you on the record to appear tomorrow morning ... for the continuation of your deposition. ...

MR. VALENTINE: I will not attend because I have very important—

THE COURT: Will you [be] available the following day?

MR. VALENTINE: I don't know if I can be available the following day.

THE COURT: What day next week are you available?

MR. VALENTINE: I will not attend still saying, Judge, that this matter is sub judice and that you have no—

THE COURT: I understand that. But I have overruled that. The question is—

MR. VALENTINE: No, you can't overrule that, sir. I will not attend. I am going to say it again plainly. You gave a decision. I appealed against Kathleen Roberts' decision. I appealed against it. Then you said that my appeal to you was denied. Then I appealed against your decision, sir.

THE COURT: Please, I have heard you. I am directing you to appear to have your deposition taken 1 week from today ... . If you do not appear at that time your case will be dismissed.

Valentine did not appear for his deposition on October 26. ...

The severe sanction of **dismissal with prejudice** may be imposed even against a plaintiff who is proceeding pro se, so long as a warning has been given that noncompliance can result in dismissal. "[A]ll litigants, including pro ses, have an obligation to comply with court orders."

The record in this case reveals Valentine's sustained and willful intransigence in the face of repeated and explicit warnings from the court that the refusal to comply with court orders to appear for his deposition would result in the dismissal of his action. We see no abuse of discretion in the court's imposition of that sanction in the circumstances of the present case.

Case Questions

1. Did the plaintiff understand his duties with regard to discovery?
2. Did the plaintiff understand the phrase *sub judice*?

Case Glossary

sub judice Before the court for consideration and determination.

dismissal with prejudice An order of dismissal which does not declare that the dismissal is "without prejudice"; a final judgment on the merits of the case.

used to encourage settlement. The judge may urge the attorneys to focus on real issues and suggest areas for compromise. Attorneys may show a willingness to settle in the pretrial hearing that they were reluctant to show previously. The judge may express some impatience with frivolous claims and issues and ask the attorneys to submit written arguments on questions of law.

Depending on the judge, the attorneys may come away from the conference with a clear idea of where the judge stands on the law and even the judge's attitude toward the merits, weaknesses, and defenses with regard to the claim. It is not that the judge prejudges the lawsuit, but a frank discussion of the case takes place in which the judge can act as a mediator to resolve the dispute and obviate the necessity for going to trial. It is often in the interests of all present to forgo the time and expense of trial. At the pretrial conference, the adversaries finally come face to face with the one person whose job it is to resolve the dispute.

Procedure at Trial

Trial is conducted as an orderly sequence of steps. The model presented here is followed quite generally in federal and state courts.

Jury Selection

The means and manner of selecting a jury vary considerably among jurisdictions, and even different judges differ in the extent to which they wish to control the process. The jury pool is typically selected from the list of registered voters within the jurisdiction, a number of whom are called for jury duty when the court is in session. From a number larger than the number of jurors required in a case, the jury will be selected by an examination called *voir dire,* during which the attorneys and/or the judge will ask the prospective jurors questions with regard to their qualifications to serve in the case. In addition to statutory disqualifications, jurors who are prejudiced with regard to the parties or subject matter of the case or who cannot reasonably be expected to judge the facts impartially may be excluded from the jury. An attorney who wishes to exclude such a juror makes a *challenge for cause.* These are unlimited in number, on the theory that no party should be tried by a biased jury. Cases that receive widespread publicity prior to trial may involve lengthy *voir dire* in the attempt to find impartial jurors, though the problem is usually encountered in sensational criminal trials.

In addition to challenges for cause, each party is allowed a specific number of *peremptory challenges*, which allow the parties to exclude jurors they suspect are unsympathetic to their side of the case but who are not otherwise disqualified. Attorneys do not give reasons for exercising peremptory challenges.

Jury selection is extremely important. Cases commonly go to trial because there are two believable versions of the facts or simply because the facts could be viewed to favor either side. A case may be won or lost on the basis of the jury selection. After all, a decision on the value of "emotional distress" or an award of punitive damages is arbitrary and subjective.

The *Eaton* case, a land line dispute involving jury disqualification, is the sort of case in which the parties sometimes end up paying more for the litigation than the land is worth.

Conduct of the Trial

With the jury selected, the trial begins with *opening statements* by each side, plaintiff first and then defendant, who may reserve opening remarks until later. Opening statements are designed to inform the jury of the nature of the case and the facts each side proposes to show or dispute. In a bench trial (a nonjury trial), opening statements are usually waived because the judge ordinarily does not need to be prepared in this way.

The plaintiff then presents the evidence that forms the *case-in-chief*. The plaintiff has the burden of proof, meaning that there must be

Garland EATON
v.
James H. GRINDLE et al.
Supreme Court of Georgia.
236 Ga. 324, 223 S.E.2d 670 (1976)

Appellant brought suit in the Superior Court of Lumpkin County to resolve a land line dispute. After a jury trial the dispute was resolved in appellant's favor. Appellee filed a motion for new trial on the ground that a juror at the trial was disqualified as a third cousin of the appellant's wife. The motion was sustained and a new trial granted. At the second trial, a jury returned a verdict for appellee. Appellant filed an amended motion for new trial contending that unknown to him one of the jurors, Jewell Justus, was the husband of a third cousin of Alma Grindle, a named defendant. The trial court overruled the motion, ruling that Jewell Justus and Alma Grindle were related in the eighth degree, and therefore not within the prohibited degree. Appellant appeals this ruling.

The relevant Code section provides that "All trial jurors in the courts of this State shall be disqualified to act or serve, in any case or matter, when such juror is related by consanguinity or affinity to any party interested in the result of the case or matter, within the sixth degree, as computed according to the civil law . ..." The trial court computed the degree of kinship by counting each ancestor starting with the juror, through the common ancestor and ending with the defendant. However, the civil law degree of kinship is ascertained by counting from the juror to the common ancestor to the interested party. Therefore, the correct method of computation is to count the "steps" or generations from one ancestor to the next counting each "step" or generation as one degree, and not to count each ancestor as a degree. If the sum is within the sixth degree, the juror is disqualified to serve in the matter.

The record shows that the juror's wife is the third cousin of the defendant, making their great-grandfather the common ancestor. This results in third cousins being related in the sixth degree, a prohibited degree under [state statute]. The question then becomes whether Jewell Justus is related within the sixth degree as is his wife or in the seventh degree, counting the "step" between the husband and wife as a degree, as the trial court held. The statute is applicable to jurors and interested parties related by consanguinity or affinity, i.e., by blood or by marriage. The husband is related to his wife's kindred by affinity in the same degree that she is related by consanguinity. Therefore, the juror Jewell Justus is directly related to his wife's father by way of marriage, making it a direct "step" from the wife's father to Mr. Justus without first counting the "steps" to the wife from her father and then from her to her husband.

We hold that the juror Jewell Justus is related to the defendant Alma Grindle within the prohibited sixth degree, and was disqualified to serve as juror in the matter.

We further hold that the disqualified juror's presence on the jury was not harmless. We cannot say as a matter of law that the evidence here demands a verdict for appellees since two successive jury trials in the matter have resulted in opposite verdicts.

Judgment reversed. All the Justices concur.

Case Questions

1. Diagram the kinship relations in this case.
2. Is the reckoning problem helped by counting the steps between relatives rather than the relatives themselves? Check your diagram.
3. Is there a step between husband and wife?

sufficient proof of the allegations of the complaint to sustain a verdict in favor of the plaintiff if the evidence is believed. This is called making a *prima facie* case.

Questioning of witnesses proceeds with the party calling the witness conducting a *direct examination,* followed by *cross-examination* by the other side. Cross-examination aims at showing flaws in the witness's testimony or discrediting the witness. The initial party then has the opportunity to *redirect* questions concerning issues raised "on cross." This is followed by *recross.*

When the plaintiff finishes the case-in-chief, the defendant produces witnesses favorable to the defense, who are questioned in similar fashion, with the defense conducting the direct examination. The plaintiff then has the opportunity to present evidence rebutting the defendant's presentation, followed by rebuttal by the defendant.

Finally, each side makes a *summation,* or *closing argument,* before the jury, with the defendant usually first (in opposite order of opening statements). The function of the closing argument is to summarize the evidence and present an interpretation of the facts consistent with the evidence that favors the party making the argument. Considerable latitude is given the attorneys in their closing arguments, provided they stay within the scope of the evidence presented and conduct themselves properly.

Verdict and Judgment

Before the jury retires to deliberate the facts, the judge *charges* them, that is, gives them instructions. Paralegals assist in the research and preparation of jury instructions. The jury returns when it reaches consensus and reads the verdict before the court. The judge then asks each juror if he or she concurs in the verdict. After dismissing the jury, the judge may enter judgment on the verdict immediately or wait for a period, during which the parties may make posttrial motions.

In a nonjury trial, the judge is the trier of fact, so no verdict is entered, though the judgment should include findings of fact beyond what would be appropriate in a jury trial. Final judgment is in written form, dated and signed by the judge and filed with the court records.

The Rules of Evidence

Evidentiary rules form an independent subject for study that cannot be treated in satisfactory fashion here. In general, the rules of evidence are designed to exclude evidence that is irrelevant, repetitious, or unreliable. They help to prevent filibustering (delaying tactic) by attorneys representing losing causes. But the rules also reveal a distrust of the jury. Much that is excluded could be helpful in learning the truth, but is not admissible because of questions of reliability, thus questioning the jury's ability to weigh the import of unreliable evidence. Because the jury may find facts based only on the evidence that it hears and sees, it often receives a limited picture of the circumstances of the case.

The ancient forerunner of the modern jury was composed of members of the community who knew the defendant and could judge the veracity of the plaintiff's claim. Today the jurors are strangers to the parties as well as the facts and are limited by the rules of evidence in what they can know of the case.

Two examples of evidentiary rules may illustrate this problem. First, one rule of evidence holds that a nonexpert witness, or layperson, may not give opinion testimony. A person qualifying as an expert, let us say a psychiatrist, may express an opinion on the facts of the case as long as the opinion is within the expert's field of expertise. As a result, an eyewitness friend of the defendant may not declare that the defendant was "insane," whereas a psychiatrist who entered the case long after the events took place may talk at length about how Oedipal conflicts caused the defendant to act as he did.

Second, the *hearsay rule* excludes from testimony out-of-court statements made by a person not present in court ("My friend told me that Joe had been drinking"). There are more than a dozen major exceptions to the hearsay rule, but it excludes what might otherwise be extremely relevant evidence on the grounds of unreliability and the lack of opportunity to cross-examine the person who made the statement.

Motions

Parties to a case have at their disposal numerous motions that ask the court to take particular action by granting or denying the motion. Because the ruling on each motion requires the exercise of legal judgment, and therefore raises a question of law, denial of a motion may be the basis for appeal by the movant (person making the motion), and granting the motion may provide a basis for appeal by the nonmoving party on the grounds of prejudicial error. The discussion here is confined to a handful of motions that are designed to terminate the case favorably to the moving party if granted. They have several names but much in common; their differences depend largely on their timing, and so they are often classified as pretrial, trial, and posttrial motions.

Fact/Law Distinction

The purpose of trial must be kept in mind in order to understand the function of these motions. Trial refers to trying facts. Assuming a typical jury trial of a damage suit, the plaintiff must prove the elements of a cause of action and the amount of the damages. The jury must find facts supporting each element and fix the dollar amount of damages in order for the plaintiff to recover. The only issues before the jury are those of disputed fact. If no facts are in dispute, the jury has no function. The parties may stipulate the truth of certain facts, thus taking those fact questions out of dispute. For example, in a suit for damages, the defendant might acknowledge liability for compensation to the plaintiff, not disputing the amount claimed as compensation by the plaintiff, but arguing that punitive damages are not allowed under the circumstances of the case. Whether punitive damages are allowable is a legal question. If the judge agrees with the defendant's argument, there would be no task for the jury; if the judge disagrees, the jury must determine whether the facts of the case warrant punitive damages according to the instructions given the jury by the judge. If the jury finds punitive damages appropriate, the amount must be fixed by the jury.

The simple model of dispute resolution describes a two-step process in which (1) facts are determined from the evidence presented and (2) law is applied to the facts to establish the prevailing party and the form of relief, if any, to be awarded. This assumes, first, that facts will be found—this is almost always the case, but on rare occasions the jury finds it impossible to reach a consensus, resulting in a mistrial. The model also assumes that the law is there to be found and applied. This is somewhat problematic, because the judge will always make conclusions of law, but the peculiarities of a given case may present novel legal issues not easily answered on the basis of existing law.

If no material facts are in dispute, the only task before the court is to apply the law. Whether there are facts in dispute is a question of law for the judge. The judge may take the case out of the hands of the jury or take a fact question away from jury determination by converting it into a question of law. This sleight of hand is justified with language such as, "reasonable persons could not disagree ... ." The rationale here is that the jury is needed only if some doubt exists with regard to the facts. If the judge concludes that no doubt exists, even though the parties dispute the facts, the question can be decided "as a matter of law" ("reasonable persons could not disagree"). Disputed facts should normally go to the jury; a judge who oversteps the authority to decide facts will be reversed on appeal.

In its simplest form, the conversion of a fact question into a question of law is seen in the taking of *judicial notice*. The court may relieve a party of the burden of proving a fact by taking judicial notice of that fact. Ordinarily notice is taken on the basis of common knowledge of a fact (it is dark in Omaha at midnight; Mario Cuomo was governor of New York in 1989). Of course, self-evident facts are rarely disputed, so the court does not need to bother with such questions, but sometimes facts that seem clear are nevertheless disputed, as when a party attempted to argue that wine is not intoxicating and the judge took judicial notice of the fact that wine is an intoxicating beverage.

In the 1940s, the great silent film actor Charlie Chaplin was sued by Joan Berry over paternity of her daughter, Carol Ann Berry. Chaplin agreed to pay support for the child if blood tests indicated he could be the father. To the contrary, the blood tests indicated he could *not* have been the father. Carol Ann had blood type B, while Joan had A and Charlie had O. Because Carol Ann must have inherited B from a parent who had a B or AB type blood, Charlie could not have been the father. Joan won a suit that was characterized by histrionics, including putting Charlie and Carol Ann side by side to show a family resemblance. The court refused to take judicial notice of the blood tests as conclusive and sent the case to the jury, which concluded that Charlie was the father. Although judicial notice is usually reserved for matters of common knowledge, the question arises as to whether the court should take fact-finding away from the jury when scientific certainty compels a factual conclusion. Compare *State v. Gray*.

Note that bastardy, usually called paternity, proceedings are "quasi-criminal" proceedings used to establish paternity for related civil suits. The court uses preponderance of the evidence rather than guilt beyond a reasonable doubt as the standard of proof.

Dismissal Motions

On motion, a judge may end a case because one side has no legal basis for its claims or because no material fact is in dispute and it is time to enter judgment. Because the granting of such motions cuts short further discussion and presentation of facts and denies a person's "day in court," the court uses a strict test. Although it is phrased somewhat differently according to the motions, generally it states that the court will test the motion by looking at the case "in the light most favorable to the nonmoving party." This test must be examined by considering the motions.

The Demurrer

The first dismissal motion that can arise in a case is one made by the defendant attacking the complaint by a "motion to dismiss for failure

STATE of Ohio *ex rel.* Hope A.
STEIGER, Complainant,
v.
Bruce GRAY, Defendant.
Juvenile Court of Ohio, Cuyahoga County
145 N.E.2d 162 (1957)

Complainant, an unmarried woman, filed a complaint in bastardy alleging that the defendant is the father of her child born to her December 1, 1956.

Defendant himself did not testify on his own behalf. He called but one defense witness—Dr. Roger W. Marsters, a clinical pathologist, who had been appointed by the court to conduct the blood grouping tests of the child, the complainant and the defendant, as requested by the defendant. ...

Dr. Marsters' qualifications as an expert serologist were not questioned by the complainant. He testified that he carefully tested the blood specimens of the complainant, the defendant and the child "for the International OAB, M and N, and C, D, E, and c blood factors by using known blood controls along with the unknowns". ...

"The data on the International OAB blood group factors are inconclusive because the mating of a type A individual with a type O individual may produce offspring of either type A or type O.

"The data on the M–N factors are inconclusive,. ...

"The data on the Rh blood factor D are inconclusive,. ...

"The data on the Rh blood factor E are inconclusive,. ...

"The data on the [Rh] factor c are inconclusive,. ...

"The data on the Rh factor C however indicate that an exclusion of paternity is established on this basis. Both Hope Steiger and Bruce Gray are negative for the C factor and therefore lack this particular blood antigen. On the other hand Baby Norma June Steiger is C-positive and therefore possesses this particular blood antigen. Since these blood factors can only be inherited from the parents and since both of these adults lack the C, then some other man than Bruce Gray must be the father of this child.

"In conclusion, an exclusion of paternity is established by the demonstration of the C factor in this child, Norma Steiger, without the presence of this particular blood factor in the blood of either of these two adults, Hope Steiger or Bruce Gray."

Dr. Marsters stated that he and his associates made five separate blood tests and that all proper safeguards were taken to protect the integrity and accuracy of the blood grouping tests. The accuracy of his conclusion of the exclusion of defendant as the father of the child was not rebutted by any counter medical evidence submitted by complainant. ...

This court further believes that the near unanimity of medical and legal authorities on the question of the reliability of blood grouping tests as an indicator of the truth in questioned paternity cases justifies the taking of judicial notice of the general recognition of the accuracy and value of the tests when properly performed by persons skilled in conducting them. The law does not hesitate to adopt scientific aids to the discovery of the truth which have achieved such recognition. ...

I hold, further, that because this great weight must be accorded to the blood grouping test results as testified to by Dr. Marsters, complainant has failed to prove the guilt of the defendant by a preponderance of the evidence.

Accordingly, I find the defendant not guilty as charged in the complaint.

Case Questions

1. Why did the defendant not testify in his own behalf?
2. On what does the court base its justification for taking judicial notice?

to state a claim upon which relief can be granted." This is quite a mouthful, so it is abbreviated to "motion to dismiss for failure to state a claim," "motion to dismiss for failure to state a cause of action," or, borrowing from equity, a "demurrer." Granting this motion stops the action dead in its tracks. With a demurrer, the defendant argues that the complaint is legally insufficient, that it does not state a cause of action, or that the law has no remedy for the grievance asserted by the plaintiff.

The test used by the court for a demurrer is as follows: If all the allegations of the complaint were true, the complaint would still not allow the plaintiff any relief. In a sense, the demurrer says, "So what?" Some essential ingredient is missing. The *Georgia High School Association* case in Chapter 7 is a case that *should* have been dismissed if the trial court judge had taken the position the appellate court did; namely, that the plaintiffs had no property rights that were infringed by the referee's bad call. The law does not allow relief for such a case—no cause of action exists.

The assumption of the truth of a plaintiff's allegations is made only for the purpose of testing the demurrer. By making the demurrer, the defendant does not admit the allegations are true for any other purpose. If the demurrer is denied (the usual outcome), the defendant may proceed to dispute the facts alleged.

Summary Judgment

A motion for summary judgment can be both a trial and a pretrial motion. As a pretrial motion, it is made at some point before trial, when it appears that one side must win. For example, although the complaint may appear to state a cause of action, after all pleadings have been filed and discovery has taken place, the plaintiff's case may reveal some fatal weakness, so the defendant moves for summary judgment. In such a case, the test to be applied is whether, viewing the case in the light most favorable to the plaintiff, the nonmoving party, the plaintiff could not win. Again, if material facts are in dispute, the motion will be denied.

Motion for a Directed Verdict

At trial, after the plaintiff has presented its case-in-chief, the defendant may make a motion for a directed verdict. Construing all the evidence in the light most favorable to the plaintiff, the motion will be granted if it appears that the plaintiff has not provided sufficient proof to prevail. If granted, judgment is entered for the defendant and the case is over. Usually there are sufficient facts that a jury might find in the plaintiff's favor, so the case will continue. The motion for directed verdict is made routinely, and almost as routinely denied, so that the defendant preserves the right to appeal on the basis of its denial. Even if the plaintiff's case is weak, the judge may be reluctant to take the factfinding away from the jury.

At the close of all the evidence, both sides commonly make motions for a directed verdict. At first glance, it might seem that one would be granted, but because each is measured in terms most favorable to the nonmoving party, if there is a reasonable dispute over the facts, the evidence could be interpreted to support either side. Thus, both motions are denied and that task is left to the jury.

In a nonjury trial, the judge is the factfinder, so the appropriate motions are called motions for summary judgment, as the judge may immediately enter judgment. Formerly judges directed the juries to enter verdicts, which explains the "directed verdict" label of the motion, but this is no longer done. A motion for a directed verdict is also called a motion for nonsuit in some jurisdictions.

Motion for Judgment Notwithstanding the Verdict

After the jury has returned a verdict, either party may make a motion for judgment notwithstanding the verdict, usually referred to as a motion n.o.v., from the Latin *non obstante veredicto* ("notwithstanding the verdict"). This will be granted if the judge finds as a matter of law that the verdict is against the manifest weight of the evidence. On occasion a jury will return a verdict that appears absurd on the basis of the record, or the jury's factfinding may be legally inconsistent. For example, the jury may find that the plaintiff was negligent as well as the defendant, giving the defendant an absolute defense to the suit (in a state that recognizes contributory negligence), and yet award compensation to the plaintiff. In such a case, the judge would enter a judgment in favor of the defendant on a motion for judgment n.o.v.

The aforementioned motions terminate the proceedings if granted. Usually they are denied; in most instances a case should not proceed to trial if one side's case is fatally flawed—the case should have been settled short of trial. Nevertheless, the expense of trial is a threat that is used for bargaining, and sometimes both sides are so stubborn in the negotiating process that trial is held regardless of the merits of the case. When the dispute is based on novel or controversial interpretations of the law, the trial may be primarily a prelude to appeal. Negotiations may continue during trial and prior to appeal. In addition, there are posttrial motions designed to set aside the judgment or to ask for a new trial. These and other pretrial procedures will be left to further study. Specific devices of civil procedure vary considerably from one jurisdiction to another, and it is best to learn the peculiarities of the jurisdiction in which one intends to practice.

Res Judicata and Collateral Estoppel

Although it is possible to obtain a new trial if an appellate court has determined that prejudicial error in the first trial justifies relitigating the case, the losing plaintiff does not have the right to a retrial simply by filing the cause of action again. This is the essence of the principle of *res judicata*, Latin for "the thing has been decided." A party may not bring a suit over and over again until a favorable result is achieved. *Res judicata* is an affirmative defense that bars further suit. It is also called *merger and bar*, referring to the principle that the claim of the winning plaintiff is "merged" in the judgment of the court and enforceable by the judgment, but the claim is "barred" from further suit when the plaintiff loses.

Although this seems straightforward, a number of problems complicate the principle. Overlapping state and federal jurisdictions allow a claim in either or both courts. State and federal law may cover similar subjects in different ways. The problem then becomes whether a suit brought in one court is really the same case as that later brought in another. And, because the law provides different causes of action that can arise from the same events (e.g., threatening someone with physical harm might be grounds for assault or intentional infliction of mental distress), the question can arise as to whether one suit bars the later suit.

There are important conflicting policies in claim preclusion (*res judicata*). On the one hand, fairness would prevent a defendant from being forced to defend the same case more than once. On the other hand, the plaintiff should have full access to the courts. The court will not invoke *res judicata* if there is a difference in the parties to the claim or if the case involves issues different from those brought in the first case. This discussion seriously oversimplifies *res judicata*, which can become very complex with multiple parties and multiple claims.

Collateral estoppel is directly related to *res judicata*; it is a bar to the relitigation of specific issues that have been previously adjudicated, even though the suits may not satisfy the requirements of *res judicata* (if all the issues in a new suit are identical to those in the prior suit, collateral estoppel and *res judicata* may both be said to apply). Occasionally a new suit raises issues presented in a former case as well as additional issues not barred by the prior suit. Nevertheless, those issues raised in the former suit and decided in it may not again be raised, because of collateral estoppel.

Res judicata and collateral estoppel are simple in principle but often difficult in application.

Summary

Civil procedure has both theoretical and practical importance. Theoretically, examination of our system of civil procedure reveals an adversarial system in which the fairness of the procedural rules takes on special significance. Reliance is placed on procedure to achieve justice. Practically, the legal practitioner must understand the procedure of the jurisdiction, both to enforce the rights of clients and to protect them from the maneuvers of the opposing side.

Lawsuits are initiated by the filing of a complaint and service of process on the defendant. In order to determine the rights of the parties, the court must have personal jurisdiction over them. In restricted cases, a suit may be filed against a thing (*in rem* jurisdiction). When there is a choice of courts having jurisdiction over a case, proper venue is determined by the rules and the circumstances of the parties.

Most American jurisdictions follow code pleading, which is a statutory refinement of common law, and equity pleading, which requires that a complaint state a cause of action, to which the defendant files a responsive pleading called an answer. In some cases the plaintiff then files a pleading responding to the answer.

An important feature of pretrial procedure is the discovery process, in which the parties enjoy great latitude in learning about the case for the other side through deposition, interrogatories, requests for documents, and so on.

Key features of the jury trial are jury selection and presentation of evidence. Each side has ample opportunity to present evidence and challenge the evidence for the other side. The plaintiff carries the burden of proving the elements of the cause of action.

Each side has at its disposal several motions at the pretrial, trial, and posttrial stages. The most important of these are motions that test the validity of the case for the other side, such as a motion for summary judgment. When granted, these motions terminate the litigation at that point.

Review Questions

1. Why is it necessary to be thoroughly familiar with the rules of civil procedure in one's jurisdiction?

2. Why is *voir dire* so important?

3. How does a defendant attack a complaint for legal insufficiency?

4. Why are depositions important?

5. What causes the most delay in reaching trial?

6. How does the pretrial hearing encourage settlement?

7. How does the paralegal play a part in discovery?

8. What is the difference between *res judicata* and collateral estoppel?

9. How does venue differ from subject matter jurisdiction?

10. On what basis can the judge keep a case from going to the jury?

SOURCES OF CRIMINAL LAW

Source	Comment
Constitutions	The United States and every state have a constitution. The United States Constitution is the supreme law of the land. Amendment of the federal constitution requires action by both the states and United States Congress.
Statutes	The written law created by legislatures, also known as codes. State statutes may not conflict with either their own constitution or the federal constitution. State statutes are also invalid if they conflict with other federal law, and the federal government has concurrent jurisdiction with the states. Statutes of the United States are invalid if they conflict with the United States Constitution or if they attempt to regulate outside federal jurisdiction. Legislatures may change statutes at will.
Common Law	Law which evolved as courts, through judicial opinions, recognized customs and practices. Legislatures may alter, amend, or abolish the common law at will. In criminal law, the common law is responsible for the creation of crimes and for establishing defenses to crime.
Regulations	Created by administrative agencies under a grant of authority from a legislative body. Regulations must be consistent with statutes and constitutions and may not exceed the legislative grant of power. The power to make rules and regulations is granted to "fill in the gaps" left by legislatures when drafting statutes.
Ordinances	Written law of local bodies, such as city councils. Must be consistent with all higher forms of law.
Model Penal Code	Written under the direction of the American Law Institute. It was drafted by experts in criminal law to be presented to the states for their adoption. It is not law until a state has adopted it, in whole or part. More than half the states have adopted at least part of the Model Penal Code.
Court Rules	Rules created by courts to manage their cases. Court rules are procedural and commonly establish deadlines, lengths of filings, etc. Court rules may not conflict with statutes or constitutions.

Reprinted from *Criminal Law and Procedure*, 2nd ed., © 1996, Delmar Publishers and Lawyers Cooperative Publishing.

CHAPTER 9

THE LAW OF CRIMINAL PROCEDURE

The Constitutional Basis of Criminal Procedure

Criminal procedure follows many of the patterns of civil procedure, but major differences are largely due to the special provisions of the U.S. Constitution, which are usually echoed in state constitutions. The Constitution, and especially the first ten amendments (the Bill of Rights), expresses a basic code of criminal procedure by enumerating rights of the citizens against government intrusion and rights of those accused of crimes. The provisions of the Constitution have been subject to intense scrutiny by state and federal courts, particularly since the 1950s. Criminal procedure cannot be understood without reference to these rights. The following excerpts from the Constitution highlight these rights, with brief annotations or explanations of the terms emphasized in **boldface**.

Excerpts from the Constitution of the United States

ARTICLE I

Section 9:

(2) The privilege of the **Writ of Habeas Corpus** shall not be suspended, unless when in Cases of Rebellion or Invasion the public Safety may require it.

(3) No **Bill of Attainder** or **ex post facto Law** shall be passed.

ARTICLE III

Section 2:

(3) The trial of all Crimes, except in Cases of Impeachment, shall be by **Jury**; and such Trial shall be held in the State where the said Crimes shall have been committed; but when not committed within any State, the Trial shall be at such Place or Places as the Congress may by Law have directed.

AMENDMENT IV

The right of the people to be secure in their persons, houses, papers, and effects, against **unreasonable searches and seizures**, shall not be violated, and **no warrants shall issue, but upon probable cause, supported by oath or affirmation, and particularly describing the place to be searched, and the persons or things to be seized.**

AMENDMENT V

No person shall be held to answer for a capital, or otherwise infamous crime, unless on a presentment or **indictment of a grand jury**, except in cases arising in the land or naval forces, or in the militia, when in actual service in time of war or public danger; nor shall any person be subject for the same offense to be **twice put in jeopardy** of life or limb; nor shall be compelled in any criminal case to be a **witness against himself, nor be deprived of life, liberty, or property, without due process of law**; nor shall private property be taken for public use, without just compensation.

AMENDMENT VI

In all criminal prosecutions, the accused shall enjoy the **right to a speedy and public trial**, by an **impartial jury** of the State and district wherein the crime shall have been committed, which district shall have been previously ascertained by law, and to be informed of the **nature and cause of the accusation**; to be **confronted with the witnesses against him**; to have **compulsory process** for obtaining witnesses in his favor, and to have the **assistance of counsel for his defense**.

AMENDMENT VIII

Excessive bail shall not be required, nor excessive fines imposed, nor **cruel and unusual punishments** inflicted.

AMENDMENT XIV

... No State shall make or enforce any law which shall abridge the privileges or immunities of citizens of the United States; nor shall any State deprive any person of life, liberty, or property, without **due process** of law; nor deny to any person within its jurisdiction the **equal protection** of the laws. ...

Annotations

A **writ of habeas corpus** is brought by a petition, the purpose of which is to challenge the lawfulness of a detention by the government. This includes institutions other than prisons, although most habeas corpus petitions are brought by imprisoned criminals. It is often used as a form of federal review after state appeals have failed.

A **bill of attainder** is a law that singles out a person or a very small group of persons for penal sanctions. An example of such a law would be one that made it a crime to be the Grand Wizard of the Ku Klux Klan.

An **ex post facto law** is a penal law that operates retroactively. For example, under such a law a person could be charged with a crime for an action that was not a crime at the time it took place, or a person's sentence for a crime could be increased to a greater sentence than was permissible at the time the crime occurred.

The right to a **jury** trial applies to all criminal prosecutions. Disciplinary actions in prisons do not fall into this category.

The right to be free from **unreasonable searches and seizures** is designed primarily to protect citizens from excessive intrusions by government and police into their homes and persons, but interpretation of search and seizure has extended its application to places of business as well. The reasonableness of a search must necessarily remain a subjective judgment.

"... **no warrants shall issue, but upon probable cause, supported by oath or affirmation, and particularly describing the place to be searched, and the persons or things to be seized.**" Warrants are carefully scrutinized by criminal defense attorneys to determine whether they conform to this constitutional requirement. If the warrant or the search exceeds constitutional limits, the evidence seized may be excluded from trial, which is often fatal to the case for the prosecution. For example, drugs illegally seized may not be used as evidence at trial, so the prosecution then has no case.

A **grand jury indictment** requires a hearing before a special body of citizens gathered to review the prosecutor's evidence in support of taking the accused to trial. If the grand jury concludes that there is probable cause to believe the accused committed the crime, it issues an indictment, which is a written accusation by the grand jury charging the accused with a criminal act. It is also referred to as a *true bill,* but when the grand jury does not indict, it is called a *no bill.* The grand jury proceeding is controlled by the prosecutor to such an extent that a chief judge of the New York Court of Appeals remarked that a grand jury would indict a ham sandwich if the prosecutor recommended it.

> A grand jury, although composed of citizens, is different from the petit jury which serves at trial. The grand jury has been used as an investigatory tool of the prosecutor's office on many occasions, as where the federal prosecutor investigated activities of the Black Panther Party, whose leaders had indicated an intent to kill President Nixon and had advocated sabotage by Black soldiers in Vietnam. Since witnesses before the grand jury are not represented in the hearings by their attorneys and since the grand jury cannot convict, the prosecutor enjoys a freedom from the usual limitations imposed at trial, [so] the grand jury can be used oppressively.
>
> In 1734, William Cosby, the English governor of New York, sought to have the publisher of a radical newspaper with extremely limited circulation indicted for criminal libel. The grand jury twice refused to indict. Thereafter, the publisher, Peter Zenger, was charged with libel, and one of the most celebrated trials in American history followed. [After a dramatic trial characterized by hostility between an arrogant judge appointed specially by Governor Cosby and a brave and unrelenting defense attorney, Mr. Zenger was found by the jury to be *not guilty,* an historic victory for the people and the cause of freedom of speech and of the press.] It was with this and similar precedents fresh in their memories that our founding fathers incorporated into the Fifth Amendment the requirement that no person shall be held to answer for an infamous crime except upon the presentment or indictment of a grand jury.

Today, courts across this country are faced with an increasing flow of cases arising out of grand jury proceedings concerned with the possible punishment of political dissidents. It would be a cruel twist of history to allow the institution of the grand jury that was designed at least partially to protect political dissent to become an instrument of political suppression.

Bursey v. United States, 466 F.2d 1059 (9th Cir. 1972).

Double jeopardy prevents a person from being tried twice for the same crime. Jeopardy attaches once the accused has been put on trial before judge or jury; until that time, the case may be postponed without violating this provision. Double jeopardy applies to bringing the same charges in the same jurisdiction even if the courts are different (e.g., a lower criminal court versus a higher criminal court). This does not apply to state and federal jurisdictions. In the famous case of the three civil rights workers who were killed in Mississippi, an acquittal of homicide in the state court was followed by prosecution and conviction in federal court for depriving the victims of their civil rights.

A person cannot be held to be a **witness against himself**. This is usually referred to as the *privilege against self-incrimination,* generally restricted to a testimonial privilege; that is, a person may not be required to testify to matters that would tend to incriminate him or her. Blood tests, fingerprints, and most documents that might incriminate are are not considered "testimony" and are not covered by this privilege. This provision of the Fifth Amendment is the basis for the *Miranda* rights, particularly the right to remain silent during a police interrogation. The privilege against self-incrimination in the Fifth Amendment is zealously guarded by the U.S. Supreme Court, as the *Griffin* case demonstrates.

"[No person may ...] be deprived of life, liberty or property, without due process of law" is an important feature of criminal law because of the inclusion of the words *life* and *liberty*, as the primary means of punishing criminals are execution and incarceration. Any criminal procedure can be scrutinized for fairness on the basis of the due process clause. Although the Fifth Amendment applies to federal action, a similar clause in the Fourteenth Amendment applies to the states, subjecting state action to review by federal courts.

The defendant has a **right to a speedy and public trial**. Most state and federal jurisdictions have by statute fixed a time period within which a criminal case must be brought. If the prosecutor exceeds the time limit, the accused may not be tried. The right to a public trial is designed to prevent abuse that might occur in a closed hearing. When appropriate, and with the court's approval, the defendant may waive this right and close the trial to the public.

The right to an **impartial jury** is fundamental to our criminal justice system, as police and prosecutor assume an accusatorial role. Great pains are often taken to guarantee that the jury is untainted by pretrial publicity or acquaintance with the facts of the case.

GRIFFIN
v.
CALIFORNIA
U.S. Supreme Court
380 U.S. 609 (1965)

Petitioner was convicted of murder in the first degree after a jury trial in a California court. He did not testify at the trial on the issue of guilt, though he did testify at the separate trial on the issue of penalty. The trial court instructed the jury on the issue of guilt, stating that a defendant has a constitutional right not to testify. But it told the jury:

> As to any evidence or facts against him which the defendant can reasonably be expected to deny or explain because of facts within his knowledge, if he does not testify or if, though he does testify, he fails to deny or explain such evidence, the jury may take that failure into consideration as tending to indicate the truth of such evidence and as indicating that among the inferences that may be reasonably drawn therefrom those unfavorable to the defendant are the more probable. ...

Petitioner had been seen with the deceased the evening of her death, the evidence placing him with her in the alley where her body was found. The prosecutor made much of the failure of petitioner to testify:

> ... He would know how she got down the alley. He would know how the blood got on the bottom of the concrete steps. He would know how long he was with her in that box. He would know how her wig got off. He would know whether he beat her or mistreated her. ...
> These things he has not seen fit to take the stand and deny or explain.
> And in the whole world, if anybody would know, this defendant would know.
> Essie Mae is dead, she can't tell you her side of the story. The defendant won't.

The death penalty was imposed and the California Supreme Court affirmed. ...

The question remains whether, statute or not, the comment [on defendant's refusal to testify] rule, approved by California, violates the Fifth Amendment.

We think it does. It is in substance a rule of evidence that allows the State the privilege of tendering to the jury for its consideration the failure of the accused to testify. No formal offer of proof is made as in other situations; but the prosecutor's comment and the court's acquiescence are the equivalent of an offer of evidence and its acceptance. The Court in the *Wilson* case stated: "... It is not every one who can safely venture on the witness stand though entirely innocent of the charge against him, ... will often confuse and embarrass him to such a degree as to increase rather than remove prejudices against him. It is not every one, however honest, who would, therefore, willingly be placed on the witness stand. The statute, in tenderness to the weakness of those who from the causes mentioned might refuse to ask to be a witness, particularly when they may have been in some degree compromised by their association with others, declares that the failure of the defendant in a criminal action to request to be a witness shall not create any presumption against him."

... What the jury may infer, given no help from the court is one thing. What it may infer when the court solemnizes the silence of the accused into evidence against him is quite another. That the inference of guilt is not always so natural or irresistible is brought out in the *Modesto* opinion itself: "Defendant contends that the reason a defendant refuses to testify is that his prior convictions will be introduced in evidence to impeach him and not that he is unable to deny the accusations. It is true that the defendant might fear that his prior convictions will prejudice the jury, and therefore another possible inference can be drawn from his refusal to take the stand."

... We take that in its literal sense and hold that the Fifth Amendment, in its direct application to the Federal Government, and in its bearing on the States by reason of the Fourteenth Amendment, forbids either comment by the prosecution on the accused's silence or instructions by the court that such silence is evidence of guilt.

Reversed.

MR. JUSTICE STEWART, with whom MR. JUSTICE WHITE joins, dissenting. ...

We must determine whether the petitioner has been "compelled ... to be a witness against himself." Compulsion is the focus of the inquiry. Certainly, if any compulsion be detected in the California procedure, it is of a dramatically different and less palpable nature than that involved in the procedures which historically gave rise to the Fifth Amendment guarantee. When a suspect was brought before the Court of High Commission or the Star Chamber, he was commanded to answer whatever was asked of him, and subjected to a far-reaching and deeply probing inquiry in an effort to ferret out some unknown and frequently unsuspected crime. He declined to answer on pain of incarceration, banishment, or mutilation. And if he spoke falsely, he was subject to further punishment. Faced with this formidable array of alternatives, his decision to speak was unquestionably coerced.

Those were the lurid realities which lay behind enactment of the Fifth Amendment, a far cry from the subject matter of the case before us. I think that the court in this case stretches the concept of compulsion beyond all reasonable bounds, and that whatever compulsion may exist derives from the defendant's choice not to testify, not from any comment by court or counsel.

Case Questions

1. The case refers to a right not to testify; the Fifth Amendment is commonly described as stating a privilege. What is the difference between a right and a privilege in this context?
2. Why does the majority consider the remarks of the judge and prosecutor sufficiently prejudicial to require a new trial?.
3. What reasons does the *Modesto* case give justifying an innocent defendant's refusal to testify? For what other reasons might an innocent person refuse to testify?
4. Why does the defense dwell on the word *compulsion* in reference to self-incrimination?

The defendant must be informed of the **nature and cause of the accusation** in order to prepare a defense. This simply spells out the notice requirement that would otherwise be implied by the due process clause.

The right of the defendant to be **confronted with the witnesses against him** is a protection against anonymous accusers and ensures the right to cross-examine witnesses.

Compulsory process refers to the power of the defendant in a criminal case to force witnesses to attend trial under a subpoena issued by the court. If appearance were voluntary, the defendant would be at a severe disadvantage.

In England, at common law, defendants in felony cases were forbidden to have an attorney. The Sixth Amendment was intended to do away with this prohibition. The right to effective **assistance of counsel** for the defendant has become a cherished right only in the last few decades. For many years, the right to counsel was considered applicable only to federal cases and then only when the accused could afford to pay or was accused of a capital offense (*Powell v. Alabama*, 287 U.S. 45 [1932])—until the famous exchange between Gideon and the Florida judge:

> *The Court:* Mr. Gideon, I am sorry, but I cannot appoint Counsel to represent you in this case. Under the laws of the State of Florida, the only time the Court can appoint Counsel to represent a Defendant is when that person is charged with a capital offense. I am sorry, but I will have to deny your request to appoint Counsel to defend you in this case.
>
> *The Defendant:* The U.S. Supreme Court says I am entitled to be represented by Counsel.

Gideon v. Wainwright, 372 U.S. 335 (1963).

Mr. Gideon was not exactly correct when he made this statement, but after he presented his own defense and was convicted, he took the case to the U.S. Supreme Court, which agreed with him. *Argersinger v. Hamlin*, 407 U.S. 25 (1972) extended the right to petty offenses involving possible imprisonment. A defendant who cannot afford an attorney must be furnished one by the government.

The right to be free from the imposition of **excessive bail** is self-explanatory; what is excessive may be judged relative to what is usual bail under similar circumstances. This is a limitation on the judge's discretion.

The right against the imposition of **cruel and unusual punishments** is also a relative concept. This particular principle has been viewed as an evolving standard—what was not considered "cruel and unusual" fifty years ago may be considered uncivilized and barbaric by today's standards.

The **due process** clause demands fair procedure and reasonable laws; it is a standard that the courts can invoke when injustice is apparent.

The **equal protection** clause imposes a test of equality before the law against discriminatory practices. There must be no difference in treatment in the statement of the law itself or in its application. In recent years the differential impact of the laws with regard to minorities has raised equal protection claims; for example, it has been shown statistically that blacks receive a disproportionate number of death sentences.

The Exclusionary Rule

The exclusionary rule is a special feature of criminal procedure that has developed from a series of U.S. Supreme Court interpretations of the Fourth, Fifth, and Fourteenth Amendments. It applies to excluding evidence illegally obtained by the government and enforces the adversarial principle in criminal proceedings. Because of the disparity between the power and resources of the government and the relative powerlessness of the criminal defendant, a number of protections, such as those enumerated in the Constitution, are afforded the defendant to equalize the respective positions in a criminal proceeding. The exclusionary rule operates to protect the defendant from abusive procedures by a more powerful opponent.

Basically, the exclusionary rule excludes from trial evidence obtained in violation of the defendant's constitutional rights. It first arose in *Weeks v. United States,* 232 U.S. 383 (1914), which held that evidence illegally obtained by federal officers could be excluded from evidence, but *Weeks* failed to apply the principle to the states. *Wolf v. Colorado,* 338 U.S. 25 (1949) held that search and seizure provisions of the Fourth Amendment were applicable to the states under the due process clause of the Fourteenth Amendment, but did not exclude illegally obtained evidence from state prosecutions. *Wolf* was overruled in 1961 by *Mapp v. Ohio,* 367 U.S. 643, which held that the products of a search violating Fourth Amendment rights may not be used in state prosecutions.

Suppose the police exact a confession from a suspect through torture. Should the confession be presented to the jury and the defendant allowed to disavow the confession because it was involuntary? Should the jury be allowed to weigh the relevance of the confession in light of the circumstances under which it was obtained? Our law answers in the negative. Coerced confessions have no place in the trial. This principle needs little justification; it is a reasonable interpretation of the meaning and intent of the due process clause of the Fourteenth Amendment.

In *Miranda v. Arizona*, 384 U.S. 486 (1966), Chief Justice Warren wrote an opinion that linked the right to counsel of the Sixth Amendment with the privilege against self-incrimination of the Fifth Amendment, both applicable to the states under the Fourteenth Amendment due process clause. The four dissenters argued that the Fifth Amendment was historically unconnected to the exclusion of involuntary confessions, but Warren and his four brethren prevailed, and police have been reading Miranda rights ever since. (Warren pointed out that these rights had been FBI policy for some time.) The precise requirements were spelled out in Chief Justice Warren's majority opinion:

> Our holding will be spelled out with some specificity in the pages which follow but briefly stated it is this: the prosecution may not use statements, whether exculpatory or inculpatory, stemming from custodial interrogation of the defendant unless it demonstrates the use of procedural safeguards effective to secure the privilege against self-incrimination. By custodial interrogation, we mean questioning initiated by law enforcement officers after a person has been taken into custody or otherwise deprived of his freedom of action in any significant way. As for the procedural safeguards to be employed, unless other fully effective means are devised to inform accused persons of their right of silence and to assure a continuous opportunity to

exercise it, the following measures are required. *Prior to any questioning, the person must be warned that he has a right to remain silent, that any statement he does make may be used as evidence against him, and that he has a right to the presence of an attorney, either retained or appointed.* The defendant may waive effectuation of these rights, provided the waiver is made voluntarily, knowingly and intelligently. If, however, he indicates in any manner and at any stage of the process that he wishes to consult with an attorney before speaking there can be no questioning. Likewise, if the individual is alone and indicates in any manner that he does not wish to be interrogated, the police may not question him. The mere fact that he may have answered some questions or volunteered some statements on his own does not deprive him of the right to refrain from answering any further inquiries until he has consulted with an attorney and thereafter consents to be questioned [emphasis added].

In most jurisdictions, a *motion to suppress* (physical evidence or a confession) is a pretrial motion that tests the applicability of the exclusionary rule to the circumstances of the case. If the prosecution's case relies on such evidence, the granting of the motion will be followed by a dismissal of the charges or a motion by the defense for a judgment of acquittal. The motion to suppress is the defense's first line of attack in cases in which confessions or physical evidence are critical elements. A surprising majority of criminal defendants confess in spite of being advised of their right to remain silent and their right to an attorney. When first contacted, the criminal defense attorney's first words of advice are likely to be: "Do not say anything to the police until I get there."

The criminal courts have been inundated for many years by drug crimes. In most of these, the defense's best attack is to suppress the evidence, so search and seizure appeals abound. Search and seizure law has come to draw extremely fine lines between proper and improper searches.

Plea Bargaining

The criminal justice system cannot be appreciated without an understanding of the custom of plea bargaining. The prosecuting attorney and the defense attorney usually engage in a form of negotiation, which until recent years has been a largely unofficial part of criminal procedure. Nearly all convictions are the result of negotiation. The defendant agrees to plead guilty in return for beneficial treatment by the prosecution. The prosecution may agree to drop some of the charges, reduce the offense—say, from first-degree murder to second-degree murder or from burglary to criminal trespass—thereby lessening the penalty, or recommend a lenient sentence or probation, which recommendation is usually accepted by the judge.

The present system could not work without plea bargaining. If every defendant demanded a jury trial, there would not be enough courts and prosecutors to try all the cases. Less than 5 percent of criminal cases go to trial (the same is true of civil cases). The presumption is that in most cases a trial would result in a conviction, thus encouraging defendants to make the best deal they can. Nevertheless, the custom of plea bargaining has come under severe criticism because negotiation takes place outside of public and judicial scrutiny and suggests a degree of collusion between prosecutors and defense attorneys.

Plea bargaining is nevertheless an entrenched part of the criminal justice system. When it breaks down, the defendant may look for a means to challenge his or her treatment. The *Redondo-Lemos* case reveals several facets of criminal procedure. The defendants focus on what they call gender discrimination in plea agreements. They were handed this argument by the trial judge, but the court of appeals insisted on close scrutiny of the law.

UNITED STATES of America,
Plaintiff-Appellant,
v.
Gilberto REDONDO-LEMOS,
Defendant-Appellee.

UNITED STATES of America,
Plaintiff-Appellant,
v.
Angel NOLASCO-COTA,
Defendant-Appellee.

UNITED STATES of America,
Plaintiff-Appellant,
v.
Sergio ALCARAZ-PERALTA,
Defendant-Appellee.
United States Court of Appeals,
Ninth Circuit
27 F.3d 439 (9th Cir. 1994)

[In the first appeal, referred to as *Redondo-Lemos I*, the district judge *sua sponte* raised the issue of discrimination in plea bargaining between males and females. The judge found that male drug carriers were treated more harshly in plea bargains than females and therefore gave the male defendants a sentence below the statutory minimum. The court of appeals agreed that this

was proper, but reversed the case because there was not enough evidence to show intentional discrimination—there was only enough to establish a **prima facie case**, shifting the burden of proof.]

On remand, the district court conducted an evidentiary hearing that consisted largely of testimony by Assistant United States Attorneys (AUSAs), each of whom explained the reasons for various prosecutorial decisions. The court nonetheless found that the U.S. Attorney's Office ... had engaged in intentional discrimination on the basis of gender. The court therefore again sentenced defendants below the statutory minimums for the offenses of which they were convicted. The government appeals.

* * *

The AUSA handling the Redondo-Lemos prosecution offered, in exchange for a guilty plea, to recommend the lowest sentence allowed by the Guidelines and still within the mandatory minimum. She testified that she assessed the strength of her case, followed the factors set out in the [Attorney General's Memorandum], was not motivated by defendant's gender and knew of no office policy of plea bargaining on the basis of gender. ...

In the ten other cases which concerned the district judge, the responsible AUSAs testified that they based their plea bargaining decisions on the strength of the evidence, the legality of the stops and searches, the defendant's cooperation, the level of the defendant's involvement, and special circumstances surrounding particular defendants. ...

The district court rejected these explanations as "mere general assertions that [the AUSAs] did not discriminate." As such, the district court held, they were not sufficient to rebut the prima facie case of intentional discrimination that we held was established. In so ruling, the court overlooked the fact that the prima facie case does no more than shift to the party accused of discrimination the burden of articulating a legitimate, non-discriminatory explanation for its conduct. By offering gender-neutral explanations for its plea bargaining decisions, the government fully carried this burden.

Defendants argue, however, that the government's explanations couldn't rebut the presumption of discrimination raised by the prima facie case because the district court just didn't believe them. But, at the rebuttal stage, it doesn't matter whether the district court believed the AUSAs were "actually motivated by the proffered reasons." The question is only whether the government introduced evidence "which, taken as true, would permit the conclusion that there was a nondiscriminatory reason for the adverse action." The government introduced more than enough evidence of this sort. At that point the presumption of discriminatory intent raised by the prima facie case "simply drop[ped] out of the picture." The question remained whether the evidence—without the benefit of any presumption—supported a finding of discrimination.

* * *

In *Redondo-Lemos I,* we authorized an unusual variant of the prima facie case: As an exercise of supervisory authority, the district judge could raise the matter sua sponte and the aggrieved defendant could proceed as if he (the defendant) had established a prima facie case of discrimination. A district judge, however, is not a witness; his observations in the courtroom are not proof. A judge who notices what he thinks may be a problem need not—indeed, cannot—present evidence of what he has seen and heard; he cannot be deposed or cross-examined; he cannot very well weigh his own credibility. The district judge's observations can serve as a springboard for further inquiry, but they are not evidence.

* * *

[T]he AUSA's observation that, when faced with a choice, couples usually select the woman to care for the children reflects no policy of gender discrimination. While government endorsement or adoption of private discriminatory conduct that affects third parties can amount to a violation of equal protection, it cannot be so where the parties affected are also the very ones making the decision. The government's compassionate practice of allowing one parent to stay with children who otherwise would be effectively orphaned is not rendered unconstitutional because the government allows the parents to decide which one is best suited to be the care-giver.

Nor do the statistics support a finding of intentional discrimination. [The court notes that the general statistics on male-female differences in sentencing did not take into account any individual circumstances of these cases and therefore failed to meet the burden required to establish intentional discrimination.]

In *Redondo-Lemos I,* we stressed the extreme deference the courts must give to prosecutorial charging decisions. We reiterate this note of caution today. While a district judge has the authority and the responsibility to take a hard look at evidence of invidious discrimination by the U.S. Attorney's Office, he must accord a presumption of constitutionality to prosecutorial decisions, and approach the inquiry with appropriate respect for the judgments exercised by officers of a coordinate branch of government. This is especially true where, as happened here, the government responds fully and promptly to the district judge's concerns by presenting live testimony from those who made the prosecutorial decisions. The government amply demonstrated that it acted on the basis of sound, non-discriminatory criteria, and the defendants produced no evidence capable of carrying their burden of proof.

The case is therefore remanded to the district court with instructions that it sentence defendants to the mandatory minimums for their respective offenses.

REVERSED and REMANDED.

Case Questions

1. How and why does the burden of proof shift back and forth in this case?
2. Does the government deny that males and females are treated differently in sentencing?
3. It would seem that the government is blaming any gender discrimination here on choices made by the defendants rather than the government. Is this a hollow argument? Can the government put its stamp of approval on those choices (for compassionate reasons)?
4. Does the court strain to defend plea bargaining?

Case Glossary

sua sponte   Own motion; a term referring to a disposition made by a court during the course of a proceeding, without a party having requested it.

prima facie case   A cause of action or defense that is sufficiently established by a party's evidence to justify a verdict in his or her favor, provided the other party does not rebut that evidence.

The Steps in Processing a Crime

The steps in criminal procedure tend to follow a more consistent routine than those of civil procedure because of legal limitations. The burden of proving guilt beyond a reasonable doubt, as opposed to "a preponderance of the evidence," forces police and prosecutor to monitor cases carefully. The exclusionary rule makes evidence or confessions unlawfully obtained inadmissible at trial and thus requires that great care be taken in investigation, arrest, interrogation, and search and seizure of evidence, lest the case fail for improper procedure. The constitutional right to a speedy trial forces police and prosecutor to organize investigation, charges, and trial within a limited timeframe. In addition, the constitutional protections afforded an accused require that cases be carefully prepared to avoid infringement of the accused's rights.

The following is an outline of the steps involved in the criminal process, which are followed virtually universally in criminal cases, though the terminology may differ from one jurisdiction to another:

1. Detection of crime.
    a. Report of crime.
    b. Police investigation.

2. Identification of a suspected criminal.

3. Arrest.
    a. Arrest without a warrant before the filing of a complaint.
    b. Arrest with a warrant after the filing of a complaint.

4. Initial appearance before a magistrate.
    a. Inform the accused of the charges and legal rights.
    b. Set bail or the terms of release from custody.
5. Preliminary hearing.
    a. Determine probable cause that accused committed a crime.
    b. Release accused or bind over for grand jury.
6. Indictment.
    a. Grand jury decides whether accused should be tried, or
    b. Prosecutor indicts by "information."
7. Arraignment before the court.
    a. Accused informed of charges brought.
    b. Accused enters plea.
        i. If plea of guilty or *nolo contendere*, the defendant may be sentenced.
        ii. If plea of not guilty, accused requests or waives jury.
8. Pretrial preparation.
    a. Pretrial motions.
    b. Discovery.
    c. Plea bargaining.
9. Trial.
    a. Acquittal results in release of defendant.
    b. Conviction leads to sentencing.
10. Optional posttrial motions, appeals, and habeas corpus.

Detection of Crime

The initial intervention of law enforcement officers is prompted by the report of a suspected crime by victims or witnesses or the police themselves, who may witness a crime or discover one during a police investigation into suspected criminal activities. The criminal act may be apparent from the circumstances, as when police encounter bank robbers in the act of robbing a bank, or there may simply be suspicious activities that require investigation or surveillance.

Although it may be clear that a crime has been committed, the identity of the perpetrator may not be immediately apparent. The objective of police inquiry is to establish facts to support the conclusion that a crime has been committed and that a specific person or persons committed that crime. Detection of crime is simply the first step; the police must also furnish the prosecutor with sufficient evidence to form the basis for a probable conviction of the offender.

Statements made in the absence of Miranda warnings in the course of a custodial interrogation may be excluded from evidence at trial. What exactly is a *custodial interrogation* has been the subject of numerous cases, including the *Bruder* case.

PENNSYLVANIA
v.
Thomas A. BRUDER, Jr.
U.S. Supreme Court
488 U.S. 9, 102 L. Ed. 2d 172,
109 S. Ct. 205 (1988)

In the early morning of January 19, 1985, Officer Steve Shallis of the Newton Township, Pennsylvania, Police Department observed Bruder driving very erratically along State Highway 252. Among other traffic violations, he ignored a red light. Shallis stopped Bruder's vehicle. Bruder left his vehicle, approached Shallis, and when asked for his registration card, returned to his car to obtain it. Smelling alcohol and observing Bruder's stumbling movements, Shallis administered field sobriety tests, including asking Bruder to recite the alphabet. Shallis also inquired about alcohol. Bruder answered that he had been drinking and was returning home. Bruder failed the sobriety tests, whereupon Shallis arrested him, placed him in the police car and gave him Miranda warnings. Bruder was later convicted of driving under the influence of alcohol. At his trial, his statements and conduct prior to his arrest were admitted into evidence. On appeal, the Pennsylvania Superior Court reversed, on the ground that the above statements Bruder had uttered during the roadside questioning were elicited through custodial interrogation and should have been suppressed for lack of Miranda warnings. The Pennsylvania Supreme Court denied the State's appeal application.

In *Berkemer v. McCarty,* which involved facts strikingly similar to those in this case, the court concluded that the "noncoercive aspect of ordinary traffic stops prompts us to hold that persons temporarily detained pursuant to such stops are not 'in custody' for the purposes of Miranda" ... .

The facts in this record, which Bruder does not contest, reveal the same noncoercive aspects as the *Berkemer* detention: "a single police officer ask[ing] respondent a modest number of questions and request[ing] him to perform a simple balancing test at a location visible to passing motorists." Accordingly, *Berkemer's* rule, that ordinary traffic stops do not involve custody for purposes of Miranda, governs this case. The judgment of the Pennsylvania Superior Court that evidence was inadmissible for lack of Miranda warnings is reversed.

Case Questions
1. Where does the court draw the line between a custodial and a noncustodial stop?
2. From the language of the case, can we infer that an interrogation did or did not take place?

Arrest and Complaint

Arrest is not an easy term to define in all circumstances and cases, but it generally refers to detaining someone for the purposes of having him or her answer to an allegation of a crime. The *complaint* is the formal allegation that the accused has committed a crime.

Legal process begins with a complaint. The complaint may be filed before or after arrest. When an arrest is made without a warrant during the commission of a crime, the complaint is filed at the defendant's initial appearance before the court or magistrate. When a crime has been completed and the police have information linking a person to the crime, the complaint is filed and an arrest warrant issued, which then serves as the basis for arresting the suspect.

In either case, an initial determination must be made as to whether there is *probable cause* to believe that a crime has been committed and that the defendant committed it. The complaint is accompanied by sworn statements, *affidavits,* which must present sufficient allegations to persuade the magistrate that a warrant should issue. If an arrest is made without a warrant, the arresting officer must have probable cause to believe that the suspect has committed a crime.

The arrest powers of police are limited by constitutional and statutory requirements. When police exceed their authority in making an arrest, they may subject themselves to civil suit by the arrestee for the tort of false arrest or to a civil rights suit. An arrest made in the good faith belief that it is lawful and under the authority of a warrant and conducted with reasonable force is the ideal standard against which allegedly improper arrests are tested. There is a large body of constitutional cases on arrest, because arrest commonly involves incidental searches and the discovery of evidence later used in prosecution.

Initial Appearance

State and federal statutes require that an arrestee be brought before a magistrate without undue delay, commonly within twenty-four hours. This is called *initial* or *first appearance* and is designed to protect individuals from being jailed without charges or bonds in the absence of scrutiny by an impartial magistrate. The accused will be informed of the charges and legal rights, especially the right to an attorney, and that an attorney will be appointed at state expense if the accused does not have funds to pay an attorney.

Bail is set at the initial appearance. The purpose of bail is to assure the defendant's appearance at further hearings. The Eighth Amendment prohibits excessive bail, and the defendant may request a hearing to reduce the bail. Under federal law, the court must set the least restrictive conditions to assure appearance. Defendants are frequently released on their own recognizance if, for instance, the defendant has steady employment, has a stable residence, presents little threat to society, and the nature of the crime suggests little likelihood that the defendant will flee the jurisdiction. Extreme circumstances may justify a denial of bail. The court may impose certain conditions on release, such as restrictions on travel.

Preliminary Hearing

A preliminary hearing is frequently called to examine the basis for the charges against the defendant, although this is frequently waived by the defendant. Because in the American system the prosecutor enjoys unrestricted authority over whether to prosecute, the preliminary hearing provides a defendant the opportunity to challenge the prosecution's case before the court. The preliminary hearing does not determine guilt, but examines the legal basis for the charges against the defendant. The judge determines whether there is sufficient evidence to send the case to the grand jury or whether to release the defendant instead. Not all states require a grand jury indictment, so the preliminary hearing may be the only opportunity to challenge the charges prior to trial.

Indictment and Information

Although the Constitution requires a grand jury for "infamous crimes" and many states require a grand jury indictment for felonies, many cases are brought on the basis of an "information," which is a written accusation by a public prosecutor. The practice differs from jurisdiction to jurisdiction, but the defendant must be formally charged by an indictment or information.

Grand jury hearings are not truly adversarial; they are secret hearings in which the prosecutor is given wide latitude to present the case for the guilt of the defendant. The grand jury does not decide guilt, but determines whether probable cause exists that the defendant committed the crime. If the grand jury finds no probable cause, the defendant is discharged; otherwise, the defendant is indicted and the case goes to trial.

Arraignment

After indictment or upon an information, the defendant is brought before the court to answer the charge. At arraignment, the defendant makes a plea. In minor crimes (misdemeanors), the arraignment may be part of the preliminary hearing—the defendant is informed of the charges and asked to make a plea. Felonies requiring a grand jury and indictment separate the preliminary hearing and the arraignment, which follows the indictment.

The defendant has three pleas available:

1. *Not guilty.* A plea of not guilty results in a trial. The defendant may waive a jury, but the Constitution guarantees the right to a jury trial in criminal cases.

2. *Guilty.* The defendant admits commission of the crime and submits to the sentence of the court. Guilty pleas are usually the result of a plea negotiation between the prosecution and the defense attorney, with the acquiescence of the defendant.

3. *Nolo contendere.* (not available in some jurisdictions; often not available in felony cases). *Nolo contendere,* literally "I do not wish

to contest," is equivalent to a guilty plea except that it does not admit guilt. It is treated the same as a guilty plea for the purposes of sentencing, but it cannot be used in later civil or criminal cases as an admission of guilt.

The court has discretion to accept a guilty or *nolo contendere* plea. The court may require a defendant to plead guilty or not guilty rather than *nolo contendere* and may also in its discretion refuse to accept a guilty plea. If the defendant refuses to make a plea, the court will assume this refusal to be a plea of not guilty and set the case for trial.

A special plea of "not guilty by reason of insanity" is available in many jurisdictions; this subject is more fully covered in Chapter 10. This plea admits commission of the acts with which the defendant is charged but negates the critical element of criminal intent on the basis of the defendant's insanity.

Pretrial

In many respects the pretrial phase is reminiscent of civil procedure. Pretrial motions are available, such as the motion to suppress evidence. Discovery procedures are similar except for protections against self-incrimination. Plea bargaining bears some resemblance to the strategies for negotiating settlements in civil cases.

Ethical dilemmas in life and in law involve not only determining the right course of action, but also sometimes doing what appears to be morally wrong because it is ethically right, as illustrated by the *Belge* case. It concerns the issue of attorney-client confidentiality. With a few exceptions, lawyers may not reveal statements made to them by clients in confidence without the consent of the clients. This allows clients to truthfully disclose facts to the attorney without fear that these facts will be disclosed to others.

Trial

In most respects the criminal trial is conducted in the same way as a civil trial. The prosecutor has the burden of proving the case. Each side presents its witnesses and cross-examines witnesses for the other side. There are opening statements, closing arguments, and so on. The major difference in the nature of the proceedings comes from the much higher standard that the prosecutor must meet, that of proving guilt beyond a reasonable doubt. Another major difference is that the defendant may not be compelled to testify. In one respect this right is illusory. It is human nature to expect the defendant to take the witness stand and declare innocence. If a criminal defendant declines to testify, the judge will instruct the jury that they should not draw any conclusions from this since the defendant is

PEOPLE
v.
BELGE
390 N.Y.S.2d 867 (1976)

[In 1973 Robert Garrow, who was charged with child molestation, was represented by attorney Frank Armani. On July 28 of that year, Garrow encountered four young campers in the Adirondacks and held them at gunpoint. He then stabbed and killed one of them, Philip Domblewski. The three remaining campers later identified Garrow, who was captured several days later. Garrow requested that Armani represent him and Armani asked the help of Francis Belge in the defense. Both attorneys were appointed by the court as defense attorneys.

The attorneys persuaded Garrow to reveal the facts of his past, guaranteeing him that his disclosures were confidential and could not be revealed without his consent. Garrow admitted to three other killings, one involving a sixteen-year-old high school girl whom he had raped and killed and buried near a cemetery. He had also killed two university students who were camping, killing the young man first and then abducting his female companion for three days, raping her, and finally killing her and leaving her body in an abandoned mine shaft.

In an effort to check their client's story, Armani and Belge went to find the bodies of the two women and found them where Garrow said he had left them. Armani was uncertain as to his duties under the circumstances (parents of the two women were then attempting to find them); he posed a hypothetical situation similar to his dilemma before an appellate judge. The judge concluded that such information was confidential and advised Armani that he might be disbarred for disclosing it.

The attorneys attempted to plea bargain in Garrow's behalf, offering to provide information on unsolved crimes if Garrow's charges were reduced from murder to second-degree manslaughter. The offer was refused and the attorneys ultimately decided that, given three eyewitnesses to the Domblewski killing, Garrow's best defense was insanity. Garrow's personality and background of extensive abuse as a child made the insanity plea plausible. At trial Garrow also admitted to the other killings, but was nevertheless convicted of Domblewski's murder.

Following Garrow's testimony, Armani and Belge held a press conference to disclose their knowledge of the prior crimes and discovery of the bodies, but insisted that they had no choice but to keep the information secret, despite the continuing agony suffered by the families of the victims. The public was outraged by the attorneys' behavior and both were summoned before a grand jury on charges that they had violated New York law requiring a decent burial and reporting of death without medical attendance. Belge was indicted by the grand jury, but the case was later dismissed by the trial judge on the grounds that Belge was protected by his duty of nondisclosure and "the interests of justice." This decision was affirmed on appeal.]

Case Questions

1. Could the defense attorneys have ethically disclosed the whereabouts of the bodies through another means?
2. What limits on confidentiality could be imposed that could have changed the attorneys' conduct in this case?

exercising a constitutional right. Human nature, however, slants jurors toward a negative inference when the defendant refuses to take the opportunity to urge his or her innocence.

Sentencing

Sentencing procedures differ widely among the states. Historically, judges had wide discretion in sentencing because the range of imprisonment was broad (e.g., "one to ten years"). But some states have adopted guidelines that establish customary sentences for crimes. The judge must justify imposing a sentence more severe than the guidelines or risk reversal on appeal. Some crimes in some states now call for mandatory minimum imprisonment, limiting the judge's discretion. Federal prosecutions follow sentencing guidelines as well.

There are a number of alternatives to incarceration. In recent years, judges have become reluctant to send convicted criminals to jail. This is partly because our jails are full and partly because numerous studies have shown that incarceration tends to breed career criminals rather than prepare them for a return to society. It is now rare for a person on first conviction of nonviolent lesser crimes to be sent to prison.

Among alternatives to incarceration, the oldest is probation. Probation is ordered for a fixed period of time, during which the probationer is subject to stringent conditions, the violation of which may result in incarceration. The probationer is monitored by a probation officer, who ideally not only checks for violations of probation but also serves as a personal counselor to aid the probationer in obtaining employment and making appropriate choices in conduct and career.

A convicted criminal may be sentenced to perform community service. The accused may also avoid conviction by having the judge withhold adjudication under specified conditions. Some jurisdictions allow pretrial diversion, which postpones and usually obviates the need for trial if the accused meets certain conditions, typically the performance of community service. The criminal justice system recognizes that incarceration can be detrimental not only to the criminal but also to society. In addition, the effect of conviction may be a serious impediment to a person's career, so young first offenders are often treated leniently.

Prison alternatives are frequently the result of plea bargaining and offer the judge considerable discretion in the treatment of offenders. This feature of the criminal justice system distinguishes it from civil procedure. In criminal cases, the court is not concerned simply with the determination of guilt and the award of penalties, but also with the regulation of conduct and the protection of society.

Appeal

In most respects criminal appeals are similar to those in civil procedure. Appellate courts, however, jealously guard against infringements of basic constitutional rights, such as involuntary confessions and illegal searches and seizures, in an effort to ensure fairness to the accused. The right to counsel is the subject of many appeals. Indigent defendants are appointed counsel from the public defender's office or private counsel. Public defenders typically have heavy case loads and may not always be able to devote as much attention to each case as it deserves. Private attorneys often serve on a *pro bono* basis and are under pressure to devote their time to paying clients. This may or may not result in neglect of criminal cases, but those who are convicted often use this argument to claim ineffective assistance of counsel, in an effort to obtain a new trial.

Although prejudicial error is the basis for reversal of rulings on the law, jury instructions, and so on, as in civil cases, the test of error in factfinding is necessarily different in a criminal trial because the test is guilt beyond a reasonable doubt. On appeal, a verdict of guilty is tested against a standard that asks whether "no trier of fact could have found proof beyond a reasonable doubt." Like "clearly erroneous" and "substantial evidence," this test shows great deference to factfinding at trial and makes it difficult to challenge on this basis.

Habeas Corpus

The writ of habeas corpus provides prisoners with a remedy not available in civil cases. Because it challenges the lawfulness of detention, habeas corpus is often used as a means to obtain review of a case in addition to appeal.

The *Whiteside* case shows how a clever defendant can manipulate attorneys, the law, and the Constitution. Criminal defense requires great attention to ethical conduct, but sometimes a client can put an attorney in a position in which there is no easy course to pursue.

Summary

Criminal procedure is similar to civil procedure in the steps it follows from pretrial to trial, in the presentation of evidence, and in the adversarial nature of the proceedings. There are important differences, however, many of which are based on constitutional rights of the accused. The Bill of Rights forms a skeletal code of criminal procedure that has been elaborated through appellate decisions. Among the more important rights guaranteed an accused are the privilege against self-incrimination, the right to an attorney even for those who cannot afford one, the right to a speedy and public trial, the right to be free of cruel and unusual punishment, and the right against the imposition of excessive bail.

Criminal procedure involves initial steps to assure that the accusation of crime is well grounded: the requirement of probable cause for

WHITESIDE
v.
SCURR
U.S. Court of Appeals, Second Circuit
744 F.2d 1323 (2d Cir. 1984)

The problem presented on the merits in this case is what kind of action defense counsel, representing a defendant in a criminal case, may constitutionally pursue when counsel believes that the client intends to testify falsely. This issue implicates both due process and effective assistance of counsel considerations and has been extensively debated, but by no means resolved, by several courts and many commentators.

* * *

Our ... analysis does not deal with the ethical problem inherent in appellant's claim. We are concerned only with the constitutional requirements of due process and effective assistance of counsel. As the ABA Model Rules [state], the Constitution prevails over rules of professional ethics, and a lawyer who does what the sixth and fourteenth amendments command cannot be charged with violating any precepts of professional ethics. This is a very controversial matter and we commend counsel for conscientiously attempting to address the problem of client perjury in a manner consistent with professional responsibility.

* * *

In the present case the state supreme court found that "counsel was convinced with good cause to believe [appellant's] proposed testimony would be deliberately untruthful," and that counsel had based this belief upon an independent investigation and prior discussions with appellant. ... For the purposes of our analysis, we presume that [Whiteside] would have testified falsely. We recognize, of course, that criminal defendants' privilege to testify in their own defense does not include the right to commit perjury. However, the fact that appellant would have committed perjury does not mean that appellant has waived his right to a fair trial, due process or effective assistance of counsel.

... Counsel's actions prevented appellant from testifying falsely. We hold that counsel's action deprived appellant of due process and effective assistance of counsel. ... "[W]e are acutely aware of the anomaly presented when mistrial must result from counsel's bona fide efforts to avoid professional irresponsibility. We find no escape, however, from the conclusion that fundamental requisites of fair trial have been irretrievably lost."

The Constitution guarantees a fair trial through the Due Process Clauses, but it defines the basic elements of a fair trial largely through the several provisions of the Sixth Amendment, including the Counsel Clause ... .

... The Sixth Amendment recognizes the right to the assistance of counsel because it envisions counsel's playing a role that is critical to the ability of the adversarial system to produce just results. An accused is entitled to be assisted by an attorney, whether retained or appointed, who plays the role necessary to ensure that the trial is fair. ...

Counsel's ability to serve as an effective advocate, in turn, depends upon the defendant's ability to disclose information fully and in confidence to counsel. When an attorney unnecessarily discloses the confidences of [the] client, [the attorney] creates a chilling effect which inhibits the mutual trust and independence necessary to effective representation.

... Counsel's actions, in particular the threat to testify against appellant, indicate that a conflict of interest had developed between counsel and appellant, even though this conflict was admittedly precipitated by appellant's intention to testify falsely. At this point counsel had become a potential adversary and ceased to serve as a zealous advocate of appellant's interests. ...

Counsel's actions also impermissibly compromised appellant's right to testify in his own defense by conditioning continued representation by counsel and confidentiality upon appellant's restricted testimony. ...

We wish to stress that our task is not at all to determine whether counsel behaved in an ethical fashion. That question is governed solely by the Iowa Code of Professional Responsibility, as it was in effect at the time of the trial in this case, and as it has been authoritatively interpreted by the Supreme Court of Iowa. The Supreme Court of Iowa is the last word on all questions of state law, and the Code of Professional Responsibility is a species of state law.

* * *

Here, counsel went so far in his (at least initially) commendable zeal to avoid deceiving the court that he became an adversary to his own client. In this situation, we believe that appellant did not receive the effective assistance of counsel.

Accordingly, the judgment of the district court is reversed and the case is remanded to the district court with directions to grant the petition for writ of habeas corpus if the state does not begin new trial proceedings within a period to be determined by the district court.

Case Questions

1. If Whiteside's attorney had followed the ABA standard, would the unorthodox line of questioning and the failure to mention the defendant's testimony make it obvious to an astute judge and prosecutor that the defendant had perjured himself?
2. Inspect *Lowery v. Cardwell*, 575 F.2d 730 (9th Cir.) (cited in *Whiteside*). Could a clever defendant use perjury both to gain an acquittal and to appeal a conviction?
3. Both the Iowa Supreme Court and the U.S. Court of Appeals commended Whiteside's attorney for his ethical stand, yet his conduct resulted in "ineffective assistance of counsel" and a reversal of Whiteside's conviction. Does this make sense?
4. If an attorney allows a client to perjure himself or herself in a criminal trial, is the attorney providing effective assistance of counsel while committing an ethical violation?

arrest and for warrants (arrest or search warrants); of initial appearance before a magistrate after arrest; of preliminary hearing; and of grand jury indictment and arraignment.

The major differences between criminal and civil trials are the right of the accused in a criminal trial not to be compelled to testify, the exclusion of improperly obtained evidence, and the burden of proof on the prosecution to prove guilt beyond a reasonable doubt.

Review Questions

1. Why do grand juries usually indict the defendants brought before them?

2. When is the privilege against self-incrimination usually exercised?

3. What is a custodial interrogation?

4. Who usually brings a petition for a writ of habeas corpus?

5. Which principle in the Bill of Rights is considered by the courts to express an evolving standard, which may be more strict as time passes?

226 FOUNDATIONS OF LAW

6. The exclusionary rule has frequently been criticized because it allows guilty persons to go free merely to discipline the police. What counterarguments can you make to this charge?

7. At what point should a police officer inform persons of their Miranda rights?

8. What advantages are there to pleading *nolo contendere*?

9. Should the role of the criminal justice system be to punish or rehabilitate the offender?

10. Should plea bargaining be abolished?

11. What is the difference in the burden of proof between criminal and civil cases?

Exercises

1. Do the statutes in your state express a speedy trial standard? What are the time periods, and when do they start to run?

2. Find your state constitution and compare its protections for criminal defendants with those expressed in the U.S. Constitution.

3. Under what circumstances are grand jury indictments required in your state? May a criminal case be brought on an "information"?

4. Who handles the criminal defense of indigents in your state?

DEATH ROW PARALEGALS

Mark Curriden

The mission of Malikkah Rollins, Ellie Hopkins and Chris Cox is to save their clients from the electric chair. The three are paralegals at the Georgia Appellate Resource Center, a public agency that represents inmates on death row.

It's a job that requires 60-hour work weeks, except when a client is under a death warrant. It's a stressful job. One hundred and ten inmates on death row look to these paralegals to save their lives.

The Caseload

Each paralegal handles about 15 to 20 cases at a time. Three or four of those are are always on the active, highly intensive list. A case usually arrives on their desk a few weeks or months after the the direct appeal has failed. Sometimes they do not hear about a case until weeks or days prior to the first scheduled execution date (which is never carried out; routine stays are issued so that new appeals can be filed).

They start by pulling the case file at the Georgia Supreme Court, which contains a summary of all the facts of the case and the names of the defense lawyers. They then visit the original defense lawyer to see if he or she has a copy of all of the pre-trial hearings, pre-trial motions, trial testimony and arguments made on appeal. They also review old newspaper clips for information about the case and trial. The record they accumulate will amount to tens-of-thousands of pages of court records—documents they must read along with all recent court rulings and articles about death penalty defense work. "We must know the law and what the courts are looking for before we know what to search for."

Their Clients

Security around the prison is intense. The prison is surrounded by electric barbed wire and guards armed with shotguns. To get to death row, the paralegals must have security clearance, leave all personal items at the front gate and walk through a long tunnel where guards escort them to a holding area. The main goal of the first visit is to gain the trust of the inmate, and explain the efforts that will be made on their behalf. Over a period of a few days, each paralegal tries to get as much information out of the inmate as possible, while assuring him that everything possible will be done. Because many of the defendants did not take the witness stand during the trial, the inmates are telling their stoty for the first time.

The Investigation

The goal in every death row case is to reconstruct each facet of the trial. They start with the state's main witnesses. Of course, there are the police detectives, but they are seldom any help. Family members of the victim are usually none too eager to cooperate either. They each travel thousands of miles a year going across the country tracking down witnesses and leads. A major goal is to identify and find confidential informants or sources used by the police during the investigation. For example, if the police used informants to develop the case and the paralegals are able to prove that there really was no snitch or that the informant lied, the evidence may be inadmissible and the conviction could be in jeopardy.

In a growing number of cases, much of the paralegals' attention is focused on how the jury was selected and what happened during the deliberations. "One of the first things we do is investigate a possible Batson violation." (A Batson violation refers to the 1986 U.S. Supreme Court case *Batson v. Kentucky* where the court ruled that prosecutors could not use their peremptory strikes to remove black people from the jury pool just because of their race. *Batson* had been an issue in several previous death penalty cases from Georgia.) The next step is to interview each juror who sat in judgement of their client to see if anything unusual occurred during deliberations.

The third and final angle to investigate is any mitigating circumstances. This involves extensive interviews with the inmate's family. They also look into each defendant's educational history for evidence of mental illness or retardation. Besides family members, they interview old teachers, ministers, next-door neighbors and family doctors.

The Final Appeal

When the state moves forward with its plan to execute their client, the paralegals work feverishly to firm up their evidence for presentation in court. Dozens of copies of each brief and affidavits from witnesses must be filed at the various court clerks' offices. Then there's the hard part—dealing with the client. "They look to us to help them prepare to die."

Reprinted with permission from *Legal Assistant Today* magazine.

CHAPTER 10

CRIMINAL LAW

CHAPTER OUTLINE

Introduction

With a basic knowledge of criminal procedure, we can now turn to the substantive law of crimes. Because substantive criminal law varies from state to state, a concise catalog of American crimes is not possible. Instead, this chapter concentrates on underlying issues related to criminal concepts of fault and culpability involved in the criminal act and in criminal intent, especially the latter.

Criminal Law and the Paralegal

Paralegals are currently underutilized in criminal work. Much of criminal work involves plea bargaining and trial work that can be done only by an attorney. Also, many criminal defense attorneys work as sole practitioners or in small firms where a large staff is not cost-efficient. The most promising area for paralegals is public employment, assisting prosecutors and public defenders. In addition, many government agencies have positions in which legal training and skills are useful. No understanding of American law is complete, however, without studying the basics of criminal law.

Definition

There is no adequate substantive definition of crime. The condemnation of heinous acts against persons, such as murder, is a common feature of human societies; but property crimes, crimes against the state, and regulatory crimes—and the penalties for their violation—reflect arbitrary decisions of rulemakers that vary considerably from nation to nation and even from one American state to another, depending on perceived needs to regulate behavior. The criminal law as presently constituted is a compilation of specific prohibited acts. In a sense, a *crime* may be defined simply as an act that violates the criminal law. In the American legal system, a line has been drawn between acts that are regulated by criminal law process and those for which redress is sought through the civil law process depending on whether punishment or compensation is sought. In many instances, a specific act may give rise to both civil and criminal legal actions.

Thus, *criminal law* may be defined as the list of crimes promulgated by the state. This list is essentially arbitrary in the sense that the state may penalize conduct that was formerly not criminal and may decriminalize conduct that was formerly criminal. Slavery was once legal in the United States; now it is not. Using cocaine was once legal; now it is not. It was once criminal to libel the president; now it is not.

Criminal law may be practically defined by concentrating on procedural distinctions. Crime is defined as a "wrong against society." This really means that the means to redress that wrong are monopolized by the state. Our system has evolved to put the redress of criminal conduct wholly in the hands of public officials, so we have created agencies of police, prosecutors, and judges to accomplish the task. A criminal case can be distinguished from a civil case by the fact that it is brought by the public prosecutor, enforcing a criminal statute.

In short, a crime is a crime because the legislature (or in some cases the court) says it is a crime.

Crime and Morality

There is a cliché that says, "You can't legislate morality." This is patently false, as that is exactly what law, especially criminal law, does. However, if the statement really means that immorality cannot be eliminated by passing criminal laws, then the statement is correct.

To say that a crime is a wrong against society is to assert that it is immoral; otherwise, it might merely be a wrong against a person and of little consequence to the public at large. There are certain offenses, like murder, which are virtually universally condemned in our society, and others, such as using marijuana, over which there is widespread disagreement. As social mores change, so too will the law. In part, the criminal law is a reflection of societal values, but it is also an effort by lawmakers to control and regulate conduct they consider politically undesirable. In the latter sense, the criminal law may impose morality rather than merely reflect it.

Mala in Se and *Mala Prohibita*

Some crimes, such as murder, are considered inherently wrong (*mala in se*). Others, which are not wrong in themselves but are nonetheless penalized (usually as a regulatory measure, such as failure to file an income tax return), are called *mala prohibita*. The recent proliferation of the latter offenses is derived from the growth of a highly bureaucratized and regulated political organization in the form of the state.

Consider the difference in nature between driving while intoxicated and driving with an expired automobile registration. The former represents a danger to the public and is *mala in se,* whereas the latter is primarily designed for revenue collection and recordkeeping and is *mala prohibita.*

In simpler times, a person could rely, with good reason, on the shared values of society to avoid breaking the moral injunctions of the law. Today, the bewildering complexity of a regulated society requires its members to consult the requirements of the law at every turn. The moral basis of the penal law has become obscure.

The confusion is exacerbated by rules penalizing offenses that are not criminal, a development of recent decades. Parking violations may no longer be misdemeanors (smaller crimes), as they were in the past. That ne'er-do-well who lets his auto registration expire will most certainly pay an extra fee when he renews, but why is he penalized? He was not caught, not charged, not convicted; he incurred no extra administrative expense. No doubt the late fee is called a *civil penalty,* something of a contradiction in terms. It is not labeled criminal, but it looks like a wrong and certainly not a private wrong, which would be a tort and covered by compensation law (see Chapter 11).

In short, a crime is not a crime if the legislature says it is not a crime.

Note on the Model Penal Code

The American Law Institute, which publishes the *Restatement of Torts* and the *Restatement of Contracts,* is also responsible for the Model Penal Code, an additional attempt to encourage uniformity in state law. Some areas of criminal law present a bewildering assortment of treatments among the states, and the Model Penal Code is often a leader in these areas rather than merely a restatement of the law. Many state laws are a hodgepodge of custom, past practice, and reformulation of the common law of crimes. The Model Penal Code attempts a more consistent and coherent statement of criminal law, but it has no official standing in state law that departs from it. Nevertheless, it is perhaps the most modern statement of American criminal law and is occasionally referred to here. It is an important research resource for those examining the law and is often quoted in judicial opinions.

Fault

Fault is as much a part of public wrongs (crimes) as it is of private wrongs (torts). In criminal law, however, the element of intent to do wrong is far more important than in tort law or contract law, where the law's attention is drawn to the injured party. Criminal law is primarily concerned with **punishment** of the criminal and the **deterrence** of crime; Anglo-American law aims at punishing those who deserve it. Traditionally, two components have been required to hold a person responsible for a crime: criminal act and criminal intent.

Criminal Act and Criminal Intent

To find a person guilty of a crime, there first must be a criminal act or *actus reus,* conduct that the law prohibits or absence of conduct that the law requires. With most crimes there must also be criminal intent or *mens rea* (literally, "criminal mind"). Before defining these requisites for a crime, consider the following cases:

1. A prostitute, knowing she has AIDS, continues to ply her trade and is charged with attempted murder.

2. Four seamen adrift in a lifeboat for twenty days decide that one of them must be sacrificed and eaten in order to save the rest. A young cabin boy in weakened condition is killed and eaten. The others are charged with murder.

3. A parent who belongs to a religious sect that believes that physical illness must be cured by prayer and faith refuses medical aid for a child suffering from leukemia. When the child dies, the parent is charged with manslaughter.

4. A young woman is kidnapped by a revolutionary gang, put in a closet for several weeks, and occasionally raped by her kidnappers. For several months she is subjected to political indoctrination and finally agrees to participate in a bank robbery with her abductors to get funds to continue the revolutionary cause. When finally found, she is charged with bank robbery.

5. A man meets a young woman in a bar; when asked by the bartender for identification proving her age, she shows a driver's license and is served a beer. She states to the man that she is twenty, and he believes it. Later they go to his apartment and have sexual relations. He is later charged with the crime of statutory rape, "sexual relations with a person under the age of 18."

BALLENTINE'S

punishment   The penalty for violating the law, which may include imprisonment, fine, or forfeiture.

deter   To discourage; to prevent from acting.

6. A woman believes her husband to be dead and remarries. When her first husband reappears, she is charged with bigamy.

7. A man picks up the wrong suitcase at an airport, believing it to be his, but later finds out his mistake and returns the suitcase. He is charged with theft.

8. A physician assists a terminally ill person to commit suicide by preparing and providing the means to end her life in a painless and comfortable way. He is charged with murder.

9. A game warden makes an image of a deer and puts it in the woods. When hunters shoot at the deer, the game warden arrests them for hunting deer out of season.

10. A man shoots a person intending to kill. It later turns out that the victim was already dead, although the shooting would have killed him if he had still been alive. The shooter is charged with homicide.

Criminal Act

Under early English law, most crimes were treated in the courts as common law crimes. Today, most crimes are statutory, though many of these are simply statutory refinements of the old common law crimes (e.g., murder, rape, burglary, embezzlement, etc.). In an earlier, settled, agricultural society, values relating to wrongs against persons and property were widely shared and understood, so that the courts could turn to customary values and religious principles to define criminal misconduct. Today, in our diverse and complex society, it is not always clear exactly what should be prohibited and what should not. The underlying policy of the criminal law is that a person should not be punished for conduct not expressly prohibited by the law. This requires the articulation of criminal law by the legislatures rather than the courts. All states have criminal statutes, and most do not allow conviction for common law crimes. Judges are not supposed to impose their perceptions of wrongful conduct; they must find that the conduct falls clearly within a criminal statute in order to hold a person guilty of a crime. Ultimately, a court must determine the meaning of the statute as it applies to a particular incident; but, as already noted, criminal statutes are strictly construed.

Actus reus requires that the criminal act be **voluntary**. At first blush, this would seem to be a feature of the mental state of the accused, part of the criminal intent (*mens rea*). *Voluntariness,* however, refers to whether the act was a product of free will, and does not address issues of motivation

---

BALLENTINE'S

voluntary   A word applied to an act freely done out of choice, not brought about by coercion, duress, or accident.

specific to *mens rea*. Examples of involuntary acts are those occurring during sleep, unconsciousness, or hypnosis and those caused by reflexes or convulsions.

Thoughts alone are not criminal; an act must occur. In general, speech is protected by the First Amendment, but speech is conduct and sometimes constitutes a crime, as with inciting to riot or promoting a conspiracy.

The failure to act, an omission, may also constitute *actus reus* in cases in which the law imposes a duty to act; for instance, when a parent fails to provide nourishment to a child or a person with knowledge of a felony fails to report such knowledge (misprision of a felony). Failure to meet a *moral* obligation to act is not a crime if there is no *legal* duty to act. Historically, American law has not recognized a duty to rescue; a person may stand by and watch another drown, even if saving the drowning person offers no risk to the potential rescuer. A duty arises only if the rescuer was in some way responsible for the peril or enjoys a status requiring rescue, such as a lifeguard.

Because criminal act is typically shown by physical evidence, it presents far fewer problems than criminal intent, in which a mental state must usually be inferred from the circumstances of the events of the crime.

Criminal Intent

An act may be voluntarily accomplished without entailing *mens rea*. The man who mistakenly took the wrong suitcase at the airport acted voluntarily but without criminal intent. The nature of the intent required for guilt varies significantly from one crime to another, and some strict liability crimes require no proof of criminal intent.

General Intent

The broadest form of intent is called *general intent,* to be distinguished from *specific intent,* discussed in the next section. General intent is the traditional form of *mens rea* derived from the common law. It requires that the actor intended a harmful act, but not that the specific result was intended. This may extend to reckless and negligent acts in which the actor acted with a "conscious disregard of a substantial and unjustifiable risk of harm" (recklessness) or, though lacking conscious disregard, nevertheless acted when a "reasonable person would have recognized a substantial and unjustifiable risk" (negligence). A person throwing a firecracker into a crowd of people would be guilty of resulting harm covered by a crime requiring only general intent.

Criminal intent is more convincingly shown if malice can be proven. General intent is a somewhat cloudy area because of the variety of harmful acts and the mysteries of the human mind and human motivation. With a few exceptions requiring powerful deterrents, the law and judicial decisions reflect a desire not to punish involuntary, innocent, and accidental acts. The elements that make up a specific crime indicate the intention required.

Specific Intent

As a rule of thumb, statutes that use the words "knowingly," "willfully," or "maliciously" require *specific intent*. These statutes are most easily satisfied when the defendant intended the precise results of the wrongful act (e.g., shooting someone in the head at close range). Defendants will naturally assert a lack of intent or knowledge, but the courts and juries are disinclined to accept such assertions. It may be enough that a knowledge of a high risk was present, as measured by what a reasonable person would know. The problem is that this is a subjective measure, that is, what the defendant knew or intended. Because only the defendant knows for certain what his or her knowledge and intent were, the defendant theoretically is the most reliable witness as to that intent. However, in practice the defendant's statements are highly unreliable because self-interest often distorts the truth. What was intended may be inferred from the defendant's conduct, and the defendant's self-serving statements may be treated with skepticism. The *Jewell* case demonstrates the court's reluctance to accept a defendant's self-serving assertions.

Mens rea is a confusing area of criminal law because it attempts to define subjective knowledge, volition, and intent. To paraphrase one justice's comments about the definition of contracts, perhaps the definition of *mens rea* consists of the totality of the cases that define it. As a practical matter, this means that applying criminal intent to a given case requires fitting that case into similar cases of the past. It then becomes clear that the method of the common law prevails even in an area that ostensibly has been preempted by statute.

Long ago, *mens rea* may have appeared to be a relatively simple concept, but as we come to know more about the complexity of the human psyche, the legal concept has become more and more difficult to state with certainty. In questionable cases, a great deal of research into precedents may be appropriate.

All the research in the world, however, means little to the jury. Through its deliberations, the jury mysteriously arrives at conclusions about the defendant's intent. The jury is likely to pay more attention to common sense and experience than the technicalities of the jury instructions. In the *Jewell* case, some jurors must have asked, "Why did he have a secret compartment in his trunk? Surely he must have known, or at least guessed, there was marijuana in the secret compartment."

**UNITED STATES of America,
Plaintiff-Appellee
v.
Charles Demore JEWELL,
Defendant-Appellant
U.S. Court of Appeals, 9th Circuit
532 F.2d 697 (9th Cir. 1976)**

[This is an appeal from a conviction for violating the Comprehensive Drug Abuse Prevention and Control Act of 1970. Jewell was found to have knowingly transported marijuana in the trunk of his car from Mexico to the United States. The marijuana was concealed in a secret compartment behind the back seat of his car. Jewell insisted that he did not know the marijuana was in the secret compartment. Whether he knew or did not know was a fact question for the jury. If he knew, he was guilty of the crime; but the trial judge was concerned that even a lack of knowledge could have been the result of "deliberate ignorance" and gave the following instruction to the jury:

> The Government can complete their burden of proof by proving, beyond a reasonable doubt, that if the defendant was not actually aware that there was marijuana in the vehicle he was driving when he entered the United States his ignorance in that regard was solely and entirely a result of his having made a conscious purpose to disregard the nature of that which was in the vehicle, with a conscious purpose to avoid learning the truth.

Jewell appealed on the grounds that this instruction was not an accurate statement of the law with regard to criminal intent and that the jury should have been instructed that to find guilt, they must find that he knew he was in possession of marijuana. The court of appeals upheld the trial court's jury instruction with the following reasoning:]

The substantive justification for the rule is that deliberate ignorance and positive knowledge are equally culpable. The textual justification is that in common understanding one "knows" facts of which he is less than absolutely certain. To act "knowingly," therefore, is not necessarily to act only with positive knowledge, but also to act with an awareness of the high probability of the existence of the fact in question. When such awareness is present, "positive" knowledge is not required.

* * *

[D]efining "knowingly" makes actual knowledge unnecessary. "[T]hose who traffic in heroin will inevitably become aware that the product they deal with is smuggled, *unless they practice a studied ignorance to which they are not entitled.*"
... Holding that this term [knowingly] introduces a requirement of positive knowledge would make deliberate ignorance a defense. It cannot be doubted that those who traffic in drugs would make the most of it. This is evident from the number of appellate decisions reflecting conscious avoidance of positive knowledge of the presence of contraband—in the car driven by the defendant or in which he is a passenger, in the suitcase or package he carries, in the parcel concealed in his clothing.

* * *

The conviction is affirmed.
Kennedy, J., dissenting: [T]he "conscious purpose" jury instruction is defective in three respects. First, it fails to mention the requirement that Jewell have been aware of a high probability that a controlled substance was in the car. It is not culpable to form "a conscious purpose to avoid learning the truth" unless one is aware of facts indicating a high probability of that truth. ...

The second defect in the instruction as given is that it did not alert the jury that Jewell could not be convicted if he "actually believed" there was no controlled substance in the car. ...

Third, the jury instruction clearly states that Jewell could have been convicted even if found ignorant or "not actually aware" that the car contained a controlled substance. This is unacceptable because true ignorance, no matter how unreasonable, cannot provide a basis for criminal liability when the statute requires knowledge.

Case Questions

1. Why did the majority not adopt the dissent's approach?
2. In a portion of the dissenting opinion omitted above, the dissenting judge declared his approval of the Model Penal Code § 2.02(7), which reads:

    Requirement of Knowledge Satisfied by Knowledge of High Probability. When knowledge of the existence of a particular fact is an element of an offense, such knowledge is established if a person is aware of a high probability of its existence, unless he actually believes that it does not exist.

    Does this imply the dissent's conclusion that "true ignorance, no matter how unreasonable, cannot provide a basis for criminal liability when the statute requires knowledge ..."?

3. Perhaps when Jewell spoke with his attorney, the attorney said, "The statute requires that you *knowingly* transported controlled substances. You didn't know that what was in the secret compartment was *actually* marijuana, *did* you?" And suppose Jewell responded, "I didn't actually *see* marijuana put in the car; I didn't actually *know* there was marijuana in there." Can attorney and client then in good conscience go to court and base their defense on lack of knowledge? Is it unethical for the attorney to lead the client in this way?

4. Is not subjective knowledge always arguable? If Jewell actually knew there was marijuana placed in the secret compartment, but he left his car for an hour, would he *know* the marijuana was still there if he did not check to see? Does this deliberate ignorance principle furnish a reasonable alternative to the philosophical problem of knowledge?

5. Does the rule in *Jewell* accord with the principle of strict construction of criminal statutes?

6. Do you think the jury would have found differently if it had been instructed as the dissent suggested?

Preparation of a jury case must pay at least as much attention to the mentality of the jury as to the law.

Specific Problems of Criminal Intent

The nature and degree of criminal intent required varies from crime to crime. In some instances, intent refers simply to the knowledge the accused must have. For example, crimes involving theft commonly require that the defendant intended to deprive someone permanently of property, knowing that the property belonged to another. Such a requirement would save our airport suitcase mistake because there was neither an intent to permanently deprive nor a knowledge of true ownership at the time of the taking.

Crimes against property, such as burglary, embezzlement, and larceny, are usually economically motivated, so intent can readily be inferred. Unless these involve violence or large amounts of money, they receive only modest attention in the press, which tends to focus on bizarre and violent crime. As a result, the popular conception of crime is distorted.

Other crimes require special ingredients for criminal intent that make them quite distinct. Murder, rape, and conspiracy are examples.

Murder

Murder is the unlawful killing by one human being of another with malice aforethought. It is distinguished from manslaughter (also called murder in the second degree) by the requirement of "malice afore-thought," often referred to as premeditation or malice prepense, depending on one's preference for Old English, new Latin, or French. The requirement of premeditation removes from this most heinous of crimes homicides that are accidental but blameworthy (i.e., caused by culpable negligence) and those occurring in a moment of passion or anger. At the very least, murder requires some reflection about what one is doing or sufficient time between the beginning of the act and its completion to provide an opportunity to desist from following through. Obviously, a planned killing satisfies premeditation. In other cases, proof of premeditation typically takes the form of showing that the accused thought about what he or she was doing and then did it.

Murder cases present a very distorted picture of the criminal law. One reason is the requirement of evil intent; another is the availability of the death penalty in most states. Because of our fear of sending an innocent person to the gallows, a mistake that can never be corrected, the propriety of conduct by the police and prosecution and the conduct of the trial are scrutinized to a degree unusual in other cases. Because of media attention to these cases, the public forms a strange picture of the criminal law and criminal procedure.

Rape

Forcible **rape** is the most serious of sex crimes. At present there is little uniformity either in terminology or definition among the states with regard to sex crimes. On the one hand, we have seen a strong movement toward decriminalizing consensual sexual relations, but different states have shown different approaches depending on whether the partners are married, heterosexual, or homosexual. On the other hand, there

--------------------------------BALLENTINE'S--------------------------------

rape Sexual intercourse with a woman by force or by putting her in fear or in circumstances in which she is unable to control her conduct or to resist ... . Under the common law definition of the crime, only a female can be raped and only a male can perpetrate the crime. In recent years, however, courts in several states have held that the rape statutes of their jurisdictions are gender-neutral and apply equally to perpetrators of either sex.

has been a movement to refine the definitions of sex crimes to protect specific categories of victims—the young, the elderly, the mentally and physically handicapped. Because this is presently a dynamic area of legislation, we encounter a lack of uniformity among the states.

With regard to the mental state required for forcible rape, the problem is compounded by its nonconsensual element. Not only the defendant's mental state is at issue but also the victim's. It is a defense to forcible, as opposed to statutory, rape that the alleged victim consented to the sexual act. Because sexual relations usually occur in private without witnesses, ascertaining the mental states of perpetrator and victim presents difficult problems of proof.

An essential element of rape is the use of force. What constitutes force is problematic, and the relationship between force and consent raises additional questions. If a man holds a knife to a woman's throat and asks her if she wants to have sexual relations, is her affirmative answer consent? Consent under duress is not consent at all.

To illustrate problems inherent in rape, consider the following hypothetical cases, which are drawn from two actual cases but are highly embellished:

1. A woman and a man meet in a bar; the woman is scantily clad, with a hemline that barely conceals that she is wearing no underwear. She agrees to have sexual intercourse with the man for money, and they go off in his van. She later accuses him of rape. She has prior convictions for prostitution, and on a prior occasion charged rape against another man under roughly similar circumstances. The defendant is wanted in another state on a rape charge.

2. Man and woman meet in a singles bar. The woman is dressed provocatively and plays the temptress. After many drinks, they end up in her apartment. She puts on a nun's habit and declares she is a virgin and married to God. Then she takes her clothes off, and they have intercourse; all the while she is saying "No. No. No. I'm a virgin" (which she is not). It turns out later that the woman is psychotic, with multiple personalities, and the man is of below-average intelligence. He acknowledges overcoming some slight efforts of physical resistance on her part.

In both of these illustrations, a rape may have occurred, but the factual issues raised would make it very difficult for a jury to convict, relying on proof of guilt beyond a reasonable doubt. Rape is a serious crime that occurs with significant frequency in our society and is likely to leave victims with permanent emotional damage, yet it is difficult to prove and usually goes unreported. The commands of the criminal law have failed to control primal urges toward violence and sex. Recently, focus has changed toward victim-oriented services and enlightened treatment of victims in court.

Conspiracy

Conspiracy presents problems for both *mens rea* and *actus reus*, in that it addresses the planning of crime rather than its actual commission.

(1) *Definition of Conspiracy.* A person is guilty of conspiracy with another person or persons to commit a crime if with the purpose of promoting or facilitating its commission he:

(a) agrees with such other person or persons that they or one or more of them will engage in conduct which constitutes such crime or an attempt or solicitation to commit such crime; or

(b) agrees to aid such other person or persons in the planning or commission of such crime or of an attempt or solicitation to commit such crime.

* * *

(5) *Overt Act.* No person may be convicted of conspiracy to commit a crime, other than a felony of the first or second degree, unless an overt act in pursuance of such conspiracy is alleged and proved to have been done by him or by a person with whom he conspired.

(6) *Renunciation of Criminal Purpose.* It is an affirmative defense that the actor, after conspiring to commit a crime, thwarted the success of the conspiracy, under circumstances manifesting a complete and voluntary renunciation of his criminal purpose.

Model Penal Code § 5.03.

Under these rules, one may effectively be charged with conspiracy for participating in the planning of a bank robbery even if one did not plan to participate in the actual bank robbery, conduct that society may appropriately condemn as criminal; but the crime of conspiracy may cast a wide net to include many persons marginally associated with others engaged in criminal conduct.

The *Lauria* case involves call girls and the telephone answering service they used. One may wonder why the police and prosecutor were anxious to find the owner of the answering service guilty of conspiracy to commit prostitution. The answer may lie in an effort to find another crime against the call girls. When the conspiracy count against Lauria failed, it also failed against the call girls.

Attempt

The attempt to commit a crime is also a crime. In its simplest form, an attempt is a crime that failed. The deterrent aspect of the criminal law should apply with equal force to attempts as to successful crimes (for instance, it would seem useful to deter bank robbers whether or not they are successful). The punitive aspect of the criminal law, however, has traditionally been more lenient with attempted crimes, which are usually of lesser grade or carry a lesser sentence. Model Penal Code

The PEOPLE of the State of California,
Plaintiff and Appellant

v.

Louis LAURIA et al.,
Defendants and Respondents
California District Court of Appeal,
Second District, Division 2
251 Cal. App. 2d 471, 59
Cal. Rptr. 628 (1967)

In an investigation of call-girl activity the police focused their attention on three prostitutes actively plying their trade on call, each of whom was using Lauria's telephone answering service, presumably for business purposes. ...

On April 1 Lauria and the three prostitutes were arrested. Lauria complained to the police that this attention was undeserved, stating that Hollywood Call Board had 60 to 70 prostitutes on its board while his own service had only 9 or 10, that he kept separate records for known or suspected prostitutes for the convenience of himself and the police. On a subsequent voluntary appearance before the Grand Jury Lauria testified he had always cooperated with the police. But he admitted he knew some of his customers were prostitutes ... .

Lauria and the three prostitutes were indicted for conspiracy to commit prostitution, and nine overt acts were specified. Subsequently the trial court set aside the indictment as having been brought without reasonable or probable cause. The People have appealed, claiming that a sufficient showing of an unlawful agreement to further prostitution was made. ...

Under what circumstances does a supplier become a part of a conspiracy to further an illegal enterprise by furnishing goods or services which he knows are to be used by the buyer for criminal purposes? ...

Both the element of *knowledge* of the illegal use of the goods or services and the element of *intent* to further that use must be present in order to make the supplier a participant in a criminal conspiracy.

Proof of *knowledge* is ordinarily a question of fact and requires no extended discussion in the present case. The knowledge of the supplier was sufficiently established when Lauria admitted he knew some of his customers were prostitutes and admitted he knew that Terry, an active subscriber to his service, was a prostitute. ...

The more perplexing issue in the case is the sufficiency of proof of *intent* to further the criminal enterprise. The element of intent may be proved either by direct evidence, or by evidence of circumstances from which an intent to further a criminal enterprise by supplying lawful goods or services may be inferred. ...

Essentially, the People argue that knowledge alone of the continuing use of his telephone facilities for criminal purposes provided a sufficient basis from which his intent to participate in those criminal activities could be inferred.

1. Intent may be inferred from knowledge, when the purveyor of legal goods for illegal use has acquired a stake in the venture. ...

In the present case, no proof was offered of inflated charges for the telephone answering services furnished the codefendants.

2. Intent may be inferred from knowledge, when no legitimate use for the goods or services exists. ...

However, there is nothing in the furnishing of telephone answering service which would necessarily imply assistance in the performance of illegal activities. Nor is any inference to be derived from the use of an answering service by women, either in any particular volume of calls, or outside normal working hours. ...

3. Intent may be inferred from knowledge, when the volume of business with the buyer is grossly disproportionate to any legitimate demand, or when sales for illegal use amount to a high proportion of the seller's total business. ...

No evidence of any unusual volume of business with prostitutes was presented by the prosecution against Lauria. ...

With respect to misdemeanors, we conclude that positive knowledge of the supplier that his products or services are being used for criminal purposes does not, without more, establish an intent of the supplier to participate in the misdemeanors. With respect to felonies, we do not decide the converse, viz. that in all cases of felony knowledge of criminal use alone may justify an inference of the supplier's intent to participate in the crime. ...

Under these circumstances, although proof of Lauria's knowledge of the criminal activities of his patrons was sufficient to charge him with that fact, there was insufficient evidence that he intended to further their criminal activities, and hence insufficient proof of his participation in a criminal conspiracy with his codefendants to further prostitution. Since the conspiracy centered around the activities of Lauria's telephone answering service, the charges against his codefendants likewise fail for want of proof.

In absolving Lauria of complicity in a criminal conspiracy we do not wish to imply that the public authorities are without remedies to combat modern manifestations of the world's oldest profession. Licensing of telephone answering services under the police power, together with the revocation of licenses for the toleration of prostitution, is a possible civil remedy. The furnishing of telephone answering service in aid of prostitution could be made a crime. Other solutions will doubtless occur to vigilant public authorities if the problem of call-girl activity needs further suppression.

The order is affirmed.

Case Questions

1. Why is knowledge of a criminal purpose not sufficient for conspiracy?
2. Did the state fail to establish Lauria's criminal intent? What were the issues with regard to intent?

§ 5.05(1) treats attempts as equal to the crime attempted, and a few states have adopted this policy. *Mens rea* can become confused in the area of attempt, as the *Guffey* and *Dlugash* cases demonstrate.

Strict Liability

Underlying the *mens rea* requirement is the traditional legal principle in criminal law of a *presumption of innocence*. *Mens rea* imposes a burden on the prosecution to show that the defendant acted out of evil intent. In recent years, however, legislatures have sometimes imposed strict criminal liability, thereby either eliminating the burden of proving *mens rea* or shifting to the defendant the burden of proving innocent motive.

Some precedent for strict liability can be found in the common law felony-murder rule, under which a person can be found guilty of murder without proof of premeditation if a person is killed during the perpetration of a felony. Some justification in the rule can be found in an attempt to deter the use of unreasonable force in the commission of a felony, but on rare occasions the rule has been applied with peculiar results, as when one of the felons is killed by police and the other co-felons are held accountable for felony-murder. The felony-murder rule has been subject to much criticism and is severely qualified in some jurisdictions.

IIII IIII

STATE
v.
GUFFEY et al.
Springfield Court of Appeals, Missouri
262 S.W.2d 152 (Mo. Ct. App. 1953)

[Missouri Conservation agents set up a stuffed deer hide in a field about fifty yards from the roadside, then lay in wait for "some citizen who might come that way, see the tempting bait and with visions of odoriferous venison cooking in pot or pan, decide not to wait until" the beginning of deer season. The defendants drove by with a spotlight and noticed the deer; the car stopped, followed by a shotgun blast. The defendants were arrested, and despite their testimony that they were out frog-hunting and shot at the "deer" thinking it was a wolf, were convicted of the misdemeanor of pursuit and taking of wildlife against rules and regulations.]

Bearing these definitions [of *pursue*] in mind, it seems to us that the State has wholly failed to make its case when it stands upon the proposition that defendants "pursued" a deer. In the first place there was no deer. The hide of a doe long since deceased filled with boards, excelsior and rods with eyes made of a reflective scotch tape, was not a deer within the meaning of the statute ... . The

dummy, such as it was, was a stationary affair, it could not run, could not jump, it could not flee from the rifle slug of a hunter. It was not wild and it had no life.

* * *

Undoubtedly the words "pursued"... and "pursue" as used in [the statute] mean to follow with the intention of overtaking, or to chase.

* * *

The State's evidence shows that one of the defendants did shoot the dummy but did they pursue, chase or follow a *deer* by shooting this stuffed defunct doe hide? It was not a deer. If the dummy had been actually taken (it could not be pursued), defendants would not have committed any offense. It is no offense to attempt to do that which is not illegal. ... Neither is it a crime to attempt to do that which it is legally impossible to do. For instance, it is no crime to attempt to murder a corpse because it cannot be murdered.

* * *

If the State's evidence showed an attempt to take the dummy, it fell far short of proving an attempt to take a deer. We hold that the State wholly failed to make a case.

Case Questions

1. Did the state's case fail because of an absence of *actus reus* or *mens rea*?
2. In part of the case omitted, the court examined the meaning of the word "pursue" in great detail. Why was this necessary?

IIII IIII

Another example of traditional strict liability is covered in the crime of statutory rape, in which sexual relations with a person under a certain age eliminates the defense of consent and in many states denies the defendant the defense of a good faith belief that the victim was above the prescribed age. Again, a reasonable objective of protecting young and innocent or naive girls from predatory older males is used to justify strict liability. The so-called "sexual revolution" and the apparent promiscuity of American youth have caused many legislatures to tinker with the traditional age of consent, lowering the age of the

The PEOPLE of the State of New York,
Appellant
v.
Melvin DLUGASH,
Respondent.
Court of Appeals of New York
41 N.Y.2d 725, 363 N.E.2d 1155 (1977)

[Dlugash, Bush, and Geller had been drinking until three o'clock in the morning. Several times Geller, in whose apartment the incident occurred, had demanded that Bush pay $100 toward the rent since Bush had moved in with Geller. Bush threatened to shoot Geller if he would not shut up, and on the final demand Bush fired three shots at Geller, one of which went through Geller's lung and into his heart. A few minutes later, Dlugash fired several shots into Geller's head. When the investigating detective asked Dlugash why he did this, he said at first he did not really know, but when asked the third time, Dlugash said, "well, gee, I guess it must have been because I was afraid of Joe Bush." At trial, medical experts testified that the chest wounds would have killed Geller without prompt medical attention, but it was not clear whether Geller was still alive when Dlugash fired into his head. Dlugash did not testify at trial, but after the jury found him guilty of murder, he moved to set the verdict aside on the grounds that he was certain Geller was dead before Dlugash shot him, and his shots were made because Bush held a gun on him and said he would kill Dlugash if Dlugash did not shoot the body. On appeal ... , it was held that the state failed to prove beyond a reasonable doubt that Geller had been alive at the time Dlugash shot him; and also held him not guilty of attempted murder. The highest court came to a somewhat different conclusion:]

The criminal law is of ancient origin, but criminal liability for attempt to commit a crime is comparatively recent. At the root of the concept of attempt liability are the very aims and purposes of penal law. The ultimate issue is whether an individual's intentions and actions, though failing to achieve a manifest and malevolent criminal purpose, constitute a danger to organized society of sufficient magnitude to warrant the impositions of criminal sanctions. ... [One] concern centers on whether an individual should be liable for an attempt to commit a crime when, unknown to him, it was impossible to successfully complete the crime attempted. ... The 1967 revision of the Penal Law approached the impossibility defense to the inchoate crime of attempt in a novel fashion. The statute provides that, if a person engages in conduct which would otherwise constitute an attempt to commit a crime, "it is no defense to a prosecution for such attempt that the crime charged to have been attempted was, under the attendant circumstances, factually or legally impossible of commission, if such crime could have been committed had the attendant circumstances been as such person believed them to be." This appeal presents to us, for the first time, a case involving the application of the modern statute. We hold that, under the proof presented by the People at trial, defendant Melvin Dlugash may be held for attempted murder, though the target of the attempt may have already been slain, by the hand of another, when Dlugash made his felonious attempt.

[There follows a long discussion of the facts followed by the conclusion that the Appellate Division was correct in overturning the conviction for murder. The court then discusses the history of impossibility theory, concluding that legal impossibility was a defense, citing *Guffey*, "it is no crime to attempt to do that which is legal," while factual impossibility was not a defense ("Thus, a man could be held for attempted grand larceny when he picked an empty pocket.")]

In the belief that neither of the two branches of the traditional impossibility arguments detracts from the offender's moral culpability, the Legislature substantially carried the code's treatment of impossibility into the 1967 revision of the Penal Law. Thus, a person is guilty of an attempt when, with intent to commit a crime, he engages in conduct which tends to effect the commission of such crime. It is no defense that, under the attendant circumstances, the crime was factually or legally impossible of commission. ... Thus, if defendant believed the victim to be alive at the time of the shooting, it is no defense to the charge of attempted murder that the victim may have been dead.

* * *

The jury convicted the defendant of murder. Necessarily, they found that defendant intended

to kill a live human being. Subsumed within this finding is the conclusion that defendant acted in the belief that Geller was alive. Thus, there is no need for additional fact findings by a jury. ...

The Appellate Division erred in not modifying the judgment to reflect a conviction for the lesser included offense of attempted murder. ...

Case Questions

1. Consider the following fact situations:
   a. A person shoots a corpse in the head, knowing that the corpse is dead.
   b. A person shoots a corpse in the head, believing the corpse to be alive.
   c. A person intending to kill shoots at a figure in a bed, but there is no one there.
   d. A person shoots at someone, intending to kill, but misses.

   Which of these actions is the law of attempts designed to punish? Which would be attempts under the reasoning of *Dlugash*?

2. *Dlugash* refers to a New Jersey case in which the defendant agreed to perform an abortion, then illegal, upon a female undercover police investigator who was not pregnant. The defendant was found guilty, and it was "no defense that the defendant could not succeed in reaching his goal because of circumstances unknown to him." Is this reasoning sound?

3. The court cites another case in which it was held that "men who had sexual intercourse with a woman, with the belief that she was alive and did not consent to the intercourse, could be charged for attempted rape when the woman had, in fact, died from an unrelated ailment prior to the acts of intercourse." Is this reasoning sound?

4. What if the police have a sting operation and buy drugs from someone who believes the police to be drug dealers but sells them powdered sugar instead of drugs, intending to cheat the drug dealers? Has the seller committed a crime? An attempted crime?

victim when defenses are not allowed, providing for different grades of crime depending on the relative ages of the participants. Gender equality has also confused the issue. If a fourteen-year-old boy and a fourteen-year-old girl have sexual intercourse, who is the perpetrator and who is the victim? The states have come up with fifty different solutions to this problem.

The growth of strict liability, however, has occurred primarily in regulatory statutes. On the one hand, strict liability has been justified when a class of persons, such as the young, seem to warrant special protection, or when the danger to the public is particularly hazardous—as with alcohol, firearms, drugs, poisons. On the other hand, legislatures can be justly accused of relaxing the *mens rea* requirement simply to make conviction easier.

The Insanity Defense

No discussion of *mens rea* would be complete without mention of the insanity defense. A criminal defendant may plead "not guilty by reason of insanity." This plea acknowledges the commission of the criminal act but negates criminal intent because of the defendant's insanity. The policy basis for the defense is to hold accountable for crimes only those persons who freely chose to commit crimes. An additional reason for the defense is the inappropriateness of putting insane persons in with the general prison population. The insanity defense is very much like the defense of an involuntary act or the absence of criminal intent. The difference lies in acknowledging insanity, which typically results in commitment to a mental institution if insanity is proven.

The principal problem with insanity is defining it. Understanding the subjective states of the human mind is difficult even for psychologists and psychiatrists with extensive training and experience. Although some persons may be found to be insane by almost any measure, the line between sanity and insanity cannot be drawn with accuracy, yet the law requires that the line be drawn.

The English rule originating in the nineteenth-century *M'Naghten* case (10 Cl. & F. 200, 8 Eng. Rep. 718 [1843]) is still followed, with some modifications, in many American jurisdictions. Daniel M'Naghten suffered delusions that the Prime Minister was out to get him; M'Naghten shot and killed the Prime Minister's secretary, mistakenly believing the secretary to be the Prime Minister. Public outrage over M'Naghten's acquittal ultimately led to a consideration of the insanity defense by the House of Lords (England's "Supreme Court"). Consensus resulted in what is often called the "right-wrong test," namely, whether the accused suffered from a defect of mind such that he did not understand the nature of his act or did not know that it was wrong. This is a difficult test to meet because it requires a very serious mental imbalance.

The fields of psychology and psychiatry in the twentieth century have shown that we are much less in control of our minds and actions than was formerly believed, so other insanity tests have been adopted that lower the threshold of insanity for legal purposes. The issue of legal accountability for acts committed by someone with diminished mental capacity is very murky at present.

Insanity defenses frequently involve several highly paid expert witnesses. Prosecution witnesses testify that the defendant was sane at the time of the act, while defense witnesses argue precisely the opposite; the jury must attempt to arrive at the "truth" of defendant's mental state as described by experts who reconstruct that mental state after the fact.

A satisfactory resolution of these and other problems related to the insanity defense does not appear to be forthcoming.

Summary

Although the practice of criminal law tends to focus on problems of proof and other procedural issues, the substantive law of crimes is largely the concern of legislative enactments. There is considerable variability in the definitions of specific crimes from state to state. A general definition of crime is difficult to state, but crime may be identified procedurally by recourse to statutes that define crimes and delegate authority to police and prosecutors for the resolution of misconduct so labeled.

The criminal law penalizes conduct that offends the moral sentiments of the people. However, in our diverse society, moral commands are not always a matter of consensus. In addition, lawmakers provide criminal and civil penalties to encourage people to conform to an increasingly regulated state.

Traditionally, a crime requires both a criminal act and criminal intent on the part of the actor. The criminal act is defined by the elements of specific crimes, and it is up to the courts to determine whether a particular act falls within the prohibitions of the law.

Criminal intent, or *mens rea,* requires that the defendant in a criminal case be shown to have had a specific state of mind at the time of commission of the criminal act. Because subjective states of mind are difficult to ascertain, the intent of the defendant is a frequent issue in trials. Specific crimes often require or infer a specific state of mind. Questions of motivation, willfulness, premeditation, accident, knowledge, and intent are fact questions for the jury that may be quite confusing to resolve. The insanity defense is particularly problematic because of the inconsistency of legal and psychiatric definitions of insanity.

Review Questions

The following questions are designed both to test your understanding of the key points in the chapter and to make an initial inquiry into the substantive crimes of your state jurisdiction. Typically, statutory law is found in one long section or sections on the subject and is readily found from the index. The statutes themselves may be examined, but answers to the difficult questions presented would usually call at least for resort to the statute or code annotations, which give brief summaries of the rules found by the courts.

1. A prostitute, knowing she has AIDS, continues to ply her trade and is charged with attempted murder. It can be a crime to attempt a crime. What does the law of your state say about attempts? What is the likely outcome of this case? Is there a criminal act? Is there *mens rea*?

2. A parent who belongs to a religious sect that believes physical illness must be cured by prayer and faith refuses medical aid for a child suffering from leukemia. When the child dies, the parent is charged with manslaughter. Would it make a difference if the leukemia were medically incurable, though the child's life might have been prolonged with medical treatment? Does the parent's action fit into any definition of homicide found in your state's statutes? How does the First Amendment's freedom of religion fit into the case?

3. A young woman is kidnapped by a revolutionary gang, put in a closet for several weeks, and occasionally raped by her kidnappers. For several months she is subjected to political indoctrination and finally agrees to participate in a bank robbery with her abductors to get funds to continue the revolutionary cause. When finally found, she is charged with bank robbery. (This hypothetical case is based on the famous Patty Hearst case, in which she was convicted and went to prison. There was a serious question as to whether Patty Hearst was acting voluntarily or intentionally.) What do you think?

4. A man meets a young woman in a bar; when asked by the bartender for identification proving her age, she shows a driver's license and is served a beer. She states to the man that she is twenty, and he believes it. Later they go to his apartment and have sexual relations. He is later charged with the crime of statutory rape, "sexual relations with a person under the age of 18." What is the age (or ages) for statutory rape in your state? Does the defendant have a defense with regard to his reasonable belief in the age of the girl?

5. A woman believes her husband to be dead and remarries. When her first husband reappears, she is charged with bigamy. Bigamy has traditionally been a strict liability crime. What is it in your state? Should it be in this case?

6. A physician assists a terminally ill person to commit suicide by preparing and providing the means to end her life in a painless and comfortable way. He is charged with murder. Depending on state law, the physician could be an accomplice or conspirator in the crime of suicide. Does your state have a law covering "causing or aiding suicide"? Are the elements of murder or some lesser homicide present in the case?

SETTLE OR TAKE IT TO COURT

Stephanie A. Danielson

Statistics prove that more personal injury claims are settled than are resolved in the courtroom. Therefore, the legal assistant's role in the settlement process is as vital as it is in trial preparation. ...

The idea of settling a case prior to trial often represents an attractive alternative available to the parties. It may be to the defendant's advantage to consider settlement when liability in a case might go either way, particularly if the the plaintiff would make a sympathetic court witness. Conversely, if the responsible insurance carrier tenders a settlement offer for policy limits, it would seem in plaintiff's best interests to abandon the prospect of trial. That is, unless the supervising attorney feels that a jury award in excess of the policy limits is collectible. In addition, in order to to maximize settlement offers, some insurance carriers suggest structured settlements [in which] an annuity is bought and paid out over a certain time period.

Settlement can be initiated by either plaintiff's counsel or the liability insurance carrier. A legal assistant should not engage in settlement negotiations and all offers must be conveyed by the attorney to the client. The client holds the ultimate decision in determining whether a settlement agreement is reached on his or her own behalf. However, in many states, settlement agreements made on behalf of infants must be approved by the court. These hearings are referred to as "friendly hearings," as the matter has been settled and awaits court approval.

Many personal injury firms find settlements to be advantageous to their practice in terms of cash flow. Without the threat of a "no-cause" verdict or appeal of a jury award, settled cases help bring in attorneys' fees expeditiously. The legal assistant skilled in preparing cases for settlement is therefore a definite asset. Additionally, the paralegal should be attuned to the supervising attorney's workload and make the attorney aware of cases that may be ripe for settlement.

Generally speaking, a case is ready for settlement consideration once the injured party has been released from treatment, although some attorneys prefer to defer negotiations until six months after that release. This is so that a degree of permanent disability can be established.

Preparing the File

You can start preparing for settlement from the time the client's file is opened in the office. It is up to you, under the direction of the supervising attorney, to ensure that medical records are requested, wage-loss forms are solicited, and proper investigation of the accident is conducted.

Preliminarily, maintain a checklist of items that are pertinent to potential settlement. Make sure the file contains the following documentation:

- Accident Report
- Witness Statements
- Medical Treatment Records
- Pre-Existing Conditions
- Special Damages
- General Damages
- Possible Liens
- Wrongful Death Cases

Once you and the supervising attorney have determined that the case is ready for settlement talks, draft a demand letter for transmittal by the supervising attorney to the insurance carrier.

In a catastrophic case, the attorney may feel a demand letter is not visual enough. The use of a settlement brochure is not uncommon in such an instance. A settlement brochure may be done in either print or video, which has the most dramatic effect. Settlement brochures are reserved for cases with substantial value. They are expensive but are essential in alerting insurance adjusters to the value of cases.

Settlement brochures present photographic documentation of the plaintiff prior to the incident in question, and point out the differences from then to now. Video versions allow family members and friends to express their feelings about the changes in the plaintiff, without the fear of the courtroom.

A settled claim generally concludes with the execution of a standard release form to the defendant. Needless to say, a successful settlement makes for happiness for all without the necessity and stress of the courtroom.

Reprinted with permission from *Legal Assistant Today* magazine.

CHAPTER 11

TORTS, PERSONAL INJURY, AND COMPENSATION

Introduction

The traditional term for the field of personal injury and compensation law is *torts*. Generally, torts have specific legal labels, each considered a different cause of action, such as **trespass, slander, negligence,** and **products liability**. They often seem to have little in common except that the law recognizes that private interests can be subject to injury, the remedy of which is typically compensation if responsibility for the injury can be attributed to another party. The difference in terminology reflects a difference in attitude. "Torts" suggests a set of fixed, labeled causes of action; "compensation for injuries" reflects a more flexible category recognizing new interests as tort law evolves. For example, electronic eavesdropping has come to be recognized as an impermissible intrusion on privacy subsumed under the cause of action invasion of privacy. Despite the more descriptive and realistic "compensation for injuries," "torts" continues to be favored for saving seven syllables or twenty keystrokes.

Definition

In the word *tort* we have a rare example of legal custom providing a doctrinaire but reliable definition: "A tort is a private wrong not arising out of contract." Unfortunately, the definition states what a tort is *not* without stating exactly what it *is*. It is not a public wrong, that is, it is not a crime and it is not based on a contract.

Tort versus Crime

Legal scholars have argued whether in ancient times crime and tort were separable. In modern times, the distinction between the two is

---

BALLENTINE'S

trespass   An unauthorized entry or intrusion on the real property of another.

slander   A false and malicious oral statement tending to blacken a person's reputation or to damage his or her means of livelihood.

negligence   The failure to do something that a reasonable person would do in the same circumstances, or the doing of something a reasonable person would not do. Negligence is a wrong generally characterized by carelessness, inattentiveness, and neglectfulness rather than by a positive intent to cause injury.

product liability   The liability of a manufacturer or seller of an article for an injury caused to a person or to property by a defect in the article sold. A product liability suit is a tort action in which strict liability is imposed. The manufacturer or seller of a defective product may be liable to third parties ... as well as to purchasers, as privity of contract is not a requirement in a product liability case.

clear because the rise of the modern state resulted in the assumption of authority by the state over misconduct it deemed criminal. Public wrongs are often characterized as "wrongs against society." It is doubtful that the victim of a rape or robbery meditates on the social impact of the crime. Nevertheless, in our legal system the public has a legitimate interest in preventing such crimes.

Distinguishing tort from crime is clearest from a procedural standpoint. If the public prosecutor seeks a remedy (usually punishment) for misconduct, the wrong is public—it is a crime. If the victim sues in his or her own right for compensation, the wrong is private, a cause of action in tort. If conduct constituting a public wrong causes injury to person or property, there is nearly always a private action in tort available to the injured party in addition to prosecution available to the state. The public and private actions are independent of each other and are procedurally distinct. In some cases the causes of action may have similar names—battery is a criminal offense as well as a civil cause of action in tort. The crime of rape, in contrast, fits best into the civil cause of action called battery (some states have renamed the crime "sexual battery").

Not all torts involve criminal conduct. Because crimes ordinarily require intentional conduct, unintentional infliction of injuries, such as through negligence (e.g., causing an auto accident, medical malpractice) and liability for unsafe products (products liability), is usually not criminal even though the wrongdoer, a **tortfeasor**, may be subject to severe financial liability in tort.

Civil cases can be distinguished from criminal cases by the titles of the cases. *Montagu v. Capulet, Hatfield v. McCoy* are civil cases, whereas *Commonwealth v. Ripper, People v. Samson, State v. Miranda* (when defendant appeals to the U.S. Supreme Court, it becomes *Miranda v. Arizona, Ripper v. Massachusetts*) are criminal cases. This distinction is not infallible, however, as states may be involved in civil cases as well.

Tort versus Contract

Private wrongs fall into two categories: tort and contract. Because torts are "private wrongs not arising out of contract," noncontract actions based on wrongful conduct are necessarily torts. The reason for defining tort by what it is *not* can be attributed to the fact that the field of torts consists of a number of causes of action that have little in common, whereas contract actions are predicated on the existence of a valid contract.

The legal significance of this distinction rests on the source of the duty imposed on the defendant. In contract cases, the duties are created by the agreement between the parties and do not exist without it. If a

tortfeasor   a person who commits a tort.

young man offers to mow a neighbor's lawn for ten dollars and the neighbor agrees, the neighbor is obligated by this contract under the law to pay the ten dollars if the man mows the lawn. On the other hand, if the young man simply mows the lawn in the neighbor's absence without any agreement and then demands payment, the neighbor has no obligation to pay; there was no contract. In fact, going on the neighbor's land without consent could technically constitute the tort of trespass.

Rights and duties in tort action, by contrast, are based on obligations imposed by law. For example, our law recognizes an individual's right to a good reputation and a corresponding duty on others not to spread lies that injure an individual's reputation. If such an injury occurs, the injured party may sue in tort under a cause of action for **defamation**. Liability is based on the breach of duties established by law (statutes and cases) rather than on an agreement between the parties found in the terms of a contract.

In a cause of action for breach of contract, the court looks to the contract to determine whether it is valid and enforceable under contract law and then, if valid, to the terms of the contract to determine precisely what obligations were created. If one party failed to fulfill promises made in the contract, liability may be imposed for a resulting injury to the other party. In principle this is simple, but life is complex, so a large body of law has developed to fit this principle to a variety of circumstances (discussed fully in Chapter 12). It should be kept in mind that the law sets the rules for the enforcement of contracts, but the specific duties on which suits are based are to be found in the private agreement of the parties, the contract itself. In a sense, the duty imposed by the law of contracts simply embodies a policy that the law favors the fulfillment of promises made between private parties.

In a cause of action for tort, duties to be enforced must be found in the law. A basic policy of protecting person, property, reputation, or the like is not sufficient. The court needs guidance to determine whether liability should be imposed under the unique circumstances presented by a given case. This is the reason that the common law has been extremely important in the development of tort law. Whenever possible, the court will look to similar cases from past decisions to determine how the duties have been defined. If duties have been established by statute, these may serve as the basis for judicial enforcement in tort. In fact, legislatures often create or redefine tort actions. For example, Congress provided in 42 U.S.C. § 1983 (Civil Rights Act of 1871) for private actions to be brought against state officials who wrongfully deprive individuals of their civil rights.

BALLENTINE'S

defamation   Libel or slander; the written or oral publication, falsely and intentionally, of anything that is injurious to the good name or reputation of another person.

Often tort actions arise between persons who have relations such that the cause of action may appear to be a contract action. For example, medical malpractice cases arise in a contract relationship—a physician agrees to furnish services in return for payment, a rather typical exchange of promises between parties to a contract. If the physician negligently treats a patient, thereby causing injury, the patient may sue for malpractice in tort based on the duties imposed by law on the physician rather than the duties expressed by the terms of the contract. Although this seems to be a wrong arising out of contract, in fact, the court looks to the law rather than the contract to determine the duties between the parties. There is also a tort called "wrongful interference with contractual relations," which occurs when a person *not* a party to a contract improperly disrupts the contractual relationship of others, as when a theater owner persuades a singer to break a contract at another theater. Obviously the tort is predicated on a contract, but in this case the contract is not one between the plaintiff and the defendant.

Elements of Tort

As suits for personal injury developed over the centuries, the courts distinguished types of wrongful conduct. It seemed clear that the intentional infliction of physical injury, for example, was quite different in nature from an injury to reputation, so each required its own definition. Even the *threat* of physical injury (**assault**) was distinguished from the *infliction* of injury (**battery**). The definitions of specific causes of action in tort were framed in terms of elements (crimes are also defined by elements). To succeed in a tort action, the plaintiff must allege sufficient facts in a complaint to satisfy each element of a particular cause of action. If the plaintiff fails to do this, the complaint may be dismissed for failure to state a cause of action (the defendant would make a motion to dismiss "for failure to state a claim upon which relief can be granted"). Of course, the plaintiff must prove these allegations at trial to win the case.

Battery provides a time-tested example of the elements of a tort. It has been defined traditionally as an "unconsented, unprivileged, offensive contact." The definition contains the elements of battery as well as the defenses to battery.

—————————————————————————BALLENTINE'S—————————————————————————

assault   An act of force or threat of force intended to inflict harm upon a person or to put the person in fear that such harm is imminent; an attempt to commit a battery. The perpetrator must have, or appear to have, the present ability to carry out the act.

battery   The unconsented-to touching or striking of one person by another, or by an object put in motion by him or her, with the intention of doing harm or giving offense. Battery is both a crime and a tort.

Elements:

1. Intent
2. Bodily contact (extended to clothing, etc.)
3. Offensive in nature

Defenses:

1. Consent to the contact
2. Privilege

Battery is rooted in injury caused by fists or weapons but has been extended generally to offensive bodily contacts, such as sexual touching. It must be intentional and not simply accidental or careless, which might constitute a cause of action for negligence. There must be a contact and not merely a threat of contact (assault). The contact must be offensive. Although a particular form of contact may ordinarily constitute a battery, consent may prevent recovery, as with prizefighters and football players. The contact may be privileged, as when a parent strikes a child as a reasonable disciplinary measure or a policeman subdues a criminal with reasonable force.

Tort Law: An Evolving Field

Preparation of a tort suit begins with the search for an appropriate cause of action and an examination of whether a client's case fits comfortably within the elements of one or more torts. Tort law has experienced and continues to experience an evolution in both its definition as a whole and the definition of specific causes of action. Not only does our notion of appropriate conduct change, but opportunities for injury change as well.

For example, the tort labeled "intentional infliction of mental distress" is a product of the twentieth century, undergoing considerable growth and refinement. Courts of the past were reluctant to compensate for emotional suffering unless accompanied by some physical injury, but modern courts have come to recognize emotional injuries as compensable when caused intentionally by malice or outrageous conduct. Harassing telephone calls, unscrupulous bill collectors, impersonal public

---

BALLENTINE'S

defense   In both civil and criminal cases, the facts submitted and the legal arguments offered by a defendant in support of his or her claim that the plaintiff's case, or the prosecution's, should be rejected. The term "defense" may apply to a defendant's entire case or to separate grounds, called *affirmative defenses*, offered by a defendant for rejecting all or a portion of the case against him or her.

and private bureaucracies, and perhaps even the lowering of standards of courtesy on many fronts have all contributed to a recognition that the potential for serious harm to one's emotional well-being is a fact of modern life. The courts have come to impose a legal duty on conduct that custom has always disapproved but not legally condemned. The recognition of intentional infliction of mental distress is not designed to compensate for every insult or affront nor to encourage the overly sensitive to sue. Nevertheless, some individuals engage in conduct aimed at causing suffering in ways that the courts feel compelled to condemn. (Example: A man was held liable when he jokingly told a woman that her husband had been in a serious accident and persuaded her to rush down to the hospital.)

Each new tort must start with a dispute before a judge, who will be inclined to recognize right and duty when faced with a compelling set of facts. Tort law has evolved to be highly individualized, based on a recognition of an individual's right to be free from unjustified intrusions on person, personality, personal dignity, and private property. Establishment of a new right of action occurs when an appropriate case demands the redress of a harm that is socially acknowledged and fits within the basic policy of general tort law. In short, the court is unwilling to refuse an injured party a remedy even if the case does not fit precisely into the elements of some traditional cause of action. Whether this will give rise to a cause of action depends on whether other courts agree, and allow the precedent to stand, or whether they criticize it, thus cutting short its life.

Extraneous Factors Influencing Tort Law

The law develops in a social, economic, and political context. As Oliver Wendell Holmes declared in 1881, "the life of the law has not been logic; it has been experience." Lawmaking is not simply a process of refining abstract rules, nor is the process of deciding disputes controlled by the simple expedient of applying abstract rules to concrete events. Tort law has a strong component of logic and common sense. The rights represented by tort law generally reflect what most Americans consider their rights should be (e.g., a person can use force against another person in self-defense). In a sense, tort law more than any other area of law reflects our social values with regard to interpersonal conduct. Nevertheless, there are some special factors that play a large part in tort suits and influence actual outcomes that have little to do with the values expressed in substantive principles.

Before reading the *Frito-Lay* case, you might wish to review the principle of comparative negligence discussed in Chapter 4. *Frito-Lay* is an example of the least responsible party paying the major share for the injury. Note also that Frito-Lay is liable under the doctrine of respondeat superior, not because the company was in any way directly at fault. Although tort law presumably assigns liability based on fault, Frito-Lay sorely tests the credibility of that concept. Is the result based on fact or sympathy?

FRITO-LAY, INC.
v.
Toni CLOUD and The State of Indiana
Court of Appeals of Indiana
569 N.E.2d 983 (1991)

Frito-Lay, Inc. appeals the judgment in the amount of $924,000.00 in favor of the plaintiffs, Toni Cloud and her parents, ... entered upon a jury verdict after a [thirteen-]day trial. The Clouds brought suit in negligence against Frito-Lay and the State of Indiana seeking compensation for the serious personal injuries Toni suffered in an automobile accident involving Toni and a Frito-Lay employee, Robert Hammond, who was driving Frito-Lay's delivery van at the time of the accident. The Clouds alleged that Hammond was negligent in his operation of Frito-Lay's van. Frito-Lay **stipulated** that if Hammond were found liable, it would be liable under the theory of respondeat superior. The Clouds also sued the State of Indiana for the negligent construction and maintenance of the intersection where the accident took place. The jury found Toni Cloud to be 49% at fault, the State 30% at fault, and Frito-Lay 21% at fault for the accident. The State—being exempt from the principles of comparative fault—is exonerated from liability by Cloud's contributory negligence.

The jury found that Cloud's damages amounted to [$4.4 million]. Frito-Lay's 21% of this amount results in the verdict against it in the amount of $924,000.00.

We have found reversible error in the trial court's instruction of the jury concerning both the issues of liability and damages. Therefore, we must reverse and remand to the trial court for a new trial on all issues. We also address some of the other issues raised by Frito-Lay because we anticipate that they will resurface on the retrial of this matter.

FACTS

The facts in the light most favorable to the verdict indicate that early in the morning of November 6, 1986, [sixteen-]year-old Toni Cloud attempted to pull out from County Road 1000 onto State Road 56 in Jefferson County, Indiana. After stopping at the stop sign, she failed to yield and pulled out onto the preferred State highway directly into the path of Hammond's Frito-Lay van traveling within the speed limit. Hammond's Frito-Lay van struck Cloud's car injuring both Cloud and Hammond.

* * *

The injuries Toni suffered in the accident were nearly fatal. ...

The accident happened at the intersection of County Road 1000 and State Road 56. It is virtually undisputed that this intersection is extremely dangerous. ...

Nearly every fact related to the accident is vigorously disputed.

* * *

It is difficult to determine from the briefs which accident scenario represents the evidence in the light most favorable to the verdict. We believe the following scenario represents the Clouds' assertions. The absence of skid marks on the highway indicates that Hammond was inattentive at the wheel and did not use his brakes before the collision. Cloud's accident reconstruction expert placed Hammond's speed at 50 mph at the time of impact. Evidence was presented that a reasonably prudent Frito-Lay van driver would not have been driving in excess of 40 mph and that had Hammond been driving 40 mph he could have easily avoided the accident by—among other actions—swerving to the right around Toni's car. ...

DECISION

[The court agreed with Frito-Lay that the trial court should have instructed the jury with regard to the sudden emergency doctrine, relating to the duty of care of one confronted by a sudden emergency.]

[The court agreed with Frito-Lay's contention that separately instructing the jury to find damages for Toni Cloud's loss of enjoyment of life and also for future mental suffering improperly allowed her to collect twice for the same injury.]

* * *

Whether the trial court abused its discretion by denying Frito-Lay's motion to **bifurcate** the trial?

* * *

Frito-Lay has mounted a compelling argument in favor of the bifurcation of the issues of liability and damages in the present case. It asserts that the jury was inundated with evidence that inevitably created sympathy for [the sixteen-year-old], junior varsity cheerleader, now gravely disabled accident victim, Toni Cloud. Such heart-rending evidence included testimony regarding Toni's youth, social nature, lost career opportunities, the gruesomeness and severity of the injuries to her brain and body, and the severe and permanent neuropsychological and economic effects of these injuries. Frito-Lay asserts further that the order of the presentation of evidence regarding liability and damages was intertwined for no reason other than to evoke the jury's sympathy for the Clouds and prejudice the jury's ability to render a verdict in favor of Frito-Lay on the issue of liability. ...

We are of the opinion that [the] Clouds' arguments against bifurcation almost entirely amount to mere subterfuge. ...

We cannot imagine a case more appropriate for bifurcation than the case at bar. ...

* * *

Whether the trial court erred in instructing the jury regarding the rights of motorists to assume that other drivers will obey traffic laws and the respective obligations of Hammond and Cloud to maintain a proper lookout?

Frito-Lay raises several issues with regard to the trial court's instruction of the jury regarding Hammond's right to assume that Cloud would not disregard the stop sign and pull out in front of him and the respective obligations of both Hammond and Cloud to maintain a proper lookout. ...

[In a prior case, we] held that, unless a party has notice to the contrary, he has the right to assume others who owe him a duty of reasonable care will exercise such care. The exercise of ordinary and reasonable care does not require the preferred driver to be constantly aware of the actions of the nonpreferred drivers in plain view. Motorists are not required to anticipate extraordinary hazards or to constantly expect or search for unusual dangers. The motorist on the preferred road is under no duty to anticipate that the motorist on the nonpreferred road who is stopped at a stop sign will pull out in front of his vehicle.

* * *

We have examined the instructions given to the jury and the instructions tendered by Frito-Lay. As a general proposition, we agree with Frito-Lay that the trial court has failed to adequately instruct the jury regarding the respective rights and obligations of the preferred driver and the nonpreferred driver. ...

Based on the above, we reverse and remand for proceedings consistent with this opinion.

Case Questions

1. Why was the state of Indiana not liable?
2. Why did Frito-Lay want the trial bifurcated? Why did the court of appeals agree?
3. Can a person be liable for failure to drive defensively?
4. What are preferred and nonpreferred drivers?

Case Glossary

stipulation An agreement by the parties to a lawsuit with respect to certain uncontested facts. A stipulation avoids the need to present evidence regarding the matters it covers; it is entered into to save time and expense.

bifurcated trial A trial that is divided into two parts to provide separate hearings for different aspects of the same matter.

The Doctrine of *Respondeat Superior* (Vicarious Liability)

The English legal historian Plucknett attributes the birth of this doctrine to Lord Holt, who, in deciding a case in 1691, stated: "Whoever employs another is answerable for him, and undertakes for his care to all that make use of him." Until that time, the doctrine of *respondeat superior,* which places liability on the employer for injuries caused by an employee within the scope of employment, had only been applied to certain public officials when their underlings could not pay damages. Nothing inherent in tort law requires this principle, which is a peculiarity of Anglo-American common law. It contradicts a fundamental principle of tort law, namely, that fault should be the basis for liability. Nonetheless, an employer may be liable without acting wrongfully.

The influence of *respondeat superior* on modern tort litigation is great. Personal injury cases are costly to litigate, and it is futile to sue a defendant who has limited resources. If, however, a person is injured by someone working on the job for a large corporation, the suit becomes economically feasible. The resources of employees are generally far more limited than those of their employers. As a practical matter, juries tend to be less concerned about the pocketbooks of large businesses than they are about those of workers.

As a result, the availability of compensation may depend more on who may be liable than on the legal merits of the case. When we read in the newspapers of unusually high awards, we can be relatively certain that some "deep pocket" was available to be sued. *Respondeat superior* creates many deep pockets.

Insurance

The rise of the modern insurance industry has abetted tort litigation. The basic principle of insurance is pooling risk. A homeowner who buys fire insurance contributes a small amount to a large pool for protection against the possible but unlikely prospect of a fire. Although the risk of fire is small, the result if it occurs is likely to be financial catastrophe for the uninsured. The insurance company is the pooling agency, collecting payments and maintaining funds from which the unlucky are reimbursed for their losses. The homeowner usually has a homeowner's policy that includes protection against suits from those who may in some way be injured on the homeowner's property. Loss from a fire may be a simple economic loss that can be fairly easily established, but it is quite different when the child next door wanders over and drowns in the swimming pool. The value of that child's life is not easy to fix and will likely produce a protracted negotiation between the insurance company and the bereaved parents (through their attorneys). Insurance companies differ greatly in their willingness to make reasonable settlement offers, so the threat of lawsuit is often necessary; when a settlement cannot be reached, the dispute may be resolved by trial.

The presence of insurance encourages lawsuits for the very reason *respondeat superior* does—the insurance company has great financial resources. The economic costs of this system are great—attorneys reap large rewards, insurance companies make handsome profits, and injured parties suffer through long delays to receive their (presumably) just compensation.

Given the realities of the economic system and tort law, however, alternative choices are often too risky. For example, physicians commonly pay enormous premiums for malpractice insurance. One might think that a competent, diligent physician need not carry insurance, as the likelihood of suit is minimal. But dedicated, ethical physicians are more concerned with treatment than with liability. Under the law they are held to a high standard of professional care. A simple error of judgment may result in death or serious permanent injury. The potential injuries are so severe that a physician practices without insurance at the peril of financial ruin. The alternative is to practice medicine with the primary purpose of avoiding liability, something neither the medical profession nor the public finds desirable.

Contingency Fees

The prominence of personal injury lawsuits in the practice of law is encouraged by the custom of contingency fees. This is a contract between the lawyer and the client under which the lawyer receives compensation measured by the settlement negotiated with the defendant or the award determined by the court. Rather than charging an hourly fee or a fee fixed in advance, the attorney agrees to represent the client for a percentage of the award. Typically the minimum fee is one third for a settlement, forty percent if the case goes to trial.

Ethically, contingency fees have always been suspect. They not only encourage suits if the potential award is great, but they also give the attorney an interest in the lawsuit, which presents a temptation for the attorney to act on the basis of personal gain rather than in the interests of the client or the law. The contingency fee arrangement is a peculiarly American institution and is not allowed in most countries. The justification for the arrangement most often given is that most injured parties could not afford to pursue a lawsuit if they were forced to pay attorneys as the case proceeds. They would be forced by economic circumstances to settle for much less than their injuries are worth. The individual of limited resources suing an insurance company or a large corporation with sufficient funds to pay attorneys to delay awards indefinitely is necessarily at a great disadvantage. The contingency fee arrangement somewhat equalizes the disparity between the parties. One must question, however, whether this is a natural or artificial product of the tort law.

Contingency fees encourage some sorts of lawsuits and discourage others. If an injury is severe and permanent, especially if it is disabling or disfiguring, compensation may be very great and thus justify the costs of litigation. If the defendant has no financial resources, a lawsuit is unlikely.

Fault

The concept of fault is central to the development of legal theories of tort. Ultimately the resolution of a tort suit involves the question of a transfer of wealth from the defendant to the plaintiff. If someone suffers an injury or a loss, should there be a source of compensation? The law looks to the cause of the injury. If caused by an "act of God," as when someone is struck by lightning, the law cannot allocate compensation, because there is no party at fault.

In contrast, if the cause of the injury can be attributed to human forces, liability may be appropriate. At that point a question of fairness arises. Would it be fair for this person or this organization to surrender some of its resources to the injured party? An affirmative answer to this question is easiest when the injury can be shown to have been caused directly by wrongful conduct of another party to an injured party who is utterly blameless. Unfortunately, causation and blameworthiness are frequently obscure or difficult to prove. What should be the result, for example, when a commercial airline crashes, killing all aboard, but the cause of the crash cannot be determined? Should a widow of one of the passengers be compensated for her loss by the airline? Our sympathies are naturally with the widow, but should the airline compensate her even though she cannot prove fault on the part of the airline? The famous case of *Cox v. Northwest Airlines, Inc.,* 379 F.2d 893 (7th Cir. 1967) resolved this issue through the often-criticized principle of *res ipsa loquitur* ("the thing speaks for itself"). *Res ipsa* is used to infer negligence, specifically a failure of due care, when it would appear that the injury would not have occurred if due care had been exercised. An airplane does not crash without some fault attributable to those in control of it (is this really true?). In this case the principle could be applied without pangs of conscience. The deceased was clearly blameless. The airline was in control of the airplane. In other words, it seems fair that the airline should pay, essentially making the airline the insurer of its passengers; but the fact that fault was established in the absence of proof is troubling to those demanding logic and consistency in the law. Put another way, would it not be better simply to charge airlines (and other common carriers) with the duty to ensure the safety of their passengers rather than apply the questionable principle of *res ipsa loquitur*? Practically speaking, the doctrine of *res ipsa loquitur* is merely a device to get the issue of negligence to the jury.

A different problem of fault was encountered in another famous case, *Summers v. Tice,* 33 Cal. 2d 80, 199 P.2d 1 (1948). Summers was injured in a hunting party when two of his companions fired simultaneously at a quail, hitting Summers in the eye. It was not possible to determine which hunter's shot was responsible for Summers's injury. Logically one was at fault, while the other was not, but the California Supreme Court held both liable because both were negligent in firing in Summers's direction, even though only one could have been the actual *cause* of the injury. "To hold otherwise would be to exonerate both from liability, although each was negligent, and the injury resulted from someone's negligence." The court refused to make Summers suffer the burden of his injuries simply because he could not prove which companion fired the shot that hit his eye.

A similar problem is encountered in the DES (diethylstilbestrol) cases in which an antimiscarriage drug has been alleged to be the cause of cancer in the later life of children born to women who took the drug while pregnant. Assuming the truth of the allegations and assuming that the several drug companies who marketed the drug were legally responsible for the later injuries, who should pay when the medical records, prescriptions, and the mother's memory do not establish which company sold the drug that caused the cancer? One solution proposed to this problem is *enterprise liability* (also known as *market share liability*). Because several companies produced the drug, liability could be pooled among the companies according to their shares of the market for the drug (if one company sold 15 percent of the drug, it would pay 15 percent of the damages). Although enterprise liability is still controversial, it reflects the capacity of tort law to find novel remedies for unusual situations.

Enterprise liability also represents the modern trend in tort law away from the technicalities of finding fault toward emphasizing the search for compensating the innocent victim. The courts and legislatures have been increasingly sensitive to the plight of the consumer, the workforce, the motorist, the homemaker, the man on the street.

Unfortunately, the principles that have arisen do not correct the inequities of the legal system itself. Compensable injuries go uncompensated when the economics of litigation prove an impediment. If there is no "deep pocket," or the injuries are less than the costs of litigation, personal injury attorneys will decline to pursue a case.

The legal profession has the ethical responsibility to provide services to the public in general, not just in cases in which legal fees are readily obtained. The American Bar Association has shown concern for this very problem, but it is up to attorneys to shoulder the responsibility or assist in finding a solution. One promising alternative in this regard is in the growing body of well-trained paralegals. Many of the services provided by attorneys could be provided by paralegals at a much lower cost—not only do paralegals provide their services at a lower fee, they can operate within restricted areas with lower overhead. Full utilization of paralegals by lawyers can significantly reduce costs to clients. Economic necessity together with ethical obligation should result in a growth area for paralegals. This would serve the public and enhance the image of the legal profession. For paralegals this would be a welcome development; helping the nonwealthy may be more personally rewarding than protecting the rich and corporate America. And no one will ever say "Let's kill all the paralegals."

Should a business enterprise be liable for the intentional torts of a third party on its premises? That is the question in the *Goggin* case. It represents both the search for fault and the plaintiff's search for an affluent defendant.

One of the defenses to negligence is **assumption of risk**, under which the plaintiff voluntarily encounters a known risk (e.g., someone employed to detonate explosives). In *Goggin,* the court not only finds the defendant free of negligence for the harm caused by a third party but also suggests that the plaintiff knew what he was getting into. At the same time, the court acknowledges that the owners of premises open to the public have duties with regard to the safety of patrons. The case raises interesting issues with regard to the assignment of fault.

Fault and Three Areas of Tort Law

Tort law covers a variety of areas of injury to person and property, but three areas constitute the bulk of tort litigation:

--------------------------------BALLENTINE'S--------------------------------

assumption of risk   The legal principle that a person who knows and deliberately exposes himself or herself to a danger assumes responsibility for the risk, rather than the person who actually created the danger.

Harold J. GOGGIN
v.
NEW STATE BALLROOM
Supreme Judicial Court of
Massachusetts, Suffolk
355 Mass. 718, 247 N.E.2d 350 (1969)

On March 17, 1960, the plaintiff, accompanied by a lady companion, entered the New State Ballroom in Boston at approximately 8:45 P.M. in anticipation of an evening with Terpsichore. Having paid the admission of $2 each and checked clothing, they commenced dancing when the music began. At this time there were approximately 900 people in the hall. The dance floor was waxed and polished and was about 125 feet long with a width of 90 feet. By 9:30 P.M. the crowd had grown to 1,200, and by 10 P.M. it had increased to the point where there were 1,800 to 1,900 people on the dance floor. These dancers were "noisy and boisterous, kicking their feet, bumping into people and doing some real kicking." This kicking occurred in connection with the execution of such dances as the "cha cha and jitterbug," and was accompanied by "bumping." The plaintiff, however, "only danced the waltz and refrained from the cha cha or the jitterbug." ... While the plaintiff's partner claimed she saw no attendants, there was testimony from the defendant's manager that two police officers, plus a sergeant, were on duty "along with two employees of the Ballroom who were on the dance floor." This detail was evidently insufficient to aid the plaintiff, for at 10 P.M. "he was dancing the waltz with his partner in a corner as there was one fellow he was trying to keep away from. When it is crowded like that you really can get bumped." He and his partner remained in the corner "but this fellow kept coming and all of a sudden, bang! 'We were pushed right over!'" The plaintiff went down, his head hit the floor, and his partner fell on top of him and ripped her dress in the descent. The plaintiff had been no stranger to the physical activity which took place at the ballroom for he was a regular attendant there on every Saturday evening between March 17, 1959, and

March 17, 1960. He also repaired to the ballroom during that period on any holiday nights that fell on a weekday.

On this evidence the defendant moved for a directed verdict on a count in an action of tort brought by the plaintiff wherein he alleged that he was on the defendant's premises by invitation, that he had paid an admission, and that he was injured by reason of the defendant's negligence in its failure to conduct its establishment in an orderly manner and in compliance with statutes, ordinances and rules relating to it. The motion was denied, there was a verdict for the plaintiff, and the defendant is here on an exception to that denial.

The law in these circumstances has been often stated. The defendant, which opened its ballroom to the public in furtherance of its business, owed the duty to the plaintiff [**business invitee**], who paid to enter, of reasonable care that no injury occur to the plaintiff through the actions of a third person whether such acts were accidental, negligent or intentional. ... The defendant, however, was not an insurer of the plaintiff's safety ... . Its liability in this instance must arise from its knowledge, or the fact that it should have known of or anticipated, in the exercise of reasonable care, the disorderly or rowdy actions of third persons which might lead to injury to the plaintiff ... . Furthermore, where in a ballroom such as this conditions existing at the time of the accident are open and obvious to any person of ordinary intelligence, the defendant is under no duty to warn the plaintiff even where a substantial crowd has gathered. ...

The plaintiff in this case chose on an evening not noted for restraints on exuberance in the city of Boston to go with his lady to a public dance hall where he knew the patrons were lovers of the cha cha and the jitterbug. He knew these dances involved muscular contortions and a degree of abandon not associated with a minuet. A certain amount of innocent bumping in a large crowd would be unavoidable. That the bump which floored the plaintiff may have been deliberate was, in our view, not such a happening that the defendant was bound to anticipate it. It was unusual and not reasonably to be apprehended and affords no basis for treating the defendant as negligent. ... The vagaries of fashions in the dance and their consequences are better left subject to the judgment of those who engage in them or frequent establishments where they may be found, absent circumstances which may in the light of the principles herein discussed provide a basis for liability. ...

Exceptions sustained. Judgment for the defendant.

Case Questions

1. To what duty does the court hold the ballroom with regard to the plaintiff invitee?
2. Is there language in the case suggesting assumption of risk?

Case Glossary

business invitee A person who comes upon premises at the invitation of the occupant, and who has business to transact. If a business invitee is injured as a result of some hazard on the premises, he or she is more likely to be able to hold the owner or occupant responsible at law than would a social guest or a trespasser.

---

1. Intentional torts
2. Negligence
3. Strict liability (represented primarily by the booming area of products liability)

The most ancient category is intentional torts; negligence flowered in the nineteenth and twentieth centuries; and products liability has come to fruition only in recent decades. It is not possible here to discuss any of these in sufficient detail to suggest a mastery of them, which must be left for later study. They are discussed primarily with regard to the different ways in which they relate to concepts of fault in its historical legal evolution.

Intentional Torts

A number of causes of action are lumped together as intentional torts. Many of them are quite ancient, such as battery, assault, trespass, false imprisonment, and the like. Some are recent in origin, such as invasion of privacy and intentional infliction of mental distress. Their common bond is the essential element of intent. Intent to do some harm (sometimes the intent to do specific harm) must be alleged and be proven for the plaintiff to prevail. Neither malicious motive nor criminal intent is required for an intentional tort, though

malicious prosecution specifically requires a showing of malice. Absence of malice may in some cases be a defense against libel.

The requirement of intent demands a proof of fault against the defendant and requires a willful act on the part of the defendant. The law of intentional torts assumes that human beings act from free will and can conform their conduct to societal rules. When they fail to do so, resulting in harm to others, they will be held responsible for their acts to the injured party. If a harmful act was intended, punitive damages are often awarded in addition to compensation. Punitive damages are not ordinarily awarded for nonintentional torts.

The plaintiff must prove intentional conduct, but the defendant has the opportunity to rebut intent. Intent is commonly inferred from the events that gave rise to the injury. In the colorful case of *Katko v. Briney*, 183 N.W.2d 657 (Iowa 1971), an Iowa farmer protected his wife's often-vandalized, unoccupied farm house by wiring a shotgun to a bedroom door to go off when someone opened the door. Katko, a trespasser looking for old bottles, had the misfortune of opening the door and suffered permanent injury to his leg. Briney's attempt to negate intent by stating on the witness stand that he "did not intend to injure anyone" was not believed by the jury, which found that he had acted maliciously and awarded Katko $20,000 in compensatory and $10,000 in punitive damages.

Conversely, when a five-year-old child pulled a lawn chair out from under a woman about to sit in it, the Supreme Court of Washington held that it was insufficient that the child's act was intentional and incurred a risk and remanded the case to the trial judge to determine whether the child realized with a "substantial certainty" that the harmful contact would result (*Garrett v. Dailey*, 46 Wash. 2d 197, 279 P.2d 1091 [1955]). Liability was thus predicated on the knowledge and understanding of a five-year-old. (On remand the trial court found that the child did in fact have such knowledge.)

In addition to intent, a plaintiff must allege and prove all the other elements of the specific cause of action, as discussed earlier.

Negligence

The Industrial Revolution of the nineteenth century and the automobile of the twentieth both caused a marked increase in serious personal injuries. These injuries were caused by machines and the human beings

---

BALLENTINE'S

malicious prosecution A criminal prosecution or civil suit commenced maliciously and without probable cause. After the termination of such a prosecution or suit in the defendant's favor, the defendant has the right to bring an action against the original plaintiff for the tort of "malicious prosecution."

that control them. Injury was usually accidental rather than intentional, so the traditional notions of intentional fault required elaboration.

A complete listing of the names of the causes of action in tort would be dominated by intentional torts, but the cases brought for personal injuries would be dominated by the single cause of action called *negligence.* Most people are injured accidentally and not intentionally. In negligence law, liability arises through a different notion of fault than intent. In a sense, negligence is simply culpable carelessness. Poor judgment, momentary inattention, and lack of foresight often result in injury. Negligence law sought and found a measure by which the failure to exercise due care could be categorized as fault and thereby incur liability.

The standard of care is embodied in the *reasonable man* test. Tradition uses the generic male for the standard, but today the test is more properly put as "what a reasonably prudent *person* would have done under the circumstances." Whether someone should be found at fault and held liable is measured by a standard of care based on reasonableness rather than subjective mental state or intent.

Negligence has four elements:

1. Duty (standard of care)
2. Breach of the duty (conduct falling below the standard of care)
3. Causation (the breach must be the cause of the injury)
4. Injury

The breach of the duty establishes fault. Because negligence applies to the myriad injuries incurred daily through oversight and carelessness, it is not possible to cover in the elements the precise circumstances that give rise to liability; they are simply too numerous. The reasonable man standard acknowledges that what may be prudent conduct in one situation may not be prudent in another. The test must be applied on a case-by-case basis, with the standard of care determined by the jury. The "reasonable man" is a hypothetical person of ordinary understanding but prudent in conduct; individuals are not expected to exercise extraordinary care, nor are they excused by the fact that most people are often careless. It would undoubtedly be negligent not to fence in a swimming pool in a neighborhood full of small children, but perhaps not imprudent not to do so on a country estate with no neighboring children; it is up to the jury to decide what is reasonable and prudent.

The standard of care for negligence may vary from the reasonable man standard. Thus, if a statutory standard fits the case, it usually serves for the standard of care. For example, if a motorist runs a stop sign and causes an accident, the breach of the standard of care is satisfied by a statute that requires a full stop at stop signs, so the jury need not question whether a reasonably prudent person stops at stop signs.

For professionals, the standard of care is measured by professional standards in the community in which the professional practices or by a national standard for specialists. It would hardly do for a jury to decide what a reasonably prudent person would do when performing brain surgery. At present, paralegals are not professionals in this legal sense, so negligence on their part ordinarily would result in a suit against the supervising attorney. Should a paralegal who has been certified as a legal assistant by NALA be subject to suit if the paralegal represents himself or herself as a "Certified Paralegal"? At present, many states are questioning whether paralegals should be licensed, which would presumably make them professionals and subject to suit for their negligent mistakes.

Contributory Negligence/Comparative Negligence

With the rise of negligence suits in the nineteenth century, the requirement of fault (breach of the standard of care) also gave rise to a defense based on fault. It did not seem just to allow recovery if the plaintiff shared some responsibility for causing the injury. A plaintiff's fault was called *contributory negligence* and constituted a complete defense to a suit for negligence. The courts soon realized that the result of using this doctrine was not always just. In some cases the minor fault of the plaintiff would not allow recovery. Railroad workers, for example, often worked under dangerous conditions in which a moment's inadvertence could result in serious injury or death. It was not sufficient for the widow and children to prove that the employer had been responsible for the dangerous conditions; if the employee had not been careful, there could be no recovery.

Legislatures responded to dangers in the workplace with **workers' compensation**, and many courts and legislatures responded with *comparative negligence*. Under comparative negligence schemes, many of which are statutory, fault is apportioned; that is, if the plaintiff is negligent as well as the defendant, the plaintiff's award is reduced by the plaintiff's percentage of fault. Thus, if the jury, under the judge's instructions, determines that 80 percent of the fault rests with the defendant, while 20 percent is the fault of the plaintiff, the plaintiff is entitled only to 80 percent of the amount of the injuries. If the jury

---BALLENTINE'S---

workers' compensation acts   State statutes that provide for the payment of compensation to employees injured in their employment or, in case of death, to their dependents. Benefits are paid under such acts whether or not the employer was negligent; payment is made in accordance with predetermined schedules based generally upon the loss or impairment of earning capacity. Workers' compensation laws eliminate defenses such as assumption of risk, contributory negligence, and fellow servant. ... Occupational diseases are compensable under these acts as well.

values the plaintiff's injuries at $50,000, the plaintiff would receive $40,000. The percentages are arbitrary approximations, but the jury must estimate them if it finds fault on both parties. Many states will not allow the plaintiff to recover if the jury assigns 50 percent or more of the fault to the plaintiff. Automobile accidents often involve injuries to both drivers, each of whom claims the other was at fault. The final award can differ greatly depending on whether the jurisdiction uses contributory negligence or comparative negligence ("pure" or modified).

Strict Liability/Products Liability

The Age of Technology has confounded the concept of fault in tort. The American consumer acquires a bewildering assortment of machines, appliances, and pharmaceutical drugs, as well as other products that pose unseen dangers. Manufacturers may exercise reasonable precautions to make their products safe and certainly do not intend to injure their customers, so it is difficult to assign fault under theories of negligence or intentional tort. The purchase of products creates a contractual relationship, but ordinary contract remedies do not contemplate compensation for personal injury.

Earlier in the twentieth century, judges were troubled by innocent victims of defective products who could not prove fault on the part of the producer. As America became a mighty industrial power, courts became less concerned about protecting business from ruinous lawsuits and more concerned about the hapless victims of their products. It did not seem just that a company could reap large profits from sales of its products without compensating those injured by them. A number of cases strained at the concept of fault to protect innocent parties, and in 1963 Justice Traynor of the California Supreme Court wrote the opinion in *Greenman v. Yuba Power Products, Inc.*, 59 Cal. 2d 57, 377 P.2d 897, which announced the birth of products liability. Greenman had purchased a combination power tool for his home workshop that one day inexplicably ejected a piece of wood, striking him in the forehead. Justice Traynor reasoned that traditional requirements of proof of fault were no longer tenable and set the standard for the plaintiff in the case as follows:

> To establish the manufacturer's liability it was sufficient that plaintiff proved that he was injured while using the Shopsmith in a way it was intended to be used as a result of a defect in design and manufacture of which plaintiff was not aware that made the Shopsmith unsafe for its intended use ...

Perhaps no case in the common law has had a more immediate and far-reaching effect on American law. The *Restatement of Torts* responded two years later with § 402A, which elaborated on the *Greenman* decision. Section 402A was adopted in some form by state after state in rapid succession. In a few short years, numerous cases served to refine the principles of products liability. Never has such a vast body of law so quickly fixed a cause of action so firmly in the law.

This was a revolution in tort law waiting to happen. Traynor could appeal to precedent in **implied warranty** theory, which held sellers responsible for the fitness for use of the products they sell. The consumer reasonably relied on the seller to deliver a product fit for use. Implied warranties were in addition to the express warranties given by the seller. The advent of the automobile made implied warranties important because the purchaser was rarely in a position to determine whether the product was properly designed or assembled.

The adoption of the cause of action for products liability was justified on policy grounds, which were stated succinctly by Judge Jacobson in a concurring opinion in *Lechuga, Inc. v. Montgomery,* 12 Ariz. App. 32, 467 P.2d 256:

> It is apparent from a reading of the Restatement, and the leading cases on this subject, that the doctrine of strict liability has evolved to place liability on the party primarily responsible for the injury occurring, that is, the manufacturer of the defective product. This, as Justice Traynor stated in his concurring opinion in *Escola v. Coca Cola Bottling Co. of Fresno,* 24 Cal. 2d 453, 150 P.2d 436 (1944), is based on reasons of public policy: "If public policy demands that a manufacturer of goods be responsible for their quality regardless of negligence there is no reason not to fix that responsibility openly." 150 P.2d, at 441.
>
> These public policy considerations have been variously enumerated as follows:
>
> 1. The manufacturer can anticipate some hazards and guard against their recurrence, which the consumer cannot do. ...
> 2. The cost of injury may be overwhelming to the person injured while the risk of injury can be insured by the manufacturer and be distributed among the public as a cost of doing business. ...
> 3. It is in the public interest to discourage the marketing of defective products. ...
> 4. It is in the public interest to place responsibility for its reaching the market. ...

———————————————————— BALLENTINE'S ————————————————————

implied warranty   In the sale of personal property, a warranty by the seller, inferred by law (whether or not the seller intended to create the warranty), as to the quality or condition of the goods sold.

Under the Uniform Commercial Code, the most important implied warranties are the implied warranty of merchantability and the implied warranty of fitness for a particular purpose. In any sale of goods, a warranty of merchantability (fitness for general or customary purposes) is implied if the seller normally sells such goods. An implied warranty of fitness for a particular purpose exists when the seller has reason to know the purpose for which the buyer wants the goods and the buyer is relying on the seller to furnish goods suited to that purpose.

5. That this responsibility should also be placed upon the retailer and wholesaler of the defective product in order that they may act as the conduit through which liability may flow to reach the manufacturer, where ultimate responsibility lies. ...

6. That because of the complexity of present day manufacturing proceeses and their secretiveness, the ability to prove negligent conduct by the injured plaintiff is almost impossible. ...

7. That the consumer does not have the ability to investigate for himself the soundness of the product. ...

8. That this consumer's vigilance has been lulled by advertising, marketing devices and trademarks. ...

Inherent in these policy considerations is not the nature of the transaction by which the consumer obtained possession of the defective product, but the character of the defect itself, that is, one occurring in the manufacturing process and the unavailability of an adequate remedy on behalf of the injured plaintiff.

In addition to implied warranty as a ground for products liability, the principle of **absolute liability** for extrahazardous activities furnished precedent. Under this principle, parties engaged in especially dangerous activities, such as the use of explosives, were held liable regardless of fault. The policy grounds were similar. It appeared to the courts unjust that innocent parties could be injured through the direct cause of another's activities and be left without a remedy simply because those engaged in the activities had exercised due care.

Nevada was late in recognizing liability for extrahazardous activities, having adopted products liability first, even though the latter was partially drawn from principles enunciated in the former. The *Valentine* case cites the grandfather of strict liability, *Rylands v. Fletcher*, an English case decided in 1868. *Valentine* is an interesting example of the closeness of these two forms of strict liability as an incident of modern industrial society.

Behind liability for dangerously defective products and extrahazardous activities lies a foreseeability issue. Clearly, engaging in activities that present a significant risk to the public makes injury foreseeable in a general sense, even if neither the victim nor the manner of occurrence is precisely foreseeable. And when a manufacturer makes products that are potentially dangerous, the risk of injury has a degree of foreseeability. The law now holds that those who incur risks should bear the cost of the injuries that result. Foreseeability lurks everywhere in tort law. Because of the nature of lawsuits, the foreseeability issue always arises from hindsight—what may seem foreseeable in looking back on the course of events may not have been remotely foreseen at the beginning.

BALLENTINE'S

absolute liability   Liability for an injury whether or not there is fault or negligence.

Michela D. VALENTINE
v.
PIONEER CHLOR ALKALI COMPANY
Supreme Court of Nevada
109 Nev. 1107, 864 P.2d 295 (1993)

Appellants ("the Valentines"), on behalf of their son, brought this action in negligence and strict liability for ultrahazardous activity in the state district court. The Valentines asserted that the respondent ("Pioneer") released liquified chlorine or chlorine gas into the environment, thereby injuring their son. Pioneer removed the action to the United States District Court for the District of Nevada. ... Pioneer then moved to dismiss the Valentines' cause of action in strict liability for failure to state a claim upon which relief could be granted.

* * *

Nevada recognizes the doctrine of strict tort liability for defective products. However, this court has not yet decided whether strict liability should also extend to abnormally dangerous activities.

The doctrine of strict liability for ultrahazardous or abnormally dangerous activities was first articulated in *Rylands v. Fletcher* ... . In *Rylands*, the defendant built a water reservoir on his property above abandoned mine shafts. The water burst through into one of the shafts and flooded the plaintiff's coal mine. Although the defendant was unaware of the shafts and was found not negligent, the English House of Lords nonetheless concluded that the defendant was liable ... . The

doctrine of *Rylands* has been explained and codified in the *Restatement (Second) of Torts*, section 519 (1977): "One who carries on an abnormally dangerous activity is subject to liability for harm to the person, land or chattels of another resulting from the activity, although he has exercised the utmost care to prevent the harm."

In response to the first question certified to this court, we now adopt the *Rylands* doctrine of strict liability as articulated in section 519 of the *Restatement (Second) of Torts*. Such a holding is consistent with our reasoning in strict products liability cases.

Section 520 of the Restatement ... sets forth six factors relevant to a determination of whether an activity is abnormally dangerous: (a) existence of a high degree of risk of some harm to the person, land or chattels of others; (b) likelihood that the harm that results from it will be great; (c) inability to eliminate the risk by the exercise of reasonable care; (d) extent to which the activity is not a matter of common usage; (e) inappropriateness of the activity to the place where it is carried on; and (f) extent to which its value to the community is outweighed by its dangerous attributes.

[The court concluded that it was not the proper court to determine factually whether the activity at bar was abnormally hazardous.] ... If the district court determines that Pioneer was engaged in an abnormally dangerous activity, strict liability will obtain. If, however, the district court determines that Pioneer's activity did not constitute an abnormally dangerous activity, strict liability will not apply.

Case Questions

1. What is the difference between extrahazardous, ultrahazardous, and abnormally dangerous activities?
2. Would the facts of *Rylands v. Fletcher* pass the modern Restatement test for abnormally dangerous?

The foreseeability issue is both argued and ignored, but further study is beyond the scope of our present discussion.

Damages

A person who loses an arm, a leg, or an eye or is left paraplegic suffers a loss of lifestyle as well. The courts have long considered a reduction in earning potential to be recoverable, but recently attorneys have argued, sometimes successfully, that injured parties should collect for "hedonic" losses, meaning essentially a decrease in enjoyment of life. Imagine an artist made blind by another's wrongful conduct. The artist may lose not only a career and earnings, but also much of the meaning and enjoyment of life. The next few years will tell how far courts are willing to go in recognizing such losses as compensable.

The *McDougald* case expresses the nature of **compensatory damages**. **Hedonic losses** are discussed and their limitations established in the context of a comatose plaintiff.

Punitive (or Exemplary) Damages for Intentional Tort

If compensatory damages aim at returning the plaintiff to the condition enjoyed before the wrongful injury by way of monetary compensation, punitive damages are reserved to punish the outrageous conduct of the defendant. They have nothing to do with compensation and are a windfall to the plaintiff (after paying 30 or 40 percent of the award to the plaintiff's attorney, the windfall is likely to be erased).

Summary

Tort has traditionally been defined as "a private wrong not arising out of contract." This definition distinguishes between public wrongs, which are classified as crimes, and private wrongs, which are designed to redress wrongful conduct causing injury to a private party. The public prosecutor is responsible for bringing actions in criminal cases; private parties bring actions on their own behalf to redress a wrong. The definition also distinguishes between torts and contract causes of action. In contract, the legal obligations are created by mutual agreement of the parties; the law

---
BALLENTINE'S

compensatory damages   Damages recoverable in a lawsuit for loss or injury suffered by the plaintiff as a result of the defendant's conduct. Also called *actual damages*, they may include expenses, loss of time, reduced earning capacity, bodily injury, and mental anguish.

hedonic damages (losses)   Damages awarded by some courts for loss of enjoyment of life or of life's pleasures.

Emma McDOUGALD et al., Respondents,
v.
Sara GARBER et al., Appellants.
Court of Appeals of New York
73 N.Y.2d 246, 536 N.E.2d 372,
538 N.Y.S.2d 937 (1989)

This appeal raises fundamental questions about the nature and role of nonpecuniary damages in personal injury litigation. By nonpecuniary damages, we mean those damages awarded to compensate an injured person for the physical and emotional consequences of the injury, such as pain and suffering and the loss of the ability to engage in certain activities. **Pecuniary damages ...** compensate the victim for the economic consequences of the injury, such as medical expenses, lost earnings and the cost of custodial care.

The specific questions raised here deal with assessment of nonpecuniary damages and are (1) whether some degree of cognitive awareness is a prerequisite to recovery for loss of enjoyment of life and (2) whether a jury should be instructed to consider and award damages for loss of enjoyment of life separately from damages for pain and suffering. We answer the first question in the affirmative and the second question in the negative.

* * *

On September 7, 1978, plaintiff Emma McDougald, then 31 years old, underwent a Caesarean section and tubal ligation at New York Infirmary. Defendant Garber performed the surgery; defendants Armengol and Kulkarni provided anesthesia. During the surgery, Mrs. McDougald suffered oxygen deprivation which resulted in severe brain damage and left her in a permanent comatose condition. This action was brought by Mrs. McDougald and her husband, suing derivatively, alleging that the injuries were caused by the defendants' acts of malpractice.

A jury found all defendants liable and awarded Emma McDougald a total of $9,650,102 in damages, including $1,000,000 for conscious pain and suffering and a separate award of $3,500,000 for loss of the pleasures and pursuits of life. The

balance of the damages awarded to her were for pecuniary damages—lost earnings and the cost of custodial and nursing care. Her husband was awarded $1,500,000 on his derivative claim for the loss of his wife's services. On defendants' posttrial motions, the Trial Judge reduced the total award to Emma McDougald to $4,796,728 by striking the entire award for future nursing care ($2,353,374) and by reducing the separate awards for conscious pain and suffering and loss of the pleasures and pursuits of life to a single award of $2,000,000. Her husband's award was left intact. On cross appeals, the Appellate Division affirmed and later granted defendants leave to appeal to this court.

* * *

We conclude that the court erred, both in instructing the jury that Mrs. McDougald's awareness was irrelevant to their consideration of damages for loss of enjoyment of life and in directing the jury to consider that aspect of damages separately from pain and suffering.

* * *

We begin with the familiar proposition that an award of damages to a person injured by the negligence of another is to compensate the victim, not to punish the wrongdoer. The goal is to restore the injured party, to the extent possible, to the position that would have been occupied had the wrong not occurred. To be sure, placing the burden of compensation on the negligent party also serves as a deterrent, but purely **punitive damages**—that is, those which have no compensatory purpose—are prohibited unless the harmful conduct is intentional, malicious, outrageous, or otherwise aggravated beyond mere negligence.

Damages for nonpecuniary losses are, of course, among those that can be awarded as compensation to the victim. This aspect of damages, however, stands on less certain ground than does an award for pecuniary damages. An economic loss can be compensated in kind by an economic gain; but recovery for noneconomic losses such as pain and suffering and loss of enjoyment of life rests on "the legal fiction that money damages can compensate for a victim's injury." We accept this fiction, knowing that although money will neither ease the pain nor restore the victim's abilities, this device is as close as the law can come in its effort to right the wrong. We have no hope of evaluating what has been lost, but a monetary award may provide a measure of solace for the condition created.

Our willingness to indulge this fiction comes to an end, however, when it ceases to serve the compensatory goals of tort recovery. When that limit is met, further indulgence can only result in assessing damages that are punitive. The question posed by this case, then, is whether an award of damages for loss of enjoyment of life to a person whose injuries preclude any awareness of the loss serves a compensatory purpose. We conclude that it does not.

Simply put, an award of money damages in such circumstances has no meaning or utility to the injured person. ...

We recognize that, as the trial court noted, requiring some cognitive awareness as a prerequisite to recovery for loss of enjoyment of life will result in some cases "in the paradoxical situation that the greater the degree of brain injury inflicted by a negligent defendant, the smaller the award the plaintiff can recover in general damages." The

force of this argument, however—the temptation to achieve a balance between injury and damages—has nothing to do with meaningful compensation for the victim. Instead, the temptation is rooted in a desire to punish the defendant in proportion to the harm inflicted. However relevant such retributive symmetry may be in the criminal law, it has no place in the law of civil damages, at least in the absence of culpability beyond mere negligence.

Accordingly, we conclude that cognitive awareness is a prerequisite to recovery for loss of enjoyment of life. We do not go so far, however, as to require the fact finder to sort out varying degrees of cognition and determine at what level a particular deprivation can be fully appreciated. With respect to pain and suffering, the trial court charged simply that there must be "some level of awareness" in order for plaintiff to recover. We think that this is an appropriate standard for all aspects of nonpecuniary loss. ...

Accordingly, the order of the Appellate Division, insofar as appealed from, should be modified, with costs to defendants, by granting a new trial on the issue of nonpecuniary damages of plaintiff Emma McDougald, and as so modified, affirmed.

Case Questions

1. What seems to be the difference in purpose between compensatory damages and punitive damages?
2. What is the inherent weakness in nonpecuniary damages as compensation?
3. What would be required to allow recovery for hedonic losses in New York? Did Emma McDougald meet the test?

Case Glossary

pecuniary damages Damages capable of being calculated in terms of their monetary value.

punitive damages Damages that are awarded over and above compensatory damages or actual damages because of the wanton, reckless, or malicious nature of the wrong done by the plaintiff. Such damages bear no relation to the plaintiff's actual loss and are often called *exemplary damages*, because their purpose is to make an example of the plaintiff to discourage others from engaging in the same kind of conduct in the future.

of contracts simply establishes the requisites for enforcement. In tort law, obligations are imposed by law. Tort law establishes protected private interests relating to person, property, reputation, and so on that are not premised on a contractual relationship, though one may exist (e.g., doctor-patient in medical malpractice).

There are numerous causes of action in tort, each having elements, each of which must be present for the court to accept a lawsuit based on a specific cause of action. However, tort law is a continually evolving field. New causes of action arise with some regularity, and courts exercise flexibility in allowing cases that do not fit into textbook definitions if conduct is clearly wrongful and injury is apparent.

Many factors influence the course of tort law independent of the interest sought to be protected. New law cannot be made by the courts unless disputes are brought, yet the economics of litigation usually influence which suits may be economically rewarding for a plaintiff.

Among the factors facilitating suit is the doctrine of *respondeat superior,* which holds an employer liable for the wrongful acts of an employee, thus making suits feasible when the wrongdoer/employee has limited funds and the employer has substantial resources. Similarly, the widespread use of insurance presents the opportunity for collecting full compensation for injuries sustained, which might not be possible if the defendant were uninsured and without assets.

In personal injury cases, customary practice includes the use of contingency fee arrangements whereby attorneys receive as their compensation a percentage of the settlement or award at the termination of the case. A great many cases could not be brought if the injured party were required to provide compensation to a lawyer as the case progressed.

Although these factors address practical questions, they affect the development of tort law, as certain sorts of cases are frequently pursued while others remain impractical.

Traditionally, the basis for requiring a defendant to compensate an injured plaintiff was fixing fault on the defendant for a wrongful act. The degree of fault required for a particular tort distinguishes between major categories of tort. The common element of intentional torts is an intentional act, whereas in negligence the standard is not what the defendant intended but the failure to act in a reasonable and prudent manner, the so-called "reasonable man" standard.

The relatively new field of products liability establishes liability without the necessity of proving fault. Manufacturers, in particular, are held liable for distributing dangerously defective products despite a lack of intent to harm or care in production. Although products liability has developed primarily over the last three decades, its roots can be found in much older theories of implied warranty and absolute liability for extrahazardous activities.

An important aspect of tort law is damages, or monetary compensation. Determining the amount of compensation depends on what can be included, but the object is to put the injured party in the position occupied before the wrongdoing occurred, that is, compensation for the difference in the plaintiff's life that the injury imposed. In some cases punitive damages may be available to punish the wrongdoer. These go beyond actual compensation and require malicious or outrageous conduct on the part of the defendant.

Review Questions

1. In the aftermath of a barroom brawl, two lawsuits arise. One is titled *State v. Holmes* and the other *Gonzalez v. Holmes*; the defendant is the same in both. Which is a criminal case and which a civil case? Several stages later, one of the cases is retitled *Holmes v. California*. Which case name has changed, and why has it changed?

2. At a New Year's Eve party, Beau Jangles attempts the Mexican Hat Dance blindfolded and bumps into a guest, causing physical injuries. Would Beau be more likely to be liable for battery or negligence? Why?

3. Why is it necessary in medical malpractice cases for the plaintiff to call a physician as a witness, even though that witness may have no firsthand knowledge of the events of the case?

4. Why are contingency fee arrangements allowed in personal injury cases but not in divorce cases?

5. *Black's Law Dictionary* defines "champerty" as "a bargain by a stranger with a party to a suit, by which such third person undertakes to carry on the litigation at his own cost and risk, in consideration of receiving, if successful, a part of the proceeds or subject sought to be recovered." Champerty was originally a crime. Is a contingency fee arrangement different from champerty?

6. Which of the policy grounds for products liability enumerated in *Lechuga, Inc. v. Montgomery* do you find most persuasive?

7. The most common form of legal advertising falls in the area of personal injury cases. The ABA and state bar associations for many years restricted advertising as unethical. What arguments can you make for and against advertising legal services in the personal injury field?

8. One state passed a law to prevent attorneys from free access to police accident reports after police complained that attorneys were searching reports for potential clients. How does this practice differ from advertising (soliciting clients versus advertising)?

9. Mental state is considered an important feature of torts. The measure of the difference between intentional torts and negligence is sometimes stated as that between an objective and a subjective measure of mental state. Which uses an objective and which uses a subjective measure?

10. If a pharmacist negligently fills a prescription for birth control pills with tranquilizers, should the pharmacist pay for the costs of raising the child born nine months later?

Exercises

1. Go to a law library, preferably one used by practitioners rather than an academic law library, and locate materials on torts. What areas are represented, and what proportion does each area comprise (e.g., how many texts or manuals are there on products liability, negligence, malpractice, etc.)? To what extent can coverage be explained by extraneous factors influencing tort litigation?

2. Find out if your state follows a contributory or comparative negligence principle. If it follows the comparative negligence principle, determine what formula applies. Then determine what the award would be in your state for the following:

   In *Hadley v. Baxendale,* the jury determines that defendant Baxendale was 40 percent responsible for the auto accident on which the suit was based, while plaintiff Hadley was 60 percent at fault. Hadley's injuries were determined to be $50,000.

   What would be the award if the apportionment of fault were reversed (Baxendale 60 percent and Hadley 40 percent)?

3. Under the doctrine of *respondeat superior,* an employer may be liable for the negligence of an employee while the employee is acting in the scope of employment. "An employee acts in the scope of his employment when he is doing something in furtherance of the duties he owes to his employer and where the employer is, or could be, exercising some control, directly or indirectly, over the employee's activities."

   In an interview with a new client, she tells you that she was injured in an accident by the driver of a United States Telephone and Telegraph truck at 8:00 P.M. on October 31. The driver was wearing a U.S. T & T uniform; sitting inside the truck beside the driver were two children dressed as clowns.

   An oral deposition has been scheduled for the driver. Make up ten questions you would ask to determine whether *respondeat superior* would be applicable.

CONTRACTING FOR A ROOM

Contracts touch every aspect of life and even paralegals who are not involved in contract or business law must be familiar with them. Something as simple and commonplace as booking a hotel room provides a good illustration of the contract process.

As with all contracts, a contract for a room between an innkeeper and a guest must satisfy the essential elements—contractual capacity, mutuality, legality, consideration, proper form, and genuine consent.

Most contracts for hotel rooms begin with an invitation to negotiate from a would-be guest who inquires as to room availability and price. An offer is often thereafter made by the guest or the hotel. If it is accepted the necessary mutuality exists.

If the hotel and guest are savvy, they will put their agreement in writing. Misunderstanding as to dates, duration of stay, and special needs of the guest are thereby avoided.

The agreement for one or more rooms between the hotel and guest can take many forms including:

- *Walk-in:* A guest without a reservation requests and receives accommodations.
- *Confirmed reservation:* The hotel has agreed, usually in writing, to the guest's reservation request.
- *Guaranteed reservation:* The guest promises to pay for the room, even if the guest never takes possession of it.
- *Prepaid reservation:* Payment of the first day's charge is made by a guest to the hotel, a travel agency, or through a computer network.
- *Blanket reservation:* A block of rooms is held for a particular group, with individual members of the group requesting individual room assignments from that block.

Reprinted from *Hotel, Restaurant, and Travel Law: A Preventive Approach,* 4th ed., © 1993, Delmar Publishers.

CHAPTER 12

CONTRACTS AND COMMERCIAL LAW

Introduction

There are two fundamental, conflicting conceptions of contractual obligations. The earlier, pre-nineteenth century conception embodied equitable principles emphasizing fairness and concepts of property, especially relying on transfer of title. The nineteenth century gave rise to the modern law of contracts, in which the obligations of contracts were cast in the light of the agreement itself, the bargain relationship, and the intent of the parties.

The title theory of exchange works well for the simultaneous exchange of things of fixed value, as when one pays for groceries at the supermarket. The will theory is more effective for **executory contracts**, that is, contracts relying on promises of future performance. For example, if a food processor contracts with farmers to buy crops for delivery at a fixed price in the future, principles of transfer of property rights at the making of the contract prove very awkward, whereas an examination of the bargain and the intent of the parties usually provides a basis for the enforcement of promises. The will theory is far more suitable for merchants and manufacturers in a commercial society and was gradually adopted by nineteenth-century courts, which viewed the encouragement of commerce and manufacturing as an important instrument of national growth.

A mechanical adherence to the will theory, however, encourages ruthless competition, so many of the adjustments to contract law in the twentieth century have been designed to ensure fairness in the market and protection against unfair exploitation. Equitable concepts of fairness are used by the courts to prevent the excesses of the unscrupulous. In addition, legislatures have been active in passing laws, such as recent consumer-oriented legislation, to protect a vulnerable public.

Contract Law and the Paralegal

Most contract obligations are discharged by performance of the parties according to the terms of the agreement. When full performance is not feasible, the parties usually compromise their differences without recourse to law or litigation. Except for the specialist in commercial litigation, lawyer and paralegal alike are most often concerned with

---
BALLENTINE'S

executory contract   A contract yet to be performed, each party having bound himself or herself to do or not to do a particular thing.

making, rather than breaking, contracts. Aiding contract negotiation and drafting contracts constitutes most of the work. Precision and clarity of language are the skills most needed for drafting and should be taught as part of a legal writing course (but often are not).

It may appear that we devote an inordinate amount of space in this chapter to contract formation and the conflicting principles that surround it. The reason for this concentration is twofold:

1. Paralegals are generally more concerned with the formation of contracts than any other aspect.
2. The law governing contract formation is complex and confusing, despite being commonly presented in business law texts as consistent and logical.

Although the approach here may seem unduly theoretical for a text for practitioners, the object is to avoid the morass of confusion presented by comprehensive contract texts and the omissions and simplifications of texts on business law.

Definition

Like so many legal concepts, contract is not easily defined. If, as Grant Gilmore has persuasively argued, contract is dead and is being reabsorbed into tort, present definitions may look silly to future generations. Nevertheless, there is a difference between tort and contract in determining obligations from mutual agreements of the parties as opposed to obligations imposed by the law of torts. Even this distinction becomes seriously blurred when a court imposes terms or conditions on parties that they never bargained for and never agreed to.

Tort and contract often overlap. In *Demakos*, a tenant sued a landlord for injuries incurred by other tenants and their visitors. The landlord sought recovery from his insurance company. Although insurance contracts are ordinarily construed in favor of the insured, when the language is clear it is given effect. In contracts, the rights and duties are created by agreement.

The important feature of contract law is not the contract itself, but the contractual relations it creates, and it is the regulation of relationships that is the subject of this chapter. If a court declares a contract void because one of the parties was coerced into agreement, it is saying something not about the nature of contracts but about the nature of contractual relationships. With this caveat in mind, let us look at some definitions of *contract*.

George DEMAKOS, et al.,
Appellants,
v.
TRAVELERS INSURANCE COMPANY,
Respondent
Supreme Court, Appellate Division,
Second Department
613 N.Y.S.2d 709 (1994)

In an action, inter alia, for a judgment declaring the rights of the parties under a liability insurance policy, the plaintiffs appeal from an order and judgment (one paper) ... which granted the motion of the defendant insurer for a declaration that it had no duty to defend or indemnify the plaintiffs in an underlying negligence action and to dismiss the plaintiffs' cause of action for damages.

ORDERED that the order and the judgment is affirmed, with costs.

After being sued by a tenant for physical injuries caused by cigarette smoke which allegedly seeped into the tenant's premises from the pool and billiard club in the basement of the building, the insured landlord sought coverage from the insurer under his business liability insurance policies. The insurer disclaimed, based on the pollution exclusion clauses in the policies. Thereafter, the insured brought the instant action. Upon the insurer's motion, the Supreme Court held that the language of the pollution exclusion was clear and unambiguous and that the complaint in the underlying personal injury action fell within the four corners of the exclusion. We agree.

The two identical exclusion clauses in the two policies in effect at the time stated that the insurer was not liable under the policy for any physical or property damage caused by pollutants. The policies also defined the term pollutant to include vapor, smoke, and fumes. The complaint in the underlying personal injury action alleged damages as a result of smoke and noxious fumes and vapors seeping through the basement. The exclusion is unambiguous, and the underlying complaint falls within the exclusion.

Case Questions

1. Why are insurance contracts construed in favor of the insured?
2. To what does the court look to determine what rights and duties are owed?

A contract is a promise or set of promises for the breach of which the law gives a remedy, or the performance of which the law in some way recognizes as a duty.

Restatement (Second) of Contracts § 1 (1981).

"Contract" means the total legal obligation which results from the parties' agreement as affected by this Act and any other applicable rules of law.

Uniform Commercial Code (UCC) § 1-201(11).

The *Restatement* takes the traditional view of contract as an exchange of promises (e.g., "I promise to pay you $10,000 if you promise to give me title to your automobile") that the law recognizes as enforceable. The UCC avoids promissory language and describes a contract as an enforceable agreement. At any rate, it is clear that individuals may make promises or agreements, some of which are legally enforceable and are called contracts.

The *Restatement* definition of contract reflects the will theory mentioned previously, which will henceforth be referred to as the *classical* approach to contracts, reflecting developments in contracts in the nineteenth and early twentieth centuries. It comprises what most paralegals and lawyers need to know about contracts (along with the UCC) in order to draft contracts. Classical contract theory treats the essentials of contract formation in terms of discrete elements necessary to make a valid contract, namely, offer, acceptance, and consideration. It attempts to treat contract law as logical, precise, and self-contained.

Unfortunately, when the promises made at the formation stage are not fulfilled, issues of fairness and morality arise that are not so neatly resolved. A body of law that conflicts with classical theory has evolved to deal with contractual relations. This approach might be called the *moral* or *reliance theory* and is embodied in the somewhat obscure language of § 90 of the first *Restatement:*

> A promise which the promisor should reasonably expect to induce action or forbearance of a definite and substantial character on the part of the promisee and which does induce such action or forbearance is binding if injustice can be avoided only by enforcement of the promise.

In many cases, this principle allows the court to weigh the fairness of enforcement or nonenforcement of contract claims. Although theories of reliance and moral obligation may be of little significance in drafting contracts, they are important once a contract dispute arises. Failure to appreciate that there are two competing theories of contract inevitably leads to confusion. The classical model will be addressed with the issue of contract formation, and the reliance model will be introduced in connection with breach of contract and contract remedies.

Contract Formation: The Classical Model

The requirements of contract formation established in the nineteenth century cast the bargain relationship in idealized form. Parties to contracts were seen as individuals negotiating from equal positions of power, freely arriving at a "meeting of the minds," in which the agreement that constituted the contract was complete and its subject matter and terms were understood by both parties. When such was the case, if one of the parties failed to fulfill contractual promises, it would be necessary only for the court to apply the appropriate remedy for the injured party. Under this scheme, the court inquired into whether the elements of offer, acceptance, and consideration were present; it then interpreted the terms of the contract.

Offer

Contract negotiations typically begin with an offer; the party making the offer is the *offeror*. The contract is not complete until an offer has been accepted by an *offeree*. An offer requires:

1. Intent to make an offer on the part of the offeror
2. Definite terms
3. Communication to the offeree.

The failure of any of the requisites of an offer may nullify contract formation.

What appears to be an offer may fail because it lacks intent on the part of the offeror. Offers are often distinguished from invitations to negotiate or even solicitations for offers. "No reasonable offer refused," "Would you go as high as $1000?," or "I might sell it for as little as $500" are illusory offers in this category. The circumstances of the offer may also indicate that intent is lacking, as when the offer is made in jest, anger, or intoxication ("I'd sell that money-sucking car for two cents!"). The offeror's post hoc claim that a serious offer was not intended is not sufficient to avoid the contract; the test is whether a reasonable person would conclude from the circumstances that a serious offer had been made.

The offer may be made in terms so indefinite as to render the contract unenforceable; no meeting of the minds was present. Indefiniteness of price, for example, is usually fatal ("just pay me a fair price"). [The UCC takes exception to the indefinite price rule in the sale of goods when certain conditions are met. *See* UCC § 2-305.]

A valid and intended communication must be made to the offeree. The classic example in this category is the offer of a reward. Someone not aware of an offer of a reward who returns a lost dog is not legally entitled to the reward.

Acceptance

An offer does not bind the offeror until it is accepted by the offeree. Prior to acceptance, the offeror may revoke the offer, so acceptance subsequent to revocation does not bind the offeror. Acceptance requires:

1. Communication to the offeror
2. Acceptance of the terms of the offer.

Because a valid acceptance creates a contract, it is essential that the acceptance be communicated to the offeror. Acceptance has traditionally been classified in two forms:

1. Acceptance by a return promise ("I will pay the $4,000 you are asking for your car").
2. Acceptance by performance required by the offer (acceptance of the offer of a reward for lost property is made by returning the property, not by promising to return the property).

When an offer calls for a return promise, it is called a *bilateral contract*. When the offer calls for acceptance in terms of performance, it is called a *unilateral contract*. Because most contracts are bilateral, it is important for the offeror who insists on performance (rather than a promise to perform) to make this condition quite clear. To "I will pay you $500 to clear my lot by Thursday, October 20" should be added "If you cannot finish by the end of Thursday, do not undertake the job because I will not pay."

The offeror is *master of the offer* and may set specific terms or manner of acceptance. When the offer is silent as to the manner of acceptance, the law has developed a complex set of rules governing the communication of acceptance, to which the UCC has made exceptions with regard to sales of goods.

A valid acceptance requires that the offeree agree to the specific terms of the offer. This is the so-called *mirror image rule,* which has been changed drastically for sales of goods covered by the UCC. If the offeree attempts to change the terms of the offer, the attempted acceptance will be treated as a counteroffer rather than an acceptance, and the offeror and offeree change places. If the offeror offers to sell "my first edition of *Moby Dick* for $500," offeree's response of "I'll pay $400" is a counteroffer rather than an acceptance, and the purchaser has become the offeror and the owner the offeree ("I accept your offer of $400" would constitute acceptance and create a contract). Similarly, "I will pay $500 if you furnish a certificate of authenticity" is a counteroffer because it has added a term not present in the original offer.

The meeting-of-the-minds/mirror-image formula is technically simple, but transactions in the real world often defy its application. For example, in something as simple as the first edition sale, when the offeree appears with the personal check for $500, the offeror may insist on cash or a cashier's check. When they agreed on $500, did this mean "cash"? Can the offeror insist on cash? Does the offer to clear land "by" Thursday mean "before" Thursday (midnight Wednesday) or "on" Thursday (before Friday). An apparent meeting of the minds rarely includes every last detail of performance, and the courts do not require perfection in offer and acceptance; but those who draft contracts must be particularly careful in the precision of their language and use their imaginations to include essential terms and conditions of the contract.

The goal of the attorney may conflict with that of the contracting parties. The attorney aims at protecting a client and providing a contract, the terms of which are sufficiently clear that litigation can be avoided, or if litigation is necessary, so that the court could apply the contract terms as originally intended. The contracting parties, in contrast, are interested in a mutually satisfactory result. Professor Stewart Macaulay has noted that businesspersons are often more concerned about flexibility, cooperation, and continuing good relations than they are about technical problems of contract law. A good legal team should not assume that contracting parties are adversaries—contract relations are ordinarily created because both sides have found a mutual benefit in working together.

If a contract is formed by a "meeting of the minds," what happens when one of the parties later claims the intentions were different? If anyone could avoid a contract simply by asserting a secret intent at the time of making the contract, no contract could be reliable. The courts have developed an "objective" standard for assessing the intent of the parties similar to the reasonable man standard of torts: What would a reasonable person have inferred from the circumstances and conduct of the parties? Such a standard was applied in *Lucy v. Zehmer*.

W.O. LUCY and J.C. Lucy
v.
A.H. ZEHMER and Ida S. Zehmer
Supreme Court of Appeals of Virginia
196 Va. 493, 84 S.E.2d 516 (1954)

This suit was instituted by W.O. Lucy and J.D. Lucy, complainants, against A.H. Zehmer and Ida S. Zehmer, his wife, defendants, to have specific performance of a contract by which it was alleged the Zehmers had sold to W.O. Lucy a tract of land owned by A.H. Zehmer in Dinwiddie county containing 471.6 acres, more or less, known as the Ferguson farm for $50,000. J.C. Lucy, the other complainant, is a brother of W.O. Lucy, to whom W.O. Lucy transferred a half interest in his alleged purchase.

The instrument sought to be enforced was written by A.H. Zehmer on December 20, 1952, in these words: "We hereby agree to sell to W.O. Lucy the Ferguson Farm complete for $50,000, title satisfactory to buyer," and signed by the defendants, A.H. Zehmer and Ida S. Zehmer.

The answer of A.H. Zehmer admitted that at the time mentioned W.O. Lucy offered him $50,000 cash for the farm, but that he, Zehmer, considered that the offer was made in jest; that so thinking, and both he and Lucy having had several drinks, wrote out "the memorandum" quoted above and induced his wife to sign it; that he did not deliver the memorandum to Lucy, but that Lucy picked it up, read it, put it in his pocket, attempted to offer Zehmer $5 to bind the bargain, which Zehmer refused to accept, and realizing for the first time that Lucy was serious, Zehmer assured him that he had no intention of selling the farm and that the whole matter was a joke. Lucy left the premises insisting that he had purchased the farm.

* * *

The defendants insist that the evidence was ample to support their contention that the writing sought to be enforced was prepared as a bluff or dare to force Lucy to admit that he did not have $50,000; that the whole matter was a joke;

that the writing was not delivered to Lucy and no binding contract was ever made between the parties.

It is an unusual, if not bizarre, defense. When made to the writing admittedly prepared by one of the defendants and signed by both, clear evidence is required to sustain it.

In his testimony Zehmer claimed that he "was high as a Georgia pine," and that the transaction "was just a bunch of two doggoned drunks bluffing to see who could talk the biggest and say the most." That claim is inconsistent with his attempt to testify in great detail as to what was said and what was done. It is contradicted by other evidence as to the condition of both parties, and rendered of no weight by the testimony of his wife that when Lucy left the restaurant she suggested that Zehmer drive him home. The record is convincing that Zehmer was not intoxicated to the extent of being unable to comprehend the nature and consequences of the instrument he executed, and hence that instrument is not to be invalidated on that ground. It was in fact conceded by defendants' counsel in oral argument that under the evidence Zehmer was not too drunk to make a valid contract.

The evidence is convincing also that Zehmer wrote two agreements, the first one beginning "I hereby agree to sell." Zehmer first said he could not remember about that, then that "I don't think I wrote but one out." Mrs. Zehmer said that what he wrote was "I hereby agree," but that the "I" was changed to "We" after that night. The agreement that was written and signed is in the record and indicates no such change. Neither are the mistakes in spelling that Zehmer sought to point out readily apparent.

The appearance of the contract, the fact that it was under discussion for forty minutes or more before it was signed; Lucy's objection to the first draft because it was written in the singular, and he wanted Mrs. Zehmer to sign it also; the rewriting to meet that objection and the signing by Mrs. Zehmer; the discussion of what was to be included in the sale, the provision for the examination of the title, the completeness of the instrument that was executed, the taking possession of it by

Lucy with no request or suggestion by either of the defendants that he give it back, are facts which furnish persuasive evidence that the execution of the contract was a serious business transaction rather than a casual, jesting matter as defendants now contend.

* * *

If it be assumed, contrary to what we think the evidence shows, that Zehmer was jesting about selling his farm to Lucy and that the transaction was intended by him to be a joke, nevertheless the evidence shows that Lucy did not understand it but considered it to be a serious business transaction and the contract to be binding on the Zehmers as well as on himself. The very next day he arranged with his brother to put up half the money and take a half interest in the land. The day after that he employed an attorney to examine the title. The next night, Tuesday, he was back at Zehmer's place and there Zehmer told him for the first time, Lucy said, that he wasn't going to sell and he told Zehmer, "You know you sold that place fair and square." After receiving the report from his attorney that the title was good he wrote to Zehmer that he was ready to close the deal.

Not only did Lucy actually believe, but the evidence shows he was warranted in believing, that the contract represented a serious business transaction and a good faith sale and purchase of the farm.

In the field of contract, as generally elsewhere, "We must look to the outward expression of a person as manifesting his intention rather than to his secret and unexpressed intention. 'The law imputes to a person an intention corresponding to the reasonable meaning of his words and acts.'"

* * *

"The law, therefore, judges of an agreement between two persons exclusively from those expressions of their intentions which are communicated between them." ... [T]he law imputes to a person an intention corresponding to the reasonable meaning of his words and acts. ... [I]t is immaterial what may be the real but unexpressed state of his mind.

So a person cannot set up that he was merely jesting when his conduct and words would warrant a reasonable person in believing that he intended a real agreement.

Whether the writing signed by the defendant and now sought to be enforced by the complainants was the result of a serious offer by Lucy and a serious acceptance by the defendants, or was a serious offer by Lucy and an acceptance in secret jest by the defendants, in either event it constituted a binding contract of sale between the parties.

* * *

The complainants are entitled to have specific performance of the contract sued on. ...
Reversed and remanded.

Case Questions

1. Zehmer had bought the farm eleven years before for $11,000 and had refused an offer seven years prior by Lucy for $20,000. If the contract had been for $10,000, would the court have enforced it?
2. What if Lucy had known the contract was a joke but proceeded as if it had not been? Would the facts have been any different?
3. Could Zehmer have succeeded if he argued that he was drunk at the time, claiming intoxication as a defense?

Consideration

Consideration is a somewhat anomalous requirement for contract formation. It is the symbolic proof that the contract was the result of bargaining. In its broadest conception, consideration is represented by the exchange of something of value. Many form contracts include a pro forma recital of consideration, typically one dollar or ten dollars, to satisfy the consideration requirement. Although this is artificial and often illusory (no money actually changes hands), many courts developed the doctrine that the sufficiency of consideration is not to be questioned.

The bargain aspect of consideration is exemplified by § 71 of the *Restatement*: "To constitute consideration, a performance or a return promise must be bargained for." The "something of value" may simply be a return promise. The original purpose of consideration appears to have been the refusal to enforce promises of gifts when the promisee does nothing in return. If Grandmother says to Grandson, "When you reach 25, I'll give you $10,000," and Grandson replies, "I'll be glad to receive it," the appearance is that of acceptance; but when Grandmother's junk bonds become worth twenty cents on the dollar, the court is loath to enforce the agreement, arguing that Grandson neither conferred a benefit on Grandmother nor suffered a "detriment" by forbearing to do something he was entitled to do, so there was no consideration on his part for the contract. In contrast, when Uncle promised Nephew $5,000 on his twenty-fifth birthday if until that time Nephew would refrain from drinking and smoking, the court may find consideration, in that Nephew suffered a legal detriment by forbearing doing something he had a legal right to do. Courts have on occasion found consideration based on "love and affection" to support the promise of a gift when a relative has provided aid and support. It would seem that the courts have attempted to avoid unfairness by invoking the existence of consideration or its absence and have stretched logic to justify their conclusions. Any other explanation suggests a logic and consistency to the concept of consideration that is not corroborated by the cases.

Love and affection have on occasion been construed to be consideration to support enforcement of a contract between persons in close relationships, even though material consideration is lacking. The *Rose* court, however, was unwilling to find consideration on this basis.

Leah ROSE, Plaintiff-Appellant,
v.
Samuel ELIAS, Defendant-Respondent.
Supreme Court, Appellate Division,
First Department
177 A.D.2d 415, 576 N.Y.S.2d 257 (1991)

Order ... entered May 14, 1990, which granted defendant's motion to dismiss the complaint for failure to state a cause of action, unanimously affirmed, without costs.

Defendant, a married man, promised in writing to purchase an apartment for the plaintiff, his female companion, in return for the "love and affection" that she provided to him during the prior three years. We agree with the [lower] court that the love and affection provided by plaintiff were insufficient consideration for defendant's promise to purchase an apartment for her.

Nor is a cause of action stated by virtue of plaintiff's claim that she forbore job opportunities at defendant's oral request, since defendant's written promise to provide an apartment for plaintiff was unambiguous and complete, and it is apparent that the parties did not view plaintiff's

forbearance from accepting job opportunities as consideration for the promise. " 'Nothing is consideration ... that is not regarded as such by both parties.' "

The defendant asserted that his relationship with the plaintiff was primarily a sexual relationship, and plaintiff did not deny that sexual relations were a part of the relationship. Plaintiff admitted that the proposed purchase of an apartment was intended to facilitate a "comfortable" life together with the defendant. "Agreements tending to dissolve a marriage or to facilitate adultery are closely scrutinized to determine whether the main objective of the agreement is aimed to produce that result." The [lower] court concluded that the words "love and affection" in the circumstances presented suggest adultery, and thus illegal consideration. Since there was found to be no severable legal component of the consideration for defendant's promise, the court correctly ruled in the alternative that the contract was void as against public policy.

We have considered plaintiff's arguments based on theories of estoppel and unjust enrichment, and find them to be without merit.

Case Questions

1. Is there more here than a promise to make a gift?
2. How critical to this decision is the fact that defendant was married?

Consideration is an artificial legal concept rarely of concern to those engaged in the bargaining relationship. Gilmore traces the rise of the concept to Holmes's *The Common Law,* where it appears mysteriously without authority. The effect of the consideration requirement is to negate many contracts that would be enforceable without it. It is a device that can be used by a court to declare that contract formation was flawed and therefore unenforceable. It is probably of little practical importance to the attorney except as a strategy on behalf of a client trying to avoid enforcement of a contract. Nevertheless, when custom dictates a recital of consideration, it is wise to follow established practice.

Consideration is important in option contracts. Because offers may be revoked prior to acceptance, one way to keep an offer open is to pay for it. A person may purchase an option on land, for example—by paying $1,000 for an option to purchase land for $50,000 before January 1. In this way, the offer to sell the land may not be revoked until the expiration of the option (January 1). Because consideration has been paid, a contract has been formed. Of course, if January 1 passes without action, the contract ends, as do the duties of the parties.

Limitations on Contract Formation

Even when offer, acceptance, and consideration are present, the law will not recognize a contract if the bargaining process was flawed by misconduct (fraud, misrepresentation, duress, or undue influence), defect in agreement (mistake), the incapacity of one of the parties (minority or mental incompetence), or illegal purpose. In addition, the law requires that certain contracts must be in writing to be enforceable (Statute of Frauds). Each of these is treated in summary fashion here.

Contract Induced by Misconduct of One of the Parties

Although parties have great latitude in the promises they exchange in a bargaining relationship, the absence of a bargain may be found if one of the parties was deceived as to the bargain or deprived of free will in bargaining.

Fraud and misrepresentation are generally distinguished on the basis of intentional false representations (fraud) and innocent false representations (misrepresentation). If a used car dealer sells a 1979 model as a 1980 model, while knowing it to be a 1979 model, it would be fraud; if the dealer believed it to be a 1980 model, it would be misrepresentation. In either case, the innocent party should have the option to accept the contract or to **rescind** it, returning the car and receiving the return of payments made. Such contracts are *voidable,* meaning the innocent party may avoid the contract by returning to the conditions prior to the agreement. This is distinguished from contracts that are *void* (see "Illegality," later in this section).

A contract is also voidable if it can be shown that one of the parties could not exercise free will in the bargaining process (duress). Duress occurs when one party is threatened with harm to induce agreement. The threatened harm is ordinarily physical or emotional harm directed against the party, the party's family, or the party's property. Usually economic pressure is not sufficient to constitute duress, nor is the threat to bring lawsuit ("If you don't sell, I'll foreclose").

Undue influence occurs when relentless pressure so weakens a party's will that the bargain is not freely obtained. Undue influence also occurs when the parties have a confidential relationship such as close family relations, attorney-client, physician-patient, or the like.

Mistake

Mutual, or bilateral, mistake of fact makes the contract voidable by either party. For example, in one famous case, the violinist Efrem Zimbalist purchased two violins believed by both purchaser and seller to have been made by Guarnerius and Stradivarius. Zimbalist was able to void the contract when the violins proved to be nearly worthless. This example somewhat oversimplifies the complex and confusing area of mistake.

Lack of Capacity to Form a Contract

Lack of capacity may be due to lack of legal competence based on status (minor), lack of mental capacity to form contracts, or temporary incapacitation (intoxication).

In most states, the age of majority is eighteen. Until reaching the age of majority, persons are not legally competent, which includes an incapacity to bind themselves contractually. Exceptions are sometimes made for **emancipated minors.** Contracts with minors may be avoided

---

BALLENTINE'S

rescind   To effect a rescission. Properly used, "rescind" means to annul a contract from the beginning, not merely to terminate the contract as to future transactions.

emancipated minor   A person who has not yet attained the age of majority who is totally self-supporting or married. A parent emancipates [a] minor child when he or she surrenders control and authority over the child and gives [the child] the right to [the child's] earnings. Emancipation also terminates the parent's legal duty to support the minor child.

by the minor, but can be **ratified** upon reaching the age of majority. Contracts for "necessaries," such as food and clothing, are usually enforceable against minors.

The invalidity of contracts involving lack of mental capacity is based on the notion that lack of capacity prevents an individual from understanding the bargain. A person may display peculiarities that indicate mental illness yet understand fully the subject matter and obligations entered into by contract, in which case the contract may not be avoided. A person determined to be mentally incompetent by legal authority is not legally competent, and contracts with such persons are in some states void from their inception.

Inability to understand the nature and purpose of contractual obligations may also be established by the intoxication of one of the parties at the time the contract was formed. Intoxication includes all drugs that affect one's mental state and ability to understand the consequences of the bargain. The intoxicated person may later affirm or disaffirm the contract. There is significant variation among jurisdictions as to proof and legal effect of intoxication.

There is a story about Sophocles, the great dramatist of ancient Athens, who had amassed significant wealth from prizes for his plays. When he reached the ripe old age of eighty, his children, then in their fifties, grew tired of waiting for their inheritance and brought Sophocles before the court of Athenian citizens to have him declared senile so that they could manage his wealth. As his only defense, Sophocles read to those assembled a play he had just written. The jury found him to be of sound mind, and his children had to wait another ten years to collect their inheritance. Sophocles would undoubtedly have enjoyed the result in the *Hanks* case.

Illegality

Agreements to do an unlawful act, including tortious as well as criminal acts, or for an unlawful purpose, are deemed void by the courts and will not be enforced. A number of problems, such as what exactly is unlawful and how to handle a contract that is in part unlawful and in part lawful, have had different results in different jurisdictions.

BALLENTINE'S
---

ratification   The act of giving one's approval to a previous act, either one's own or someone else's, which, without such confirmation, would be nonbinding. A person may ratify a contract by expressly promising to be bound by it. Ratification may be implied from a person's conduct; it may also take place as a result of accepting the benefits of a transaction. Ratification is the confirmation of an act that has already been performed, as opposed to the authorization of an act that is yet to be performed.

HANKS

v.

McNEIL COAL CORPORATION et al.
Colorado Supreme Court
114 Colo. 578, 168 P.2d 256 (1946)

Lee A. Hanks, who was a prosperous farmer and businessman in Nebraska, came to Colorado with his family in 1918, at first settling on a farm in Weld county, which included the coal lands involved in this proceeding; then, in 1920 moving to Boulder where he purchased a home, engaged in the retail coal business, and thereafter resided. ... Shortly after 1922 Lee Hanks discovered that he was afflicted with diabetes, and members of his family noticed a progressive change in his physical and mental condition thereafter. He became irritable and easily upset, very critical of his son's work, and increasingly interested in the emotional type of religion. He began to speculate in oil and other doubtful ventures with money needed for payment of debts and taxes. About 1934 he sent his son what he denominated a secret formula for the manufacture of medicine to cure fistula in horses, which was compounded principally of ground china, brick dust, burnt shoe leather and amber-colored glass. If the infection was in the horse's right shoulder, the mixture was to be poured in the animal's left ear, and if on the left shoulder then in the right ear. In 1937 Mr. Hanks started to advertise this medicine through the press under the name of Crown King Remedy. Thereafter he increasingly devoted his efforts and

money to the compounding and attempted sale of this concoction, his business judgment became poor and he finally deteriorated mentally to the point that on May 25, 1940, he was adjudicated insane and his son was appointed conservator of his estate.

[Before being adjudicated insane, in 1937, Hanks sold property to the coal company, which he had learned was hauling coal over his lands. His son, the conservator of his estate brought this suit to avoid the contract.]

... The legal test of Hanks' insanity is whether "he was incapable of understanding and appreciating the extent and effect of business transactions in which he engaged."

... One may have insane delusions regarding some matters and be insane on some subjects, yet capable of transacting business concerning matters wherein such subjects are not concerned, and such insanity does not make one incompetent to contract unless the subject matter of the contract is so connected with an insane delusion as to render the afflicted party incapable of understanding the nature and effect of the agreement or of acting rationally in the transaction.

... Patently Hanks was suffering from insane delusion in 1937 with reference to the efficacy of the horse medicine, but there is no evidence of delusions or hallucinations in connection with this transaction or with his transaction of much of his other business at that time; there is no basis for holding voidable his sale here involved on the ground of his insanity.

Case Questions

1. What difference would it have made if Hanks had been adjudicated insane prior to the sale?
2. Of what significance was the horse medicine?

Statute of Frauds

An oral contract binds the parties as much as a written one, though a written contract provides more certain evidence of the terms of a contract than personal recollection of what was orally agreed. In 1677 the

Statute of Frauds was enacted, making certain contracts unenforceable unless written. In 1677 the law of contracts was poorly developed, as were the laws of evidence and proof; the statute was an attempt to prevent fraudulent abuse of legal process. The Statute of Frauds remained largely intact during the creation of American law, often with only minor modifications. Although the statute identified five categories in which a written contract was required, two remain of major importance in the practice of law: (1) contracts for the conveyance of interests in land; (2) contracts not to be performed within one year. The UCC has created its own version of the Statute of Frauds, requiring certain contracts be in writing, the most notable of which covers the sale of goods for more than $500 and the sale of other forms of personal property valued at more than $5000.

Today the Statute of Frauds can actually invite fraud, as, for instance, when a person attempts to avoid an obligation by invoking the statute while at the same time benefiting from another's performance. The courts have displayed considerable creativity in getting around the statute when the interests of justice are not served by strict adherence to it.

Compensatory Damages for Breach of Contract

Because contract law is modeled largely on business relations, and contractual relations are created by the parties to the contract, the remedy for breach of contract is quite different from that in tort. Injuries that are not foreseeable or not within the contemplation of the parties are not a usual element of compensatory damages. Physical or emotional injuries are not recoverable except where tort principles have invaded contract territory (e.g., malpractice and products liability).

The overriding policy in compensatory damages for breach of contract is to put the "nonbreaching party in the position he would have been in had the contract been performed." This may include lost profits if they are roughly ascertainable and within the contemplation of the parties. It may mean paying the cost of completion, as with unfinished construction contracts, or cost of replacement, or the difference between contract price and market price. Damages are often rephrased as "giving the nonbreaching party the benefit of his bargain." Several different measures of damages have developed for different categories of contracts, and the Uniform Commercial Code provides its own special rules. The diversity of rules is designed to ensure that the nonbreaching party does not suffer a loss or enjoy a windfall. Although breach represents the fault aspect of contract law, the breaching party is to be protected rather than penalized (punitive damages are rare in contract cases).

This brief summary of damages ignores numerous complicating factors, such as **anticipatory breach**, **substantial performance**, and cases in which both parties breach, which are normally covered in some detail in contract and business law texts.

Problems with the Classical Model

Classical contract theory, which developed during the period before and after the turn of the century, constructed a logical set of rules based on offer, acceptance, and consideration for the formation of contract and compensatory damages for the resolution of contract disputes. This scheme is satisfactory for a great many contracts, but the diversity of contract relationships creates a variety of situations that defy mechanical solutions:

1. *A person promises to make a gift.* A brother offers his sister the free use of his second home on a permanent basis. She sells her own house and moves her belongings and family. Brother later gets a good offer on the house and reneges on his promise. Under classical consideration principles, the sister has no enforceable contract rights.

2. *Charitable pledges.* A church solicits pledges from its parishioners to build a new annex, then enters into a building contract. Was there consideration to support enforcing the pledges?

3. *Confidential professional relationships.* Doctor and patient enter a contract for treatment, but the treatment is negligently performed. Compensatory damages for breach of contract do not compensate for the injuries sustained.

4. *Indefinite oral contracts.* Buyer and seller agree to transfer title to an automobile, but time and place of performance are not mentioned.

5. *Unilateral contracts requiring performance as acceptance when promisee has begun to perform and promisor revokes the offer.* Property owner offers $2,500 to roofer when roof is completed to "owner's satisfaction." Roofer moves trucks and men out to do the work, only to find that owner has hired someone else.

————————BALLENTINE'S————————

anticipatory breach The announced intention of a party to a contract that he or she does not intend to perform his or her obligations under the contract; an announced intention to commit a breach of contract.

substantial performance The doctrine that there is adequate consideration to support a contract if there has been substantial performance of the contract.

6. *Contracts in which the parties leave the details to be worked out later.*

7. *Performance without a contract.* Contractor blacktops the wrong driveway while owner stands by and watches silently, later disclaiming any liability in the absence of a contract.

8. *Contracts for which compensatory damages create an unfair result.* Seller of house lot refuses to deliver deed as required by contract because a second buyer has offered a higher price. First buyer's costs attributable to the breach of contract are minimal.

9. *Inducements to contract cause a party to incur costs relying on the inducement, but the contract is never completed.* Offer of hardware franchise induces potential franchisee to sell business at loss and work as manager/trainee to learn business. Franchisor later refuses to enter contract.

10. *Strict adherence to the Statute of Frauds will have grossly unfair results.* Seller and buyer agree orally to transfer land for a fixed price. Buyer clears the land and puts in a foundation for a house, and seller decides not to sell. Under the statute, the contract is unenforceable.

11. *Manufacturer claims no responsibility for person injured by a product because purchaser bought the product from a dealer and had no contractual relation with manufacturer.*

Fault

Historically, judges were naturally reluctant to leave an innocent injured party without a remedy. This presented no problem if the contract was clearly enforceable and one party had breached. If a damages remedy fully compensated the injured party, an easy and just result was available. The breaching party was at fault under contract law, and liability was fixed. In many cases, such as those previously listed, contract principles were unavailing. Judges employed a number of devices to avoid unjust results, some of them old, notably equitable remedies and principles; some of them new; and some of them fictitious.

When fault under common-law contract theory was unworkable, the courts frequently resorted to the developing law of torts. Negligence theory provided a ready remedy for professional malpractice, especially medical malpractice, where compensatory contract damages were inappropriate because the injury was not loss of profits but disability, death, or pain and suffering. The duty of due care was imposed by law rather than by contract, so these cases jumped the fence from contract to tort at an early date without much resistance from the courts. The foreseeability of serious injury from medical malpractice, viewed either from a contract or a tort law perspective, gives strength to the imposition of liability. A high standard of professional care also places the burden on the physician in the doctor-patient relationship, a standard easily implied to the contract.

The shift of products liability from contract to tort was more tortuous (forgive the pun). Although Justice Traynor finally justified the imposition of tort liability for defective products on policy grounds (see Chapter 11), his landmark decision in *Greenman v. Yuba Power Products* rested on a line of cases developed from Judge Cardozo's opinion in *MacPherson v. Buick Motor Co.,* 217 N.Y. 382, 111 N.E. 105 (1916) dispensing with the **privity of contract** requirement and holding the manufacturer as well as the dealer liable. Products liability ultimately rested on the principle of implied warranty, the law imposing duties beyond the express terms of the contract. Although products liability is said to be strict liability without the need to prove fault, the plaintiff must show that the product was "dangerously defective when it left the manufacturer" and that the user was using the product in the manner for which it was designed. In many cases, the plaintiff's burden of proof is not significantly less than showing a manufacturer's negligence.

In other cases, fault in the sense of a legal wrong (e.g., breach of contract, tortious conduct) may be absent, but concepts of commercial morality, such as "good faith," present convenient analogies.

Equitable Remedies

When compensatory damages are inadequate, equitable remedies may be available. Some exist as alternative remedies if certain defects in contract formation can be shown (rescission and reformation). Others ask for something other than money (specific performance and injunctive relief).

Rescission and Reformation

Rescission aims at destroying the contract and its obligations and putting the parties back in their positions prior to the agreement. Grounds for rescission are defects in formation already mentioned: illegality, undue influence, insanity, and so on. Reformation aims at correcting the contract to reflect the actual intent of the parties, usually where mutual mistake exists.

BALLENTINE'S

privity of contract   The legal relationship between the parties to a contract. In some circumstances, a party must be in privity of contract with another party in order to assert a claim.

What happens when the purchaser gets less than what was agreed? It depends on the subject matter of the contract. In a contract for the sale of goods, when the goods are unique or irreplaceable, the purchaser should not be required to accept a substitute. The *Tunick* case involves a purchaser dissatisfied with the goods tendered and unwilling to accept a nearly identical substitute.

DAVID TUNICK, INC., Plaintiff,

v.

E.W. KORNFELD and Galerie Kornfeld Und Cie, Defendants,

v.

David TUNICK, Counterclaim Defendant.
United States District Court, S.D. New York.
838 F. Supp. 848 (S.D.N.Y. 1993)

This action arises from Mr. E. W. Kornfeld's and Galerie Kornfeld und Cie's (collectively "Kornfeld" or "defendants") sale of a signed Picasso print to plaintiff, David Tunick, Inc. Plaintiff alleges that defendants sold David Tunick, Inc. a print entitled Le Minotauromachie (the "Print") which defendants represented was signed by Pablo Picasso (the "Signature") but which, in fact, bears a forged signature. As a result, plaintiff brought this action alleging breach of warranties, fraud, reckless misrepresentation, breach of the duty of honesty and fair dealing, and breach of fiduciary duty. ...

* * *

Defendants seek summary judgment on plaintiff's first claim for relief ... [which] alleges that "Defendants have breached their express warranties to plaintiff (a) that the [Signature on the Print] is authentic and (b) that the [Print] had been signed in 1942 and had gone directly from Picasso to a private collector whose widow consigned it to Defendants for sale at the auction." Defendants contend that plaintiff is unable to demonstrate that the Signature is not genuine. Further, defendants contend that, even if the Signature is not authentic, plaintiff's refusal to accept a replacement print of *Le Minotauromachie*, that also was allegedly signed by Pablo Picasso, defeats plaintiff's ability to recover for breach of warranty.

... [D]efendants in their reply memorandum concede that ... the authenticity of the Signature is in dispute ... .

Defendants' second contention, that even if the Signature is not authentic, plaintiff's refusal to accept a replacement print ... defeats plaintiff's ability to recover for breach of warranty, appears to raise an issue of first impression. Plaintiff claims that, immediately upon learning that the Signature was forged, it demanded rescission of the sale and tendered the Print to defendants. Plaintiff thus revoked acceptance of the Print in accordance with Section 2-608 of the Uniform Commercial Code as enacted in New York ("N.Y.U.C.C."). Under the N.Y.U.C.C., a purchaser who in good faith revokes his acceptance of goods, has the same rights and duties with regard to the goods involved as if he had rejected them. One duty imposed upon the buyer ... is that:

(1) Where any tender or delivery by the seller is rejected because it is non-conforming and the time for performance has not yet expired, the seller may seasonably notify the buyer of his intention to cure and may then within the contract time make a conforming delivery. (2) Where the buyer rejects a non-conforming tender which the seller had reasonable grounds to believe would be acceptable with or without money allowance the seller may if he seasonably notifies the buyer have a further reasonable time to substitute a conforming tender.

Defendants allege, and plaintiff does not contest, that shortly after Mr. Tunick informed Mr. Kornfeld that he believed the Signature to be a forgery, Mr. Kornfeld offered to exchange the Print for another print ... which also was allegedly signed by Pablo Picasso. Defendants contend that, in so doing, defendants exercised their right ... to substitute conforming goods for the allegedly non-conforming tender rejected by plaintiff. Plaintiff rejected defendants' offer to replace the Print with another print ... and filed suit in this Court. Defendants aver that, because Mr. Kornfeld's offer met the standards of [the] N.Y.U.C.C., plaintiff could not properly reject the offer and look to alternative remedies. Plaintiff disputes the applicability of [the] N.Y.U.C.C. to prints. Plaintiff avers that: In the world of fine art ... there can be no legally meaningful doctrine of functional equivalence or substitution. ... Prints vary, sometimes widely, in many ways and no two are the same. Purchasers obviously buy prints for different reasons. ... Their choice of one print over another will be motivated by objective reasons, subjective reasons, whim, fancy and impulse.

Defendants' argument is novel. No court in this Circuit or in New York appears to have been presented with the question of whether a nonconforming tender of a work of art may be cured by an offer of a different but similar work. Furthermore, the legislative history of the relevant Uniform Commercial Code section is of no aid in answering this question. Indeed, this issue requires consideration of whether prints are substitutable for one another: Are two prints, printed from the same plates and by the same artist, sufficiently similar that one can be said to be a perfect substitute for another? Moreover, is any such similarity sufficient to burden a good faith purchaser of a print with the duty to accept, as fulfillment of a contract to purchase that print, another print that the purchaser did not view or bid upon?

After carefully considering this issue, I find that two prints, by the same artist and from the same plates, are not interchangeable. [Thus, the] N.Y.U.C.C. ... does not, as a matter of law, obligate a buyer to accept in lieu of a non-conforming print, a substitute print from the same series of prints.

First, two prints from a series produced by an artist each possess distinctive qualities that may impact their aesthetic and economic value. Often, differences in the quality of impressions are observable as the plate used to make the prints wears during the course of printing. ... In addition, the price of a given print may be inflated by "some 'autograph' quality or quality of impression" not shared by other prints in the same series. ... Similarly, depending on the type of printing method used, coloration and contrast may vary among prints in a series. Each of these factors can substantially impact the value of a given print.

Second, prints, like other types of artwork, are fragile and their value can be diminished by the manner in which they are treated over time. Prints that are improperly stored easily can become damaged, fade or blur. ... Any such occurrence substantially impacts the economic value of the print. ...

Third, prints, unlike petroleum or produce, are not purchased for strictly utilitarian reasons. A print is selected by a purchaser because the traits of that print please the purchaser's aesthetic sensibilities. Thus, whether prints in a series are largely similar or slightly different is of no critical importance. The real fact to be considered is that the purchaser chose a given print because he viewed it as uniquely beautiful, interesting, or well suited to his collection or gallery. Nothing else will satisfy that collector but that which he bought. For these reasons, prints are not interchangeable.

... In the case at bar, plaintiff did not enter into a contract to purchase a print of *Le Minotauromachie* signed by Picasso; rather, plaintiff bid for and purchased the specific print of *Le Minotauromachie* that Mr. Tunick viewed prior to the auction, which was signed by Picasso and in the condition Mr. Tunick observed at the time of purchase. In this context it would be fundamentally unfair, and unsound policy, to impose on plaintiff a duty to accept another—inherently different—print ... as a substitute for the one plaintiff actually viewed, bid for, and purchased.

Case Questions

1. What are the rights of seller and buyer under the UCC when nonconforming goods are tendered?
2. Why is the other print not an acceptable substitute?

Specific Performance

Specific performance asks the court to order the breaching party to perform rather than compensate, that is, to deliver the goods or the deed to real property. This remedy is available when goods are unique, such as a Stradivarius violin (land is always considered unique, hence the availability of specific performance for enforcing real property sales contracts). This remedy, however, is premised on a valid contract and does not cure formation and consideration problems.

Injunctive Relief

Injunctive relief is sometimes available to order someone not to do something that is prohibited by a contract (e.g., to prevent someone from building a carport in a development where deed restrictions require garages and prohibit carports). Such relief also is premised on valid contractual obligations.

Liberal Construction of Consideration

One means of avoiding the arbitrariness of the classical model of contract formation was to construe consideration in the broadest possible terms in order to create a contract. This method was a favorite of Judge Cardozo of the New York Court of Appeals. Cardozo enforced a father's promise to pay an annuity to his daughter following her marriage by finding consideration in her forbearance from breaking off the engagement. *DeCicco v. Schweizer*, 221 N.Y. 431, 117 N.E. 807 (1917). In another case, he found consideration for a pledge to a college endowment campaign in an implied duty of the college to memorialize the donor. *Allegheny College v. National Chatauqua Bank*, 246 N.Y. 369, 159 N.E. 173 (1927). In both of these cases, classical theory should have found a promise to make a gift without consideration on the part of the promisee.

When consideration was designed to deny contracts even when offer and acceptance were present, the liberal construction of consideration undercut its importance. When a powerful moral, as opposed to legal, obligation was present or when a promisee changed position in reliance on a promise, judges at first strained to find consideration.

Moral Obligation and Reliance Theory

Consider the following examples taken from those listed earlier:

1. Contractor makes a contract with Thomas to blacktop Thomas's driveway at 116 Spring Street for $2000. Contractor mistakenly blacktops Henry's driveway at 114 Spring Street (the two houses are in an urban subdivision where the houses bear a striking similarity to each other). Variations on the facts might be: Henry is away on vacation while the blacktopping occurs and has no knowledge of it until he returns; Henry watches through his window but remains silent, all the while knowing that Thomas was planning to blacktop and that Contractor is mistaken.

2. George, the owner of a small business, opens negotiations with a national hardware chain for a franchise. Franchisor insists that George get experience as manager/trainee in one of the branches and assures George that training plus $25,000 will result in a franchise, although no guarantees are made. George sells his business, moves to another city, and works as trainee. Franchisor increases the cost of the franchise to $35,000. George sells his house to raise the money, but Franchisor decides not to grant the franchise.

Moral Obligation: Quasi-Contract

In example 1, there was no contract, but Henry has received a benefit at Contractor's expense. There was no contract, no offer, no acceptance, no consideration on Henry's part; but it would seem unfair for Henry to retain the benefit, particularly if he failed in his moral obligation to inform Contractor of the mistake. In such a situation the court may impose contractual obligations in the name of *quasi-contract,* which is not an actual contract but a "non-contractual obligation that is to be treated procedurally as if it were a contract." *Continental Forest Products, Inc. v. Chandler Supply Co.,* 95 Idaho 739, 518 P.2d 1201 (1974).

Quasi-contract is also called *contract implied in law* (distinguished from a **contract implied** in fact) and is based on the concept of unjust

---

BALLENTINE'S

implied contract   Implied contracts are of two types: *contracts implied in fact,* which the law infers from the circumstances, conduct, acts, or the relationship of the parties rather than from their spoken words; and *contracts implied in law,* which are quasi contracts or constructive contracts imposed by the law, usually to prevent unjust enrichment.

enrichment and **restitution**. Unjust enrichment is an equitable principle asserting that one receiving a benefit at another's loss owes restitution to the other. Because fairness is the goal of equity, the imposition of contractual obligations depends on the specific circumstances of each case and cannot easily be reduced to mechanical rules. Typically, quasi-contract requires that the recipient of the benefit have the opportunity to decline the benefit and yet fail to do so. In the driveway example, the court might imply such failure if Henry sat idly by and watched the work. It is doubtful that the court would impose the same obligation if Henry had no knowledge of the work (for example, if he was on vacation).

Reliance: Promissory Estoppel

Example 2 presents a different problem. Although a contract was never complete, George's course of action was determined by assurances made in the course of contract negotiations. George incurred significant costs in reasonably relying on those assurances. The national chain received no benefit at George's expense, so unjust enrichment/quasi-contract is not appropriate, but George has certainly suffered because of the chain's conduct. To impose liability on the chain, the court may resort to another equitable principle called **equitable estoppel**, under which liability is incurred if one by language or conduct leads another to do something he or she would not otherwise have done. This is the basis for the mysterious language of the first *Restatement* § 90:

> A promise which the promisor should reasonably expect to induce action or forbearance of a definite and substantial character on the part of the promisee and which does induce such action or forbearance is binding if injustice can be avoided only by enforcement of the promise.

This section applies to George's plight; it is a concise statement of *reliance theory*. Promises were made on which George relied to his detriment. Although a contract never quite passed the negotiation stage, it would be unjust for George to go without some compensation.

————————————————————————BALLENTINE'S————————————————————————

restitution   In both contract and tort, a remedy that restores the status quo. Restitution returns a person who has been wrongfully deprived of something to the position he or she occupied before the wrong occurred; it requires a defendant who has been unjustly enriched at the expense of the plaintiff to make the plaintiff whole, either ... by returning property unjustly held, by reimbursing the plaintiff, or by paying compensation or indemnification.

equitable estoppel (estoppel in pais)   [A] term applied to a situation in which a party is denied the right to plead or prove a fact because of something he or she has done or has failed to do.

Hoffman is a classic case of promissory estoppel. The plaintiff was induced into a course of conduct by the defendant with the promise of a forthcoming contract that never came. Good faith and reliance on one side were met with vacillation and chicanery on the other. Nevertheless, promissory estoppel is not the same as breach of contract, and the case was ultimately set for new trial on the issue of the amount the plaintiff should receive. Omitted from the case excerpt is the following quotation from Corbin, one of the leading contributors to the *Restatement of Contracts,* the supreme master of reliance theory, showing just how elusive promissory estoppel can be:

> Enforcement of a promise does not necessarily mean Specific Performance. It does not necessarily mean Damages for breach. Moreover the amount allowed as Damages may be determined by the plaintiff's expenditures or change of position in reliance as well as by the value to him of the promised performance. Restitution is also an "enforcing" remedy, although it is often said to be based upon some kind of a rescission. In determining what justice requires, the court must remember all of its powers, derived from equity, **law merchant**, and other sources, as well as the common law. Its decree should be molded accordingly.

Failure of the Classical Model

Out of the chaos of contract law in the nineteenth century, an effort was made by scholars, particularly Langdell and Holmes in this country, to reduce contract law to logical principles in the common law. The effort was doomed from the start because of the nearly infinite variety of promissory situations and bargaining relations. Judges were disinclined to apply mechanical formulas when the results were clearly unjust. The concepts of fairness and good faith in principles of equity provided alternative remedies in some cases, and in other cases alternatives were found in the foundations for quasi-contract and promissory estoppel. The result has been an uneasy coexistence of two contradictory conceptions of contract.

Evidence of the demise of the classical model can be found in the Uniform Commercial Code, which departs from that model at every turn. The UCC emphasizes assisting contract formation rather than restricting it. Consideration is transformed, the mirror image rule is banished, indefinite terms may be implied or determined by the custom of the marketplace, and so on.

BALLENTINE'S

law merchant   A term referring to the law governing transactions between merchants, which evolved over many years as a part of the English common law.

Joseph HOFFMAN

v.

RED OWL STORES, INC.,
a foreign corp., et al., Appellants
Supreme Court of Wisconsin
26 Wis. 2d 683, 133 N.W.2d 267 (1965)

[An agent for Red Owl Stores engaged in continuing negotiations with Hoffman, who operated a bakery but wanted to run a Red Owl supermarket. Negotiations took more than two years, during which Hoffman sold his bakery at the agent's request and bought and worked in a small grocery store. During this period, the price of the franchise was raised from $18,000 to $24,000 to $26,000. When Red Owl insisted that $13,000 put up by Hoffman's father-in-law be considered a gift, Hoffman balked.]

The record here discloses a number of promises and assurances given to Hoffman by Lukowitz in behalf of Red Owl upon which plaintiffs relied and acted upon to their detriment.

Foremost were the promises that for the sum of $18,000 Red Owl would establish Hoffman in a store. After Hoffman had sold his grocery store and paid the $1,000 on the Chilton lot, the $18,000 figure was changed to $24,100. Then in November, 1961, Hoffman was assured that if the $24,100 figure were increased by $2000 the deal would go through. Hoffman was induced to sell his grocery store fixtures and inventory in June, 1961, on the promise that he would be in his new store by fall. In November, plaintiffs sold their bakery building on the urging of defendants and on the assurance that this was the last step necessary to have the deal with Red Owl go through.

We determine that there was ample evidence to sustain the answers of the jury to the questions of the verdict with respect to the promissory representations made by Red Owl, Hoffman's reliance thereon in the exercise of ordinary care, and his fulfillment of the conditions required of him by the terms of the negotiation had with Red Owl.

There remains for consideration the question of law raised by defendants that agreement was never reached on essential factors necessary to establish a contract between Hoffman and Red Owl. Among these were the size, cost, design, and layout of the store building; and the terms of the lease with respect to rent, maintenance, renewal, and purchase options. This poses the question of whether the promise necessary to sustain a cause of action for promissory estoppel must embrace all essential details of a proposed transaction between promisor and promisee so as to be the equivalent of an offer that would result in a binding contract between the parties if the promisee were to accept the same.

Originally the doctrine of promissory estoppel was involved as a substitute for consideration rendering a gratuitous promise enforceable as a contract. In other words, the acts of reliance by the promisee to his detriment provided a substitute for consideration. If promissory estoppel were to be limited to only those situations where the promise giving rise to the cause of action must be so definite with respect to all details that a contract would result were the promise supported by consideration, then the defendants' instant promises to Hoffman would not meet this test. However, [the Restatement of Contracts] does not impose the requirement that the promise giving rise to the cause of action must be so comprehensive in scope as to meet the requirements of an offer that would ripen into a contract if accepted by the promisee. Rather the conditions imposed are:

(1) Was the promise one which the promisor should reasonably expect to induce action or forbearance of a definite and substantial character on the part of the promisee?
(2) Did the promise induce such action or forbearance?
(3) Can injustice be avoided only by enforcement of the promise?

We deem it would be a mistake to regard an action grounded on promissory estoppel as the equivalent of a breach of contract action. ...

While the first two of the above listed three requirements of promissory estoppel present issues of fact which ordinarily will be resolved by a jury, the third requirement, that the remedy can only be invoked where necessary to avoid injustice, is one that involves a policy decision by the court. Such a policy decision necessarily embraces an element of discretion.

We conclude that injustice would result here if plaintiffs were not granted some relief because of the failure of defendants to keep their promises which induced plaintiffs to act to their detriment.

* * *

Plaintiffs contend that in a breach of contract action damages may include loss of profits. However, this is not a breach of contract action.

The only relevancy of evidence relating to profits would be with respect to proving the element of goodwill in establishing the fair market value of the grocery inventory and fixtures sold. Therefore, evidence of profits would be admissible to afford a foundation for expert opinion as to fair market value.

Where damages are awarded in promissory estoppel instead of specifically enforcing the promisor's promise, they should be only such as in the opinion of the court are necessary to prevent injustice. Mechanical or rule of thumb approaches to the damage problem should be avoided.

* * *

"The wrong is not primarily in depriving the plaintiff of the promised reward but in causing the plaintiff to change position to his detriment. It would follow that the damages should not exceed the loss caused by the change of position, which would never be more in amount, but might be less, than the promised reward."

* * *

At the time Hoffman bought the equipment and inventory of the small grocery store at Wautoma he did so in order to gain experience in the grocery store business. At that time discussion had already been had with Red Owl representatives that Wautoma might be too small for a Red Owl operation and that a larger city might be more desirable. Thus Hoffman made this purchase more or less as a temporary experiment. Justice does not require that the damages awarded him, because of selling these assets at the behest of defendants, should exceed any actual loss sustained measured by the difference between the sales price and the fair market value.

Since the evidence does not sustain the large award of damages arising from the sale of the Wautoma grocery business, the trial court properly ordered a new trial on this issue.

Case Questions

1. What is the difference in the measure of damages between breach of contract and promissory estoppel?
2. The court cites and rejects the argument that promissory estoppel creates a substitute for consideration. Williston was the foremost proponent of the classical model (offer, acceptance, and consideration) in contract law. *Restatement* § 90 was written by Corbin, the foremost critic of the classical model. How does the court choose one over the other?

For the practitioner, the classical model of offer, acceptance, and consideration must be kept in mind in constructing contracts, but the full range of principles must be appreciated when an agreement fails.

The Field of Commercial Law

Contract law is the starting point for the study of commercial law, as most commercial relationships are contractual in nature. Just as the intricacies of contract law are beyond the scope of this book, so too are the various specialized areas of commercial law, each of which deserves a course by itself in law school curricula. Although they are very important to the paralegal, only a brief introduction to the subject matter of the major subfields of commercial law is presented to acquaint the paralegal with topics covered more fully elsewhere.

The Uniform Commercial Code

The Uniform Commercial Code was designed to establish a set of rules governing commercial transactions, modernizing the concepts of contract and commercial law to suit the marketplace. The UCC encouraged uniformity in state law regarding commercial transactions, and in this it has been largely successful, having been adopted with only minor variations in all states except Louisiana, which has adopted only four of its articles. Separate sections (articles) of the UCC cover the following subjects:

Sales

Commercial Paper

Bank Deposits and Collections

Letters of Credit

Bulk Transfers

Warehouse Receipts, Bills of Lading, and Other Documents of Title

Investment Securities

Secured Transactions; Sales of Accounts, Contract Rights, and Chattel Paper

Except for the specialist, the key sections of the UCC concern sales, commercial paper, and secured transactions. Of these, Article 2 (Sales) is extremely important because it clarifies and modifies existing principles of contract law, some of which have been noted earlier. The one transactional area *not* covered in detail by the UCC is real property transactions, in which long-standing principles differ widely among the states, defying attempts at unification. The UCC as incorporated in state law should be consulted on any question that comes within its coverage.

Commercial Paper

Commercial paper, or "negotiable instruments," consists of substitutes for cash used to facilitate commercial transactions. **Checks,**

————————————————————BALLENTINE'S————————————————————

check   A written order directed to a bank to pay money to the person named.

drafts, promissory notes, and **certificates of deposit** constitute commercial paper. Commercial paper is thus a signed writing representing an unconditional promise to pay money. It is regulated by Article 3 of the UCC.

Secured Transactions

A secured transaction takes place when the payment of a debt is protected by **collateral**. The most common secured transactions are (1) real property **mortgages**, in which the purchaser or owner of land borrows money, pledging interests in real property to satisfy the debt in case of default; and (2) purchase money installment contracts for personal property, such as an automobile, in which the seller retains rights of repossession in case of default. Article 9 of the UCC covers secured transactions of personal property except for interests arising by operation of law, such as **mechanic's liens**. Secured interests in real property fall outside the UCC, so the law of each state must be consulted for applicable rules.

Obligations to pay money that are unsecured are covered by the state law of debtor and creditor. Discharge of debt through bankruptcy falls within federal jurisdiction under the U.S. Constitution.

Business Organizations

Business organizations consist of variations on three forms: **corporations, partnerships**, and **sole proprietorships**. Attorneys are regularly

---
BALLENTINE'S
---

draft An order in writing by one person on another (commonly a bank) to pay a specified sum of money to a third person on demand or at a stated future time.

promissory note A written promise to pay a specific sum of money by a specified date or on demand. A promissory note is negotiable if, in addition, it is payable to the order of a named person or to bearer.

certificate of deposit A voucher issued by a bank acknowledging the receipt of money on deposit which the bank promises to repay to the depositor.

collateral Stocks, bonds, or other property that serve as security for a loan or other obligation; property pledged to pay a debt.

mortgage A pledge of real property to secure a debt. ... A written agreement pledging real property as security.

mechanic's lien A lien created by law for the purpose of securing payment for work performed or materials furnished in constructing or repairing a building or other structure.

corporation An artificial person, existing only in the eyes of the law, to whom a state or the federal government has granted a charter to become a legal entity, separate from its shareholders, with a name of its own, under which its shareholders called upon to advise clients on the choice of business organization that will best suit their needs. Personal liability, tax consequences, and financing are major considerations that affect the choice, but size of the organization, its structure, and its long-range goals are also important considerations. Paralegals frequently draft the documents that create and control business organizations. Once formed, businesses must not only conform to their own rules, but also are subject to numerous requirements of state and federal law with which the commercial lawyer and the paralegal must be familiar.

Summary

The law of contracts is concerned with private agreements that the law recognizes as enforceable. Unlike torts, the obligations to be enforced are established by the agreement rather than the law. Under the classical model of contract formation, the requisites of making an enforceable contract consisted of offer, acceptance, and consideration. In its simplest form, consideration is an exchange of promises to perform agreed-upon obligations. The contract is not complete until offeror and offeree agree upon identical terms; an attempted acceptance of an offer that alters a term of the contract is considered a counteroffer rather than acceptance.

Even when offer, acceptance, and consideration are present, contract formation is corrupted by misconduct of one of the parties, mistake, lack of contractual capacity, or illegality. Certain kinds of contracts are required to be in writing by the Statute of Frauds and the Uniform Commercial Code, the latter making significant changes in the model of offer, acceptance, and consideration.

When a contract is not fulfilled, compensatory damages are available to put the nonbreaching party in the position he or she would have been in if the contract had been performed. Punitive damages and recovery for emotional damages are not ordinarily available in contract,

---

BALLENTINE'S

can act and contract and sue and be sued. A corporation's shareholders, officers, and directors are not normally liable for the acts of the corporation.

partnership An undertaking of two or more persons to carry on, as coowners, a business or other enterprise for profit; an agreement between or among two or more persons to put their money, labor, and skill into commerce or business, and to divide the profit in agreed-upon proportions. Partnerships may be formed by entities as well as individuals.

sole proprietorship Ownership by one person, as opposed to ownership by more than one person, ownership by a corporation, ownership by a partnership, etc.

but the lines between contract and tort have become increasingly blurred, as witnessed by medical malpractice and products liability.

Strict adherence to the classical model provides little flexibility in the nearly infinite variety of contractual situations, so the courts have devised a number of ways around what appear to be unjust results. The classical model based on the common law must compete with traditional concepts of fairness emanating from equity. A number of equitable remedies are available that depart from monetary compensation. In addition, equitable principles have given rise to enforcement of moral obligations in the form of quasi-contract, whereby the law imposes a contract to avoid unjust enrichment, and promissory estoppel, whereby a party suffers a detriment in relying on inducements made by another when a contract is not enforceable under common-law principles. Although common-law contract principles and theories of moral obligation and reliance in equity exist side by side, they are intrinsically contradictory, resulting in inconsistency in contract law.

The field of commercial law covers a number of subfields such as commercial paper, secured transactions, and business organization. Much of the law in this area is statutory, including the Uniform Commercial Code, which has been adopted by most states and which provides uniformity in interstate commercial transactions.

Review Questions

1. Why is specific performance available to enforce contracts for sale of real property?

2. Why is a promise to make a gift usually unenforceable?

3. When may a contract with a minor be enforced?

4. Why is a promise to return a lost dog for which a reward has been offered not a contract?

5. If a contractor discovers that the completed contract for building a motel has itemized five chandeliers for $1000 each rather than $10,000 each as he quoted them to his secretary, what is his best remedy for correcting the mistake and still continuing the contract?

6. As an incentive to win a case, a criminal client offers his attorney a bonus of $5,000 if an acquittal is obtained. Can the attorney sue successfully for the bonus if an acquittal is in fact obtained?

7. Does the definition of a contract as "a promise or set of promises for the breach of which the law gives a remedy, or the performance of which the law in some way recognizes as a duty" give the Court discretion to decide arbitrarily what is a contract and what is not a contract?

8. Professor Corbin comments that "the chief purpose underlying the law of contract is not to carry out the will of the promisor ... the chief purpose of enforcement is the avoidance of disappointment and loss to the promisee." Is this reflected in the cases included in the chapter?

9. Does the quote from Corbin in Question 8 sound more like the classical model of contract or promissory estoppel? Why?

10. Client tells attorney he is guilty of crime charged against him. Can the attorney ethically make a contract aimed at gaining an acquittal for the client?

Exercises

1. Find the definition of an emancipated minor in your state.

2. Is an attorney-client contract confidential (in a lawsuit)?

3. Father promises to make a gift to son on son's twenty-fifth birthday. Son wants to go to college but must borrow heavily to do so. Son asks you to write father's promise in such a way as to make it legally binding so that son can pay back college loans. Write out the contract to make it legally enforceable.

4. You advertise your car for sale, and a buyer offers $5,000, which is acceptable to you, but the buyer, a stranger to you, will not have the money for a week. Draft a simple agreement that will allow you to continue to negotiate with others in case the buyer does not come up with the money.

5. Look in the newspaper for advertisements that present "illusory" offers, that is, advertisements that appear to make offers but are not capable of acceptance.

WHAT TO CONSIDER WHEN DRAFTING SIMPLE WILLS

Carla J. Carter

Even if drafting wills isn't a large part of your job description, you need to know how to do it reasonably well, if you will have to do it at all.

To do a decent job of drafting wills, there are certain basic things to know about them. You probably already have a pretty good idea of what a will is—it's one way a person can direct what happens to his property, possessions, debts, children, etc., after he dies.

Unlike real estate contracts, lease agreements, or a myriad of other legal documents, wills do not include exact dates on which they take effect. In order for the will to take effect it must be triggered by an event (the death of the testator), the timing of which is virtually impossible to predict. For this reason, each will you draft must be done correctly—you may not have a chance to fix it.

It is helpful if you can meet with the client during his initial conference with the attorney. This will allow you to gather information at the outset that you will ultimately need to draft the will. Unfortunately some attorneys often overlook what they consider to be the "mundane details" when they meet with clients—they have hired you to take care of this. It's easier for you and the client if this can all be taken care of at the initial conference.

Your office probably already has a "bank" of stock will paragraphs and clauses. You might have a wonderful word processing department which has painstakingly stored and numbered the various clauses from wills they have prepared. If this is the case, you can just pick and choose the particular clauses you need for each will. You will need to work with your word processors to develop a system that all of you can use to accomplish this with minimal effort.

There is, however, some danger in using "standard clauses." They can become so routine that they are rarely examined or read thoroughly, and they may not be appropriate to the exact situation you are working with.

Pitfalls and How to Avoid Them

Perhaps the scariest part of will drafting is the inherent pitfalls, which generally result from one of three types of errors:

- things that were left out;
- things that were left in (especially when an old will is revised); and
- things that were never even considered.

Don't rely on your secretary to proofread a will that you are responsible for drafting. That's your job, not hers. And, yes, because it's such a drag, you must read every will—that means every word, every time.

The fact that it came from a form off of a word processor doesn't mean it's accurate. Machines have been known to jumble words, drop sentences, delete clauses, etc., and you can't assume that none of these happened to the will you just drafted. Besides, forms get out of date and language can be improved.

Beware of "generic" terms—does "automobile" mean the $75,000 motor home? Does "clothing" refer to a $50,000 sable coat? Do "personal possessions" include a $25,000 stamp collection? These are good examples of the importance of knowing your client's financial status.

Remember that the only person who really knows what the will should say will be dead when it becomes effective—make sure all of its provisions are clear. Have someone else read it over for you, if you need to.

Don't put funeral arrangements in the will—by the time it's read, it will undoubtedly be too late. At the very least, make certain that the testator knows the importance of letting her relatives or a funeral director know her wishes now, so that they will be met when the time comes.

Beware of the word "or"—*don't use it if you really mean "and."* These words are not interchangeable, and using the wrong one can spell disaster.

Be sure that wills which devise property to "classes" of beneficiaries specify whether the property passes per stirpes or per capita. The language of any clauses directing an unequal distribution must be crystal clear—the executor shouldn't have to second-guess the testator's intentions.

Use your common sense. Just knowing when something doesn't feel or sound right can be your greatest asset—pay attention to it!

Reprinted with permission from *Legal Assistant Today* magazine.

CHAPTER 13

THE LAW OF PROPERTY

Introduction

The previous chapters have probably given the impression that disputes and litigation form the core of the law, but this is a false impression of the practice of law. Particularly in the area of property, litigation is rare because good "lawyerly" work prevents the need for litigation. A properly drafted and executed will should avoid all but unreasonable challenges. A carefully executed real estate transaction transfers title without loose ends and settles all important future questions about ownership.

Property law is extremely important for paralegals because it involves a great deal of work that does not require an attorney except as legal advisor and supervisor. Within the area of property law are a number of important subfields, such as real estate transactions, landlord and tenant law, estates and trusts, estate planning, planning and zoning, environmental law, and commercial leases. Other areas present specialized property law aspects, such as community property, equitable distribution, and marital estates in family law, and leases and real property transactions in contract law. Taxation is an important consideration in legal advising on all aspects of property law. There are specific causes of action in tort to protect property interests: **trespass**, **nuisance**, **ejectment**. In recent years government regulation of property by planning, zoning, and environmental law has placed severe restrictions on land use and created a need for legal specialization in these areas. Bankruptcy, **foreclosure**, mortgages, and mechanic's liens concern rights of third parties in property. In short, all of private law that is not concerned with wrongful misconduct (and much that is) revolves around property law. Perhaps in no other field of law is a more comprehensive knowledge of law required for legal advice, even on what may appear to be a relatively simple problem or transaction, as in the area of real property law.

Jeremy Bentham's dictum that property is the core of law is sound. Political systems are founded upon different ideologies of property—e.g., **capitalism**, **socialism**, **communism**. The **due process clauses** of the U.S. Constitution in the Fifth and Fourteenth Amendments protect citizens' property rights. In civil law, virtually all rights are either characterized in property terms or measured by property, for example, in money, which is a form of property.

BALLENTINE'S

trespass   An unauthorized entry or intrusion on the real property of another.

nuisance   Anything a person does that annoys or disturbs another person in his or her use, possession, or enjoyment of his or her property, or which renders the ordinary use or possession of the property uncomfortable.

ejectment   An action at common law for the right to possession of land.

foreclosure   1. A legal action by which a mortgagee terminates a mortgagor's interest in mortgaged premises. 2. The enforcement of a lien, deed of trust, or

Property Is an Abstraction

Bentham is also correct in stating that natural property does not exist. From a legal point of view, a mountain is not property, nor a lake, nor a book. Until we assign legal rights in a thing, it is not property. When a person building a new home says, "I am going out to the property," we understand a building site, a piece of land, in its natural or altered state, but we also understand that the statement asserts rights of ownership over something that has been defined on a map with boundaries, the title to which has been transferred from one hand to another and recorded in the records of the county in which it is situated. But the most important, albeit often unconscious, assertion in this use of the word *property* is that the owner has rights that the law will defend. The definition, determination, and allocation of these rights are the subject matter of property law.

The abstract nature of property may be illustrated by a few examples:

1. A retailer builds up a profitable business over many years and then decides to sell it and retire. Not only may the retailer sell the premises and the inventory of the store, but a major part of the sales price may be for "goodwill," which is valuable property.

2. A professional basketball player may be paid a very large sum of money just to have his name associated with a line of sneakers. He has property rights in his name.

---BALLENTINE'S---

mortgage on real estate, or a security interest in personal property, by any method provided by law.

capitalism An economic system in which production (manufacturing, agriculture) and distribution (transportation) are privately owned and carried on for profit.

socialism An economic system in which the state owns the means of production (manufacturing, agriculture, transportation) and in which, in theory, every citizen participates in production according to his or her ability.

communism An economic system in which the state owns the means of production (manufacturing, agriculture, transportation) and in which, in theory, every citizen participates in production according to his or her ability and shares in what has been produced according to his or her need. A primary distinction between communism and socialism is that the former is almost universally totalitarian and the latter generally democratic in greater or lesser degree.

due process clause Actually a reference to two due process clauses, one in the Fifth Amendment and one in the Fourteenth Amendment. The Fifth Amendment requires the federal government to accord "due process of law" to citizens of the United States; the Fourteenth Amendment imposes a similar requirement upon state governments.

3. A person buys a fifth-story condominium on the beach before it is built. Until constructed, ownership is of a piece of air.

4. Someone pays for a franchise to operate a fast-food restaurant.

5. An inventor registers an invention with the Patent Office, thus acquiring an exclusive property right.

6. A state university professor receives tenure, which grants a right to permanent employment at the university.

7. An Hispanic employee sues an employer for discriminating in promotions.

8. A physician challenges antiabortion statutes on the grounds that the right to practice medicine has been unconstitutionally restricted.

9. A state halts building construction on private land because Indian artifacts have been unearthed that suggest an important archeological site may be located on the land.

All these examples express valuable property rights of which the law takes cognizance. Note that the government not only restricts property rights (examples 8 and 9), but also creates them (examples 5 and 6). In fact, the government through its laws can create or destroy property rights, subject only to due process of law and just compensation for property taken for a public purpose.

The law may recognize something as property for one purpose but not for another. In New York, for example, a professional license may be "marital property," the value of which can be divided in a divorce, but it is not property for the purposes of sale or gift. In *Community Redevelopment Agency v. Abrams,* 15 Cal. 3d 813, 543 P.2d 905, 126 Cal. Rptr. 423 (1975), the California Supreme Court held that goodwill in a pharmacy that was taken in order to redevelop an urban center was not property, even though it would be property for the purposes of a private sale of the pharmacy. In relation to this last example, Professor Berger asked the unanswerable question, "Did the pharmacist lose because he had no property or did he have no property because he lost?" Goodwill is an abstract concept, but goodwill as property raises it to an even higher level of abstraction. Property itself is an abstraction of the rights that the law recognizes.

The common law tradition in property law placed responsibilities on landowners for injuries suffered by those present on the landowner's premises. The duties owed depended on the status of the injured party (e.g., trespassers were owed minimal care, whereas those encouraged or invited on the premises, such as retail customers, were owed substantial care). In *Errico*, the court found that the owner and employees of a convenience store generally owe no duty to customers to control the acts of third persons.

Juanita Donna ERRICO, Appellant,
v.
SOUTHLAND CORP., et al., Respondents.
Court of Appeals of Minnesota
509 N.W.2d 585 (Minn. Ct. App. 1994)

SYLLABUS

The owner and employees of a 24-hour convenience store generally owe no duty to a customer to control the acts of unidentified third persons which take place in the store's parking lot, or to protect the customer from those acts.

OPINION

Appellant Juanita Donna Errico (Errico) brought this negligence action against respondents Southland Corporation and several of its employees (Southland). Her complaint alleged that Southland and its employees had a duty to provide for her safety and security, and that Southland had a duty to properly supervise and train its employees in the protection of its patrons.

Errico appeals from the district court's grant of summary judgment to Southland. We affirm.

FACTS

Sometime after midnight on June 21, 1989, Errico and a friend drove into the parking lot of a 24-hour convenience store located in Minneapolis, Minnesota. At the time, the store was owned by Southland.

Errico made a purchase in the store and left, intending to use a telephone located outside the store. As she was about to use the phone, an unidentified man informed her he had to use the phone. Errico let the man use the phone.

As Errico was walking back toward her parked car, she saw an unidentified female hitting her friend, who had just returned to Errico's car after being inside the store. Errico got into the car and began to drive away. She was pulled from the car and attacked by three unidentified men and one woman. Errico claims that several store employees stood inside the store watching the attack, but that no one called the police or did anything else to try and stop it. She further claims that one employee even locked the store's front door.

After about ten minutes, Errico's assailants got into their car and left. Instead of seeking assistance from the store employees at that point, Errico pursued her assailants for several minutes in her own car, attempting to get a license plate number. She eventually pulled over and was taken to the hospital by her friend.

Stanley Pryor, a store employee who was working that evening, saw the entire assault. He admitted he simply watched and rendered no aid. He stated he did not want to get involved. Pryor acknowledged that the training he had received from Southland had not adequately prepared him to respond to such an assault.

Errico thereafter brought this negligence action against Southland and several of its employees, alleging [that] Southland had a duty to provide for the safety and security of its patrons. Errico's complaint further alleges [that] Southland had a duty to properly manage, supervise and train its employees in the protection of its patrons from criminal assaults by third persons.

Southland moved for summary judgment, arguing that since it had no special relationship with Errico or her assailants, it had no duty to control the acts of those assailants or protect Errico from those acts. Southland further argued it owed no duty to properly supervise and train its employees in the protection of its patrons.

* * *

In granting summary judgment, the district court concluded that because no special relationship existed between Southland and Errico or her assailants, Southland owed her no duty to either control her assailants or to protect her. Errico appeals.

ISSUE

Did the district court err in concluding as a matter of law that Southland owed no duty to Errico?

ANALYSIS

* * *

A defendant generally has no duty to control the conduct of a third person in order to prevent that person from causing injury to another. Whether a duty exists depends upon two factors: (1) the existence of a special relationship between the defendant and the third person which imposes a duty to control, or between the defendant and the other which gives the other the right to protection; and (2) the foreseeability of the harm.

... [A] duty to protect has been found in a number of special relationships ... . But ... the law has been cautious and reluctant to impose such a duty upon a business enterprise, and ... a mere merchant-customer relationship is generally not enough.

[Another court] examined the following basic public policy considerations: (1) the prevention of crime is a governmental function that should not be shifted to the private sector; (2) imposition of a duty to protect against the unpredictable conduct of criminals does not lend itself easily to an ascertainable standard of care; and (3) the most effective crime deterrent may be cost prohibitive for both the property owner and customer ... .

The duty advanced by Errico is essentially to provide police protection, a duty that is traditionally vested in the government. To require Southland to protect its customers from criminal acts by third persons would require it to provide a safer environment on its premises than the government can provide to those same customers in the surrounding neighborhood. We do not believe that this is a reasonable expectation for customers to have, nor is it reasonable to expect Southland to provide such protection.

DECISION

Since no special relationship existed between Southland and Errico or her unknown assailants, summary judgment was properly granted to Southland.

Affirmed.

[DISSENT]

I believe that here, Errico successfully established a special relationship that imposed on Southland a duty to Errico—a duty to respond reasonably to criminal activity on its premises. [FN: I do not find necessary (or even relevant) to this duty or to the level of care required that Southland operated a 24-hour convenience store in a high-crime neighborhood or that the store was often the scene of criminal activity or was the place from which such criminal activity was reported to the police. It is also not relevant that the police had voiced concerns to Southland about the high level of criminal activity at this store, about the fact that there was not enough security in and around the store, and about the store's practice of allowing people to loiter in its parking lot. It is enough that Southland sought customers and, by lighting its parking area, gave those customers who came some legitimate expectation of increased security.]

* * *

I do not suggest that the special relationship here requires Southland to patrol the lot or to provide armed guards; it does, however, require Southland and its employees to keep a proper lookout over activities occurring on the well-lit parking area. At a minimum, store employees, having discovered unlawful and dangerous activity in the store parking area, should call the police, rather than merely pulling up seats for a ringside view.

Thus, I believe that a special relationship existed between Southland and Errico, and that Southland had a duty to provide minimal, cost-free protection to Errico against these criminal acts of unidentified third persons. While Errico may still have a problem showing that Southland's neglect caused any injury, that issue is for a jury to decide ... .

Case Questions

1. Why would the owner of a convenience store have a lesser duty to protect than a common carrier? An innkeeper?
2. Do you agree that criminal activity is unforeseeable?
3. What duties should a property owner owe to those on its property? Does it matter if the property is used to conduct business?

Real Property's "Bundle of Rights" Model

In an effort to simplify the abstraction of property, legal scholars refer to a *bundle of rights* that a person may enjoy. This model is used to explain the complex laws of real property ownership. Real property consists of land and its improvements (buildings, fences, wells, etc.—those valuable changes that humans inflict on their land). Other things that may be owned, such as money, goods, stocks and bonds, and the like, are called *personal property* and have a much smaller bundle of rights.

The most important property rights are rights of **possession**, use, and transfer. Each of these includes other rights. The right of possession allows one not only to be present on the land but also to exclude others. The causes of action for trespass, ejectment, and nuisance are based on this right. Use rights include the right to improve the land, to exploit it for agriculture, mining, cut timber, and so on. The right of transfer or conveyance includes the right to sell, lease, or give away real property. Real property is also transferred at death by will or intestate succession; these are important rights of ownership.

The nature and duration of these rights are restricted by a number of features of property law and property rights. Consider a married couple that "owns" a home. If they acquired the home after they were married, it is likely that they have a form of co-ownership called a *tenancy by the entirety,* whereby the surviving spouse would own the entire property in the event of the other's death. Even if title to the home is held in only one name, the other may have a marital interest based on **dower** or **curtesy** or on community property rights in some states. If there is a **mortgage** on the home, someone else has a right to sell the property in foreclosure if they default on the payments, and their capacity to sell the property may be severely restricted by the terms of their mortgage.

What they can do with their land may be subject to many limitations (**restrictive covenants**) placed in their deed if the home was part of a housing development. The use of their land is limited by local, state, and federal law—they may not be able to cut down a tree or have a garage sale without a permit. If their house is on a city street, the city has an **easement** along the street that gives the city a number of rights and the owners little but duties. The electric company has an easement for lines across the property, as does the city water department. There

---

BALLENTINE'S

possession Occupancy and dominion over property; a holding of land legally, by one's self (actual possession) or through another person such as a tenant (constructive possession). The holding may be by virtue of having title or an estate or interest of any kind.

dower The legal right or interest that a wife acquires by marriage in the property of her husband. ... Dower, as such, no longer exists or has been substantially could be other private easements allowing other persons a right of way across their land. They might not own the mineral rights below the surface of their land. The city, county, state, or federal governments could take away their property to build a highway or for other public use, only providing them with just compensation. Despite these restrictions, they are taxed on the value of the entire property, which could be sold for nonpayment of the taxes.

The duration of property rights may also be limited. If possession is held by a lease, the right of possession is subject to limitations of time as well as any other conditions the lessor includes in the lease agreement. A title may be limited in duration, such as for life (life estate) or until the fulfillment of a condition. When title has a limited duration, someone other than the present possessor has a future interest in the property, so that the present possessor has duties and limitations on use for the benefit of the future interest.

The bundle of rights may be viewed as the totality of rights and restrictions on rights held by a person with regard to real property. In view of the complexities of property rights, the term *ownership* has limited usefulness in the field of real property. The law deals with rights, and the extent of a person's ownership depends on how much of the bundle a person has.

Estates in Land

In a highly commercial society such as ours, real estate is often perceived as a commodity to be bought and sold for investment or speculation.

─────────────────────────── BALLENTINE'S ───────────────────────────

modified in most states, but every state retains aspects of the concept for the protection of both spouses.

curtesy   The rights a husband had under the common law with respect to his wife's property. Today these rights have been modified in every state in various ways, but all states that retain curtesy in some form extend the same rights to both spouses.

mortgage   A pledge of real property to secure a debt. Which one of at least three possible legal principles defines the rights of the parties to a given mortgage depends upon the state in which the mortgaged property is located. In states that have adopted the lien theory, the mortgagee (creditor) has a lien on the property; the mortgagor (debtor) retains legal title and is entitled to possession unless his or her interest is terminated by a foreclosure decree. In title theory states, a mortgage transfers title and a theoretical right of possession to the mortgagee; title reverts to the mortgagor upon full payment of the mortgage debt. A third group of states employs hybrid versions of the lien and title theories, with characteristics of both.

restrictive covenant   A covenant in a deed prohibiting or restricting the use of the property.

easement   A right to use the land of another for a specific purpose.

But it is not a commodity like pencils, where monetary payment and delivery of the goods passes title from one hand to the next without either side considering problems of title. Even the simplest real estate sale involves lawyers, title companies, tax stamps, recording at the court house, realtors, closing agents, mortgage companies, and so forth. The need for all of these has a lot to do with the ancient law of estates.

The law of tort and contract is a model of common sense compared to property law. Law based on private wrong must adapt to changing values and daily life, whether personal or commercial. Property law, in contrast, reflects the accumulation of technical principles establishing ownership rights. Land law is conservative; many basic principles have changed little over the centuries.

The conservatism of land law is partly due to concern on the part of those who have property that their rights remain secure; and because, over the centuries, those with wealth in property have either made the law or had extraordinary influence over those who make the law, tinkering with the rules of property rights has been disfavored. Another reason for the conservatism can be attributed to the very law that has given us the bundle-of-rights principles. Title to land, as we have seen, is a complex matter. Intrusions into ownership rights may take place at any time—a second mortgage, a tax lien, a lease or marriage or divorce can occur during the course of possession and will affect how various rights are distributed and limited. When someone sells real estate, the buyer will want to know the status of all rights pertaining to the property in question. The current status of a piece of real property depends upon its history. A search of the history (**chain of title**) of the property may even reveal that the seller's claims of ownership are much in doubt, or that someone else claims to be the owner, or that there are restrictions that make the property unsuitable for the purchaser's intended use.

To many our land law is simply a cumbersome relic of the past, but it is self-perpetuating—its technical complexity makes it difficult to change. What may appear to be a minor change may turn out to require adjustments through the entire system, and anything that potentially casts doubt on ownership is unfavorably viewed by property owners, lawyers, and those who make the law. Modernization of land law would be a monumental task and an agonizing ordeal that few seem ready to undertake.

The result of this conservatism is land law based on an ancient system that bears little relation to present realities. At the core of land law are the common law estates, which were developed in the first centuries following the Norman Conquest in 1066. These came into being during

---

BALLENTINE'S

chain of title The succession of transactions through which title to a given piece of land was passed from person to person from its origins to the present day.

England's feudal period when a person's status in society depended almost entirely on rights in land. Society and government were built on a military model with the king at its apex. Technically all land was held by the king, but it was divided among his subjects, who thereby owed the king certain fees and military service. Thus, a certain baron might control a certain area of land and the peasants working the land and be required to furnish his overlord with fees and a specified number of knights and soldiers in time of conflict. The overlord, in turn, was similarly responsible to his overlord, and so forth up to the king. At the base of the pyramid were the peasants who worked the land, providing a portion of their crops and personal service to the landlord, who was their protector. Although no one owned the land in the modern sense of the word, the status attached to the land passed from father to eldest son (primogeniture) as long as the son was acceptable to the lord and swore fealty to him. A baron's (or count's) land was inherited by his son (land could not be passed by will until the Statute of Wills in 1540), who then became the baron.

Although the system of primogeniture and certain other features of aristocratic land ownership were not adopted in the United States, the system of common law estates continues to this day. The estates were divided between freehold and nonfreehold estates; freeholders were free men and nonfreeholders were called "villeins." Except for the last term, which has come to mean something quite different, the terms have been preserved intact. It is more common to call a nonfreehold a leasehold estate with a **lease**, a **lessor**, and a **lessee**.

Fee Simple Absolute

The inheritable freehold estates were called fees; the most important one, then and today, was the *fee simple absolute*. This estate represents the maximum bundle of rights with the fewest strings attached. Among its important features are that it is *alienable* (it can be sold or given away), *inheritable,* and *devisable* (it can be passed by will). A fee simple absolute is unconditional and has potentially infinite duration. Standard real estate sales contracts call for a fee simple absolute, and that is what purchasers want and expect, whether or not they are familiar with its name. Such

---
BALLENTINE'S

lease   A contract for the possession of real estate in consideration of payment of rent, ordinarily for a term of years or months, but sometimes at will.

lessor   The person conferring the right of possession of real property, or possession and use of personal property, under a lease. A lessor of real estate is also known as a landlord.

lessee   The person receiving the right of possession of real property, or possession and use of personal property, under a lease. A lessee of real estate is also known as a tenant.

an estate still represents what it did several hundred years ago: the complete bundle of rights to possession, use, and transferability.

Life Estate

Contrast fee simple absolute with *life estate,* which is a freehold estate that is not inheritable. A life estate is created to last for a person's lifetime. It cannot be inherited or passed by will because it ends immediately upon the death of the owner or *life tenant.* Otherwise, it has the attributes of a fee simple absolute. It can be sold, leased, given away; of course, the life tenant cannot transfer more than he has—the purchaser gets an estate that lasts only as long as the original life tenant is alive. A life estate always creates a future interest; someone must have title after the life tenant dies, which imposes a duty on the life tenant to preserve the estate or be liable for "waste." For example, a father conveys real property "to my son Michael for life, and then to my grandson George." If no other limiting language is included, when Michael dies, George will hold the property in fee simple absolute (while Michael is alive, George's future interest is called a *remainder*).

Saltzman v. Ahern presents the problem of an owner of property, here the **grantor**, delivering two **deeds** to the property to two different **grantees**. The first grantee, Ahern, brought a suit to quiet title, an appropriate action requesting the court to determine who has **title**. The Saltzmans challenged Ahern's deed, claiming it did not pass title but was an attempt to pass title at the grantor's death, the grantor having reserved a life estate in the property in the deed. In other words, the Saltzmans argued that the deed should be treated as if it were a will. As a will can be revoked at any time prior to death, the subsequent deed to the Saltzmans served as a revocation. Revocation may in fact have been the grantor's intention; but if it was, he certainly chose the wrong means for accomplishing his purpose and compounded the problem by the subsequent grant to the Saltzmans.

The Saltzmans' argument at first sight seems to strain logic, but the history of property law shows a concern for technicality that lends some support to their challenge. They make much of the fact that the

---
BALLENTINE'S

grantor The person who makes a grant; the party in a deed who makes the conveyance.

deed A document by which real property, or an interest in real property, is conveyed from one person to another.

grantee The person to whom a grant is made; the party in a deed to whom the conveyance is made.

title 1. The rights of an owner with respect to property, real or personal, i.e., possession and the right of possession. 2. A document that evidences the rights of an owner, i.e., ownership rights.

terms "warranty" and "in fee simple" were deleted from the standard printed form. At common law, the words "and his [her, their] heirs" were required for conveying a fee simple absolute because the phrase meant the conveyance of a heritable estate; without the inclusion of this phrase, only a life estate was conveyed. In Florida, as in most states, this technicality has been dispensed with, and a fee simple absolute is presumed when other qualifying language is absent. The grantor's deletion of the phrase "in fee simple" might suggest that some other estate was intended, but the grantor did not delete "and their heirs and assigns." The deletion of words of warranty might suggest that the grantor intended something other than a **warranty deed**, which warrants title and promises to defend it, but there is nothing in the deed to suggest that it is anything but a warranty deed.

Nonfreehold Estates

Nonfreehold estates are also called *leasehold estates* and are most commonly represented by formal leases, commercial or residential, which spell out rights, duties, commencement, and termination as well as rental terms. Because these are contractual in nature and do not pass title, problems are resolved under contract law and state landlord and tenant law. Oral and informal arrangements present special problems that are usually handled in small claims court, as most rentals involving substantial amounts of money are evidenced by written contracts that are the products of professional legal advice.

Co-Ownership

Title may be held by more than one owner. Mention has been made of tenancy by the entirety, which is a species of co-ownership that can be held only by husband and wife. It includes a right of survivorship, as does *joint tenancy,* which can be held by two or more people as equal owners with equal rights of use and possession. Under the right of survivorship, if one co-owner dies, the share of the deceased is owned equally by the survivors. Sale or gift prior to death defeats the right of survivorship, but an attempted gift by will fails because death terminates all property interests in a joint tenancy or tenancy by the entirety. A remaining form of co-ownership is *tenancy in common,* which does not have a right of survivorship and which permits unequal shares among the co-owners.

─────────────── BALLENTINE'S ───────────────

warranty deed   A deed that contains title covenants.

**Herman SALTZMAN and Irene P. Saltzman,
his wife, et al., Appellants,
v.
Lacey N. AHERN, Appellee
District Court of Appeal of Florida,
First District
306 So. 2d 537 (1975)**

Both appellants and appellee claim title to a parcel of real estate, each claiming under separate conveyances from a common grantor, one James M. Dudley. Appellee filed a complaint to **quiet title** and appellants counterclaimed. The trial judge granted a motion for summary judgment, quieting title in appellee and appellants appealed.

* * *

The questioned deed was executed by Dudley on August 24, 1953. A standard printed form was utilized, but the grantor deleted the word "warranty" and the "warranting clause" as well as the words "in fee simple," causing the deed to read (in material part) as follows:

"WITNESSETH, that the said grantor, in consideration of Ten ($10.00) dollars and other valuable consideration, the receipt whereof is hereby acknowledged, does give, grant, bargain, sell, alien, remise, release, enfeoff, convey and confirm unto the said grantees and their heirs and assigns the lands situate in Duval County, State of Florida, ...

"BUT RESERVING, HOWEVER, unto the said grantor a life estate in said above described lands for the period of his natural life.

"TO HAVE AND TO HOLD the same together with the hereditaments and appurtenances, unto the said grantees, and their heirs and assigns forever, subject, however, to the estate for the life of the said grantor therein."

... Appellants' sole contention is that the grantor, by making the changes in the deed form above mentioned, and by subsequently conveying the identical property to appellants' predecessors in title thereby evinced an intention that the subject deed not take effect during his lifetime but be considered instead as an attempted testamentary disposition.

In order to resolve the issue, there being no question as to execution, consideration or delivery, we must examine the deed itself. When the language of a deed is clear and certain in meaning and the grantor's intention is reflected by the language employed, there is no room for judicial construction of the language nor interpretation of the words used. ... The recitation of consideration in an instrument raises a presumption thereof and when a person executes and delivers a deed for consideration there is raised a presumption that the words employed in the deed were intended to be effective in accordance with their ordinary meaning. If a deed is, by virtue of execution, delivery, consideration and language employed, impervious to attack by the grantor executing same, then it may not be successfully collaterally attacked by another.

* * *

The judgment appealed is accordingly Affirmed.

Case Questions

1. In its opinion, the court does not delve into the circumstances of the making of the deed. What is more important here, the grantor's intent or the interpretation of his intent from the language of the deed?
2. Does the treatment here conform to contract law with regard to consideration?
3. What is the status of the Saltzmans' deed?
4. Why did the grantor deed the property twice? Is that relevant?

Case Glossary

quieting title A lawsuit brought to remove a cloud on the title so that the plaintiff and those in privity with him or her may forever be free of claims against the property.

An important example of co-ownership today is the condominium, in which owners of individual housing units are also tenants in common with regard to common areas—stairs, walkways, parking lots, etc.—and are equally obligated for their maintenance. Time-share arrangements are a relatively new phenomenon commonly associated with a condominium-like land use. Under time-share, owners are tenants in common but restricted in their use to certain time periods during the year. States in which condominiums and time-share are common have adopted comprehensive statutes governing them.

In *Armer*, Charles and Lillian bought a ranch in the country but decided not to live there. Charles's mother gave them $20,000 to pay the balance due on the ranch. Later Charles persuaded his wife to sign a **quit claim deed** (a deed relinquishing her interest in the property) made out to Charles's mother, Mrs. Hill, so that in the event both Charles and Lillian died, Mrs. Hill could own the property. In 1964, Charles **recorded** the deed without informing his wife. Charles and Lillian later divorced; the lower court found that the delivery of the deed was without Lillian's consent and held that Lillian's interest in the land remained **community property**, subject to distribution in divorce. Charles appealed.

In community property states, property acquired during the marriage is presumed to be owned equally by husband and wife.

In the *Armer* case, one imagines that the mother-in-law's gift was made during a happier period in the marriage. Later events look suspiciously like an attempt on the part of the husband and his mother to get the gift back and perhaps more. In the divorce, Lillian received property valued at $17,600 and her car, while Charles received property worth $500 and his truck, which shows that community property is not necessarily split fifty-fifty at divorce. The disproportionate award may have been influenced by the court's reaction to Charles's misconduct.

BALLENTINE'S
---

quitclaim deed A deed that conveys whatever interest the grantor has in a piece of real property ... .

record To file or deposit a document or instrument ... for recording.

community property A system of law under which the earnings of either spouse are the property of both the husband and the wife, and property acquired by either spouse during the marriage (other than by gift, under a will, or through inheritance) is the property of both.

**Charles C. ARMER and Gertrude Hill,
Appellants,
v.
Lillian ARMER, Appellee
Supreme Court of Arizona
105 Ariz. 284, 463 P.2d 818 (1970)**

It has long been the law in Arizona that property acquired by either spouse during **coverture**, whether taken in the name of the husband or wife, is prima facie community property. Such a presumption is rebuttable, but only by clear and convincing evidence. When the character of property is once fixed, the property retains such character until changed by agreement of the parties or by operation of law.

* * *

Lillian's complaint alleged that "the defendant Charles Armer, fraudulently induced and coerced plaintiff to sign a quit claim deed conveying the (Coon Creek) property to Gertrude Hill." We do not find it necessary, however, to determine whether Lillian proved the nine elements of fraud at trial. For whether or not fraud was sufficiently proved, we hold that Charles, acting as agent for both the community and for his mother, performed an unauthorized delivery of the Coon Creek deed when he had the quit claim deed notarized, delivered to Mrs. Hill, and recorded without his wife's consent.

As previously indicated, all property acquired by either spouse during coverture is presumed to be community property. Since Charles and Lillian purchased the ranch as husband and wife, and since nothing was done subsequently to change the character of the property, the Coon Creek ranch was part of the community estate of Charles and Lillian. In Arizona, the husband is recognized as the head of the family, and its agent in control and management of the community estate. While the husband has the entire management of the community during coverture, he may not encumber or dispose of community realty without his wife's consent and signature, and must act at all times for the benefit of the community. There is no statutory or implied agency on the part of the husband to dispose of community realty. Charles, as agent of the community, had no authority to alienate any interest in the Coon Creek property without Lillian's consent. Lillian had affixed her signature to the quit claim deed only on the representation by Charles that the deed would not be notarized, that it would be put in their safe deposit box, and that it would only be delivered to Mrs. Hill in the event that Lillian and Charles were killed in a common accident. The subsequent notarization of the deed, its delivery to Mrs. Hill, and the deed's recordation were unauthorized, nor did Lillian ever ratify such actions by her husband. ...

We cannot agree with the trial court's findings of fact, conclusions of law, and judgment in one other respect, wherein the court concluded that Charles and Lillian held the Coon Creek property as "tenants in common," and that therefore either party could convey his or her interest to a third party. ... We hold that the entire quit claim deed conveying the Coon Creek ranch to Mrs. Hill is null and void, and that the Coon Creek ranch remains part of the community estate of Charles and Lillian. We further hold that Mrs. Hill has no interest in the property, except that she presently holds the entire ranch in trust for Charles and Lillian.

Case Questions

1. Did Charles come out better, worse, or the same by appealing this case?
2. Does this case suggest when title passes? At the signing of the deed or its delivery?

Case Glossary

coverture The status and rights of a wife arising from the marriage relationship.

Implications

Clearly the holder of a life estate is missing some of the rights enjoyed by the owner in fee simple absolute. There are other less frequently used freehold estates that are not described here, but keep in mind that in a sale of land, the purchaser ordinarily expects a fee simple absolute, and it is the responsibility of the person examining the land's past to determine whether the asserted owner does in fact have a clear title with the full bundle of rights.

The purchaser must be informed of any encumbrances. Attorneys are called upon to search titles, that is, to examine the records to establish the present owner and the extent of ownership. If there are any of the numerous intrusions on ownership mentioned previously, the purchaser should know of these and their legal ramifications—for instance, the significance of a utility easement that allows the electric company to cross the land to serve other properties. Inconsistencies and questions should be resolved—Has an old mortgage been satisfied even though satisfaction of mortgage has not been recorded? What was the effect of the divorce of a prior owner? An attorney may be retained not only to help conduct the transaction but also to provide a title opinion describing the current status of the title. Title insurance companies, which maintain extensive records on land within the territory they cover, offer additional protection to the prudent buyer.

Title searches, title opinions, and title insurance are made necessary by the system of estates that has been inherited over the centuries. Land sales call for a methodical approach that typically follows an orderly checklist to prepare for a smooth closing at which the purchase price is exchanged for delivery of a deed to the property. Much of the work in real property transactions can and should, for reasons of cost, be done by paralegals. In fact, a person who specializes in such transactions, or even one who specializes in residential or commercial sales or leases, is preferable to a general practitioner. Experience develops an awareness of the myriad problems that may arise.

Title

The word *title* has been used frequently thus far; its definition cannot be postponed. It is an important concept but one that is often misunderstood. The definition of title is curiously absent from or cursorily treated in law texts covering real property. The concept of title is abstract to the point of mystery.

In its beginnings it was embodied in the concept of *seisin,* which originally meant possession but gradually came to signify possession under the right to claim a freehold estate. Seisin originally referred to what seems today to have been a rather mystical relationship between an owner and his land; seisin was passed from one man to another by a ritual called *livery of seisin,* symbolized by handing over a twig or a clump of dirt from the land. When seisin passed, so did the right of possession.

The concept of title is similar. Its definition takes three forms:

1. The right to ownership and possession of land
2. The means whereby an owner of land has just possession
3. The evidence of ownership of land.

Title is not a document, such as a deed, though the term is often loosely used in such a reference. A deed is simply one of many bits of evidence of title. In a sense, title is held by the one who holds the greatest number of the bundle of rights that constitute a freehold estate; a lessee does not have title despite having the right of possession.

The three definitions of title treat different aspects of title. As evidence of title, there are numerous documents that, combined in a somewhat mystical union, tell us who has title. Documents alone may not be sufficient. One in wrongful possession for a sufficient period of time may acquire title (**adverse possession**). Treating title as a means of claiming possession refers to the need on occasion for one holding title to prove title against other claimants for title or possession. Finally, the right of ownership represented by the concept of title is its most common meaning, especially when ownership is not in question. "Right of ownership" must remain abstract, because the law is normally concerned with acknowledging and enforcing specific rights.

If the concept of title is still obscure, it is because it is relative and abstract. It is used in preference to ownership because it signifies the application of all the rules that identify ownership. Perhaps it is best explained by the barb, "I don't own the house, the bank owns it." This is an obvious reference to the lender on a mortgage, who usually puts up a far greater portion of the purchase price than the actual purchaser. In most states, however, the bank merely holds a lien on the property and no part of the title. Nevertheless, the title to the land in question is encumbered by the mortgage, and no prudent purchaser would buy the land without resolving the mortgage question. (A mortgage may not prevent a sale of land, but because the mortgage is secured by the land, a failure to pay the mortgage could result in foreclosure no matter who has title.)

BALLENTINE'S

adverse possession   The act of occupying real property in an "open, notorious, and hostile manner," under a claim of right, contrary to the interests of the true owner.

Personal Property

Title to personal property does not usually raise the complex problems associated with chain of title to real property. Because tangible personal property is commonly exchanged by sale or gift, mere possession is significant evidence of exchange of title. Most problems arise with **bailments** and lost, stolen, or abandoned property, which is usually covered by well-established legal rules. The Uniform Commercial Code gives specific guidance on sale of goods and intangible personal property in the form of negotiable instruments.

What happens to an engagement ring when the marriage does not take place? Devising fair principles is not as easy as it may seem. The problem is complicated by the intersection of several fields of law:

1. Contract law. Is an engagement a contract? If the contract is breached, is restitution in the form of return of the engagement ring an appropriate remedy?
2. Tort law. There was at one time an action at common law called "breach of promise to marry" with a consequent suit for damages. Many states have abolished this cause of action. Could the engagement ring be an element of damages? Does abolishing the cause of action put the ring beyond reach?
3. Family law. Should the marriage (and engagement) contract be treated like any other contract, or should the state's interest in the sanctity of the family treat this contract specially, including the right to the engagement ring? If the state's public policy is not to force incompatible couples to marry, how should the court decide on the ring?
4. Property law. Is the engagement ring a gift? Consideration for a contract? A pledge? Has title passed?

The basic principles that developed concerning return of the ring were as follows: (1) If the donee breaks off the engagement without fault on the part of the donor, the donor is entitled to its return. (2) If the donor breaks off the engagement, the donee keeps the ring. (3) An engagement broken by mutual consent obliges the return of the ring.

In the state of New York, these common law rules applied until 1935, when the legislature abolished actions for breach of promise to marry, which was interpreted by the courts to bar an action for recovery of engagement rings. In 1965, the legislature enacted law to

---

BALLENTINE'S

bailment The entrusting of personal property by one person (the bailor) to another (the bailee) for a specific purpose, with the understanding that the property will be returned when the purpose is accomplished, the stated duration of the bailment is over, or the bailor reclaims it.

allow recovery of engagement rings when "justice so requires." This moral tone is echoed in the *Cohen* case, in which the fiance was killed in an auto accident shortly before the wedding and the personal representative of his estate attempted to recover the ring.

A somewhat similar case had occurred in Massachusetts a few years before with different results. In *De Cicco v. Barker,* 339 Mass. 457, 159 N.E.2d 534 (1959), a married man gave several rings to a woman, at least one of which, a six-carat diamond ring, was apparently an engagement ring. His wife was in the hospital at the time, and the engagement was conditioned on her death, which occurred two months later. Subsequent to the wife's death, the fiancee bought him an engagement ring but several months later broke the engagement.

She relied on the Massachusetts legislative abolishment of the cause of action for breach of promise to marry, but the court gave him the six-carat ring, stating:

> .... It is a proceeding not to recover damages, either directly or indirectly for breach of the contract to marry but to obtain on established equitable principles restitution of property held on a condition which the defendant was unwilling to fulfil. It seeks to prevent unjust enrichment

Estate Planning

An important area of law practice is estate planning, which deals with the orderly distribution of assets at death. If no provision is made in advance, the property of a deceased person, called the *estate* or *decedent's estate,* passes by intestate succession as ordered by state law. Most persons would distribute their property somewhat differently than will the state and should so provide in advance by will and/or trust. The estate planner not only assists in preparing the documents of distribution, but also advises clients on tax and other legal consequences of different distributions. Advice is not merely legal and financial, but can be very personal as well.

Wills

The primary purpose of wills is distribution of the financial assets of the deceased according to directions provided prior to death in the will itself. Many persons wish to control the use of their property long after death or want to specify in great detail how everything they own will pass to intended beneficiaries. All this can be accomplished through a will. However, unnecessary complexity not only makes administration of the estate cumbersome, but it also tends to anger and frustrate beneficiaries and encourage suits to contest the validity of the will. When

COHEN
v.
BAYSIDE FEDERAL SAVINGS AND LOAN ASSOCIATION
Supreme Court of New York
62 Misc. 2d 738, 309 N.Y.S.2d 980 (1970)

Some courts have propounded a pledge theory. Other courts state that principles of unjust enrichment govern and the most popular rationale is that the ring is given as a gift on condition subsequent. It is not always clear, however, whether it is the actual marriage of the parties or the donee's not performing any act that would prevent the marriage that is the actual condition of the "transaction."

Thus a confusing body of law has grown up around the engagement ring and, after careful consideration of these principles, this court has decided that Carol should keep the ring because that result is equitable and because "justice so requires"... .

I cannot believe that the age-old ritual of giving an engagement ring to bind the mutual premarital vows can be or is intended to be treated as an exchange of consideration as practiced in the everyday market place. Can it be seriously urged that the giving of this ring by the decedent "groom" to his loved one and bride-to-be can be treated as the ordinary commercial or business transaction requiring the ultimate in consideration and payment? I think not. To treat this special and usually once in a lifetime occasion, one as requiring quid pro quo, is a mistake and unrealistic.

[Carol Cohen's ring was worth only one thousand dollars. In *Lowe v. Quinn* the ring was valued at $60,000, which explains why she wanted to keep it and he went to the highest state court to get it back. Although she broke off the engagement, he was in a special dilemma—he was still married.]

Edwin S. LOWE, Appellant
v.
Jayne D. QUINN, Respondent
Court of Appeals of New York
27 N.Y.2d 397, 267 N.E.2d 251 (1971)

An engagement ring "is in the nature of a pledge for the contract of marriage" and, under the common law, it was settled—at least in a case where no impediment existed to a marriage—that, if the recipient broke the "engagement," she was required, upon demand, to return the ring on the theory that it constituted a conditional gift. However, a different result is compelled where, as here, one of the parties is married. An agreement to marry under such circumstances is void as against public policy, and it is not saved or rendered valid by the fact that the married individual contemplated divorce and that the agreement was conditioned on procurement of the divorce. Based on such reasoning, the few courts which have had occasion to consider the question have held that a plaintiff may not recover the engagement ring or any other property he may have given the woman. ...

[The court goes on to argue that the legislative reenactment of the right to recover an engagement ring did not apply to a situation in which either of the parties is married at the time of the gift of the ring.]

Case Questions

1. Is *Cohen* decided on the basis of contract, tort, family, or property law, as suggested in the comments prior to the cases?
2. Is *Lowe* decided on the basis of contract, tort, family, or property law, as suggested in the comments prior to the cases?

specific problems, such as a spendthrift child or spouse, warrant limitations on the distribution or use of property, a trust is often the more appropriate solution.

Will drafting is often left to paralegals, who can use the language and form of past models to express the intent of the testator, to be reviewed by the responsible attorney prior to signing by the testator and witnesses. Today drafting wills can be greatly facilitated by computers programmed with standard clauses and paragraphs that reflect the requirements of state law. In some instances an attorney or paralegal may simply follow a checklist of questions, the answers to which are entered into a computer which then prints a will. If the computer program is comprehensive, the possibility of human error is minimized.

Each state requires specific formalities for the signing and attesting of wills that must be strictly adhered to in order to create a valid will. The legal advisor's goal should be to give force to the intent of the testator in a form that will discourage and overcome legal challenge. The process of settling an estate through the court is called *probate*, and the court responsible is commonly called *probate* or *surrogacy* court.

Working with clients who wish to have wills drafted calls for delicacy, tact, common sense, and a basic understanding of human nature. Contemplation of death is unpleasant at best, and letting go of the acquisitions of a lifetime is not easy.

A special note is warranted here. Making a will for a client usually results in the attorney and staff acquiring a detailed knowledge of the client's finances and personal relationships. All of this information is strictly confidential, and all members of the legal staff must scrupulously avoid revealing any knowledge thus acquired.

Trusts

A *trust* is a device dating back to the fourteenth century, when it was used to avoid certain features of the ownership of common law freehold estates. It was enforced in the courts of equity and is still governed by equity today. A trust involves a transfer of title of real or personal property to a trustee who is charged with a duty to hold the property for the benefit of another, a beneficiary (*cestui que* trust). The trust instrument provides instructions for the trustee to follow in distributing property to the beneficiary.

By setting up a *living (inter vivos) trust,* a person can put property into the trust that will go to named parties immediately or when the donor dies. In this way the trust can be used as a will substitute and has the advantage of making possible detailed instructions on the distribution of property at the same time that it avoids probate of the property. When a trust is used as a will substitute, the donor can make himself or herself trustee and beneficiary for his or her lifetime and thereby both control and benefit from the property. Trusts can also be used to transfer property without regard to death, as with a trust fund to send one's children to college; the donor may relinquish any control (*irrevocable trust*).

The advantage of a trust over a will is that it names a trustee to carry out the wishes of the donor. Without such an arrangement, future decisions would be based on interpretations of the intent of the testator, which might prove inappropriate as times and situations change. The donor may provide for flexibility that would not be possible in an outright distribution. Also, the trustee has a fiduciary duty toward the beneficiary that can make the trustee more accountable than someone who misuses distributed property. For someone with minor children or others who cannot properly take care of their affairs, a trust can be established that provides temporarily for financial needs while preserving assets for later distribution. In short, the trust can be tailored to very special problems that would be very awkward to handle in a will.

A good deal of the work involving trusts can be efficiently done by paralegals.

Government Regulation of Real Property

Ownership of real property today is subject to many intrusions by government. Most of these take the form of restrictions on use. In addition, governments may take property under the power of eminent domain, and the federal government has authority over navigable waters. Former rights over airspace above an owner's property have been restricted primarily because of the advent of the airplane.

Eminent Domain

The Fifth Amendment to the U.S. Constitution, the repository of basic rights in criminal law, ends with the clause, "nor shall private property be taken for a public use, without just compensation." This, along with similar language in state constitutions, is the basis for the power our governments exercise called *eminent domain*. This power is used to take property for highways, parks, urban redevelopment, and protection of the environment. "Public use" has been broadly defined to cover laws allowing private railroads to acquire property for their routes, electric utilities to obtain rights of way, and so forth.

Compensation for the taking of property is often subject to dispute, but state and federal governments have procedures designed to determine fair market value and to give the opportunity to challenge assessments. The major issue in litigation has been interpretation of the word "taking." When government takes title to an entire piece of property, the problem may be simple—pay fair market value. If, however, the state builds a new highway, reducing traffic on an old highway and thereby making a filling station unprofitable, there is no "taking"—it is considered *damnum absque injuria,* a harm without a legal injury, and not compensable. Thus, some effects of government action constitute taking and some do not. The issue arose early in this century with planning and zoning.

Planning and Zoning

The most direct intrusions into a private property owner's rights have come from governmental attempts to regulate land use. For both residential and commercial owners, planning and zoning have resulted in severe restrictions on property owners' rights. The classic example of planning that is still to be found everywhere is the comprehensive zoning ordinance. Starting in the 1920s, cities and counties throughout the country adopted the practice of mapping land use zones, which restrict areas to categories of use such as residential, professional, commercial, and industrial. Generally these zones reflect contemporary uses but restrict future development. The object of zones is to diminish the effects of urban blight, save agricultural and green areas, and prevent the intrusion of incompatible uses in adjacent areas. Because zoning clearly represents the government depriving property owners of use rights they would otherwise enjoy, it was challenged as a taking under eminent domain for which no compensation was provided.

The U.S. Supreme Court in *Euclid v. Ambler,* 272 U.S. 365, 47 S. Ct. 114, 71 L. Ed. 303 (1926) upheld comprehensive zoning in the village of Euclid, Ohio, under the state's power to regulate health, safety, and welfare, but found a taking in *Nectow v. City of Cambridge,* 277 U.S. 183, 48 S. Ct. 447, 72 L. Ed. 842 (1928), where zoning effectively deprived the owner of any economically feasible use of his property (property zoned residential, though adjacent properties were occupied by industrial enterprises). The judgment relied on the Fourteenth Amendment's prohibition of deprivation of property without due process of law. Subsequent constitutional history has affirmed the resulting balancing test between the rights of communities to control land use and the rights of individual property owners to make reasonable use of their land.

Today planning has taken on additional tasks. Zoning maps are only a temporary solution to the problems that intensive growth has created in many areas. Comprehensive, long-range planning prevails in populous states, along with environmental concerns. Residential and commercial development are frequently carried out on a grand scale, and federal and state laws have been enacted to require exhaustive studies of the impact of such development on the environment and the capacity of local resources to support new building. Government has taken a serious role in controlling and directing growth. Major projects, airports, shopping malls, large residential developments, and the like are subject to intense scrutiny to assure compliance with the law, and it is unlikely that legal requirements will decrease in the future.

Lawyers find much work in this area in advising, negotiating, and facilitating cooperation between developers and local governmental bodies. Paralegals can be invaluable in the process.

Summary

Property is an abstract concept, not a natural or physical object or feature. It is best explained in terms of legal rights, such as rights to possess, exclude, and transfer. Rights can also be limited in time, such as a lease or a life estate, and in the nature of use and transferability. Rights may be restricted by a deed, by zoning ordinances, and by rights of others, such as utility easements and rights of way.

Property is divided into real and personal property. Real property, which consists of land and its improvements, is based on common law estates, which have endured for many centuries because of the basic conservatism of real property law. Under this system a person owns rights in land (the bundle-of-rights concept) rather than owning the land itself. When a person owns the maximum bundle of rights, the estate is called a fee simple absolute and corresponds to what we casually refer to as ownership. Lesser estates may be held, of which the most common is the life estate, which allows the life tenant to exercise rights over the property while alive. Upon death, the rights automatically transfer to a person who until that time held only a future interest.

Leasehold (or nonfreehold) estates involve the temporary transfer of the right of possession and are regulated by landlord and tenant laws of each state.

Title is an important concept in property law. It is not a document like a deed, but an abstraction based on the history of the ownership of property that describes the extent of rights and limitations on rights; it can be determined by examining the records of transactions dealing with a particular piece of land. Title to personal property is generally much simpler, especially when physical property is directly exchanged for cash or a cash equivalent—title passes instantaneously.

An important aspect of the practice of property law involves estate planning, preparing for the distribution of a person's estate (the totality of one's property, real and personal). The most common devices used in estate planning are wills and trusts. A will provides for the distribution of property at death. A trust may distribute property at death or during one's lifetime; it establishes a trustee who distributes property to a beneficiary according to instructions in the trust instrument.

Today property is extensively regulated by government. Particularly affecting real property are restrictions on land use covered by local government planning and zoning, but state and federal governments have become more and more active in limiting land use, especially in the area of environmental law.

Review Questions

1. Why would the owner of a vacant city lot vehemently object to the city rezoning the lot from commercial to residential?

2. What is equal ownership with right of survivorship called?

3. Why have we preserved the ancient law of estates?

4. Why is it necessary to examine the chain of title prior to a sale of real estate?

5. Where does the state's power of eminent domain come from?

6. Are stocks and bonds personal property or real property?

7. Why are real property transactions so much more complicated than personal property transactions?

Exercises

1. All states have recording acts, the purpose of which is to have a record of real estate transactions. When a deed is delivered upon the sale of real property, the purchaser ordinarily records that deed, usually with a clerk of the court. Once recorded, anyone searching the title of the land involved should discover the deed as part of the process of establishing who has title. Recording acts do not require recording but provide for the consequences of failure to record. Recording acts are designed to protect those who rely on the official records. Suppose, for instance, that in *Saltzman v. Ahern* the first grantee, Ahern's predecessor in title, did not record the deed until *after* the Saltzmans received their deed (from the original grantor as well) and recorded it. The Saltzmans' deed would be the first deed in the record. Who has title? The answer varies among the states. Check your recording statute to answer this question. Does it make a difference if the Saltzmans knew about the prior deed, that is, if they had notice of the prior deed?

2. What property transactions in your state must be in writing? Check the Statute of Frauds and the Uniform Commercial Code.

3. Is your state a title state (mortgagor/debtor holds title) or a lien state (mortgagee/creditor holds title until debt is paid)?

DISCOVERY: JUST WHAT ARE YOU LOOKING FOR?

Lindi Massey

Discovery is the longest and most tedious part of a family law case. Usually the parties have numerous assets and liabilities that need to be documented, discovered and produced for review in order to settle or try issues.

Prepare an Inventory

Normally, you should begin with an inventory which each party prepares and exchanges. The inventory will help you determine what property the parties have that needs to be appraised. It also helps you determine whether or not one of the parties has claims for, or contests any claims for, separate property or reimbursement. The inventory information (assets and liabilities) is sworn to by each party and each states under oath that to the best of his/her knowledge and belief the inventory contains the following:

- A full and complete list of all properties in their possession or subject to their control that they claim belong to the community estate, with the values thereof;
- A full and complete list of all properties in their possession or subject to their control that they claim or admit as theirs or their spouse's separate property and estate, with the values thereof;
- A full and complete list of the debts that they claim are community indebtedness.

The preparing party will also make the following reservations and qualifications:

- Any omission from this inventory is not intentional but is done through mere inadvertence and not for the purpose of misleading their spouse; and
- There may be other assets and liabilities of which their spouse is aware, and their omission from this inventory should not be construed as a waiver of their interest in those items.

In the event there is any omission, mischaracterization or undervaluation for fraudulent reasons, this document will provide your client with evidence for a future lawsuit.

After exchanging inventories, make a comparison to determine contested issues. Additionally, prepare a one-page Inventory Summary in order to determine the value of the parties' marital estate. This summary allows the attorney to determine at a glance the net worth of the estate and they can then begin settlement negotiations, using these figures. The inventory also helps in preparing deposition questions or interrogatories as well as deciding what documents need to be requested for production.

Interrogatories and Production Requests

If a settlement is not forthcoming, proceed with interrogatories and a request for production of documents.

An obvious question that you should always ask is who their witnesses, fact and expert, will be. Also, if you have separate property and reimbursement issues, you need to ask what they base their claim on, and request any documentation they have to back up their claim.

If one of the parties already has a "significant other," be sure to request information on that person, as well as information and documentation on any community funds spent on gifts or entertainment for this person. A review of the check books and credit card statements will also help you determine if community funds have been expended and need to be reimbursed to the marital estate.

When custody is an issue, ask the opposing party each and every fact they know that supports their allegation that your client would not be the best party to have managing conservatorship or joint managing conservatorship of the children. Get their list of why your client is such a bad person and why the opposing party is such a good person. If their story changes at time of trial, these answers can help your attorney impeach their testimony.

In requesting production of documents, ask for copies of everything that substantiates the opposing party's figures on the inventory and the answers to the interrogatories. There is no limit to what you can request to be produced but, of course, the opposing counsel can file a protective order in an effort to trim your request, extend the time to produce and protect privileged information.

Reprinted with permission from *Legal Assistant Today* magazine.

CHAPTER 14

FAMILY LAW

Historical Roots of Family Law

Probably no area of law has changed more in American history than family law. Family and family life have changed radically and the law has changed along with them. Regulation of the family by legislatures and courts has followed a tortuous course. The degree to which the state should intrude into family relationships has always been controversial. For example, public policy supports the protection of children from abuse and neglect, but traditional values also protect parental authority against interference by the government.

Regulation of the family involves limiting choices by law in an area of human life where choices are jealously guarded. Should individuals be free to marry, divorce, and bear children at their whim? In our society, some would place severe restrictions on each of these; others would insist that each is purely a matter of individual choice and not a concern of government.

Whereas other areas of law, such as the law of property, may be seen as a logical evolution from ancient English roots, family law is largely an American creation, consciously departing from English legal traditions. For example, Connecticut allowed absolute divorce long before England did. Divorce is really an American legal institution.

The archetypal family consists of a father, a mother, and children. Although there are contemporary pressures to define *family* in much broader terms, the legal foundations of family law are premised on legitimizing a sexual relation between husband and wife that encourages child-bearing and child-rearing. American courts have, throughout their history, regarded themselves as the protectors of the family, often invoking rules on purely moral grounds.

The moral basis of family law was formalized when the Church assumed responsibility for regulating domestic relations in the late Middle Ages. At that time, marriage became a sacrament, subjecting the marital relationship to regulation by the Church. Our family law originated in the **canon law**, the law of the ecclesiastical courts. Because America did not employ ecclesiastical courts or canon law, the area of domestic relations was subsumed under the courts of equity, except in colonies, like Connecticut and Massachusetts, which refused to adopt courts of equity. At the founding of the American republic, the division between courts of equity and common law courts was still very strong. There was no common law tradition of family law except for property rights, and the common law was most appropriately charged with formal legal matters such as the remedies for injury to person or property, for crimes, and for breach of contract.

BALLENTINE'S

canon law   Christian religious law, particularly that of the Roman Catholic church.

Despite the American rejection of ecclesiastical law, the marriage contract retains some elements of its former sacred character. In former times, the betrothal was the critical event in marriage, as marriage partners were chosen by the parents of the bride and groom as part of a family alliance that benefited the respective families as well as the couple. In recent times, the wedding has become the significant event, as people have become free to choose their own partners. Both church and state have retreated from their former authority, leaving individuals free to form and dissolve the marital union.

Law and Marriage

The legal requirements for marriage are minimal. The bride and groom must meet minimum age requirements; for the moment they must ordinarily be of different sexes; they must have legal capacity to contract marriage; they must not be married to someone else; and they must not be closely related by blood. In short, it is easy to get married. Lawyers are rarely consulted.

Divorce, in contrast, is far more complicated. The principal subjects of family law are in one way or another concerned with divorce and its aftermath: child **custody**, **child support**, spousal support (**alimony**), **community property**, and **equitable distribution**.

Marriage as Contract

The marriage itself is traditionally viewed as a contractual arrangement, because the parties voluntarily assume the relationship of husband and

---
BALLENTINE'S
---

custody   As applied to persons, physical control. ... Custody carries with it the obligation on the part of the custodian to maintain and care for the person in his charge for the duration of their relationship.

child support   1. Money paid, pending divorce and after divorce, by one parent to the other for the support of their children. 2. The obligation of parents to provide their children with the necessities of life.

alimony   Ongoing court-ordered support payments by a divorced spouse. ... Alimony is not child support.

community property   A system of law under which the earnings of either spouse are the property of both the husband and the wife, and property acquired by either spouse during the marriage (other than by gift, under a will, or through inheritance) is the property of both.

equitable distribution   Some jurisdictions permit their courts, in a divorce case, to distribute all property obtained during the marriage on an "equitable" basis, that is, without regard to whose name the property is in.

wife, but the most important duties are those imposed by law rather than the agreement of the parties. For example, husband and wife are obligated to provide mutual support for each other and support and nurture for their children. Individuals may avoid these duties by agreement only under special circumstances allowed by the law.

Although marriage has long been characterized as a contract, it has not been an ordinary contract in the eyes of the law, that is, one that could be freely made, altered, and broken. The sacred aspect of the family and procreation argued for a sacred contract. In recent decades, however, the state, which in America had assumed responsibility for domestic regulation, moved toward making the marriage contract much more like other contracts, in which the contracting parties controlled the relationship. Many of the features of family law can be explained by the tension between the special regard with which we view marriage and the family and the objective contractual rights and duties which the law imposes on family relationships.

> It is also to be observed that, although marriage is often termed by text writers and in court decisions as a civil contract—generally to indicate that it might be founded upon the agreement of the parties, and does not require any religious ceremony for its solemnization—it is something more than a mere contract. The consent of the parties is of course essential to its existence; but when the contract to marry is executed by the marriage, a relation between the parties is created which they cannot change. Other contracts may be modified, restricted, or enlarged, or entirely released upon consent of the parties. Not so with marriage. Once the relation is formed, the law steps in and holds the parties to various obligations and liabilities. It is an institution, in the maintenance and purity of which the public is deeply interested, for it is the foundation of the family and of society, without which there would be neither civilization nor progress.

Maynard v. Hill, 125 U.S. 190, 210 (1888).

Marriage as a Partnership

From an economic standpoint, the marriage contract establishes an ongoing, cooperative unit like a business partnership. In some instances the reciprocal nature of the business is clear, as when the wife works as a secretary to support her husband while he gets through law school, with the understanding that once the husband's practice is prospering, the wife will quit working and bear and raise the couple's children. Success of the partnership depends upon each spouse meeting the terms of the contract. Other marriage partners may be business partners in an objective sense, that is, they may jointly manage their own commercial enterprise. Often the division of profits does not take place in the way unmarried partners would ordinarily conduct a business, but in every other respect the differences may be insignificant. Perhaps the majority of marriages do not have the usual characteristics of a business venture, but nearly all marriages involve important cost and savings sharing for mutual benefit, similar to a business enterprise.

Divorce may be treated like the dissolution of a business partnership. To the extent that property assets have been acquired by the joint efforts of the spouses, this model may, when used with caution, effect a fair distribution of the marital property.

Children

Family law, often called **domestic relations**, might more properly be titled the law of intimate relations, especially in this period in our society when couples exercise considerable freedom in the partners they choose and the lifestyles those partnerships express. Even though we have moved away from the traditional marriage-and-children model of adult relationships, the idealized model of the family continues to be a heterosexual union having as its major motivation the creation and nurture of children. Children add a dimension to family law that distinguishes it from other areas of law: Family law commonly deals with the welfare of human beings who have not reached the age of legal competence (majority), who are vulnerable to abuse or exploitation, and who must be protected by society through its legal institutions when the family, the primary social institution, fails. Problems in other areas of law are often neatly handled by the transfer of wealth from one pocket to another; family law involves issues that are not readily measured in dollars and cents.

Family Law and the Adversarial Process

American legal procedure has developed around an adversarial process in which disputing parties arm themselves with legal representatives and ultimately try their cases before an impartial judge if the lawyers and the parties cannot reach an agreement. The sides are viewed as hostile and the lawyers are duty-bound to fight for the interests of their clients. This model quite naturally tends to focus and intensify the dispute, one of the reasons the states attempted to soften the process by adopting **no-fault divorce** statutes. Divorcing couples with minor

---

BALLENTINE'S

domestic relations   The field of law relating to domestic matters, such as marriage, divorce, support, custody, and adoption; family law.

no-fault divorce   A term for the requirements for divorce in jurisdictions in which the party seeking the divorce need not demonstrate that the other party is at fault. The requirements differ from state to state.

children pose a serious problem for the legal system. We assume that parents will care for the interests of their children, but divorcing parents often aggravate the damage the divorce causes to children by drawing them into a continuing dispute.

Annulment

An examination of annulment is valuable because it reveals the requirements for a valid marriage. An action for annulment challenges the validity of the original marriage contract. Annulment is uncommon today largely because the adoption of no-fault divorce statutes has made divorce easier than annulment. Nevertheless, for religious or other reasons, some individuals may prefer to seek annulment.

The most important aspect of the difference between annulment and divorce relates to the grounds for ending the marriage. Annulment is based on a defect in existence when the marriage was contracted. Divorce is based on grounds arising during the marriage itself. For instance, it is often possible to obtain an annulment if one of the parties to the marriage was impotent or sterile at the time of the marriage (usually assuming this fact was unknown to the other party); impotence or sterility developing after the marriage contract would not ordinarily be grounds for annulment—the complaining party would be forced to resort to divorce to get out of the marriage.

Divorce terminates the marriage from the time of the final decree, but annulment operates retroactively to invalidate the marriage from its beginning. This is so because the cause of action for annulment asserts some impediment to the formation of the marriage contract itself—if the contract was invalid, no marriage resulted. One of the important consequences of annulment is the general unavailability of alimony, which most American courts award only upon dissolution of a valid marriage.

Void or Voidable?

Under traditional contract theory, some contracts are deemed void and some are merely voidable. A *void contract* is one that was never valid; a *voidable contract* is valid until a court declares it invalid. Through the passage of time and removal of the impediment to validity, a voidable contract may become enforceable. Marriage contracts are similarly subject to the void–voidable distinction. Because of the special nature of the marriage contract, the grounds for invalidity are somewhat different from other contracts.

Marriages generally considered void include:

1. *Bigamous marriage*, when one of the parties is already married
2. *Incestuous marriage*, within a prohibited relationship for marriage (e.g., brother-sister)
3. *Mental incompetence*, when one of the parties lacks mental capacity to contract marriage
4. *Nonage*, when at least one of the parties is below the minimum age to marry.

Marriages may be merely voidable on the ground of *formalities*, that is, failure to meet the formal requirements for a licensed marriage; and *fraud*. Fraud, which accounts for the largest number of attacks on marriages through annulment proceedings, includes three categories:

1. *Fraud with regard to essentials of marriage.* Many courts have adopted the rule that fraud as to the essentials of marriage must be of an extreme nature. This is often referred to as the *Massachusetts rule*, derived from *Reynolds v. Reynolds*, 85 Mass. (3 Allen) 605 (1862), in which an annulment was granted to a husband whose wife had represented herself as chaste even though she was already pregnant by another man. An annulment was granted to the husband.
2. *Fraud with regard to inability or unwillingness to have children.* Perhaps the oldest ground for annulment known to our law has to do with sex and procreation. When one spouse misrepresents his or her ability to have children, the law traditionally permits annulment.
3. *Fraud on the court or legal process.* Certain cases of collusion between parties involve fraud on the legal system rather than fraud on the other party. This occurs with sham marriages, wherein some purpose other than marriage, cohabitation, and procreation is intended, such as marrying to qualify for a visa or legitimizing a child. When there was no intent to consummate the marriage and the marriage was not in fact consummated, annulment may be available.

Consequences of Annulment

Historically, annulment treated the marriage as if it had never occurred, but the harshness of this rule has been softened in recent times. In particular, annulment should not bastardize the offspring of an annulled marriage. The Uniform Marriage and Divorce Act (UMDA)

§ 207(c) states: "Children born of a prohibited marriage are legitimate." (The UMDA was drafted by the National Conference of Commissioners on Uniform State Laws to propose legislation for the states that would cover the principal subject of marriage and divorce. Several states have adopted the Act and many judicial opinions cite it as supporting authority.)

Alimony is another matter. Under the common law, it was the duty of the husband to provide for the wife and this extended to legal separations (i.e., divorce from bed and board), as well as absolute divorce. This duty, however, depended upon a valid marital contract and was therefore inconsistent with annulment. A number of states have passed legislation allowing alimony following annulment under restricted circumstances, as when the receiving spouse is an innocent party.

Antenuptial (Premarital) Agreements

Dower and **curtesy** under the common law, and their modern representatives such as **elective share**, provide that a surviving spouse is entitled to a large share of the decedent's estate despite testamentary provisions (the laws of intestacy apply when no valid will exists). Community property or equitable distribution favor a fifty-fifty split in case of divorce. In most states, the only way to decrease this share upon death or divorce is through an agreement signed before the marriage: an *antenuptial* or *premarital agreement*. Until the twentieth century, such agreements were judicially disapproved as violating public policy, which disfavored any agreement tending to promote divorce. As the twentieth century draws to a close, most states have reversed this policy and now enforce antenuptial contracts, especially when financial disclosure precedes the contract and coercive conduct is absent.

Antenuptial agreements are private contracts setting the terms of the marital contract in advance. Both their popularity and their use have increased in recent years. In the practice of law, the important

---
BALLENTINE'S
---

dower   The legal right or interest that a wife acquires by marriage in the property of her husband. ... Dower, as such, no longer exists or has been substantially modified in most states, but every state retains aspects of the concept for the protection of both spouses.

curtesy   The rights a husband had under the common law with respect to his wife's property. Today these rights have been modified in every state in various ways, but all states that retain curtesy in some form extend the same rights to both spouses.

elective share   In some states, the share a surviving spouse may elect to take in the estate of the deceased spouse. In such jurisdictions, it replaces dower. An elective share is also referred to as a *statutory share*.

features of antenuptial agreements are concerned with the distribution of property at death or divorce. Jurisdictions that approve antenuptial agreements have tended to treat them in most respects like other contracts. Their validity may be challenged on traditional contract grounds, such as voluntariness, fraud, and conscionability. Some jurisdictions, however, have been reluctant to treat antenuptial agreements like other contracts, expressing traditional public policy concerns for the stability of the family and protection of its members.

Certain situations are ready-made for antenuptial agreements, as when someone remarries and wants to ensure that a major portion of his or her assets will be preserved for children of a prior marriage. Spouses, most commonly women, who sacrifice to put their spouses through a long and expensive education, may want to protect themselves in case of divorce so that they recoup their investments.

Postmarital Contracts

Postmarital contracts may be labeled *postnuptial agreements*, *separation agreements*, or *property settlement agreements*. Postnuptial agreements executed while the marriage is still harmonious are subject to the same public policy challenge as antenuptial agreements, and they lack the consideration essential to a valid contract. Separation agreements and property settlements executed in contemplation of an impending divorce are generally exempt from these attacks. The modern trend in most states increasingly favors recognition of the validity of postmarital agreements.

A major issue regarding agreements submitted to the courts in divorce proceedings concerns whether the agreement is merged into the final decree, so that it loses its separate existence as a contract. On the answer to this question rests the availability of a suit or petition for modification to change or extend the terms of the agreement at a later date. The means of enforcement also depend on whether the agreement is said to be merged in the decree. If merged, contempt of court is available to enforce compliance, on the ground that noncompliance defies the order of the court. Without merger, traditional contract actions may be necessary to remedy noncompliance. If the agreement is merged so that its terms are ordered by the court, those orders may be modified like other orders (custody and support) emanating from the court. If the agreement is not merged, the contract may only be modified by mutual agreement of the parties. The common exception to this concerns children, whose interests most courts will not allow to be bargained away.

Divorce: Property Settlements

The principal legal issues at divorce are the division of property and rights and duties with regard to children. These issues should be explicitly resolved in the property settlement or marital settlement agreement. Although the judge in a divorce case is ultimately responsible for recognizing the agreement or setting its provisions, most judges will avoid making difficult choices if at all possible. Because the judge in a divorce case is vested with great discretion, lawyers are extremely reluctant to take chances on the vagaries of judicial choice and advise their clients against such a course. This means that the lawyers will hammer out a property settlement, often through extended negotiations with obstinate spouses. The negotiations are limited by principles enunciated by state legislatures and the courts.

The distribution of assets at divorce is treated differently in different states, but the underlying goal is fairness to both parties. In the past, a major theme of distribution was the effort to protect dependent spouses. More recently, this has been restated in terms of valuing home-making in the distribution of marital assets. Now that wives have taken their place in the workforce, the valuation of respective contributions has an added feature. The questions that arise in this context concern classification and valuation. Fairness requires that the courts be open to a variety of economic claims that were rare a few decades ago. For example, is a spouse entitled to share in the value of a professional license acquired by the other spouse during the marriage? Are future pension benefits classified as property, or marital property, or something else? What if one of the spouses dissipates marital assets (say, through gambling or extravagance)—does this entitle the other spouse to a larger share of what is left? The answer to these questions is yes in *some* states. Regardless of the nature of the property which is subject to distribution, its valuation is a major problem when market value is less than obvious.

In community property states (Arizona, California, Idaho, Louisiana, New Mexico, Nevada, Texas, and Washington), property acquired during the marriage is owned equally, so disputes in divorce concern whether property is community or *separate property*. The latter consists of property owned prior to the marriage or acquired during the marriage by gift, will, or inheritance. Separate property can be transmuted into community property by transfer or gift or by commingling funds so as to render them untraceable as separate property.

Community property embodies a partnership model that has been borrowed in so-called common law states with the label *equitable distribution*. This scheme is designed to treat the partners fairly, especially considering domestic contributions equal to financial contributions.

Although equitable distribution generally takes a broad, inclusive view of marital property, the distinction between marital and separate property is similar to community property. It would be a mistake, however, to conclude that divorces in any of the states involved will result in either a fifty-fifty split in property or a division regarded as fair by both sides.

Under basic community property theory, property acquired during marriage is owned equally by husband and wife, because they are a community. What exactly may be included varies somewhat from state to state. In the *Lynch* case, the court argues that the rules may be drastically opposed in different states.

LYNCH
v.
LYNCH
Court of Appeals of Arizona
164 Ariz. 127, 791 P.2d 653 (1990)

A man who won the lottery before the pending dissolution of his marriage seeks to reverse the trial court's grant of half his winnings to his wife. We hold that the winnings were community property and affirm ... .

Michael Lynch (husband) and Bonnie Lynch (wife) were married in 1968. Their only child was born in 1971. The couple separated in 1985, and within a year husband began living with a woman named Donna Williams. Wife filed for dissolution shortly after.

Wife's petition was uncontested, and at a default hearing on February 10, 1987, wife testified that the marriage was irretrievably broken. A decree of dissolution is ordinarily entered at the conclusion of a default hearing. However, on February 10, the trial court took the matter under advisement and, on February 19, vacated the hearing because husband had received untimely notice. ...

On February 21, husband and Donna Williams won a $2.2 million jackpot in the Arizona State Lottery. Each owned half a share of the winning ticket. Wife then filed an amended petition in the unconcluded dissolution seeking half of husband's share. This time husband answered, the case went on to trial, and in the ultimate decree of dissolution the trial court awarded wife half of husband's lottery share.

Husband has appealed the trial court's ruling on three grounds. ... By each argument, he attempts to establish that the parties acquired no community property after February 10, 1987, when the invalid default hearing was held. First, he argues that a marital community lasts only as long as the parties' will to union and that these parties' will to union had ended by the time of wife's testimony on February 10 that the marriage was irretrievably broken. Second, he argues that, by this testimony, wife waived her community interest in his future acquisitions. Last, he contends that, because wife's lawyers gave untimely notice of the February 10 hearing, wife is estopped from denying that the marital community ended on that date.

COMMUNITY DURATION

When an Arizona spouse acquires an asset before marital dissolution, Arizona law treats the asset as community property unless it falls within one of several statutory exceptions. ... A marriage endures in Arizona—and thus the acquisition of community property continues—"until the final dissolution is ordered by the court."

In some jurisdictions, acquisition of community property ceases when spouses begin to live separate and apart. In Arizona, however, demarcation by decree "avoids the factual issue of when the couple began living apart, and provides appropriate treatment for the on-again off-again manner in which some couples try to resolve their differences and patch up their marriages."

An Arizona couple that wishes to end the acquisition of community property before (or without) dissolution has a statutory means to do so. [State statute] provides for entry of a decree of legal separation that terminates "community property rights and liabilities ... as to all property, income and liabilities received or incurred after [its] entry." In the absence of a decree of legal separation, however, acquisition of community property continues in Arizona until the decree of dissolution is filed.

[The court then rejected husband's argument based on the will-to-union doctrine, a Spanish rule which holds that property acquired after the union of the wills has ceased would not be community property. On the facts, the court found some basis to doubt that the will to union had really ceased.]

WAIVER

Husband makes the related argument that wife waived any interest in his further acquisitions on February 10 when she testified that the marriage was irretrievably broken, expecting a decree of dissolution to issue on that date. We disagree. Waiver is the intentional relinquishment of a known right. Wife surely waived her interest in husband's acquisitions beyond the dissolution of their marriage, but her waiver went no further. She did not relinquish what might accrue to the marital community if the marriage lasted beyond its anticipated end. ...

CONCLUSION

This case displays the hand of chance. Fortune favored husband with a jackpot, but, because his marriage had not ended, fortune dealt his wife a share. Though the lottery was a windfall, spouses marry for better or for worse and share no less in windfalls than in labor's wages. Husband claims that his marriage ended equitably, though not formally, before the winning ticket was acquired. We have given our reasons for rejecting his arguments. The judgment of the trial court is affirmed.

Case Questions

1. Why wasn't a default entered on February 10, 1987? What would its effect have been if it had been entered? Do you think Bonnie Lynch could have challenged a default if entered?
2. Bonnie Lynch's attorney made a mistake in the hearing notice procedure. Was she mad at him?

Alimony

The traditional term for spousal support was *alimony*. In many jurisdictions it is called *maintenance,* and all three terms may be used interchangeably in many states. For some, alimony has a negative connotation because it is associated with an earlier time when a husband had a lifelong duty to support his dependent wife, whether married or divorced. Because of equal rights guaranteed by the Constitution, alimony today requires that a husband may receive alimony if a wife can. In recent times, courts and legislatures have come to disfavor both permanent alimony and alimony in general. Most awards of alimony today come in the form of periodic payments lasting a few months or years, classified as *rehabilitative alimony* and designed to return a homemaker to the job market (i.e., to help a dependent spouse get through the post-divorce period of adjustment to self-sufficiency). **Lump-sum alimony** is occasionally awarded, often to provide compensation for contributions by one spouse, such as one spouse who worked to put the other through a professional education.

Alimony is part of a more comprehensive plan dividing the resources and obligations of the spouses. The distribution of assets and child support are the other two important economic ingredients of this plan.

Alimony is characterized by a high degree of discretion on the part of the judiciary, although most states have provided more or less detailed guidelines for judges to weigh when awarding alimony. Alimony is principally based on the need of the recipient and the other spouse's ability to pay. Need is a relative concept, depending to a large degree on the standard of living enjoyed during the marriage. Alimony is usually terminated by the death of either party or by remarriage of the recipient. Depending on the jurisdiction, this may be waived in the property settlement agreement.

A post-divorce procedure in the form of a petition for modification is available to increase or decrease alimony or to extend or shorten the period during which payments are made. The key element in a successful suit for modification is proof of *changed circumstances* justifying modification. For the recipient of alimony to obtain an upward modification, it must be shown also that the payor has the ability to pay the increased amount.

The *Brown* case traces the history of alimony in Florida over more than a century. Although the dates may differ from state to state, the path from a preference for permanent periodic monthly payments for a divorced wife to the general disfavor in which alimony is held today is echoed in state after state. In most instances, changes in the law of alimony directly reflect the changing status of women in our society.

Child Support

After divorce, one parent usually becomes the primary caregiver of the children. When one parent is responsible for the physical custody of the children more than the other, the primary caregiver is entitled to contribution for providing more than his or her share of support. Today both parents are obligated to support their children, and that obligation is measured in terms of their respective ability to pay and the needs of the children. Legal issues with regard to child support range

-----------BALLENTINE'S-----------

lump-sum alimony   An award of alimony in gross, that is, an award of one lump sum to be paid either in installments or as a lump sum.

BROWN
v.
BROWN
First District Court of Appeal of Florida
300 So. 2d 719 (Fla. Dist. Ct. App. 1974)

For at least forty years prior to the recent enactments repealing divorce and instituting dissolution of marriage (commonly referred to as no fault), the courts awarded a divorced wife periodic alimony almost as a matter of constitutional right. In *Phelan v. Phelan*, 12 Fla. 449 (1868) the Supreme Court [said:] "Permanent alimony is not a sum of money or a specific proportion of the husband's estate given absolutely to the wife. It is a continuous allotment of sums payable at regular periods for her support from year to year."

This definition of permanent alimony was reaffirmed in ... 1948[, in a case holding that a wife was entitled to periodic alimony based upon her needs and her husband's ability to pay. The court refused to apply retroactively a newly enacted statute permitting the award of lump-sum alimony.]

The next development in the law of alimony was the appearance of the doctrine of special equity. As early as 1919, the Supreme Court ... , after noticing that the wife, mother of six children, had contributed generously in funds and by her personal exertion and industry through a long period of time to the acquisition and development of [the] home and other property and the establishment of [a] fortune, held that the wife possessed a special equity in the property which she aided in acquiring and possessing.

In 1932, the Supreme Court utilized the doctrine of special equity to relieve a wife from the harshness of the statutory prohibition of awarding alimony to an adulteress.

* * *

[The court was again confronted with the question of lump-sum alimony in 1968. [T]he original final judgment for payment of periodic alimony by the husband to the wife was amended to provide lump-sum alimony payable in monthly installments.]

In 1955, Justice Roberts, speaking for our Supreme Court, announced:

> Times have now changed. The broad, practically unlimited opportunities for women in the business world of today are a matter of common knowledge. Thus, in an era where the opportunities for self-support by the wife are so abundant, the fact that the marriage has been brought to an end because of the fault of the husband does not necessarily entitle the wife to be forever supported by a former husband who has little, if any, more economic advantages than she has.

This pronouncement marks the entry in the jurisprudence of this state of the concept of rehabilitative alimony. Rehabilitative means the restoration of property that has been lost. The concept of rehabilitative alimony appeared in the statutory scheme of this state in 1971 when the legislature made a major change ... . The salient provisions are:

> ...[T]he court may grant alimony to either party, which alimony may be rehabilitative or permanent in nature. In any award of alimony, the court may order periodic payment or payments in lump sum or both. ...
>
> In determining a proper award of alimony, the court may consider any factor necessary to do equity and justice between the parties.

In 1966, [another Florida district court] clearly stated the rule that prevailed as to awarding alimony prior to the dissolution of marriage act in 1971 as: "The accepted principles are that a divorced wife is entitled to alimony which will permit her to live in a manner commensurate with that provided by her husband during coverture, if he has the ability to pay."

Post 1971 alimony

[In 1972], the trial court found (as is probably true in more than 90 percent of marriage failures) that although neither party was without fault, "the preponderance of the equities lies with appellant husband and he is entitled to a divorce from appellee wife on the ground of habitual intemperance and indulgence in alcoholic beverages." [The court reversed an award of $100 per month permanent alimony with the following statement:]

They now occupy a position of equal partners in the family relationship resulting from marriage, and more often than not contribute a full measure to the economic well-being of the family unit. Whether the marriage continues to exist or is severed through the device of judicial decree, the woman continues to be as fully equipped as the man to earn a living and provide for her essential needs. The fortuitous circumstance created by recitation of the marriage vows neither diminishes her capacity for self-support nor does it give her a vested right in her husband's earnings for the remainder of her life. ...

"The new concept of the marriage relation implicit in the so-called no fault divorce law enacted by the legislature in 1971 places both parties to the marriage on a basis of complete equality as partners sharing equal rights and obligations in the marriage relationship and sharing equal burdens in the event of dissolution."

... Either spouse may contribute either by working in the market place or by working as a homemaker. The fact that in one marital venture a spouse is gainfully employed in the market place and pays a housekeeper to rear the children and keep house is not distinguishable from the spouse who devotes his or her full time to the profession of homemaker. The primary factual circumstance is each spouse's contribution to the marital partnership. In the case sub judice, the wife has been short changed. The wife has not been adequately compensated for the contribution that she made as a full time mother and homemaker to the equal partnership marriage. We hold that the trial court abused its discretion in awarding the wife a pittance of the material assets accumulated in the husband's name during 21 years.

McCORD, Judge (specially concurring):

[Rehabilitative alimony is defined as] financially supporting an ill spouse until his or her health is restored, or financially supporting a spouse until he or she can be trained for employment, or, in some circumstances, until the spouse has a reasonable time to recover from the trauma of the dissolution.

Case Questions

1. Why does Judge McCord's definition of rehabilitative alimony fit the commonly accepted meaning of the phrase better than the definition given in the main opinion?
2. How does the evolution of alimony reflect the changing status of American women?

from the basic questions of how much support should be paid and how to collect arrearages to questions of who should pay and what should be covered. Legislation in this area has focused on establishing precise guidelines for payment and the means to enforce them.

Parental Duty to Support

As the duty of support was first legally recognized, it applied only to the father. In the twentieth century, the duty of support was extended to mothers as *secondarily* liable for support. This concept was destined to fail as focus on the equal protection clause of the Fourteenth Amendment was applied with greater force to legal distinctions based on gender. Eventually, the law required equal duty of support from mother and father.

Unmarried fathers are also obligated to support their offspring. Adoptive parents are legally bound to support their adoptive children—adoption severs the legal bond between a child and its natural parents and treats the child as having the same legal relationship to its adoptive parents as a natural child would have. There is even a trend toward recognizing stepparents' legal obligations to support their stepchildren.

Need and Ability to Pay

Like alimony, child support is based on (children's) *need* for support and (parents') *ability to pay*. Even when the mother is the primary custodian of the children, her resources may be considered in the amount ordered to be paid by the father, as she is obligated to support her children, too. Similarly, when the father has custody of the children, the mother may be ordered to pay child support to the father. Unlike alimony, the resources of the beneficiary have only a limited impact on the award. A child's resources (e.g., a trust set up by grandparents) do not ordinarily reduce the parental obligation for furnishing necessaries.

Need is a relative concept. The courts do not limit parental contributions to necessaries after divorce. In this instance, the child of divorce may be entitled to more (and usually receives less) than the child of an intact family, who has only a right to necessaries. The rationale is that a child should not be required to drastically reduce an accustomed lifestyle simply because one of the parents has moved to other quarters.

Setting and Enforcing Child Support

During the 1980s and 1990s, both states and the federal government made a major effort at reducing welfare costs by collecting child support arrearages. A federal law made crossing state lines to avoid paying child support a federal crime. The motivation for government action was not a simple and direct response to the woeful record of support payments, although statistics in that regard demanded attention and action. The governments aimed to reduce the governments' share in welfare payments to single-parent families. In many instances, public assistance provided support when parents (fathers in particular) failed to meet their legal support obligations. New laws provided means for collecting arrears that could then be credited to welfare amounts that had been paid, mostly through Aid to Families of Dependent Children (AFDC).

These efforts were begun primarily through the Office of Child Support Enforcement (OCSE) of the U.S. Department of Health and Human Services, beginning in 1974, and are presently collecting several billion dollars yearly. The federal government furnishes funds for state enforcement programs at the same time that it imposes requirements on the states that receive the funds. Amendments to the law (the Federal Enforcement Initiative of 1974) in 1984 and 1988 have added more requirements and made more drastic the means of enforcement. AFDC applicants assign their uncollected support rights to the state and must assist efforts to collect. Both the states and the federal government maintain records to assist in locating parents in arrears.

Under the new requirements imposed on the state, new laws must require employee withholding of child support from paychecks of those in arrears. Arrears in excess of $1,000 must be deducted from state and federal income tax refunds. Under the 1988 amendments, new orders for support or orders modifying support will cause support payments to be automatically deducted from paychecks whether the payor is in arrears or not. The 1988 amendments also provide new standards for paternity and provide federal funds for paternity testing, in an obvious effort to make unwed fathers financially responsible for their offspring.

Child Support Guidelines

One of the most far-reaching requirements of the 1984 amendments provided: "Each state, as a condition for having its State plan approved under this part, must establish guidelines for child support award amounts within the state. The guidelines may be established by law or by judicial or administrative action." Although need and ability to pay are the foundation for determining the amount of child support the noncustodial parent must pay, a powerful movement toward establishing statutory (sometimes judicial) guidelines has resulted in numerous schemes, from criteria to formulas to lengthy tables, by which to calculate child support.

Interstate Enforcement—URESA

The Uniform Reciprocal Enforcement of Support Act (URESA) and its latest revised version (RURESA), was produced by the National Conference of Commissioners on Uniform State Laws. URESA was formulated because of the national problem with interstate enforcement of child support orders. URESA provides a means of enforcement when defaulted payments have not been reduced to judgment, as well as provisions for when the defaulting obligor has been ordered in contempt of court. It is a means by which the recipient of child support payments may bring an action in his or her own state that will be tried in the state of the debtor. This solves the problem of lack of personal jurisdiction over the debtor by the state of the creditor and saves the creditor the expense of traveling to the debtor's state.

A complaint is filed in the appropriate court in the creditor's state. The complaint is forwarded to the court having jurisdiction over the debtor-defendant and the case is tried there, with a local official representing the creditor.

Once the case is decided, the state ordering compliance receives the payments and forwards them to the court of the creditor. Failure to pay subjects the debtor to the usual sanctions (contempt, garnishment, etc.) available in the state with personal jurisdiction over the defendant.

Unwed fathers may also be subject to URESA. If paternity has already been adjudicated, they may be treated the same as divorced fathers. URESA also provides for the responding state to adjudicate paternity.

Child Custody

Battles over custody of children may be the most intense of all legal encounters. The introduction of no-fault divorce did not seriously change the volatile nature of custody cases, which pose special problems. Those most deeply affected—namely, minor children—are not parties to the lawsuit. In custody battles, children often become pawns in a political struggle between men and women. Complicating this situation is the fact that the court departs from its usual role of resolving a dispute over *past* events and must predict the best course of action for the *future* welfare of the children.

Historical Overview

The English common law carried on the Western European tradition of Roman law, which gave the father absolute control over his children. Because the father-husband enjoyed and exercised legal rights in behalf of the family, his duty of support was balanced by custodial rights. In America, where divorce was early recognized, issues of custody and support became problems for ordinary people. As the revolutionary family was cast in the companionate mold, with the wife responsible for home and children, the father's right to custody was disputed and lost, particularly for children of tender years.

It was not until the twentieth century that this custodial double standard was challenged. The movement for equality of women caused two ideological changes in the legal view of custody. First, if the sexes are equal and should have equal rights, as embodied in the equal protection clause of the Fourteenth Amendment, the tender years doctrine could no longer stand. Second, as the country grew more prosperous and new opportunities for employment of women became available, judicial opinions began to argue that women were no longer unable to join men in the workplace. The custodian of the children then became a matter of choice, giving rise to the ultimate standard, the best interests of the child.

The most recent turn in this story has been a shift from parental rights toward parental responsibilities. The best interests of the child standard emphasizes rights of the child rather than those of the parents. This change of focus has encouraged extensive study of children of divorce, single-parent families, and adopted and foster children, all of which we now have in large supply. Psychological and sociological studies have influenced both statute and court decisions. Child custody is but one part of a larger picture in which many of our youth appear to be at risk.

Many states have attempted to reduce the injury that divorce does to children by adopting *joint custody* as the preferred form of parental responsibility. Formerly, *sole custody* was granted to one parent, who made all decisions for the children, while the other parent was granted visitation rights. Under the joint custody scheme, both parents share in the decision-making over the vital concerns of the children, and both have frequent contact with the children. There is a fundamental weakness in the premise of joint custody: We are asking two individuals who were unable to cooperative effectively while married to cooperate after the destructive ordeal of divorce. Fortunately, most parents continue to love their children long after they have lost their love for each other, and may be able to cooperate for the sake of the children. That, at least, is the hope that joint custody offers.

Best Interests of the Child

Case after case insists that the polestar of custody decisions is the best interests of the child. This is a significant departure from the older common law paternal rights approach, but the common law rule really acted as a presumption in favor of the father and existed in an era when divorce was rare. Today, despite the best-interests standard, custody decisions are made in the context of presumptions, preferences, and legislative and judicial guidelines. For example, the tender years doctrine, popular during the latter part of the nineteenth century and most of the twentieth, expressed a presumption or preference, depending on the state, that young children should be in the custody of their mother. Even in jurisdictions that have clearly abolished the tender years doctrine by judicial decision, the mother of small children asserts an unspoken claim which judges are likely to heed. After all, the suckling infant will not be forcibly weaned in the name of parental equality. Other policies underlying custody decisions include the wishes of the child; avoidance of splitting siblings; minimizing dislocation of children from school, community, and extended family; and protecting parents' rights against third parties.

Formerly, the adultery of the mother could cause her to lose custody; a strict moral code was in force, including a double standard censuring extramarital conduct on the part of the wife and mother. Not only was a woman at fault with regard to the divorce itself, but the moral code presumed that her conduct would have a bad impact on the children. This sometimes overcame the preference in favor of awarding custody to the mother. More recently, however, sexual misconduct has generally been abandoned as grounds to deny custody, unless the father can demonstrate that the mother's sexual behavior has a detrimental impact on the children. The issue continues to be cloudy, however, because judges have very different perceptions of improper sexual conduct and different beliefs about the impact of parental sexuality on children.

Modification

Custody awards may be modifiable, like alimony and child support, but modification is more difficult to obtain than alimony and child support because of judges' reluctance to switch custody and remove a child from a stable environment. Many states have adopted provisions prohibiting modification of custody for two years following a custody order, absent a showing of danger to the child posed by its environment. The most common form of modification attack addresses the sexual misconduct of a custodial mother—the moral leper approach used to gain custody at divorce. When the single mother begins to court, the ex-husband may use this to seek custody (and sometimes as a device to negotiate reductions in support payments). Formerly, courts concluded without proof that extramarital sexual encounters by the mother automatically created an immoral environment for children. Sensitivity in the courts to the impropriety of a sexual double standard, along with a focus on the welfare of the child rather than the rights of the parents, has reversed this custom. Today, a mother's sexuality does not justify modification of custody without a clear showing that the mother's conduct has an injurious effect on the children.

The Natural Father

When children are born to unmarried parents, a special set of problems arises. On the one hand, there is no body of law from which to fashion rights of the unofficial family. On the other hand, the recognition of Fourteenth Amendment equal protection rights has generated a continuing inquiry into discrimination against the relationships within a nonmarital family. As a general rule, nonmarital relationships should not invoke different treatment. The unwed father should have the same rights as the man married to a child's mother. Although it may pose a moral issue for some, the nonmarital family does not pose a legal quandary when it is an intact family or when an intact family splits up. In many cases, however, the illegitimate child is the product of a relatively brief relationship, sometimes terminating before the child's birth. This may constitute abandonment of a relationship that was never established except biologically.

Uniform Child Custody Jurisdiction Act

The outcome of custody disputes can be radically different in different states. In the past, a parent could grab the kids, run to another state, and thwart the other parent's custodial rights not only by hiding but also by making recovery of the children dependent on a cumbersome process in which state jurisdiction became a legal issue of considerable complexity. The Uniform Child Custody Jurisdiction Act (UCCJA) was proposed to ameliorate this situation, discourage child snatching, and provide a uniform basis for jurisdiction that could be applied reciprocally by the states.

The UCCJA resolves three problems that arose in the past. First, jurisdiction was commonly premised on the physical whereabouts of the child, which encouraged child snatching and interstate flight as well as forum-shopping. Second, parents often attempted to undo custody orders by seeking modification in another state. Although full faith and credit applied to the original order, this did not prevent another state from assuming jurisdiction for the sake of modification. Third, the UCCJA promotes swift enforcement of the custody orders of other states.

Adoption

Adoption creates bonds of parent and child between persons who did not previously have this relationship. Ordinarily this involves the severance of legal bonds between a child and its natural parent or parents and the substitution of a new parent or parents, with all the legal consequences of the parent-child relationship.

Adoption was not recognized in England until 1926. The American law of adoption traces its roots to Massachusetts statutes in 1851. Until recently, adoption was primarily concerned with finding children for childless couples; providing parents for children was an incidental benefit. As the focus of public policy turned away from parental rights toward the interests of children, some reorientation in adoption has taken place.

An early issue in the law of adoption was the degree to which judicial intervention was appropriate. Today governmental administrative agencies concern themselves with the adoption process and legislatures have enacted increasing numbers of laws to regulate the adoption process.

Government has entered the adoption process in favor of children with special needs, creating subsidies for parents to adopt children when their resources would otherwise be insufficient. The National Conference of Commissioners on Uniform State Laws published the Uniform Adoption Act in 1953 and revised in 1969, and the Department of Health, Education, and Welfare proposed a model act for the states called "An Act for the Adoption of Children."

The Parties

Other than the status of adulthood, the states place few statutory requirements on the prospective adopting parent. Administrative or judicial approval, however, is another matter. The law has been reluctant to grant anyone a *right* to adopt, but clear preferences may be found in the law and in the decisions approving and disapproving particular adoptions. An examination of some of the most common situations clarifies the adoption picture:

1. *Blood relatives.* By custom, orphans became the wards of their close relatives. For divorced parents with minimal resources or for working single mothers, parental duties may be overwhelming, and children are often placed in the care of grandparents or aunts and uncles. Although these may be purely temporary placements, with legal custody remaining with the parent or parents, the desire to adopt may arise for many reasons. With orphans, de facto adoption may be followed by legal adoption. The court or agency look for the same factors applicable to custody disputes—wholesome environment, continuity of care (same home, school, neighborhood, etc.), keeping siblings together.

2. *Foster parents.* Children who have been placed in the care of strangers may remain with them via adoption even though the foster care administered through the state is commonly conditioned on the **foster parents** not attempting adoption.

3. *Stepparents.* One of the most common relationships involved in adoption is **stepparent-stepchild**. A typical scenario: A stepfather

---

BALLENTINE'S

foster parent   A person who rears a foster child.

step-parent   A wife, in her relationship to her spouse's child by a former marriage; a husband, in his relationship to his spouse's child by a former marriage.

stepchild   A son or daughter of one's spouse by a former spouse.

is actively involved in raising his wife's children by a former marriage, with the natural father mostly or completely absent and perhaps totally neglecting support obligations. The greatest stumbling block to such an adoption is denial of consent by the natural parent. Although this may be overcome by a court finding that abandonment or neglect has severed the bonds between parent and child, the law so strongly favors continuance of the biological bond as a legal bond that lack of consent in many instances is fatal to the adoption process. Adoption severs the natural parents' rights with regard to the child, something the court is extremely reluctant to do.

4. *Childless strangers.* Couples unable to bear children are most likely to go to adoption agencies or lawyers to seek children to adopt. Adoption agencies are usually extensively regulated and subject to statutory restriction. Potential adoptive parents are in theory carefully scrutinized both for the environment they can provide and their capacity to be good parents. The process may be lengthy and cumbersome, so many couples employ attorneys to facilitate the process.

5. *Unwed (nonmarital) fathers.* Until recent years, fathers of illegitimate offspring had no rights or legal relationship with their children. With the advent of financial responsibility through paternity suits, the fathers could expect to have rights as well. Visitation rights were forthcoming and custody was possible when the mother died or her custody was detrimental to the child. Still, because the father had not married the mother and usually had not otherwise acknowledged paternity, his rights inevitably threatened the maternal bond. Courts and legislatures have created a balancing act between recognition of the special place of the mother without depriving the father of rights.

Surrogacy

Because of the *Baby M* case in 1988, much public attention was directed at so-called *surrogacy contracts*. In surrogacy contracts, the natural father takes custody of the child while the mother relinquishes custody in favor of adoption by the natural father's wife. Conception is ordinarily achieved by artificial insemination with the contracting father's sperm or by implanting a fertilized ovum in the surrogate mother. In the former case, the childbearer is the genetic mother, but not in the latter case. Although in theory surrogacy contracts are simple, their subject matter is unique. From one point of view, they seem to be agreements to sell babies, and thus clearly illegal. In contrast, because the natural fathers are assuming custody, they cannot be said to be buying something to which they have no right. These contracts have also been considered offensive because they imply that womens' bodies may be rented for a period of time, suggesting exploitation of the poor by the rich. Additionally, surrogacy involves the psychobiology of rending an infant from its natural mother, whose feelings and state of mind have undoubtedly changed considerably from the time of contracting. For all these (and perhaps other) reasons, the *Baby M* case, in which a surrogate mother changed her mind after the birth of the child, prompted a diversity of intense emotional and intellectual responses, and state legislatures hurriedly passed legislation to regulate surrogacy contracts.

Summary

Family law has undergone continuous revision since the founding of American law, changing to keep up with American society. The principal subject of family law is divorce, although annulment remains an alternative. Divorce inevitably raises the issues of distribution of marital property, spousal and child support, and child custody. Although these are the most litigated issues of family law, in most instances their resolution occurs outside of court during lawyers' negotiations. This is due in part to the uncertainty created by the vast discretion judges exercise when forced to decide domestic relations issues.

Adoption and premarital, or antenuptial, agreements pose additional areas of legal concern in family law.

Review Questions

1. Why does a judge in a divorce proceeding have so much discretion?
2. How has family law changed as a result of the changing status of women?
3. Why is annulment less common than in the past?
4. What is the difference between a void marriage and a voidable marriage?
5. Why would someone need or want an antenuptial agreement?
6. What is the primary issue in child custody decisions?
7. What are some of the policies affecting child custody decisions?
8. Why is alimony less favored now than formerly?
9. What is community property?
10. What is equitable distribution?

Exercises

1. Determine whether your state has a no-fault divorce statute and whether it still allows divorce to be based on fault as well.

2. Does your state divide property at divorce on the basis of community property, equitable distribution, or some other scheme?

3. What is the law regarding surrogacy contracts in your state?

4. How do you go about getting married in your state? What are the legal requirements for marriage? Who may not marry?

THOUSANDS OF ADMINISTRATIVE LAW OPPORTUNITIES AWAIT YOU ...

Here is one example of a nontraditional paralegal career in administrative law:

Company: Federal Deposit Insurance Corporation (FDIC)
City: Washington, D.C.
Department: Legal Division, Liquidations Branch, Closed Bank Litigation & Policy Section
Title: Paralegal Specialist
Salary Range: $44,000–$58,000
Benefits:
    Insurance: Medical, dental, life
    Financial: 401(k), United States government pension plan
    Vacation: 1–3 years: 1 day per month, 3–15 years: 1.5 days per month, 15+ years: 2 days per month
    Sick time: One day per month
    Misc: Limited tuition reimbursement

JOB DESCRIPTION

Responsibilities:

- Assist in the preparation of memoranda which are used to determine appropriate legal advice given by section attorneys to Regional Field Offices, Consolidated Field Office, the General Counsel, DOL, DOR, and the FDIC Board of Directors and Chairman. Usually, the subject of these memoranda is of a highly complex nature.

- Draft legal documents to evaluate and implement closed bank litigation policies for Division of Liquidation and Board Resolution, which are reviewed by the section attorneys.

- Assist in the preparation of responses to congressional inquiries and to inquiries from outside legal counsel.

- Assist in the preparation of internal position papers analyzing novel or unique factual issues and recommending an appropriate policy for the corporation. The memoranda are reviewed by section attorneys, assistant general counsel, or senior counsel, as appropriate.

- Conduct legal research and prepare legal memoranda and directives for review by section attorneys.

- Assist section attorneys in coordinating activity between the Department of Justice, regional field offices, consolidated field offices and in the consolidated field offices to ensure that consistency is preserved on the various special issues that affect the FDIC in its litigation throughout the country.

- Monitor the decisions rendered by the federal courts in order to alert section attorneys to adverse or inconsistent opinions by the courts and to keep abreast of any changes that might affect the interests of the corporation.

- Assist other GS-7 through GS-11 law clerks, paralegals, and legal technicians in preparing memoranda and court documents used in the purchase and assumption transactions and bridge bank transactions.

- Prepare the Reserve for Potential Losses Report, which is furnished to the Government Accounting Office, in order to audit corporate activity within the Bank Insurance Fund and Savings Association Insurance Fund.

Reprinted from *Life Outside the Law Firm: Non-Traditional Careers for Paralegals,* © 1995, Delmar Publishers.

CHAPTER 15

ADMINISTRATIVE LAW AND PROCEDURE

CHAPTER OUTLINE

Introduction

Administrative law refers to the law that governs administrative action by government. It regulates the relationship between the citizen and the government. Although it is poorly understood by laypersons and many practitioners, it has a greater impact on the daily lives of Americans than any other area of law. Most people have few, if any, brushes with criminal law; few are often involved in personal injury law; contract and property law are matters of occasional concern for the nonbusinessperson. But the rules and regulations of government agencies are encountered throughout a lifetime. The water we drink, the air we breathe, the places we work, the schools we attend, the social security system, and a host of other facets of our lives are subject to regulations by agencies governed by administrative law.

The Field of Administrative Law

Administrative law is a phenomenon of the twentieth century. In theory, it can be traced back through the centuries, but the field as it is defined today emanates principally from the U.S. Constitution as it has come to be interpreted in this century. The federal Administrative Procedure Act, first enacted in 1946, may have been the most important event in administrative law, although its provisions drew heavily on prior case law. Because administrative law is relatively young, it is still dynamic and changing. Our **bureaucracy** has expanded and blossomed, particularly in the years since Roosevelt's New Deal. The greatest expansion has come in social services agencies, such as social security, the Veterans Administration, Medicare, and the social welfare agencies. The new agencies and the expanding scope of government activities have presented numerous problems that have encouraged the growth of administrative law and the litigation that often shapes it. Charting new ground for law has left a confusing array of cases and rules that makes administrative law a great challenge.

Substantive Law

The study of administrative law is generally confined to procedural law because of the impossibility of learning the substantive law. Each

---

BALLENTINE'S

bureaucracy The operation of government by bureaus and departments directed by levels of officials rigidly following rules and routines.

agency as its own set of substantive rules and regulations, sometimes a product of the legislature and sometimes the legislative product of the agency itself. The regulations of the Social Security Administration bear little resemblance to those of the Securities and Exchange Commission or the Environmental Protection Agency, and their regulations are collected in the *Code of Federal Regulations,* which is a huge compendium that no one has ever mastered. It would be a major undertaking simply to gain a relatively complete understanding of the rules and regulations of the Social Security Administration.

Procedural Law

Administrative procedural law encompasses most of what is usually meant when the term *administrative law* is used. There are certain principles governing administrative action regardless of the agency concerned. Administrative agencies pose a special problem for the law because most agencies engage in all three governmental functions. Although they belong to the executive branch of government, most agencies engage in rulemaking, which is the administrative agency equivalent of legislation; and most large agencies (and many small agencies) have an adjudicatory function as well.

Administrative procedure is particularly concerned with the legislative (rulemaking) and adjudicatory functions of agencies. Because these involve state or federal action, they are constrained by the due process clauses of the Fifth and Fourteenth Amendments requiring fundamental fairness in substance and procedure. What makes administrative procedural law different from the procedural principles that apply in suits between private parties derives from the nature of the parties involved.

Every administrative law case potentially involves weighing the important interests of the individual against the interests of society as represented by government. A prime example is sovereign immunity from suit. In the nineteenth century, the courts and some state legislatures concluded that it made no sense for a private citizen to sue the government. At that time, of course, government was small, offered few services, and intruded very little into private affairs. A democratic government was perceived as benevolent, as representing the people, so it was illogical for the people to sue themselves. By the 1960s and 1970s, it had become apparent that a democratic government could indeed be intrusive and abusive, and that sovereign immunity was often viewed as a license for government to run roughshod over private interests.

Administrative Law and the Paralegal

The study of administrative law is a worthwhile endeavor for the paralegal student for a number of reasons. Only by studying administrative law can a person gain a deep understanding of the basic process of upholding the rights of the citizen against the intrusions of government. It is also a rewarding education into constitutional law. But the study of administrative law can also be very practical. Litigation against the government increases as the scope of government activities increases, and there seems to be no end to this increase. Administrative law cases frequently involve lengthy litigation with copious amounts of research that should be done by paralegals for reasons of cost efficiency. In addition, many agencies, such as the Social Security Administration and other social service agencies, permit claimants to be represented by anyone of their choosing. The California Bar Association in 1989 issued an opinion allowing paralegals employed by law firms to represent the firm's clients in administrative hearings. This affords paralegals an opportunity to do trial work. Many legal aid offices employ paralegals to represent indigents at administrative hearings. Administrative law thus presents a promising area for employment of paralegals. Although many (perhaps most) paralegals will never handle administrative law work, many others will be administrative law specialists.

Independent Regulatory Agencies

Administrative law questions ultimately concern the power of government to regulate and the right of private parties to challenge regulation. Most of the major principles of the law of administrative procedure grew out of challenges to government regulation of business against government agencies established for the purpose of regulating business.

The discussion of administrative law in this chapter uses federal administrative procedure as its model. Most states have adopted comprehensive administrative procedure statutes, modeled on the federal act with modifications. Nevertheless, administrative law at the federal level has tended to lead the way—the federal Administrative Procedure Act (APA) predates state acts by two to four decades. Congress and the federal courts naturally became involved at an earlier stage because of the creation of independent regulatory agencies with national authority and great power.

Independent regulatory agencies were originally created to control the devastating effects of cutthroat competition in certain industries. The first great agency to be created was the Interstate Commerce Commission, created in 1887. Since that time Congress has periodically created new agencies; there now exist a dozen major independent regulatory agencies and more than fifty smaller ones. Regulating an industry is essentially anticompetitive and counter to a pure market model of free enterprise. Americans, especially politicians, often speak of free enterprise as if it has always characterized—and continues to characterize—the American economy. Even a cursory review of world history shows that free enterprise unregulated by government probably never existed, though the United States may have come closest to the model at one time or another. In a legal sense, we have been more committed to a *fair* market than a *free* market. It is the nature of government to allocate and distribute power and wealth, which makes it inevitable that business will be taxed and regulated.

The Interstate Commerce Commission (ICC) is a good illustration of the rationale of regulation. The ICC was formed to serve the railroad industry and the public. Vicious competition combined with monopolistic practices often undermined individual companies on the one hand and allowed excessive rates on the other. The industry was unstable at a time when the railroads were a major vehicle for economic growth of the country. Railroads are different from some other businesses in that they must operate on fixed routes—the investment in land and track must result in a level of use that will repay the investment. If 100 railroads build tracks from Chicago to St. Louis, none of them will make money until most have abandoned the route. The ICC was charged with regulating routes and rates in such a way that the railroads could make a reasonable profit charging rates that business and the public could afford so that everyone would benefit. Regulatory schemes are not perfect—sometimes they benefit the country and sometimes they are a burden—but the fact remains that some business activities are so central to the national economy that the government is unlikely to relinquish control.

Some activities must be controlled because they are by nature monopolistic. Public utilities are the prime example. The furnishing of water, sewer, gas, and electricity is an activity that can only be accomplished efficiently by one company serving a community, locality, or region. In fact, these activities are often performed by government. Where they are not, public service commissions monitor their activities and particularly their rates. Because these activities provide absolutely essential services to the community, government does not allow the utilities a free rein.

Independent agencies may be distinguished on the federal level by the following rule of thumb: an independent agency is one whose head cannot be removed by the president without cause. By contrast, cabinet chiefs (the secretaries of state, labor, defense, etc.) occupy their positions at the pleasure of the president. Although the president must obtain Congress's approval for appointment, he can remove a cabinet secretary at any time. The president may remove the chiefs or commissioners of the independent regulatory agencies only upon showing just cause for their removal.

Since the Roosevelt New Deal era, Congress has moved away from creating new industry-regulating agencies toward the establishment of social service agencies such as the Social Security Administration, the Occupational Safety and Health Review Commission, established by the Occupational Safety and Health Act (OSHA), and the Consumer Product Safety Commission (CPSC).

The importance of independent regulatory agencies for administrative law is twofold. First, the creation of these agencies brought into question the authority of Congress to delegate its legislative powers granted by the Constitution. Second, authority was delegated to administrative agencies with a degree of independence from the executive branch of government of which they were a part. Because the agencies often regulated national industries and administrative activities, the regulations they promulgated, the enforcement procedures they used, and their activities were frequently challenged by business interests that could afford to pursue their remedies all the way to the U.S. Supreme Court. As the initial legal issues were basic constitutional questions, many of the fundamental principles of administrative procedure were formulated in the context of the regulation of business.

Thus, many of the landmark cases in administrative law seem remote from daily life. For example, *United States v. Morgan,* 313 U.S. 409 (1941), involved the fixing of rates for buying and selling livestock at the Kansas City Stock Yards, but it went to the U.S. Supreme Court four times and ultimately set standards for the extent to which litigants could inquire into the decisionmaking of high level policymakers. *Abbott Laboratories v. Gardner,* 387 U.S. 136 (1967), concerned Food and Drug Administration regulation of drug labeling, but set forth the fundamental interpretation of judicial review under the APA, namely, that agency action is presumptively reviewable by the courts.

Research and argument in administrative procedural law differ from other areas of law because the cases deal with a myriad of agencies. Whereas in most private law cases, especially substantive questions of law, the researcher looks for cases with a similar fact pattern (argument in a slip-and-fall case will usually revolve around prior slip-and-fall decisions), administrative procedure arguments are constructed from a line of precedent-setting cases that bear no fact resemblance other than the procedural issue raised.

Delegation of Legislative Authority

In the nineteenth century, the courts frequently repeated the doctrine that Congress could not delegate its legislative authority, on the ground that the Constitution restricted this authority to Congress. In actual fact, Congress from the very beginning delegated its authority to administrative agencies, but the courts did not strike down such delegation until 1935, when a broad delegation of authority under the National Industrial Recovery Act was held by the U.S. Supreme Court to be unconstitutional in two cases. Since that time, the nondelegation doctrine has been all but dead, though it was partially resurrected in *Immigration and Naturalization Service v. Chadha,* 462 U.S. 919 (1983). The principle is still occasionally raised in administrative law cases with state agencies.

Judicial Review of Agency Action

Critical topics in the field of administrative law are judicial review and the scope of judicial review. These issues address basic questions concerning whether a dispute over agency action is a matter for the courts, who may bring such an action, and what exactly the courts should consider. These problems are constitutional ones. Because the U.S. Constitution establishes the doctrine of separation of powers, it was thought in the nineteenth century that the courts had no authority to question actions by the executive branch of government. An opposing constitutional premise, however, is that the executive branch may not violate the Constitution; and because the federal courts are responsible for interpreting the Constitution, logically the courts should be the forum for preventing the executive branch from exceeding its constitutional authority.

The demise of the doctrine of nonreviewability was signaled by *American School of Magnetic Healing v. McAnnulty,* 187 U.S. 94 (1902), in which the postmaster general prohibited the school from using the mail. It was clear that the postmaster general did not have such authority, and the court was faced with either dismissing the case for nonreviewability, thereby allowing the postmaster general unbridled authority, or reviewing the case and limiting the postmaster general to his legal authority. There really was no choice; our democratic legal principles could not allow a public official to act unlawfully. The postmaster general lost, and judicial review assumed respectability. Thereafter, the doctrine of judicial review was formulated in a series of cases that culminated in the enactment of Chapter 7 of the APA, which states in relevant part:

§ 701. Application; definitions

(a) This chapter applies, according to the provisions thereof, except to the extent that—

   (1) statutes preclude judicial review; or
   (2) agency action is committed to agency discretion by law.

§ 704. Actions reviewable

———————————— |||| ————————————

Agency action made reviewable by statute and final agency action for which there is no other adequate remedy in a court are subject to judicial review.

What exactly these two sections mean in combination has been the subject of much commentary and will undoubtedly continue to require clarification. What is clear, in theory if not always in fact, is that § 701(a)(1) means that Congress may specifically exempt some agency action from court review by statute, but when review is specifically authorized by statute, review is available. If Congress states that action cannot be reviewed, it cannot be reviewed; if Congress states action can be reviewed, it can be reviewed. This is simple enough except that Congress is usually silent with regard to review. In that case, § 704 would seem to indicate that review is available, except where "agency action is committed to agency discretion by law," a proviso that is less than crystal clear. *Abbott Laboratories v. Gardner,* 387 U.S. 136 (1967), resolved the issue by ignoring the lack of clarity in the language of the APA and stating that the APA expresses a "presumption of reviewability." The courts and Congress seem content with that principle and have left the debate over the nuances of the APA to legal scholars.

The *Barry* case provides an example of judicial review of an agency's actions. Note that that claimant went through a series of administrative procedures and hearings before he was able to get into court.

Scope of Review

The reluctance of the early courts to review administrative action was due in part to a desire to avoid retrying the facts. When an agency had made a determination of rights, especially if a hearing had been provided, the courts saw no need to conduct another hearing. When facts were found by the agency, the courts did not want to engage in a new round of factfinding. In addition, the agency was presumably better at finding facts because it employed experts in the field for which it was established. It was reasoned, for example, that the ICC was better able to understand the intricacies of the railroad business than ordinary judges and juries, so the courts were reluctant to interfere with policymaking by the agencies entrusted with that function.

The resolution of this problem came about through the gradual transformation of judicial review into an appellate procedure, with the agencies serving in the place of trial courts (conducting the hearings, finding fact, and applying rules) and the court of appeals reviewing agency determinations much like an appellate court reviews an appeal from a trial court. Today, nearly all judicial review in both state and federal courts takes place at the appellate level.

Kevin BARRY
v.

Donna E. SHALALA,
Secretary of Health and Human Services
United States District Court
840 F. Supp. 29 (S.D.N.Y. 1993)

This is an action to review a decision of the Secretary of Health and Human Services (the "Secretary") denying plaintiff's claim that the money he received from panhandling be excluded in calculating the amount of his disability benefits. [Supplemental Security Income (SSI) is paid as a disability benefit under the Social Security Act. The amount paid is reduced by the recipient's income; the degree of reduction depends on the nature of the income.]

BACKGROUND

Plaintiff Kevin Barry is a disabled individual who suffers from paralysis of his dominant right arm, a personality disorder and organic brain syndrome resulting from a history of drug abuse. In March 1990, Barry applied for Supplemental Security Income ... based on disability. From the time of his application and through August 1990, Barry supported himself by walking down a line of cars stopped at a traffic light ... on a daily basis and asking people for money. As a result of these panhandling activities, Barry earned $250 per month. ... [T]he Secretary treated plaintiff's income from panhandling as "unearned" income, and therefore reduced the amount of monthly benefits by $230, reflecting plaintiff's monthly panhandling income minus the $20 general income disregard set forth in the Social Security Act ... and Regulations. This calculation was affirmed ... . Subsequently, ... , the Administrative Law Judge upheld the Secretary's calculation, finding that the money plaintiff collected from panhandling was unearned income. This decision became the final decision ... when the Appeals Council denied plaintiff's request for review.

DISCUSSION

I. Standard of Review
The Report accurately sets forth the standard of review of the Secretary's decision. "The findings of the Secretary as to any fact, if supported by substantial evidence, shall be conclusive." 42 U.S.C. § 405(g). "This deferential standard of review is inapplicable, however, to the Secretary's conclusions of law. 'Where an error of law has been made that might have affected the disposition of the case, this court cannot fulfull its statutory and constitutional duty to review the decision of the administrative agency simply by deferring to the factual findings of the ALJ.' "

II. The Social Security Act and 1972 Amendments

... The amount of benefits provided to eligible individuals is determined on the basis of the individual's current income, and is calculated by subtracting the individual's nonexcludable income from a statutory benefit level.

In order to determine whether an individual's income is excludable, income is separated into two categories under the Act: earned and unearned. Earned income is defined as, among other things, "net earnings from self-employment." ... Unearned income is defined as "all other income, including ... gifts." ...

In calculating the SSI benefit amount, the first $20 of monthly income, whether earned or unearned, is excluded. For those individuals under age 65 who are disabled but not blind, the balance of any earned income is subject to an additional exclusion of $65, and then a final exclusion of one-half of the remainder thereof. *As these additional exclusions do not apply to unearned income, however, plaintiff's SSI benefits are greater if his panhandling income is treated as earned, rather than unearned, income* [emphasis added].

III. The Report

In her Report [the ALJ] determined that, as the money plaintiff received from panhandling is a gift rather than self-employment income derived from a trade or business, the money constitutes unearned income ... . [The ALJ] initially considered and dismissed plaintiff's contention that the money he received from panhandling is not a gift because he provided certain "services" to the individuals who gave him money. ...

IV. Plaintiff's Benefits

... Plaintiff contends that his income is earned as it consists of self-employment income from a trade or business. ...

The definition of "trade or business" under the Internal Revenue Code was analyzed by the United States Supreme Court ... . Although the [C]ourt acknowledged that "resolution of this issue 'requires an examination of the facts in each case,' " ... it held that, as a general rule, "to be engaged in a trade or business, the taxpayer must be involved in the activity with continuity and regularity and that the taxpayer's primary purpose for engaging in the activity must be for income or profit." The Court also emphasized that "[s]kill was required and was applied."

In this case, plaintiff's panhandling activities fall squarely within the ... definition of "trade or business." Plaintiff begged for money with continuity and regularity, as well as with the purpose of obtaining income. He treated panhandling as a "serious business. Like any structured activity, he reported to a particular location every day and performed a particular set of behaviors." In addition, the Court finds that plaintiff's activities required a degree of skill in selecting the optimum location and convincing members of the public to contribute money. In short, plaintiff's panhandling operation required considerable effort. Accordingly, the Court finds that plaintiff's income constitutes earned income under the Act.

CONCLUSION

For the reasons set forth above, plaintiff's motion for judgment on the pleadings is granted and defendant's motion ... is denied. This case is hereby remanded to the Secretary to calculate and pay the underpayment due for the period of March through August 1990.

Case Questions

1. Does review of agency findings of fact and conclusions of law follow the same standards as if this had been a trial?
2. What difference does it make whether Barry's panhandling is classified as earned or unearned income?
3. Did Barry get a trial?

In this way, the courts have limited the scope of judicial review to the legal questions with which appellate judges are competent and comfortable. Issues of jurisdiction, the interpretation of statutes, and due process raise questions that the courts treat on a daily basis. When factfinding is questioned, the courts borrow the substantial evidence test used for appellate review of jury factfinding. By limiting the scope of review, the courts remove themselves from making policy decisions and assume responsibility for monitoring the fairness of procedure.

A celebrated example of this was *Environmental Defense Fund, Inc. v. Ruckelshaus,* 439 F.2d 584 (D.C. Cir. 1971), in which the Secretary of Agriculture was sued by an environmental group in an effort to ban the pesticide DDT. Judge Bazelon separated the questions of fact from the questions of law. He declined to examine the conclusion of the secretary that DDT did not present an "imminent hazard," which would warrant summary suspension—this was a fact question left to the determination of the agency. However, the issue raised by EDF concerning whether the standard of proof used by the secretary conflicted with legislative intent in the applicable statute was a legal question appropriate for judicial determination. In this way, the court avoided making policy as to whether DDT should be banned and restricted the scope of review to whether the agency acted properly within the statute.

Rulemaking

The major innovation made by the APA was § 553, "Rule Making." With acceptance of Congress's authority to delegate its legislative powers, a standard was needed to ensure that those powers were exercised with procedural fairness. *Rulemaking* is simply the name applied to the agency's legislative function. In some cases, Congress specifically charges an agency with rulemaking authority; sometimes Congress is silent, but rulemaking authority is implied from the agency's statutory mission; and occasionally Congress denies an agency rulemaking authority (the Federal Trade Commission, for example, is an investigatory rather than a regulatory agency).

When an agency engages in rulemaking, it must follow the procedure of the APA, or the rule is invalid and unenforceable. The steps required by the APA are simple:

§ 553. Rule Making

(b) *General notice of proposed rule making shall be published in the Federal Register, unless persons subject thereto are named and either personally served or otherwise have actual notice thereof in accordance with law. The notice shall include—*

(1) *A statement of the time, place, and nature of public rule making proceedings;*

(2) *reference to the legal authority under which the rule is proposed; and*

(3) *either the terms or substance of the proposed rule or a description of the subjects and issues involved.*

* * *

(c) *After notice required by this section, the agency shall give interested persons an opportunity to participate in the rule making through submission of written data, views, or arguments with or without opportunity for oral presentation. After consideration of the relevant matter presented, the agency shall incorporate in the rules adopted a concise general statement of their basis and purpose. ...*

(d) *The required publication or service of a substantive rule shall be made not less than 30 days before its effective date [with exceptions].*

Although § 553 presents some burden to the agencies, the steps are not cumbersome. Basically it requires public notice of proposed rules and an opportunity for public input. Legally there is nothing to prevent an agency from making rules despite major opposition as long as it follows the procedure. The innovation of § 553 is in requiring that the process be public and provide for public participation. The weaknesses and unpopularity of a proposed rule may thus be brought into the open. An agency cannot long defy the public interest without a response from Congress and the president, who ultimately control the power that the agency exercises.

Section 553 has some significant exceptions. Internal housekeeping rules, those concerning personnel and internal management, are not covered by it. So-called "interpretative rules" need not go through the § 553 procedure. In a loose sense, interpretative rules are those that carry out the meaning of a statute, interpreting it rather than adding to it. The distinction between interpretative and legislative or substantive rules is far from clear—a technical question that several cases have confused rather than clarified. The question seems purely academic until an agency attempts to make an interpretative rule without going through § 553 procedure, only to find a complaining party asserting that the rule is substantive and therefore invalid for lack of proper procedure. If the court agrees with the complaining party and concludes that the rule is substantive (legislative), the failure to follow § 553 procedure makes the rule invalid.

When Congress specifically authorizes an agency to make rules under § 553, those rules are said to have the "binding force of law," meaning that the courts will accord them the same respect as if the rules had been passed by Congress. Interpretative rules do not enjoy this stature, though as a practical matter they ordinarily are enforced by the courts.

The Right to Be Heard

Section 553 leaves to the agency the discretion to allow oral presentation and argument and its scope, but some rules call for more than the mere opportunity for written submission of argument. Some questions are better left to an adjudicatory process by the agency.

An isssue that often arises in suits against governmental bodies is whether the plantiffs have *standing*, that is, do they have the right to sue, or, as it is described in *Norris*, do they have a "legally congnizable interest"?

As discussed in earlier chapters, legislation and adjudication are different processes appropriate to different situations. In the administrative field, two cases arising in Colorado have been used repeatedly as examples of this distinction. In *Bi-Metallic Investment Co. v. State Board*

Donald L. NORRIS, et al., Petitioners/Plaintiffs,
v.
Town of WHEATLAND, et al.,
Respondents/Defendant.
Supreme Court, Monroe County, N.Y.
613 N.Y.S.2d 817 (1994)

After eighteen months of divisive debate about the future of their police department, the Town of Wheatland voters elected two board members and a supervisor who stood for its abolition. Upon taking office in January 1994, the Town Board, by a three to two vote, immediately approved the Wheatland Police Department for only three months. On March 3, 1994 the Town Board proposed, and on March 30, 1994 passed, Local Law No. 1 abolishing the Wheatland Police Department as of June 1, 1994.

This action was brought ... seeking to set aside and annul the decision of the Wheatland Town Board pursuant to Local Law No. 1. The Petitioners, which include the Wheatland Police Chief and 41 residents of the town, allege the Town Board acted improperly by: 1) not procedurally complying with the appropriate provisions of the State Enviornment Quality Review Act (SEQRA) and by failing to consider the "socioeconomic effect" of the Local Law; 2) acting arbitrarily and capriciously; 3) failing to comply with the requirements of the Municipal Home Rule Law; 4) not referring the Local Law to a referendum; and 5) one of the Board Members voting in favor of the Local Law No. 1 not being a resident of the Town of Wheatland at the time of the vote.

In rejoinder, the respondents deny the allegations of the petition and questioned whether the petitioners have standing to bring the action.

STANDING

... "It is established law that to be entitled to seek judicial review of an administrative determination, the petitioning party must have a legally cognizable interest that is or will be affected by the determination. A showing of special damage or actual injury is not necessary to establish a party's standing."

Unlike a zoning matter, the abolition of a town police department is all-pervasive. To require a showing of special damage or actual injury to one resident vis-à-vis another is unlikely and counteracts the intent of SEQRA, which is "to assure that those charged with decision-making responsibility are aware of their obligations to protect the environment for the use and enjoyment of this and all future generations." Furthermore, to deny standing in this matter would be to insulate governmental action from scrutiny. In a matter affecting a town-wide service, either all residents have standing, or none do. In this matter, any resident of the Town of Wheatland has standing.

* * *

[In a lengthy discussion of whether the Board had properly complied with the procedural requirements related to abolishing the police force, the court concluded that it had.]

SEQRA COMPLIANCE-SUBSTANTIVE

It must now be reviewed whether the Town Board, as lead agency, by issuing a Negative Decision, " ... determine(d) either that there will be no environmental effect or that the identified environmental effects will not be significant," and did the Town Board " ... take a hard look at all relevant impacts ... in making this decision and document its reasons in writing."

Those supporting the retention of the Police Department provided the Town Board with reports, letters and testimony which raised questions as to the environmental, economic and social effects on the community. In addition, there existed a thorough and comprehensive task force report supporting the retention.

In response, the Town Board undertook the following steps: 1. The Town solicited comments from all the Town Supervisors in Monroe County who relied on the Monroe County Sheriff's Department for their police services. The request for information specifically related questions concerning response time, community involvement, professionalism and effectiveness. 2. The Town contacted the Monroe County Sheriff's Office and requested information concerning its ability to provide police services to the Town of Wheatland. Sheriff Andrew Meloni, in part, stated: "I am confident that the Monroe County Office of Sheriff has all the necessary resources to provide professional, effective and efficient services to the Town of Wheatland." 3. The Supervisor conducted a review of crime statistics, the capacity of Monroe County Sheriff's Office, the degree of activities of various districts of the Monroe County Sheriff's Office and the ability of the Monroe County Sheriff's Office to handle the Town of Wheatland. The Town of Wheatland invited the public to comment on issues including environmental significance of the proposed action and heard all parties wishing to address the issue and received and filed all documents concerning this subject. The Town Board also held a public informational meeting on March 1, 1994 at which the public addressed questions to Undersheriff O'Flynn.

The Court's role in reviewing SEQRA determinations is to, first, review the agency procedures to determine whether they were lawful. As set forth above, the only procedural defect, an inadvertent reference to a hearing, has been satisfactorily resolved. Second, courts may review the record to determine whether the agency identified the relevant areas of environmental concern, took a "hard look" at them, and made a "reasoned elaboration" of the basis for its determination. When doing so the Courts are to remember that an

agency's substantive obligations under SEQRA must be viewed in light of a rule of reason. Although agencies have considerable latitude in evaluating environmental effects and choosing among alternatives, "[n]othing in the law requires an agency to reach a particular result on an issue, or permits the courts to second-guess the agency's choice, which can be annulled only if arbitrary, capricious or unsupported by substantial evidence."

[T]he court finds that the Wheatland Town Board identified the relevant areas of environmental concern, took a hard look at them and made a "reasoned elabortion" for the basis of its determination.

* * *

ARBITRARY AND CAPRICIOUS

Considering its extensive experience with and regard for local police, this Court does not necessarily agree with the Board's abolition of the Police Department. However, it cannot be said that the Board's actions, as set forth in the legislative findings, are unsupportable or were arbitrary or capricious. Ultimately, in the representative democracy of Wheatland, New York, the wisdom of the abolition of the police department by the Town Board can be reviewed by the voters on November 7, 1995.

Case Questions

1. Can a town through its elected representatives abolish the police force?
2. On what basis do the plaintiffs have standing?
3. Why is the statute (SEQRA) at issue here?

of Equalization, 239 U.S. 441 (1915) the state had increased the valuation of all real estate in Denver by 40 percent. The court denied a suit for an injunction by the company, holding that no hearing was necessary. The court distinguished the earlier case of *Londoner v. Denver*, 210 U.S. 373 (1908), in which it had required a hearing ("by argument however brief, and, if need be, by proof, however informal") on the assessment of the plaintiff's land for the cost of paving a street. The distinction was made on the difference between policy that treated the entire community equally (*Bi-Metallic*) and a decision in which a few persons were affected individually (*Londoner*). In other words, the decision to set valuations in general is a legislative question, whereas assessing costs individually and differentially is an adjudicative question, as the individual may have special reasons why the assessment is unfair. Highly particularized disputes of this sort call for a hearing.

Although the court may allow a town to abolish its police force, it may also require local governmental bodies to expend monies on entitlements, as in *Rothschild*.

ROTHSCHILD
v.
GROTTENTHALER
United States Court of Appeals, Second Circuit
907 F.2d 286 (2d Cir. 1990)

DISCUSSION

This case presents a matter of first impression: Whether section 504 of the Rehabilitation Act of 1973 requires a public school district receiving federal financial assistance to provide sign-language interpreter services, at school district expense, to deaf parents of non-hearing impaired children at certain school-initiated activities. Defendant-appellant School District routinely invites plaintiffs-appellees Kenneth and Karen Rothschild, whose children are enrolled in the School District, to parent-teacher conferences, meetings with School District personnel and other events designed for parental involvement. The Rothschilds are interested in participating in these activities. They contend, however, that absent the services of a sign-language interpreter, they are denied an equal opportunity to participate in these activities because they cannot effectively communicate with teachers and other School District personnel. They claim that the School District's failure to make a reasonable accommodation that would afford them an equal opportunity to participate in school-initiated activities incident to their children's education consititutes a violation of section 504 of the Rehabilitation Act. We agree.

Our inquiry begins, as it must, with the language of section 504. That section, in pertinent part, provides: "No otherwise qualified individual with handicaps in the United States, as defined in section 706(8) of this title, shall solely by reason

of her or his handicap, be excluded from the participation in, be denied the benefits of, or be subjected to discrimination under any program or activity receiving Federal financial assistance ... ." In this Circuit, it is settled that a private right of action against recipients of federal financial assistance may be implied from section 504. To establish a prima facie violation of section 504, a plaintiff must prove that: 1) he or she is a "handicapped person" as defined in the Rehabilitation Act; 2) he or she is "otherwise qualified" to participate in the offered activity or to enjoy its benefits; 3) he or she is being excluded from such participation or enjoyment solely by reason of his or her handicap; and 4) the program denying the plaintiff participation receives federal financial assistance. Once a prima facie violation of section 504 has been established, "the defendant must present evidence to rebut the inference of illegality."

In the present case, the School District concedes that the Rothschilds are handicapped persons within the meaning of the Rehabilitation Act and that the School District receives federal financial assistance. The School District does not seriously contest that the Rothschilds are denied the opportunity to participate in school-initiated activities concerning their children's education by reason of their handicaps. Rather, the heart of the School District's argument is that the Rothschilds are not "otherwise qualified" for the offered activities. According to the School District, "Section 504 does not apply to plaintiffs because public schools are for children, not their parents and Section 504 was designed to protect children, not their parents." The School District seriously misapprehends the import of section 504.

"Section 504 was enacted to prevent discrimination against all handicapped individuals ... in relation to Federal assistance in employment, housing, transportation, education, health services, or any other Federally-aided programs."

* * *

Under these circumstances, it seems to us that the Rothschilds are being unfairly "excluded from participation in a federally funded program 'solely by reason of [their] handicap. ' "

* * *

As "otherwise qualified handicapped individuals," the Rothschilds are entitled to "meaningful access to" the activities that the School District offers parents. However, our determination must be "responsive to two powerful but countervailing considerations—the need to give effect to the statutory objectives and the desire to keep § 504 within manageable bounds." Accommodations to permit access to handicapped persons should not impose "undue financial and administrative burdens." Thus, a recipient of federal financial assistance should not be "required to make 'fundamental' or 'substantial' modifications to accommodate the handicapped." A recipient may, however, be required to make "reasonable" modifications to accommodate an otherwise qualified handicapped individual. "[S]ection 504 of the Rehabilitation Act requires some degree of positive effort to expand the availability of federally funded programs

to handicapped persons otherwise qualified to benefit from them."

Mindful of the need to strike a balance between the rights of the Rothschilds and the legitimate financial and administrative concerns of the School District, the district court limited the scope of activities for which the School District would be required to provide a sign-language interpreter. It stated: "We take pains, however, to emphasize that the [school] district's obligation, and, correspondingly, the plaintiffs' entitlement, is limited to 'school-initiated conferences incident to the academic and/or disciplinary aspects of their child's education.' " To the extent that the plaintiffs wish to voluntarily participate in any of the plethora of extra-curricular activities that their children may be involved in, we think they, like other parents, must do so at their own expense. The reasonableness of providing the Rothschilds with sign-language interpreters at certain school-initiated activities is demonstrated by the contemplation of such an accommodation in related DOE regulations promulgated pursuant to section 504 ... . The School District's refusal to modify its program to accommodate the Rothschilds' handicap is "unreasonable and discriminatory." The Rothschilds' entitlement to sign-language interpreter services provided at School District expense is limited, however, to those activities directly involving their children's academic and/or disciplinary progress.

Case Questions

1. What test is applied to determine whether someone is a handicapped person?
2. Describe the two conflicting interests that the court is concerned with.

What Kind of a Hearing?

The right to a hearing in administrative law does not necessarily mean an on-the-record, trial-type, or evidentiary hearing. Such events present a significant burden to an agency, which may devote significant resources and time when the full complement of rights and procedures must be respected. The extent of a person's rights in a hearing run the gamut from extremely informal meetings to hearings that are virtually indistinguishable from trials. The extremes are represented by *Goss v. Lopez,* 419 U.S. 565 (1975), and *Goldberg v. Kelly,* 397 U.S. 254 (1970). *Goss* involved ten-day suspensions of high school students. The U.S. Supreme Court held that they were entitled to a hearing, but the rights of the students were limited to (1) notice of the charges against them; (2) explanation of the evidence against them; and (3) the opportunity to present their side of the facts. By contrast, *Goldberg* concerned the right of a welfare recipient to a hearing prior to termination of benefits. The court held that she was entitled to a hearing before termination, including the following rights in connection with the hearing:

1. Notice with reasons for the termination
2. Confrontation of witnesses against her
3. Oral argument
4. Cross-examination of adverse witnesses
5. Disclosure of evidence for the other side
6. Representation by an attorney
7. Determination on the record
8. Statement of reasons relied on for decision
9. Impartial decision maker

Practically speaking, this is a catalog of the rights ordinarily enjoyed in a civil trial.

Administrative Hearings

Most agencies provide procedural steps within the agency for processing grievances and complaints. Judicial review is premised on "final agency action," which requires some authoritative determination of rights; the APA allows agencies to require that a claimant exhaust some or all of these steps prior to seeking judicial review. Prior to the APA, claimants were required to exhaust all administrative remedies before judicial review, and many states still require this.

Agencies are hierarchical bureaucracies and typically provide aggrieved parties the opportunity to pursue review of determinations from lower levels all the way to the top of the bureaucratic pyramid. Someone once counted thirty-three steps in the social security system that would have to be completed to fully exhaust the administrative remedies available. It is unrealistic to think that the reviewing court would reverse a consistent determination through all these steps except on the ground that the procedure itself was constitutionally defective.

Hearings at the highest level are held by hearing officers called *administrative law judges,* who are employed by the government to hold recorded hearings, make findings of fact, and recommend action to the highest level of the agency. In most instances, the agency will follow the recommendations of the administrative law judge.

Liability of Government and Its Officers

Recent decades have seen a major change in liability for agency action. When sovereign immunity was in its heyday, the only remedy for a person injured by official action was a suit against the public employee who caused the injury. Even there, the courts developed a doctrine of official immunity for injuries caused by "discretionary" acts within the scope of the employee's duties. Policy makers and planners were thus immunized for most of their acts.

The death knell of sovereign immunity for tort suits came with enactment of the Federal Tort Claims Act (FTCA) in 1947. The FTCA continued the judicial doctrine of discretionary immunity, and exempted a number of intentional torts, but held the federal government "liable, respecting the provisions of this title relating to tort claims, in the same manner and to the same extent as a private individual under like circumstances." This formally enacted a judicial doctrine that had developed to disallow governmental immunity when the activities were the same as those performed by private enterprise, the so-called "governmental–proprietary function test." The states gradually followed suit, though they did so with a variety of statutes, many of which retained varying degrees of immunity.

With the availability of suits against the government, the courts became more protective of government officers. Not only was the discretionary immunity expanded, but also a form of *qualified immunity* was invented that immunized from suit officers acting in good faith and under a reasonable belief that their actions were proper. This was a logical result of the dilemma in which public officers, especially police, found themselves when acting pursuant to statutory authority, only to have a court hold the statute unconstitutional. For example, a police officer makes an arrest under a state statute, but the statute is found by the court to be unconstitutional, so the arrest was illegal and the officer subject to suit for false arrest and false imprisonment. If the standards of the doctrine are met, the officer enjoys qualified (as distinguished from absolute) immunity.

42 U.S.C. § 1983

To protect former slaves from abuse at the hands of white authorities following the Civil War, Congress passed the Civil Rights Act of 1871, from which 42 U.S.C. § 1983 reads:

> Every person who, under color of any statute, ordinance, regulation, custom, or usage, of any State or Territory, subjects, or causes to be subjected, any citizen of the United States or other person within the jurisdiction thereof to the deprivation of any rights, privileges, or immunities secured by the Constitution and laws, shall be liable to the party injured in an action at law, suit in equity, or other proper proceeding for redress.

The broad provisions of this act were rarely used until 1961, when a suit brought against Chicago police officers and the City of Chicago was successful (*Monroe v. Pape*, 365 U.S. 167). *Monroe* held, however, that the city was not a "person" under the act and could not be sued; but in 1978 the U.S. Supreme Court overruled *Monroe* and allowed a suit against the City of New York in *Monell v. Department of Social Services*, 436 U.S. 658. Since *Monell*, § 1983 suits have proliferated and are a constant concern of local governments, especially for the conduct of their police; a § 1983 suit was even brought against the governor of Ohio over the National Guard shootings of Kent State University students during antiwar demonstrations in 1970. (The U.S. Supreme Court held that the governor had qualified immunity.) The broad scope of the language of § 1983 and its expanding application have made it a frequent basis for litigation.

Although the scope of 42 U.S.C. § 1983 has been greatly expanded with regard to suing state and local governments, suits against government officals have confronted an increasing recognition of absolute and qualified immunities. The courts have been steadfast in upholding absolute immunity of judges acting in their judicial capacity. *Stump v. Sparkman* expresses the most extreme application of judicial immunity. The mother of a "somewhat retarded" daughter petitioned Judge Stump of an Indiana Circuit Court for an order permitting the daughter to be sterilized. Judge Stump met with the mother in chambers and wrote and signed the order. The sterilization procedure was performed, the daughter being told that her appendix was being removed. When the daughter married two years later, she soon discovered what had happened. She sued Judge Stump under § 1983. The U.S. District Court held the judge enjoyed immunity from suit, but the Court of Appeals reversed and the case reached the U.S. Supreme Court on certiorari.

STUMP
v.
SPARKMAN
U.S. Supreme Court
435 U.S. 349 (1978)

The governing principle of law is well established and is not questioned by the parties. As early as 1872, the Court recognized that it was "a general principle of the highest importance to the proper administration of justice that a judicial officer, in exercising the authority vested in him, [should] be free to act upon his own convictions, without apprehension of personal consequences to himself." For that reason the Court held that "judges of courts of superior or general jurisdiction are not liable to civil actions for their judicial acts, even when such acts are in excess of their jurisdiction, and are alleged to have been done maliciously or corruptly." Later we held that this doctrine of judicial immunity was applicable in suits under § 1 of the Civil Rights Act of 1871, 42 U.S.C.A. § 1983, for the legislative record gave no indication that Congress intended to abolish this long-established principle.

* * *

Perhaps realizing the broad scope of Judge Stump's jurisdiction, the Court of Appeals stated that, even if the action taken by him was not foreclosed under the Indiana statutory scheme, it would still be "an illegitimate exercise of his common law power because of his failure to comply with elementary principles of procedural due process." This misconceives the doctrine of judicial immunity. A judge is absolutely immune from liability for his judicial acts even if his exercise of authority is flawed by the commission of grave procedural errors. ...

Disagreement with the action taken by the judge, however, does not justify depriving that judge of his immunity. Despite the unfairness to litigants that sometimes results, the doctrine of judicial immunity is thought to be in the best interests of "the proper administration of justice ... for it allows] a judicial officer, in exercising the

authority vested in him [to] be free to act upon his own convictions, without apprehension of personal consequences to himself." The fact that the issue before the judge is a controversial one is all the more reason that he should be able to act without fear of suit. ...

Mr. Justice STEWART, with whom Mr. Justice MARSHALL and Mr. Justice POWELL join, dissenting.

It is established federal law that judges of general jurisdiction are absolutely immune from monetary liability "for judicial acts, even when such acts are in excess of their jurisdiction, and are alleged to have been done maliciously or corruptly." It is also established that this immunity is in no way diminished in a proceeding under 42 U.S.C.A. § 1983. But the scope of judicial immunity is limited to liability for "judicial acts," and I think that what Judge Stump did on July 9, 1971, was beyond the pale of anything that could sensibly be called a judicial act.

* * *

When the Court says that what Judge Stump did was an act "normally performed by a judge," it is not clear to me whether the Court means that a judge "normally" is asked to approve a mother's decision to have her child given surgical treatment generally, or that a judge "normally" is asked to approve a mother's wish to have her daughter sterilized. But whichever way the Court's statement is to be taken, it is factually inaccurate. In Indiana, as elsewhere in our country, a parent is authorized to arrange for and consent to medical and surgical treatment of his minor child. And when a parent decides to call a physician to care for his sick child or arranges to have a surgeon remove his child's tonsils, he does not, "normally" or otherwise, need to seek the approval of a judge. On the other hand, Indiana did in 1971 have statutory procedures for the sterilization of certain people who were *institutionalized.* But these statutes provided for *administrative proceedings* before a board established by the superintendent of each public hospital. Only if after notice and an evidentiary hearing, an order of sterilization was entered in these proceedings could there be review in a circuit court.

* * *

Mr. Justice POWELL, dissenting.

While I join the opinion of Mr. Justice STEWART, I wish to emphasize what I take to be the central feature of this case—petitioner's preclusion of any possibility for the vindication of respondent's rights elsewhere in the judicial system.

* * *

But where a judicial officer acts in a manner that precludes all resort to appellate or other judicial remedies that otherwise would be available, the underlying assumption of the *Bradley* doctrine is inoperative. ... The complete absence of normal judicial process foreclosed resort to any of the "numerous remedies" that "the law has provided for private parties."

Case Questions

1. Was Judge Stump's order a judicial act?
2. Judicial immunity was again tested in the U.S. Supreme Court in 1988 in *Forrester v. White,* 108 S. Ct. 538, in which a female probation officer was fired by Judge White, who was responsible for hiring and firing probation officers. Ms. Forrester sued under § 1983 on the grounds that she had been discriminated against because of her sex. Writing the opinion of the Court, Justice O'Connor applied the "judicial function" test that asserts absolute immunity for a judge's actions while exercising a judicial function. Justice O'Connor concluded that Judge White's authority over personnel was an administrative function separate from his judicial function, rendering him amenable to suit for improper actions in his administrative function, and the suit was allowed to proceed. Can you reconcile *Forrester* with *Stump?*

Summary

Administrative law covers the rules relating to legal action taken against the administrative agencies of the government. Although each agency has its own substantive rules and regulations, procedural law has evolved, and is still evolving, first from the Constitution and more recently from the enactment of federal and state administrative procedure legislation.

The last hundred years have witnessed reversals in the major areas of administrative law. In the nineteenth century, sovereign immunity was doctrine throughout the United States—officers could be sued but not the government. It was presumed that Congress could not delegate its legislative authority to other government agencies. There was a presumption of nonreviewability of administrative action by the courts. All of these doctrines met their demise in the twentieth century. Rather than challenging legislative delegation, the courts have concentrated on the question of whether the agencies adhere to legislative intent. Rather than refusing to review, the courts have limited the scope of review along lines similar to appellate review. With the erosion of sovereign immunity, the courts have expanded the liability of government and narrowed the liability of public officers.

The enactment of the Administrative Procedure Act in 1946 put administrative law on a firm footing. The major innovation of the APA was its provisions for rulemaking, requiring public notice and the opportunity for public input prior to the promulgation of agency rules.

Administrative law was forced to change as government changed from performing relatively few services into an immense bureaucracy regulating every aspect of our daily lives. Administrative law changed to hold government more accountable to the public.

Review Questions

1. What determines whether an agency of government is an independent regulatory agency?

2. Why do courses on administrative law concentrate almost exclusively on administrative procedure?

3. What is the legal source for federal rulemaking?

4. Where may the substantive rules of federal administrative agencies be found?

5. Why are public utilities subject to regulatory agencies?

6. What special role can the paralegal play in administrative law that is not available in private law cases?

7. Where does the "presumption of reviewability" come from?

8. What is meant by "judicial review" in administrative law?

9. When is oral argument available in § 553 rulemaking?

10. Can a person sue a city under 42 U.S.C. § 1983?

Exercises

1. Does your state have a comprehensive statute for administrative procedure? How do its rulemaking provisions compare to Chapter VII of the federal Administrative Procedure Act?

2. Locate the rules and regulations of a state or federal agency and determine the steps necessary to exhaust its administrative remedies.

A QUICK LOOK AT THE INTERNET

- History: the Internet evolved from a U.S. Defense Department communications network creation that was designed in 1969 to withstand the fallout of nuclear war.
- There is no "Internet Company" that owns or manages the Internet; rather, it is a free-existing entity that anyone with a computer and a modem can access through various "gateway" companies.
- Costs are minimal: about $20 per month plus phone charges.
- About 25,000 educational, research, and corporate computer networks are now on the Internet, and 20 million people are believed to have access.

One of the Internet's biggest draws is that e-mail can be sent to literally anyone in the world who is also connected. A drawback has been difficulty of use; the language, UNIX, is generally known only by "techies" and researchers. Luckily, the National Center for Supercomputing Applications (NCSA) in Illinois created "Mosaic"—an application that allows the "Windows generation" to point and click their way through what had been a horrible maze for non-tech users. There are also numerous publications that guide users through the Net, and even software programs that get you ready to "surf."

If you have a modem, communications software, and a telephone, you can access any number of databases around the world through the Internet. However, unless you are equipped with a complex, high-end hardware computer system like those used by research universities and government agencies, you will need help gaining Internet access. Such help is provided by both major service companies—America Online, CompuServe, and Prodigy—and smaller, independent companies that can be found in most major metropolitan areas. Along with Internet access, these companies offer easy-to-use search tools that help guide subscribers through the Internet maze. Smaller access companies, which are typically more expensive (about $40 per month), generally offer more local telephone numbers and higher-speed access to their subscribers than the giants are able to offer. But this is beginning to change. Today, these small companies' major advantage is the "hand-holding" they provide to those not-so-familiar users of the Net. Many also offer free "home page" addresses for their clients—a graphic or other announcement that you have reached a specific party on the Net—a feature that is especially attractive to growing companies.

Using the Internet to "Network"

What would legal research be without on-line services? Simply punch a few computer keys and access thousands of case decisions, ethics opinions, news updates, and more. If you're not sure what we're talking about, it's time to plunge into cyberspace. Lexis, Westlaw, the National Association of Legal Assistants (NALA), and now the National Federation of Paralegal Associations (NFPA) all offer access to legal information super-databases.

But today, on-line services are about more than research. Thousands of people now find jobs through the Internet and other on-line services, posting their resumes on numerous electronic job bulletin boards and networking through e-mail. Job-related databases on the Internet include: Worldwide news groups (search "misc.jobs.misc"), Telnet's Career Connections ("telnet career.com"), Usenet job listing groups, NFPA's "paralegals.org" ("HTTP: www.paralegals.org").

"The very fact that a candidate seeks jobs this way demonstrates a willingness to use technology and to be in touch with the cutting edge," says *The On-Line Job Search Companion* author James Gonyea, speaking to *Working Woman* magazine (March 1995).

Don't hesitate to use the newest technology when making your next career move.

Legal Research? "Go-fer" It

An easy way to access thousands of resources on the Internet when you haven't a clue where to look is to simply "gopher" it.

The Internet gopher system was originally developed by technology wizards at the University of Minnesota. Today, gopher software enables Internet users to access remote computer databases where structured "menus" exist to guide you to the infosrmation you need. (Most service providers—i.e., CompuServe, America Online, Prodigy, etc.—provide gopher capabilities as part of their service.)

The American Association of Law Libraries runs a gopher that can really help to speed your legal research called "AALLNET." To reach the AALLNET gopher you "telnet" (i.e., call their host computer by typing in "$ telnet" followed by their Internet address). For AALLNET type: "$ telnet lawlib.wuacc.edu" (lawlib.wuacc.edu is the AALLNET address).

Reprinted with permission from *Legal Assistant Today* magazine.

CHAPTER 16

LAW IN THE AGE OF COMPUTERS

Introduction

Any person preparing to become a paralegal must look into the future. Opportunities for employment and advancement will be driven by economics and performance. The aspiring paralegal should be sensitive to the needs of the profession and the requirements for paralegal jobs. The uncertainty of the future is compounded by rapidly developing technology, primarily in the computer field. Much of the paralegal's work is decidedly technical, and technicians who do not prepare themselves for changes in technology can become as obsolete as the machines that are sent to the junkpile each year. Although paralegal employment is projected to increase through the end of the century, the number of paralegal training programs has already multiplied significantly. There will be many opportunities, but the competition will be stiff. In this context, those with the most credentials will have the advantage. It behooves the paralegal-in-training to keep abreast of developments in the field and in office technology.

Future Trends for Paralegals

In her book, *Paralegal,* Barbara Bernardo predicted ten future trends in the paralegal field. Several of these warrant discussion:

1. "Greater emphasis will be placed on education." The paralegal field appears headed inevitably toward recognition as a profession, and professional status inevitably requires educational credentials. This is supported by the fact that lawyers have both a bachelor's degree and a law degree and the fact that legal problems reflect the full diversity of our complex society. Paralegals will be expected to be more than technicians; they will be educated professionals. In the recession of the early 1990s, numerous reports surfaced of new law school graduates accepting positions as paralegals. The general economy affects law firms as well. A paralegal student should consider whether it is better to take a course on bankruptcy or construction (building) law.

2. "More sophisticated and substantive legal work will be performed by paralegals." Anyone who has been in the legal field over the past two decades cannot help but have noticed a radical change in lawyers' attitudes toward paralegals. Twenty years ago, most lawyers doubted that a person without law school training could adequately conduct legal research or draft legal documents. Tens of thousands of paralegals have convinced them otherwise. Many lawyers now see paralegals as essential members of the legal team

who perform most of the same tasks as lawyers—and perform them just as well. As legal specialization increases, paralegal specialization increases; the result is that paralegals become virtually indispensable. Imagine an attorney specializing in workers' compensation with a paralegal who has assisted for five years and understands every facet of the field, as well as the attorney's work routine and strategies. Losing that paralegal is like a death in the family. This increased dependence on paralegals will result not only in increased status for the paralegal, but increased compensation as well.

3. "Recognition of the paralegal profession by the general public will continue to increase." Twenty years ago, very few people, even some lawyers, were familiar with the term *paralegal*. This has changed dramatically; paralegal is a commonly considered career choice for those seeking careers and is known to every career counselor. Tens of thousands of legal clients have dealt directly with paralegals and have gained respect for them. Some businesses have begun to question high legal fees with, "Couldn't this have been done by a paralegal?"

4. "New career alternatives." In business and government, a great many tasks call for an understanding of the law. In many cases, hiring a paralegal is cost-effective when hiring an attorney would not be feasible. Those with paralegal training are employed as insurance adjustors, real estate appraisers, bank trust department employees, office managers, and the like. As the field becomes more appreciated, employers of all sorts will come to consider paralegals as valuable alternatives to those with more general education.

5. "More paralegals will start their own businesses." The California movement toward permitting or licensing independent paralegals has spread to all regions of the country. Given the bar's stated mission of providing legal services to all sectors of the society, the inevitable conclusion is that some services can be provided economically only by paralegals who can charge less and keep overhead down. Rosemary Furman proved that a variety of legal services can be provided at minimal cost to clients; perhaps she was simply ahead of her time—the problems her activities raised could have been minimized by licensing and regulation. As far as paralegals are concerned, unauthorized practice of law is currently being redefined.

The New Technology of the Law Office

Because lawyers excel in the art of verbal dialogue, persuasion, and negotiation, it is not surprising that this profession was slow to acquire the new technology that has proliferated in science and business.

Today, the degree to which a law office is electronic depends largely on the economy of scale—a law firm with 200 employees can efficiently run systems that would be utterly extravagant for a five-person firm. Of course, the most important change in the modern law office is the proliferation of the computer. The following list describes the advantages with which computers have provided the modern law firm:

1. Computers can store vast amounts of data and information in a very small space and can access that information very quickly. Something as simple as retrieving a file can be done with a few keystrokes instead of searching a file cabinet. Although this may mean five seconds as opposed to a minute, when multiplied over and over again, the savings in time and convenience becomes very great. The incorporation of CD-ROM drives is revolutionizing law libraries; one CD can replace a bookcase full of books, and search time is reduced to a fraction of the time it takes to look through printed material.

2. Computers can conduct searches with lightning speed. Two dramatic examples of this are WESTLAW and LEXIS, two legal databases that contain all the reported appellate decisions of American courts as well as the federal district court opinions. In an actual search, in less than two minutes WESTLAW searched every state and federal case for the terms "homosexual marriage" and "same-sex marriage." The speed was partially due to the extreme rarity of cases—there were only three—but such a search conducted manually would take hours for even the most adept researcher. Intraoffice files that are on disk can likewise be searched with comparable time savings.

3. Computers eliminate many human errors. With unusual exceptions, computers do not make mistakes, though the human beings who program them and the users who enter information and data on them can make mistakes. More and more, computers are being programmed to anticipate human error in data entry. A simple example is spell checking—some programs will check the spelling of each word as it is typed. There are also programs to check whether the legal citations in a document are in the correct form. Ultimately computer software will check to see if a named case and the citation that follows it are correct (i.e., a case dictionary that includes the correct citation for the case).

4. Computers as word processors are now indispensable in the law office. Long-time practitioners can remember when letters and documents were constantly retyped because of typographical errors or the need to change a phrase or a sentence after rereading. Editing a document is now child's play by comparison. Word processing software now has so many features that few users are even aware of all the things that can be done. Indexing and outlining can be done with speed and accuracy.

5. Standard forms have taken on a new meaning with computers and word processors. Lawyers have always relied on forms for drafting simple documents, but now the forms can be put on computer. In some instances drafting can be accomplished simply by filling in the blanks. In other cases (for example, drafting a will), programs have been devised in which the attorney or paralegal may simply run through a set of questions and enter information into the computer, which can then print out a will. The will can be printed immediately, including even relatively complex wills if the will-drafting program is truly sophisticated. When the program is error-free, the result is error-free, eliminating mistakes that might inadvertently occur otherwise.

6. Computers are at their best when dealing with numbers. For example, there are numerous tax programs that are error-free if the correct numbers are entered; figures can be changed, and the numbers throughout the entire tax form will be recalculated.

7. Computers are orderly, and they force the workers in the law office to be orderly. Recordkeeping becomes a simple and mechanical process. Billing programs abound and have made a traditionally sloppy process an orderly one, which has made firms more profitable. A positive side effect has been to protect attorneys from accusations of excessive charges. For instance, a large firm can install a program that mechanically times telephone calls and records them in a client's file, thus providing an unassailable record for billing purposes.

8. Computers are indispensable in support of complex litigation, which collects massive documentation that may be indexed, filed, tracked, and accessed with an efficiency that was unthinkable a few years ago. Computers are not only faster and more efficient than manual filing systems, but they also have retrieval capacities not possible with manual filing. For example, the computer can quickly find every document in a file that contains the name of a witness or a business entity; it can order any set of documents chronologically, alphabetically, or numerically.

The advent of computers in the law firm has increased the learning time necessary for the law office staff. Back in the 1970s, paralegal programs often struggled with the issue of whether to teach typing. Not only did such classes appear nonacademic, but they also suggested that the program was teaching legal secretaries rather than paralegals. At that time, paralegals were also fighting for recognition as career specialists. Today, computers pose a very different scenario—they are indispensable and computer skills are indispensable. The curriculum problem remains, though: should computer skills be taught within the program, or be learned outside of the paralegal curriculum? Nonetheless, the modern paralegal must be comfortable with computers. This does not mean familiarity with every software program, but rather the ability to learn and adjust to the programs likely to be found in the law office, especially word processing and research.

Coming Events in Law Office Automation

The law office library as it presently exists will soon disappear. Those venerable rows of the reporter series will be replaced by compact disks, which can store enormous amounts of text in a very small space. The compact disks can be read by the computer so that the law library becomes part of the working files of the law office.

When technology improves and the price plummets, optical character readers (OCRs) will be universally used. These permit text in written form (hardcopy) to be scanned and entered into computer files for retrieval or editing, without the need to type in text. Preparation of reports, legal memoranda, and trial and appellate briefs will be accomplished with unimaginable speed and enhanced accuracy.

The combination of computer and telecommunications will revolutionize many aspects of practice. Computers can exchange data and information with each other; fax machines may become a relic of the past. It is conceivable that court reporters may simply monitor a device that translates the spoken word into print that can be sent by telephone to the firm's computer. A copy of a deposition or a trial could be available within hours of its completion.

Specialization

Recent decades have witnessed increasing specialization among lawyers, and there is no end to this trend in sight. The largest law firms have doubled and tripled in size and even created branches in different cities. This enables lawyers to specialize in very restricted fields where the market provides a sufficient number of clients. Where in the past a lawyer might simply have specialized in property law, there are now lawyers who specialize in government defense contracts, commercial leases, and condominiums. Even smaller firms may develop narrow specialties once they have developed a client base and may form informal referral arrangements with other firms that have different specialties. The advantage of narrow specialization is that an attorney may acquire a nearly total grasp of the field, keeping abreast of each new case and every statutory revision.

Paralegals have tended to be even more specialized than lawyers. In a small firm, a single paralegal may serve a few lawyers, but in larger firms, paralegals specialize in restricted fields and in restricted tasks. A paralegal may be assigned exclusively to real estate closings or deposition analysis if the volume of work warrants. From a business standpoint, this specialization is very effective because it encourages efficiency, accuracy, and speed. Paralegals are better able to concentrate on one task at a time than lawyers, who must frequently interrupt their work to respond to client requests.

Unless there is a continuing local market for a particular specialization, it is difficult for paralegal training programs to offer significant specialized training. Law firms often train their paralegals to perform specialized tasks, but some actively recruit specialists when a vacancy occurs. It is difficult for the paralegal-in-training to prepare for an employment requiring specialization.

Alternative Dispute Resolution

Litigation is a costly and cumbersome process. Disputing parties are turning to more efficient forms of dispute resolution. In commercial cases, disputes often arise between parties who wish to resolve their differences without injury to their business relationship. Litigation tends to drive the parties apart because the process is adversarial and expensive. Two frequently used alternative means for resolving disputes are arbitration and mediation. Both of these suggest rich opportunities for paralegals in the future.

Arbitration

Arbitration has traditionally been linked to labor-management disputes, but it is fast becoming a commonly used method to settle commercial disputes. If the disputing parties agree, a third party or parties can be chosen to hear both sides and render a decision on the merits of the dispute. Many contracts provide for arbitration in lieu of litigation in case of a breach. The ground rules can minimize the costs commonly associated with discovery and delays in settlement. If the original contract does not provide for arbitration, parties may nevertheless agree, once a dispute has arisen, to settle their differences through arbitration. The American Arbitration Association is composed of retired judges who serve as arbitrators. The arbitration procedure may imitate a trial-type hearing, but a lesser degree of formality and technicality can make arbitration faster and cheaper than a trial. It is essential, in arbitration, that the parties waive their rights to trial by agreeing to be bound by the decision of the arbitrator. Occasionally nonbinding arbitration is employed; this is really a form of mediation, as discussed later. It is important to remember that private parties may agree to any mutual rights and duties that are lawful. Theoretically, disputing parties could agree to pick the first person they meet in the street to arbitrate their dispute. In this context, the opportunities for using paralegals are self-evident at all levels, but their use in minor disputes clearly would be cost-effective.

Mediation

Mediation is not binding on the parties; it has a very different design than arbitration. The function of a mediator is to assist disputants in working out their problems. The mediator does not take sides, but works to minimize unproductive hostilities and to maximize means of cooperation. Mediation is nonadversarial. It has been used extensively in divorce and child custody problems, helping the parties to learn to cooperate to settle the terms of their break-up. Because it is not binding, it is not always successful, but the advantage of mediation in divorce cases is that it empowers the parties to take control of their lives. It may even establish a method for future cooperation that is essential if the parties must continue to deal with each other with regard to their children.

Mediation is appropriate in a multitude of other situations in which the goal is long-term cooperation despite the present dispute. Public institutions such as schools and school boards may avail themselves of mediation to open lines of communication with their constituents and avoid the adversarial roles that litigation promotes. Mediation in commercial disputes can also be a much more comfortable procedure than the adversarial process.

Many states have encouraged mediation and have established mediation training programs. The various states differ on licensing or qualifying mediators. Many lawyers engage in mediation, and some have even forsaken the practice of law in favor of careers as mediators. Psychologists and other mental health professionals have entered the mediation field as well. Neither the practice of law nor mental health training fits the mediation model precisely, though, because the role of the mediator is neither to solve individual emotional problems nor to take sides in an adversarial role. The paralegal as mediator has not yet been recognized, but the paralegal would seem to be an obvious choice because the paralegal has or can easily acquire the knowledge of the law necessary for mediating a dispute. (In divorce mediation, for example, a marital settlement agreement cannot be attempted without some understanding of its tax consequences.) The paralegal, while working for an advocate, does not take on the role of advocate, but is more likely to assume the role of liaison between client and attorney. It might well be that the ideal mediator would be a paralegal with counseling and mediation training.

Legal Databases

Discussion of legal technology would not be complete without mention of legal databases. Although there are a number of specialized databases, the most commonly used, broad-based data-bases are WESTLAW and LEXIS. There are some differences between these, which their marketers are only too happy to point out, but their primary use is similar. Every month, each adds some new materials, but the advantage of these databases is that cases and statutes are stored in very powerful systems that permit quick access to legal materials.

Aside from the time they save finding and searching through books, they have one major advantage over traditional library research: the computer can quickly scan huge numbers of cases for quite specific words and phrases. For example, suppose the researcher is involved in a case in which a defective ball-joint is the alleged cause of an auto accident. WESTLAW or LEXIS could collect reported decisions that include the word "ball-joint." Because "ball-joint" is not a legal term, it will not be found in any of the indexes for cases. When the researcher is looking for cases with factual similarities, such a tool is invaluable. A search can be further narrowed to finding "ball-joint" in the same sentence or paragraph with "Chevrolet" or "defective." These legal databases can quickly provide materials that would be difficult and time-consuming to find through traditional manual searches.

To put this in perspective, a note must be added about legal research, a subject otherwise left to other texts and courses. Much of legal research aims at building a legal argument based on decided cases bearing some resemblance to the present case. Although legal arguments are based on legal, rather than factual, issues, the more similar a cited case is in its fact situation to the case at hand, the more compelling is the precedent. Legal materials are extensively cross-indexed so that often the first task of research is to find a pertinent case, then pursue the leads that case presents until a full complement of cases bearing on the issues is assembled. With unlimited time, anyone with a modicum of instruction can find all the pertinent cases; the problem is finding them with the least waste of time. Legal databases are unbeatable in this respect. At present the cost (per minute) of using these databases is fairly high, but for the researcher who knows how to use them efficiently, a two-minute search can easily save two hours in the law library, a considerable savings for the client.

Summary

In the late 1980s, employment estimates for the paralegal field placed it at the very top of occupations, and these projections did not even take account of the possibilities for new and expanding opportunities for paralegals. Paralegals will be employed in many areas not clearly foreseen. Legal specialization and expanding law office technology will require expansion of legal staff in directions only vaguely discernible at present. The prospects for paralegals appear more promising in number than those for lawyers. It is essential that a person preparing for the paralegal profession take note of new developments in the practice of law and in the law office and be prepared for the many changes that will inevitably occur.

APPENDIX A

HOW TO READ A CASE

Introduction

Reported judicial decisions have a style and format all their own. This discussion is designed to acquaint readers with the form and the nature of judicial decisions. Although judges have considerable freedom in how they write opinions, some uniformity of pattern comes from the similarity of purpose for decisions, especially decisions of appellate courts, which frequently serve as authority for later cases.

Similarity is also a product of custom. The influence of West Publishing Company, which publishes the regional reporter series as well as the federal reporters, has been great. Some of this material repeats discussions in the first chapters of the book, but this appendix is designed to be read at almost any point during the book—the sooner, the better, as judicial decisions are interspersed throughout the text.

Which Court?

Knowing which court issued the opinion is extremely important. As a general rule, the higher the court, the more compelling its authority. The binding force of precedent depends on the relationship between the court which issues it and the court applying it. A decision of the Iowa Supreme Court has no precedential power over courts in Tennessee because each state has its own laws and legal system. Iowa courts may not dictate to Tennessee what Tennessee law is or should be. However, decisions of the Supreme Court of Tennessee, the highest court of that state, are binding precedent on other state courts in Tennessee—lower courts must follow the law as stated by a higher court in their jurisdiction.

Federal and State Courts

The United States has two parallel legal structures. Each state has its own set of laws and courts. In addition, the federal government has a separate legal authority through courts located in every state. Federal courts are not superior to state courts but parallel to them, having authority over different types of cases. For example, the U.S. Constitution restricts authority over patents and copyrights to the federal government. Thus, a patent case will be heard in federal court but not in a state court. In contrast, there are both federal and state civil rights laws, so a particular case might be filed in one or the other. When federal and state courts have concurrent jurisdiction of this sort, exercise of authority is governed by custom or law; but when state and federal law overlap and conflict, state law must yield to federal law.

Trial and Appellate Courts

State and federal courts are divided into trial and appellate courts. Most cases originate in trial courts, where evidence is presented, witnesses are questioned, and a judgment determining the rights of the parties is entered. If one of the parties to the case is dissatisfied with the result, the case may be appealed; an appellate court is petitioned to review the proceedings of the lower, or trial, court to determine if errors were made that would justify changing the outcome of the case.

The federal system provides a model followed in general terms by a majority of state systems. The U.S. District Court is the primary federal trial court. The next higher federal court is the United States Court of Appeals. It is called an intermediate appellate court because it is subordinate to the highest court, the U.S. Supreme Court.

Most states name their highest court Supreme Court; New York, a notable exception, calls its highest court the Court of Appeals and uses the designation Supreme Court for lower courts. Some states do not have intermediate appellate courts. There is also considerable variety in state trial courts and the names applied to them.

The careful researcher always takes note of the court issuing a decision because the higher the court, the greater the force of its decision. The decision of a court is binding on lower courts within its jurisdiction, meaning that the rules it lays down must be followed by lower courts faced with the same issue.

For Whom Are Judicial Opinions Written?

In evaluating any written material, the reader should assess the audience the writer is addressing and the writer's goals. Judges write decisions for two reasons. The first is to inform the parties to the dispute who won and who lost, giving the rules and reasoning the judge applied to the facts. The second is to inform the legal profession, attorneys and judges, of the rules applied to a given set of facts and the reasons for the decision.

Attorneys and Judges Read Judicial Opinions

Very few laypersons ever enter a law library to find and read cases. The people found in the county law library are usually lawyers, paralegals, and judges. Cases are rarely intended to be entertaining, and judges are not motivated to make their cases "reader-friendly." Their tasks are quite specific. Because any case may serve as precedent, or at least form a basis for subsequent legal arguments, judges are especially concerned with conveying a precise meaning by carefully framing the rules and providing the reasoning behind them. The higher the court, the greater this concern will be. Imagine writing an opinion for a highly skilled, highly intelligent readership that critically analyzes every word and phrase, an opinion that may well affect important rights of citizens in the future.

Judicial writing is different from most other kinds of writing in that its goal is neither simply to pass on information nor to persuade the reader of the author's point of view. The judge is stating the law, making a final judgment, but must do so with caution so that the statements are not misinterpreted or misused. An appreciation of the judge's dilemma is essential to critical evaluation of cases.

The Effect of Setting Precedent

The cost of litigation is great, and appeal of a decision incurs significant additional cost. It makes sense to appeal if the losing party reasonably concludes that the lower court was incorrect in its application of the law. It would be quite foolish to spend large sums of money to go to the higher court if the chances of winning were slim and the stakes were small. This means that the cases we read from appellate courts, and especially from the highest courts, generally involve questions with strong arguments on both sides. The judges of these courts are faced with difficult decisions and must respect the reasonable arguments of both sides in deciding which side will prevail.

Clarity versus Confusion

Judicial writing is often difficult and obscure, but such criticism of judicial writing often neglects to recognize that not only are the issues difficult to present with clarity, but also that often the importance of narrowing the application of the decision encourages tortuous reasoning. For example, when faced with a landmark case of reverse discrimination (a white applicant for medical school was denied admission, while less-qualified minority students were admitted), the U.S. Supreme Court was expected to lay down a rule concerning the constitutionality of such admissions programs. Those expectations were disappointed. The Justices wrote divergent opinions that made it very difficult to discover exactly what the rule was. At the time the issue was quite controversial, and the decision potentially could have affected efforts by the Administration and Congress to help the position of disadvantaged minorities. Any precedent of the court would have far-reaching consequences. Although the plaintiff won and subsequently entered medical school, there was some confusion as to why he won. The effect of the decision was to stifle future efforts to pursue reverse discrimination cases. Each Justice of the court viewed the problem in a different light, and the result was a resolution of the dispute without a clear picture of the rule to be applied in such cases.

Thus, the reader of cases should be aware that the complex reasoning of a judge's writing is not always due to the complexity of the issues, but may also be caused by the judge's desire to narrow the effect of the precedent.

Most appellate decisions are the product of three or more judges. A unanimous or majority opinion is not the reasoning of a single person. The author of an opinion must take into consideration the views of the judges who join in the opinion. In some cases, especially with the nine Justices of the U.S. Supreme Court, achieving a majority involves negotiation—one Justice may vote with the majority only if a key point in his or her reasoning is included or only if the rule is narrowed to cover a limited number of situations. The author of the opinion may thus be stating someone else's reasoning or opinion, or may be stating the argument to appease a Justice who is reluctant to join in the opinion. The politics of decision making may make it quite difficult to write a cohesive opinion that makes everyone happy.

Doing Justice to the Parties

It is a mistake to assume that judges are dispassionate, totally rational, and objective interpreters of the law. The notion that judges reason directly from the facts to the law in a rather mechanical fashion neglects the obvious fact that judges are human beings doing their best to dispense justice. We must suspect that in any given case, the judge or judges form an opinion as to which side should win and then select rules and arguments to support that side. (If justice clearly favors one side, it is usually not difficult to frame a convincing legal argument for that side to win.)

Sometimes a strict application of the law causes a very undesirable result. The Kentucky Court of Appeals was faced with such circumstances in *Strunk v. Strunk,* 445 S.W.2d 145, in which a man was dying of a kidney problem and his brother was the only appropriate donor for a life-saving kidney transplant. The problem was that the brother with the healthy kidneys was severely mentally retarded and therefore legally incompetent to consent to the operation. The issue facing the court was whether the mother of the two brothers could consent to the operation, acting as the guardian of the retarded brother. Kentucky precedents (cited by the dissenting judges, but ignored by the majority) seemed to show clearly that a guardian's authority did not extend to making such a decision. Faced with a heart-rending life-or-death decision, four of seven judges deciding the case ignored prior precedents. Three of the judges disagreed, and one wrote a vigorous dissenting opinion. The reasoning of the majority opinion was weak, but it is difficult to fault the judges under the circumstances.

The Format for a Reported Decision

The cases found in the reporters generally follow a uniform format with which researchers must become familiar. The first part of the case has no official authority. Authoritative statements begin with the actual text of the opinion.

Format Preceding the Opinion

West Publishing Company publishes the reporter series for which it has established a uniform format. The first page of *United States v. National Lead Co.*, 438 F.2d 935 (8th Cir. 1971) (Figure A-1) illustrates all the elements.

The Citation

The heading of the page indicates the citation "**UNITED STATES v. NATIONAL LEAD COMPANY**" and "**Cite as 438 F.2d 935 (1971).**" This is the name of the case and where it can be found, namely, on page 935 in Volume 438 of the Federal Reporter, Second Series. Note that this differs from the official citation, *United States v. National Lead Co.*, 438 F.2d 935 (8th Cir. 1971), that would be used in legal texts and opinions. The official citation indicates that the case was decided by the U.S. Court of Appeals for the Eighth Circuit.

The Caption

Figure A-2 shows the caption of the case, which names the parties. Note that the citation names only one party for each side, whereas the caption

FIGURE A-1

UNITED STATES v. NATIONAL LEAD COMPANY
Cite as 438 F.2d 935 (1971)

UNITED STATES of America,
Plaintiff-Appellant,
v.
NATIONAL LEAD COMPANY, a
Corporation, and Chemical
Workers' Basic Union Local 1744,
AFL-CIO , Defendants-Appellees.
No. 20427.
United States Court of Appeals,
Eighth Circuit. Feb. 26, 1971.

Action by government against company and union for alleged violations of Civil Rights Act of 1964. The United States District Court for the Eastern District of Missouri, Roy W. Harper, Senior District Judge, 315 F.Supp. 912, denied government's motion for preliminary injunction, and government appealed. The Court of Appeals, Bright, Circuit Judge, held that although, under facts, some of vestiges of employer's past discrimination seemed preserved in employer's transfer and promotion procedures, in view of fact that actual impact of this discrimination upon black employees possessing seniority dating back prior to end of discrimination was unclear, and in view of fact that an appropriate solution was not readily apparent from partial development of facts, denial of relief by way of a preliminary injunction was not error.

Affirmed and remanded.

1. Civil Rights 3

Employment policies which appear racially neutral but build upon bias that existed prior to enactment of 1964 Civil Rights Act to produce present discrimination are actionable. Civil Rights Act of 1964, § 701 et seq., 42 U.S.C.A. § 2000e et seq.

2. Civil Rights 3

Policy of 1964 Civil Rights Act is not fulfilled by a showing that black employees may enjoy substantially equal pay with others in similar capacities; the test is whether all employees possess an equal opportunity to fully enjoy all employment rights. Civil Rights Act of 1964, §§ 703(h), 706(g), 42 U.S.C.A. §§ 2000e–2(h), 2000e–5(g).

3. Injunction 137(4)

Although, under facts, some of vestiges of employer's past discrimination seemed preserved in employer's transfer and promotion procedures, in view of fact that actual impact of this discrimination upon black employees possessing seniority dating back prior to end of discrimination was unclear, and in view of fact that an appropriate solution was not readily apparent from partial development of facts, denial of relief by way of a preliminary injunction was not error. Civil Rights Act of 1964, §§ 701 et seq., 707(a) 42 U.S.C.A. §§ 2000e et seq., 2000e–6(a).

4. Injunction 147

In view of evidence disclosing that in recent years blacks had filled three of six vacancies for guard positions and that employer planned no immediate expansion of present guard force or filling of any existing vacancies, no need for preliminary injunction was shown with respect to guard force. Civil Rights Act of 1964, §§ 701 et seq., 707(a), 42 U.S.C.A. §§ 2000e et seq., 2000e–6(a).

Jerris Leonard, Asst. Atty. Gen., Daniel Bartlett, Jr., U. S. Atty., David L. Rose, Stuart P. Herman, Attys., Dept. of Justice, Washington, D. C., for plaintiff-appellant.

Edward Weakley, Howard Elliott, Boyle, Priest, Elliott & Weakley, St. Louis, Mo., for National Lead Co.

Harry Moline, Jr., Thomas, Busse, Cullen, Clooney, Weil & King, St. Louis, Mo., for Chemical Workers' Basic Union, Local 1744, AFL-CIO.

Before GIBSON and BRIGHT, Circuit Judges, and McMANUS, Chief District Judge.

BRIGHT, Circuit Judge.

The United States by its Attorney General brings this action seeking in-

FIGURE A-2

UNITED STATES of America
Plaintiff-Appellant,
v.
NATIONAL LEAD COMPANY,
a Corporation, and Chemical Workers'
Basic Union Local 1744, AFL-CIO,
Defendants-Appellees.

No. 20427.
United States Court of Appeals
Eighth Circuit.
Feb. 26, 1971.

---

includes a codefendant, a union local of the AFL-CIO. The caption also indicates the status of the parties with regard to the suit as "Plaintiff-Appellant" and "Defendants-Appellees." We can surmise from this that the United States brought the original suit as plaintiff and then also the appeal, apparently having lost the original suit.

Commonly the caption simply states "appellant" and "appellee," and the reader must discover from the text who brought the suit originally. It is important to note who is appellant and who is appellee because many opinions refer to the parties by those terms. In *National Lead,* Judge Bright refers to "the government" and "National Lead," which makes reading much less confusing.

Below the parties we find "No. 20427," the docket number, which is a number assigned to the case upon initial filing with the clerk of the court and by which it is identified prior to assigning it a volume and page number in the reporter series. This number is important when attempting to research the case prior to its official publication. Below the docket number is the name of the court issuing the decision and the date of the decision.

The Syllabus

Following the caption is a brief summary of the case called the *syllabus* (Figure A-3). Although this is sometimes written by the court or a reporter appointed by the court, it is a narrow condensation of the court's ruling and cannot be relied upon as the precise holding of the court. The syllabus can be useful in obtaining a quick idea of what the case concerns—a summary of the issue and the holding of the court. Frequently legal researchers follow leads to cases, which upon reading prove to be unrelated to the issue being researched. Reading the syllabus may make reading the entire opinion unnecessary. However, if the syllabus suggests that the case may be important, a careful reading of the entire text of the opinion is usually necessary.

FIGURE A-3

Action by government against company and union for alleged violations of Civil Rights Act of 1964. The United States District Court for the Eastern District of Missouri, Roy W. Harper, Senior District Judge, 315 F.Supp. 912, denied government's motion for preliminary injunction, and government appealed. The Court of Appeals, Bright, Circuit Judge, held that although, under facts, some of vestiges of employer's past discrimination seemed preserved in employer's transfer and promotion procedures, in view of fact that actual impact of this discrimination upon black employees possessing seniority dating back prior to end of discrimination was unclear, and in view of fact that an appropriate solution was not readily apparent from partial development of facts, denial of relief by way of a preliminary injunction was not error.

Affirmed and remanded.

Headnotes

Figure A-4 illustrates the *headnotes,* which are statements of the major points of law discussed in the case. With limited editing, the headnotes tend to be nearly verbatim statements lifted from the opinion. The headnotes are listed in numerical order, starting at the beginning of the opinion, so that the reader may look quickly for the context of a point expressed by a headnote. For example, the part of the text that deals with a particular point made in the headnote will have the number of the headnote in brackets, e.g., [4], at the beginning of the paragraph or section in which it is discussed. This is very helpful when researching lengthy cases in which only one issue is of concern to the researcher.

To the right of the headnote number is a generic heading, such as "Civil Rights," and a *key* number. Because this reporter is published by West Publishing Company, it uses an indexing title and number that can be used throughout the many West indexes, reporters, and encyclopedias.

Although syllabi and headnotes are useful, they are not authoritative.

FIGURE A-4

3. Injunction   137(4)

Although, under facts, some of vestiges of employer's past discrimination seemed preserved in employer's transfer and promotion procedures, in view of fact that actual impact of this discrimination upon black employees possessing seniority dating back prior to end of discrimination was unclear, and in view of fact that an appropriate solution was not readily apparent from partial development of facts, denial of relief by way of a preliminary injunction was not error. Civil Rights Act of 1964, §§ 701 et seq., 707(a) 42 U.S.C.A. §§ 2000e et seq., 2000e-6(a).

4. Injunction   147

In view of evidence disclosing that in recent years blacks had filled three of six vacancies for guard positions and that employer planned no immediate expansion of present guard force or filling of any existing vacancies, no need for preliminary injuction was shown with respect to guard force. Civil Rights Act of 1964, §§ 701 et seq., 707(a), 42 U.S.C.A. §§ 2000e et seq., 2000e-6(a).

Attorneys for the Parties

Figure A-5 shows the *attorneys for the parties* as well as the judges sitting on the case. These are listed just above the beginning of the opinion, shown in Figure A-6.

FIGURE A-5

> Jerris Leonard, Asst. Atty. Gen., Daniel Bartlett, Jr., U.S. Atty., David L. Rose, Stuart P. Herman, Attys., Dept. of Justice, Washington, D.C., for plaintiff-appellant.
>
> Edward Weakley, Howard Elliott, Boyle, Priest, Elliott & Weakley, St. Louis, Mo., for National Lead Co.
>
> Harry Moline, Jr., Thomas, Busse, Cullen, Clooney, Weil & King, St. Louis, Mo., for Chemical Workers' Basic Union, Local 1744, AFL-CIO.
>
> Before GIBSON and BRIGHT, Circuit Judges, and McMANUS, Chief District Judge.

FIGURE A-6

> BRIGHT, Circuit Judge.
> The United States by its Attorney General brings this action seeking in-

Format of the Opinion

Following the names of the attorneys and a list of the judges sitting on the case, the formal opinion (that is, the official discussion of the case) begins with the name of the judge writing the opinion, for example, "Bright, Circuit Judge," in *National Lead*. The author of the opinion has considerable freedom in presentation. Some opinions are written mechanically; a few are almost poetic. The peculiarities of any particular case may dictate a special logical order of its own. Nevertheless, the majority of opinions follow a standard format. When this format is followed, reading and understanding are simplified, but no judge is required to make an opinion easy reading. The following format is the one most frequently used.

Procedure

Most opinions begin with some reference to the outcome of the trial in the lower court and the basis for appeal. In a criminal case, for example, the opinion may state that the defendant was found guilty of aggravated assault and is appealing the judge's ruling to admit certain evidence over the defendant's objections that the evidence was prejudicial to the defendant's case. Often the remarks about procedure are brief and confusing, especially if the reader is not familiar with procedural rules. If the procedure is important to the opinion, a more elaborate discussion is usually found in the body of the opinion. Many things in the opinion become clear only upon further reading, and many opinions must be read at least twice for a full understanding. An opinion is like a jigsaw puzzle—the reader must put the parts together to see the full picture.

The Facts

Most of the text of an opinion in appellate decisions is concerned with a discussion of the law, but because a case revolves around a dispute concerning events that occurred between the parties, no opinion is complete without some discussion of the events that led to the trial. Trials generally explore these events in great detail and judge or jury settle the facts, so appellate opinions usually narrow the fact statement to the most relevant facts. In an interesting case, the reader is often left wanting to know more about what happened, but the judge is not writing a story. The important element in the opinion is the application of law.

The Issue

Following a summary of relevant facts, many writers describe the questions of law that must be decided. Rarely, this is made quite clear: "The only issue presented to the court is … " Unfortunately, few writers pinpoint the issue in this fashion, so the reader must search the text for the issue. At this point it is appropriate to introduce a favorite term used by attorneys: caveat. This means "warning" or, literally, "Let him beware."

Caveat: The issue is the most important element in an opinion. If the issue is not understood, the significance of the rule laid down by the court can easily be misunderstood. This point cannot be emphasized too strongly. Law students study cases for three years with one primary goal: "Identify the issues." Anyone can fill out forms, but a competently trained person can go right to the heart of a case and recognize its strengths and weaknesses.

The Discussion

The main body of the text of an opinion, often 90 percent of it, discusses the meaning of the issue(s) and offers a line of reasoning that leads to a disposition of the case and explains why a certain rule or rules must apply to the dispute. This part of the opinion is the most difficult to follow. The writer has a goal, but the goal is often not clear to the reader until the end. For this reason, it is usually helpful to look at the final paragraph in the case to see whether the appellate court affirmed (agreed with the lower court) or reversed (disagreed with the lower court). Many judges seem to like to hold the reader in suspense, but the reader need not play this game. By finding out the outcome of the decision, the reader can see how the writer of an opinion is building the conclusion. By recognizing the issue and knowing the rule applied, the reader can see the structure of the argument. The discussion section is the writer's justification of the holding.

The Holding

The holding states the *rule of the case,* that is, the rule the court applies to conclude whether the lower court was correct. The rule is *the law,* meaning that it determines the rights of the parties unless reversed by a higher court. It binds lower courts faced with a similar dispute in future cases. It is best to think of the holding as an answer to the issue.

Let us give a real-life example. A woman is suing for wrongful death. Her husband was killed in an auto accident, and she is attempting to collect damages based on the income her husband would have received had he lived, in which income she would have shared. Since the death, however, she has married an affluent man, and her lifestyle has not diminished. The issue is whether the jury can be informed of her remarriage. The court holds that the fact of her remarriage may not be kept from the jury. The court also holds that evidence of her new husband's earnings may *not* be presented to the jury. In this instance the holding goes a bit beyond the issue and clarifies it. (This particular issue has been answered quite differently in different states.) The reasoning for the holding is as follows: There is no justification for deliberately deceiving the jury about the woman's marital status. However, her current husband's earnings are irrelevant to the damage she suffered in losing her former husband. Fairness on this issue is difficult.

Evaluating Cases

Once the purpose, style, and structure of appellate decisions are grasped, mastering the content is a matter of concentration and experience. Researching cases generally has one or more of the following three goals:

1. Finding statements of the law.
2. Assessing the law in relation to the client's case.
3. Building an argument.

Finding the Law

Research of cases is done for a number of reasons. The principles that apply to a dispute may be unknown, unfamiliar, or forgotten. With experience, legal professionals come to develop a knack for guessing how a dispute will be decided and can even predict what rules will be applied. Once the issues of a case are recognized, a reasonable prediction of a fair outcome can be made. This is, however, merely tentative; the researchers must check their knowledge and memory against definitive statements of the law. In some instances a statute clearly defines the rights and duties that pertain to the case at hand; in others the elaboration of the law in the cases leaves little room for doubt. Frequently, however, the issue in a client's case is complex or unique, and no case can be found that is directly "on point." Ideally, research will result in finding a case that contains a fact situation so similar to that of the client that an assumption can be made that the same rule will apply. A case with a factual background identical to that of the client is said to be *on point,* as illustrated in the following example.

Suppose Laura Lee, while waiting for a bus, was hit and injured by an automobile. The driver had lost control because of a defective steering mechanism. Laura was seriously injured and the driver has minimal insurance (and may not have been at fault). The issue is whether the manufacturer of the automobile is liable. The owner could sue the automobile manufacturer, but can a bystander sue as well? A search reveals several cases involving bystanders who were injured by defective brakes and were able to sue the manufacturer for products liability. Although the facts are not identical, these cases are on point, because the issue is not what kind of defect caused the accident but whether a bystander can sue.

Distinguishing Cases

In some instances the facts of a dispute are used to *distinguish* it from similar cases. For example, in researching Laura Lee's case, a case is encountered in which a bystander was injured by an automobile with a defective steering mechanism. In that case, the bystander did not collect damages from the manufacturer. The case was distinguishable because the driver was intoxicated. The driver's negligence was not merely passive, such as procrastinating in obtaining repairs, but was actively caused by his intoxication. The intoxication was the true cause of the injury, so it would have been unfair to place liability on the manufacturer. (The manufacturer would probably be sued anyway simply because it has the resources to compensate for the injury.)

Only experience and knowledge of the law will develop the keen sense it takes to separate cases that are on point from those that are distinguishable. It is often the advocate's job to persuade on the basis of threading a way through a host of seemingly conflicting cases.

Summary

Judicial opinions are unique as a literary form in that their statements of law as defined by the court become precedent for future legal arguments and decisions. Judges must not only do justice to the parties but also must remain aware that their decisions determine rights of other parties in the future. Complex issues often result in opinions that are difficult to follow. Controversial issues may cause judges to be evasive in their conclusions.

A standard publishing format is followed in reported judicial decisions. In addition, custom has dictated a format for the text of the opinion itself. Judges are under no requirement to follow this format, and it is up to the reader to ferret out the issues and follow the reasoning.

APPENDIX B

NALA CODE OF ETHICS AND PROFESSIONAL RESPONSIBILITY

It is the responsibility of every legal assistant to adhere strictly to the accepted standards of legal ethics and to live by general principles of proper conduct. The performance of the duties of the legal assistant shall be governed by specific canons as defined herein in order that justice will be served and the goals of the profession attained. The canons of ethics set forth hereafter are adopted by the National Association of Legal Assistants, Inc., as a general guide and the enumeration of these rules does not mean there are not others of equal importance although not specifically mentioned.

Canon 1. A legal assistant shall not perform any of the duties that lawyers only may perform nor do things that lawyers themselves may not do.

Canon 2. A legal assistant may perform any task delegated and supervised by a lawyer so long as the lawyer is responsible to the client, maintains a direct relationship with the client, and assumes full professional responsibility for the work product.

Canon 3. A legal assistant shall not engage in the practice of law by accepting cases, setting fees, giving legal advice or appearing in court (unless otherwise authorized by court or agency rules).

Canon 4. A legal assistant shall not act in matters involving professional legal judgment as the services of a lawyer are essential in the public interest whenever the exercise of such judgment is required.

Canon 5. A legal assistant must act prudently in determining the extent to which a client may be assisted without the presence of a lawyer.

Canon 6. A legal assistant shall not engage in the unauthorized practice of law.

Canon 7. A legal assistant must protect the confidences of a client, and it shall be unethical for a legal assistant to violate any statute now in effect or hereafter to be enacted controlling privileged communications.

Canon 8. It is the obligation of the legal assistant to avoid conduct which would cause the lawyer to be unethical or even appear to be unethical and loyalty to the employer is incumbent upon the legal assistant.

Canon 9. A legal assistant shall work continually to maintain integrity and a high degree of competency throughout the legal profession.

Canon 10. A legal assistant shall strive for perfection through education in order to better assist the legal profession in fulfilling its duty of making legal services available to clients and the public.

Canon 11. A legal assistant shall do all things incidental, necessary or expedient for the attainment of the ethics and responsibilities imposed by statute or rule of court.

Canon 12. A legal assistant is governed by the American Bar Association Model Code of Professional Responsibility and the American Bar Association Model Rules of Professional Conduct.

Reprinted with permission of the National Association of Legal Assistants, Inc., 1601 South Main, Suite 300, Tulsa, OK 74119. Copyright ©1975.

APPENDIX C

NFPA AFFIRMATION OF PROFESSIONAL RESPONSIBILITY

NFPA Mission Statement

The National Federation of Paralegal Associations, Inc. ("Federation") is a non-profit, professional organization comprised of state and local paralegal associations throughout the United States. The Federation affirms the paralegal profession as an independent, self-directed profession which supports increased quality, efficiency and accessibility in the delivery of legal services. The Federation promotes the growth, development and recognition of the profession as an integral partner in the delivery of legal services.

NFPA has adopted an Affirmation of Professional Responsibility, which is the code of ethics for its members. The Affirmation sets forth guidelines for paralegals in the delivery of legal services and affirms their responsibility to the public and their dedication to the development of the paralegal profession. NFPA has also taken steps to become a leader in the improvement of paralegal education programs throughout the country.

PREAMBLE

The National Federation of Paralegal Associations recognizes and accepts its commitment to the realization of the most basic right of a free society, equal justice under the law.

In examining contemporary legal institutions and systems, the members of the paralegal profession recognize that a redefinition of the traditional delivery of legal services is essential in order to meet the needs of the general public. The paralegal profession is committed to increasing the availability and quality of legal services.

The National Federation of Paralegal Associations has adopted this Affirmation of Professional Responsibility to delineate the principles of purpose and conduct toward which paralegals should aspire. Through this Affirmation, the National Federation of Paralegal Associations places upon each paralegal the responsibility to adhere to these standards and encourages dedication to the development of the profession.

I. PROFESSIONAL RESPONSIBILITY

A paralegal shall demonstrate initiative in performing and expanding the paralegal role in the delivery of legal services within the parameters of the unauthorized practice of law statutes.

Discussion: Recognizing the professional and legal responsibility to abide by the unauthorized practice of law statutes, the Federation supports and encourages new interpretations as to what constitutes the practice of law.

II. PROFESSIONAL CONDUCT

A paralegal shall maintain the highest standards of ethical conduct.

Discussion: It is the responsibility of a paralegal to avoid conduct which is unethical or appears to be unethical. Ethical principles are aspirational in character and embody the fundamental rules of conduct by which every paralegal should abide. Observance of these standards is essential to uphold respect for the legal system.

III. COMPETENCE AND INTEGRITY

A paralegal shall maintain a high level of competence and shall contribute to the integrity of the paralegal profession.

Discussion: The integrity of the paralegal profession is predicated upon individual competence. Professional competence is each paralegal's responsibility and is achieved through continuing education, awareness of developments in the field of law, and aspiring to the highest standards of personal performance.

IV. CLIENT CONFIDENCES

A paralegal shall preserve client confidences and privileged communications.

Discussion: Confidential information and privileged communications are a vital part of the attorney, paralegal and client relationship. The importance of preserving confidential and privileged information is understood to be an uncompromising obligation of every paralegal.

V. SUPPORT OF PUBLIC INTERESTS

A paralegal shall serve the public interests by contributing to the availability and delivery of quality legal services.

Discussion: It is the responsibility of each paralegal to promote the development and implementation of programs that address the legal needs of the public. A paralegal shall strive to maintain a sensitivity to public needs and educate the public as to the services that paralegals may render.

VI. PROFESSIONAL DEVELOPMENT

A paralegal shall promote the development of the paralegal profession.

Discussion: This Affirmation of Professional Responsibility promulgates a positive attitude through which a paralegal may recognize the importance, responsibility, and potential of the paralegal contribution to the delivery of legal services. Participation in professional associations enhances the ability of the individual paralegal to contribute to the quality and growth of the paralegal profession.

Courtesy of National Federation of Paralegal Associations, Inc. All rights reserved.

APPENDIX D

THE CONSTITUTION OF THE UNITED STATES OF AMERICA

We the People of the United States, in Order to form a more perfect Union, establish Justice, insure domestic Tranquility, provide for the common defence, promote the general Welfare, and secure the Blessings of Liberty to ourselves and our Posterity, do ordain and establish this Constitution for the United States of America.

ARTICLE I

Section 1 All legislative Powers herein granted shall be vested in a Congress of the United States, which shall consist of a Senate and House of Representatives.

Section 2 (1) The House of Representatives shall be composed of Members chosen every second Year by the People of the several States, and the Electors in each State shall have the Qualifications requisite for Electors of the most numerous Branch of the State Legislature.

(2) No Person shall be a Representative who shall not have attained to the age of twenty-five Years, and been seven Years a Citizen of the United States, and who shall not, when elected, be an Inhabitant of that State in which he shall be chosen.

(3) Representatives and direct Taxes shall be apportioned among the several States which may be included within this Union, according to their respective Numbers, which shall be determined by adding to the whole Number of free Persons, including those bound to Service for a Term of Years, and excluding Indians not taxed, three fifths of all other Persons. The actual Enumeration shall be made within three Years after the first Meeting of the Congress of the United States, and within every subsequent Term of ten Years, in such Manner as they shall by Law direct. The Number of Representatives shall not exceed one for every thirty Thousand, but each State shall have at Least one Representative; and until such enumeration shall be made, the State of New Hampshire shall be entitled to chuse three, Massachusetts eight, Rhode Island and Providence Plantations one, Connecticut five, New York six, New Jersey four, Pennsylvania eight, Delaware one, Maryland six, Virginia ten, North Carolina five, South Carolina five, and Georgia three.

(4) When vacancies happen in the Representation from any State, the Executive Authority thereof shall issue Writs of Election to fill such Vacancies.

(5) The House of Representatives shall chuse their Speaker and other Officers; and shall have the sole Power of Impeachment.

Section 3 (1) The Senate of the United States shall be composed of two Senators from each State, chosen by the Legislature thereof, for six Years; and each Senator shall have one Vote.

(2) Immediately after they shall be assembled in Consequence of the first Election, they shall be divided as equally as may be into three Classes. The Seats of the Senators of the first Class shall be vacated at the Expiration of the second Year, of the second Class at the Expiration of the fourth Year, and of the third Class at the Expiration of the sixth Year, so that one third may be chosen every second Year; and if Vacancies happen by Resignation, or otherwise, during the Recess of the Legislature of any State, the Executive thereof may make temporary Appointments until the next Meeting of the Legislature, which shall then fill such Vacancies.

(3) No Person shall be a Senator who shall not have attained to the Age of thirty Years, and been nine Years a Citizen of the United States, and who shall not, when elected, be an Inhabitant of that State for which he shall be chosen.

(4) The Vice President of the United States shall be President of the Senate, but shall have no Vote, unless they be equally divided.

(5) The Senate shall chuse their other Officers, and also a President pro tempore, in the Absence of the Vice President, or when he shall exercise the Office of the President of the United States.

(6) The Senate shall have the sole Power to try all Impeachments. When sitting for that Purpose, they shall be on Oath or Affirmation. When the President of the United States is tried, the Chief Justice shall preside: And no Person shall be convicted without the Concurrence of two thirds of the Members present.

(7) Judgment in Cases of Impeachment shall not extend further than to removal from Office, and disqualification to hold and enjoy any Office of honor, Trust or Profit under the United States: but the Party convicted shall nevertheless be liable and subject to Indictment, Trial, Judgment and Punishment, according to Law.

Section 4   (1) The Times, Places and Manner of holding Elections for Senators and Representatives, shall be prescribed in each State by the Legislature thereof; but the Congress may at any time by Law make or alter such Regulations, except as to the Places of chusing Senators.

(2) The Congress shall assemble at least once in every Year, and such Meeting shall be on the first Monday in December, unless they shall by Law appoint a different Day.

Section 5   (1) Each House shall be the Judge of the Elections, Returns and Qualifications of its own Members, and a Majority of each shall constitute a Quorum to do Business; but a smaller Number may adjourn from day to day, and may be authorized to compel the Attendance of absent Members, in such Manner, and under such Penalties as each House may provide.

(2) Each House may determine the Rules of its Proceedings, punish its Members for disorderly Behaviour, and, with the Concurrence of two thirds, expel a Member.

(3) Each House shall keep a Journal of its Proceedings, and from time to time publish the same, excepting such Parts as may in their Judgment require Secrecy; and the Yeas and Nays of the Members of either House on any question shall, at the Desire of one fifth of those Present, be entered on the Journal.

(4) Neither House, during the Session of Congress, shall, without the Consent of the other, adjourn for more than three days, nor to any other Place than that in which the two Houses shall be sitting.

Section 6   (1) The Senators and Representatives shall receive a Compensation for their Services, to be ascertained by Law, and paid out of the Treasury of the United States. They shall in all Cases, except Treason, Felony and Breach of the Peace, be privileged from Arrest during their Attendance at the Session of their respective Houses, and in going to and returning from the same; and for any Speech or Debate in either House, they shall not be questioned in any other Place.

(2) No Senator or Representative shall, during the Time for which he was elected, be appointed to any civil Office under the Authority of the United States, which shall have been created, or the Emoluments whereof shall have been encreased during such time; and no Person holding any Office under the United States, shall be a Member of either House during his Continuance in Office.

Section 7   (1) All Bills for raising Revenue shall originate in the House of Representatives; but the Senate may propose or concur with Amendments as on other Bills.

(2) Every Bill which shall have passed the House of Representatives and the Senate, shall, before it become a Law, be presented to the President of the United States; If he approve he shall sign it, but if not he shall return it, with his Objections to that House in which it shall have originated, who shall enter the Objections at large on their Journal, and proceed to reconsider it. If after such Reconsideration two thirds of that House shall agree to pass the Bill, it shall be sent, together with the Objections, to the other House, by which it shall likewise be reconsidered, and if approved by two thirds of that House, it shall become a law. But in all such Cases the Votes of both Houses shall be determined by Yeas and Nays, and the Names of the Persons voting for and against the Bill shall be entered on the Journal of each House respectively.

If any Bill shall not be returned by the President within ten Days (Sunday excepted) after it shall have been presented to him, the Same shall be a Law, in like Manner as if he had signed it, unless the Congress by their Adjournment prevent its Return, in which Case it shall not be a Law.

(3) Every Order, Resolution, or Vote to which the Concurrence of the Senate and House of Representatives may be necessary (except on a question of Adjournment) shall be presented to the President of the United States; and before the Same shall take Effect, shall be approved by him, or being disapproved by him, shall be repassed by two thirds of the Senate and House of Representatives, according to the Rules and Limitations prescribed in the Case of a Bill.

Section 8 (1) The Congress shall have Power To lay and collect Taxes, Duties, Imposts and Excises, to pay the Debts and provide for the common Defence and general Welfare of the United States; but all Duties, Imposts and Excises shall be uniform throughout the United States;

(2) To borrow Money on the credit of the United States;

(3) To regulate Commerce with foreign Nations, and among the several States, and with the Indian Tribes;

(4) To establish an uniform Rule of Naturalization, and uniform Laws on the subject of Bankruptcies throughout the United States;

(5) To coin Money, regulate the Value thereof, and of foreign Coin, and to fix the Standard of Weights and Measures;

(6) To provide for the Punishment of counterfeiting the Securities and current Coin of the United States;

(7) To establish Post Offices and post Roads;

(8) To promote the Progress of Science and useful Arts, by securing for limited Times to Authors and Inventors the exclusive Right to their respective Writings and Discoveries;

(9) To constitute Tribunals inferior to the supreme Court;

(10) To define and punish Piracies and Felonies committed on the high Seas, and Offenses against the Law of Nations;

(11) To declare War, grant Letters of Marque and Reprisal, and make Rules concerning Captures on Land and Water;

(12) To raise and support Armies, but no Appropriation of Money to that Use shall be for a longer Term than two Years;

(13) To provide and maintain a Navy;

(14) To make Rules for the Government and Regulation of the land and naval Forces;

(15) To provide for calling forth the Militia to execute the Laws of the Union, suppress Insurrections and repel Invasions;

(16) To provide for organizing, arming, and disciplining, the Militia, and for governing such Part of them as may be employed in the Service of the United States, reserving to the States respectively, the Appointment of the Officers, and the Authority of training the Militia according to the discipline prescribed by Congress;

(17) To exercise exclusive Legislation in all Cases whatsoever, over such District (not exceeding ten Miles square) as may, by Cession of particular States, and the Acceptance of Congress, become the Seat of the Government of the United States, and to exercise like Authority over all Places purchased by the Consent of the Legislature of the State in which the Same shall be, for the Erection of Forts, Magazines, Arsenals, dock-Yards, and other needful Buildings;—And

(18) To make all Laws which shall be necessary and proper for carrying into Execution the foregoing Powers, and all other Powers vested by this Constitution in the Government of the United States, or in any Department or Officer thereof.

Section 9 (1) The Migration or Importation of such Persons as any of the States now existing shall think proper to admit, shall not be prohibited by the Congress prior to the Year one thousand eight hundred and eight, but a Tax or Duty may be imposed on such Importation, not exceeding ten dollars for each Person.

(2) The Privilege of the Writ of Habeas Corpus shall not be suspended unless when in Cases of Rebellion or Invasion the public Safety may require it.

(3) No Bill of Attainder or ex post facto Law shall be passed.

(4) No Capitation, or other direct, Tax shall be laid, unless in Proportion to the Census or Enumeration herein before directed to be taken.

(5) No Tax or Duty shall be laid on Articles exported from any State.

(6) No Preference shall be given by any Regulation of Commerce or Revenue to the Ports of one State over those of another; nor shall Vessels bound to, or from, one State, be obliged to enter, clear or pay Duties in another.

(7) No Money shall be drawn from the Treasury, but in Consequence of Appropriations made by Law; and a regular Statement and Account of the Receipts and Expenditures of all public Money shall be published from time to time.

(8) No Title of Nobility shall be granted by the United States: And no Person holding any Office of Profit or Trust under them, shall, without the Consent of the Congress, accept of any present, Emolument, Office, or Title, of any kind whatever, from any King, Prince or foreign State.

Section 10 (1) No State shall enter into any Treaty, Alliance, or Confederation; grant Letters of Marque and Reprisal; coin Money; emit Bills of Credit; make any Thing but gold and silver Coin a Tender in Payment of Debts; pass any Bill of Attainder, ex post facto Law, or Law impairing the Obligation of Contracts, or grant any Title of Nobility.

(2) No State shall, without the Consent of Congress, lay any Imposts or Duties on Imports or Exports, except what may be absolutely necessary for executing its inspection Laws: and the net Produce of all Duties and Imposts, laid by any State on Imports or Exports, shall be for the Use of the Treasury of the United States; and all such Laws shall be subject to the Revision and Controul of the Congress.

(3) No State shall, without the Consent of Congress, lay any Duty of Tonnage, keep Troops, or Ships of War in time of Peace, enter into any Agreement or Compact with another State, or with a foreign Power, or engage in War, unless actually invaded, or in such imminent Danger as will not admit of Delay.

ARTICLE II

Section 1 (1) The executive Power shall be vested in a President of the United States of America. He shall hold his Office during the Term of four Years, and, together with the Vice President, chosen for the same Term, be elected, as follows:

(2) Each State shall appoint, in such Manner as the Legislature thereof may direct, a Number of Electors, equal to the whole Number of Senators and Representatives to which the State may be entitled in the Congress: but no Senator or Representative, or Person holding an Office of Trust or Profit under the United States, shall be appointed an Elector.

The Electors shall meet in their respective States, and vote by Ballot for two Persons, of whom one at least shall not be an Inhabitant of the same State with themselves. And they shall make a List of all the Persons voted for, and of the Number of Votes for each; which List they shall sign and certify, and transmit sealed to the Seat of the Government of the United States, directed to the President of the Senate. The President of the Senate shall, in the presence of the Senate and House of Representatives, open all the Certificates, and the Votes shall then be counted. The Person having the greatest Number of Votes shall be the President, if such Number be a Majority of the whole Number of Electors appointed; and if there be more than one who have such Majority, and have an equal Number of Votes, then the House of Representatives shall immediately chuse by Ballot one of them for President; and if no Person have a Majority, then from the five highest on the List the said House shall in like Manner chuse the President. But in chusing the President, the Votes shall be taken by States, the Representation from each State having one Vote; a quorum for this Purpose shall consist of a Member or Members from two thirds of the States, and a Majority of all the States shall be necessary to a Choice. In every Case, after the Choice of the President, the Person having the greatest Number of Votes of the Electors shall be the Vice President. But if there should remain two or more who have equal Votes, the Senate shall chuse from them by Ballot the Vice President.

(3) The Congress may determine the Time of chusing the Electors, and the Day on which they shall give their Votes; which Day shall be the same throughout the United States.

(4) No Person except a natural born Citizen, or a Citizen of the United States, at the time of the Adoption of this Constitution, shall be eligible to the Office of President; neither shall any Person be eligible to that Office who shall not have attained to the Age of thirty five Years, and been fourteen Years a Resident within the United States.

(5) In Case of the Removal of the President from Office, or of his Death, Resignation, or Inability to discharge the Powers and Duties of the said Office, the Same shall devolve on the Vice President, and the Congress may by Law provide for the Case of Removal, Death, Resignation or Inability, both of the President and Vice President, declaring what Officer shall then act as President, and such Officer shall act accordingly, until the Disability be removed, or a President shall be elected.

(6) The President shall, at stated Times, receive for his Services, a Compensation, which shall neither be increased nor diminished during the Period for which he shall have been elected, and he shall not receive within that Period any other Emolument from the United States, or any of them.

(7) Before he enter on the Execution of his Office, he shall take the following Oath or Affirmation:—"I do solemnly swear (or affirm) that I will faithfully execute the Office of President of the United States, and will to the best of my Ability, preserve, protect and defend the Constitution of the United States."

Section 2 (1) The President shall be Commander in Chief of the Army and Navy of the United States, and of the Militia of the several States, when called into the actual Service of the United States; he may require the Opinion, in writing, of the principal Officer in each of the executive Departments, upon any Subject relating to the Duties of their respective Offices, and he shall have Power to grant Reprieves and Pardons for Offenses against the United States, except in Cases of Impeachment.

(2) He shall have Power, by and with the Advice and Consent of the Senate, to make Treaties, provided two thirds of the Senators present concur; and he shall nominate, and by and with the Advice and Consent of the Senate, shall appoint Ambassadors, other public Ministers and Consuls, Judges of the supreme Court, and all other Officers of the United States, whose Appointments are not herein otherwise provided for, and which shall be established by Law: but the Congress may by Law vest the Appointment of such inferior Officers, as they think proper, in the President alone, in the Courts of Law, or in the Heads of Departments.

(3) The President shall have Power to fill up all Vacancies that may happen during the Recess of the Senate, by granting Commissions which shall expire at the End of their next Session.

Section 3 He shall from time to time give to the Congress Information of the State of the Union, and recommend to their Consideration such Measures as he shall judge necessary and expedient; he may, on extraordinary Occasions, convene both Houses, or either of them, and in Case of Disagreement between them, with Respect to the Time of Adjournment, he may adjourn them to such Time as he shall think proper; he shall receive Ambassadors and other public Ministers; he shall take Care that the Laws be faithfully executed, and shall Commission all the Officers of the United States.

Section 4 The President, Vice President and all Civil Officers of the United States, shall be removed from Office on Impeachment for, and Conviction of, Treason, Bribery, or other high Crimes and Misdemeanors.

ARTICLE III

Section 1 The judicial Power of the United States, shall be vested in one supreme Court, and in such inferior Courts as the Congress may from time to time ordain and establish. The Judges, both of the supreme and inferior Courts, shall hold their Offices during good Behaviour, and shall, at stated Times, receive for their Services, a Compensation, which shall not be diminished during their Continuance in Office.

Section 2 (1) The judicial Power shall extend to all Cases, in Law and Equity, arising under this Constitution, the Laws of the United States, and Treaties made, or which shall be made, under their Authority;—to all Cases affecting Ambassadors, other public Ministers and Consuls;—to all Cases of admiralty and maritime Jurisdiction;—to Controversies to which the United States shall be a party;—to Controversies between two or more States;—between a State and Citizens of another State;—between Citizens of different States;—between Citizens of the same State claiming Lands under Grants of different States, and between a State, or the Citizens thereof, and foreign States, Citizens or Subjects.

(2) In all Cases affecting Ambassadors, other public Ministers and Consuls, and those in which a State shall be Party, the supreme Court shall have original Jurisdiction. In all the other Cases before mentioned, the supreme Court shall have appellate Jurisdiction, both as to Law and Fact, with such Exceptions, and under such Regulations as the Congress shall make.

(3) The Trial of all Crimes, except in Cases of Impeachment, shall be by Jury; and such Trial shall be held in the State where the said Crimes shall have been committed; but when not committed within any State, the Trial shall be at such Place or Places as the Congress may by Law have directed.

Section 3 (1) Treason against the United States, shall consist only in levying War against them, or in adhering to their Enemies, giving them Aid and Comfort. No Person shall be convicted of Treason unless on the Testimony of two Witnesses to the same overt Act, or on Confession in open Court.

(2) The Congress shall have Power to declare the Punishment of Treason, but no Attainder of Treason shall work Corruption of Blood, or Forfeiture except during the Life of the Person attainted.

ARTICLE IV

Section 1 Full Faith and Credit shall be given in each State to the public Acts, Records, and judicial Proceedings of every other State. And the Congress may by general Laws prescribe the

Manner in which such Acts, Records and Proceedings shall be proved, and the Effect thereof.

Section 2 (1) The Citizens of each State shall be entitled to all privileges and Immunities of Citizens in the several States.

(2) A Person charged in any State with Treason, Felony, or other Crime, who shall flee from Justice, and be found in another State, shall on Demand of the executive Authority of the State from which he fled, be delivered up, to be removed to the State having Jurisdiction of the Crime.

(3) No Person held to Service of Labour in one State, under the Laws thereof, escaping into another, shall, in Consequence of any Law or Regulation therein, be discharged from such Service or Labour, but shall be delivered up on Claim of the Party to whom such Service or Labour may be due.

Section 3 (1) New States may be admitted by the Congress into this Union; but no new State shall be formed or erected within the Jurisdiction of any other State; nor any State be formed by the Junction of two or more States, or Parts of States, without the Consent of the Legislatures of the States concerned as well as of the Congress.

(2) The Congress shall have power to dispose of and make all needful Rules and Regulations respecting the Territory or other Property belonging to the United States; and nothing in this Constitution shall be so construed as to Prejudice any Claims of the United States, or of any particular State.

Section 4 The United States shall guarantee to every State in this Union a Republican Form of Government, and shall protect each of them against Invasion; and on Application of the Legislature, or of the Executive (when the Legislature cannot be convened) against domestic Violence.

ARTICLE V

The Congress, whenever two thirds of both Houses shall deem it necessary, shall propose Amendments to this Constitution, or, on the Application of the Legislatures of two thirds of the several States, shall call a Convention for proposing Amendments, which, in either Case, shall be valid to all Intents and Purposes, as Part of this Constitution, when ratified by the Legislatures of three fourths of the several States, or by Conventions in three fourths thereof, as the one or the other Mode of Ratification may be proposed by the Congress; Provided that no Amendment which may be made prior to the Year One thousand eight hundred and eight shall in any Manner affect the first and fourth Clauses in the Ninth Section of the first Article; and that no State, without its Consent, shall be deprived of its equal Suffrage in the Senate.

ARTICLE VI

(1) All Debts contracted and Engagements entered into, before the Adoption of this Constitution, shall be as valid against the United States under this Constitution, as under the Confederation.

(2) This Constitution, and the Laws of the United States which shall be made in Pursuance thereof; and all Treaties made, or which shall be made, under the Authority of the United States, shall be the supreme Law of the Land; and the Judges in every State shall be bound thereby, any Thing in the Constitution or Laws of any State to the Contrary notwithstanding.

(3) The Senators and Representatives before mentioned, and the Members of the several State Legislatures, and all executive and judicial Officers, both of the United States and of the several States, shall be bound by Oath or Affirmation, to support this Constitution; but no religious Test shall ever be required as a Qualification to any Office or public Trust under the United States.

ARTICLE VII

The Ratification of the Conventions of nine States, shall be sufficient for the Establishment of this Constitution between the States so ratifying the Same.

ARTICLES IN ADDITION TO, AND AMENDMENT OF, THE CONSTITUTION OF THE UNITED STATES OF AMERICA,

PROPOSED BY CONGRESS, AND RATIFIED BY THE SEVERAL STATES, PURSUANT TO THE FIFTH ARTICLE OF THE ORIGINAL CONSTITUTION

AMENDMENT I (1791)

Congress shall make no law respecting an establishment of religion, or prohibiting the free exercise thereof; or abridging the freedom of speech, or of the press; or the right of the people peaceably to assemble, and to petition the Government for a redress of grievances.

AMENDMENT II (1791)

A well regulated Militia, being necessary to the security of a free state, the right of the people to keep and bear Arms, shall not be infringed.

AMENDMENT III (1791)

No Soldier shall, in time of peace be quartered in any house, without the consent of the Owner, nor in time of war, but in a manner to be prescribed by law.

AMENDMENT IV (1791)

The right of the people to be secure in their persons, houses, papers, and effects, against unreasonable searches and seizures, shall not be violated, and no Warrants shall issue, but upon probable cause, supported by Oath or affirmation, and particularly describing the place to be searched, and the persons or things to be seized.

AMENDMENT V (1791)

No person shall be held to answer for a capital, or otherwise infamous crime, unless on a presentment or indictment of a Grand Jury, except in cases arising in the land or naval forces, or in the Militia, when in actual service in time of War or public danger; nor shall any person be subject for the same offence to be twice put in jeopardy of life or limb; nor shall be compelled in any criminal case to be a witness against himself, nor be deprived of life, liberty, or property, without due process of law; nor shall private property be taken for public use, without just compensation.

AMENDMENT VI (1791)

In all criminal prosecutions, the accused shall enjoy the right to a speedy and public trial, by an impartial jury of the State and district wherein the crime shall have been committed, which district shall have been previously ascertained by law, and to be informed of the nature and cause of the accusation; to be confronted with the witnesses against him; to have compulsory process for obtaining witnesses in his favor, and to have the Assistance of Counsel for his defence.

AMENDMENT VII (1791)

In Suits at common law, where the value in controversy shall exceed twenty dollars, the right of trial by jury shall be preserved, and no fact tried by a jury, shall be otherwise re-examined in any Court of the United States, than according to the rules of the common law.

AMENDMENT VIII (1791)

Excessive bail shall not be required, nor excessive fines imposed, nor cruel and unusual punishments inflicted.

AMENDMENT IX (1791)

The enumeration in the Constitution, of certain rights, shall not be construed to deny or disparage others retained by the people.

AMENDMENT X (1791)

The powers not delegated to the United States by the Constitution, nor prohibited by it to the States, are reserved to the States respectively, or to the people.

AMENDMENT XI (1798)

The Judicial power of the United States shall not be construed to extend to any suit in law or equity, commenced or prosecuted against one of the United States by Citizens of another State, or by Citizens or Subjects of any Foreign State.

AMENDMENT XII (1804)

The Electors shall meet in their respective states and vote by ballot for President and Vice-President, one of whom, at least, shall not be an inhabitant of the same state with themselves; they shall name in their ballots the person voted for as President, and in distinct ballots the person voted for as Vice-President, and they shall make distinct lists of all persons voted for as President, and of all persons voted for as Vice-President, and of the number of votes for each, which lists they shall sign and certify, and transmit sealed to the seat of the government of the United States, directed to the President of the Senate;—The President of the Senate shall, in the presence of the Senate and House of Representatives, open all the certificates and the votes shall then be counted;—The person having the greatest number of votes for President, shall be the President, if such number be a majority of the whole number of Electors appointed; and if no person have such majority, then from the persons having the highest numbers not exceeding three on the list of those voted for as President, the House of Representatives shall choose immediately, by ballot, the President. But in choosing the President, the votes shall be taken by states, the representation from each state having one vote; a quorum for this purpose shall consist of a member or members from two-thirds of the states, and a majority of all the states shall be necessary to a choice. And if the House of Representatives shall not choose a President whenever the right of choice shall devolve upon them, before the fourth day of March next following, then the Vice-President shall act as President, as in the case of the death or other constitutional disability of the President—The person having the greatest number of votes as Vice-President, shall be the Vice-President, if such number be a majority of the whole number of Electors appointed, and if no person have a majority, then from the two highest numbers on the list, the Senate shall choose the Vice-President; A quorum for the purpose shall consist of two-thirds of the whole number of Senators, and a majority of the whole number shall be necessary to a choice. But no person constitutionally ineligible to the office of President shall be eligible to that of Vice-President of the United States.

AMENDMENT XIII (1865)

Section 1 Neither slavery nor involuntary servitude, except as a punishment for crime whereof the party shall have been duly convicted, shall exist within the United States, or any place subject to their jurisdiction.

Section 2 Congress shall have power to enforce this article by appropriate legislation.

AMENDMENT XIV (1868)

Section 1 All persons born or naturalized in the United States and subject to the jurisdiction thereof, are citizens of the United States and of the State wherein they reside. No State shall make or enforce any law which shall abridge the privileges or immunities of citizens of the United States; nor shall any State deprive any person of life, liberty, or property, without due process of law; nor deny to any person within its jurisdiction the equal protection of the laws.

Section 2 Representatives shall be apportioned among the several States according to their respective numbers, counting the whole number of persons in each State, excluding Indians not taxed. But when the right to vote at any election for the choice of electors for President and Vice-President of the United States, Representatives in Congress, the Executive and Judicial officers of a State, or the members of the Legislature thereof, is denied to any of the male inhabitants of such State, being twenty-one years of age, and citizens of the United States, or in any way abridged, except for participation in rebellion, or other crime, the basis of representation therein shall be reduced in the proportion which the number of such male citizens shall bear to the whole number of male citizens twenty-one years of age in such State.

Section 3 No person shall be a Senator or Representative in Congress, or elector of President and Vice-President, or hold any office, civil or military, under the United States, or under any State, who, having previously taken an oath, as a member of Congress, or as an officer of the United States, or as a member of any State legislature, or as an executive or judicial officer of any State, to support the Constitution of the United States, shall have engaged in insurrection or rebellion against the same, or given aid or comfort to the enemies thereof. But Congress may by a vote of two-thirds of each House, remove such disability.

Section 4 The validity of the public debt of the United States, authorized by law, including debts incurred for payment of pensions and bounties for services in suppressing insurrection or rebellion, shall not be questioned. But neither the United States nor any State shall assume or pay any debt or obligation incurred in aid of insurrection or rebellion against the United States, or any claim for the loss or emancipation of any slave; but all such debts, obligations and claims shall be held illegal and void.

Section 5 The Congress shall have power to enforce, by appropriate legislation, the provisions of this article.

AMENDMENT XV (1870)

Section 1 The right of citizens of the United States to vote shall not be denied or abridged by the United States or by any State on account of race, color, or previous condition of servitude.

Section 2 The Congress shall have power to enforce this article by appropriate legislation.

AMENDMENT XVI (1913)

The Congress shall have power to lay and collect taxes on incomes, from whatever source derived, without apportionment among the several States, and without regard to any census or enumeration.

AMENDMENT XVII (1913)

The Senate of the United States shall be composed of two Senators from each State, elected by the people thereof, for six years; and each Senator shall have one vote. The electors in each State shall have the qualifications requisite for electors of the most numerous branch of the State legislatures.

When vacancies happen in the representation of any State in the Senate, the executive authority of such State shall issue writs of election to fill such vacancies: *Provided,* That the legislature of any State may empower the executive thereof to make temporary appointments until the people fill the vacancies by election as the legislature may direct.

This amendment shall not be so construed as to affect the election or term of any Senator chosen before it becomes valid as part of the Constitution.

AMENDMENT XVIII (1919)

Section 1 After one year from the ratification of this article the manufacture, sale, or transportation of intoxicating liquors within, the importation thereof into, or the exportation thereof from the United States and all territory subject to the jurisdiction thereof for beverage purposes is hereby prohibited.

Section 2 The Congress and the several States shall have concurrent power to enforce this article by appropriate legislation.

Section 3 This article shall be inoperative unless it shall have been ratified as an amendment to the Constitution by the legislatures of the several States, as provided in the Constitution, within seven years from the date of the submission hereof to the States by the Congress.

AMENDMENT XIX (1920)

The right of citizens of the United States to vote shall not be denied or abridged by the United States or by any State on account of sex.

Congress shall have power to enforce this article by appropriate legislation.

AMENDMENT XX (1933)

Section 1 The terms of the President and Vice President shall end at noon on the 20th day of January, and the terms of Senators and Representatives at noon on the 3d day of January, of the years in which such terms would have ended if this article had not been ratified; and the terms of their successors shall then begin.

Section 2 The Congress shall assemble at least once in every year, and such meeting shall begin at noon on the 3d day of January, unless they shall by law appoint a different day.

Section 3 If, at the time fixed for the beginning of the term of the President, the President elect shall have died, the Vice President elect shall become President. If a President shall not have been chosen before the time fixed for the beginning of his term, or if the President elect shall have failed to qualify, then the Vice President elect shall act as President until a President shall have qualified; and the Congress may by law provide for the case wherein neither a President elect nor a Vice President elect shall have qualified, declaring who shall then act as President, or the manner in which one who is to act shall be selected, and such person shall act accordingly until a President or Vice President shall have qualified.

Section 4 The Congress may by law provide for the case of the death of any of the persons from whom the House of Representatives may choose a President whenever the right of choice shall have devolved upon them, and for the case of the death of any of the persons from whom the Senate may choose a Vice President whenever the right of choice shall have devolved upon them.

Section 5 Sections 1 and 2 shall take effect on the 15th day of October following the ratification of this article.

Section 6 This article shall be inoperative unless it shall have been ratified as an amendment to the Constitution by the legislatures of three-fourths of the several States within seven years from the date of its submission.

AMENDMENT XXI (1933)

Section 1 The eighteenth article of amendment to the Constitution of the United States is hereby repealed.

Section 2 The transportation or importation into any State, Territory or possession of the United States for delivery or use therein of intoxicating liquors, in violation of the laws thereof, is hereby prohibited.

Section 3 This article shall be inoperative unless it shall have been ratified as an amendment to the Constitution by conventions in the several States, as provided in the Constitution, within seven years from the date of the submission hereof to the States by the Congress.

AMENDMENT XXII (1951)

Section 1 No person shall be elected to the office of the President more than twice, and no person who has held the office of President, or acted as President, for more than two years of a term to which some other person was elected President shall be elected to the office of the President more than once. But this Article shall not apply to any person holding the office of President when this Article was proposed by the Congress, and shall not prevent any person who may be holding the office of President, or acting as President, during the term within which this Article becomes operative from holding the office of President or acting as President during the remainder of such term.

Section 2 This Article shall be inoperative unless it shall have been ratified as an amendment to the Constitution by the legislatures of three-fourths of the several States within seven years from the date of its submission to the States by the Congress.

AMENDMENT XXIII (1961)

Section 1 The District constituting the seat of Government of the United States shall appoint in such manner as the Congress may direct:

A number of electors of President and Vice President equal to the whole number of Senators and Representatives in Congress to which the District would be entitled if it were a State, but in no event more than the least populous State; they shall be in addition to those appointed by the States, but they shall be considered, for the purposes of the election of President and Vice President, to be electors appointed by a State; and they shall meet in the District and perform such duties as provided by the twelfth article of amendment.

Section 2 The Congress shall have power to enforce this article by appropriate legislation.

AMENDMENT XXIV (1964)

Section 1 The right of citizens of the United States to vote in any primary or other election for President or Vice President, for electors for President or Vice President, or for Senator or Representative in Congress, shall not be denied or abridged by the United States or any State by reason of failure to pay any poll tax or other tax.

Section 2 The Congress shall have power to enforce this article by appropriate legislation.

AMENDMENT XXV (1967)

Section 1 In case of the removal of the President from office or of his death or resignation, the Vice President shall become President.

Section 2 Whenever there is a vacancy in the office of the Vice President, the President shall nominate a Vice President who shall take office upon confirmation by a majority vote of both Houses of Congress.

Section 3 Whenever the President transmits to the President pro tempore of the Senate and the Speaker of the House of Representatives his written declaration that he is unable to discharge the powers and duties of his office, and until he transmits to them a written declaration to the contrary, such powers and duties shall be discharged by the Vice President as Acting President.

Section 4   Whenever the Vice President and a majority of either the principal officers of the executive departments or of such other body as Congress may by law provide, transmit to the President pro tempore of the Senate and the Speaker of the House of Representatives their written declaration that the President is unable to discharge the powers and duties of his office, the Vice President shall immediately assume the powers and duties of the office as Acting President.

Thereafter, when the President transmits to the President pro tempore of the Senate and the Speaker of the House of Representatives his written declaration that no inability exists, he shall resume the powers and duties of his office unless the Vice President and a majority of either the principal officers of the executive department or of such other body as Congress may by law provide, transmit within four days to the President pro tempore of the Senate and the Speaker of the House of Representatives their written declaration that the President is unable to discharge the powers and duties of his office. Thereupon Congress shall decide the issue, assembling within forty-eight hours for that purpose if not in session. If the Congress, within twenty-one days af-

ter receipt of the latter written declaration, or, if Congress is not in session, within twenty-one days after Congress is required to assemble, determines by two-thirds vote of both Houses that the President is unable to discharge the powers and duties of his office, the Vice President shall continue to discharge the same as Acting President; otherwise, the President shall resume the powers and duties of his office.

AMENDMENT XXVI (1971)

Section 1   The right of citizens of the United States, who are eighteen years of age or older, to vote shall not be denied or abridged by the United States or by any State on account of age.

Section 2   The Congress shall have power to enforce this article by appropriate legislation.

AMENDMENT XXVII (1992)

No law varying the compensation for the services of the senators and representatives shall take effect, until an election of representatives shall have intervened.

GLOSSARY

absolute liability   Liability for an injury whether or not there is fault or negligence.

adjudication   The final decision of a court, usually made after trial of the case; the court's final judgment.

admiralty   The body of law that regulates the conduct of affairs on navigable waters.

adversary system   The system of justice in the United States. Under the adversary system, the court hears the evidence presented by adverse parties and decides the case.

adverse possession   The act of occupying real property in an "open, notorious, and hostile manner," under a claim of right, contrary to the interests of the true owner.

alimony   Ongoing court-ordered support payments by a divorced spouse. ... Alimony is not child support.

anticipatory breach   The announced intention of a party to a contract that he or she does not intend to perform his or her obligations under the contract; an announced intention to commit a breach of contract.

appellant   A party who appeals from a lower court to a higher court.

appellee   A party against whom a case is appealed from a lower court to a higher court.

assault   An act of force or threat of force intended to inflict harm upon a person or to put the person in fear that such harm is imminent; an attempt to commit a battery. The perpetrator must have, or appear to have, the present ability to carry out the act.

associate   A person engaged in the practice of law with another attorney or attorneys, but not as a partner or member of the firm.

assumption of risk   The legal principle that a person who knows and deliberately exposes himself or herself to a danger assumes responsibility for the risk, rather than the person who actually created the danger.

attachment   The process by which a person's property is figuratively brought into court to ensure satisfaction of a judgment that may be rendered against him or her. In the event judgment is rendered, the property may be sold to satisfy the judgment.

attorney-client privilege   Most information a client tells his or her attorney in connection with his or her case cannot be disclosed by the attorney, or anyone employed by the attorney or the attorney's firm, without the client's permission.

bailiff   A court attendant charged with maintaining order in the courtroom.

bailment   The entrusting of personal property by one person (the bailor) to another (the bailee) for a specific purpose, with the understanding that the property will be returned when the purpose is accomplished, the stated duration of the bailment is over, or the bailor reclaims it.

bankruptcy   The system under which a debtor may come into court or be brought into court by his or her creditors, either seeking to have [the debtor's] assets administered and sold for the benefit of his or her creditors and to be discharged from his or her debts, or to have his or her debts reorganized.

battery   The unconsented-to touching or striking of one person by another, or by an object put in motion by him or her, with the intention of doing harm or giving offense. Battery is both a crime and a tort.

bicameral   Two-chambered, referring to the customary division of a legislature into two houses (a Senate and a House of Representatives).

black letter law   Fundamental and well-established rules of law.

breach of contract   Failure, without legal excuse, to perform any promise that forms a whole or a part of a contract, including the doing of something inconsistent with its terms.

brief   A written statement submitted to a court for the purpose of persuading it of the correctness of one's position. A brief argues the facts of the case and the applicable law, supported by citations of authority.

bureaucracy   The operation of government by bureaus and departments directed by levels of officials rigidly following rules and routines.

canon law   Christian religious law, particularly that of the Roman Catholic church.

capitalism   An economic system in which production (manufacturing, agriculture) and distribution (transportation) are privately owned and carried on for profit.

certificate of deposit   A voucher issued by a bank acknowledging the receipt of money on deposit which the bank promises to repay to the depositor.

certiorari   (Latin) A writ issued by a higher court to a lower court requiring the certification of the record in a particular case so that the higher court can review the record and correct any actions taken in the case which are not in accordance with the law. The Supreme Court of the United States uses the writ of certiorari to select the state court cases it is willing to review. Commonly referred to as "cert."

chain of title   The succession of transactions through which title to a given piece of land was passed from person to person from its origins to the present day.

check   A written order directed to a bank to pay money to the person named.

child support   1. Money paid, pending divorce and after divorce, by one parent to the other for the support of their children. 2. The obligation of parents to provide their children with the necessities of life.

civil procedure   The rules of procedure by which private rights are enforced; the rules by which civil actions are governed.

class action   An action brought by one or several plaintiffs on behalf of a class of persons. A class action may be appropriate when there has been injury to so many people that their voluntarily and unanimously joining in a lawsuit is improbable and impracticable. In such a situation, injured parties who wish to do so may, with the court's permission, sue on behalf of all. A class action is sometimes referred to as a *representative action.*

clearly erroneous   A standard by which a trial court's findings of fact are reviewed. An appellate court will not set aside a trial court's findings of fact unless they are "clearly erroneous."

clerkship   Employment of a law student or a graduate attorney as a clerk by a licensed attorney or a judge.

closing   Completing a transaction, particularly a contract for the sale of real estate.

codification   1. The process of arranging laws in a systematic form covering the entire law of a jurisdiction or a particular area of the law; the process of creating a code. 2. The process of turning a common law rule into a statute.

collateral   Stocks, bonds, or other property that serve as security for a loan or other obligation; property pledged to pay a debt.

communism   An economic system in which the state owns the means of production (manufacturing, agriculture, transportation) and in which, in theory, every citizen participates in production according to his or her ability and shares in what has been produced according to his or her need. A primary distinction between communism and socialism is that the former is almost universally totalitarian and the latter generally democratic in greater or lesser degree.

community property A system of law under which the earnings of either spouse are the property of both the husband and the wife, and property acquired by either spouse during the marriage (other than by gift, under a will, or through inheritance) is the property of both.

compensatory damages Damages recoverable in a lawsuit for loss or injury suffered by the plaintiff as a result of the defendant's conduct. Also called *actual damages*, they may include expenses, loss of time, reduced earning capacity, bodily injury, and mental anguish.

conflict of laws (choice of laws) Area of the law that determines whether the law of some other state or country will be applied in a circumstance where the laws of more than one jurisdiction could apply and are in opposition to each other.

contingent (contingency) fee A fee for legal services, calculated on the basis of an agreed-upon percentage of the amount of money recovered for the client by his or her attorney.

contract An agreement entered into, for adequate consideration, to do, or refrain from doing, a particular thing. The Uniform Commercial Code defines a contract as the total legal obligation resulting from the parties' agreement.

convey To transfer title to property from one person to another by deed, bill of sale, or other conveyance.

copyright The right of an author, granted by federal statute, to exclusively control the reproduction, distribution, and sale of his or her literary, artistic, or intellectual productions for the period of the copyright's existence. Copyright protection extends to written work, music, films, sound recordings, photographs, paintings, sculpture, and some computer programs and chips.

corporation An artificial person, existing only in the eyes of the law, to whom a state or the federal government has granted a charter to become a legal entity, separate from its shareholders, with a name of its own, under which its shareholders can act and contract and sue and be sued. A corporation's shareholders, officers, and directors are not normally liable for the acts of the corporation.

counterclaim A cause of action on which a defendant in a lawsuit might have sued the plaintiff in a separate action … [,] stated in a separate division of a defendant's answer … .

court reporter A person who stenographically or by "voice writing" records court proceedings, from which, when necessary, he or she prepares a transcript that becomes a part of the record in the case.

criminal procedure The rules of procedure by which criminal prosecutions are governed.

cross-appeal An appeal filed by the appellee from the same judgment, or some portion of the same judgment, as the appellant has appealed from.

curtesy The rights a husband had under the common law with respect to his wife's property. Today these rights have been modified in every state in various ways, but all states that retain curtesy in some form extend the same rights to both spouses.

custody As applied to persons, physical control. … Custody carries with it the obligation on the part of the custodian to maintain and care for the person in his charge for the duration of their relationship.

decedent A legal term for a person who has died.

decedent's estate The total property, real or personal, that a decedent owns at the time of his or her death.

deed A document by which real property, or an interest in real property, is conveyed from one person to another.

defamation Libel or slander; the written or oral publication, falsely and intentionally, of anything that is injurious to the good name or reputation of another person.

default judgment A judgment rendered in favor of a plaintiff based upon a defendant's failure to take a necessary step in a lawsuit within the required time.

defense In both civil and criminal cases, the facts submitted and the legal arguments offered by a defendant in support of his or her claim that the plaintiff's case, or the prosecution's, should be rejected. The term "defense" may apply to a defendant's entire case or to separate grounds, called *affirmative defenses,* offered by a defendant for rejecting all or a portion of the case against him or her.

deter To discourage; to prevent from acting.

dicta Plural of *dictum,* which is short for ... *obiter dictum.* Dicta are expressions or comments in a court opinion that are not necessary to support the decision made by the court; they are not binding authority and have no value as precedent. If nothing else can be found on point, an advocate may wish to attempt to persuade by citing cases that contain dicta.

disbarment The revocation of an attorney's right to practice law.

discovery A means for providing a party, in advance of trial, with access to facts that are within the knowledge of the other side, to enable the party to better try his or her case.

docket A list of cases for trial or other disposition; a court calendar.

domestic relations The field of law relating to domestic matters, such as marriage, divorce, support, custody, and adoption; family law.

dower The legal right or interest that a wife acquires by marriage in the property of her husband. ... Dower, as such, no longer exists or has been substantially modified in most states, but every state retains aspects of the concept for the protection of both spouses.

draft An order in writing by one person on another (commonly a bank) to pay a specified sum of money to a third person on demand or at a stated future time.

due process clause Actually a reference to two due process clauses, one in the Fifth Amendment and one in the Fourteenth Amendment. The Fifth Amendment requires the federal government to accord "due process of law" to citizens of the United States; the Fourteenth Amendment imposes a similar requirement upon state governments.

easement A right to use the land of another for a specific purpose.

ejectment An action at common law for the right to possession of land.

elective share In some states, the share a surviving spouse may elect to take in the estate of the deceased spouse. In such jurisdictions, it replaces dower. An elective share is also referred to as a *statutory share.*

emancipated minor A person who has not yet attained the age of majority who is totally self-supporting or married. A parent emancipates [a] minor child when he or she surrenders control and authority over the child and gives [the child] the right to [the child's] earnings. Emancipation also terminates the parent's legal duty to support the minor child.

eminent domain The power of the government to take private property for a public use or public purpose without the owner's consent, if it pays just compensation.

entire output contract A contract in which the seller binds itself to the buyer to sell to the buyer the entire output of a product [the seller] manufactures, and the buyer binds itself to buy all of the product.

equitable distribution Some jurisdictions permit their courts, in a divorce case, to distribute all property obtained during the marriage on an "equitable" basis, that is, without regard to whose name the property is in. In deciding what is equitable, the court takes into consideration factors such as the length of the marriage and the contributions of each party, including homemaking.

equitable estoppel (estoppel in pais)   [A] term applied to a situation in which a party is denied the right to plead or prove a fact because of something he or she has done or has failed to do.

estate   The right, title, and interest a person has in real or personal property, either tangible or intangible.

evidentiary facts   Facts admissible in evidence.

executory contract   A contract yet to be performed, each party having bound himself or herself to do or not to do a particular thing.

finding of fact   A conclusion with respect to disputed facts in a legal action, reasoned or inferred from the evidence.

foreclosure   1. A legal action by which a mortgagee terminates a mortgagor's interest in mortgaged premises. 2. The enforcement of a lien, deed of trust, or mortgage on real estate, or a security interest in personal property, by any method provided by law.

foster parent   A person who rears a foster child.

garnishment   A proceeding by a creditor to obtain satisfaction of a debt from money or property of the debtor which is in the possession of a third person or is owed by such a person to the debtor.

grantee   The person to whom a grant is made; the party in a deed to whom the conveyance is made.

grantor   The person who makes a grant; the party in a deed who makes the conveyance.

hedonic damages (losses)   Damages awarded by some courts for loss of enjoyment of life or of life's pleasures.

house counsel   An attorney who represents a single client, usually on a full-time basis.

implied contract   Implied contracts are of two types: *contracts implied in fact,* which the law infers from the circumstances, conduct, acts, or the relationship of the parties rather than from their spoken words; and *contracts implied in law,* which are quasi contracts or constructive contracts imposed by the law, usually to prevent unjust enrichment.

implied warranty   In the sale of personal property, a warranty by the seller, inferred by law (whether or not the seller intended to create the warranty), as to the quality or condition of the goods sold.

Under the Uniform Commercial Code, the most important implied warranties are the implied warranty of merchantability and the implied warranty of fitness for a particular purpose. In any sale of goods, a warranty of merchantability (fitness for general or customary purposes) is implied if the seller normally sells such goods. An implied warranty of fitness for a particular purpose exists when the seller has reason to know the purpose for which the buyer wants the goods and the buyer is relying on the seller to furnish goods suited to that purpose.

Inns of Court   For centuries, English lawyers were trained in the Inns of Court, where students learned the law in association with legal scholars, lawyers, and judges. (The reputation of these institutions had its ups and downs, at times appearing more like young gentlemen's clubs than legal institutions.) English lawyers are divided into two groups: *barristers,* roughly equivalent to our trial lawyers, and the more numerous *solicitors,* who handle legal matters other than trial work. The Inns of Court were the traditional training ground for barristers.

integrated bar   A type of involuntary bar association that exists in some states, to which all attorneys practicing in the state must belong. Created by statute or rule of court, it is, in effect, a governmental body.

interrogatories   Written questions put by one party to another, or, in limited situations, to a witness in advance of trial. Interrogatories are a form of discovery and are governed by the rules of civil procedure.

jurisprudence   The science of law; legal philosophy.

Justice   The title of a judge, especially the judge of an appellate court.

law merchant   A term referring to the law governing transactions between merchants, which evolved over many years as a part of the English common law.

law reviews   A publication containing articles by law professors and other authorities, with respect to legal issues of current interest, and summaries of significant recent cases, written by law students.

lease   A contract for the possession of real estate in consideration of payment of rent, ordinarily for a term of years or months, but sometimes at will.

legislation   Laws ... enacted by a legislative body ... .

lessee   The person receiving the right of possession of real property, or possession and use of personal property, under a lease. A lessee of real estate is also known as a tenant.

lessor   The person conferring the right of possession of real property, or possession and use of personal property, under a lease. A lessor of real estate is also known as a landlord.

litigation   A legal action; a lawsuit.

long-arm statutes   State statutes providing for substituted service of process on a nonresident corporation or individual. Long-arm statutes permit a state's courts to take jurisdiction over a nonresident if he or she has done business in the state (provided the minimum contacts test is met), or has committed a tort or owns property within the state.

lump-sum alimony   An award of alimony in gross, that is, an award of one lump sum to be paid either in installments or as a lump sum.

malicious prosecution   A criminal prosecution or civil suit commenced maliciously and without probable cause. After the termination of such a prosecution or suit in the defendant's favor, the defendant has the right to bring an action against the original plaintiff for the tort of "malicious prosecution."

malpractice   The failure of a professional person to act with reasonable care; misconduct by a professional person in the course of engaging in his or her profession.

mandamus   (Latin) Means "we command." A writ issuing from a court of competent jurisdiction, directed to an inferior court, board, or corporation, or to an officer of a branch of government (judicial, executive, or legislative), requiring the performance of some ministerial act.

marital agreement   An agreement between two people who are married to each other ... , with respect to the disposition of the marital property or property owned by either spouse before the marriage, with respect to the rights of either in the property of the other, or with respect to support.

mechanic's lien   A lien created by law for the purpose of securing payment for work performed or materials furnished in constructing or repairing a building or other structure.

medical malpractice   A physician's negligent failure to observe the appropriate standard of care in providing services to a patient; also, misconduct while engaging in the practice of medicine.

memorandum decision   A court decision, usually consisting of a brief paragraph announcing the court's judgment, without an in-depth opinion.

mortgage   A pledge of real property to secure a debt. Which one of at least three possible legal principles defines the rights of the parties to a given mortgage depends upon the state in which the mortgaged property is located. In states that have adopted the lien theory, the mortgagee (creditor) has a lien on the property;

the mortgagor (debtor) retains legal title and is entitled to possession unless his or her interest is terminated by a foreclosure decree. In title theory states, a mortgage transfers title and a theoretical right of possession to the mortgagee; title reverts to the mortgagor upon full payment of the mortgage debt. A third group of states employs hybrid versions of the lien and title theories, with characteristics of both.

negligence   The failure to do something that a reasonable person would do in the same circumstances, or the doing of something a reasonable person would not do. Negligence is a wrong generally characterized by carelessness, inattentiveness, and neglectfulness rather than by a positive intent to cause injury.

no-fault divorce   A term for the requirements for divorce in jurisdictions in which the party seeking the divorce need not demonstrate that the other party is at fault. The requirements differ from state to state.

nuisance   Anything a person does that annoys or disturbs another person in his or her use, possession, or enjoyment of his or her property, or which renders the ordinary use or possession of the property uncomfortable.

ordinance   A law of a municipal corporation; a local law enacted by a city council, town council, board of supervisors, or the like.

partnership   An undertaking of two or more persons to carry on, as coowners, a business or other enterprise for profit; an agreement between or among two or more persons to put their money, labor, and skill into commerce or business, and to divide the profit in agreed-upon proportions. Partnerships may be formed by entities as well as individuals.

patent   The exclusive right of manufacture, sale, or use granted by the federal government to a person who invents or discovers a device or process that is new and useful.

per curiam opinion   An opinion, usually of an appellate court, in which the judges are all of

one view and the legal question is sufficiently clear that a full written opinion is not required and a one- or two-paragraph opinion suffices.

perjury   Giving false testimony in a judicial proceeding or an administrative proceeding; lying under oath as to a material fact; swearing to the truth of anything one knows or believes to be false.

physical evidence   Evidence other than testimony; demonstrative evidence.

plea bargain   An agreement between the prosecutor and a criminal defendant under which the accused agrees to plead guilty, usually to a lesser offense, in exchange for receiving a lighter sentence than he or she would likely have received had he or she been found guilty after trial on the original charge.

pleadings   Formal statements by the parties to an action setting forth their claims or defenses.

possession   Occupancy and dominion over property; a holding of land legally, by one's self (actual possession) or through another person such as a tenant (constructive possession). The holding may be by virtue of having title or an estate or interest of any kind.

prejudicial   Detrimental to a party or person or to his or her interests.

privity of contract   The legal relationship between the parties to a contract. In some circumstances, a party must be in privity of contract with another party in order to assert a claim.

pro se   Means "for one's self." Refers to appearing on one's own behalf in either a civil action or a criminal prosecution, rather than being represented by an attorney.

probate   1. The judicial act whereby a will is adjudicated to be valid. 2. a term that describes the functions of the probate court, including the probate of the wills and the supervision of the accounts and actions of administrations and executors of decedents estates.

procedure   1. The means or method by which a court adjudicates cases, as distinguished from the substantive law by which it determines legal rights. 2. A specific course of action; a particular method for doing something.

product liability   The liability of a manufacturer or seller of an article for an injury caused to a person or to property by a defect in the article sold. A product liability suit is a tort action in which strict liability is imposed. The manufacturer or seller of a defective product may be liable to third parties ... as well as to purchasers, as privity of contract is not a requirement in a product liability case.

promissory note   A written promise to pay a specific sum of money by a specified date or on demand. A promissory note is negotiable if, in addition, it is payable to the order of a named person or to bearer.

prosecutor   A public official, elected or appointed, who conducts criminal prosecutions on behalf of his or her jurisdiction.

punishment   The penalty for violating the law, which may include imprisonment, fine, or forfeiture.

punitive damages   Damages that are awarded over and above compensatory damages or actual damages because of the wanton, reckless, or malicious nature of the wrong done by the plaintiff. Such damages bear no relation to the plaintiff's actual loss and are often called exemplary damages, because their purpose is to make an example of the plaintiff to discourage others from engaging in the same kind of conduct in the future.

quitclaim deed   A deed that conveys whatever interest the grantor has in a piece of real property ... .

rape   Sexual intercourse with a woman by force or by putting her in fear or in circumstances in which she is unable to control her conduct or to resist. ... Under the common law definition of the crime, only a female can be raped and only a male can perpetrate the

crime. In recent years, however, courts in several states have held that the rape statutes of their jurisdictions are gender-neutral and apply equally to perpetrators of either sex.

ratification   The act of giving one's approval to a previous act, either one's own or someone else's, which, without such confirmation, would be nonbinding. A person may ratify a contract by expressly promising to be bound by it. Ratification may be implied from a person's conduct; it may also take place as a result of accepting the benefits of a transaction. Ratification is the confirmation of an act that has already been performed, as opposed to the authorization of an act that is yet to be performed.

record   To file or deposit a document or instrument ... for recording.

record on appeal   The papers a trial court transmits to the appellate court, on the basis of which the appellate court decides the appeal. The record on appeal includes the pleadings, all motions made before the trial court, the official transcript, and the judgment or order appealed from.

removal of case   1. In the usual sense, the transfer of a case from a state court to a federal court. 2. In the broad sense of the term, any transfer of a case from one court to another.

replevin   An action by which the owner of personal property taken or detained by another may recover possession of it.

rescind   To effect a rescission. Properly used, "rescind" means to annul a contract from the beginning, not merely to terminate the contract as to future transactions.

Restatements of the Law   A series of volumes published by the American Law Institute, written by legal scholars, each volume or set of volumes covering a major field of the law. Each of the Restatements is, among other things, a statement of the law as it is generally interpreted and applied by the courts with respect to particular legal principles.

restitution   In both contract and tort, a remedy that restores the status quo. Restitution returns a person who has been wrongfully deprived of something to the position he or she occupied before the wrong occurred; it requires a defendant who has been unjustly enriched at the expense of the plaintiff to make the plaintiff whole, either ... by returning property unjustly held, by reimbursing the plaintiff, or by paying compensation or indemnification.

restrictive covenant   A covenant in a deed prohibiting or restricting the use of the property.

seduction   [T]he act of inducing a person to have sexual relations, usually through some form of deception. Seduction is a criminal offense in some jurisdictions if it is accomplished by means of a promise of marriage.

slander   A false and malicious oral statement tending to blacken a person's reputation or to damage his or her means of livelihood.

socialism   An economic system in which the state owns the means of production (manufacturing, agriculture, transportation) and in which, in theory, every citizen participates in production according to his or her ability.

sole proprietorship   Ownership by one person, as opposed to ownership by more than one person, ownership by a corporation, ownership by a partnership, etc.

stare decisis   (Latin) Means "standing by the decision." ... [T]he doctrine that judicial decisions stand as precedents for cases arising in the future. It is a fundamental policy of our law that, except in unusual circumstances, a court's determination on a point of law will be followed by courts of the same or lower rank in later cases presenting the same legal issue, even though different parties are involved and many years have elapsed.

statutes of limitations   Federal and state statutes prescribing the maximum period of time during which various types of civil actions and criminal prosecutions can be brought after the occurrence of the injury or the offense.

step-parent   A wife, in her relationship to her spouse's child by a former marriage; a husband, in his relationship to his spouse's child by a former marriage.

stepchild   A son or daughter of one's spouse by a former spouse.

substantial evidence   Evidence that a reasonable person would accept as adequate to support the conclusion or conclusions drawn from it; evidence beyond a scintilla.

substantial performance   The doctrine that there is adequate consideration to support a contract if there has been substantial performance of the contract.

substantive law   Area of the law that defines right conduct, as opposed to *procedural law,* which governs the process by which rights are adjudicated.

supremacy clause   The provision in Article VI of the Constitution that "this Constitution and laws of the United States ... shall be the supreme law of the land, and the judges in every state shall be bound hereby."

title   1. The rights of an owner with respect to property, real or personal, i.e., possession and the right of possession. 2. A document that evidences the rights of an owner, i.e., ownership rights.

tort   A wrong involving a breach of duty and resulting in an injury to the person or property of another. ... [A] violation of a duty established by law ... . [A] private wrong that must be pursued by the injured party in a civil action.

trademark   A mark, design, title, logo, or motto used in the sale or advertising of products to identify them and distinguish them from the products of others. A trademark is the property of its owner and, when registered under the Trademark Act, is reserved for the exclusive use of its owner.

transcript   A typewritten copy of the court reporter's stenographic notes of a trial ... [;] a record of the proceedings.

treatise   A book that discusses, in depth, important principles in some area of human activity or interest.

trespass   An unauthorized entry or intrusion on the real property of another.

trust   A fiduciary relationship involving a trustee who holds trust property for the benefit or use of a beneficiary.

ultimate facts   The facts in a case upon which liability is determined or based.

uncontested   Not disputed; unopposed; not defended against; not litigated.

Uniform Commercial Code   One of the Uniform Laws, which has been adopted in much the same form in every state. It governs most aspects of commercial transactions, including sales, leases, negotiable instruments, deposits and collections, letters of credit, bulk sales, warehouse receipts, bills of lading and other documents of title, investment securities, and secured transactions.

variance   In zoning law, an exception from the strict application of a zoning ordinance, granted to relieve a property owner of unnecessary hardship.

voluntary   A word applied to an act freely done out of choice, not brought about by coercion, duress, or accident.

warranty deed   A deed that contains title covenants.

will   An instrument by which a person (the testator) makes a disposition of his or her property, to take effect after his or her death.

workers' compensation acts   State statutes that provide for the payment of compensation to employees injured in their employment or, in case of death, to their dependents. Benefits are paid under such acts whether or not the employer was negligent; payment is made in accordance with predetermined schedules based generally upon the loss or impairment of earning capacity. Workers' compensation laws eliminate defenses such as assumption of risk, contributory negligence, and fellow servant. ... Occupational diseases are compensable under these acts as well.

writ of prohibition   A writ issued by a higher court directing a lower court not to take a certain action, i.e., prohibiting it from attempting to exercise jurisdiction in a matter in which it has no jurisdiction.

zoning   The creation and application of structural, size, and use restrictions imposed upon the owners of real estate within districts or zones in accordance with ... regulations or ordinances. ... [A] form of land use regulation.

INDEX

NOTE: Italicized page numbers refer to nontext material. Italicized page numbers following the word "defined" refer to definitions at the bottom of the referenced page.